RANDOM HOUSE

FOUR SEASONS

CROSSWORD OMNIBUS

RANDOM HOUSE

FOUR SEASONS

CROSSWORD OMNIBUS

edited by Stanley Newman

Random House
Puzzles & Games

The puzzles in this book were previously published as *Random House More Vacation Crosswords* (2001), *Random House Cozy Crosswords* (2001), *Random House Bedtime Crosswords* (2002), and *Random House Back to the Beach Crosswords* (2002).

Please address inquiries about electronic licensing of reference products for use on a network, in software, or on CD-ROM to the Subsidiary Rights Department, Random House Reference, fax 212-572-6003.

This book is available for special discounts for bulk purchases for sales promotions or premiums. Special editions, including personalized covers, excerpts of existing books, and corporate imprints, can be created in large quantities for special needs. For more information, write to Random House, Inc., Special Markets/Premium Sales, 1745 Broadway, MD 6-2, New York, NY, 10019 or e-mail specialmarkets@randomhouse.com.

Random House Puzzles & Games Web site address: www.puzzlesatrandom.com

0 9 8 7 6 5 4 3 2 1

ISBN: 0-8129-3668-X

Introduction

Welcome to *Random House Four Seasons Crossword Omnibus,* featuring 400 lively but "not too tough" crosswords from earlier volumes in the handy "Vacation-size" series. Each crossword has a theme, or central idea, running through its longest answers. The title provided at the top of each page will give you a hint as to what the theme is. And the answers are all in the back, just in case.

Thanks to Laura Neilson and Adam Cohen for their help in the preparation of the manuscript.

Your comments on any aspect of this book are most welcome. You can reach me via regular mail or e-mail at the addresses below.

If you're Internet-active, you're invited to my Web site, www.StanXwords.com. It features puzzlemaker profiles, solving hints, and other useful info for crossword fans. There's also a free daily crossword and weekly prize contest. Please stop by for a visit.

Best wishes for happy solving!

Stan Newman

Regular mail: P.O. Box 69, Massapequa Park, NY 11762

(Please enclose a self-addressed stamped envelope if you'd like a reply.)
E-mail: StanXwords@aol.com

PUZZLES

1 HOUSEHOLD HELP

by Rich Norris

ACROSS

1 Reasoning
6 Magna __ laude
9 Inventor Nikola
14 Island near Venezuela
15 Genetic letters
16 Peru natives
17 Ticket writer
19 Hart and Matalin
20 Ballroom dance
22 Actor Lugosi
23 Golf score
26 Cigar residue
27 Scenic transport
29 Shocked
31 Pulled suddenly
32 Gear meshers
33 Tremor
34 Fisherman's need
37 Involved with, as a hobby
38 Available money
39 Ready for picking
40 Baseball great Mel
41 Like a defective roof
42 Black bird
43 Flaubert character
45 Errand runners
46 Vacationing traveler
48 Intention
49 *Norma* __
50 Some choristers
51 Riot-squad supply
54 Actress Vera
56 *Terminal* author
60 Episode
61 Brian of rock
62 Wrist bones
63 Pub missiles
64 __ *Rosenkavalier*
65 Made a slip

DOWN

1 On the __ (fleeing)
2 Mine find
3 Abdomen
4 Doubter's words
5 Auto oasis
6 Malfunction, as a computer
7 Military squad
8 Prepared
9 Allen or Conway
10 Give power to
11 Toolbox item
12 Eric Clapton tune
13 Analyze, as ore
18 Nearly all
21 Urban greenery
23 Barbecue site
24 Ten-percenter
25 Scarlett's love
28 Presidential nickname
30 From __ Z
31 Inferior in quality
33 Provided with lodging
35 Wagner work
36 Not too astute
38 Celebratory meal
39 Brit. flying group
41 56, to Caesar
42 Fiction genre
44 East
45 Best Picture of 1958
46 Brought under control
47 Slugger Tony
48 Shaded area
52 Tops
53 Lasting impression
55 Ave. crossers
57 Bobby of hockey
58 Expose, poetically
59 Tease

2 GET LOST!

by Patrick Jordan

ACROSS

1 Dirigible
6 Restaurant employee
10 Nile reptiles
14 Sound portion
15 Sitarist Shankar
16 Ostrich relative
17 House type
19 Large cymbal
20 Important
21 Feel antipathy toward
22 Words on a free-sample display
24 Swamp goop
25 Knickknack holder
26 Like a frisky dog's tail
29 Clearly shaped
32 Think the world of
33 Serenity
34 Gleeful shout
35 Animation
36 Fleshy root
37 Church area
38 Zodiac sign
39 Used a crowbar
40 Prickly shrub
41 Excesses
43 Caravan critters
44 Gaucho's weapons
45 Former French coins
46 Calls for
48 Spell of bad luck
49 Keats creation
52 Revered figure
53 Fitzgerald or Tormé
56 Take a shine to
57 Actress Skye
58 Mosaic units
59 Feat
60 Like some dorms
61 Put to use

DOWN

1 Lie in the sun
2 '40s actress Velez
3 Without urgency
4 DI doubled
5 Boulevard blemish
6 Largest Greek island
7 Possess
8 Holiday preceder
9 More soiled
10 Sock pattern
11 Baked molasses treat
12 Sean or William
13 Stuffing herb
18 Shiftless
23 Musical pause
24 Mythical meanie
25 Jumped with fright
26 Ivies climb them
27 "Farewell, François!"
28 Risk everything
29 Dices
30 Painting prop
31 Clothing colorists
33 Resigns
36 Period when dinosaurs appeared
37 Octopus octet
39 Animal skin
40 Aluminum ore
42 "Curses! __ again!"
43 Pros' opposites
45 Located
46 Tame
47 Singer Adams
48 Reformer Addams
49 Leer at
50 Forest foragers
51 Prefix for while
54 Dove sound
55 Veto

3 INEDIBLES

by Lee Weaver

ACROSS

1 Spider's creations
5 __ *la Douce*
9 Complain
13 Jai __
14 Kingdom
16 Melville novel
17 Used a doorbell
18 Kismet
19 Musical symbol
20 Oxlike antelope
22 Seaman's coat
24 Has to have
26 Cheer for a bullfighter
27 Less messy
29 Brave deeds
33 Slalom curve
34 Gossiper's tidbit
36 Old-style anesthetic
38 Fret and fume
40 Trivial
42 Explorer Hernando de __
43 Rips
45 Flat-topped lands
47 Harper Valley grp.
48 Like a goblet
50 Muppets creator
52 Signal an actor
53 Valuable quality
54 Opaque material used in vases
59 Sound made by taffeta
62 Concert halls
63 Spew forth
65 Canyon effect
66 Couturier Cassini
67 Frightfully strange
68 Leave out
69 Little kid
70 Religious offshoot
71 Recipe amounts: Abbr.

DOWN

1 Ending for soft or dinner
2 Airline to Israel
3 Bicycle part named for its shape
4 Official seal
5 Pique
6 Gathers (crops)
7 Filly's mother
8 __ mater
9 Egos
10 Run __ (go wild)
11 Learning method
12 Burns or Byron
15 Captain's superior
21 Bambi, for one
23 Skin soother
25 Tom-tom or snare
27 Bird's abode
28 __ Park, CO
29 Sharpened
30 Cupid, to the Greeks
31 Easy piano piece
32 Brouhaha
35 Silent performer
37 Colorful horse
39 Tornado aftermath
41 Stadium sounds
44 Self-satisfied
46 Meeting: Abbr.
49 Confused conflict
51 Most up-to-date
53 Savory jelly
54 Beside the point
55 Without purpose
56 Symbol of Wales
57 War god
58 Having no doubt
60 Send off
61 Short journeys
64 Vietnamese festival

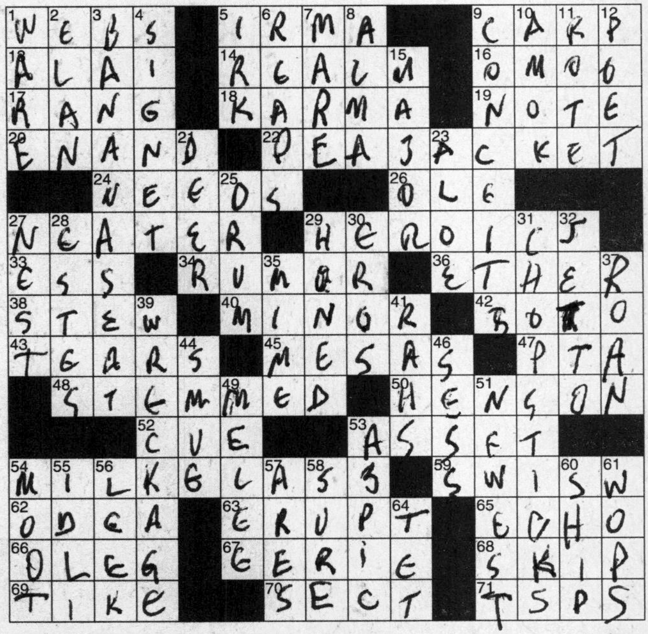

4 DOWN UNDER

by Rich Norris

ACROSS

1 Different
6 Less hospitable
11 Bank device: Abbr.
14 Selected
15 From Donegal
16 Golfer's concern
17 Meaningless triumphs
20 Take to court
21 Self-confidence
22 Idiomatic conditions
23 __ brûlée (dessert)
25 Nickname for a sharpshooter
28 Computer peripherals
31 Hardly impartial
32 __ d'oeuvre
33 __ "King" Cole
34 "Gosh, it's cold!"
35 Conclusion
36 Took a chair
38 Corker
41 More, in music
44 Set-to
46 Kid's transport
47 Thoughtful
50 Vehicle with a rumble seat
52 Forcible ejection
54 Turkish coins
55 Cartoonist Peter
56 Noodles
58 Fort Worth sch.
61 Act of desperation
65 WWII command
66 In flames
67 Home on the range
68 President pro __
69 Competed at Indy
70 Approvals

DOWN

1 '60s protest singer Phil
2 Biblical pronoun
3 One of five in stud poker
4 Immigrant's subj.
5 Investigate anew, as a case
6 Coastal resort areas
7 Novelist Leon
8 Cut into cubes
9 N.Y. hours
10 Frat letter
11 Trues up
12 One way to color fabric
13 __ up (erred)
18 Part of NOW
19 *M*A*S*H* character
24 Hosp. employees
26 Recede
27 Broadcast
28 That girl
29 Pro's opposite
30 Super Bowl I MVP
37 Where to find old saws
38 Driving breaks
39 Presidential nickname
40 For every
41 Turn on a point
42 Chemical ending
43 Exclamation of disgust
45 Ralph of *The Waltons*
46 Character-building org.
47 Aspen abode
48 Make bubbly
49 Kidnapper's demand
51 Like an uninsulated room
53 Of the eye
57 Farmland unit
59 Alberta native
60 Southwestern natives
62 Patriotic org. since 1890
63 "__ body meet a body . . ."
64 Charge

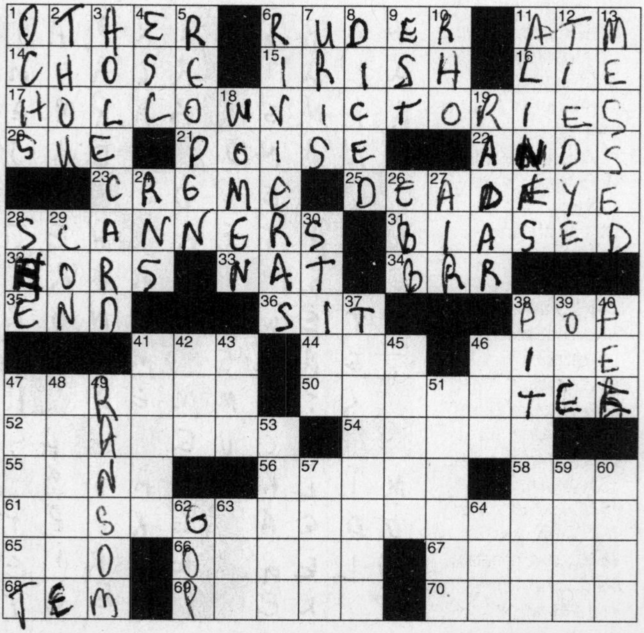

5 HANDYMAN'S SPECIAL

by Rich Norris

ACROSS

1 Underground chamber
5 Comic Soupy
10 Queens stadium
14 "Ah, me!"
15 Surrogate
16 Marshal Wyatt
17 Office-supply item
19 French friend
20 Night before
21 Less restrained
22 High points
23 Resolves, as an argument
25 Lake boat
27 Possesses
28 Prepare a present
31 Suit
34 Social group
35 Kimono belt
36 Not "fer"
37 Residences
38 Christmas
39 Tavern
40 Desert mounds
41 Pigeon homes
42 Sufficiency
44 Perfect, at NASA
45 Ninny
46 Jostled, as in a crowd
50 Actress Bo
52 Proportion
54 Eggs
55 Director Kazan
56 Up-front
58 Feels poorly
59 Herculean types
60 Philosopher Descartes
61 Depend (on)
62 Kitchen emanations
63 Picnic crashers

DOWN

1 Sidewalk eateries
2 __ and kicking
3 Manservant
4 Compass reading
5 Germ cells
6 City on the Rhône
7 Metallic deposit
8 Deep knee bends, e.g.
9 Former UAR member
10 Manatee
11 Create with effort, as an agreement
12 Southernmost Great Lake
13 Gorillas and gibbons
18 E natural's alias
22 Poker buy-in
24 Highly diluted
26 PMs
28 Full of spirit
29 Qualified
30 Dessert options
31 __ Wawa (Radner character)
32 Mild oath
33 Safety run-through
34 Caring (about)
37 Anti-Communist grp.
38 __ Ono
40 Dip, as a doughnut
41 Computer language
43 Somewhat anxious
44 Foreigners
46 Anesthetic of old
47 Interlaced
48 Incident
49 Bumpers and Evans
50 Letter opener
51 Nobelist Wiesel
53 Word form for "air"
56 "I see it all now!"
57 Historical period

6 SUPER EGOS

by Patrick Jordan

ACROSS

1 Sheep shelters
6 Pillow coverings
11 June honoree
14 Speechify
15 Hiawatha's craft
16 Playwright Levin
17 Incredible Hulk's alter ego
19 One-fifth of DX
20 Compact
21 Pressman, at times
23 __ *Choice* (Streep film)
27 Lanky and awkward
28 Waiting lines
29 Angry disposition
31 Absolute
32 Days, in Dijon
33 Football filler
36 Gets one's dander up
37 Bruno of *City Slickers*
38 Unit of force
39 German article
40 Goes a-wandering
41 Fine rains
42 Segments
44 Play merrily
45 Turn pale
47 1971 Woody Allen film
48 Greene of *Bonanza*
49 Assimilate
51 Pose a question
52 Wonder Woman's alter ego
58 Last letter
59 Checks text
60 Pepe LePew's quest
61 Commit a blunder
62 "__ Pass Go . . ."
63 Military chaplain

DOWN

1 Corn eater's leftover
2 NHL legend Bobby
3 Sigma follower
4 List-ending abbr.
5 More disreputable
6 Reads quickly
7 Skater Brinker
8 Author Rice
9 He liked to harry Larry
10 '40s Saturday movie features
11 Robin's alter ego
12 Disney's Little Mermaid
13 Milk farm
18 Quilting events
22 SSW opposite
23 Tentacled mollusk
24 Unconventional
25 Spider-Man's alter ego
26 Shades
27 Like some horror films
29 Nuclear-reactor centers
30 Major airports
32 Early jazz
34 Within: Pref.
35 Takes a breather
37 Former *People's Court* judge
38 Prima donna
40 Lost ground
41 Dangerous female
43 Traveler's stop
44 Dogpatch creator
45 Conflagration
46 One finishing second
47 Flaunt one's feats
49 Eve's eldest
50 Aware of
53 Nuptial vow
54 "__ Yankee Doodle Dandy . . ."
55 Show agreement
56 Common canine
57 Before, to Byron

7 IN THE CARDS

by Lee Weaver

ACROSS

1 __ mater
5 Bakery worker
9 Money rolls
13 Canine comment
14 Out of cash
15 At the summit
16 A way over water
18 Painter Magritte
19 Employ
20 Seine feeder
21 __ and groaned
23 Window sills
25 Iron-fisted
27 Ruffles feathers
29 Wearing down
33 Potato coverings
36 Designer Cassini
38 Entreaty
39 "A Bushel __ Peck"
40 Prepare Parmesan
41 Airline to Israel
42 Observed
43 St. Louis landmark
44 Macaroni, e.g.
45 Wrap with bandages
47 Heroic story
49 "I cannot __ lie"
51 Votes in
55 *American* __ (Gere film)
58 Mets' stadium
60 Reverence
61 Not "fer"
62 Betraying no emotion
65 Cartoon bear
66 Water pitchers
67 Male deer
68 Guitarist Clapton
69 Cincinnati team
70 Toll road

DOWN

1 Very bad
2 Not tight
3 Sounded like a Guernsey
4 Behind, on a ship
5 Novelist Murdoch
6 Ciphers
7 Heart test, for short
8 Appear again
9 Tolstoy classic
10 "__ o'clock scholar"
11 Finished
12 Went fast
14 Fast
17 Some South Africans
22 Spanish gold
24 Bar order
26 Acquire molars
28 Reddish-brown horse
30 Troubles
31 Orderly
32 Celebration
33 Back talk
34 Was aware of
35 Brainstorm
37 Varnish ingredient
40 Horse going full tilt
44 Rice dish
46 Neighbor of Penna.
48 Jury members
50 Popped the question
52 Desert plants
53 Pinch playfully
54 Riverbank plant
55 Singer Marvin
56 Composer Stravinsky
57 Role for Caron
59 Towel word
63 Be obligated
64 Viper

8 BED TIME

by Rich Norris

ACROSS

1 Type of coffee
6 Actor Baldwin
10 Royal Russian ruler
14 Chan portrayer
15 Influence
16 Inter __
17 Military scout's position
20 Stadium cheer
21 Anger
22 Easily bent
23 Not proficient in
26 Beginnings
27 Digger's tool
29 British currency
30 Reed instruments
31 Beatles film
32 Mauna __
35 Stravinsky work
39 Flier out of Stockholm
40 Plant appendages
41 Tripoli's country
42 Cod and May
44 Banquet delicacy
45 Took it easy
48 Reno or Leigh
49 Squared up
50 Always, to a poet
51 End of a British alphabet
54 Forty-something concern
58 Electric co., e.g.
59 Applaud
60 Main artery
61 Rational
62 Isn't serious
63 In disarray

DOWN

1 Portal
2 Site of a Napoleon exile
3 Money holders
4 Chemical ending
5 HST was his third VP
6 Not connected
7 Guitar relative
8 Inventor Whitney
9 Zoom photos
10 Opened, as a keg
11 Feeds the pigs
12 Bridal path
13 Is valued
18 Tiny bottle
19 Former senator Sam
24 Declare
25 He loved Lucy
26 Takes to the links
27 Fleet fliers
28 "Very funny!"
29 Unskilled workers
31 Cut down
32 Fifths for bridge?
33 Irish New Age singer
34 Ice-cream thickener
36 Cassette player
37 Prepare for the future
38 __ *gauche* (left bank: Fr.)
42 Light source
43 Jump on the ice
44 Motor vehicles
45 Fictional Uncle
46 Madonna role
47 Escorted
48 Versatile vehicles
50 Relative of "Zounds!"
52 Victuals
53 6/6/44
55 __ Baba
56 Actress Dawber
57 44 Across, essentially

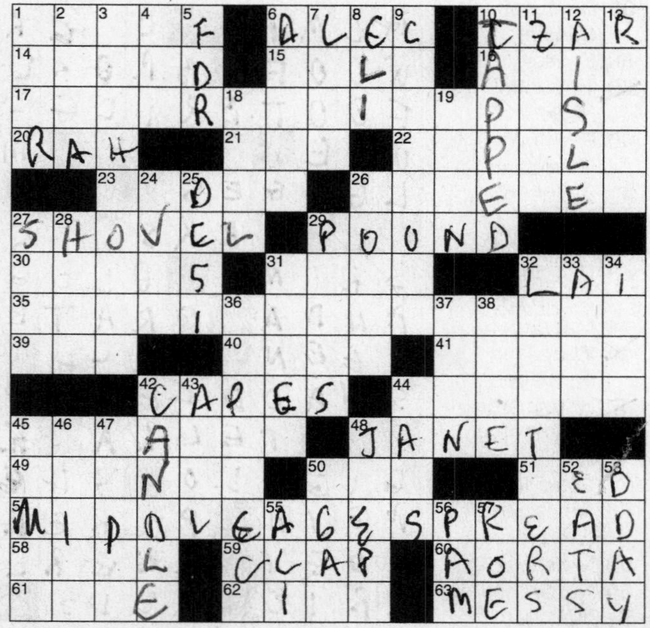

9 BRIDAL WEAR

by Rich Norris

ACROSS

1 Daunt
5 Press down
9 Soothing ointment
13 Farm animals
14 Banks' storage rooms
15 Words of understanding
16 Immigrant's homeland
18 German philosopher
19 Bandleader Brown
20 Angry
21 Lunar event
23 Golfer Ballesteros
24 Solo of *Star Wars*
25 Yanni et al.
33 Baker or Bryant
34 Walk to and fro
35 Speck
36 *Adam* __ (Eliot novel)
37 John Paul and predecessors
39 Thomas __ Edison
40 Mine material
41 Green gem
42 Aviator
43 Worried about another
47 Bed-and-breakfast
48 Do damage to
49 Temporary solution
53 PC panic button
54 Imitate
57 Singer Guthrie
58 Edit
61 Coral formation
62 Golfer Wadkins
63 Beer alternatives
64 Starting with
65 Watched warily
66 Untainted

DOWN

1 Gullible one
2 Wheel holder
3 Brit's last letters
4 Bus. letter abbr.
5 In __ (together)
6 Toward the stern
7 Insignificant
8 Fortune-tellers
9 Two-piece suit of a sort
10 Without delay: Abbr.
11 Camera part
12 Apportion, with "out"
14 Urbane
17 Alpha's opposite
22 Tie, as shoes
23 Fill to excess
25 Wealthy person
26 January, in Juárez
27 More spacious
28 Raised
29 MS. enclosure
30 Stray from the script
31 Imaginative
32 Fix one's eyes
37 Having collateral value
38 Pindar product
39 Reunion attendee
41 *Fear of Flying* author
42 Compel
44 Swindle
45 Concluding words
46 Unpleasantly grating
49 Poet Teasdale
50 Very, in Vichy
51 Toast topping
52 Broadway production
54 Rights org.
55 Ship's parking place
56 Choice word
59 One, in France
60 Short snooze

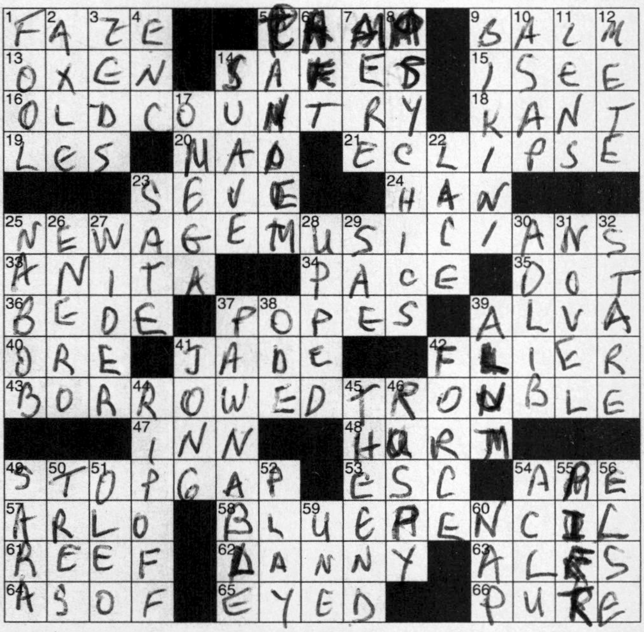

10 IN A HURRY

by Fred Piscop

ACROSS
1 Train unit
4 Auctioneer's cry
8 Packs down, as dirt
13 Commotions
15 Sloth's home
16 Dizzying design
17 Basketball tactic
19 Newspapers, radio, etc.
20 Store, as grain
21 Fight official
23 Bump into
24 Evening bash
25 Dander
27 Train system
34 Ruth __ Ginsburg
37 Composer Ned
38 Witness' vow
39 Secondhand
40 Filled to the gills
41 Oscar Madison type
42 __ up (finalize)
43 Singer Blades
44 Ridiculous
45 Cornmeal mush
48 Microscopic
49 Alex Trebek's birthplace
53 Niger neighbor
56 Cheerleader's syllable
59 Wiped out
60 "You __ kidding!"
62 Plaster ingredient
64 One of the Fab Four
65 Celestial bear
66 Author Bellow
67 Wolfed down
68 Resting on
69 Gun owner's org.

DOWN
1 Bistros
2 *A Bell for* __
3 Martini's partner
4 *Silkwood* star
5 Metal in the rough
6 Shake-spearean king
7 Fake out, in hockey
8 Comic Arnold
9 Primitive fellows
10 Whipped up
11 __-dieu (kneeling bench)
12 Immediately, to a surgeon
14 Tended the sauce
18 Make indistinct
22 Shot, as a gun
26 Butt into
28 Baseballer Hideki
29 Was excessively fond
30 Tendency
31 Pie-cooling place
32 Worshiped one
33 Shakespeare's Sir __ Belch
34 Florida governor
35 On the briny
36 Morning moistures
40 "Great!"
41 Omens
43 Deli bread
44 Lewis Carroll creature
46 Sudden pain
47 Polar covering
50 Flu variety
51 Voice an objection
52 __ Rogers St. Johns
53 Farmyard female
54 Pavarotti piece
55 Mardi Gras follower
57 Greenish blue
58 Damaged
61 Freight weight
63 "Equal" word form

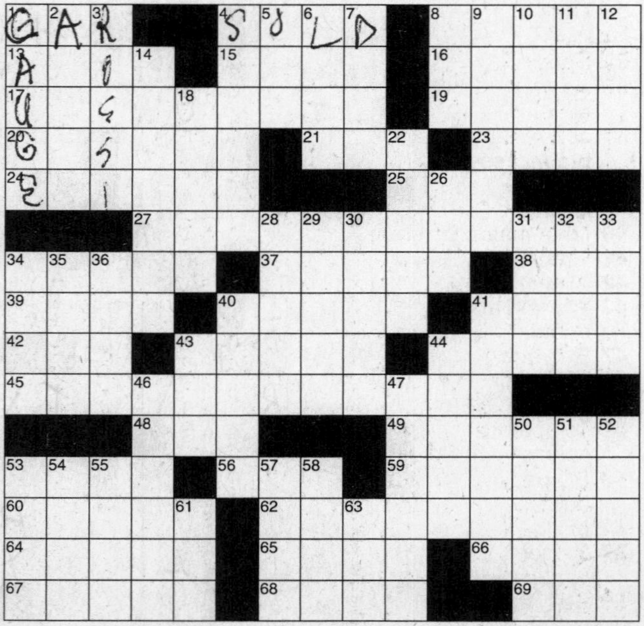

11 A MODEST PROPOSAL

by Peter Gordon

ACROSS

1 "Shoo!"
6 Went too fast
10 Sharp blow in karate
14 Scarlett of *Gone With the Wind*
15 Mata __ (infamous spy)
16 Angel topper
17 Large ocean vessel
18 "I cannot tell __"
19 Had a debt
20 It's given when asking 48 Across
23 Sailor's affirmative
24 Auto
25 Grown up
29 Winnie-the-__
31 Actress Thurman
34 Too big, weightwise
35 Flirt's signal
36 Got __ the ground floor
37 Asks 48 Across
40 ". . . lived happily __ after"
41 Musical composition
42 The U of UV
43 Actor Billy __ Williams
44 Poker-pot starter
45 Except
46 Dessert served à la mode
47 Common conjunction
48 Proposal
56 Walk in water
57 __ fide
58 "Old MacDonald" refrain
59 Singer Fitzgerald
60 Israeli submachine guns
61 Spot on clothing
62 Ran in the washing machine
63 Butterfly catchers
64 Bombay garments

DOWN

1 Bottom of a shoe
2 Beard's place
3 Sounded a bell
4 Neighborhood
5 Thatcher of Britain
6 Put to __ (outdo)
7 Fair-skinned
8 Moran of *Happy Days*
9 Competitor of Tab
10 Church singing group
11 Goldie of *Private Benjamin*
12 Designer Cassini
13 Pea's home
21 CBS logo
22 Cheerleader's sound
25 Bike that has an engine
26 None of the __
27 Native American home
28 Where Gorbachev ruled: Abbr.
29 Arouse, as interest
30 Burden
31 Join together
32 Secures with cables
33 Karenina et al.
35 Cried
36 "__ be a cold day in July . . ."
38 Sweetheart
39 Woman's summer garment
44 Feel poorly
45 Spanish article
46 Say "Not guilty"
47 Accumulate
48 Room divider
49 Keep the engine running
50 Seep slowly
51 Pound or gallon
52 Moreno or Hayworth
53 1998, for example
54 1003, in old Rome
55 Long periods of time
56 Spider's creation

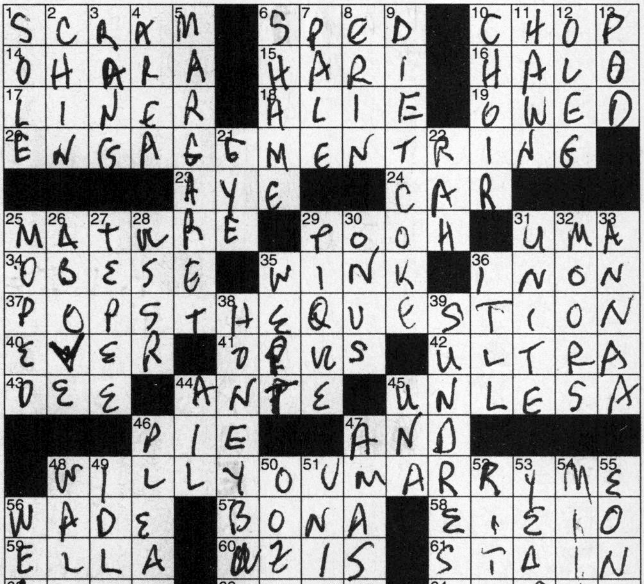

12

THREE-RING CIRCUS

by Patrick Jordan

ACROSS

1 Heathen
6 The Ugly Duckling, eventually
10 Pedestal part
14 Rub out
15 Quote as an example
16 Crooner Paul
17 First-ring performer
20 "Piece of cake!"
21 Gardener's tool
22 First host of *The Price Is Right*
23 Bumped into
24 Foundation garment of yore
25 Tropical fruit
29 Tony Musante's TV tec
30 Have being
31 Toy with a tail
32 Frying medium
36 Second-ring performer
39 Minus
40 Gaucho's weapon
41 Cartoon adventurer Quest
42 ". . . __ forgive our debtors"
43 Reno and Leigh
44 Megalomaniacs, e.g.
47 Promgoer's rental
48 Beatty of *Reds*
49 Feeling blue
50 Lane of songdom
54 Third-ring performer
57 Declare openly
58 *Return of the Jedi* creature
59 Book of photos
60 Fork-tailed seabird
61 Emulates a seamstress
62 Jury members

DOWN

1 Tennis champ Sampras
2 La Scala solo
3 Comedian's stock-in-trade
4 Very pale
5 After taxes
6 Move along quickly
7 Clean with a rag
8 Enjoyed brunch
9 Rookie
10 Formal dances
11 Foot-leg connector
12 Clay pigeon
13 Work hard for
18 Actress Perlman
19 Angelic atmosphere
23 Legend
24 Terra __ (potting material)
25 Lemon skin
26 Wheel shaft
27 Slapstick movie missiles
28 Egyptian vipers
29 Championship
31 Recognized
32 Simba or Leo
33 Bancroft or Boleyn
34 Tenant's payment
35 Prohibition supporters
37 Attendance-book notations
38 Trojan War hero
42 Prayer response
43 Jujitsu offshoot
44 Purple hue
45 Knight clothing
46 Sketched
47 Fuel receptacles
48 "Huh?"
49 Winter fall
50 Having skill
51 Pig in a '96 film
52 Become indistinct
53 Shade trees
55 Astonishment
56 Short snooze

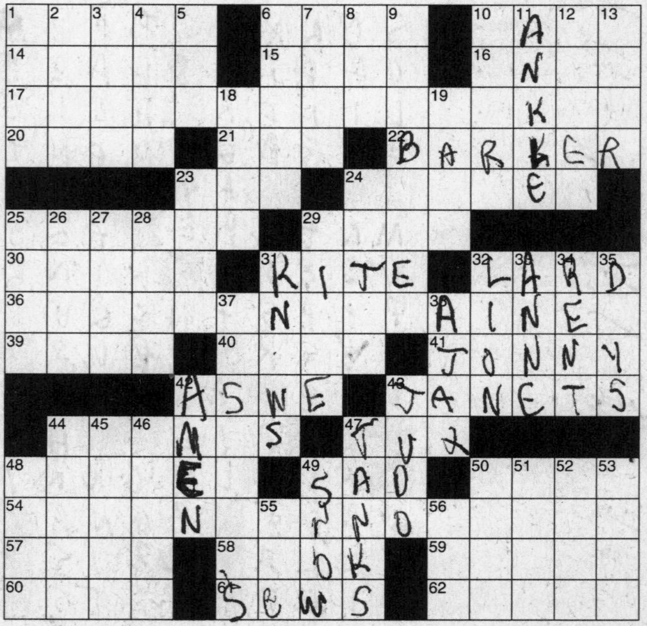

13 AROUND THE ROOM

by Rich Norris

ACROSS

1 The second Mrs. Trump
6 Tavern
9 Slide on ice
14 Self-evident truth
15 Gold: Sp.
16 __ Gables, FL
17 Very frustrated
20 "For __ a jolly good fellow"
21 Take advantage of
22 "This __ Love" (Rodgers & Hart tune)
23 Immigrant's subj.
24 MGM lion
25 Clobber, as in a contest
34 Part of SEATO
35 Life of __ (ease)
36 Word form for "earth"
37 Military melody
38 Lawn intrusions
39 Charitable offerings
40 Supplement, with out
41 Seven, in Seville
42 Info
43 Causes shame
47 Writer Fleming
48 Scale notes
49 Kidnapper's demand
52 Every
53 Covert WWII org.
56 Bill holders
59 __ Martin (007 auto)
60 Waikiki welcome
61 Put up
62 Shoals
63 Senator Kennedy
64 Charges for use

DOWN

1 Speed-of-sound number
2 Wheel connector
3 Social reformer Jacob
4 Actor Herbert
5 Sneak attack
6 Tibia, for one
7 S.A. country
8 Campus recruiting grp.
9 Stage sets, collectively
10 Act obsequiously
11 Saudi, for one
12 Story
13 Architectural add-on
18 Tropical spot
19 Angels' headgear
23 Greek letters
25 Defeated at chess
26 Japanese city
27 Tom's dad, in the rhyme
28 Turns loose
29 Deceive
30 Like days of yore
31 Dome-shaped hut
32 Metronome setting
33 Gardener, at times
38 Separate grain and chaff
39 Puts in
41 Sprinkles salt, perhaps
44 What "-ish" means
45 Agatha contemporary
46 Merchant
49 Swell, as a river
50 Build the pot
51 Become liquid
52 Zealous
53 Word on a store sign
54 Religious group
55 Fast fliers: Abbr.
56 Kids' card game
57 Born: Fr.
58 Assayer's concern

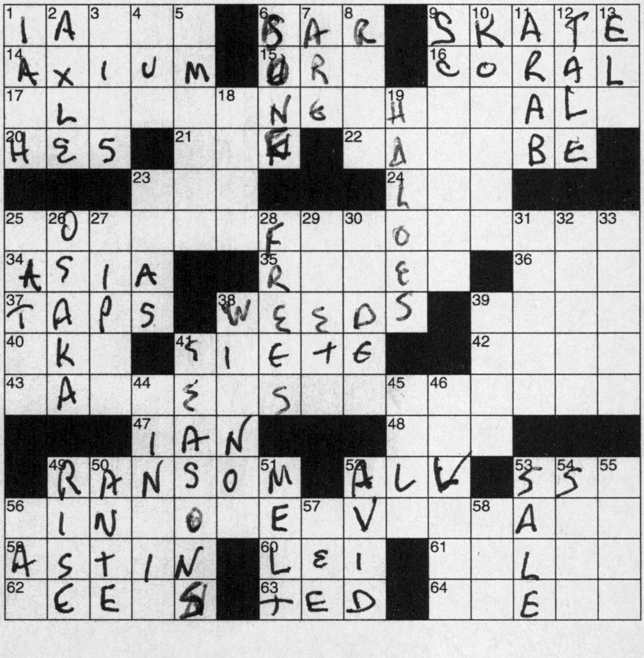

14 HANDY

by Bob Lubbers

ACROSS
1 Director Howard
4 Fatty
11 Deed
14 I love: Lat.
15 Chooses
16 Funny Charlotte
17 ". . . rain __ sleet . . ."
18 Sign of nerves
20 Search for water
22 Bridge coup
23 Track-and-field contest
24 Very long time
25 Hindsight phrase
27 Pickpocket's assets
33 Hodgepodge
34 EPA concern
35 Flora-filled lobbies
39 Estuary
40 Tours
42 Blow it
43 Fender dings
45 __-War (racehorse)
46 To-do
47 Boxing style of old
50 Previously
53 XIII x IV
54 Achieve
55 Zola novel
59 Movie award
62 Garden experts
65 Coach Parseghian
66 Pub drink
67 Make like new
68 Midmorning
69 Baseballer Cobb et al.
70 Upset with
71 "Dig in!"

DOWN
1 Author Ayn
2 Melville novel
3 From Oslo
4 Agree
5 Morning droplets
6 Seine sights
7 Ring out
8 Word form for "eight"
9 One of the Little Rascals
10 Psychic's sense
11 Composer Harold
12 Sahara beast
13 In a peevish mood
19 "It's __ Unusual Day"
21 London district
26 Monks
27 *Hawaii Five-O* star
28 Nastase of tennis
29 Chemin de __ (casino game)
30 Part of Caesar's boast
31 Kim of *Picnic*
32 Miller or Ford
36 Make a copy of
37 *"Dies __"*
38 Part of B.A.
40 Despot
41 Costello or Gehrig
44 Steak cut
46 Competes in the slalom
48 Tenant
49 Storage space
50 Sired, Biblically
51 Before the deadline
52 Releases
56 Chan rejoinder
57 Party snacks
58 Cookie man Wally
60 Zone
61 Carry on
63 Atomic energy org.
64 Bikini top

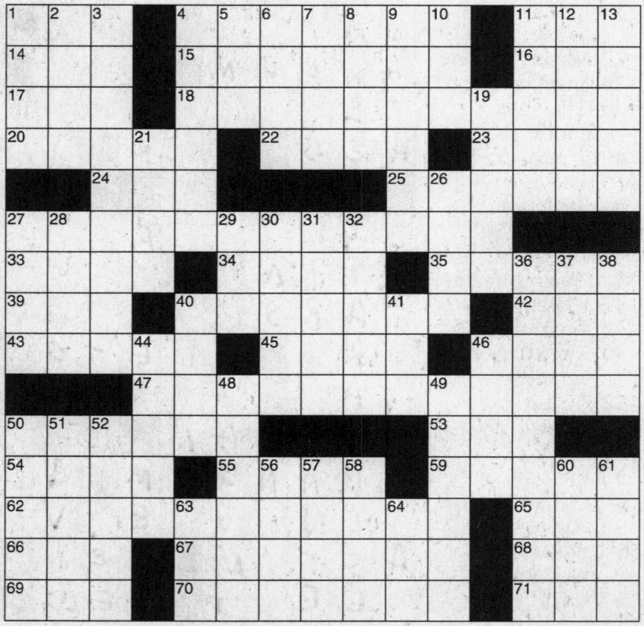

15 CAPITALISTS

by Patrick Jordan

ACROSS

1 Deteriorates
5 Got a perfect score on
9 Green sauce
14 Admit openly
15 Ice-cream holder
16 Be of use to
17 New Mexico Indian
18 The item here
19 Told a knee-slapper
20 *Steel Magnolias* costar
23 Actor Stephen
24 Nancy Reagan's son
25 Citrus fruit
26 Swindle
27 Sicilian spouter
28 __ constrictor
31 Chinese, e.g.
34 Fuzzy member of Skywalker's army
35 Drescher of *The Nanny*
36 *From Here to Eternity* costar
39 Bettor's concern
40 Calhoun of filmdom
41 Della or Pee Wee
42 Put into words
43 Baseball gear
44 Wedding attire, for short
45 African nation
46 That girl
47 Boxing stats
50 Paint-dripping artist
54 Explorer __ de León
55 *Cheers* character
56 Vicinity
57 Caruso or Domingo
58 Enjoying a cruise
59 Butcher's wares
60 Defeats a dragon
61 Soapmaking substances
62 Source of ruin

DOWN

1 Shaver's need
2 Small egg
3 Skater Harding
4 Do the butterfly
5 Director's command
6 *George M!* subject
7 Writer Bagnold
8 Without a definite purpose
9 *The __ Game* (Doris Day musical)
10 Call forth
11 Munro's pen name
12 Secures a shoelace
13 Ancient
21 Fork feature
22 Closely twisted
26 Some house pets
27 Water pitchers
28 Soft cheese
29 Clumsy sorts
30 Poker payment
31 Andy's radio partner
32 Fizzy quaff
33 500-mile race, for short
34 Appealing to feelings
35 Show off one's biceps
37 Some exams
38 Merciless
43 Pastry purveyors
44 Bush Sr. Supreme Court appointee
45 *Star Trek* doctor
46 Shopping binge
47 Divided country
48 Arctic or Indian
49 Ray with winglike fins
50 Rock singer Billy
51 Ballerina Pavlova
52 Overly inquisitive
53 Ewe's child
54 NHL stats

16 FANCY FOOTWORK

by Bob Lubbers

ACROSS
1 LAPD alert
4 Missouri Indian
9 Peel
14 Jack of *Barney Miller*
15 Levies
16 Peter O'__
17 Spanish aunt
18 Leader
20 Ms. Lauder
22 Readied a golf ball
23 Takes umbrage at
26 Tranquilized
31 Anchor setter
33 Lessen the value
34 __ Lanka
36 Fodder storages
38 What IOUs indicate
39 Baby seals
41 Thighbone
43 Jai __
44 Pullman berth
46 Nasser successor
48 Curved shape
49 Actor Keanu
51 Football's "Broadway Joe"
53 Comparatively calm
55 Countries
58 Business transaction
60 Portable quarters
61 Car-battery hookup
67 Write
68 Actress Stevens
69 Arab chief
70 Asner and Ames
71 Half of a '60s rock foursome
72 Actions
73 Deli bread

DOWN
1 Fall flower
2 Self-possession
3 Sea captain
4 Outrages
5 *To __ With Love*
6 "It's __-win situation!"
7 Lady's man
8 Senator Kefauver
9 Encrusted
10 2,000 pounds
11 Howard of *American Graffiti*
12 __ du Diable
13 For each
19 Marsh grass
21 Wide shoe
24 End-of-workweek shout
25 Monica of tennis
27 Vicinity
28 Restaurant nuisance
29 Kett and James
30 Arnaz Sr. and Jr.
32 Director Polanski
34 Pony prodders
35 Delhi dollar
37 Khartoum is its capital
40 Golfer Ballesteros
42 Avatar of Vishnu
45 Performs
47 Rags
50 Omen examiner
52 Ascot, e.g.
54 Sped
56 Impoverished
57 Have a feeling
59 Flimsy, as an excuse
61 Conrad's Lord
62 Actress Merkel
63 Movie production giant
64 Little green orb
65 Small buzzer
66 Conducted

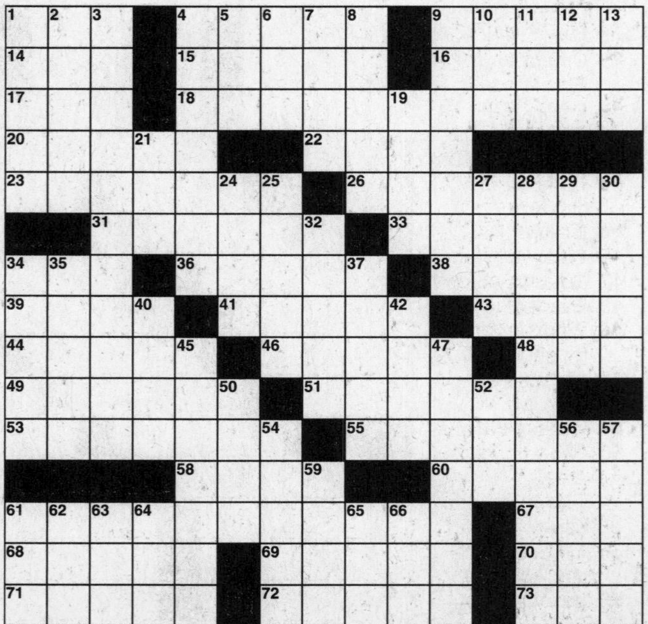

17 VEGETARIAN DIET

by David Davidson

ACROSS

1 Says further
5 "__ Old Cowhand"
9 Puccini opera
14 Urgent
15 Two-wheeled vehicle
16 Corn-oil products
17 Blabbed all
20 Repair videotape
21 Refrigerator-door device
22 Move aimlessly
23 Gear teeth
24 One glued to the tube
29 Bell and Barker
32 Initiation
33 I, to Claudius
34 Wine holder
35 Flabbergast
36 Harness races
38 Former Atlanta arena
39 Sharp-tasting
40 Spicy-tasting
41 Used diligently
42 Secret agent
43 Brats' weapons
46 Horse brake
47 Treasury Dept. agency
48 Fluttering trees
51 Unprincipled sort
55 Anne Bancroft film of 1964
59 Chorus member
60 Circus stage
61 Travel randomly
62 Mean-spirited
63 *The __ of Night*
64 Spectacular

DOWN

1 Billboard displays
2 Party spreads
3 Faucet flaw
4 Auction off
5 Martian feature
6 Got by
7 High-school course
8 Ultimate degree
9 Trinidad's partner
10 Designer Cassini et al.
11 Connery or Penn
12 Funnel shape
13 Aide: Abbr.
18 Easy to lift
19 Hams it up
23 Quitter's word
24 Prices
25 Ready to use
26 Loan shark's offense
27 Penny
28 Blows the whistle
29 '50s first lady
30 Lou Grant portrayer
31 Loses traction
34 Big name in guns
36 Religious belief
37 Horse color
41 Deputized group
43 Severe circumstances
44 Looking to add staff
45 Citrus fruit
46 Tend to an overgrown plant
48 Memo abbr.
49 Mets' stadium
50 Signing-ceremony needs
52 Give a hoot
53 On the summit
54 Jeansmaker Strauss
56 Opposite of post-
57 Tease
58 __ room (den)

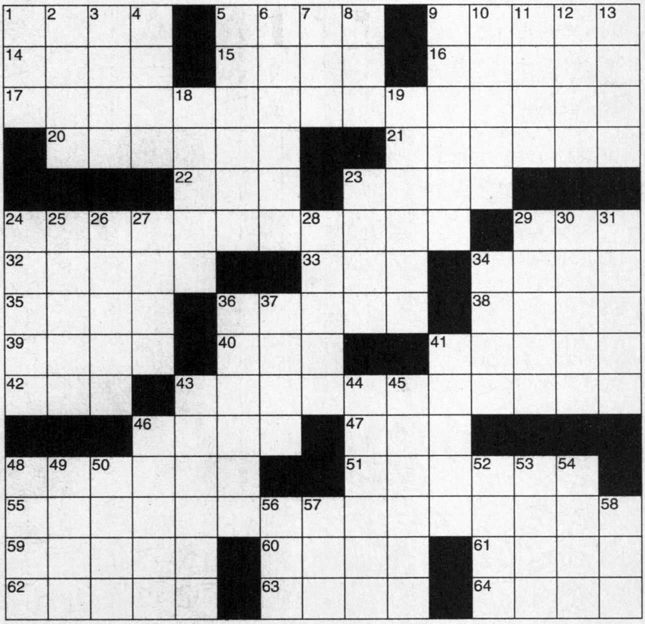

18 PLAYING THE MARKET

by Rich Norris

ACROSS

1 Powerful businessman
5 '97 Marlins, e.g.
11 High-school subj.
14 Pledge
15 NFL team
16 Heavy weight
17 Football strategies
19 Estimated-tax payee
20 Quaint motel
21 *Wheel of Fortune* purchase
22 Pay to play
23 Familiar literary figure
27 Chit
28 Help-wanted abbr.
29 Hungarian composer
30 Miami-__ county
32 Stored up
36 Summit
37 Suitable spot
38 "If __ a Hammer"
42 Physical one
44 Inlet
45 Role player
48 __ *Abner*
50 Kitten's cry
51 Boatswain or gunner
56 Came down to earth
57 Canoe paddle
58 CD-__
59 Type
60 Slave
65 Kicker's aid
66 Ready to roll
67 Singer Adams
68 Grads-to-be: Abbr.
69 *Seinfeld* character
70 Church passage

DOWN

1 Pigeon English?
2 Use a microwave
3 Disposition
4 Big beast, briefly
5 Debate side
6 Wise, so to speak
7 Islam's Almighty
8 "It don't __ thing . . ."
9 Richard of *Stir Crazy*
10 Former draft org.
11 Tenures
12 Aztec conqueror
13 Magazine filler
18 "__ upon a time, . . ."
22 Like lemon juice
23 Bathday cake
24 Reeves of *Speed*
25 Funny one
26 Pub pint
27 Actress Lupino
31 Take forcibly
33 Ludwig's lament
34 Geological ledge
35 Letter embellishment
39 Like Mom's apple pie
40 Declare
41 Morning condensation
43 "Are you a man __ mouse?"
45 Expects
46 Talk-show participant
47 Kids' wheels
49 Train line to NYC
52 Peter of Herman's Hermits
53 Ballroom dance
54 *Law &* __
55 Commandment word
60 1988 Hanks film
61 Actor's union: Abbr.
62 Palindromic preposition
63 Put the kibosh on
64 Vietnamese New Year

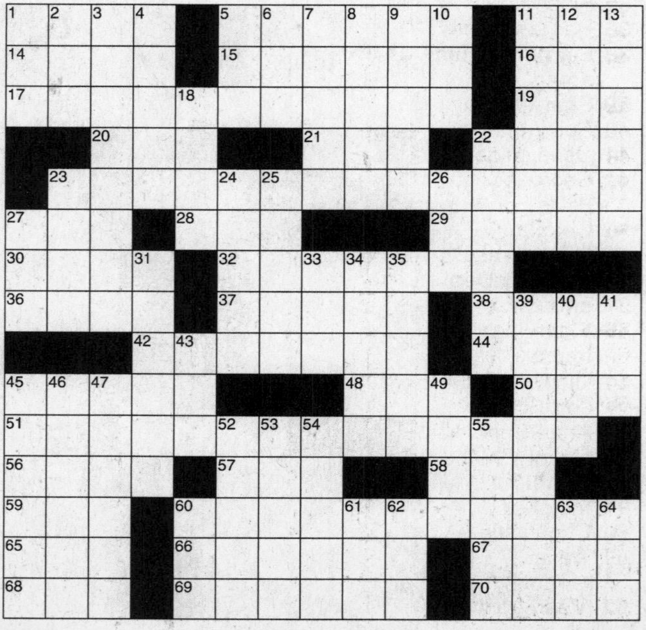

19 WHERE'S THE ENTRÉE?

by Rich Norris

ACROSS
1 Male sheep
4 Current unit
8 Support-group offshoot
14 Latin 101 word
15 Buck add-on
16 Traffic circle
17 Something simple
19 Infant's bed
20 Fireplace flakes
21 Period of youthful inexperience
23 Carter's successor
25 Greek philosopher
26 Massage
28 Process, as film
33 __ *homo* (behold the man)
37 Chart
39 Dodge
40 Cancels prior increases
44 Fire indicator
45 Title of honor
46 For fear that
47 Homeowner's clearance
50 One of the Dwarfs
52 Stinging insect
54 Sword holder
59 "Nothing to it!"
64 Stan's sidekick
65 Make
66 Personal taste, so to speak
68 Physician, for one
69 Actor Kristofferson
70 Goof up
71 Roy Rogers movies, e.g.
72 Panasonic rival
73 Q-U connection

DOWN
1 Traffic controllers' device
2 Entertain
3 Coffee flavoring
4 Poughkeepsie college
5 Gold: Sp.
6 Gehrig and Costello
7 November birthstone
8 Mysterious
9 Rule, as a kingdom
10 Just __ (not much)
11 Nothing, to Juan
12 Paris airport
13 Louis and Carrie
18 Beer barrel
22 Was in charge of
24 Without sensation
27 Sheep sound
29 Sinful
30 Shoe tie
31 Praiseful poems
32 Annoyer
33 Prefix for while
34 Robin Cook book
35 Backup cause
36 Part of BPOE
38 Mac alternatives: Abbr.
41 Bay-salt source
42 Young goat
43 Paid players
48 Hologram producers
49 Sixth sense, for short
51 Selective
53 Selects
55 Santa subordinate
56 Make changes to
57 Stadium levels
58 Tin Man's desire
59 Canyon phenomenon
60 Locale
61 Do an usher's job
62 Clinton alma mater
63 Continental prefix
67 Sewing-basket item

20 IT'S A PUZZLE

by Fred Piscop

ACROSS

1 Train for boxing
5 36 inches
9 Tots up
13 "Gay" city
14 Nobelist Wiesel
15 Romance lang.
16 Deck out
17 King of beasts
18 Actress Foch
19 Intense PR campaign
21 Hoofbeat
22 I love: Lat.
23 *The Pink Panther* star
25 Shouted out
30 Mauna __
31 United
32 Metal sources
34 Immigrant from Japan
38 Irving Berlin tune
42 Aromatic chemical
43 Ward of *Sisters*
44 From __ Z
45 *Platoon* setting
47 __ out (reached a low point)
50 The mold in Brie, e.g.
54 *Fortune 500* orgs.
55 *Bonanza* brother
56 Defender/ author Alan
62 Tiny parasite
63 "__ Plenty o' Nuttin' "
64 Sierra Nevada lake
65 __ *on the Fourth of July*
66 Walking stick
67 Chan portrayer Warner
68 Leave out
69 Hash-house side order
70 Racetrack quote

DOWN

1 Marquis de __
2 Urge
3 Satellite-dish ancestor
4 Change the title of
5 Cheerleader's routine
6 *Et* __ (and others: Lat.)
7 Runs amok
8 Washington of *Malcolm X*
9 Writer Upton
10 Serving a purpose
11 Lord's home
12 Insults, in a way
13 Actress Dawber
20 Element #5
24 Solo
25 Clinton's birthplace
26 Responsibility
27 Riga resident
28 Valentine's Day figure
29 Star in Cygnus
33 Normandy campaign town
35 Thailand, once
36 Novel suffix
37 Arrow Shirt rival
39 *West Side Story* building
40 Where Farsi is spoken
41 Devise, as a plot
46 *M*A*S*H* figures
48 Excessively affected
49 Ozzie Nelson's real first name
50 Stallone role
51 Distinct style
52 Word form for "father"
53 Fit for a king
57 Gossip queen Barrett
58 Crockpot concoction
59 "If __ a Hammer"
60 A whole bunch
61 Z, to a Brit

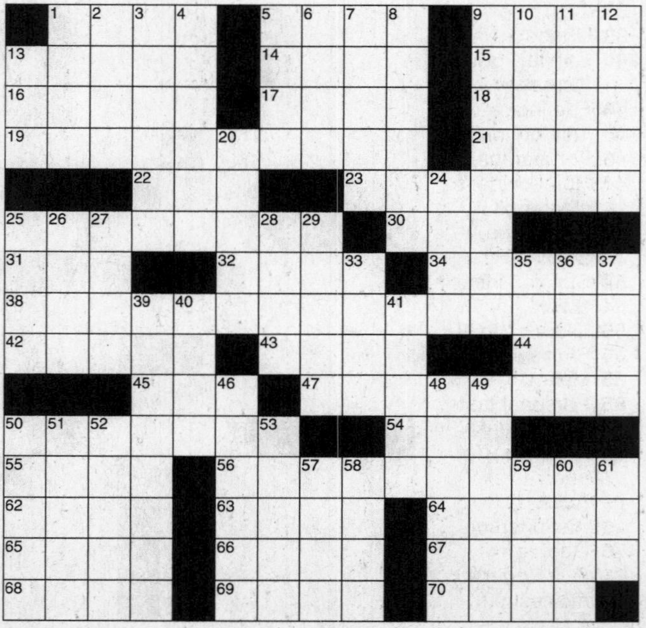

21 MONDAY MORNING QUARTERBACK

by Fred Piscop

ACROSS

1 Palindromic address
5 Dad
9 Fresh as a __
14 Bring to ruin
15 Smooth out
16 Word form for "straight"
17 Heed the drill sergeant
20 Do some tailoring
21 Samovars
22 "Common Sense" writer
23 Englander, for short
24 Arthur of tennis
25 Some college offerings
32 Senator Kefauver
33 German article
34 %: Abbr.
35 Slightly
36 Temporary trend
37 Sheet of ice
38 Dernier __ (latest fashion)
39 Raised platform
41 Tabriz native
42 Do a relay-race job
46 Choir voice
47 Evict
48 Ulan __
50 First-rate
51 Actress Charlotte
54 Creative logic
57 Bizarre
58 Bric-a-__
59 First name in fashion
60 Accumulate
61 Letter enc.
62 Like morning grass

DOWN

1 Command to a dog team
2 Heche or Rice
3 West of *Batman*
4 Floor-washing tool
5 Illinois city
6 "Let's go," in Rome
7 Cats and hamsters
8 Industrious insect
9 Former Winfrey rival
10 More bohemian
11 "Put __ writing!"
12 Blackjack dealer's device
13 Over there
18 Bailiwicks, slangily
19 Computer printer maker
23 Teaching deg.
24 Corrosive chemical
25 Fuzzy fruit
26 *Ad __ per aspera* (Kansas motto)
27 Wood coloring
28 Most insignificant
29 Egg-in-the-face sound
30 "Money-saving," in company names
31 Writer Gertrude
36 Inventory-control system, for short
37 College club
39 Actress Del Rio
40 TV workers' union
41 *The Wild Duck* dramatist
43 Receiving-department stamps
44 Uproars
45 Maria Shriver's mom
48 Oz creator
49 "__ boy!"
50 Gillette razor
51 Nettle
52 From square one
53 Like custard
54 Mauna __
55 Scale amts.
56 Sent down for

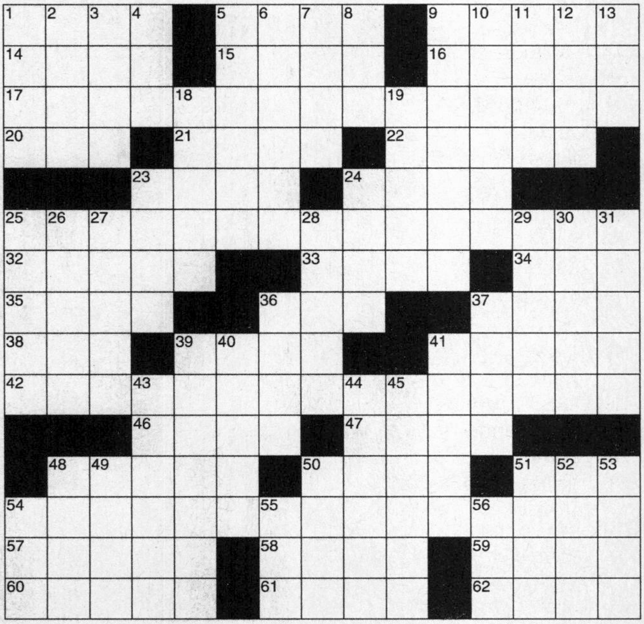

22 CALLING MRS. SPRAT

by Lee Weaver

ACROSS
1 Rile up
6 Henhouse
10 Busy bug
13 Comic actor Dudley
14 Fellow who sells space
16 Coffee server
17 Vigorous effort
19 Blaster's initials
20 Capital of the Bahamas
21 Skilled person
23 Goofs up
25 Fit to __
26 Raincoat
29 Country-club fees
31 Like some wits or cheeses
33 Canyon sound
35 Risk taking, for short
37 Set in
39 Biblical queendom
41 100%
42 Like marsh plants
43 Chopped
44 Jacob's wife
46 Take risks
47 Scarecrow stuffing
49 Fly in the ointment
51 Calculator figs.
52 Pueblo Indian
53 Arizona river
55 Tames, as a bronc
58 Arm art
62 Lummox
63 Art-gallery hanging
65 Turkish official
66 Take five
67 Chair builder, i.e.
68 *Krazy* __
69 Steak order
70 Tape over

DOWN
1 Solemn response
2 Vincent Lopez theme
3 Oodles
4 Notched, as a leaf
5 Just desserts
6 Horseless carriage
7 Music halls
8 Bridge expert Sharif
9 Ziti and cannelloni
10 Vegetable variety
11 Sea bird
12 Suffix for differ
15 Nor's partner
18 Spiritual advisors
22 Like some stockings
24 Flower part
26 Interlock
27 __ and pains
28 Have a gabfest
30 Tennis star Monica
32 Peter, in Spain
34 Titania's husband
36 Trolley sound
38 Creates batik
40 Laptop accessory
45 Caribbean republic
48 More cunning
50 Quick look
54 Fragrant oil
55 Head-over-heels
56 Singer Fitzgerald
57 Practice punching
59 Ike Turner's ex
60 Small bills
61 Folklore villain
62 Acorn product
64 Tomahawk

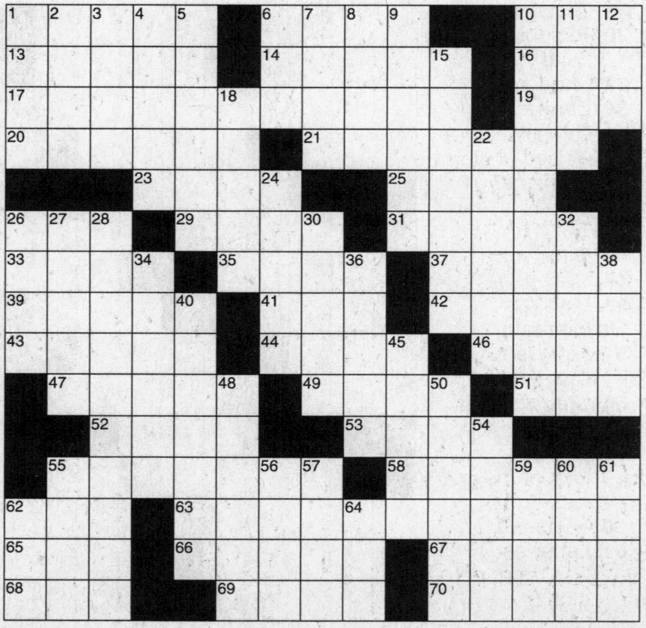

23 PLAYING DIRTY

by Fred Piscop

ACROSS

1 Mao __-tung
4 Hay units
9 Stick on
14 45 inches
15 Love, in Italy
16 Summa cum __
17 Intention
18 Composer Erik
19 Killer whales
20 Liven up the party, like a dirty baseball player?
23 It's divided by the Urals
24 Actor Liam
27 Go a few rounds
28 Hind part
31 Border
32 Period of history
35 Nasty
37 Wood-shop tool
38 Offer bargains, like a dirty hockey player?
41 Cockpit abbr.
43 Run away from
44 Poodle, e.g.
45 Arguable
47 Word form for "within"
49 Struggle for air
53 Go into a cocoon
55 Boxer Duran
58 Neaten the property, like a dirty football player?
61 Had one's say
63 Senator from North Carolina
64 Cent. parts
65 Computer-file acronym
66 Borden spokescow
67 Director Spike
68 Show as similar
69 Opt
70 Aurora's counterpart

DOWN

1 Picks on
2 Blow it
3 New York city
4 Army posts
5 Cremona violinmaker
6 Mandrake's partner
7 A Great Lake
8 Escape slowly
9 Unaccompanied
10 Mockeries
11 Purplish flowers
12 Wyo. neighbor
13 Failing-paper marks
21 Playwright Capek
22 Pro bono
25 Like an unmatched sock
26 Pince-__ glasses
29 Officiated at Shea
30 Sea: Fr.
33 WWII Brit. flyers
34 Out like a light
36 Cpl., e.g.
38 Faucet
39 Biddy
40 Provoked
41 Hi-fi component
42 Bud's buddy
46 *The Jazz Singer*, notably
48 Threat words
50 Sock style
51 Binaural
52 Sheriffs' helpers
54 Promotional link
56 Of a resistance unit
57 Surrounded
59 Amish pronoun
60 __ to pay (great trouble)
61 "My Gal __"
62 Air-pump letters

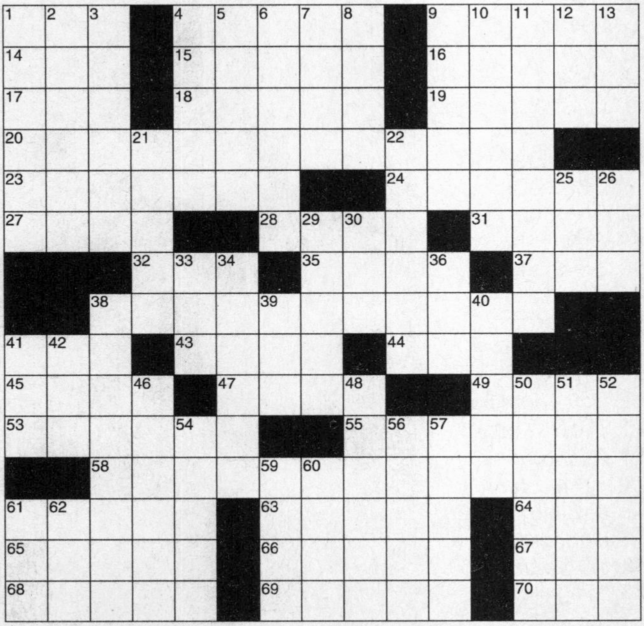

24 HIGHWAY ALERT

by Bob Lubbers

ACROSS
1 Dispense
6 Not that
10 "__ the night before . . ."
14 Knight shirt?
15 "Stop!"
16 Chaplin's wife
17 Lunch-stop alert
19 Russian river
20 Rocks, in a bar
21 Air out
22 Most basic
24 Conveyed title
26 Actor Albert
28 Mideast airline
30 Free time
34 Tiff
37 1996 Tony-winning musical
39 Wander off
40 Bulls, in Barcelona
42 Get it
43 Actress Hasso
44 Northern islander
45 Croat foe
47 Profits
48 Garden bloomer
50 Id
52 Arkin and Alda
54 Daniel and Debby
58 National song
61 Cambridge prep
63 NY summer setting
64 Local knowledge
65 Brake alert
68 Thought
69 "Sorry!"
70 Spooky
71 __ off (angry)
72 Aerie
73 Gave medication

DOWN
1 Tasty
2 Cost
3 TV host
4 "Smoking or __?"
5 Nonsense
6 Comparative word
7 Mary and Gary
8 Seine sight
9 Unvarying
10 Maps alert
11 Eroded
12 Literary collections
13 Old sailor
18 Chest liner
23 Out of kilter
25 Traffic flow alert
27 Changes
29 Abate
31 Prod
32 Carry on
33 "The __ of Texas . . ."
34 RBI, e.g.
35 Gondolier's propeller
36 Zone
38 Born: Fr.
41 Evening wrap
46 Dizzy Gillespie's bag
49 Delilah's wooer
51 Wished (for)
53 Oozes
55 Approaches
56 Comic Murphy
57 Fiery horse
58 Landed
59 Ecliptic intersection
60 Elm or oak
62 Try out
66 First to get socked?
67 Classic Olds

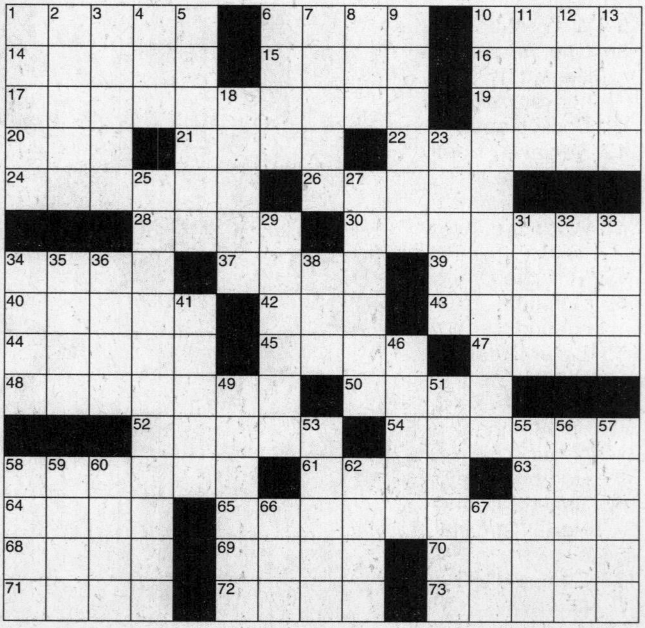

25 SAY IT WITH MUSIC

by Rich Norris

ACROSS
1 Pencil puzzles
6 Deeply engrossed
10 Knee-ankle connector
14 Texas mission
15 Design using acid
16 Corrida competitor
17 Kidnapper's missive
19 Charitable offering
20 Dead heat
21 Abound (with)
22 Brief period of subpar performance
24 *Pygmalion* playwright
25 Hingis rival
26 Toyota model
29 Square dance parties
33 Parting word in Spain
34 Indians or Braves
35 Delta House, e.g.
36 Prevaricator
37 Signals a cab
38 Capital of Peru
39 Kitchen add-on
40 Possessive pronoun
41 Bottle size
42 Dramatic reorganizations
44 Least at risk
45 Choice word
46 *Of __ and Men*
47 Villain's plan
50 Polio vaccine discoverer
51 Historic period
54 Breakfast chain, familiarly
55 Meeting place for the unattached
58 Postal district
59 Arkin of *Chicago Hope*
60 Shouts
61 Water pitcher
62 Loose garment
63 Work hard

DOWN
1 Shopping area
2 Jai __
3 Western writer Grey
4 Printer's measures
5 Gives comfort to
6 Agree to more issues?
7 Tiny particle
8 Interest amt.
9 Statements accepted as fact
10 Bread
11 Ship's area
12 __ *la Douce*
13 Like a busybody
18 One of a daily trio
23 Hula hoops, for one
24 Ball game official
25 Hockey objectives
26 Narratives
27 Archie's spouse
28 Cowboy's rope
29 Will designees
30 Compose, as a letter
31 Identifies
32 Get going
34 Brownish gray
37 Helped out vacationing friends, say
41 Toadies
43 Shade tree
44 Place for a cooling pie
46 Molten rock
47 Shoe box word
48 Eats
49 Improve, as skills
50 Unforeseen problem
51 Competent
52 Festive affair
53 Once, once
56 Altar agreement
57 Alter, as a hem

26 RIGHT AT HOLMES

by Patrick Jordan

ACROSS

1 Bambi, at first
5 Laundry
9 Cobra or copperhead
14 Garfield's nemesis
15 Vicinity
16 Gave comfort to
17 One of Judy's daughters
18 Persia, nowadays
19 Has a bawl
20 Sherlock Holmes accessory
23 Word before deck or dial
24 "You, over there!"
25 Flock females
26 Roofer's goo
27 Short Englishman?
28 SST or DC-10
31 Love, in Lyon
34 Ear-to-ear expression
35 It's played in chukkers
36 Sherlock Holmes accessory
39 Old Testament scribe
40 Limp as __ (flaccid)
41 Abbe and Nathan
42 Maiden name indicator
43 Literary figure
44 Affectedly modest
45 Cartoon collectibles
46 Collar type
47 Headed up
50 Sherlock Holmes accessory
54 LBJ, by birth
55 Inning sextet
56 James Bond's 46 Down
57 Licorice flavoring
58 Request for help
59 Barbershop call
60 More adorable
61 Pianist Hines
62 Prohibition supporters

DOWN

1 Pleats
2 "Toodle-oo, Toulouse!"
3 Shrink with age
4 Within reach
5 Eatery employee
6 Orderly grouping
7 Aquarium performer
8 Strong desire
9 Confidential matter
10 DEA officers
11 Largest continent
12 Stay fresh
13 Ames and Asner
21 Puppeteer Lewis
22 Hagman role, 1978-91
26 Albacore or bluefin
27 Director De Palma
28 Rivers or Lunden
29 End of a threat
30 Prepare the salad
31 Prayer finale
32 Hedge arrangement, perhaps
33 Foul-tempered fellow
34 Physics lab spinner
35 Stage production
37 Breaks down
38 Cheerlessness
43 *My Fair Lady* lyricist
44 Concerning a catalyst
45 Come to a halt
46 Alma __
47 Metric measure
48 Strong adhesive
49 Fender nicks
50 5 Down's offering
51 Sign over a theater door
52 Luau dance
53 Remain undecided
54 Tic-toe connection

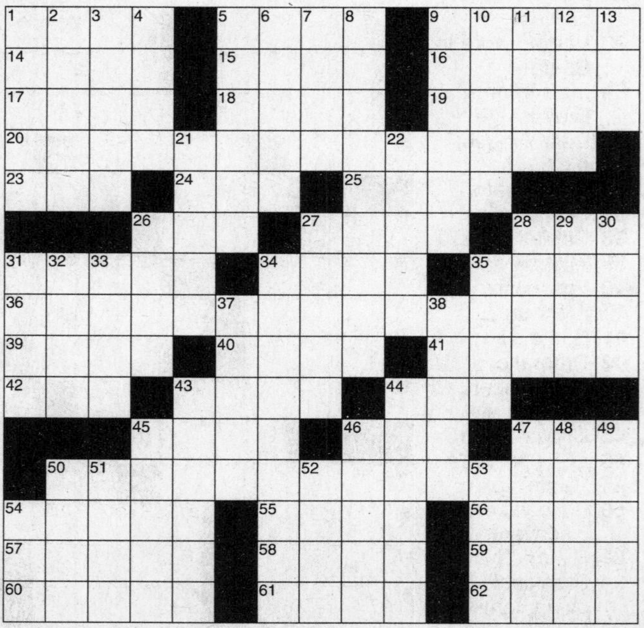

27 MESSED-UP MENU

by Fred Piscop

ACROSS

1 Walked nervously
6 Hood's knife
10 Big top
14 "It's __ country!"
15 Type size
16 Margarine
17 Sore loser's reaction
19 __ Bator
20 Calendar abbr.
21 Hit broadside
22 Sweet-tasting
24 Raring to go
26 Up to one's ears
28 Caress
29 Group of atoms
33 South Pacific republic
36 Way, way off
38 Trio trebled
39 Like some rural bridges
41 __ ceremony (was a stickler)
43 *__ of Two Cities*
44 Trumpet accessory
46 Hawaiian coffee center
47 In need of company
49 AT&T rival
51 Cohort of Doc
52 Tournament stage, for short
56 Music-score phrase
59 Caution sign
60 "Not __ bet!"
61 Mata __
62 Last ones in?
66 Sermon subject
67 Follow
68 Iroquois speakers
69 Rock star Jagger
70 Words of approximation
71 __-Coeur (French cathedral)

DOWN

1 Italian dish
2 Run __ of the law
3 Malevolent
4 Poetic adverb
5 Extent
6 Unwanted e-mail
7 Cheer starter
8 Road hazard
9 Feudal bondman
10 Tenacious one
11 Singer Fitzgerald
12 Within reach
13 Actor Curtis
18 Caner's material
23 __ HOOKS (sign on a crate)
25 Cause for crying, perhaps
26 Internists' org.
27 Most awful
30 Nullify
31 Trotsky of Russia
32 Sicilian volcano
33 Young stallion
34 Occupied with
35 Actress Harlow
37 __ fatale
40 Fable creator
42 Philadelphia school
45 Auto reversal, slangily
48 City north of Lisbon
50 Hags
53 Subject for Aristotle
54 Actress Stevens
55 Mosconi maneuver
56 "Beg pardon!"
57 *Rikki-Tikki-__*
58 Comic Idle
59 WWII town
63 Paddle
64 "My country __ of thee . . ."
65 Time period

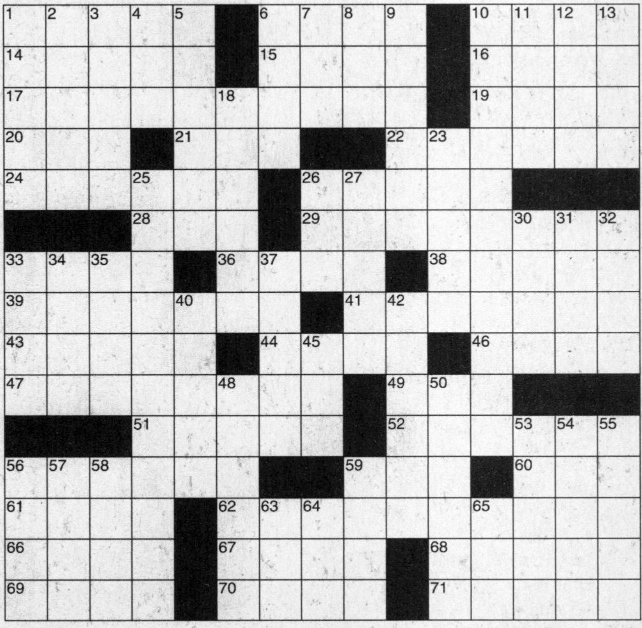

28 CAESAR'S LAW

by Bob Lubbers

ACROSS

1 Stair part
6 Gangster's gal
10 Spree
14 Wipe clean
15 Busy as __
16 Gen. Robert __
17 Discombobulating
19 Kelly or Tierney
20 Three __ match
21 Nastase of tennis
22 Use one's noodle
24 Tautened
26 Brief period
28 Lyric poems
30 Partied
34 GI offense
37 Singer McEntire
39 Banish
40 Turkic speaker
42 Flat fish
43 Where Basques live
44 Bishop's headdress
45 Ripening agent
47 Historical periods
48 Temporary fix
50 Raise (up)
52 Emits coherent light
54 Dudley Moore film
58 Bradbury beings
61 Head, in France
63 *A Chorus Line* finale
64 Hex
65 D.C. suburb
68 Aleutian island
69 Hebrides island
70 Greek writer
71 Olds oldies
72 Appear menacingly
73 British guns

DOWN

1 Transplant a seedling
2 Papas or Dunne
3 Transparent wrap
4 Sixth sense
5 Hinged (on)
6 Dress style
7 Theater awards
8 Author Deighton
9 Stowe villain
10 Trial commentator
11 Pub potations
12 Nevada city
13 Sharp
18 Church leader
23 Sprites
25 Pit of the stomach
27 Bedtime recitation
29 Mexican shawl
31 Truth-twister
32 Director Kazan
33 Family rooms
34 Dol. dispensers
35 Bide one's time
36 Palindromic name
38 Capture
41 Lear's daughter
46 Lasso
49 Set upon
51 Sports sites
53 Pool worker
55 Clydesdale, e.g.
56 Marriage
57 Harvests
58 Slightly open
59 Beer-label word
60 Division word
62 Test
66 Old card game
67 Investigator: Abbr.

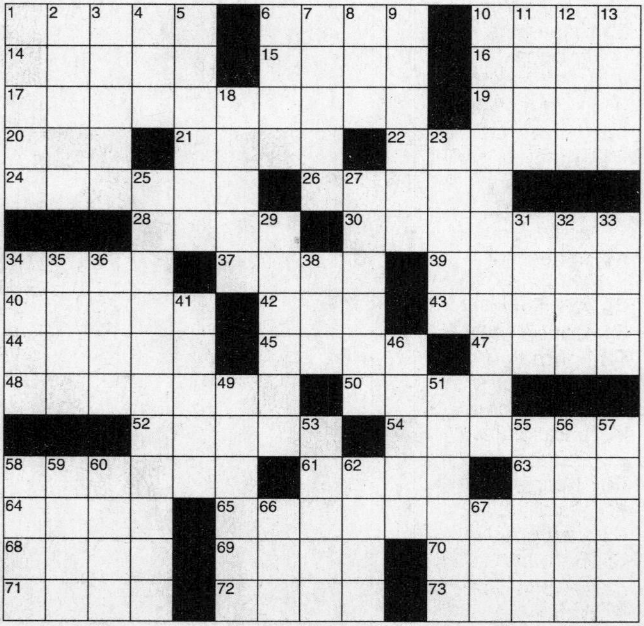

29 GENE KELLY FILMS

by Bob Lubbers

ACROSS

1 Tra follower
5 __ Rabbit (Harris character)
9 Slack-jawed
14 Algerian port
15 Learning method
16 Mideast heights
17 Classic of '41
20 Dig in
21 Columnist Barrett
22 Grammar concerns
23 Filmmaking unit
24 __ *Gotta Have It* (Spike Lee film)
25 Female honorific
28 Fr. holy women
29 Sounds of understanding
32 Overact
33 Draft drink
34 Pitcher Hershiser
35 Classic of '43
38 Osiris' wife
39 Molecule component
40 Grazing land
41 Average grade
42 ". . . __ o'clock scholar"
43 Large eel
44 "How sweet __!"
45 Praise
46 "On the double!"
49 Smooch
50 Bandleader Brown
53 Classic of '52
56 Take the helm
57 Center
58 Poet Pound
59 __ Haute, IN
60 Meadow moms
61 Chick's sound

DOWN

1 Earring site
2 Zone
3 Endure
4 Strong insect
5 Shields who played Susan
6 TV honcho Arledge
7 Singer James
8 Boxing off.
9 Nods
10 Ball dresses
11 "Oh, my!"
12 Peel
13 Means justifiers
18 Constitution drafter
19 Different ones
23 Bye-byes
24 Fulton's propellant
25 Army corpsman
26 Entertain
27 *The Many Loves of __ Gillis*
28 Attach, as a button
29 Red-headed ape
30 Hesitate
31 Trickier
33 Computer storage units
34 Filmdom's first Charlie Chan
36 Parcel out carefully
37 Awaken
42 Garb
43 Processes a check
44 Actress Stevens
45 European quart
46 "Hey, you!"
47 Ceremony
48 Unique thing
49 Be sure of
50 Loll about
51 The Auld Sod
52 Gingery cookie
54 Drink cooler
55 10-percenter

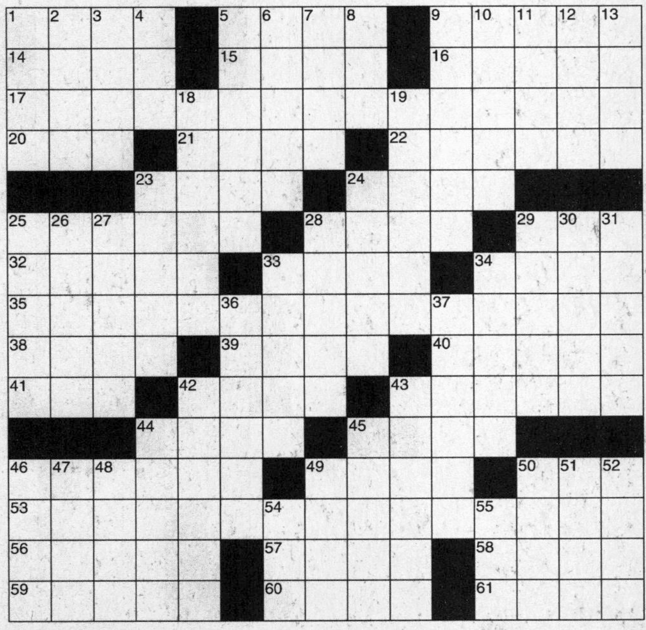

30 ONOMATOPOETIC

by Patrick Jordan

ACROSS

1 Gelatin shaper
5 Vaccine developer Jonas
9 Reducing resort
12 Tommie of baseball
13 Inventor's inspiration
14 Sign up for more issues
16 Heightened enforcement
18 Put on cloud nine
19 Daytime drama
20 Left suddenly
22 Profound
24 "And giving __, up the chimney . . ."
25 Motown or Polygram
28 Storch's *F Troop* role
31 Boxing official
34 Lupino and Tarbell
35 '40s pinup queen Betty
36 Lumberman's need
37 Mover's truck
38 Portable music maker
39 Gerard of *Buck Rogers*
40 Urge, with "on"
41 United nations
42 Survey
43 Tierra __ Fuego
44 Property claims
45 Enjoys the evening meal
46 Wild way to run?
48 Crystal-ball gazer
50 Felix Unger's quality
54 Rental agreements
58 "Fame" singer Cara
59 Warhol, for one
61 Brutish
62 Wrinkle remover
63 *Born Free* heroine
64 Fireplace residue
65 Necessity
66 Unkempt sort

DOWN

1 PC alternatives
2 Fairy-tale baddie
3 Sitcom producer Norman
4 Makes a choice
5 Move like a crab
6 Toil and trouble
7 Improper, in a way
8 *Citizen* __
9 Red-flowered garden plant
10 Folk-singer Seeger
11 Filled with reverence
14 Incorporate back into the city
15 *Sesame Street* cutie
17 Critic Pauline
21 Spain's king
23 Conditional release
25 Dwelt
26 Old saying
27 Asian nation
29 Street urchin
30 Mother superior
32 Force to leave
33 Topples
35 __ the wind (run quickly)
38 Hogwash
42 Seagoing thieves
45 Fawn or stag
47 In pristine condition
49 Spiral-horned antelope
50 "Proud Mary" singer Turner
51 Levin and Gershwin
52 Short drive
53 Miffed
55 Place to cool a pie
56 Exxon, formerly
57 Attempt
60 "The Tell-Tale Heart" author

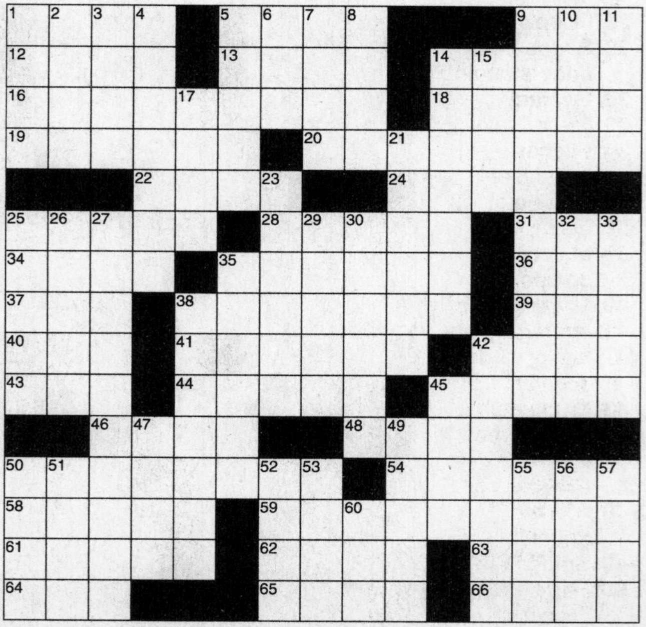

31 CUT IT OUT

by Norma Steinberg

ACROSS

1 Former Iranian ruler
5 House animals
9 Book of the Bible
13 Drab
14 Gen. Robert __
15 Slumber
17 First name in jazz singing
18 Breadth
19 Loren's husband
20 Survey taker's aid
22 Magazine edition
23 Former gas brand
24 Slither
25 Israeli dance
28 Lots
30 Malayan mammals
32 Sound from the pasture
33 Nixon chief of staff
37 Genie's boss
39 Come out even
41 Pastrami source
42 Part of a min.
44 *Simpsons* voice Julie
45 Auto racing org.
48 Germ
49 Fashionably loose
51 Racetrack advisor
53 Mockery
54 Eating implement
59 Driver's reversal
60 Vatican's city
61 DC workplace safety monitors
62 Sci-fi character
63 Valhalla bigwig
64 Skip
65 Snoozes
66 Garden annoyance
67 Use a keyboard

DOWN

1 On __ (experimentally)
2 Corridor
3 "__ want is a room somewhere . . ."
4 Pile
5 Mexican money
6 Texas border town
7 British café
8 Drop in the mailbox
9 Have hopes
10 Narrow escape
11 On edge
12 Organize
16 Dessert choice
21 Chef James
24 Dagger partner
25 Healthy
26 Moonstone
27 Equestrian equipment
29 DMV datum
30 Smidgen
31 Actress Spacek
34 Mrs. Shakespeare
35 Frosted
36 Teut.
38 Vital: Abbr.
40 Stays to the end
43 Part of CRT
46 Spies
47 Apartment sharer
49 Twirler's stick
50 Curaçao's neighbor
52 Overturn
53 Animal hair
54 Boast (about)
55 Whistle sound
56 "The Lord __ shepherd . . ."
57 Poker token
58 Actress Jackson

32 $$$$

by Patrick Jordan

ACROSS
1 Seeger or Sampras
5 Wheat bundle
10 Herringlike fish
14 Chopped down
15 __, *Dolly!*
16 One-dimensional object
17 Delicious dish
19 "__ boy!"
20 Inventor Whitney
21 Sacred chests
22 Throat feature
24 Unruffled
26 Toadstools and truffles
27 Give new meaning to
30 Autumn chill
33 Pompous people
36 Hollywood Blvd. crosser
37 Taj Mahal site
38 Adams or Kennedy
39 Cobbler's replacements
40 Secluded valley
41 Field of expertise
42 Barely gets by
43 Ranks contestants
44 Highway: Abbr.
45 Laborious effort
47 Seaside cities
49 How Harpo performed
53 Hindu deity
55 Part of a process
57 Status __
58 Singer Paul
59 *The Good Earth* novelist
62 Use a swizzle stick
63 Emulated a siren
64 Expose
65 Sound quality
66 Soaps star Slezak
67 Gravity-powered toy

DOWN
1 Looks inferior by comparison
2 Banish
3 Lukewarm
4 Sullivan and Wynn
5 Had in common
6 Mild oath
7 Antlered animals
8 Pub order
9 Chinese cookie ingredients?
10 Street talk
11 *Billboard* list item
12 Member of the opposition
13 Monty Hall offering
18 British buddies
23 United
25 Gladiator's workplace
26 Least coarse
28 Calls forth
29 Office clerk, sometimes
31 Made angry
32 Reviews unfavorably
33 Slightly open
34 Prepare the laundry
35 Graduate's parchment
37 Ten-percenter
39 Turn 7 into 42
43 Bisque and borscht
45 Directional suffix
46 Ferdinand's wife
48 Chicago hub
50 Social peer
51 "Filthy" money
52 Like some oxen
53 Seemingly limitless
54 Division word
55 Ranee's wrap
56 Arduous journey
60 Pt. of EEC
61 Gun pellets

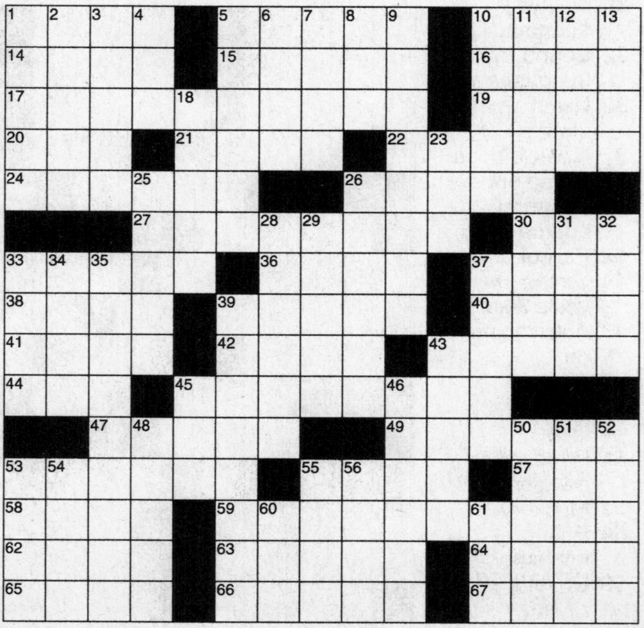

33 BACK TO SCHOOL

by Rich Norris

ACROSS

1 Cookbook meas.
4 Roof overhangs
9 Lhasa's land
14 Female sheep
15 Fissure
16 Frat quarters
17 Exactly what's expected
20 Poet Lazarus
21 Fragrance
22 Tombstone, Arizona's newspaper
26 Holy place
31 Fast flier: Abbr.
32 Unrefined one
34 Despotic ruler
35 Drummed out
37 New Haven collegians
38 Not relevant
42 Workweek-ending utterance
43 Form a queue
44 Make an accusation
47 Require
48 Rotation meas.
51 Derisive shouting
53 Accumulate
55 Medicine holder
57 James of jazz
58 Acted dignified
65 Safe place
66 Make it stick, so to speak
67 Actress Basinger
68 "My word!"
69 Flower part
70 USNA grad

DOWN

1 Conical homes
2 Everglades areas
3 Allow
4 Author Umberto
5 JFK posting
6 Large container
7 Sonic bounce
8 Timetables, briefly
9 Complex, as a predicament
10 Debtor's letters
11 Prickly seed casing
12 Sharp curve
13 Golf gadget
18 Lucrative, as a contract
19 Paint layer
23 Border (on)
24 Ritzy
25 Business-lunch locale
27 Move sneakily
28 After-bath application
29 Brigade
30 Ararat and Everest: Abbr.
33 Varnish ingredient
35 Put up for sale
36 Shore features
38 Look amorously at
39 Put in the archives
40 Borscht ingredient
41 Self-defense method
42 __ Mahal
45 Presumed truths
46 City near Tulsa
48 Shoot the scene again
49 Adds
50 Spurts of activity
52 Shows horror
54 Fam. member
56 Mythology, e.g.
58 "__ Loves You" (Beatles song)
59 Witch, to Shakespeare
60 Eggs
61 Unite in marriage
62 Swabber's need
63 One of the Gabors
64 Animation frame

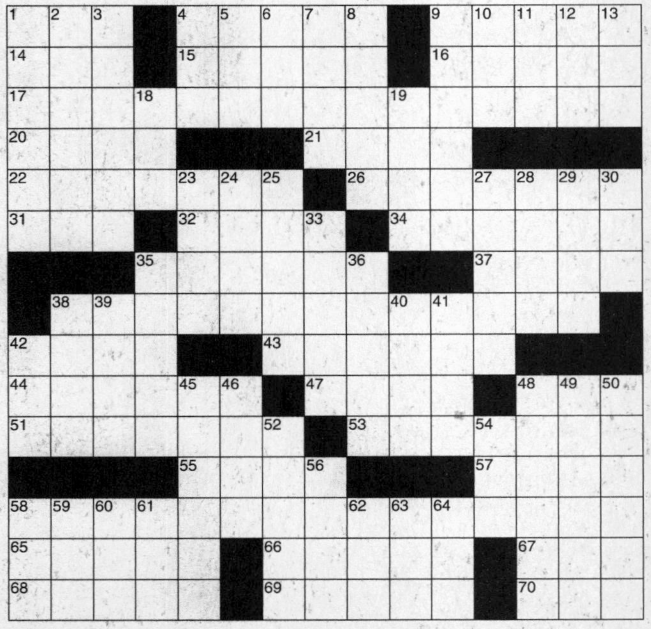

34

WING DING

by Bob Lubbers

ACROSS

1 Hale or Alda
5 City near Sacramento
9 Farm unit
13 "*Arriverderci* __"
14 Golf club
15 Bar seat
16 Curved part of a lamp
18 Bagel centers
19 Marked down
20 Rise up
22 Not fem.
25 More ticked
28 Petty quarreler
32 Torrential downpour
33 Son of Jacob
34 __ over (studied)
36 Howard or Reagan
37 Meat cut
38 Jazz pianist Hampton __
39 Mini-play
40 Eng. network
41 Peach __ (dessert)
42 Baseball great Pee Wee
43 '40s actor Jack and kin
45 CARE and CORE
47 Sports centers
48 Greek letters
49 Group of nine
51 Elfin
56 Make amends
58 Keen of sight
61 More factual
62 Gen. Robert __
63 Francis or Murray
64 Vittles
65 __-do-well
66 Low in fat

DOWN

1 Jason's ship
2 Diving bird
3 Famous cookie baker
4 Shuttle group
5 One-dimensional
6 Mine find
7 Disney dwarf
8 Signs, as a contract
9 Musically keyless
10 Abruptly
11 Caviar
12 '97 PGA champ Ernie
15 Didn't hoard
17 Playwright Rice
21 Ocean movements
23 Part of a flower's calyx
24 Lever of a sort
26 Concern for self
27 Edouard's earnings
28 Pacific discoverer
29 Barometric line
30 Lose one's nerve
31 Barbie's boyfriend
35 Attain
38 German author Hermann
39 DC legislator
41 Nastier
42 WWII riveter
44 __ glory (elated)
46 Painter's tool
50 High-schooler
52 Blue shade
53 Actress Daly
54 Olin or Horne
55 Paradise
56 Chowed down
57 Song syllable
59 Pub serving
60 "Golly!"

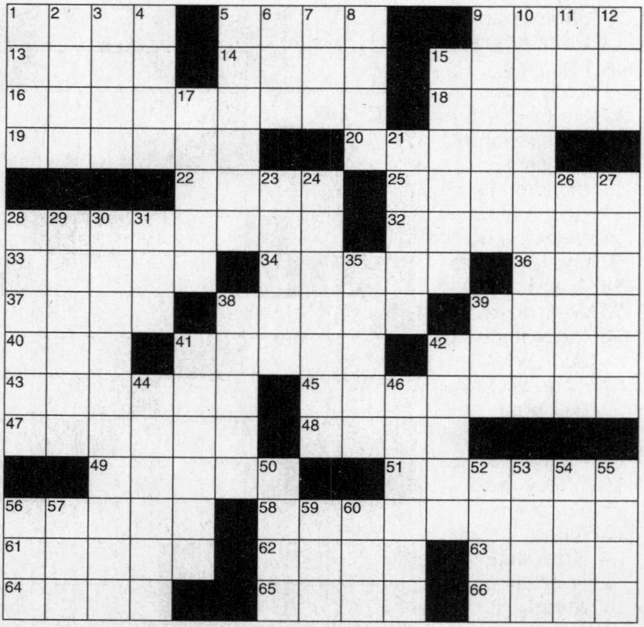

35 HOME SWEET HOME

by Lee Weaver

ACROSS
1 Puts in stitches
5 Walking speed
9 Long-ago days
13 Chowder ingredient
14 Rolls up, as a flag
16 Turkish official
17 Norway's capital
18 Fabric
19 Opposed to
20 Goes for a stroll
22 Certain raffle reward
24 Greek cheese
26 Prepare to propose, perhaps
27 Soaring aloft
29 Ready for a nap
33 Worldwide workers' grp.
34 Ruffled feathers
37 Bring together
38 Pulls along behind
40 Carpenter's tool
42 Chew like a beaver
43 Fish holder
45 Wealthy one
47 Members of the AMA
48 Section of New York City
50 Trunks
52 Hanger-on
55 Feline remark
56 Nightclub entertainment
60 Prescription amounts
63 Humdinger
64 Boring tool
66 Asian cuisine
67 Help a felon
68 Flat and tasteless
69 Party giver
70 Beer barrels
71 Puts a stop to
72 Tapered sword

DOWN
1 Coal boat
2 Famous lioness
3 Shy person
4 Fire-prevention bear
5 Sgt.'s trainee
6 New Year's Eve word
7 Swindler
8 Rocker John
9 Throughout 1998, e.g.
10 Word form for "all"
11 "Puttin' on the __"
12 Buffalo's lake
15 Tear in little pieces
21 Mix the batter
23 Lima's country
25 Blue dye
27 Plant life
28 Secluded valley
30 Browse from outside
31 Telescope sights
32 Evergreens
33 Desire
35 Zsa Zsa's sister
36 Something owed
39 Causes for SRO signs
41 Weaver's tool
44 Sly look
46 Raised racehorses
49 Scenery around Taos
51 Apply balm to
53 Coal passage
54 Golf great Ben
56 Clamorous criticism
57 Auto-service job
58 Designer Cassini
59 Join, as metals
61 Smooth the way
62 Building location
65 Domicile: Abbr.

36 NATIONALISM

by Fred Piscop

ACROSS

1 Long-tailed parrot
6 Guitarist Atkins
10 "Long, Long __"
13 Lower in prestige
14 Common Market prefix
15 Dry as dust
16 Ballroom dance
18 Church section
19 Villa d'__ (Italian landmark)
20 Congers
21 Ambitionless one
22 Spouse's assent
24 Altar words
25 *Medical Center* star
31 "Me too!"
35 Digs up
36 __ *Jury* (Spillane novel)
37 Bird-feeder filler
39 Two-dimensional measure
40 Most meager
42 Scornful look
43 Place for fine dishes
46 12-mo. periods
47 More easily understood
52 Pizza perimeter
55 Stable newborn
57 "Merry old" king of rhyme
58 Clinton cabinet member
59 Road-sign ad sponsor of yore
61 Getting __ years
62 "Right away" letters
63 Tiny openings
64 Favorite
65 Hair goos
66 *Cabaret* director Bob

DOWN

1 Pal, to a Britisher
2 Treat badly
3 Grocery-store vehicles
4 Popped the question
5 Like Willie Winkie
6 Et __ (and so forth)
7 Toss
8 Cupid, to the Greeks
9 Preschooler
10 Asian inland sea
11 United Way request
12 Frankfurt's river
15 From a tiny European nation
17 Slangy "sure!"
21 Flash of inspiration
23 Environmental prefix
24 Currier's partner
26 Because of
27 Come to a conclusion
28 Raison d'__
29 You, once
30 Pre-1917 autocrat
31 Phonograph record
32 Where to scratch
33 Bangkok resident
34 "Charge of the Light Brigade" poet
37 Parts of mins.
38 Immigrant's course: Abbr.
41 Small pie
42 Fr. holy woman
44 Rascals
45 Scat queen Fitzgerald
48 "Gesundheit!" preceder
49 Crowd noises
50 Santa's subordinates
51 Singer Della
52 Farm yield
53 Philosopher Descartes
54 Condo division
55 Weld
56 Spoken exam
59 Sack
60 Tanning-lotion letters

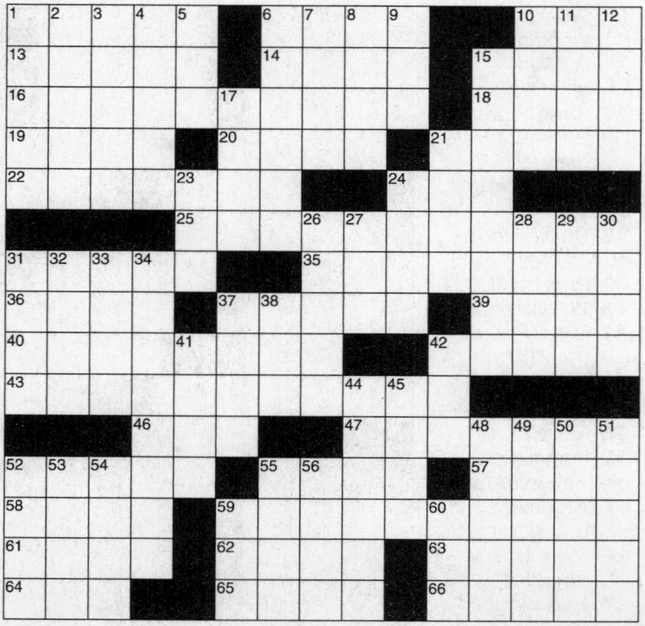

37 AVENUES OF SUCCESS

by Rich Norris

ACROSS

1 Ear part
5 Without equal
9 Valuable quality
14 Working hard
15 Not carefully considered
16 Blender setting
17 Former Iranian monarch
18 Bear up there
19 Photograph, for one
20 Educational TV show
23 Actress Dunne
24 Solves, in a way
28 Sharp curve
29 Melt
33 Fixes Junior's laces
34 Desert destination
36 One of the Brontës
37 Onetime comic strip
42 Antidrug cop
43 Musical paces
44 Novelist Leonard
47 Per __ (daily)
48 CIA forerunner
51 Quality-control personnel
53 Soak in the tub
55 1949 Joan Crawford film
59 Bizet creation
62 Singer Adams
63 Robin Cook bestseller
64 Former Knicks coach Pat
65 Ash Wednesday starts it
66 Panache
67 Athletic events
68 Vietnam neighbor
69 Reading rooms

DOWN

1 TV dog
2 Additional people
3 Prejudgments
4 Actor Hawke
5 Test answer
6 Galley propellers
7 "Hey, you!"
8 Archaeological fragment
9 Each
10 Aggregate
11 Madrid Mrs.
12 Brain scan: Abbr.
13 Golf gadget
21 Words of agreement
22 Suffix for mountain
25 Eat well
26 Start of a counting-out rhyme
27 Compass dir.
30 *2001* computer
31 __ were (so to speak)
32 Partner of dined
35 Eighteen-wheeler
37 Festive affair
38 Sleeve fillers
39 Having beaten the rap
40 Imitate
41 Backbreaking dance
42 Bottom line
45 Passes along
46 Baseball stat
48 *My Favorite Year* star
49 Tribal magician
50 Family cars
52 Get a whiff of
54 Took a circuitous path
56 Invention beginning
57 El __ (Pacific Ocean current)
58 Obtains
59 Assn.
60 Singer Zadora
61 Shade tree

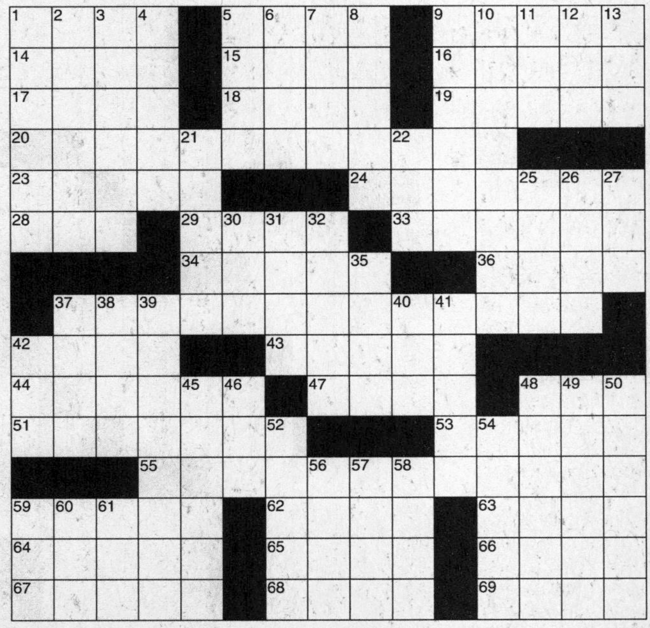

38 KNOCKING AROUND

by Frances Hansen

ACROSS

1 Break the rules
6 Overcook the meat
10 Svelte
14 *It Happened One Night* director
15 Zeus' consort
16 Toothpaste holder
17 Raps
20 Chest muscle, for short
21 Flying stinger
22 Guarantees a pension
23 Walk in water
24 Does a farm job
26 Peggy Lee song
29 County subdivision
33 Have __ with (know well)
34 Pianist Claudio
35 "All the Things You __"
36 Raps
40 Inhabitant: Suff.
41 Charge
42 Word form for "fire"
43 Riffraff
45 A real hound
47 Organic compound
48 Vaulter's aid
49 "__ woman never yields . . .": Stendhal
52 Cotton cloth
53 Go before the camera
56 Raps
60 Bathday cake
61 Bit of burlesque
62 Erin of *Happy Days*
63 Scot toppers
64 Consecrated
65 Noisy inhalation

DOWN

1 Initials on Sputnik
2 __ Krishna
3 Grist for DeMille
4 Give weapons to
5 Seat of the Kuomintang
6 Comic Chevy
7 Second Beatles film
8 Rainbow shape
9 Bowl yell
10 Accent
11 Big galoots
12 "Oh, sure!"
13 Military meal
18 Bubkes, in Barcelona
19 Broad way
23 Decrease
24 Lots of people
25 Man __ (racehorse)
26 Earvin Johnson's nickname
27 Baker or Bryant
28 Phileas Fogg portrayer
29 Vestige
30 '80s Secretary of State and kin
31 Actress Papas
32 Little bird
34 __ *of Divorcement* (Hepburn's first film)
37 Small piano
38 Woody's boy
39 Metalworker's aid
44 __ *Fables*
45 Broadway stinkeroo
46 Causes concern
48 High fidelity?
49 Rt.-hand person
50 "Hold it!"
51 Midmorning
52 Ex-Yankee Rizzuto
53 Flier's word form
54 Movie mogul
55 Outdoor accommodation
57 Sibilant silencer
58 Ring decision
59 Long time

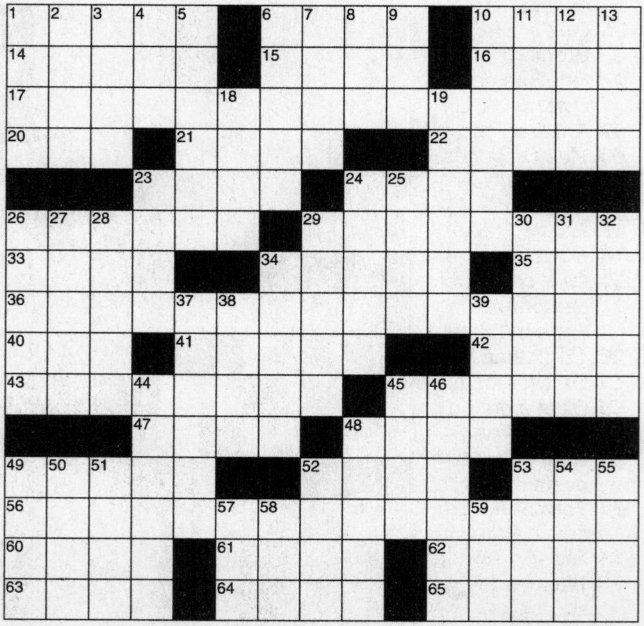

39 REPTILIAN

by Rich Norris

ACROSS
1 Balsa vessels
6 La __ (Italian opera house)
11 Used to be
14 D-sharp equivalent
15 Biblical peak
16 Chemical ending
17 Paul Hogan role
20 Fraidy-cat
21 Rapunzel feature
22 Pop the question
24 Inventor Nikola
27 Italian wine region
28 Office furniture
31 Lawyers' grp.
33 Countdown starter
34 Bring into play
36 Gather together
38 Mottled inlay material
42 Some turns
43 Proclaim
45 Acorn source
48 RR stop
49 Brazilian dance
50 Unravel, as rope fiber
52 Walkway material
56 Sort of: Suff.
57 Savage
59 Round the bend too fast
62 Treacherous one
67 Have lunch
68 Societal no-no
69 Choir members
70 Literary monogram
71 Trap
72 Title documents

DOWN
1 VCR function: Abbr.
2 Continent south of Eur.
3 Attends in hordes
4 Tijuana treat
5 Put away
6 Talia of *Rocky*
7 Winter maladies
8 Exist
9 Took command of
10 Border (on)
11 Most sprawling
12 "__ Fideles"
13 Escorts
18 "Can't Help Lovin' __ Man"
19 Powerful D.C. lobby
22 Summer quaff
23 E-mailed
25 Unconvincing, as an excuse
26 Cause embarrassment to
29 Malden or Marx
30 Locations
32 Fireplace flakes
35 Storage areas
36 Beast of burden
37 Flu preventers
39 Type of type: Abbr.
40 Cover with clear plastic
41 Attorneys' degs.
44 Morse code sound
45 Compensate for
46 Playing fields
47 Jujitsu relative
51 Talk too much
53 Role player
54 Sierra Nevada resort lake
55 Poet's preposition
58 __ *Make a Deal*
60 "Zounds!"
61 Perry's creator
63 Scottish John
64 Hoop grp.
65 Turf
66 Former draft org.

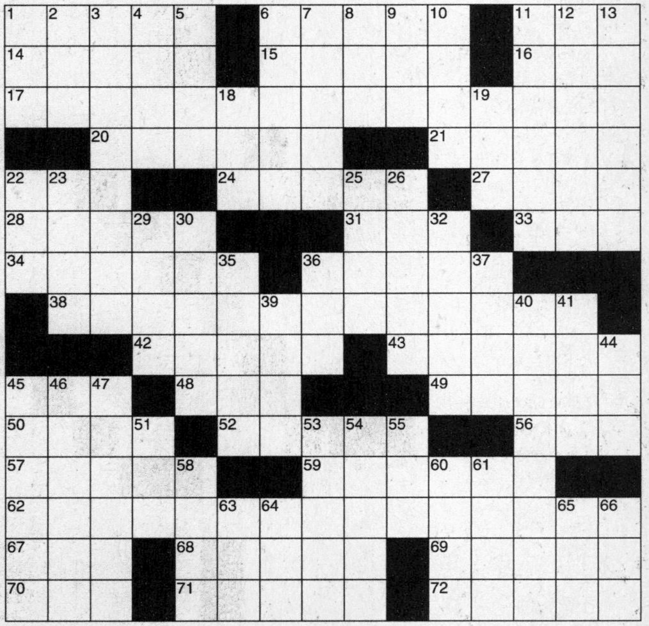

40 BIG FOUR

by Herbert Lyle

ACROSS
1 Select
5 Insertion mark
10 Man from Dundee
14 Eastern Indian
15 Worship
16 Big book
17 Vaudevillian
20 Unified
21 Ill humor
22 Public
23 Pine Tree State
25 Cupidity
27 Pure
29 Gwyneth's former beau
30 "__ bin ein Berliner"
33 Desi's daughter
34 Torments
35 Road-service agcy.
36 Rock group?
37 __ de menthe
38 Agitated state
39 Scale note
40 Irish county
41 Brit's filament
42 Supplement, with "out"
43 Tries to get elected
44 Noblemen
45 Kind
47 Moses' spy
48 Temporary currency
50 Stable fare
51 Do garden work
54 On a spree
58 Half of M.A.
59 Confused fight
60 Was imitative
61 Amusing Martha
62 Takes a look
63 Military meal

DOWN
1 Monterrey money
2 Mill material
3 Gossip-column subject
4 Beer barrel
5 Popular pet
6 Confuse
7 Took a bus
8 Period
9 Half a score
10 Canyon or Martin
11 Billing for a funnyman
12 Actor Sharif
13 Oasis abode
18 Have __ (nosh)
19 Fordham females
24 Without change
25 Wash problem
26 Appraise
27 Shut up
28 Impresario Sol
29 Max, Buddy, and "Bugs"
31 Terrier type
32 Can't stand
34 Ad name
37 Whodunit board game
38 Progenitor
40 Moved slowly
41 Less than faithful
44 Soaks in the tub
46 Dishwasher cycle
47 Feed a party
48 Practice punching
49 Singer Irene
50 Impolite look
52 Is obligated to
53 Where hairs may split
55 Bad boy
56 Born: Fr.
57 Campbell's lid

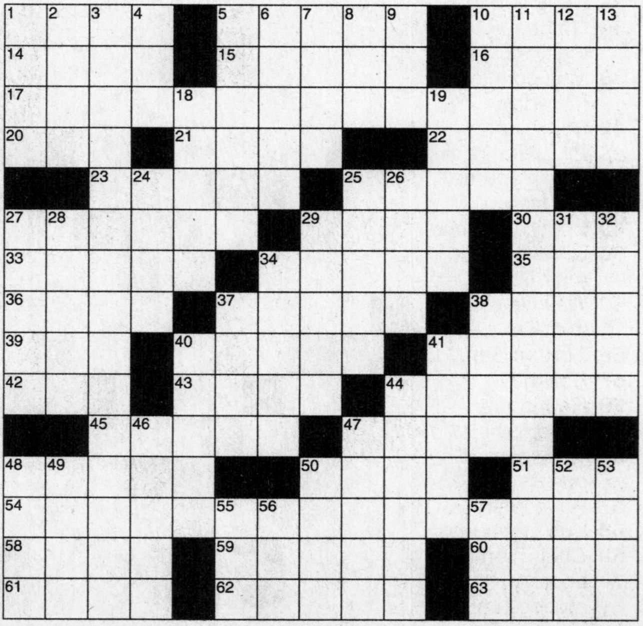

41 IRE EDUCATION

by Richard Silvestri

ACROSS
1 Rum cake
5 Manager's special
9 Burns' "sweet" stream
14 Latin 101 word
15 Wicked
16 Newswoman Sawyer
17 Like an angry clockmaker?
19 Rhymester Nash
20 Yoko __
21 Narrow street
22 Get a lungful
23 Like skim milk
25 Turned on again
27 News clipping
29 Caller
33 Take a sip
36 Creative spark
38 Temporary superstar
39 Help in a heist
40 Put right
41 Steffi of tennis
42 Vegetable spread
43 Booty
44 Process ore
45 + & #
47 *Casa* room
49 Inventor Howe
51 Harass
55 __ Island, NY
58 In a bit
60 Log splitter
61 Eyelashes
62 Like an angry ironworker?
64 Rags-to-riches author
65 Designer von Furstenberg
66 Portend
67 All geared up
68 Show flexibility
69 Russian city

DOWN
1 Twirler's tool
2 __ acid (protein component)
3 Breakfast meat
4 Make inquiries
5 Composed
6 Stratford's river
7 The Birdman of Alcatraz was one
8 Keebler worker
9 Hunk
10 Like an angry soldier?
11 Fake fanfare
12 "The __ lama . . ."
13 State bird of Hawaii
18 Delight
22 Homeric work
24 Like an angry escape artist?
26 Occurrences
28 Champagne cocktail
30 Ran fast
31 Face shape
32 Huge amount
33 New Mexico town
34 With skill
35 Have the looks of
37 __ volente
40 Bushed
44 Jargon
46 Infamous cow owner
48 Teem
50 NCO, familiarly
52 Swamp critter
53 Ooze out
54 Drive back
55 Lasting impression
56 Finish the bathroom
57 Aquatic plant
59 Marshal Kane's deadline
62 Fly catcher
63 Cable network

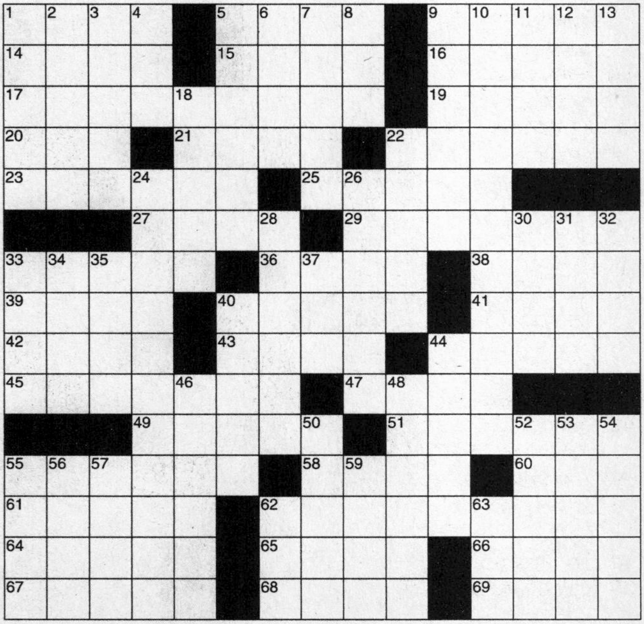

42 MEET THE BUMSTEADS

by Fred Piscop

ACROSS

1 "Voila!"
5 Hawaiian carving
9 Like many bleacherites
14 Frankenstein's assistant
15 Cassini of fashion
16 Actress Verdugo
17 BLONDIE
20 *Full Metal Jacket* setting
21 Follower of Lao-tzu
22 Ridiculous
26 "Smoking or __?"
27 Watch Junior
30 DAGWOOD
33 Fad disk
34 Pied Piper follower
35 Potato pancake
36 Sit-in participant
40 Word form for "eye"
43 Big goon
44 Bribe
47 COOKIE
52 Yodeler's perch
53 Took the reins
54 Bits of saber-rattling
55 Remove, as a splinter
58 Western treaty grp.
59 ALEXANDER
65 Ain't right?
66 Close at hand
67 Singer Adams
68 *Hollywood Squares* regular
69 Sporty cars of yore
70 Metric prefix

DOWN

1 Soft metal
2 Improve, as beef
3 Tony Blair's street
4 Indo-Europeans
5 *High* __ (Anderson play)
6 Kind
7 Retained
8 Galapagos critter
9 Start anew, as a relationship
10 Priestly garb
11 Scrams
12 Bed-and-breakfast
13 Pop
18 Skip over
19 Time for lunch
22 Fuse word
23 __ Canals
24 Infamous emperor
25 Middle of QED
28 "That's gross!"
29 Everyday article
31 Prepare vegetables
32 Armed conflict
36 Arafat's org.
37 Ball game
38 Primer pooch
39 New Age musician John
40 Son-gun link
41 BTU relative
42 A whole bunch of
44 By the shore
45 Horse's tidbit
46 WWII boats
48 Appear to be
49 Shaping wood, in a way
50 Walked on
51 Brought up
56 Proceed along
57 The way out
59 Gal of song
60 Like some humor
61 Freudian topic
62 Some A.L. players
63 Diminutive suffix
64 Mauna __

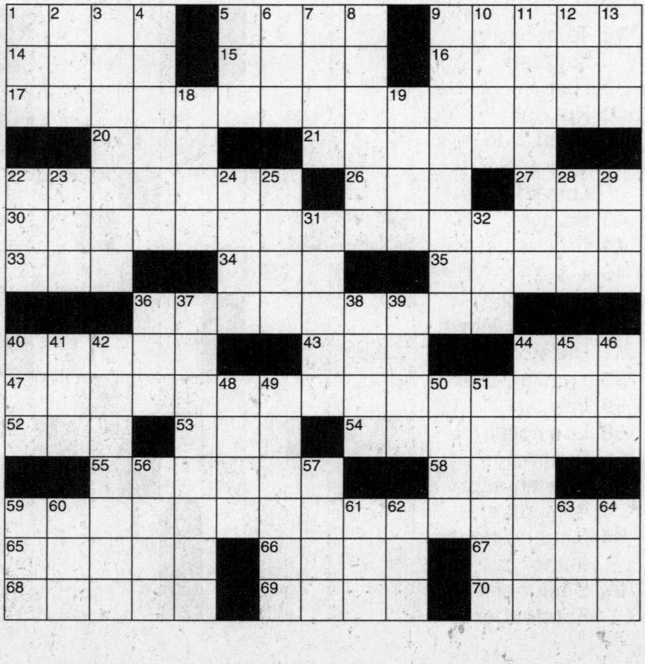

43 RINGERS

by Bob Lubbers

ACROSS

1 Ore. neighbor
6 Choreographer de Mille
11 WWII craft
14 Spanish province
15 Fortunetellers
16 "Eureka!"
17 Hotel employee
19 Still
20 Marked with stripes
21 Certain
22 Swiss peak
25 Canoe propeller
26 Tunnel-building soldier
28 Tub toy
30 Gambles
33 Public transports
34 Bela of *Dracula*
36 Edmonton athlete
38 Romantic situation
43 Indian princess
44 Aviator Earhart
45 Beefy bovine
48 Science magazine
50 River blockers
51 Eye layer
53 Explorer Johnson
55 Christmas or New Year's
56 "I __ my wit's end!"
57 Proclaims loudly
61 __ Palmas, NM
62 '70s version of *Amateur Hour*
66 Summer, in Soissons
67 Allude (to)
68 Useful
69 Angler's need
70 Cosmetician Lauder
71 Curvy turns

DOWN

1 Taxi
2 St. crosser
3 __ *Abner*
4 Troubles
5 Ipso __
6 Hope (to)
7 __ load of (notice)
8 Tidy
9 Lake Indians
10 Employee's ID, often
11 Easy baskets
12 Actress North
13 Spuds
18 Fiery steed
21 Showed disdain toward
22 Qualified
23 Vulgarian
24 Geraldine or Patti
27 Off midships
29 Flood
31 Carved pole
32 Knight's title
35 Entrap
37 Connection
39 Zodiac sign
40 Happy
41 Peruvian capital
42 Not very challenging
45 Bluff climber
46 Salad ingredient
47 Wiped away
49 "__ Mr. Nice Guy!"
52 Sore spots
54 Debate
58 Took off
59 Writer James
60 Fast planes
62 Three: It.
63 Towel inscription
64 Bullfight cheer
65 Director Craven

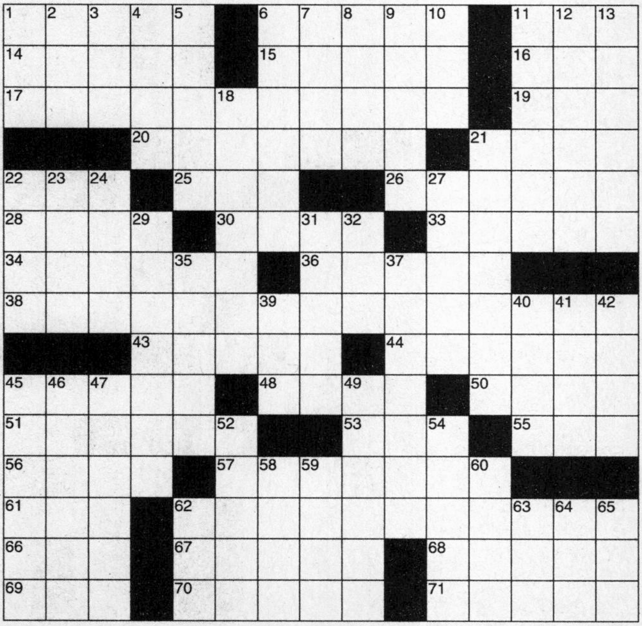

44 UNDER PRESSURE

by Brendan Quigley

ACROSS

1 Legal scholar
7 Mythical bird
10 Burn to a crisp
14 Popular record label
15 Yes: Fr.
16 Residence
17 Autumnal door decoration
19 Writer Hunter
20 Close fit
22 Half a dance name
25 6th-century date
26 Wood connector
27 Popular candy bar
32 Hitting the right notes
33 Reagan Secretary of State
34 Satire magazine
37 Kids' cereal
38 Fingerprint part
40 U2 lead singer
41 German article
42 *Grapes of Wrath* name
43 Inert gas
44 Puppy love, perhaps
47 Going on, to Sherlock
50 Ship's heading: Abbr.
51 DiCaprio, to pals
52 Side dish
57 RBI, e.g.
58 Dishes at an Egyptian restaurant
62 Author Morrison
63 Sorority letter
64 New Orleans school
65 State of irritation
66 Do better than
67 Linger

DOWN

1 __ alai
2 Decorative vase
3 Get free (of)
4 "__ bigger than a breadbox?"
5 With solemnity
6 Confuse
7 Carrot, for one
8 Couple's pronoun
9 Five, in France
10 Comic Marin
11 Float in the air
12 Dazzle
13 Extend, as a lease
18 In fashion
21 Ocean rescuers: Abbr.
22 20 fins
23 Painter Matisse
24 Invite to join
28 Nickname for a cowboy
29 '70s sitcom
30 '50s Mideast initials
31 Zip
34 Business biggie
35 Win by __
36 Hawaiian crooner
38 Despair
39 Harrison, in *Star Wars*
40 "It's freezing!"
42 Ballerina's leap
43 Gets the better of
44 Small bird
45 African antelopes
46 Makes into law
47 Aides: Abbr.
48 Thin mattress
49 Man from Muscat
53 Proof of purchase: Abbr.
54 Big Apple neighborhood
55 Funny comment
56 Oahu dance
59 For example
60 Rock producer Brian
61 Lott, for one: Abbr.

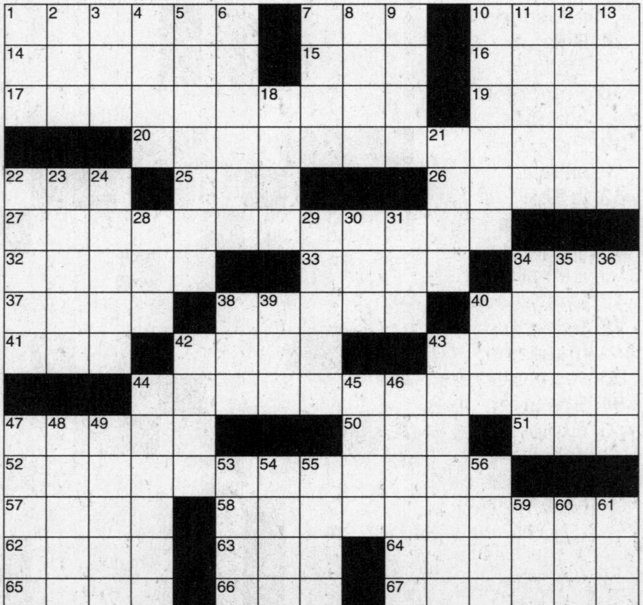

45 GETTING THERE

by Rich Norris

ACROSS

1 Glow
5 Metabolism descriptor
10 Walking stick
14 Grouch
15 "__ Entertain You"
16 Some time ago
17 Financial independence, so to speak
19 Banquet, e.g.
20 Reduce drastically, as prices
21 Blocking progress
23 Plastic wrap
26 Actor Mineo
27 Commercially popular
30 That girl
31 Gives an autograph
35 News org.
36 Sgt., for one
38 Home entertainment purchase
39 Politically moderate
43 Lined up
44 Chinese principle
45 Depot: Abbr.
46 Commuter's problem
47 The word, maybe
49 Sea plea
50 Helium, for one
52 Gold or silver
54 *Daily Planet* employee
58 Protuberances
62 Part of MIT
63 Well-traveled route
66 Run away
67 Bert's pal
68 Rubik of cube fame
69 Observer
70 Copter component
71 Stock-exchange membership

DOWN

1 Perfect serves
2 River to the Caspian Sea
3 Tabula __ (clean slate)
4 Bottomless chasm
5 Sandwich initials
6 __ Lingus
7 Beer holder
8 So be it
9 Baltic natives
10 More attractive
11 One more time
12 "Final Four" org.
13 Hard to hang on to
18 Former Iranian ruler
22 Waste maker of adage
24 Continue, as a subscription
25 With the bow, in music
27 Summery forecast
28 State one's case
29 Word before basin or wave
32 Flagrant
33 "Cool!"
34 Fast-food drinks
37 Frequently, in poems
38 Bellow
40 Racing vehicle
41 Faithful
42 Bring under control
48 Educator Horace
51 Curved sword
52 Intended
53 Runs gracefully
54 Animation
55 No more than
56 "Aha!"
57 Infamous emperor
59 Challenge
60 Sicilian spouter
61 Photographed
64 Uncle: Sp.
65 Suffix for mountain

46 LIGHTS OUT

by Bob Lubbers

ACROSS
1 Adroit
5 They contain qts.
9 Politico Les
14 Dynamics start
15 "Oh, sure!"
16 Recycling aim
17 Lose one's light, perhaps
19 Latin music
20 Tosses trash
22 Smear
23 Sully
26 Invalidates
28 Enthusiasm
29 June honoree
32 Vincent van __
33 Takes on cargo
35 South Pacific island
37 Writer Le Shan
40 Alamogordo event
41 Keogh relative
42 Ninnies
44 Still
45 Artist's prop
47 Pie-fight sound
48 Lyric poems
50 __ *semper tyrannis*
52 Continental prefix
53 Saskatchewan neighbor
56 Bigger
58 Buddies
59 Pennsylvania city
62 ". . . the bombs bursting __"
64 Lose one's light, perhaps
68 "__ bleu!"
69 Monster
70 Buckeye State
71 Scouting outings
72 Free ticket
73 Sally or Ayn

DOWN
1 Small amount
2 Moray
3 To and __
4 Barge connectors
5 Talented
6 Come up against
7 __ majesty (high crime)
8 Strict
9 __ *gratia artis*
10 Sailor's tote
11 Lose one's light, perhaps
12 Bring forth
13 Approaches
18 Feel poorly
21 __ lily (Utah state flower)
23 Put off
24 Make happy
25 Lose one's light, perhaps
27 Urges
30 Sale stipulation
31 Is bold
34 Have the helm
36 French Sudan, today
38 *The Wreck of the Mary* __ (1959 film)
39 Actress Mary
43 "Smooth __" (Sade song)
46 Film terrier
49 Covet
51 Genetic replicas
53 Prone to imitation
54 Sun porch
55 Journalist Joseph
57 In addition
60 Roman garb
61 Yours and mine
63 Musical notes
65 "So that's it!"
66 ATM ID
67 Grass square

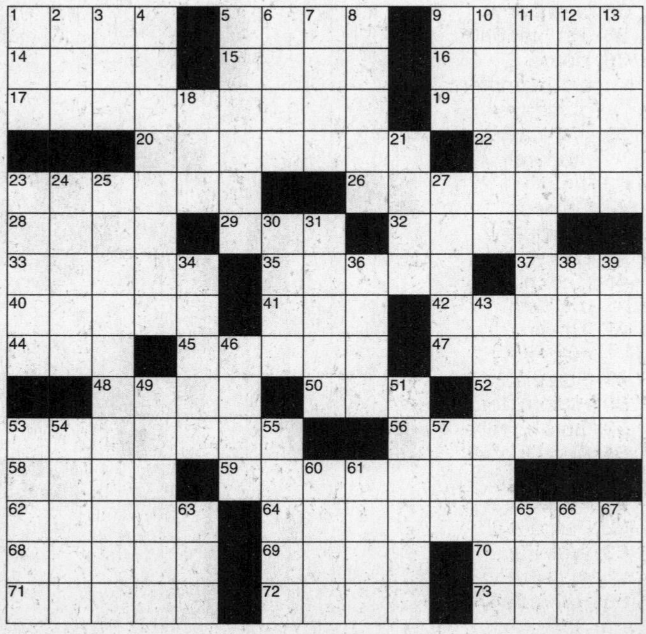

47 MASS MEDIA

by Trip Payne

ACROSS

1 Find fault
5 Impetuous
9 Historical periods
13 Opera solo
14 Comic DeGeneres
16 Get excited
17 Housing cost
18 Photographer's request
19 Sicilian volcano
20 Ad on the airwaves
23 "Just the Two __"
24 Coral island
25 Farmer's field
28 Plated
32 Confused
34 "Mayday!"
35 __ good example
39 *Sacramento Bee* and *Indianapolis Star,* for two
43 List shortener
44 Actress Arthur
45 Worth
46 Business bigwig
49 So far
50 Scents sense
54 Sassy
56 Sitcoms, news, etc.
63 Just hanging around
64 Tropical fruit
65 Gabor and Peron
66 __-do-well
67 UFO pilot
68 Shaker contents
69 Soviet news agency
70 French blessed ones, for short
71 Big game

DOWN

1 *The Alienist* author
2 Zone
3 Lemon cover
4 Backyard part
5 Save
6 Just about
7 Svelte
8 Steering gear
9 Build
10 3:1, e.g.
11 Part of a chronicle
12 Procrastinate
15 Born: Fr.
21 "In the merry month __"
22 Physicist's unit
25 Fill a hold
26 Coup d'__
27 It's east of the Urals
29 Dam spot
30 __ Alamos, NM
31 Uncommon sense
33 Plumbing joint
35 Mineral bath
36 Hard to hold
37 Undeniable
38 "I'd hate to break up __!"
40 Cagers' grp.
41 Brain-wave chart: Abbr.
42 States
46 1055, to Caesar
47 Orbital extreme
48 Dovetail sections
50 Be frugal
51 Euripedes drama
52 They, to Monet
53 Glances from Groucho
55 Not those
57 "__ Yankee Doodle Dandy"
58 Maglie and Mineo
59 "What's __ for me?"
60 Shape of Bush's office
61 Intersection sign
62 Jet set?

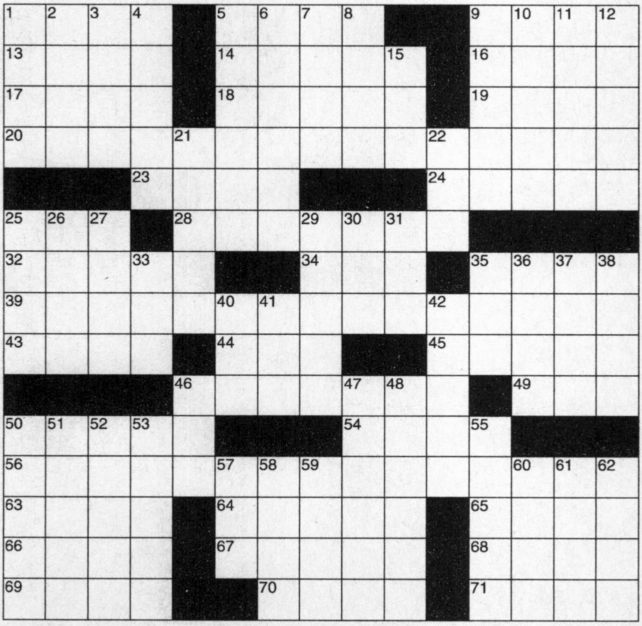

48 SHIP SHAPE

by Fred Piscop

ACROSS
1 Open a keg
4 Make suitable
9 Writer Sontag
14 __ *Mine* (George Harrison book)
15 Guitar with a resonator
16 Set things square
17 __ sequitur
18 Macaroni shape
19 1993 treaty
20 Boxing classification
23 Divination deck
24 Madrid Mrs.
25 "Get the point?"
28 Fox's quality
31 Excellent grade
34 Cashless deal
37 Nick of *48 HRS.*
38 Underhand pitcher
44 Clock-changing month
45 Weight allowance
46 Made cloudy
48 Most saucy
54 Bank acct. earnings
55 Cut short
58 Lena of *Stormy Weather*
59 Airborne messenger
64 Olympic ski champ Phil
66 Laundered
67 __-Magnon
68 Construction piece
69 Welcoming word
70 Countdown start
71 Bill of sitcoms
72 Curvy letters
73 Alums.-to-be

DOWN
1 Colors lightly
2 Lacking principles
3 Extreme want
4 "__ Fideles"
5 Kemp's running mate
6 I.e., e.g.
7 Sterns' opposites
8 Minaret, for one
9 Acted the ratfink
10 Provo's state
11 Low-pressure pitch
12 Kitchen intruder
13 Teachers' org.
21 Charged bit
22 Singer Janis
26 Suffix meaning "small"
27 Watchful one
29 Bygone map letters
30 Loretta of *M*A*S*H*
32 Pig-poke connector
33 Lon of Cambodia
35 Santa __, CA
36 Offender, in copspeak
38 Indian attire
39 Very familiar with
40 Trousers, so to speak
41 A thousand grand
42 Pub selection
43 Nectar gatherer
47 German article
49 Thick-skinned herbivores
50 __ out (dress up)
51 Puts up
52 "SKNXX-X" source
53 Mortise partners
56 Cubbyhole
57 Strikes out
60 Yemeni, e.g.
61 __ Martin (cognac brand)
62 Fam. members
63 White as a sheet
64 Tape-recorder adjunct: Abbr.
65 Blood-classification system

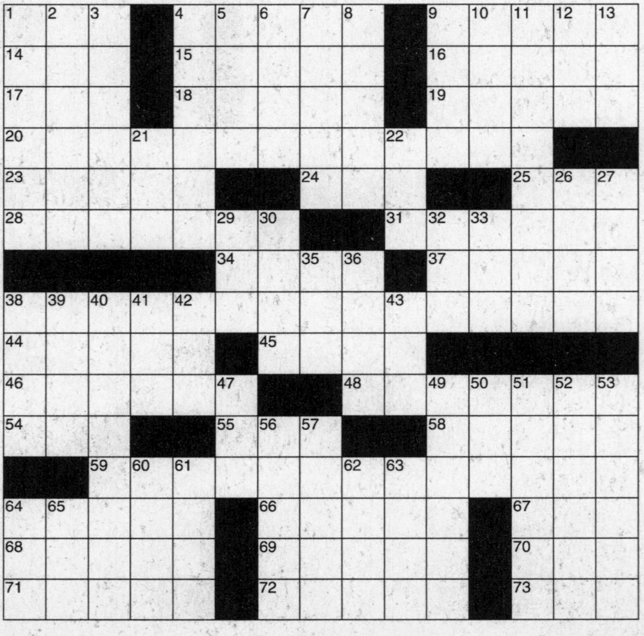

49 NATIONAL LEAGUE

by Rich Norris

ACROSS

1 In shape
5 Frog's sound
10 Bad habit
14 Actress Russo
15 Mountie's mount
16 Love, to Livy
17 "__ boy!"
18 Glacial ridge
19 Practice pugilism
20 Nashville celebrities
23 High-class
24 Agent: Abbr.
25 Tiebreakers, briefly
27 Banned insecticide
28 Fountain treat
32 Smartly dressed
34 Court challenge
36 1981 Beatty film
37 Teamster, e.g.
40 Have a craving for
42 Parody
43 Lowers in esteem
46 To-do
47 In shape
50 Big __, CA
51 Mineral spring
53 Gull relatives
55 Argues in court
60 Part of a sound system
61 Took steps
62 Don't include
63 Egg cell
64 Land on the Sea of Japan
65 Minus
66 Becomes solid
67 Nor'easter, e.g.
68 Italian noble name

DOWN

1 Made an outline
2 Handed down, as a story
3 Know somehow
4 Stood for
5 Cook, Cajun-style
6 Western actor Calhoun
7 Galena and feldspar
8 Up and about
9 Wailed
10 Still-life subject
11 Not suitable
12 Went downhill, perhaps
13 Mess up
21 Speeds, to Solti
22 Coll. student's concern
26 Some coll. students
29 Mil. address
30 Camera attachment
31 Brings under control
33 Get ready
34 Farm denizens
35 Easter preceder
37 Not like Dickens' Dodger
38 1501, in old Rome
39 Reynolds and Lancaster
40 Used to be
41 Not at all nurturing
44 Superlative suffix
45 Pipes up
47 Optician's wares
48 Give no ground
49 Dangerous fly
52 Broad-ended necktie
54 Where to find an "élève"
56 Prepares to fire
57 Other, in Andalusia
58 Poetic adverb
59 Red-wrapped cheese
60 Be greedy

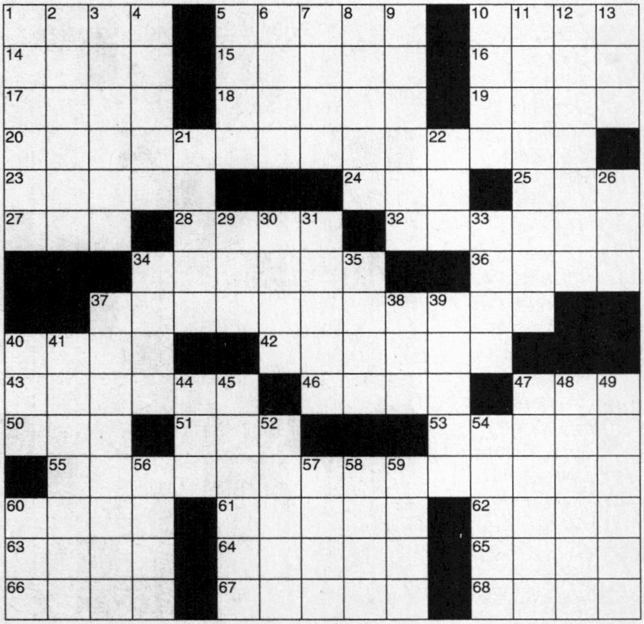

50 KID STUFF

by Trip Payne

ACROSS

1 Thin __ (very skinny)
8 Make good as new
14 Christmas stamp subject
15 Problematic situation
16 Boys Don't Cry song of '86
18 Principal
19 Repent of
20 Five-star nickname
21 Not exactly hard rock?
23 Bleep
26 Mascara applicator
27 Agreement
28 Arthur and Benaderet
31 Terminus
32 Categorize
33 Guys
35 How pros do things
37 Settle
38 Look up to
39 "Smooth Operator" singer
40 Kid's toy
41 "__ Smile Be Your Umbrella"
42 Funny stuff
43 Birthplace of seven Presidents
44 Few and scattered
46 Board material
47 2002 Winter Olympics host
50 French article
51 Keats creations
52 Dungeons and Dragons, e.g.
58 Coined word of a sort
59 Mad
60 Part of ASAP
61 Salad preparers

DOWN

1 "What Kind of Fool __?"
2 Noticed
3 Eden pair
4 Artist Searle
5 Actress Potts
6 __ uproar
7 Chem. classroom
8 Prepares potatoes, perhaps
9 *Xanadu* band
10 Church bench
11 Word form for "both"
12 Phrase in transactional analysis
13 Comic Martha
15 Overawe
17 Put up
21 Say "*&%@#!"
22 *Messiah* composer
23 Actor Elwes
24 Too large
25 Transferred employee's benefit, for short
27 Global extreme
29 Nevertheless
30 __-faire
32 Rein, essentially
33 G-men
34 Rebel of 1857
36 Cats and dogs
37 Fad
39 Sarah Vaughan's nickname
42 Prodigious
43 Alphas' opposites
45 Mel or Steve
46 Boundaries
47 Brutus' bear
48 *The __ of Katie Elder*
49 MacGraw and Baba
51 Aware of
53 Psyche section
54 Arafat's grp.
55 Relative of -arian
56 French sea
57 Bradley and Ames

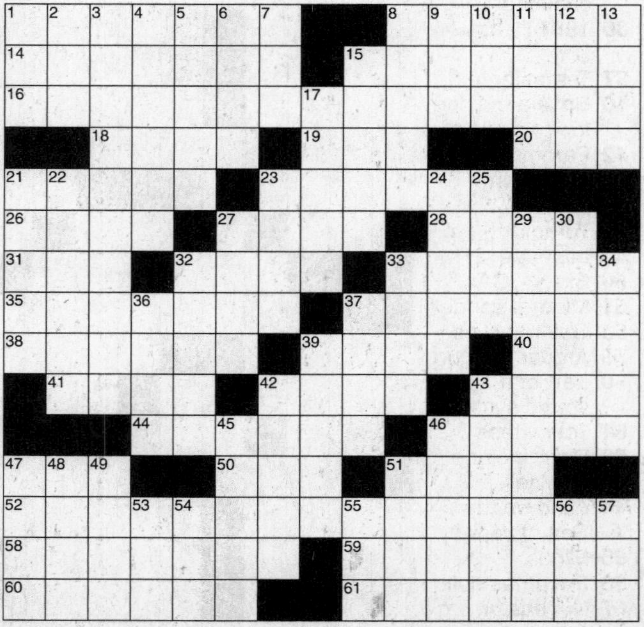

51 RH FACTOR

by Rich Norris

ACROSS

1 Incline
6 Grabbed onto
10 Composer Khachaturian
14 Decimal fraction
15 Hodgepodge
16 Destiny
17 False clue
19 Old Pontiac models
20 Anger
21 Urban tourist attraction
22 Does a tailor's job
23 Anesthetize
25 Abraham's wife
27 Author Ferber
28 Former draft org.
31 Gary of *Apollo 13*
34 One in a pool
37 Flood control devices
38 Traffic component
41 Traffic hindrance
43 UFO pilots
44 Cause to laugh
46 Followed, as a dog
48 Scenic views
50 Swell, '90s-style
51 Praiseful poems
55 Israeli dances
57 Medical staff member
59 Bounce back
61 __ longue
64 Actress West
65 Sticky stuff
66 Southfork structure
68 Sticky stuff
69 Actress Sommer
70 Less common
71 House's grounds
72 Letter starter
73 Computer operators

DOWN

1 Long step
2 Looked impolitely
3 Like the llama
4 High degree
5 Musical motif
6 __ d'oeuvre
7 Nobelist Wiesel
8 *Peanuts* boy
9 Doctrines
10 Kabul native
11 Price increase
12 Tiny particle
13 Disorderly condition
18 Seeks solace from
24 Paint carefully
26 Chain of hills
29 Former Iranian monarch
30 Passover dinner
32 Collection
33 Curvy letter
35 Toward the back
36 Actress Perlman
38 Cleveland cager, briefly
39 French friend
40 Commuting time
42 Somewhat antiquated
45 Condescended
47 E-mail address element
49 Holy
52 Shy and modest
53 Classroom tool
54 Curls one's lip
56 Layered rock
58 India's first prime minister
59 Like French toast
60 Soft-drink selection
62 "Times of Your Life" singer
63 Bakery employee
67 Western alliance since '48

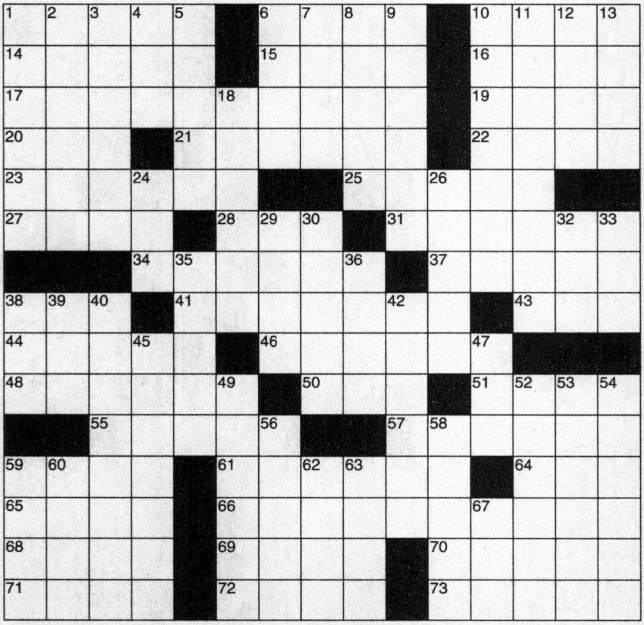

52 *OW!*

by Lee Weaver

ACROSS
1 Modern music style
4 Congressional contributors
8 Sunbather's goal
11 Morally bad
13 In regard to
15 Artist Salvador
16 Walt Kelly's possum
17 Gossipy
18 CEO, e.g.
19 Not yet paid
21 Keystone Kops comedy
23 Shipshape
25 Slangy refusal
26 Like an overcast night
30 Small scented bag
34 Go one better than
35 Nile dam
37 Steps over a fence
38 Slugger Slaughter
40 Seer's deck
42 Show signs of waking
43 Tight-fisted one
45 The entire range
47 Naval officer: Abbr.
48 Dramatic snippets
50 Women of distinction
52 Assembles a shirt
54 Affectionate
55 Batter's bane
60 Car dud
63 Beef cut
64 Glaringly vivid
66 Ready to be harvested
67 In a tizzy
68 Andes beast
69 Russian autocrat
70 Gym pad
71 Musher's vehicle
72 School-zone sign

DOWN
1 Taken-back car
2 State solemnly
3 Unknown purchase
4 Wok, for example
5 Burrows and Vigoda
6 Monk's hood
7 Brooke Shields TV role
8 Prepare to take off
9 Actor Guinness
10 Shaving mishap
12 Solitude seeker
14 Printer's errors
15 Discovers
20 Festive occasion
22 Mineral springs
24 Give it a try
26 Stair parts
27 Gin's companion
28 Pirate's booty
29 Actress Bernhardt
31 Chancy
32 Leave out in pronunciation
33 Payment conditions
36 Alaskan seaport
39 Somehow aware of
41 Matted earth
44 Offend the nose
46 Saw or hammer
49 Terrific
51 Without energy
53 Spiritual essences
55 Bridge coup
56 Roman robe
57 Laugh-a-minute type
58 Russian river
59 *Newsweek* rival
61 Australian gem
62 Rex's sleuth
65 June honoree

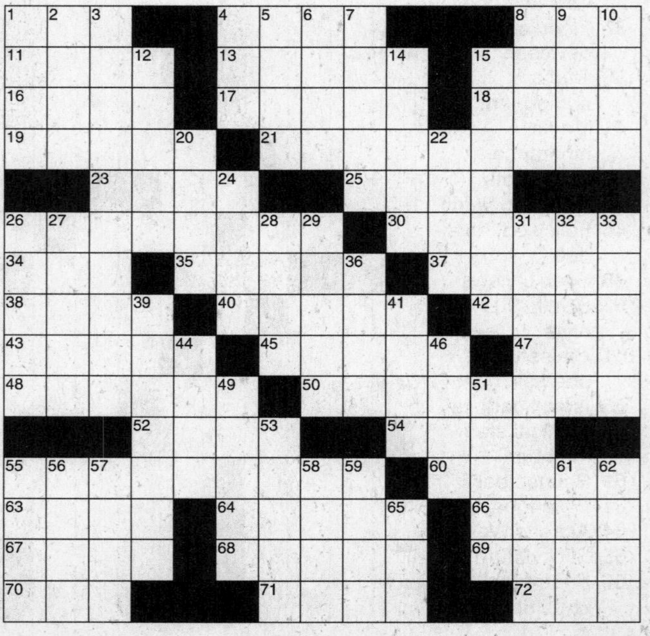

53 GET A HORSE!

by Rich Norris

ACROSS
1 Muslim pilgrimage
5 Get in a stew
9 Telegraph inventor
14 A Great Lake
15 Like a poor excuse
16 Madonna role
17 Gaze (at)
18 Send forth
19 Lengthy narratives
20 19th-century mail system
23 "__ been had!"
24 Peggy and Spike
25 Fused, as metal
27 Came together
30 Madrid museum
32 "Hold on Tight" rock group
33 Sordid quality
37 New England's highest peak
41 Cafe locales
42 Prefix with light or night
43 Thurber character Walter
44 Fine-tune
47 King's seat
50 Baseball family name
51 Amazed exclamation
52 1980 Clint Eastwood film
58 Composed a letter
60 Winnie-the-__
61 Italian farewell
62 Came to a close
63 Razor name
64 *National Velvet* author Bagnold
65 Does a casino job
66 Camera attachment
67 Flu fighters

DOWN
1 Beatles movie
2 Buck add-on
3 Singer Celine
4 Hyde's alter ego
5 Showed some muscle
6 Stairs alternatives
7 Mideast potentate
8 Nantes noggin
9 Interfered with
10 Eggs
11 Uncompromising
12 Barrel part
13 Made more manageable
21 Wide shoe width
22 Hindu religious teacher
26 Protracted
27 Valuable stones
28 *The Time Machine* race
29 Garish, as attire
30 Like Dennis the Menace
31 Stadium sounds
33 Common condiment
34 Words from Caesar
35 Scatters seed
36 Agitated state
38 Verne captain
39 Motel furnishings
40 Dampen the daffodils
44 Pearl City partings
45 Driver's license abbr.
46 Breakfast beverages
47 Did a AAA job
48 Mezzo-soprano Marilyn
49 Valerie Harper role
50 Oak starter
53 October birthstone
54 Musical symbol
55 Queue
56 Animal house
57 Luke Skywalker's teacher
59 __ Aviv

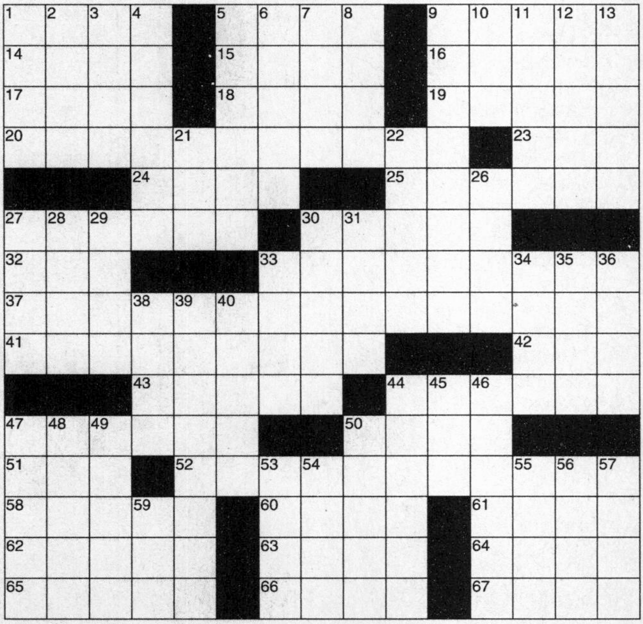

54 TERMS OF ENDEARMENT

by Patrick Jordan

ACROSS
1 Litter critters
5 Muscle spasm
10 Nintendo rival
14 "__ sow, so shall . . ."
15 Sound portion
16 Did an impression of
17 Western U.S. cash crop
19 Told a whopper
20 Orchestral gong
21 Delays in progress
23 '60s Tarzan Ron
24 3 on a phone
26 Soybean container
27 Like some peanuts
33 Faint
36 Lessen one's courage
37 Screen siren Gardner
38 Printed material
39 Sheriff's assistants
40 Former spouses
41 Miner matter
42 Be worthy of
43 From Erin
44 Never-Never Land visitor
47 Plus
48 Conclude
49 Prefix for center or cycle
52 Crosses between corners
57 Humidor contents
59 Alda or Thicke
60 1955 song for The Penguins
62 Greater quantity
63 Fix one's shoelaces
64 On the sheltered side
65 Road curve
66 Three Stooges actions
67 Took off

DOWN
1 Fake jewelry
2 Routine
3 Variety of owl
4 Senate position
5 Hacks
6 Regret
7 Fruity refreshers
8 Tiny amount
9 Put off
10 Buffet selections
11 De Mille specialty
12 Socially awkward sort
13 States further
18 Heaviest noble gas
22 Yawl or yacht
25 Felt hat
27 Extremely popular
28 PLO VIP Arafat
29 Sound of windblown leaves
30 Danny DeVito vehicle
31 Preceding nights
32 100-yard contest
33 Put into the hold
34 *The Way We* __
35 Draft animals
39 Street vendors
40 Work unit
42 Caged talker
43 Second-most populous country
45 Began to be understood
46 Furlong's 7,920
49 Hole-in-one on a par-3
50 Smooth, as feathers
51 Speck in the sea
52 Door part
53 Lotion ingredient
54 Knitting need
55 Film critic Pauline
56 Sp. maiden
58 Chew away (at)
61 Waiter's reward

55 ECHOES

by Norma Steinberg

ACROSS
1 Truth twister
5 Term of respect
9 Glaswegian
13 Author Ferber
14 Armbone
15 Location
16 Ophthalmologist's office?
18 Endures
19 Showman Hurok
20 Inquires
21 Soaks in the tub
22 Giggle
24 Ascertain
25 Zeus or Hermes
26 Singer Brewer
27 Kind of tea
30 Bivouac shelters
31 Part of a Web site address
34 Coffee brewers
35 Collide
36 Bloke
37 Prefix for "before"
38 "__ or When"
39 Sharpens
40 Plato's hometown
42 Allen Dulles' org.
43 Unanchored
44 Praying __
47 Restaurant patrons
48 Sharp taste
49 Regret
51 Perfect
52 Stylish Eastern leader?
54 Bumps into
55 Exude slowly
56 Poker buy-in
57 Singer Nelson __
58 One-on-one battle
59 Tennis ranking

DOWN
1 Minus
2 Dingbat
3 Viewpoint
4 "Yay!"
5 Disarranged
6 Identical
7 Picnic pests
8 Actress West
9 Blackboards
10 Piggy bank?
11 Two quartets
12 Mrs. Dick Tracy
15 Dinnerware
17 California/Nevada lake
21 Bed on a train
23 Personalities
24 Thick
26 Lachrymal drops
27 Baby boxer
28 "To __ is human . . ."
29 Baker's dough?
30 Senator Lott
32 Feedbag bit
33 GI cops
35 Professional cooks
36 Casual talk
38 Rotates
39 Offstage areas
41 Pact
42 Nullify
43 Lent a hand
44 Indian corn
45 Actress Dunne
46 Group of rooms
47 Ten-cent piece
48 Commandments pronoun
50 __ out a living
52 Massachusetts cape
53 Owns

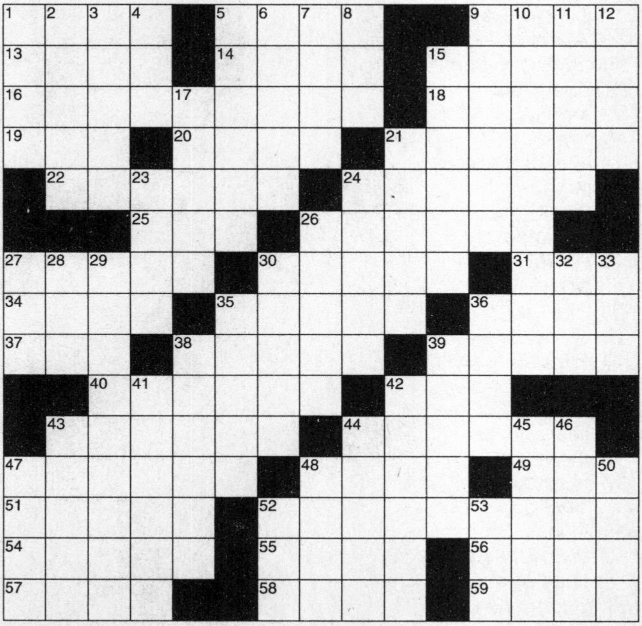

56 LITERARY GENRES

by Fred Piscop

ACROSS

1 Cracked open
5 Donaldson of ABC
8 Red Cloud, for one
14 Russian parliament
15 Singer Zadora
16 Like some films
17 Hubbubs
18 Special-interest grp.
19 Be stealthy
20 School-lunch entree, to kids
23 Young-__ (kids)
24 Tap outflow
25 Writer Loos
27 Recipe meas.
30 -arian relative
32 More smooth-talking
36 Norway's patron saint
38 Asian salt sea
40 Scandinavian coin word
41 Catalan, for one
44 Sunspot center
45 Welles role
46 Neck and neck
47 Bean product
49 "What a dope I am!"
51 Thirsty
52 Winter forecast
54 Musical notes
56 Shriver of tennis
59 Distressing experience
64 Region of Spain
66 French friend
67 Scandinavian chain
68 It's basic
69 "__ overboard!"
70 Pal of Kukla and Ollie
71 Firmly planted
72 Old hand
73 Columbo portrayer

DOWN

1 Edenite
2 Punch's pal
3 Andy's pal
4 Dreadlocked one
5 Pollen source
6 Light as a feather
7 Lava's relative
8 Soup ingredient
9 Clamping together, as one's teeth
10 Once around the track
11 Westernmost Aleutian
12 Mr. Trotsky
13 Summer beverages
21 Biblical judge
22 Ethelred I's domain
26 Concerning
27 Donut shape
28 Replay effect
29 Namby-__
31 *Enterprise* fan
33 Interweave
34 Ham-and-__ (oaf)
35 Like a bassoon's sound
37 Works the land
39 Menu words
42 Spackler's target
43 Elementary particle
48 Nikita successor
50 That guy's
53 Chaplin persona
55 Like a stuffed shirt
56 '50s late-night host
57 Folksy Guthrie
58 Great white relative
60 Poet Khayyám
61 Gumbo essential
62 True-to-life
63 Pinstriped player, for short
65 Hood's weapon

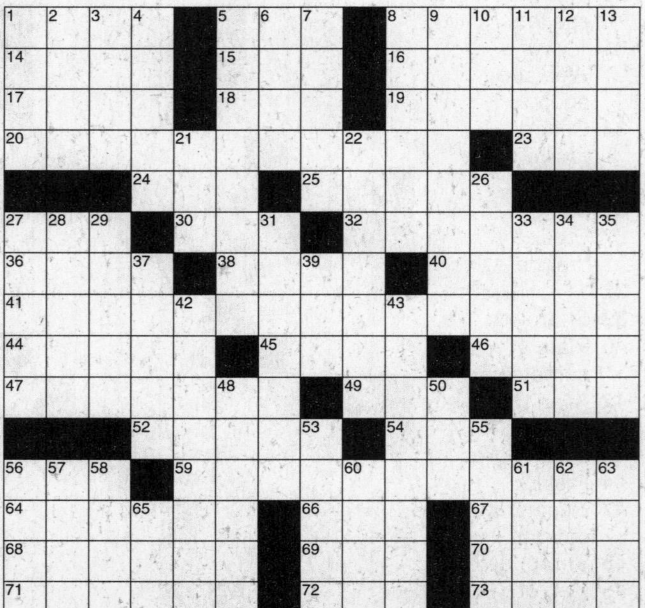

57 AT THE DAIRY

by Norma Steinberg

ACROSS
1 Feudal laborer
5 Boutique
9 Turkish leader of old
14 Blue-green color
15 Immaculate
16 French actor Delon
17 Disarrange
18 At a distance
19 Panache
20 Monarchs, e.g.
23 Dairy animal
24 Declare
25 Appreciate a joke
27 Sap
30 Words from the podium
33 And so forth: Abbr.
36 Mortgaged up to here
38 Claudius' adopted son
39 Rulers
41 Historical period
42 Lawyer's work
43 Locale
44 Salad item
46 Lamb's mama
47 Shed
49 Watt's power
51 Butcher's wares
53 Necklace closings
57 Drink like a cat
59 Earth's place
62 Rejoice
64 Ballerina's skirt
65 Trumpet
66 Michael Caine role
67 Bound
68 Comic Idle
69 Put off
70 *Coffee, Tea, __?*
71 Netting

DOWN
1 South American dance
2 Peter Shaffer play
3 Oxidizes
4 Skipped meals
5 No-frills
6 __ and puff
7 Spoken
8 Danger
9 Turn down
10 Model Carol
11 Photographer's request
12 Hawaiian city
13 Again
21 "To __ human . . ."
22 __ *of Eden*
26 Actress Rowlands
28 Brainstorm
29 Square ones
31 Ship's employees
32 Stockings
33 Israeli airline
34 Ripped
35 Choice used car
37 Fisherman's need
40 Aarhus resident
42 Blackboard adjunct
44 Portnoy's creator
45 Sequester
48 Rag
50 Uproar
52 Heated argument
54 Cussed
55 "I Love __"
56 Harmonious relationship
57 Primary role
58 Rod between wheels
60 American naturalist
61 Line-__ veto
63 Be deceitful

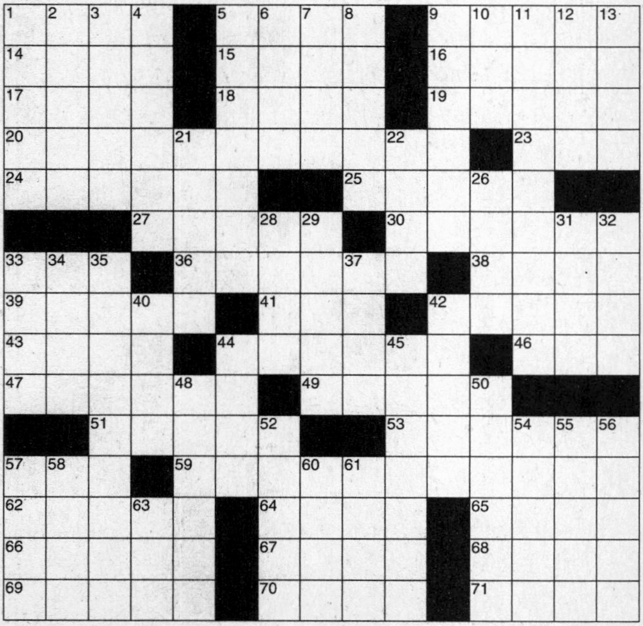

58 FASTENATION

by Fred Piscop

ACROSS
1 Stop up
4 Had faith
9 Like two peas in __
13 Author Levin
14 Vestment
15 *Desk Set* star
16 Pitcher's ploy
18 Out of the sack
19 Goya subjects
20 Test answer
22 Patty Hearst's kidnappers
23 Has a crush on
25 Stable adjunct
27 *Get __ Ya-Ya's Out!* (Stones album)
28 Greek P
30 Like
31 European airline
33 Dada father
35 "__ Blu Dipinto di Blu"
36 Pamper
40 Recline
41 Madras mister
42 Writer LeShan
44 Best: Sp.
47 "That's obvious!" in teen talk
49 Juilliard subj.
51 *Legends of the Fall* star
54 Bummed out
56 Rail splitter's unit
57 *Middlemarch* author
59 Skate's kin
60 Turn aside
62 Anxious one, perhaps
64 Hockey great Potvin
65 Fragrant compound
66 Norwegian coin
67 __-European
68 Pilot-light spot
69 Nancy Drew's boyfriend

DOWN
1 Alarm
2 Video-game emporia
3 Oregano kin
4 Ship's rope
5 Govt. finance group
6 "La Vie en Rose" chanteuse
7 Dazzling effect
8 Perry's aide
9 Uris hero
10 Send along
11 Spotted cat
12 Faraday creation
15 Traveled like Spock
17 Canal site
21 Rare-earth metal
24 Kind of crude
26 Lunar valley
29 Jazz legend Kid __
32 Like some rocket propellants
34 Desktop items, for short
37 Conch cousins
38 Former California fort
39 Saskatchewan River city
43 Tight, budgetwise
44 Part of a Beatles title
45 Established
46 Leftover
48 Guadalajara guy
50 Singed
52 Trident's trio
53 Acclaimed one
55 Ill-fated Heyerdahl craft
58 Bandleader Puente
61 Road-picture destination
63 *My Name is Asher __*

59 SOAPDISH

by Norma Steinberg

ACROSS

1 Fido's friend
6 Obi
10 Auctioneer's call
14 Singer Baker
15 Director Kazan
16 Singer Laine
17 Part of a wedding vow
18 Satirist Sahl
19 Alan Arkin's son
20 ABC soap
23 Agenda
24 "Positively!"
25 Smith of *Charlie's Angels*
29 Drenched
30 Jai __
31 Soupçon
34 Fools
39 ABC soap
42 Vista
43 Openwork material
44 Donated
45 Devonshire drink
47 Wandered
49 ID documents
53 Roebuck, e.g.
55 ABC soap
59 Thick slice
60 Litter's smallest
61 Conspicuous
64 Muscle quality
65 Low-cholesterol spread
66 Tense, so to speak
67 Washstand pitcher
68 Threaten
69 Feeds the pigs

DOWN

1 Cry from the grandstands
2 Yoko __
3 Italian wine
4 Harrow's rival
5 Seldom
6 Large trucks
7 Overhead
8 Father
9 Actress McDaniel
10 Parboil
11 Nostalgic tune
12 Furlough
13 Like the Capitol
21 Actress Lavin
22 Ready to pour
25 Binges
26 Actor Baldwin
27 Chaplin prop
28 Mortgage, for example
29 "__ on first?"
32 __ mater
33 Girl's pronoun
35 Billboard
36 For men only
37 Roof overhang
38 Winter toy
40 Take another shot
41 Destroy documents
46 Real-estate account
48 Quiver contents
49 Tomato product
50 Permit
51 Runway vehicle
52 Coal remnant
53 Barry Levinson movie
54 Rocker John
56 Maui dance
57 Satan's realm
58 Pianist Peter
62 Salesperson, for short
63 Gridiron scores: Abbr.

60 IN THE 7-11

by Fred Piscop

ACROSS

1 NHL member
5 The Forbidden City
10 "You're it!"
13 Clearheaded
15 Lets up
16 Be in debt
17 Kids' card game
19 Give no stars to
20 Say it ain't so
21 Isolate
23 Telecom giant
25 Suffix for sonnet
27 Changes the dimensions of
28 Dream-period acronym
29 Slender
31 Double twist
32 Working away
34 De Mille specialty
36 "Who's there?" response
40 Prepare for a fancy party
43 Flip-chart holder
44 Sign gas
45 Restraints, as on spending
46 As well
48 Respond to reveille
50 Deuce, in tennis
51 No-cal fat substitute
55 Jury-___ (improvise)
56 Corn holder
57 Dissolute man
59 Deep cut
61 "What ___, chopped liver?"
62 Oldtime emporia
66 Beach acquisition
67 City near Venice
68 Euphrates River land
69 Bit of a joule
70 Hits the tarmac
71 Sports channel

DOWN

1 Special attention, for short
2 It's north of Afr.
3 Military schools
4 '50s slugger Johnny
5 Hilo souvenir
6 Macbeth trio
7 Son of Jacob
8 Small sofa
9 Ninja, e.g.
10 Fall birthstone
11 In the know
12 Ladies' men
14 Units of force
18 Lace place
22 Peony part
23 A, as in eggs
24 Numerical prefix
26 Wisconsin college
30 Cut at a 45-degree angle
33 Dangerous fly
35 Loft-y group?
37 Rat finks
38 TV, radio, etc.
39 Ruhr Valley city
41 Suffering from spring fever, maybe
42 Naval rank
47 Frozen-potatoes name
49 "Good grief!"
51 Give a valedictory
52 Politico Alexander
53 Getting with great strain
54 A Chipmunk
58 Put up, as money
60 Eye woe
63 Two-time loser to DDE
64 Tuck's partner
65 ___ Fernando Valley

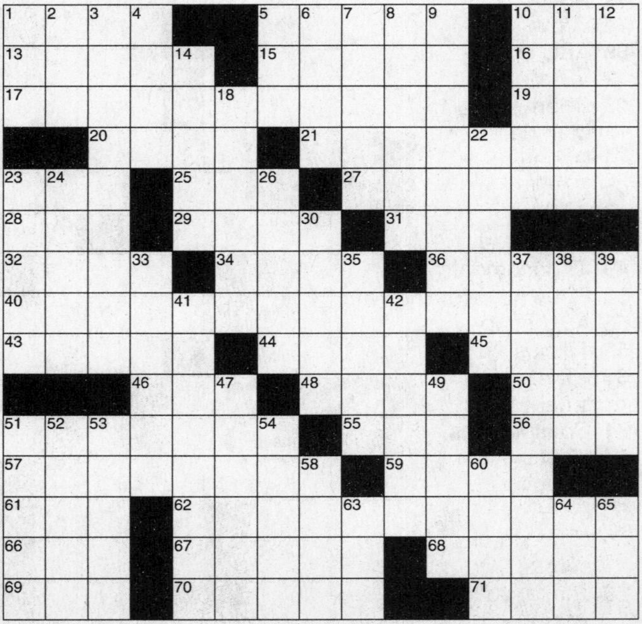

61 THIS BUD'S FOR YOU

by Lee Weaver

ACROSS

1 Plant pouches
5 Theater section
9 Pub missile
13 Arthur of tennis
14 Kind of drum
16 Composer Stravinsky
17 Yard parts
18 Mentally acute
19 Governing regulation
20 Third rock from the sun
22 Use flattery to persuade
24 Riverside plant
26 Wander off
27 Reply to the captain
29 Moves upward
33 York or Bilko: Abbr.
34 Painter of ballerinas
37 __ *Gay*
38 Carson predecessor
40 *M*A*S*H* clerk
42 U.S. Pacific island
43 Kitchen cover-up
45 Offers a challenge
47 Map abbr.
48 Keep possession of
50 Get back for
52 Speaks unclearly
55 Mix the batter
56 Regrettable conclusion
60 Weighing device
63 *Garfield* canine
64 Mountain peak
66 Olympic weapon
67 Jury member
68 Church official
69 Aquatic mammal
70 Back talk
71 Decorative evergreens
72 Cookbook abbr.

DOWN

1 Umpire's call
2 On the ocean
3 Fruit pastry
4 Parlor piece
5 Pts. of tons
6 Sounds of awe
7 Chews like a beaver
8 Everglades bird
9 Soiling
10 Water, in Madrid
11 Parker House product
12 Hard journey
15 Musical drama
21 Beer topper
23 Biblical weed
25 Colorist
27 Wide open
28 Archaic exclamation
30 Pretended disdain
31 Make jubilant
32 Identical
33 Practice punching
35 Orthodontist's org.
36 Poet Teasdale
39 Turkey cookers
41 Guns the engine
44 Aswan Dam site
46 Movie locations
49 TLC provider
51 Most pleasant
53 Answer an invitation
54 Derogatory in manner
56 Conks on the head
57 Brainstorm
58 Binds together
59 Sitcom star Carey
61 Vault
62 Sushi serving
65 Hesitation sounds

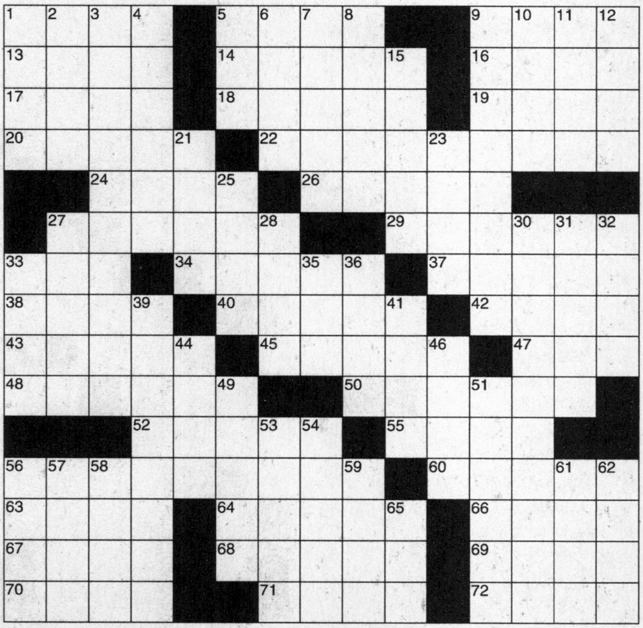

62 TORCH SONGS

by Rich Norris

ACROSS
1 April 1 victims
6 Suit
11 "Now, wait a minute . . ."
14 Da Gama destination
15 African antelope
16 Chemical suffix
17 1962 Corsairs song
19 Shaq org.
20 Wife of Zeus
21 Label word for dieters
22 Not quite shut
23 1990 Bon Jovi song
27 Malicious look
30 Italian car
31 Copenhagen residents
32 Disrespectful acts
36 Scram, oater-style
37 "__ Macabre"
39 Mine find
40 Immense
43 Reef material
45 "__ That a Shame"
46 Willie Mays' birthplace
48 1987 Bryan Adams song
52 Semi feature
53 Give a hoot
54 Map abbrs.
58 Actor Brynner
59 1972 Elvis Presley song
62 Former name of Tokyo
63 Son of Sarah
64 Actress Anouk
65 Part of a match
66 "__ luck!"
67 Bergen alter ego

DOWN
1 Go angling
2 Big spender's phrase
3 Annoying smell
4 Winsome
5 Make a statement
6 British Honduras, today
7 Make happy
8 Hockey openers
9 Female-name ending
10 NFL scores
11 *Deliverance* instrument
12 Take the bolt off
13 Prone to break down?
18 Be in the game
22 Choir member
24 __ *Misérables*
25 Drum partner
26 Needlefish
27 Head start
28 Stuck-up
29 Fascinated by
32 Resp.
33 Director Ephron
34 Sussex streetcar
35 Ward of *Sisters*
37 Slips into
38 Absolute ruler
41 Hard to find
42 Cambridge sch.
43 Jam ingredient?
44 Ohio college
46 Second-largest continent
47 Financial claim
48 President after Grant
49 Radiate
50 Parcel out
51 Grandmas
55 Heavy book
56 At any time
57 Start a lawn
59 Puppeteer Baird
60 Mil. entertainment group
61 Pump product

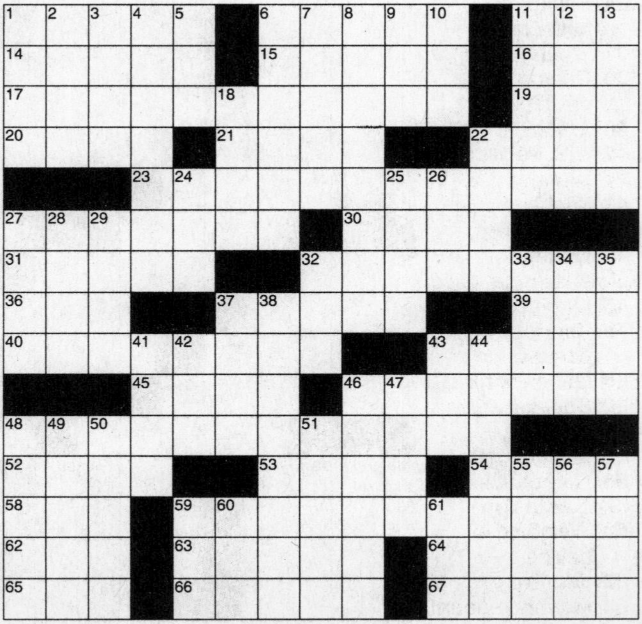

63 IT ALL ADDS UP

by Norma Steinberg

ACROSS

1 Skycap's burdens
5 Impertinence
10 Tome
14 Singer Fitzgerald
15 *Homo sapiens* member
16 Rod between wheels
17 Model's asset
19 Impolite look
20 Yoko __
21 French spot of land
22 Mideast nation
24 Part of the forehead
26 Actor McDermott
27 Furlough
29 Dresser-drawer perfumer
33 Bill of fare
36 US/European defense org.
38 Distrustful
39 "Too bad!"
40 Easel, e.g.
42 Large garage
43 Presidential candidate of 1996
45 Location
46 Threat ender
47 Cryptic
49 Poet Federico Garcia __
51 Wherewithal
53 Philip II's fleet
57 Singer Etheridge
60 Cravat
61 __ Tin Tin
62 Microwave, e.g.
63 Marabel Morgan's ideal
66 Stead
67 Author Zola
68 Singer Tennille
69 Lodge members
70 Ate well
71 Aspen, for one

DOWN

1 Had children
2 Without company
3 Doom's partner
4 Blue
5 Santiago natives
6 Immense
7 Big bird
8 Way before the bell
9 Genuflects
10 Gymnastics event
11 Yoked animals
12 No-cholesterol spread
13 *Show Boat* composer
18 Arrange alphabetically
23 Jezebel's god
25 Margin for error
26 Minutiae
28 Storage containers
30 Get better
31 Goofs
32 Actress Daly
33 Glove-compartment items
34 Gen. Robt. __
35 Antidrug cop
37 Aware of
41 Pushed off the track
44 Football holders
48 Sampled
50 Ship's staff
52 One of the Judds
54 Knight's protection
55 Actress Keaton . . .
56 . . . of __ *Hall*
57 Double agent
58 Satan's forte
59 Scallion relative
60 Yarn
64 Pewter component
65 New York Giant hero

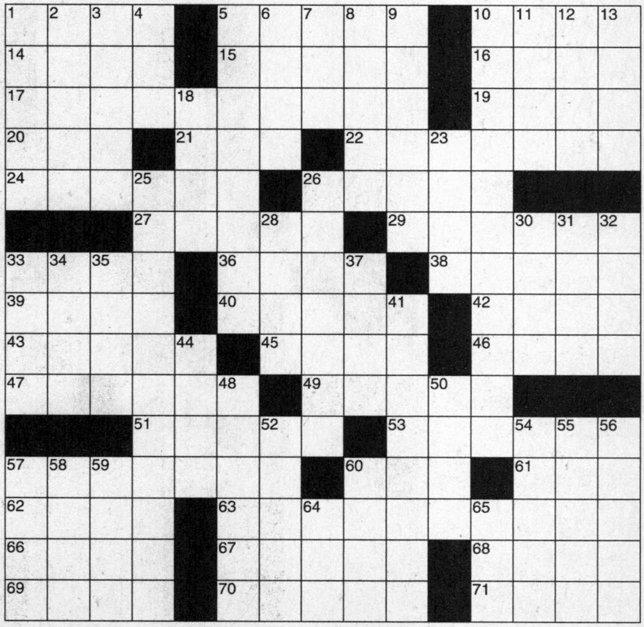

64

ATTRACTIVE FILMS

by Rich Norris

ACROSS
1 Shakespearean epithet
5 Bill of *Maude*
9 __ *diem* (seize the day)
14 On the briny
15 Shaving-cream ingredient
16 Love, in Livorno
17 "Huh?"
18 Throw the dice
19 Bag carrier
20 1952 Red Skelton film
23 Destroy gradually
24 Stimpy's pal
25 Baseball great Williams
27 Morning moisture
28 Forty winks
31 More eccentric
34 Spoke (up)
36 O. Henry technique
37 1990 Julia Roberts film
40 Hair-raising place?
42 West Coast capital
43 Put together skillfully
46 Solidify
47 Center of activity
50 Porkpie, for one
51 "Cry __ River"
53 Fight site
55 1996 Matt Dillon film
60 Story tellers
61 Fast-food drink
62 Hide's companion
63 Fry lightly
64 Long, long time
65 *In* __ (actually)
66 Al of auto racing
67 ERA, for one
68 Method: Abbr.

DOWN
1 Cried
2 Not 14 Across
3 Make new promises
4 Old-fashioned
5 Peter and Paul's partner
6 Very much
7 Spectrum component
8 Shouted
9 Roman philosopher
10 Out of control
11 Crop-raising technique
12 Twelve-year-old, e.g.
13 Always, in poetry
21 Not strict
22 Lennon's mate
26 Like Chianti
29 Fitting
30 Gerbil or canary
32 Response delay
33 Sussex streetcar
34 Campus VIP
35 Prefix meaning "badly"
37 Tablelands
38 Move one's tail
39 Corrida cry
40 Academy: Abbr.
41 Fine horse
44 Ambulance attendant: Abbr.
45 Cleans the windshield, in a way
47 Joan of Arc's crime
48 Except if
49 Red Riding Hood accessory
52 In progress
54 Goes up
56 Comic Johnson
57 Exploitative one
58 Radius neighbor
59 Cellar dweller's position
60 Shreveport coll.

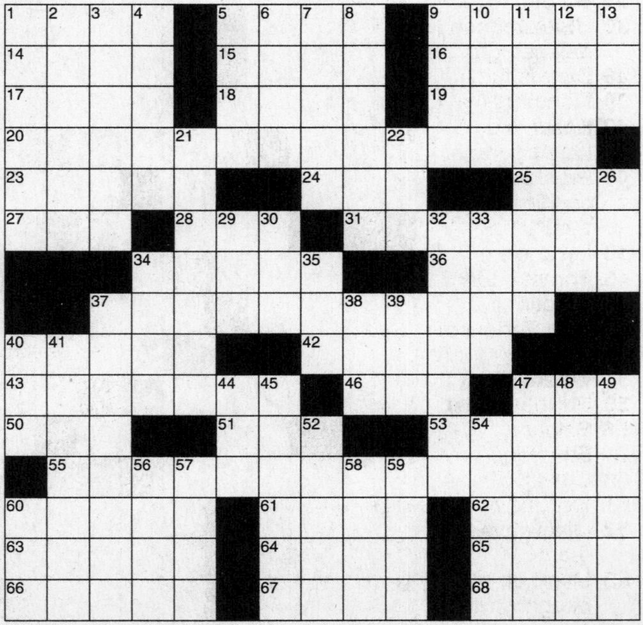

65 EXPLOSIVE

by Lee Weaver

ACROSS
1 Sleek jets
5 Pro __ (proportionally)
9 Iowa city
13 Toast topper
14 Gold unit
15 Enameled metal
16 Performance by Joel or Springsteen
18 Fly like a butterfly
19 Prepare to plant
20 Witnessed
21 Chopin pieces
23 Coined money
25 Invalidate
27 Take a break
29 "Sweet __" (quartet tune)
33 Of the moon
36 Hoarfrost
38 Steep, as tea
39 Oil cartel
40 Harder to find
41 Country byway
42 Toil away (at)
43 Cameo shape
44 More stable
45 Sign a check's back
47 Swerves off course
49 Perceives by touch
51 New York and Boston
55 Surrounded by
58 Rotate
60 Singing syllable
61 Poet Teasdale
62 Cosmologist's theory
65 Like a snail's pace
66 Having a roof overhang
67 "I cannot tell __"
68 Nashville is its cap.
69 Prophet
70 Deli loaves

DOWN
1 Some students, for short
2 Single-masted vessel
3 Conical quarters
4 Assn.
5 Marathon, e.g.
6 Sports complex
7 Sailor
8 Person present
9 All the way up, as a boom box
10 Gelatin shaper
11 Nobelist Wiesel
12 Complete collections
14 Leg joints
17 Wickerwork willow
22 Cal. column
24 Sunup
26 To wit
28 Go abroad
30 Persia, today
31 Hawaiian goose
32 Jug
33 Actor Rob
34 "__ my word!"
35 Social misfit
37 Lyricist Gershwin
40 Ornamental ribbons
44 Playground item
46 Scale notes
48 Sharp-tasting
50 Canyon of the comics
52 Boot-shaped country
53 One of the Muppets
54 Wise ones
55 Aide: Abbr.
56 Masculine
57 Bodybuilders pump it
59 Over: Ger.
63 Have, in Scotland
64 Tavern

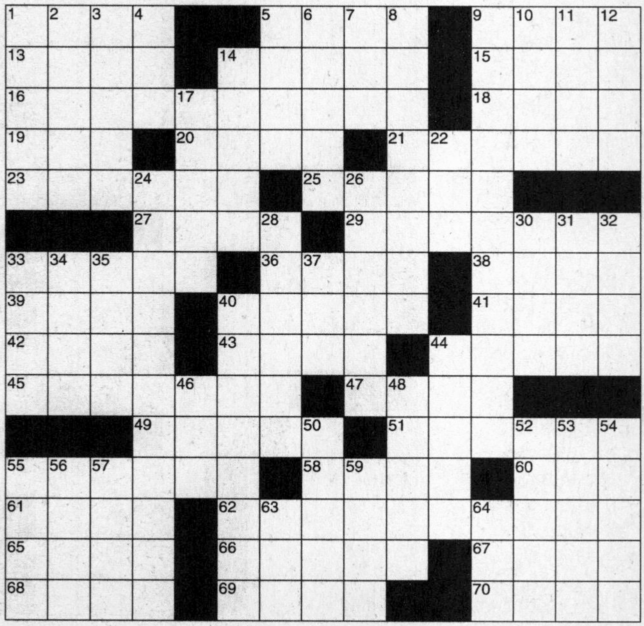

66 TIGHTENING UP

by Fred Piscop

ACROSS
1 Wolf (down)
6 Wrestling officials
10 Healthful spots
14 Repair-bill part
15 One of the Baldwins
16 Give notice
17 Greet the day
18 Robert De __
19 Astronomical bear
20 Publicity person
22 __ May Clampett
23 Blubber
24 Luther's 95
26 Kind of stew
30 Soviet space program
32 Letters at Calvary
33 Head the cast
35 Boost
39 Unfeeling
41 A Gabor
42 Lower in esteem
43 Time being
44 Novelist Jaffe
46 Cooking chamber
47 Overdramatic
49 Bobby-__ ('40s teens)
51 Potter rabbit
54 Corn portion
55 Painter Magritte
56 Philatelist's purchase
63 Blissful state
64 Shopper's bag
65 Nary a soul
66 Getz or Kenton
67 Borodin's Prince
68 Sugar-coated
69 Sacred
70 Snug
71 Annoy, so to speak

DOWN
1 Sharp blow
2 Singer Vikki
3 Irish Rose lover
4 Famous sewer
5 Painting on plaster
6 Long-limbed
7 Author Wiesel
8 Flowerless plant
9 *Star Trek* engineer
10 Concertina
11 Does some knitting
12 Usher's beat
13 Doesn't fold
21 Liberal pursuits
25 Sinuous dance
26 Hillbilly pronoun
27 Wise about
28 Suffix in accelerator names
29 Tightwad
30 "Stompin' at the __"
31 Mediterranean port
34 Jimmy Carter had one
36 Presented
37 End __ (ultimate customer)
38 Bank items on chains
40 Thumbs-up votes
45 Letters of haste
48 Occult figure
50 New Jersey city
51 Not canned or frozen
52 Caused
53 Star hoopster
54 Manicurist's material
57 Pizza order
58 All-inclusive
59 Joe Hardy's enticer
60 Dory or dinghy
61 Donald Duck, to Dewey
62 Track event

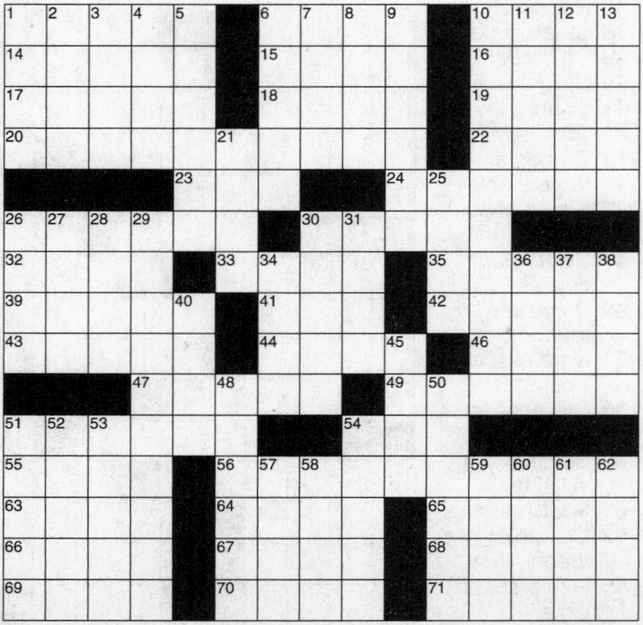

67 IN THE ROUND

by Rich Norris

ACROSS

1 Applaud
5 Warm up in the ring
9 Burn with water
14 Dan Blocker role
15 Mug for the camera
16 Comedienne Fields
17 ABA member
18 Writer Wiesel
19 Dodge
20 *The Lion King* song
23 Uproar
24 Hollywood hopeful's hope
28 Ques. response
29 High hairstyle
33 Sluggards
34 Yuletide door hanging
36 Young men
37 Philanthropic event
40 Take a risk
42 Passover dinners
43 Canada's capital
46 Housing cost
47 ACLU concerns: Abbr.
50 SWAT team rescuee
52 Flawless concept
54 Venue for Shakespeare
58 Auto racer Bobby
61 Like Mother Hubbard's cupboard
62 Icy coating
63 India's first prime minister
64 Wicked
65 Golf hazard
66 List components
67 *Ed Wood* star
68 Cabinet member: Abbr.

DOWN

1 Three-step dance
2 Sunblock, e.g.
3 Houston nine
4 College course, briefly
5 *Graf* __
6 Palm Beach sport
7 "Yeah, right!"
8 Is unsteady
9 Edberg of tennis
10 Handyman's outfit
11 One __ time (singly)
12 Jar top
13 Poor grade
21 Actress San Giacomo
22 "__ Now or Never"
25 Pushbutton predecessor
26 Ancient
27 Ed.'s concerns
30 According to
31 Honoree's spot
32 Aquatic mammal
34 Health-food store offering
35 Jekyll's alter ego
37 PC screens
38 Actor Gazzara
39 Bandleader Shaw
40 Homer Simpson expletive
41 From __ Z
44 Marine mammal
45 Past
47 Move to Arizona, maybe
48 Airport surface
49 One of the Dwarfs
51 Went out, as the tide
53 Pub projectiles
55 Roof overhang
56 Vacation excursion
57 1965 Beatles film
58 Word form for "one"
59 Court divider
60 __ *Stoops to Conquer*

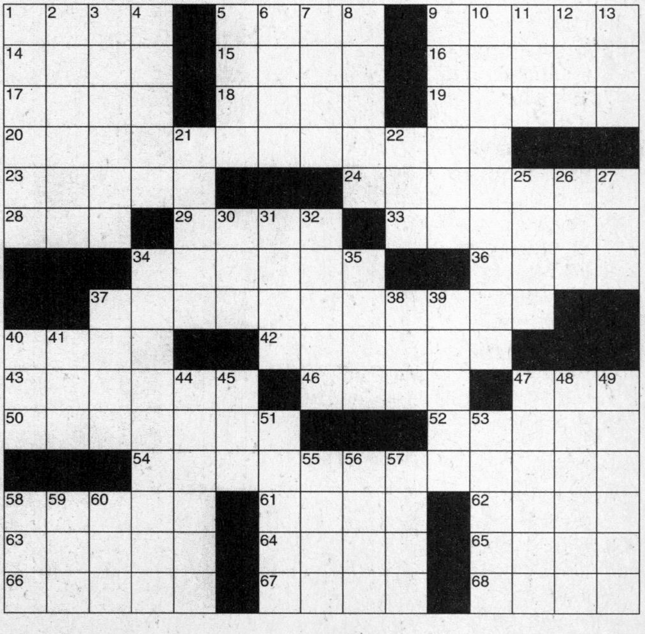

68 TAKING SIDES

by Frances Hansen

ACROSS

1 Implanted
5 Skittish
10 Social reformer Jacob
14 Siamese, today
15 "You __ mouthful!"
16 Writer Ferber
17 Dry
18 German seaport
19 Barbershop offering
20 Greet the day
22 Grace the place
24 Sanford of *The Jeffersons*
27 Part of QED
28 Fellow
30 Strong wind
31 Author Carson
34 Assn.
35 Nobel Institute site
36 Plow inventor
37 Yegg's target
39 *Amerika* author
42 "Shucks!"
43 Gnawed to a fare-thee-well
45 French actor Jacques
47 Cooling measure: Abbr.
48 French dramatist
50 Role model
51 Aurora alias
52 Property attachment
53 Donahue of *Father Knows Best*
55 Catbird's quaking cousin
58 Greet the day
61 Chesterfield, e.g.
62 Hole __ (ace)
65 Stress, perhaps
66 Printing paper size
67 Madame de __
68 "More __ You Know" (1929 song)
69 Terrier type
70 Warming drink
71 Diminutive suffix

DOWN

1 For men only
2 Czech river
3 Odets play
4 Spider's nest
5 Monogram of *Cats* librettist
6 Descartes' conclusion
7 Politically moderate
8 Nantes notion
9 One of Santa's reindeer
10 Backtracked
11 Rodgers and Hart musical
12 Monogram pt.
13 Identical
21 Half the name of a Samoan city
23 Toward the mouth
25 Soak up the sun
26 First name in scat
28 Babe in the bulrushes
29 Macaw
32 Muse of poetry
33 "__ pray" (pulpit petition)
38 Ballpark figure
40 Film critic Pauline
41 Abruzzi cathedral town
44 Hebrew eve
46 Hebrides island
49 Sign up
54 Hold forth
55 Recipe amts.
56 Fleece
57 Word form for "within"
59 Usher's offering
60 Sea eagle
63 Actor Beatty
64 Bridge expert Culbertson

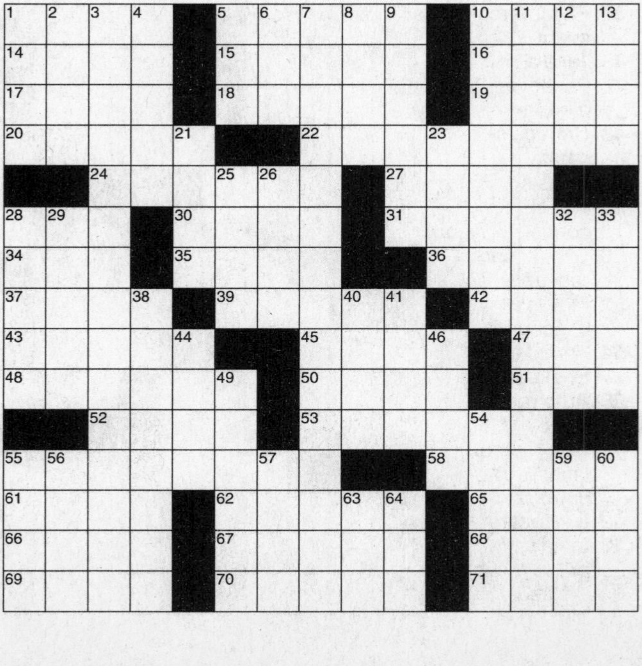

69 SKY LIGHTS

by Bill Leonard

ACROSS
1 Old Chevy
5 More impolite
10 Charts
14 Incenses
15 Accustom
16 Ancient theaters
17 Check out
18 Astronomers
20 Ceres or Juno
22 Planet discovered in 1781
23 Steak order
24 Celtic sea god
25 Cease
28 Close groups of stars
33 Word for Yorick
34 Actor Kristofferson
35 French pronoun
36 Skating surface
37 Moon lander
38 Close tightly
39 Two-year-old
40 Ooze
41 Head: Fr.
42 Peruvian plant
45 Gazes steadily
47 Pah-pah preceder
48 Practice boxing
49 Navy builder
52 Passerine bird
56 Procyon's constellation
58 Lake city
59 Moslem nation
60 Roman magistrate
61 Narrative
62 Makes a choice
63 Surfeits
64 __ stars (gets bopped)

DOWN
1 Naldi of the silents
2 Metallic rocks
3 Suit part
4 Keyboard symbol
5 Spa
6 Loosen
7 Two
8 Go wrong
9 Leo's brightest star
10 Austrian composer
11 Yemeni seaport
12 South American nation
13 Talk back
19 Mars' alias
21 Ethiopian title
25 Pub game
26 Agent Ness
27 Thanksgiving parade participant
28 Statement of belief
29 Like a wet noodle
30 Old-time anesthetic
31 Highway
32 Locations
34 Painter Paul
38 Young actresses
40 Meanings expressed by morphemes
43 Redbreasts
44 Some deer
45 Bowling marks
46 Roofing material
48 Long scarf
49 I know: Lat.
50 O.K. Corral name
51 Pre-med subj.
52 State of irritation
53 "Dies __"
54 World's longest river
55 Commands to horses
57 Cretan Mount

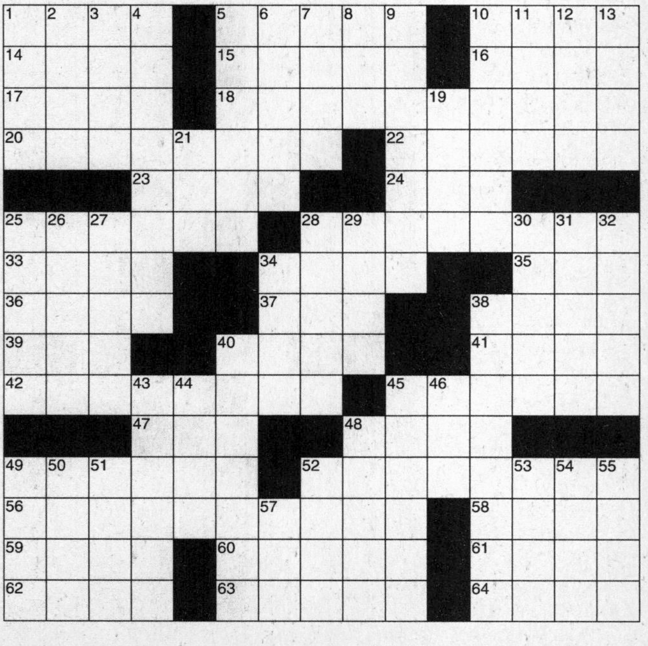

70 ON THE GRIDDLE

by Bob Lubbers

ACROSS

1 Former Palermo pelf
5 Addis __
10 Makes mistakes
14 Cain raiser
15 Royal ceremony
17 Equivocate
19 Became skilled in
20 Greek vowel
21 Linguistic suffix
24 Payable
25 Vestige
27 Hang out
29 Prepare for painting
33 Curved shape
34 Some Kenyans
36 Part of RFD
38 Face powder
43 Devil
44 Per __ (yearly)
46 Tint
48 Newspaper sections
51 Subtle atmosphere
52 Gives for a while
54 Tease
56 Came upon
57 Boat propeller
58 Manages
63 Procrastinate
68 Galley worker
69 Nobelist Wiesel
70 Espied
71 Boscs
72 Watered down

DOWN

1 Statute
2 Neighbor of Ore.
3 Churchill's "so few": Abbr.
4 Letters on a radio
5 Two-pair holding, in poker
6 Field-goal expert, e.g.
7 *Rule, Britannia* composer
8 Sort of swine
9 __ of Cleves
10 UFO crew
11 Stair parts
12 Itineraries
13 Golf Hall-of-Famer
16 Assists
18 Young feller
21 Shade tree
22 Work up lather
23 *Born Free* character
26 Western capital
28 Alit
30 Actress Papas
31 Fall bloomer
32 Paleozoic, e.g.
35 Bar rocks
37 Alias letters
39 Latin 101 word
40 Keystone character
41 Word on a quarter
42 Untainted
45 Wrestler's pad
46 Court cry
47 Not pickable
49 Chest part
50 Shankar collection
52 Barn attics
53 *Robin and the Seven Hoods* characters
55 Actor Turhan
59 Slightest sound
60 Art Deco artist
61 __-tat
62 Hodgepodge
64 Sawbuck
65 Suffix for percent
66 *Alice* name
67 "It's a mouse!"

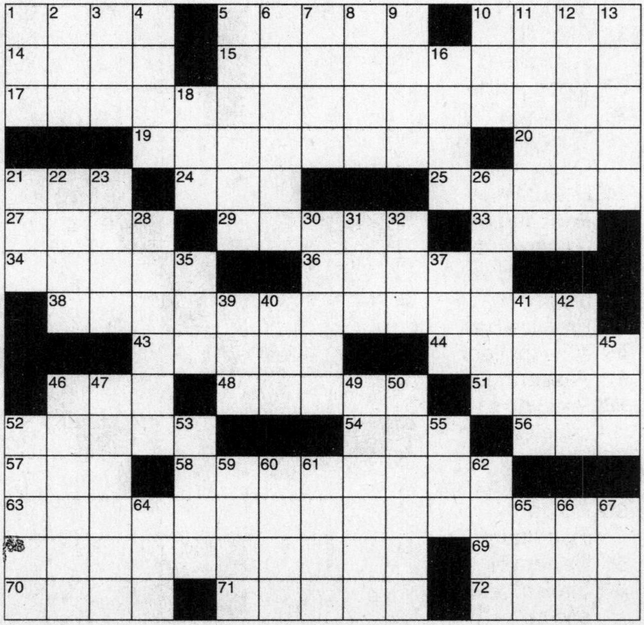

71 SO LONG FILMS

by Randy Hartman

ACROSS
1 Killer whale
5 At a __ for words
9 Propel a bike
14 Antler
15 Assert
16 Last letter, in Athens
17 Ali MacGraw film of '69
20 Stop __ dime
21 Housing cost
22 Mountain ridges
23 Temporary routes
25 Manuscript directive
26 Not hers
27 Got a hole in one
28 H.S. exam
31 Tibetan monks
34 Disney sci-fi film
35 Markdown
36 Hemingway adaptation of '57
39 Catherine __-Jones of *The Mask of Zorro*
40 Cut, in a way
41 Mighty conflict
42 She-sheep
43 Breakfast cereal
44 Sault __ Marie
45 Networks
46 Belly
50 __ *Weapon*
53 Halt
54 Feathered stole
55 Tony Curtis comedy of '66
58 Strike down
59 Out of control
60 Farm unit
61 Come to a point
62 Party bowlfuls
63 "Buenos __!"

DOWN
1 George Burns film
2 TV exec Arledge
3 Zagreb resident
4 Plus
5 Strata
6 Kilns
7 Religious group
8 Sign at the Bijou
9 Did the honors at tea
10 Irish patriot Robert
11 Money owed
12 Chills and fever
13 Highland girl
18 Fruit flaw
19 Dormant
24 Scarlett of Tara
25 Chew out
27 "Stormy Weather" composer
28 Poet Teasdale
29 Some donations
30 Pianist John
31 Be slothful
32 Some
33 Chess win
34 Lone Star State
35 Witch-trial site
37 Croon
38 Squid relatives
43 Jerry Mathers role
44 Has on hand
45 Author E.B.
46 Razor sharpener
47 Low-tech calculators
48 Hooded snake
49 Helen or Isaac
50 Endure
51 Humorist Bombeck
52 Voyage
53 Road rig
56 Mom's partner
57 Turned, as food

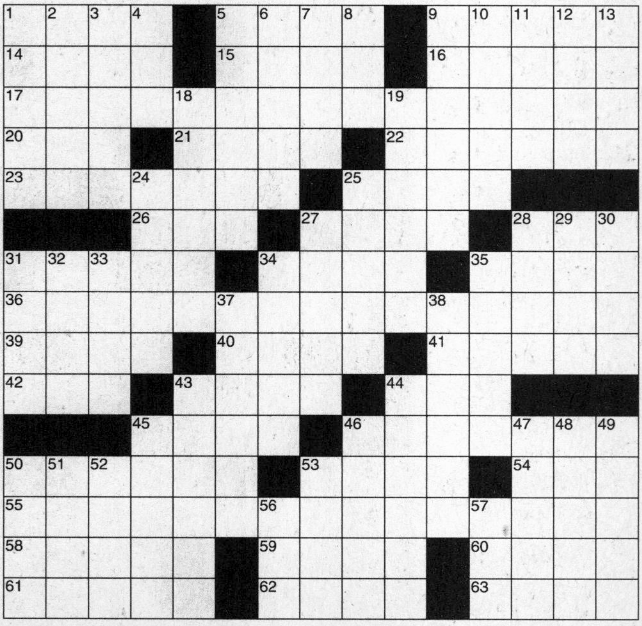

72 IN THE THICK OF THINGS

by Fred Piscop

ACROSS

1 "¿Que __?"
5 Walk through water
9 Houston player
14 Construction piece
15 Wide-eyed
16 Actor Cheech
17 It's low on a sports car
20 "Sarabandes" composer
21 Pro's charge
22 High point
23 Pilgrim to Mecca
26 Rhett Butler's last word
28 British wheels
30 Poet Levertov
34 Prefix with metric
37 "__ corny as Kansas . . ."
39 Horse opera
40 Hinterland
44 MacDowell of *Groundhog Day*
45 Char
46 __ tai
47 Loch sighting
49 Insurers incur them
52 Like a sourball
54 Be a drugstore cowboy
57 Allied victory site of 1944
60 Moo goo __ pan
62 Nettles
64 Joseph Conrad novel
68 Upper crust
69 Greek-salad cheese
70 Make bootees
71 Smarts
72 Candied tubers
73 __-serif (type style)

DOWN

1 Paparazzo's wares
2 Crosswise, nautically
3 __ Domingo
4 Virtuoso
5 Children's card game
6 In the past
7 Tip, as a hat
8 Encouraged, with "on"
9 *I __ Camera*
10 Grassy plain
11 Begin a fall
12 Solemn ceremony
13 Cameo stone
18 Wriggly
19 Crack the books
24 Part of HOMES
25 Notes from the CEO
27 Kitty cry
29 *60 Minutes* man
31 Bit of gossip
32 Antitoxins
33 ". . . __ saw Elba"
34 David Bowie's wife
35 Trig ratio
36 OTB postings
38 Poky critter
41 Twists out of shape
42 *Star Wars* princess
43 About
48 Therefore, to Descartes
50 Spock's boss
51 Brouhahas
53 Chewy candy
55 Actress Verdugo
56 Pine exudation
57 The Beatles' "__ a Woman"
58 Introduction to marketing?
59 Put down
61 Creative spark
63 Some former JFK arrivals
65 Golf prop
66 Cash dispenser, for short
67 __ Tafari (Haile Selassie)

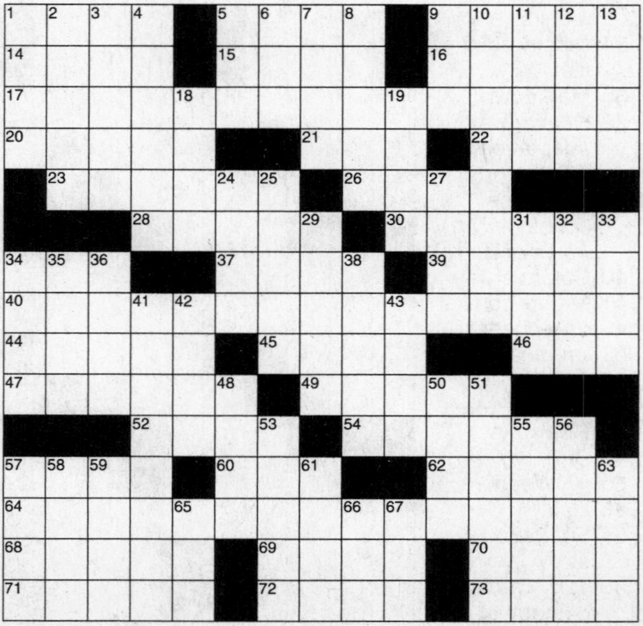

73 BUDGET BUSTER

by Patrick Jordan

ACROSS
1 Was quietly angry
6 Eye drop
10 Rock singer Joan
14 Repair a wrong
15 Diminish
16 Spiny houseplant
17 Poker player's pack
18 Annoys
19 *Duck Soup* name
20 Words from a 41 Across
23 Brother of Cain and Abel
24 Maiden-name indicator
25 Black Sea peninsula
29 Ave. crossers
30 Contemptible fellow
33 Words from a 41 Across
36 Bullring "Bravo!"
37 News article
38 Kilmer of *The Saint*
39 Movie monster
40 Backtalk
41 Nonfrugal sort
45 Morse-code character
46 Took the pennant
47 Does a double take, perhaps
48 Buddy
49 Tumult
51 Words from a 41 Across
59 Brainstorm
60 Paint layer
61 Goosebump-inducing
62 Laugh loudly
63 Director Kazan
64 Jockey's controls
65 Pretentious-looking
66 Barbie or Raggedy Ann
67 Orchard, essentially

DOWN
1 Verifiable statement
2 Beehive State
3 Additional
4 Draws to a close
5 1957 Tracy/Hepburn film
6 Chubby Checker's dance
7 Soil
8 Egyptian cross
9 Takes personally
10 Farr of *M*A*S*H*
11 Western actor Jack
12 Actress Spelling
13 Schoolbook
21 Slangy affirmative
22 For fear that
25 TV chef Julia
26 Mathematical proportion
27 Bumbling
28 *The Wizard of Oz* studio
29 Completely convinced
30 Infant's ailment
31 Up in the air
32 Obligations
34 In equilibrium
35 Has the power to
39 Swimsuit part
41 Persuade
42 Served as a security force for
43 Jazz combo, often
44 President Hoover
48 Arctic explorer Robert
49 Garden mollusk
50 Wreck completely
51 Actress Sorvino
52 Aroma
53 Kin of "Cool!"
54 Flight-school test
55 Express derision
56 Canal completed in 1825
57 Film, in France
58 Thomas Hardy heroine

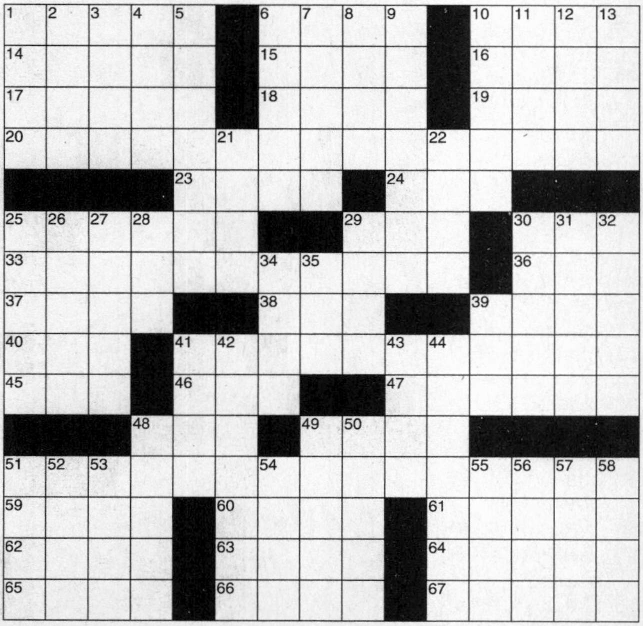

74 WEAPONRY

by Fred Piscop

ACROSS

1 Cowpokes' pals
6 Abbr. in many business names
10 Skater Lipinski
14 Allure
15 __ and file
16 Change for a five
17 Bubble-gum comics character
19 Sitarist Shankar
20 __ *and Son* (English sitcom)
21 One way to serve beans
23 Barbie's boyfriend
24 Usher's beat
25 Rigatoni relative
28 "What Kind of Fool __?"
31 1-800-FLOWERS rival
32 Oust
34 In any way
36 Pugilists' org.
39 Bullwinkle's colleague
42 Sitcom planet
43 Catty remark
44 Cultured gem
45 Baseball feats: Abbr.
46 *Krazy* __
48 "Power" word form
49 Pentium maker
52 Net holder
54 WWII life jacket
57 Stored fodders
61 __ colada
62 Basketball great Maravich
64 Perpetually
65 Creative spark
66 Thrill to pieces
67 "__ Do It" (Porter tune)
68 Words in print
69 Showed again

DOWN

1 Industrial pollutants
2 At the drop of __
3 Bulldoze
4 Football play
5 Walloped
6 Highlands hillside
7 British rule in India
8 __ close to schedule
9 __-Ball (arcade game)
10 Much more than warm
11 Diarist Nin
12 Party hearty
13 Parenthetical remark
18 Hawaiian coffee center
22 Bully's offering, maybe
25 Centigrade freezing point of water
26 Novello of old films
27 Watch sound
29 Goya's *The Naked* __
30 "No problem!"
31 Winter bug
33 House of worship
35 Pastel shade
36 Fay of *King Kong*
37 Swiss capital
38 Milan's *Teatro __ Scala*
40 "__ the season . . ."
41 Rhode Island's state tree
45 Big name in Scotch
47 Threesome
49 Drive forward
50 Wet behind the ears
51 Ism
53 Less well
55 Kebab holder
56 Rip or neap
57 "Now!" to a surgeon
58 Apparatus
59 Sundance's girlfriend
60 Caught in the act
63 Questionnaire question

75 RUN-OF-THE-MILL

by Rich Norris

ACROSS

1 Crow calls
5 Wife of Zeus
9 Madrid museum
14 Not "fer"
15 Amazed
16 '80s NBC drama
17 Columnist Barrett
18 War, to Sherman
19 Colored like the sky
20 Tax-return category
23 Tune by 63 Across
24 Ballpark beverage
25 Painter's protection
29 Way out
33 Program interruptions
36 Aligns
38 Resting atop
39 November event
43 Without delay, in a memo
44 '60s guru Timothy
45 "__ you serious?"
46 ACLU concerns
49 Get up
51 The Emerald Isle
53 Poetic feet
57 1/2, e.g.
62 Biblical spy
63 Guitarist Clapton
64 Irish folk singer
65 Military chaplain
66 Dole (out)
67 Offend the nose
68 Has __ to the ground
69 Supportive votes
70 Really upset

DOWN

1 Channing of Broadway
2 Greek marketplace
3 Like Chicago
4 Slowpokes
5 "Very funny!"
6 Wide-spouted pitcher
7 Bank (on)
8 Off-the-script comment
9 Locations
10 Hair-salon request
11 Former student, briefly
12 Challenge
13 Have debts
21 Title giver
22 Wedding-page word
26 Eggs
27 Honeycomb part
28 Leg joints
30 Capital of Samoa
31 Shoddy in quality
32 Feminine ending
33 Ice-cream thickener
34 He loved Lucy
35 Sweater problem
37 Venetian-blind component
40 Short-lived things
41 Important time
42 Pessimistic type
47 Lumberjack's shout
48 "Sold out" letters
50 Library gadgets
52 Adversary
54 Actor Sal
55 *Gaslight* star
56 Slithery reptile
57 Actor James
58 Shoppe sign word
59 On the loose
60 Comic Rudner
61 King beaters
62 Apr. 15th advisor

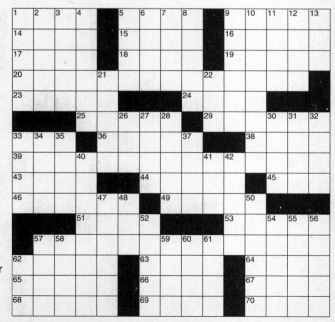

1	2	3	4	■	5	6	7	8	■	9	10	11	12	13
14				■	15				■	16				
17				■	18				■	19				
20				21					22					■
23					■	■	■	24				■	■	■
■	■	■	25		26	27	28	■	29			30	31	32
33	34	35	■	36				37	■	■	38			
39			40						41	42				
43				■	■	44					■	45		
46				47	48	■	49				50	■	■	■
■	■	■	51			52	■	■	■	53		54	55	56
■	57	58					59	60	61					
62					■	63				■	64			
65					■	66				■	67			
68					■	69				■	70			

76 MOUSE CALL

by Patrick Jordan

ACROSS
1 Skywalker's father
6 Hit the malls
10 Butter servings
14 Puccini genre
15 Frequent song subject
16 With 35 Down, Monty Python member
17 Newton or Hayes
18 PC programmer
19 Mideast bread
20 Cub Scout group
21 He appeared in 10 Disney films
24 Military vehicles
26 Got dirty
27 Isle of Capri attraction
29 Lacerates
31 Weeknightly monologist
32 Head, slangily
34 Lower the lights
37 Paradisiacal places
39 Greedy sort
40 Valerie Harper role
42 Negative votes
43 Kitchen gadget
46 Without siblings
47 Fort __, IN
48 Rouses from slumber
50 Savage
53 Find contemptible
54 She appeared in 4 Disney films
57 Galena or pitchblende
60 Step __ (rush)
61 Longest armbone
62 Composer Erik
64 Well-heeled
65 Sitcom producer Norman
66 Praise greatly
67 Dinner and a movie, maybe
68 Soaks (up)
69 Wren residences

DOWN
1 No longer valid
2 Church area
3 He appeared in 12 Disney films
4 Segment of history
5 Novotna need
6 Speaks indistinctly
7 TV emcee
8 Finished
9 Scrutiny
10 Some sodas
11 Historian Durant
12 Championship
13 Burn with water
22 Second word of many fairy tales
23 More achy
25 School founded by Henry VI
27 Singer Campbell
28 Change the decor
29 Linen fabric
30 Advantage
33 Ready for customers
34 He appeared in 6 Disney films
35 See 16 Across
36 "The Say Hey Kid"
38 "The final frontier"
41 Frost
44 Breathtaking views
45 Tortoise/hare event
47 Squirm
49 Deteriorate
50 Norwegian inlet
51 Ancient Greek region
52 Royal decree
53 Has the lead role
55 Toast topper
56 Simple task
58 Funny one
59 Marine wrigglers
63 Chestnut chopper

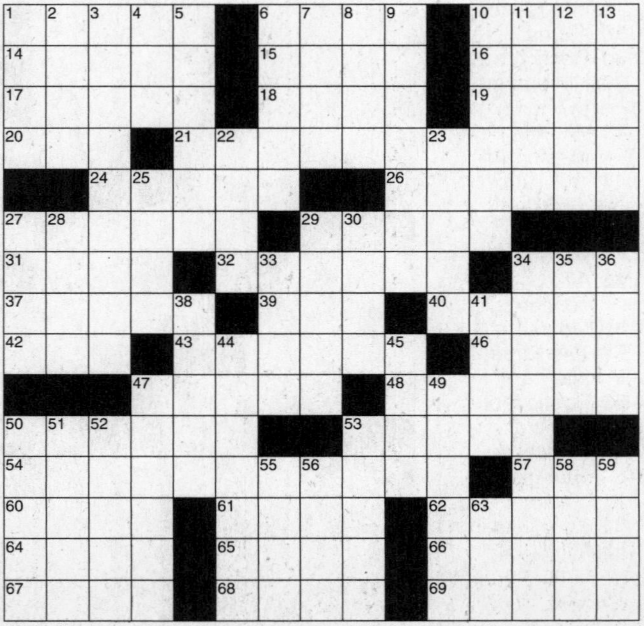

77 HEAVENLY HASH

by Patrick Jordan

ACROSS
1 Baby bleater
5 Wizardry
10 Line of fashion?
14 Solo at La Scala
15 Frigidaire competitor
16 Edison's middle name
17 African wading bird
19 Wedding-cake layer
20 Back of a boat
21 Some sculptures
23 Egyptian goddess
26 Pops like a balloon
27 Chicken-hearted sort
32 Whiskey grain
33 Upper crust
34 Disconcerted
38 Russian river
40 "Whole __ Shakin' Going On"
42 New Haven campus
43 Fracas
45 Still in bed
47 Arrest
48 Newborn, so to speak
51 Horrified
54 Actress Conn
55 Stages a Civil War battle, perhaps
58 *Lost in Space* character
62 Food fish
63 Expression of wonderment
66 Celebratory poems
67 Clear a videotape
68 Type of collar or jacket
69 Hawaiian honker
70 Holmes' creator
71 Roof coverings

DOWN
1 Glasgow girl
2 "I smell __!"
3 Mickey and Mighty
4 Spanish-speaking district
5 Sore
6 Parisian pal
7 Runs off at the mouth
8 Monogram pt.
9 Melon variety
10 Matinee time
11 Inventor Howe
12 Ward off
13 Martin and Steenburgen
18 Come next
22 Gang territory
24 "__ do for now"
25 Descendants
27 Fife accompaniment
28 Rochester's love
29 Cutlet meat
30 Preminger and Kahn
31 Made damp
35 Western novelist Grey
36 Spirited quality
37 Financial obligation
39 Beirut citizen
41 German car
44 Film lioness
46 Peter, in Pamplona
49 Drew with acid
50 Rhode Island's state flower
51 Firebug's crime
52 Crystal-lined stone
53 Singer Reddy
56 Matador's foe
57 Do in
59 First Greek consonant
60 Fragrance
61 A lot
64 Designer label initials
65 Golfer's prop

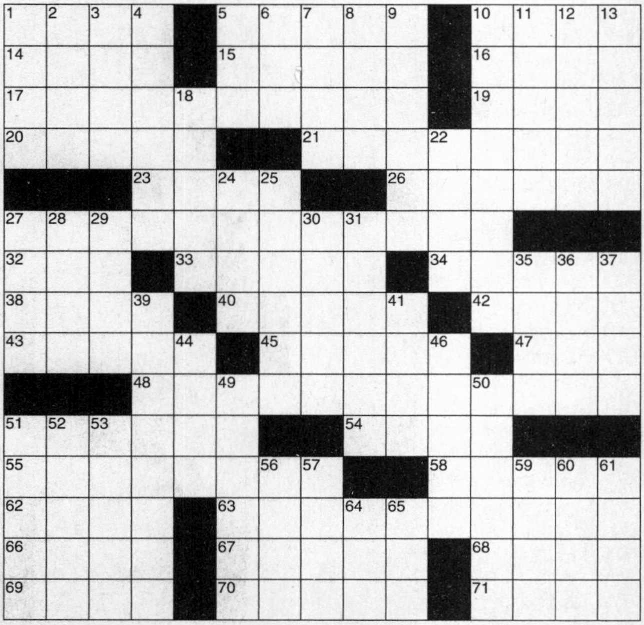

78 UP TO THE MINUTE

by Fred Piscop

ACROSS
1 Futuristic literature
6 1040, for one
10 __ Jones' locker
14 Ballpark instrument
15 Draftable
16 Lamb's pseudonym
17 Controller of body rhythms
20 Prepared baby food
21 Hotel-door posting
22 Neighbor of Ga.
23 Sax man Getz
25 Niels Bohr, for one
28 Sentinel's post
34 Ben-Gurion Airport carrier
35 One of the Osmonds
36 I love: Lat.
37 Scotland Yard unit: Abbr.
38 Old Nick
39 Styling stuff
40 Justice Fortas
41 Took notice, in a way
42 Wet blanket
43 Neophyte
46 Intaglio stone
47 Spectrum bands
48 Immigrant's subj.
50 Eloper of rhyme
53 Don't drink
58 Model's shape
61 Sidekick: Abbr.
62 Savings plans, for short
63 Chou __
64 Team that debuted in '62
65 Nada
66 Bath add-ins

DOWN
1 Whimpers
2 Reviewer, for short
3 Frankenstein's flunky
4 Mideast appetizer
5 How tuna may be packed
6 Pâté de __ gras
7 Like most of today's music
8 New Deal agcy.
9 Content starter
10 Presidential middle name
11 Jillions
12 __ versa
13 Ties up the phone
18 Chew (on)
19 Bucket of bolts
23 Tough spot
24 Like a rail
25 Kind of coffee
26 Suspect's story
27 Consumers' crusader
29 Fine fiddles
30 Jazz pianist Art
31 Pioneer's conveyance
32 Manicurist's material
33 Movado rival
38 Fill to the brim
41 Beset by hornets
42 Italian city
44 Bermuda wear
45 Shipwreck site
49 Porcine pads
50 Bogus
51 Sit for a photo
52 Give the boot to
53 Bygone despot
54 Old gas brand
55 Rock band Jethro __
56 "I smell __!"
57 Cruise keepsakes
59 Designer Claiborne
60 "Chances __"

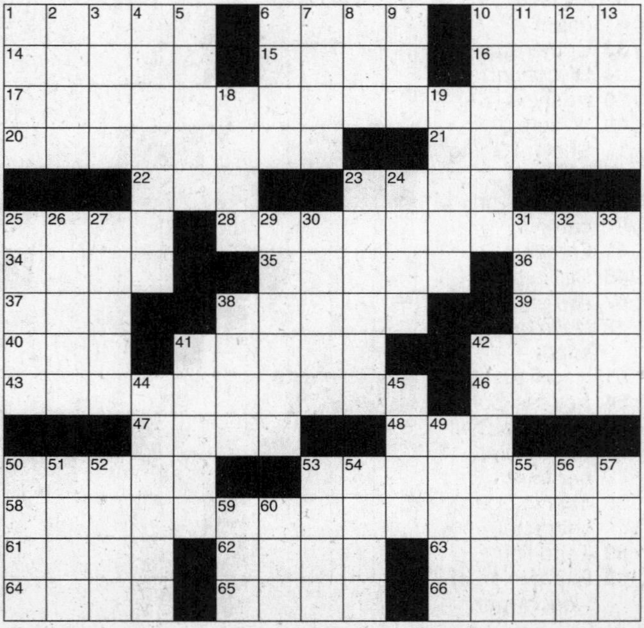

79 HOME SWEET HOME

by Lee Weaver

ACROSS

1 Drive headlong into
4 Silent-screen siren
8 More adorable
13 Be inaccurate
14 Writer Wiesel
15 Proceed nonchalantly
16 Calling on
18 Adhere closely
19 Type of potatoes
21 Auctioneer's last word
24 Daystar
25 Difficult duty
26 Corporate newsletter
33 *Nightline* host Koppel
34 Gets forty winks
35 Nemo's creator
36 Most lofty
38 Church officials
40 Utopian
41 Do a clerk's job
42 "__ on a Happy Face"
43 1910s dance
46 Boxer's signal
47 Word form for "bad"
48 Latin being
49 Posh pleasure boat
57 Street crosser
58 Turnpike structure
62 Little laugh
63 Meadow mamas
64 Ironically funny
65 '50s Ford
66 Actress Thompson
67 Soap ingredient

DOWN

1 Gun the engine
2 Nickname for Onassis
3 Bride's title: Abbr.
4 Turn down
5 Dismounted
6 Julep enhancer
7 Winged horse of myth
8 Bossy's offspring
9 Software buyer
10 Asian cuisine
11 Icicle site
12 Deli loaves
15 Public commotion
17 Tops a torte
20 Astronaut Grissom
21 Medieval style of architecture
22 New York lake
23 Prods along
26 Possesses
27 Make a decision
28 Cameo shape
29 VCR button
30 Hunts in the dark
31 Invalidates
32 Cozy up
34 Actress Carter
37 Beanie or beret
38 Neighbor of Penna.
39 Antlered animal
41 Military greetings
44 Host a roast
45 Major conflict
46 Ice mass
49 Zoo enclosure
50 Enthusiastic
51 Pleads
52 *Picnic* playwright
53 __ and void
54 Des Moines' home
55 Musher's vehicle
56 Famous lioness
59 Hole-punching gadget
60 Take a stab at
61 Hurricane center

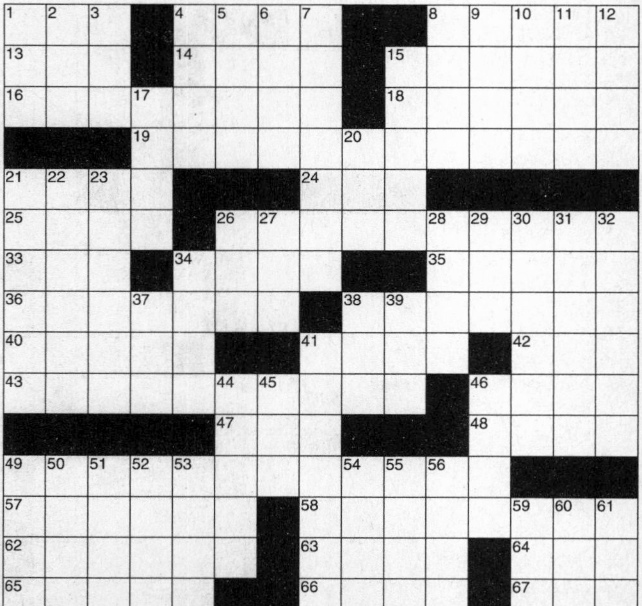

80 LISTEN CAREFULLY

by S. E. Booker

ACROSS
1 Tiny circle
4 Wood strips
9 Police alert: Abbr.
12 Momentous era
15 Disney's Little Mermaid
16 Ram's remark
17 Quarter back?
18 Edison town
20 Unornamented
21 One for the book?
22 Global speck
23 Swine
25 One more
27 Ladle, e.g.
30 Ram's remark
31 Off-Broadway award
32 __ *Arabian Nights*
34 Go get
38 Sure thing
39 Reed of sitcomdom
41 Casting slot
42 Unravels
44 Ale holders
45 Horner's surprise
46 Fields' yields
48 Industry publications
50 Facsimile
53 Binge
54 No-cholesterol spread
55 Liquefy
57 Make reparation
61 Really silly
63 Joined cloth
64 "A mouse!"
65 Effective use
66 Out on a limb?
67 Prom attendees: Abbr.
68 Conductor Zubin
69 Uninteresting

DOWN
1 Intense
2 Whitish gem
3 Augustan attire
4 Goosenecks, for instance
5 Milieu
6 BELL
7 Author Hanff
8 Highway warning
9 Embarrass
10 *Ici on __ francais*
11 Humorist Russell
13 HORSE
14 *Sun Valley Serenade* star
19 RAIN
24 Electricity distribution system
26 Klutz
27 Tip, as your hat
28 Girder
29 Elite alternative
30 Something extra
33 TUBA
35 Gave away
36 Mystery board game
37 Skirts' outskirts
40 Concerning
43 __ Lanka
47 From C to C
49 Cook one's goose
50 Thorny subjects
51 Aunt in *Oklahoma!*
52 Reaches the top
53 Choreographer Tharp
56 "They have digged __ before me": Psalms
58 Was obliged to
59 __-do-well
60 MacDonald's singing partner
62 Stage show-off

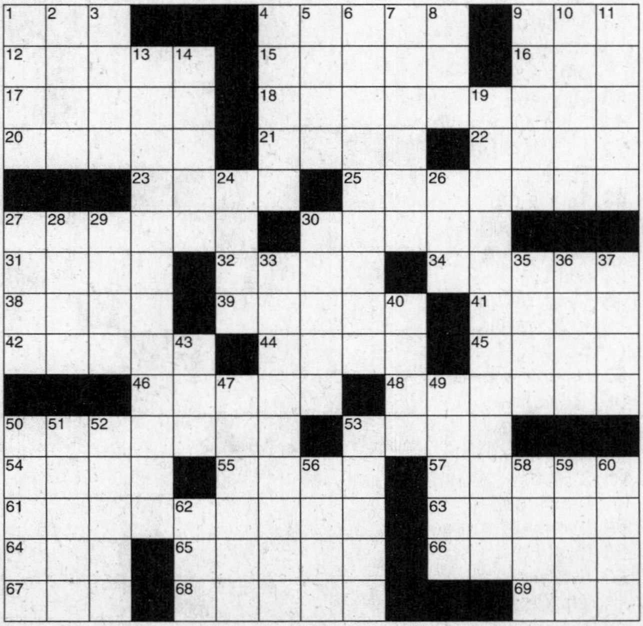

81 BOWLED OVER

by Fred Piscop

ACROSS

1 Sail support
5 Moisten the turkey
10 Shea Stadium player
13 Where vows are exchanged
15 Zones
16 "__ Maria"
17 Unneeded coins
19 Perfect score in gymnastics
20 Top-billing sharer
21 Ship's record
22 Landlord's income
23 Pub brews
25 Returns to a former condition
27 Fulton steamboat
31 "Zip-a-Dee-Doo-__"
32 Yes, to Yves
33 *Gentlemen Prefer Blondes* writer
35 Folger's rival
39 Start conducting
43 Canines and bicuspids
44 Garr or Hatcher
45 New: Pref.
46 Musical acuity
48 Renaissance preceder
51 Male graduate
55 Pigs' places
56 Microscope part
57 Cambridge coll.
59 Jalopy sound
63 "What Kind of Fool __"
64 Two images on one TV
66 Bon __ (witty saying)
67 Unaccompanied
68 Designer Donna
69 *A Chorus Line* song
70 Hostess Perle
71 Summer-camp site

DOWN

1 Opposite of fem.
2 Purina competitor
3 RR stops
4 Sauce with fish sticks
5 "__, humbug!"
6 Inland Asian sea
7 Sir, in Seville
8 Put a price on
9 Point opposite WNW
10 Alma __
11 Decathlon part
12 Campers' shelters
14 Kingdom
18 New Orleans cuisine
22 Back-to-health program
24 Pig's nose
26 Bouquet holder
27 __-of-living increase
28 Mandolin cousin
29 Irish republic
30 Drank too much
34 Part of a sandal
36 Da __, Vietnam
37 Patch place, often
38 Hubbubs
40 List components
41 Genghis __
42 Personnel departments, often
47 Wrinkle up
49 Talent
50 Star-shaped
51 Crockett's last stand
52 Sour fruit
53 Join forces
54 Farm structures
58 Color lightly
60 Trillion: Pref.
61 Dike problem
62 Feminine suffix
64 "I Want You" uncle
65 Drink with crumpets

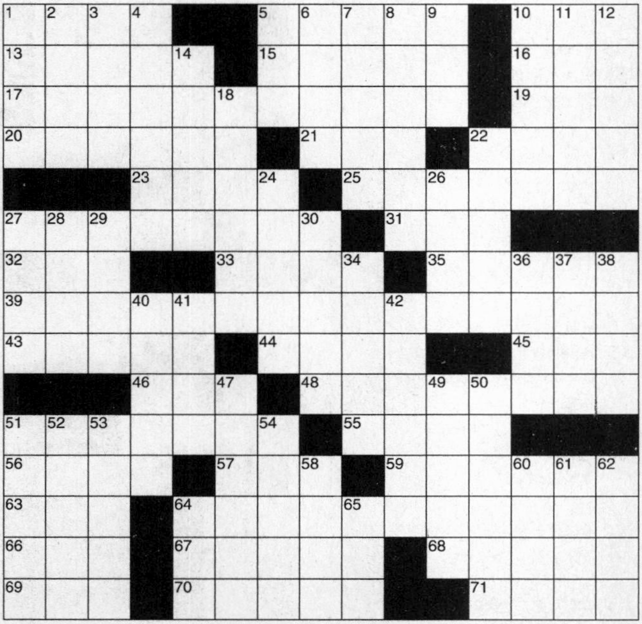

82 WEE BITS

by Bob Lubbers

ACROSS
1 Summer, on the Somme
4 La __ Opera House
9 Foundation
14 Stir
15 Expert group
16 Make joyful
17 Wrath
18 Happening
19 Evaluated
20 Alcott book
23 Gershwin brother
24 Not moving
25 Pub refresher
26 Squeal (on)
27 Fairy-tale monster
28 Mubarak of Egypt
31 Ceremony
32 Diner handout
33 Flower holders
34 Quick work
38 Jazzman Shaw
40 Skirt shape
41 Saucy
42 Stage whisper
44 Nagy of Hungary
48 Org. for Tiger Woods
49 Carney or Linkletter
50 Villainous glare
51 Sup
52 Nickels and dimes
56 Pen name
58 Norman Vincent __
59 Tic follower
60 Long gun
61 Cowboy star Lash
62 Model Carol
63 "__ ain't so!"
64 Bitter-__ (diehard)
65 Bandleader Brown

DOWN
1 Designer Gucci
2 Getting weary
3 Phillips __ Academy
4 Asian wheat
5 Grotto
6 Once again
7 Carson successor
8 *M*A*S*H* director
9 Swiss capital
10 Pie __ mode
11 Jonathan Swift, for one
12 Say repeatedly
13 Calms
21 Three, in Torino
22 New Haven student
28 That girl
29 Prov. of Canada
30 Bar food?
31 Flying Brits
32 A Stooge
33 Nabob, initially
34 Divide into castes
35 Smash
36 Mason's trough
37 Caviar
38 Pops up
39 Royal emblems
42 Pitcher's resource
43 Food basic
44 Buy a pig __ poke
45 In the head
46 Put on a feast
47 Builds
49 Valued property
50 Diaphanous
53 Lanky
54 Frying medium
55 Hint
57 __ Baba

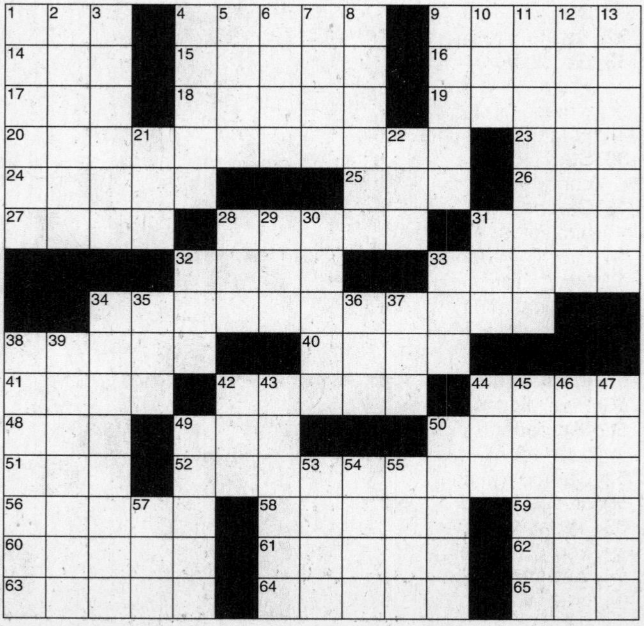

83 YOUR KIND OF MUSIC

by Norma Steinberg

ACROSS

1 Homer Simpson's son
5 Slugger's dry spell
10 Mimics
14 Famous cookiemaker
15 Danger
16 Relief pitcher's goal
17 Piece of hose
18 Sri __
19 Cabbage salad
20 Stamp-pad fluid
21 Informal conversations
23 Stuck-up sort
25 "__ the season . . ."
26 Flounder, for one
27 Stuck-up folks
32 Signal light
34 Come in second
35 Expression of wonderment
36 Theater section
37 Adds seasoning to
38 __ *18* (Uris novel)
39 Seth's mother
40 Desi's daughter
41 '30s dance
42 Sweets
44 Ladder step
45 Churl
46 Castro's predecessor
49 Bob Fosse film
54 In the know
55 Milne's bear
56 City on the Nile
57 Pinocchio, often
58 __ Raton, FL
59 Hunter Fudd
60 Bushy hairdo
61 See
62 Loses traction
63 Comic Laurel

DOWN

1 Ellington colleague
2 Surrounded by
3 Popular hymn
4 Sound of disapproval
5 Pool sound
6 Bounded
7 Vases
8 Voice-amplifying device
9 Acetate and cellophane
10 St. Francis' home
11 __ Alto, CA
12 Author Hunter
13 Makes curtains
21 Go up
22 Location
24 Become bored
27 Designer Perry
28 After the bell
29 Midafternoon to midnight stint
30 Snitched
31 Influence
32 Escaped
33 Valentine word
34 Agreement
37 Comes into view
38 Short skirt
40 Jacob's first wife
41 Lipinski feat
43 In order to
44 Shaving equipment
46 Revealed
47 Small crown
48 Kitchen coverup
49 Police alerts: Abbr.
50 Part of a bow
51 Plumb crazy
52 Radio format
53 Guitarist Hendrix
57 __ Vegas, NV

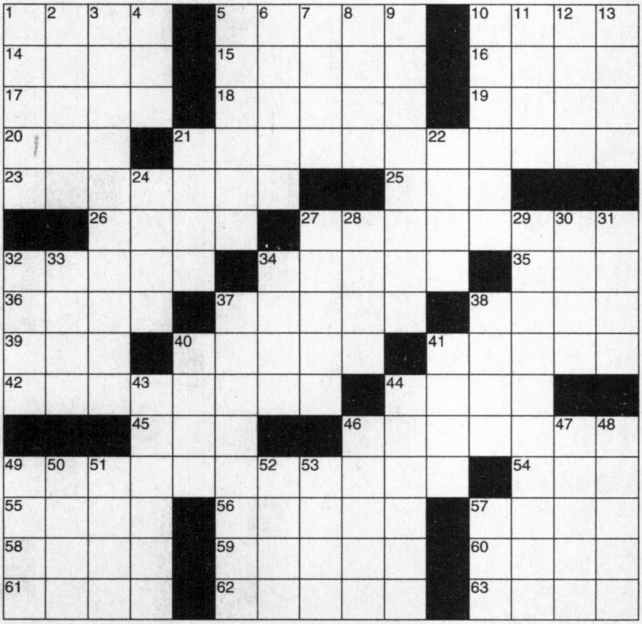

84 CLEANING UP

by Lee Weaver

ACROSS
1 Tater
5 Memo notation
9 Paul and John: Abbr.
12 Fainthearted
14 Western elevations
16 "Eureka!" is one
17 Flatter
19 Director Howard
20 Continue after interruption
21 Freedom of action
23 Tart taste
25 Swift, graceful horse
26 Perfumes, e.g.
30 Acrobatic performance
32 Nautical "yes"
33 Fender benders
35 Turn down
37 Seafood delicacy
39 Baseball stat.
40 Iroquoian Indian
41 Luau dances
43 Smooths wood
46 Put in stitches
47 Type measurements
49 Sauciness
51 Vincent Lopez theme
52 Steak order
53 Indicated a turn
57 Noxious atmosphere
61 "Wham!" relative
62 Post-battle process
64 __ premium (scarce)
65 All thumbs
66 Mortise partner
67 Boxer Baer
68 Matches a raise
69 Janet of Justice

DOWN
1 Milky Way part
2 Plumbing need
3 Refs' counterparts
4 Make thinner
5 One of a Latin trio
6 Deal in
7 China setting
8 Trattoria courses
9 Hospital worker
10 Walked heavily
11 Since, in Scotland
13 Insist upon
15 Tees and polos
18 Coppers in Coventry
22 Brownish gray
24 Inheritance units
26 Apiece
27 Waffle topping
28 Old-style letter closure
29 Purse handle
31 Makes an effort
34 More sensible
36 Fresh information
38 Pizza topping
42 Pizza topping
44 Type of stage play
45 Exacting
48 Hairdressers' hangouts
50 More tidy
53 Canned meat
54 Tiny amount
55 Olympic weapon
56 Deceive
58 Trig ratio
59 Earth's satellite
60 Part of A.D.
63 6, for a TD

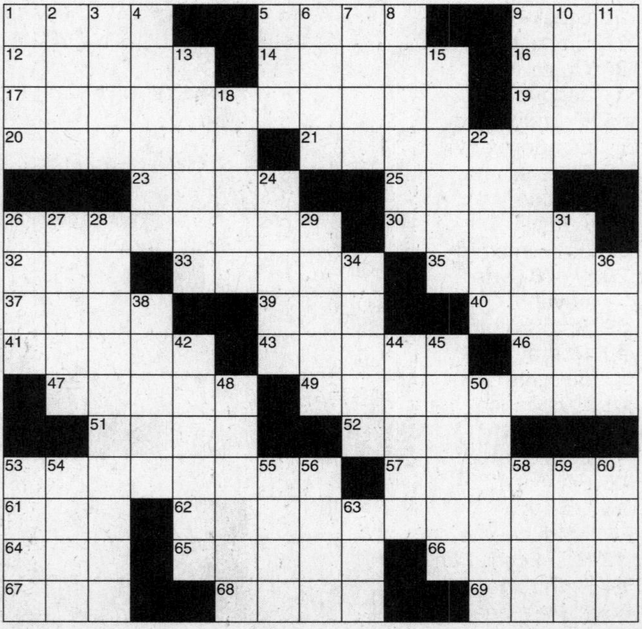

85 ANIMAL ANATOMY

by Peter Gordon

ACROSS

1 Hudson, DeSoto and LaSalle
6 The way you walk
10 Big cheese
14 Dictation pro
15 To boot
16 Northern Norwegian
17 "To Autumn" writer
18 "To Autumn," for one
19 Korea's continent
20 Quaff from Canada
23 IV units
25 Stiff __ board
26 Inconvenience
27 Vent
30 Bled, as colors
31 Hoop coup
32 *Rich Man, Poor Man* author
34 Talks amorously
38 Top with no tie
41 Church area
42 Windmill blade
43 Indian, perhaps
44 Petition
45 Wasn't a buyer
46 Boilermaker, in part
50 It's fit for pigs
52 __ *Miniver*
53 *M*A*S*H* physician
57 Bassoon relative
58 Hurler Hershiser
59 "Look, ma, no __!"
62 Toll road, for short
63 Green shade
64 Go in
65 Galley notation
66 Snakelike fish
67 Beasts of burden

DOWN

1 Present a poser
2 Western Indian
3 Drivers' union
4 Well aware of
5 Fair
6 Shows astonishment
7 Ho "Hi"
8 What *video* means
9 Cherokee chopper
10 Blurts out
11 Havens
12 Purposeful pitch
13 Bowler's pickup
21 Perched
22 Newsman Rather
23 __ Rica
24 Quite a card
28 Overdue
29 Plumbing joint
30 Hurry up
32 Hitch
33 Farm female
34 Goatee site
35 Balms
36 Mandate
37 Author Terkel
39 *Tout le monde*
40 __ *Stoops to Conquer*
44 Quilting occasion
45 Bar bottle
46 Pork portions
47 Sister's outfit
48 Got up
49 Traps game
50 Time period
51 They may be up against the wall
54 Port in Pennsylvania
55 Perlman of *Cheers*
56 Some recyclables
60 Ruby of *Do the Right Thing*
61 Prom attendees: Abbr.

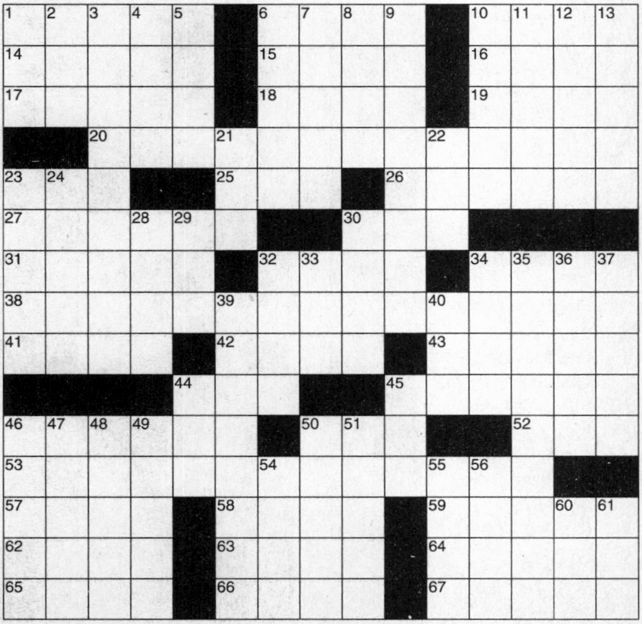

86 GRIDIRON GROUPS

by Rich Norris

ACROSS

1 Sharpens, as skills
6 Dues-paying group
10 Casino unit
14 Gussy up
15 Put on the payroll
16 Superboy's girlfriend
17 Treaty of Versailles creation
20 PC button
21 Ice sheet
22 Canadian trees
23 Eateries
25 Dutch South African
26 Hubbubs
28 Cozumel resident
32 Boston NHLer
34 Son of Seth
35 Mile High Center architect
38 Business meetings of a kind
42 N.Y. or Boston
43 Chilean coin
44 City near Gainesville
45 Curio shelf
48 Long of Louisiana
49 Very dry
51 Cartoonist Goldberg et al.
53 Spouse's kin
55 Kingly address
56 Microsoft rival
59 Assembly-line concept
62 Change one's story?
63 Agreement
64 Kate's TV pal
65 Open fabric
66 Sharp border
67 Give up

DOWN

1 Irwin of the PGA
2 Poems of praise
3 Good-for-nothing
4 Bit of work
5 Extinguish, with "out"
6 Draw straws, maybe
7 Magazine started in '36
8 Coffee maker
9 Light path
10 Like some bowties
11 Hawaiian non-native
12 *The __ Sanctum*
13 Quarterback's call
18 Kind of sch.
19 Hot sauce
24 *Clueless* remark
26 Basics
27 Rain unit
29 Noble gas
30 Letterhead abbr.
31 Miler Sebastian
33 Family members
35 Not out of the question
36 *Vogue* competitor
37 Brit's exclamation
39 Stephen of *Michael Collins*
40 Superlative suffix
41 Tylenol target
45 Visible spirit
46 Maryland's state bird
47 Home territory
49 Nasty
50 Much-impersonated star
52 Fasten, at sea
53 Bibliography word
54 Show partisanship
55 Unforeseen problem
57 Produce steam
58 '60s TV horse
60 Lge. reference work
61 Actress MacGraw

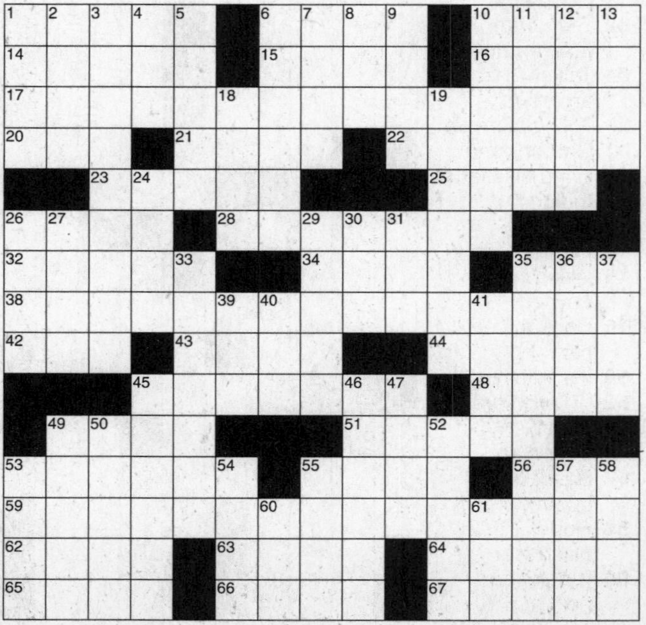

87 HOLD EVERYTHING

by Bob Lubbers

ACROSS
1 Sun-dried brick
6 __-fi
9 Shred, as cheese
14 Secret group
15 Craggy hill
16 Transplant
17 Research institute
19 Representative
20 Snow toy
21 Tolkien creature
22 Maine national park
23 "No __, Bob!"
25 Make a lap
26 Main/Kilbride film of '49
31 Shrimplike creature
33 Common article
34 Sills solo
35 Fall behind
36 Jack of *Barney Miller*
39 Hole maker
41 Plate scraping
42 Auspices
44 Friar's title
46 Gutter sites
48 Pail passers
52 Anger
53 Relieve of weapons
54 Composer Kodaly
57 "Vamoose!"
58 Least bit
62 Goes
63 Cream churn
65 Taylor of *The Nanny*
66 Former ring king
67 "Gloria __" (hymn)
68 Rare birds
69 '60s Chinese chairman
70 Without company

DOWN
1 Deeds
2 Arlene or Roald
3 Off-Broadway award
4 Toothed-belt machine
5 Wapiti
6 Fixed one's eyes
7 Idea
8 Irritate
9 Mrs. George Burns
10 Sailing race
11 Mimicked
12 Singer Braxton
13 Diminutive suffix
18 Ripped
22 Out of whack
24 Fleming and McKellen
26 Legerdemain
27 "Eureka!"
28 Valuable collection
29 Bologna bills
30 Vittles
31 USMA freshman
32 Aunt Millie's rival
37 Frequently
38 Sphere
40 Producer Norman
43 Skip around
45 Pungent salad leaf
47 Navy VIP
49 Deletes
50 *Ab* __ (from the beginning)
51 Int. trade agreement
54 Zilch
55 Draft animals
56 Bit of dialogue
59 Palindromic name
60 Revolve
61 Rose's beau
63 Loud thud
64 Pollution watchdog org.

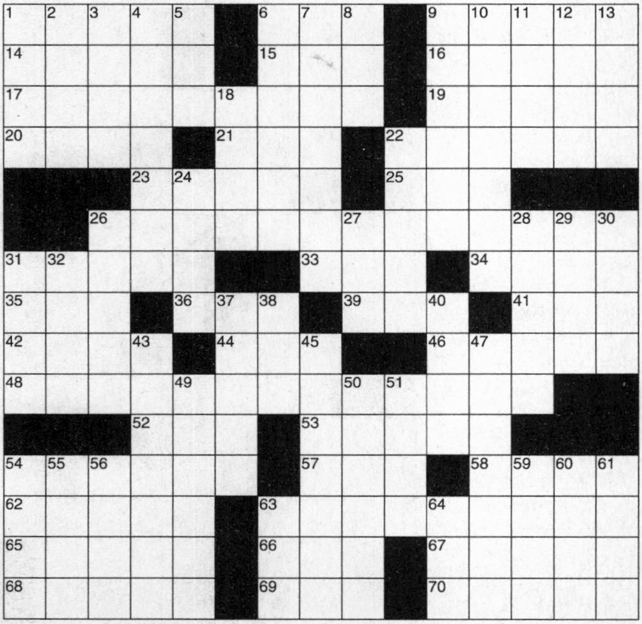

88 HIT THE DECK

by Fred Piscop

ACROSS

1 Auspices
6 Some therapy, for short
11 Old vinyl
14 Sportscaster Musburger
15 Popped up
16 Debtor's letters
17 February sweets
19 Public-house drink
20 Brosnan TV role
21 Fit of pique
22 Spectrum band
23 Social dud
25 As a group
27 Split-off group
30 Intrepid
32 Fuse unit
33 Leb. neighbor
34 Self
35 Nose-in-the-air
38 Not of the cloth
40 __-*Cop* (Reynolds film)
42 Type of terrier
43 Commotion
45 Seabird
46 MPG raters
47 Pilot's guesstimate: Abbr.
48 Like the Gobi
49 Bellicose Olympian
50 Noxious atmospheres
53 German river
55 Massachusetts cape
56 Depose
58 Overdue payment
62 Like sashimi
63 River crosser, maybe
65 "__ pig's eye!"
66 Gogol's __ *Bulba*
67 Each companion
68 Relative of -arian
69 Argus-eyed
70 Hockey great Potvin

DOWN

1 First-grade fare
2 QED center
3 Tunney of the ring
4 Start a paragraph
5 Strunk & White concern
6 Actress Charlotte
7 Elizabethan and Big Band
8 Like some toads
9 John of *The Addams Family*
10 Wedding VIP
11 Game played with dollar bills
12 Gondola propellers
13 Napped leather
18 *Babes in Toyland* composer
24 Venetian magistrate
26 Pop singer Tori
27 Delta deposit
28 Genesis twin
29 1850s conflict
31 Solitary soul
35 Flounder cousin
36 Use a keyboard
37 Pro votes
39 Goes AWOL from school
41 The Andrews Sisters, e.g.
44 *Raging Bull* subject
48 Give confidence to
49 Achieve stardom
50 Scientist Curie
51 Nonsensical
52 Of the ear
54 Missed the mark
57 Autocrat of yore
59 Tree of Knowledge site
60 Prefix with culture
61 Actors Alejandro and Fernando
64 Fast way to the UK

89 THINK BIG

by Rich Norris

ACROSS

1 Bundle of papers
6 "__ a Woman" (Beatles tune)
10 Short race
14 Sculptured forms
15 Nobelist Morrison
16 Purina competitor
17 Bred-in-the-bone
19 Toe cover
20 Former draft org.
21 EMT's skill
22 *Seinfeld* role
24 Unaffected by criticism
27 Cow of note
30 Outdoorsman's activity
31 Polaroid product
33 Giraffe feature
34 Precious stone
37 Higher than
38 Onassis' language
40 Open to view
41 Scot's negative
42 Habeas corpus, for one
43 Ad catchphrase
45 Like verse
47 Speechify
48 Extensive in scope
52 *Northern Exposure* setting
53 High school subj.
54 "The Greatest" boxer
57 Chimney passage
58 Comprehensive
62 Camping gear
63 Penitential period
64 *Paper Moon* star
65 Mlle.'s Spanish counterpart
66 Preceding periods
67 Off-the-wall

DOWN

1 Norms: Abbr.
2 Does some gardening
3 "__ Tu" (1974 song)
4 African serpent
5 Bobby of chess
6 Laundry additive
7 Like Szechuan food
8 Wind dir.
9 Heroes' helpers
10 Vietnamese seaport
11 French actor Delon
12 Backbone
13 Sank, as a putt
18 Prefix with center
23 Chain part
24 Grandstand section
25 Motion-related
26 __-Ball (arcade game)
27 Subj. for Keynes
28 Volcanic output
29 *Peter Pan* pirate
32 Pleasant
34 Ape, so to speak
35 Part of QED
36 Word on a Biblical wall
39 Comic Rudner
40 Connors rival
42 Operate effectively
44 Archer's tool of yore
45 Spanish coin
46 Deals from the bottom, say
48 Floats on the breeze
49 More under the weather
50 Frighten
51 Like Perot's party: Abbr.
54 "Just __!"
55 Plumbing problem
56 Without hurrying
59 Accelerate, with "up"
60 Individual
61 Santa __, CA

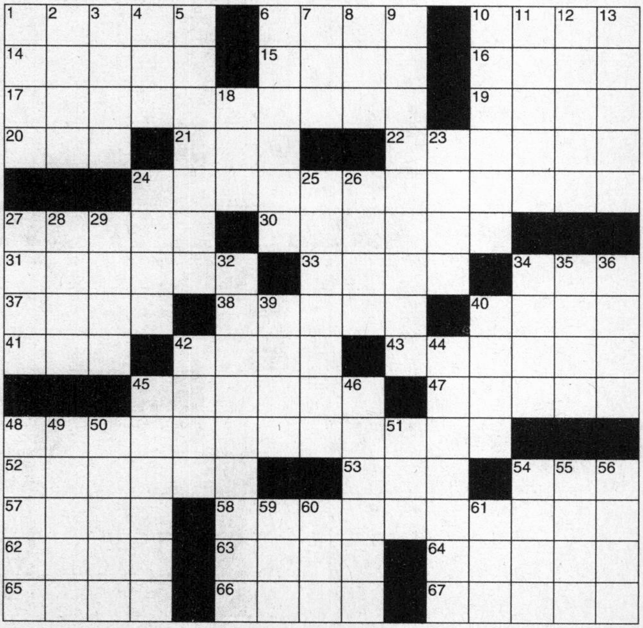

90 HERE'S THE SCOOP

by Patrick Jordan

ACROSS

1 Apparatus
5 Entreaties
10 Front of a frigate
14 Wheel shaft
15 Shire of *The Godfather*
16 Boxer's ringside wrap
17 Ice-cream variety
19 Champagne bucket
20 Tiny circus performers
21 E or G, e.g.
22 Terrier type
23 Bacon units
25 She'd rather roughhouse than play house
27 Denial from Yeltsin
29 Dismantle sail supports
32 Hits with a ray gun
35 Bistro server
39 Washington's bill
40 Inventor Whitney
41 Traveling by Airbus
42 Past
43 Musical notes
44 Videotaped over
45 Verses of tribute
46 Moving about
48 Sauce thickener
50 Where some bracelets are worn
54 Removes water, in a way
58 Denominational offshoot
60 Balladeer Burl
62 Think the world of
63 Throbbing pain
64 Ice-cream variety
66 Vibratory sound
67 Up to the time that
68 Speeds along
69 Momentarily
70 Cherry pit
71 Fencing sword

DOWN

1 Iron fishhooks
2 Rejoice
3 Birch relative
4 Wins back
5 Scoreboard nos.
6 Suburban spread
7 George or T.S. of literature
8 __-surface missile
9 Witch-trial venue
10 Alcatraz or Sing Sing
11 Ice-cream variety
12 Do the bidding of
13 Used to be
18 Catch sight of
24 Ed Norton's workplace
26 City
28 British "Bye-bye!"
30 *Come Back, Little Sheba* playwright
31 Metros and Prizms
32 Epsilon follower
33 Baba and MacGraw
34 Ice-cream variety
36 Part of TGIF
37 Wedding-cake layer
38 Create, as a scholarship
41 Quick pull
45 Begin to rust
47 New doctor
49 River to the Caspian Sea
51 Fan of The Great Pumpkin
52 Occurrence
53 Alliance formed in 1954
55 What a poor 35 Across gets
56 Fabled fox's forbidden fruit
57 Have a premonition of
58 Toothed tools
59 Canyon phenomenon
61 Recreational drive
65 Roar for a toreador

91 ELVIS QUARTET

by Ed Julius

ACROSS
1 Tasks
5 Letter on a key
10 Tory opponent
14 Mishmash
15 Buenos __
16 Socks
17 1956 Elvis tune
20 Questionable remedies
21 They stare
22 Luau musicmaker
23 Dumbbell
25 1963 Elvis tune
33 Tusk material
34 Comrade
35 Headlight setting
36 Nick at __
37 Sophia's mate
39 Even
40 Dined
41 Porter or Younger
42 Glistened
43 1958 Elvis tune
47 Disencumbers
48 Jack of *Barney Miller*
49 Celestial hunter
52 Draws
57 1962 Elvis tune
60 Gasoline, e.g.
61 Het up
62 Ticklish Muppet
63 Having oomph
64 Taunted
65 "Break __!"

DOWN
1 Adams or Tyler
2 Margarine
3 Prejudice
4 Do post office work
5 Japanese drama
6 Cadets of Colorado Springs
7 CEO, at times
8 Garden veggie
9 Inquire
10 ". . . it's __ know"
11 Table d'__
12 River to the Elbe
13 Solidifies
18 Very __ yours
19 Like a steeplechase course
23 Gherkin kin
24 1952 Olympics site
25 Singer Washington
26 1996 Madonna role
27 One exercising a franchise
28 Wrath
29 Defied
30 Language peculiarity
31 College in New York
32 German port
37 Like most colleges
38 "Woe is me!"
39 Shortened adverb
41 Cotton fabric
42 Hand-to-hand weapon
44 With humor
45 Asset holdings
46 Like some lines
49 Switch positions
50 Bounder
51 Holly
52 *Pequod* skipper
53 Neighborhood
54 Biology topic
55 Domesticate
56 Component of urban air
58 Hairpiece
59 Cycle starter

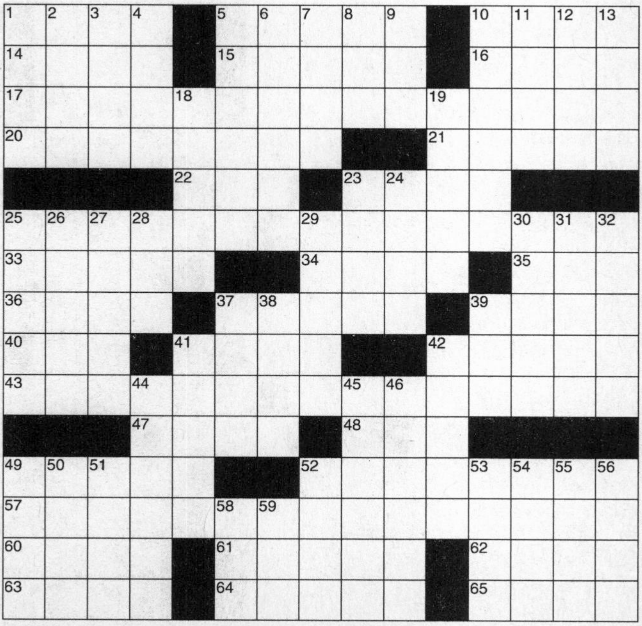

92 SHOPPING SPREE

by Bob Lubbers

ACROSS

1 Chair piece
5 Calculating subject
9 Fun's partner
14 Sites
15 Skin-cream ingredient
16 Humiliate
17 Gulf near Yemen
18 Designate
19 Put into service again
20 Store come-on
23 Patriotic org.
24 __ Alamos, NM
25 Exist
28 Stronghold
32 Long-eared equine
35 Less feral
37 Lock holder
38 Talon
39 Store come-on
42 Smirk
43 Perry's creator
44 Let up
45 Three-way joint
46 Challenges
48 Still
49 Deal maker
50 VI x L
52 Store come-on
61 Hibachi residue
62 Doozy
63 Dynamic start
64 Use a plane
65 Cain's brother
66 Agitated mood
67 Abhors
68 Examination
69 Per person

DOWN

1 Cabbage concoction
2 New Jersey town
3 Got a hole in one
4 Having prongs
5 Krishna chant
6 "Oh woe!"
7 Big book
8 Achilles' weak point
9 French waiter
10 Helps a perpetrator
11 Hawaii's "Valley Isle"
12 Exxon's ex-name
13 "As __ on TV!"
21 Buffalo NHLer
22 Steal away with one's intended
25 Skewed
26 Indian princess
27 Alex Trebek, e.g.
29 Ignore one's duties
30 Put off
31 British __
32 Assuage
33 Recipe direction
34 Bonbon, e.g.
36 Go astray
38 Auto for hire
40 Distributed the cards
41 Ethel Mertz portrayer
46 Throws
47 Supernatural
49 Source of annoyance
51 End
52 Whip
53 Workplace oversight agcy.
54 "Huh?"
55 Real-estate map
56 Cartoonist Goldberg
57 Tahiti et Martinique
58 __ cava
59 Clapton or Idle
60 *Goodbye, Columbus* author

93 GET THE POINT?

by Fred Piscop

ACROSS

1 Told a whopper
5 Bean curd
9 Marsh plant
14 Inside: Pref.
15 Off the __ (bizarre)
16 Standard partner
17 Tennis situation
18 Idle of comedy
19 Titicaca's locale
20 Sandwich partner
23 "I didn't know that!"
24 Glossy fabric
25 Snooze takers
27 Thumbs-up votes
30 Parakeet's dinner
31 Yank's foe
34 Oz pooch
36 Four-star review
39 Hard to comprehend
41 Standee's support
42 Punctilious one
43 Sleek, in auto lingo
44 Parcel's partner
45 Put out, one way
46 Ran like the dickens
48 *Get Yer __ Out!* (Rolling Stones album)
52 __ forth (sets out)
55 Horrified
59 Neighbor of Tenn.
60 Indian peace symbol
63 Japanese assassin
65 Escapade
66 Concerning
67 Windshield sticker
68 Poker payment
69 Tiny parasite
70 Bergen dummy
71 Epitome of thinness
72 Organic fuel

DOWN

1 Springs
2 *Gunga Din* setting
3 Papal bull
4 Democratic Party symbol
5 10-, 11-, and 12-year-olds
6 Rowing equipment
7 Go head over heels
8 Worrier's woe, it's said
9 Not at all dense
10 Very long time
11 '60s compact car
12 Garson of filmdom
13 Snaky curves
21 Beauregard's boss
22 He wrote of "sour grapes"
26 Maryland collegian
28 Blues singer James
29 "Pardon me!"
31 Vitamin qty.
32 Brogan width
33 Carter budget director
35 "See ya!"
37 Itinerary word
38 Quiche base
40 Combine, as resources
41 *Inside the Third Reich* writer
47 Scurrilous
49 Removed, as a tooth
50 Turkish general
51 Scampi need
52 Removes the rough spots
53 From Mars, perhaps
54 Word before battery or wind
56 Palmer's nickname
57 Not exactly, informally
58 Aviary sound
61 Memorable Welles role
62 Art Deco notable
64 Jelly holder

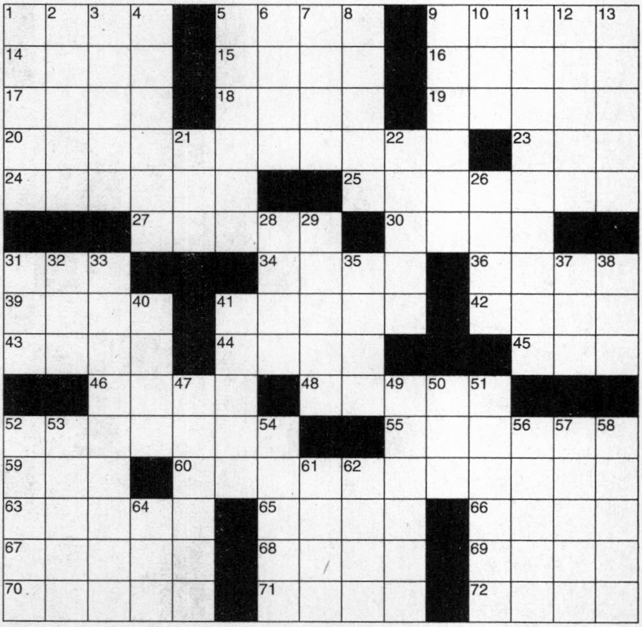

94 POST-DOCTORAL WORK

by Manny Nosowsky

ACROSS
1 Painter Chagall
5 Come apart at the seams
9 Vacuum-tube gas
14 __ close to schedule
15 Italian resort
16 __ Haute, IN
17 Physician-turned-dictator
20 Actor McQueen
21 "Eat __ eaten" (law of the jungle)
22 Not __ many words
23 Actor Baldwin
25 Bit of legalese
27 IOU
30 Physician-turned-revolutionary
35 Young fellow
36 Movie-chain name
37 Israeli money
38 Greet the day
40 Even the score
42 Skilled
43 Hid away
45 Workers' rights org.
47 Southeast Asian language
48 Physician-turned-synonymist
50 Sunbeams
51 Seeing things
52 Presidential prerogative
54 Aid in wrongdoing
57 Water, to Juan
59 From Utrecht
63 Physician-turned-educator
66 Sort of stew
67 Aroma
68 Handy bit of Latin
69 Crimean country house
70 Scale starters
71 Something owed

DOWN
1 Kitchen cleaners
2 Med. school course
3 Rodeo prop
4 Neckwear
5 Ziegfeld's nickname
6 Bullet bounce
7 ID info
8 "Leave him alone, __ bully!"
9 __ glance (quickly)
10 No longer worried
11 Look of contentment
12 Metals in the rough
13 Wolfe the detective
18 __ Monte
19 Aphrodite's equivalent
24 Author Umberto
26 Kind of therapy
27 Envelope attachment
28 "Outcasts of Poker Flat" writer
29 Knucklehead
31 *Dallas* family name
32 Cub-scout leader
33 Satisfy, as a mortgage
34 Some singers
36 Suspicious
39 Sort of sugary
41 Car in a building
44 Wild fancy
46 Hwy.
49 Rhyming newsman Charles
50 Stirred to anger
53 QB's stats
54 In the center of
55 Theda of silent films
56 Leif's pop
58 Bring to naught
60 Big bag
61 Bellyacher
62 To the __ (completely)
64 "Now I get it!"
65 Before, in poems

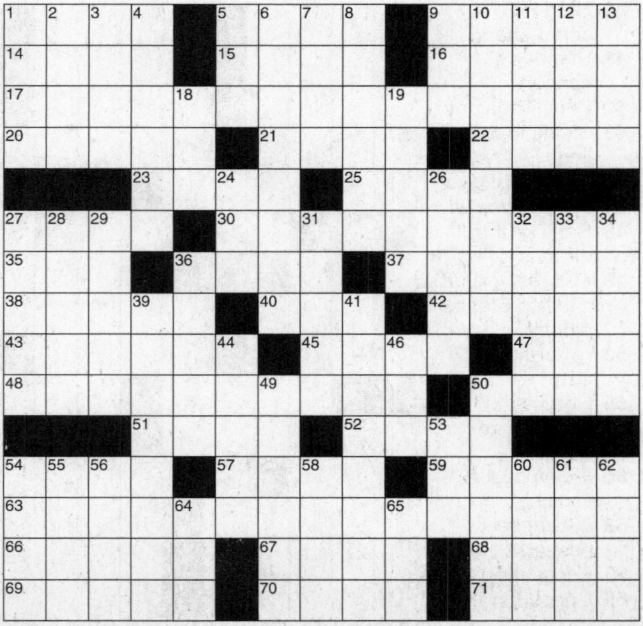

95 THE A TEAM

by Randy Hartman

ACROSS
1 On vacation
5 Car lifter
9 Hippie phrase
14 Daytona 500, for one
15 Author Hunter
16 Breathing
17 The yoke's on them
18 Yorkshire river
19 Its capital is Niamey
20 Encountered
21 Tennis star once married to Brooke Shields
23 Hatred
25 Like a debtor's ink
26 Dancer Charisse
27 Wiser companion
30 Likely
33 Raccoon cousin
35 Hokey acting
36 Surface at Vail
37 Northern metropolis
40 Maui necklaces
41 Director Kazan
42 Pays attention to
43 Hallucinogenic initials
44 African antelope
45 Kin: Abbr.
46 U-turn from SSW
47 Harbinger
50 College-football star
56 German article
57 Home of the Dolphins
58 Algerian seaport
59 Perth pal
60 Estuary
61 In the thick of
62 Large flightless birds
63 Tale
64 Numerous
65 Nile nippers

DOWN
1 Bouquet
2 Like candles
3 Vinegar, chemically
4 Craving
5 Informal clothing
6 Gung-ho
7 Chanteuse Vikki
8 Leg joint
9 Peril
10 Homeric epic
11 Jazz dates
12 Currier's partner
13 *Lois & Clark* star Hatcher
21 Sound transmission
22 Sports stadium
24 Ancient stories
27 Florida citrus center
28 Sign on
29 Trepidation
30 Yosemite photographer
31 Dawdling
32 "__ the night before Christmas . . ."
33 Cry out
34 Change for a five
36 Soldier's sword
38 U.S. Grant foe
39 Matthau's bride in *Grumpier Old Men*
44 Hatred
46 Rat, in a way
47 Deft
48 Back off
49 Attire
50 French friends
51 Fabric fuzz
52 Composer Schifrin
53 Wander
54 __ *La Douce*
55 First son
59 "Cry __ River"

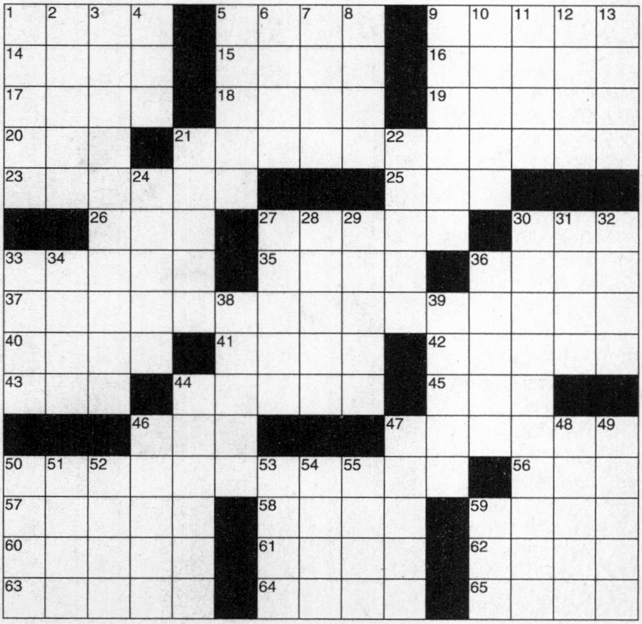

96 CHURCHILLIAN TRIO

by Fred Piscop

ACROSS

1 One __ kind (unique)
4 Conniving sort
11 Well put
14 Half a diam.
15 Venezuelan river
16 Innovator's prefix
17 Movie violence
20 Go all-out
21 Windbag's output
22 "__ to Your School" (Beach Boys tune)
23 Abrasive particles
25 Schooner filler
26 "No __" (Chinese-restaurant sign)
28 Harper Valley grp.
31 Switch positions
32 Half a dual personality
34 Shuffle
37 Togs for the treadmill
40 Xerox predecessor
43 Dame Hess
47 Cleveland cager
48 Teachers' grp.
49 Anat. or chem.
52 Granola grain
53 Take a header
55 All wound up
57 Trying to be
61 Go __ (rot)
62 Little Anthony and the Imperials song
65 Compass line
66 Looked like a villain
67 Lodge member
68 Tricky turn
69 Make like new
70 Monogram of 32 Across' creator

DOWN

1 Crystal ball, e.g.
2 In a deceptive manner
3 Accepted, as a resolution
4 Element in salt
5 Strains, as one's neck
6 "You're getting warmer," e.g.
7 Wind up
8 Flying insect
9 Canyon sound
10 Lopsided win
11 Yule-log holder
12 Using a magnifying glass
13 Craggy hill
18 Bruin Bobby
19 Racetrack slacker
22 Ebenezer's exclamation
24 Lao-__
27 Persona non __
28 Histories
29 Play about Capote
30 *Exodus* character
33 RI zone
35 Zeta follower
36 PIN requester
38 Attained
39 Nationality ending
40 Agt.'s take
41 __ Ferry, WV
42 Egg containers
44 Tyrolean tunesmith
45 Ann or Andy
46 Grabbed a bite
50 *Sergeant York* star
51 Protected from the elements
54 Pricing word
56 Sinuous swimmer
58 Gorby's realm, once: Abbr.
59 Ready to serve
60 People
61 Novice
62 __ kwon do
63 Ran into
64 Calendar divs.

97 ON THE CANVAS

by Norma Steinberg

ACROSS
1 The lion's share
5 Prohibit
8 Opposite of "to"
11 Cartoon "light bulb"
12 Truths
14 Cleansing agent
15 Defeated
18 April 15 addressee
19 ". . . __ suffer the slings and arrows . . ."
20 As a companion
21 Toon Fudd
22 Yellowish-red
23 *Catch-22* author
25 Storage area
26 Racer Andretti
27 Feeling blue
28 "Woe __!"
32 Admit defeat
36 Immense
37 For example
38 Austere
39 Have a bawl
40 Make from scratch
42 South Seas island group
45 Stands in line
46 Establish as fact
47 Assns.
48 __ Vegas
51 Fight unfairly
54 *Mila 18* author
55 Dingbat
56 West Coast sch.
57 Garden tool
58 Cozy room
59 Lanky

DOWN
1 Long skirt
2 Scent
3 Makes clothes
4 Sunbathe
5 Cashless trade
6 Thespian
7 Extreme degree
8 Stumbled upon
9 Lanky
10 Choose
12 "But Not __ " (Gershwin tune)
13 Shore
14 Imminently
16 Come next
17 Extended family
21 Prufrock's creator
23 Sounds of laughter
24 Goofs up
25 Ebenezer's exclamation
26 Cable rock station
27 Pigpen
28 Smidgens
29 Police dept. unit
30 Pierre's mom
31 Tundra beast
33 From Tel Aviv
34 No vote
35 African fly
39 Inlet
40 Milk container
41 Correct
42 Hubert's successor
43 Clarinetist Shaw
44 Throngs
45 Exclamation of surprise
48 Polish leader Walesa
49 "__ Ever Need Is You"
50 Ollie's partner
51 "What?"
52 Roulette bet
53 Except for

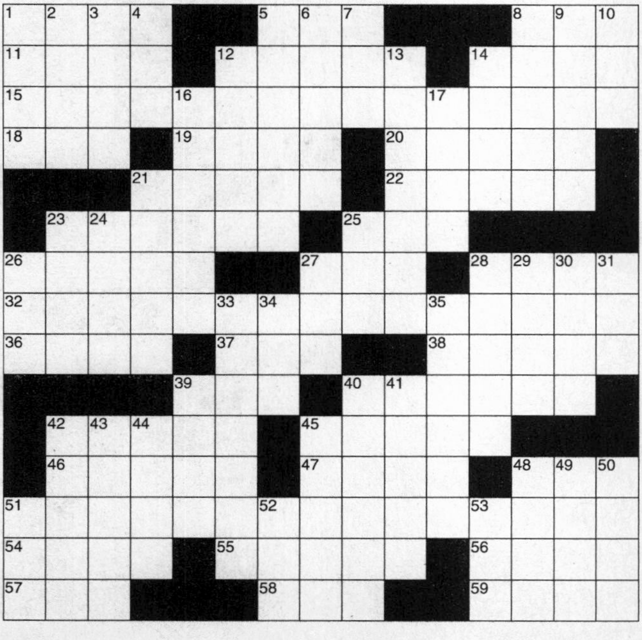

98 ROCKY IV

by Lee Weaver

ACROSS
1 Book of maps
6 School org.
9 Auction action
12 One who cajoles
14 Entered the race
15 Chills and fever
17 The __ State (New York)
18 Got
20 Pueblo Indian art
22 Prefix for hazard
25 Sounds of awe
26 Prudential rival
27 Iroquoians
30 Violin part
32 Elevate
33 Oldest national park
36 Muslim's Almighty
37 Rocker John
41 California golf locale
46 Performing mammal
50 Family chart
51 Rose oil
52 Gold bar
54 Currier's partner
56 Possesses
57 *Dick Tracy* character
61 Dacron or denim
62 Too
66 Ripening agent
67 Citrine cooler
68 More cautious
69 Superman's insignia
70 Color of Santa's suit
71 Protuberances

DOWN
1 High card
2 Selleck or Seaver
3 Race segment
4 Line of rotation
5 Blood components
6 Isaiah, for one
7 Hot sauce
8 Opposed to
9 Fisherman, at times
10 Cause to burn
11 Chaperon in Cádiz
13 Janet of Justice
16 Mystery writers' award
19 Santa __, CA
21 Adams and Johnson
22 "Yo!"
23 Carpet calculation
24 Medicinal form
28 House addition
29 Motel freebie
31 Leg joint
34 Sharpen
35 Napoleon's exile isle
38 Vietnamese festival
39 Solemn promise
40 March Madness org.
42 Military unit
43 Cut on a slant
44 Impolite look
45 Slugger's stat.
46 Greek letter
47 Incense
48 Striped stones
49 Romeo and Juliet, e.g.
53 Three times, in a prescription
55 Load cargo
58 Whopper teller
59 Lendl of tennis
60 Architect Saarinen
63 Clear out (of)
64 Loser at Gettysburg
65 Many mos.

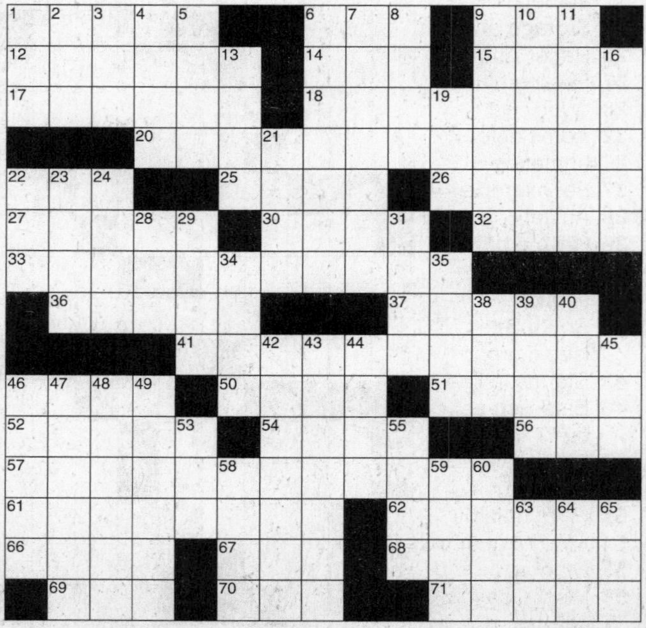

99 POETIC CONCLUSIONS

by Fred Piscop

ACROSS

1 Night vision
6 Singer Zadora
9 Reduce, as fears
14 Strike back, e.g.
15 Chapel Hill sch.
16 Mix
17 Backwards
19 Does as told
20 Confined, with "up"
21 "That's amazing!"
22 Poetic preposition
23 *Seinfeld* character
29 Author Ferber
30 Number on the sports page
31 Neither masc. nor fem.
32 Clairvoyance, for short
34 32-card game
36 Highway warning
37 Pawn in another's game
41 Layer
43 In the style of
44 Asterisk
46 A, in Worms
47 Mrs. Nick Charles
49 Left in a hurry
51 ". . . three men in __"
54 Deteriorating condition
57 Possesses
58 Complete a street
59 Trumpeter Al
61 Clear the windshield
64 Meteorologist's device
66 Hold responsible
67 Unusually smart
68 Speak at length
69 Big ship
70 Villain's snort
71 Prone to giving orders

DOWN

1 Faucet problem
2 Go back on one's word
3 Acquired deservedly
4 Varnish ingredients
5 VH-1 alternative
6 Baby foods, at times
7 Flies, e.g.
8 Flying standout
9 Cancel, to NASA
10 Big name in mail order
11 Director Spike
12 Whichever
13 Many ft.
18 Ovum
22 Heir-splitting subject
24 Carpentry tools
25 Former acorns
26 Arboreal abode
27 Natal native
28 Tiny particle
33 Literary device
35 Docket listing
37 Six-pack units
38 Big time
39 Fictional plantation
40 Model persona
42 Unlikely protagonist
45 Bureaucratic hassle
48 Not away
50 Scarcity
52 Hall-of-Fame quarterback Johnny
53 Artists' toppers
55 Raring to go
56 __-Magnon
60 Low card
61 Two-bagger: Abbr.
62 Actor Wallach
63 Summer cooler
64 Exclamation of annoyance
65 Riotous crowd

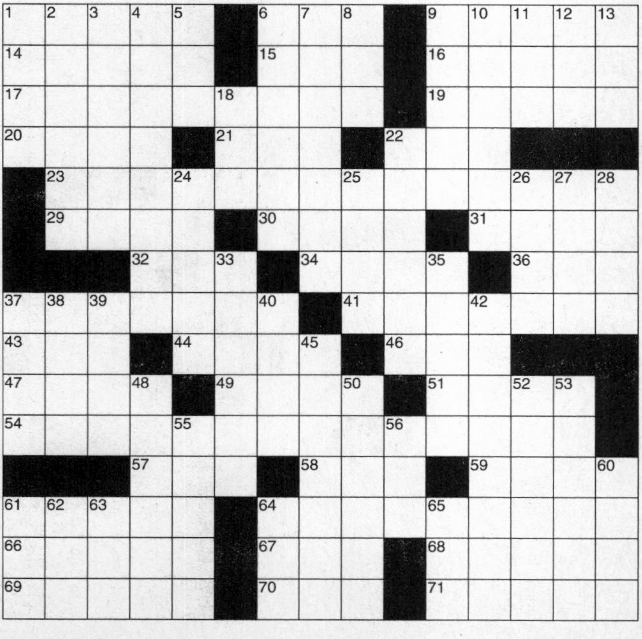

100 BEDROCK ROLL CALL

by Patrick Jordan

ACROSS

1 Dexterous
5 Fall flower
10 OOO, in love letters
14 Fairy-tale fiend
15 Indian corn
16 From the start
17 Former PBS show host
19 __ *la Douce*
20 Service charge
21 Biblical landing place
22 Take a breather
23 Shale features
25 Was a passenger
27 1960 Summer Olympics star
33 Star's brief appearance
36 Sans companions
37 Promissory initials
38 Bullring accolades
39 Prevaricator's penchant
40 Bancroft or Bronte
41 Serpentine squeezer
42 Weeper of myth
43 Kermit colleague
44 *The Feminine Mystique* author
47 Borscht veggie
48 Loosens one's laces
52 Getz of jazz
54 Church structures
58 Actor Gulager
59 Ripken et al.
60 *Andy Griffith Show* character
62 Wheel support
63 Plunders
64 "Put __ on it!"
65 Fail to attend
66 Rob of *Melrose Place*
67 English river

DOWN

1 Tips one's topper
2 Wading bird
3 Less restricted
4 Knight or Nugent
5 Ignorant of right and wrong
6 Heroic tale
7 Stadium level
8 Poet Pound
9 Fixed a tennis racket
10 Pageboy or pompadour
11 Letting out more line
12 Highly prized objects
13 Smack a skeeter
18 Mathematical proportion
24 Inspires reverence
26 Keats creation
28 City leader
29 Defendant's excuse
30 Blakley of *Nashville*
31 First video game
32 One of Donald's nephews
33 Baseball's "Georgia Peach"
34 Skin-soothing stuff
35 Pasta topping of a sort
39 Not too heavy to hoist
40 "__ Misbehavin' "
42 "Science Guy" Bill
43 Mammy Yokum's first name
45 Grammarian's concerns
46 Coercion
49 With aloofness
50 Like Ernie Keebler
51 Napped leather
52 Sting
53 Urban vehicle
55 Cambodia neighbor
56 Moderate gait
57 Poker-pot part
61 Budgetary excess

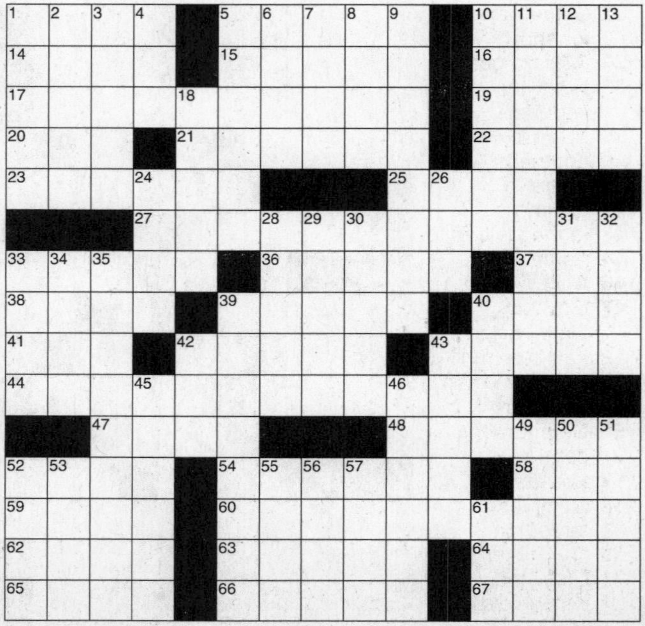

101 FIRST THINGS FIRST

by S.N.

ACROSS

1 Yodeler's place
5 "Get lost!"
10 Fill roles
14 Windless
15 Numerical goal
16 __ close to schedule
17 1/20/89, e.g.
20 Home room
21 Betz's TV wife
22 Rock bottom
23 Egg on
24 Choir member
25 In jeopardy
28 Uninteresting
29 Tiny colonist
32 Coin call
33 Elvis __ Presley
34 It may be pitched
35 Fine, so far
39 The Rams' league: Abbr.
40 Not at all nice
41 Spring up
42 Give the once-over
43 Polaroid pioneer
44 President __ of the Senate
45 Berth place
46 Job opening
47 Madame Curie
49 Ruin
50 Movie turkey
53 Cole Porter tune
56 Raised, as cats
57 Circus star
58 Chap, to Dundee
59 Give up
60 Nasal sensations
61 Fall heavily

DOWN

1 Corrosive chemical
2 Bowling area
3 Architect's work
4 Dallas sch.
5 Need oiling
6 As good as new
7 Turnpike
8 A.B.A. member
9 California's locale, to Hawaiians
10 Apt. of a sort
11 *The King* __
12 Fly high
13 Take a stab at
18 Concerto __ (Baroque work)
19 Solemn promise
23 Gold-colored
24 Crazy as __
25 Make up (for)
26 Chewy candy
27 Long arm?
28 Not limited
29 Hang around for
30 Mythology branch
31 Indian carving
33 Author's rep
36 Almond-flavored drink
37 South Seas skirt
38 Easy run
43 Beef cut
44 Wire bender
45 Joy's partner
46 Self-controlled
47 Insignificant
48 Got older
49 Floor model
50 Ring up
51 "Render __ Caesar . . ."
52 Fraught with meaning
53 English channel?
54 Hoodwinked
55 Diamond judge

102 HANDIWORK

by Shirley Soloway

ACROSS

1 Falcon feature
5 Singer Redding
9 Ferber et al.
14 Ohio city
15 Tennis star Sampras
16 Metal framework
17 Zest for life
18 Alternatively
19 Artful deception
20 New York resort area
23 On the __ (fleeing)
24 Majors and Trevino
25 Mouselike mammals
27 Firmly fixed
30 Mail again
32 Saudi Arabia's king
33 Speak highly of
35 Young fellow
36 R-V link
37 Controversial shortening
39 Sound a toreador adores
42 Gibson of *Lethal Weapon*
44 Slips into
45 Perfect match
46 Donkey, often
48 Concert instruments
50 Wool coat
52 Take wing
53 Fam. member
54 Foolish sort
60 Sheepish?
62 Dressed
63 *Born Free* lioness
64 French assembly
65 Past due
66 Stream forth
67 Golf hazards
68 Prayer end
69 Come in last

DOWN

1 Music marking
2 Caron role
3 __ *Called Horse* ('70 film)
4 Got by scheming
5 Victor Herbert work
6 Spills the beans
7 "__ deal!"
8 Look for
9 Yellowish white
10 Joanne of films
11 Settled once and for all
12 Attorney-__
13 Appears to be
21 Nighttime, in poems
22 Slalom curve
26 Cell substance: Abbr.
27 Preconditions
28 "Unforgettable" name
29 Hans Christian Andersen character
30 Gossipy tidbit
31 007's alma mater
34 Ye __ Tea Shoppe
37 Skirt slits
38 "Silence __"
40 Jar top
41 Pulver's rank: Abbr.
43 Palindromic preposition
45 North Carolinian
47 Kyoto cash
49 *Norma* __
50 "Mending Wall" poet
51 Pryer's need?
52 Rink footwear
55 Calif. sch.
56 Happy as a __
57 Seaman's saint
58 Without a warranty
59 Tropical fruit
61 Short snooze

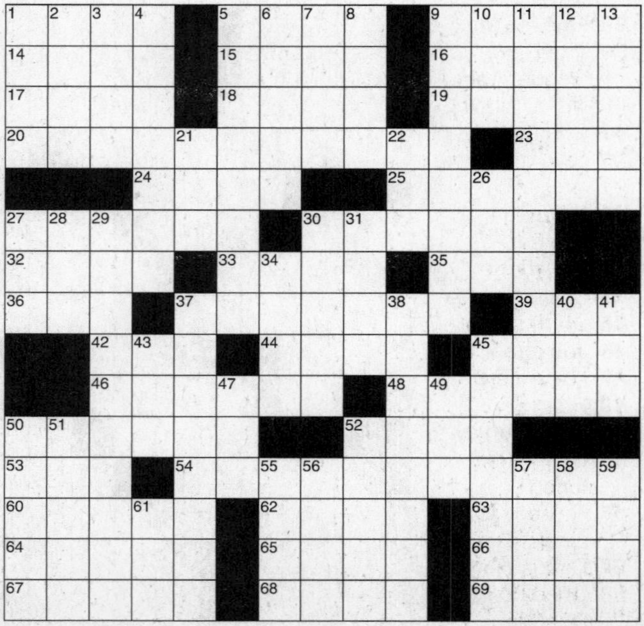

103 DOUBLE TALK

by Trip Payne

ACROSS

1 Falls behind
5 Coffee man Valdez
9 Myra Hess, for one
13 "__ Ben Adhem"
14 Molten material
15 All tied up
16 Eddie Cantor tune of '26
19 Breath-freshener brand
20 Using staff facilities
21 Genesis character
23 Flue powder
24 Go separate ways
27 Frequent title beginning
29 Skirt features
32 Nabokov novel
33 Long look
35 "What's in __?"
37 Senior golf star
40 Where the Owl and the Pussycat went
41 Barely defeated
42 Links standard
43 Quick-witted
45 Enjoy a smorgasbord
46 Juno, to the Greeks
47 Arty New Mexico town
49 Confirmation or baptism
51 Cause
54 Theater district
58 Fifties Kenyan uprising
60 Alternatively
61 Harris storyteller
62 Jogger's gait
63 Makes a sheepshank
64 Walked on
65 Saint feature

DOWN

1 Chem-class locales
2 "Rock-__ baby . . ."
3 *Wheel of Fortune* daytime host
4 Math grouping
5 Holyfield punch
6 Tropical fruit
7 "__ home is his castle"
8 Tex-Mex treats
9 Making a premiere
10 Hertz rival
11 Unimportant
12 Come to a stop
14 *Amahl and the Night Visitors* composer
17 Hankering
18 Kids' drink
22 Stock unit
24 Bloc agreement
25 Kind of committee
26 Mrs. Gorbachev
28 Eat away at
30 Brownish gray
31 False charge
33 Fifties-music revival group
34 Candice's dad
36 Poet Pound
38 Franc portions
39 Calls it a day
44 Cultured food
46 Physical condition
48 More angry
50 "Open 9 __ 6"
51 Indonesian island
52 Put-on
53 Verne protagonist
55 Pisa dough
56 Hammer or hacksaw
57 "__ bigger and better things!"
58 Happened upon
59 Blossom-to-be

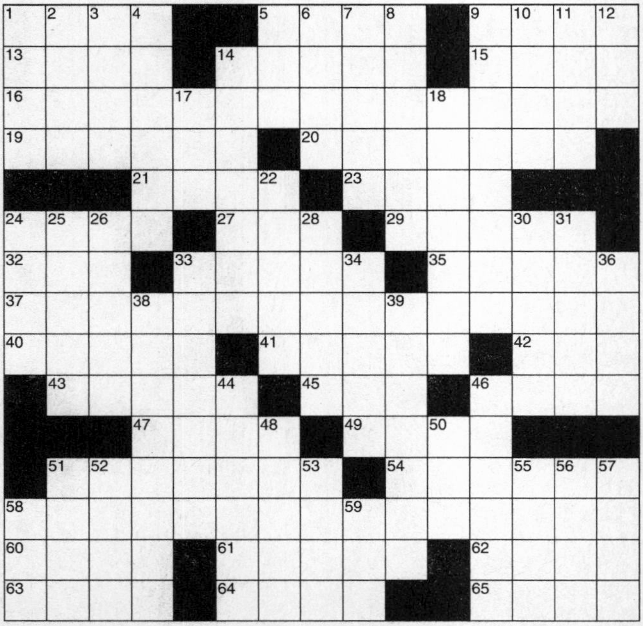

104 WHAT TIME IS IT?

by Mel Rosen

ACROSS

1 Melville madman
5 Everglades bird
9 Director __ Lee
14 Doll's word
15 Chunk-light fish
16 Spud
17 Fifties TV mayor
20 Casual footwear
21 Yes, to Yvette
22 Go one better
23 Hog haven
24 Swimsuit part
26 Throws out a line
29 Bring on board
31 Machine part
34 Abdul-Jabbar's alma mater
35 Fifties TV clown
38 Getz or Musial
39 Texas NFLer
40 Rock's partner
41 Fifties TV marionette
43 Pesky insect
44 Many mos.
45 Transgressions
46 Byron and Browning
47 What RNs dispense
48 Heavenly body
49 Chairman of the '50s
51 "This __ fine how-do-you-do!"
54 Residences
58 Fifties TV host
61 *The Addams Family* star
62 Herbert sci-fi classic
63 Analogy phrase
64 In an irritable mood
65 Part of USA
66 Enjoy gum

DOWN

1 Fuse units
2 Sound of amusement
3 Evil Idi
4 Orchestra's place
5 NATO member
6 Kramden's workplace
7 Sondheim's __ *the Woods*
8 *Elephant Boy* star
9 R-V center?
10 Ristorante course
11 "Tell __ the judge!"
12 Hang on to
13 Go astray
18 Diner sign
19 Bibliophile's pride
25 Confederate soldier
26 Easy and comfortable
27 Audition attendee
28 Side dishes
29 Heavenly headgear
30 Vexed
31 Genetic copy
32 __ once (suddenly)
33 Turns to slush
35 Will addition
36 Pride member
37 Well-suited for the workplace
42 Fashion monogram
46 Alehouses
47 "Strain the facts __ the rules": Tolstoy
48 Fencer's choice
49 Think over
50 P.M. periods
52 Malt-shop order
53 Hallelujah, I'm __!
55 Reception aid
56 Feminine suffix
57 Revue, e.g.
58 Baseball club
59 Whichever
60 Unspecified person

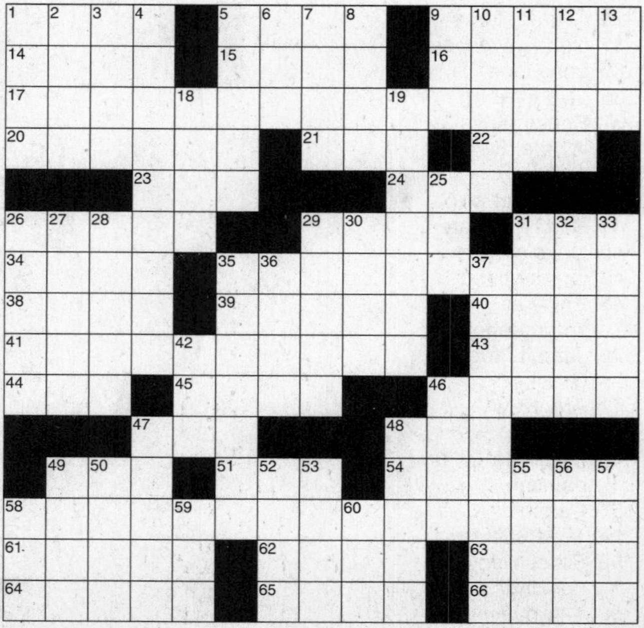

105 *TWAIN TIME*

by Mel Rosen

ACROSS

1 ASCAP rival
4 Thompson of *Family*
8 Major-__ (steward)
12 Get wind (of)
13 *Joie de vivre*
14 Wear away
16 Cuts prices on
18 Boys, in Barcelona
19 Mork's planet
20 Hungry feeling
21 Does fingerpainting
22 Cake finish
24 Biggers' detective
25 Soccer-shoe features
27 Hoarding cause, perhaps
31 Runs easily
32 Armor flaw
33 Peas purchase
34 Like __ of bricks
35 Rich cake
36 Mideast missile
37 Part of TGIF
38 Wanders about
39 Battle strategy
40 Was nurturing
42 Spread (out)
43 Sharif of films
44 Salad-dressing bottle
45 *Charlie's Angels* name
48 Sand and such
49 Came upon
52 Keep __ to the ground
53 Brand-name's protection
55 Pile up
56 Called up
57 Allegro con __
58 Midmonth day
59 Conversation filler
60 Pedigree org.

DOWN

1 Put up with
2 Night Court actress
3 Rub the wrong way
4 Family cars
5 Beside
6 Deputy __ (cartoon canine)
7 Hoofer Miller
8 Hamlet's land
9 Get situated
10 "__ Lisa"
11 Fragrance
12 Medical-insurance co.
15 Ending for host or heir
17 Barbecue adjuncts
21 Was outstanding
23 Columnist Herb
24 Promissory notes
25 Assertion
26 Numbers game
27 Minimal evidence
28 Musical notation
29 Measuring device
30 All over
32 Deal with
35 Synagogue scroll
36 Trig ratio
38 Casual comments
39 Fry lightly
41 Roman odist
42 Latter-day icebox
44 Construction-site sight
45 Musical notes
46 Thumbs-down voter
47 Scanned through
48 Mardi __
50 Author Ambler
51 WBC result
53 Numerical prefix
54 Finance deg.

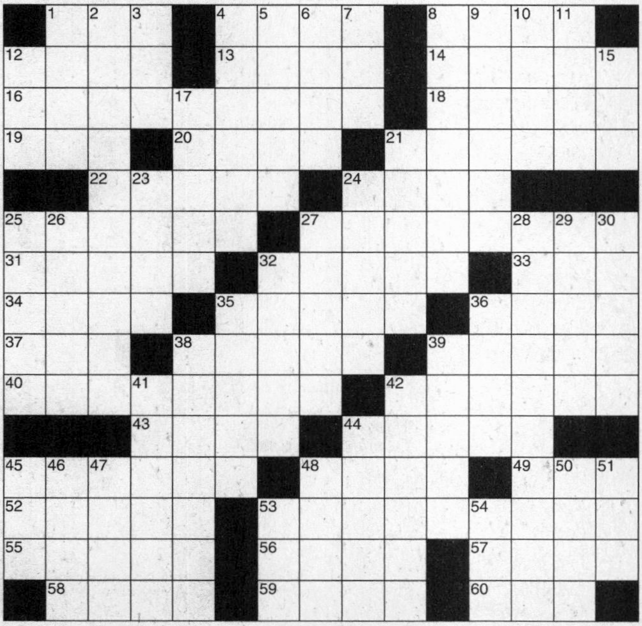

106 GLOBAL GEOMETRY

by Randy Sowell

ACROSS

1 Borders on
6 Sail support
10 Hard journey
14 Seasonal song
15 Lebanon's locale
16 Slow flow
17 London landmark
20 Pep up
21 Everlasting
22 Presidential prerogative
23 Actor Beatty
24 Nagging pain
27 __ Vegas
29 Big bankrolls
33 Bikini top
34 Author Cornelia __ Skinner
36 Small piano
38 Mysterious Atlantic region
41 Furry fish-eaters
42 Monopoly payment
43 Connecticut collegian
44 High schooler
45 Smidgen
46 Allison of '50s TV
47 Snake with a squeeze
49 Christie's *Postern of __*
52 In the wrong role
56 Charge in court
60 Cook crossed it in the 1770s
62 Defeat soundly
63 Topnotch
64 Sour expression
65 They may be split
66 __ *to Morocco*
67 Watered the lawn, perhaps

DOWN

1 Part of a French play
2 *Green Acres* structure
3 Russian river
4 Nine-__ shift
5 Dred Scott, e.g.
6 Louisiana's state flower
7 Stubborn-mule link
8 Warning devices
9 Esthetic discernment
10 Travel agent's offering
11 Chestnut horse
12 Old Testament book
13 Boat part
18 Allow
19 Proof-ending initials
24 Monastery head
25 Minotaur's home
26 Author Bret
28 Seneca's stars
29 Finish first
30 *Look Back in __*
31 Perry's aide
32 Toklas' colleague
34 __ *Man Flint*
35 Football scores: Abbr.
36 Moral wrong
37 Butter portion
39 Chess pieces
40 Visibly embarrassed
45 Arm art
46 "I will __ evil . . ."
47 Watering hole
48 Pianist Levant
50 Fly-ball's path
51 Actress Van Devere
52 Stable parent
53 Privy to
54 Poker variety
55 Abyssinians and Burmese
57 Tops a cake
58 Cheerfulness
59 Nonsocial sort
61 ". . . partridge __ pear tree"

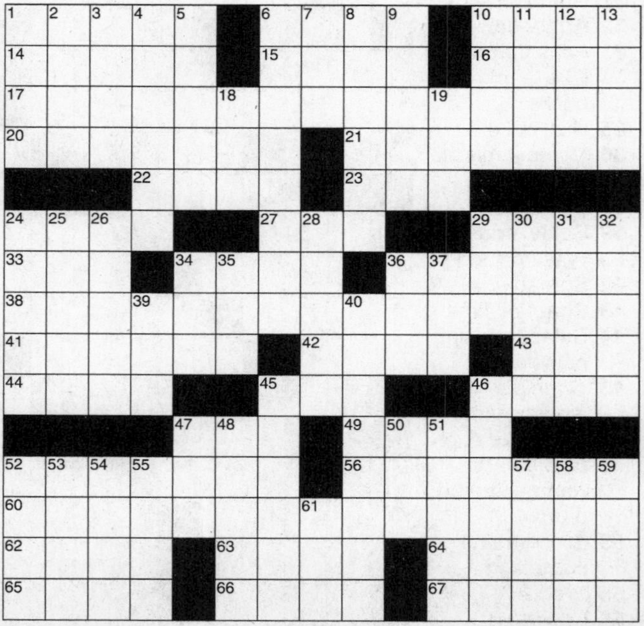

107 CALLING COSTNER

by Richard Silvestri

ACROSS
1 The West had one
5 Otherwise
9 Astor's wares
14 The third man
15 Sea swallow
16 *Cats* inspiration
17 Sherwood Forester
19 Soda-bottle size
20 Pupil's chore
21 *North by Northwest* star
23 Pick-me-up
26 Tongue-lash
28 Handcuff
31 Kitchen utensils
33 Styling shop
34 Actress Burstyn
36 Mr. DiMaggio
37 Big name in basketball
38 Pine product
39 Isolated
40 In the manner of
41 Alacrity
42 Maine senator
43 Painter Thomas Hart __
45 How ships may run
47 Our Gang girl
48 Film holder
49 Actress Burke
51 Late-night TV host Bob
56 Hold accountable
58 Sherwood Forester
61 Grounds for a medal
62 Devastate
63 Opposition prefix
64 Textile workers
65 Drop
66 Take ten

DOWN
1 Poet Sandburg
2 Large woodwind
3 Cotillion attendees
4 Wallach and Whitney
5 Kind of pride
6 Summer sign
7 Hit-show letters
8 Winds down
9 One with a large food bill
10 Donahue of *Father Knows Best*
11 Sherwood Forester
12 Boot part
13 Orch. section
18 Pitcher Ryan
22 Colorado high spot
24 Heads for the hills
25 Satellite of '62
27 Spoke monotonously
28 Sent away
29 Sherwood Forester
30 "I should say __!"
32 Spotted
33 Stick it in your ear
35 Feudal lord
38 Attacked
39 Bud's buddy
41 Cries out
42 Use crayons
44 Seismic disturbance
46 Eat one's words
50 Bushy hairdo
52 Magi's guide
53 Maintain the piano
54 New Testament book
55 Vaudeville routine
56 Hanes competitor
57 Set (down)
59 Daiquiri need
60 VI halved

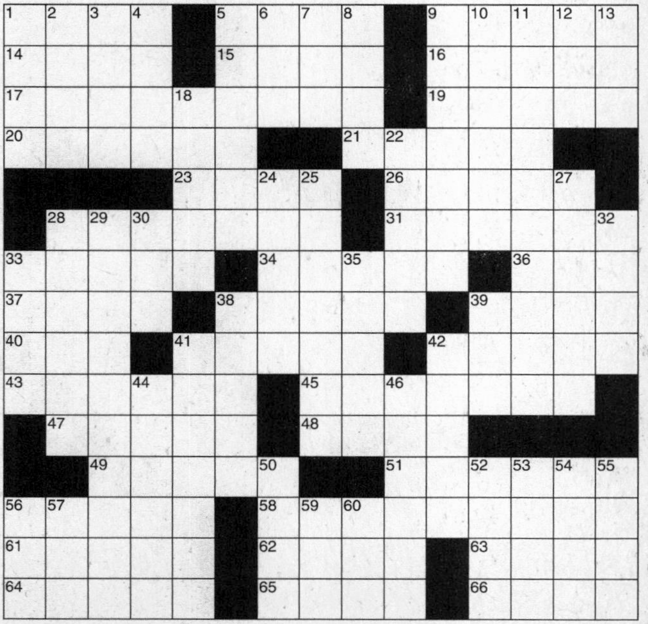

108 BASEBALL SUCCESSES

by Mel Rosen

ACROSS
1 Watered-down
5 Canyon of the comics
10 Carpet style
14 Presley's middle name
15 Out-and-out
16 Evening hour
17 Succeed without swinging?
19 Blues singer James
20 Transparencies
21 *Rhoda* star
23 Director Brooks
24 Must, informally
25 Get a move on
29 Toto's creator
30 Nay neutralizer
33 Choir members
34 Abby, to Ann
35 Economist Smith
36 Carrying a grudge
37 Impress indelibly
38 Beer-label word
39 "You must remember __"
40 Zillions of years
41 Splits up
42 __ Ridge, TN
43 Parting word
44 Potato-chip alternatives
45 Civil-rights leader Medgar
47 Joanne of films
48 Asian temple
50 Gives VIP treatment to
55 Like crazy
56 End up succeeding?
58 White as a sheet
59 Hope or Jessica
60 Step __ (hurry)
61 "No ifs, __, or buts!"
62 Not broadside
63 Vet patients

DOWN
1 Radner character
2 Rock star Clapton
3 Top-rated
4 Make a sweater
5 __ Island (Big Apple borough)
6 Beach need
7 Greek vowels
8 Kilmer of *The Doors*
9 Gray dog
10 Hagar's pooch
11 Score a lode of runs?
12 Penny, perhaps
13 Transmission choice
18 Appoints
22 24-hour cash source: Abbr.
24 Picks up
25 Is forced
26 Oahu greeting
27 Get a whiff of success?
28 Stocking stuffers
29 Safari boss
31 __ *Win* (diet book)
32 Making __ of things
34 Harness races
35 Jai __
37 Better than awful
41 Cut back
43 Media mogul Turner
44 Immovable
46 Casts a ballot
47 Don __ de la Vega (Zorro)
48 Hemingway's nickname
49 Actor Ladd
50 __ a hand (assist)
51 Flapjack chain, initially
52 Torrid, for one
53 Send forth
54 Salon jobs
57 Hightailed it

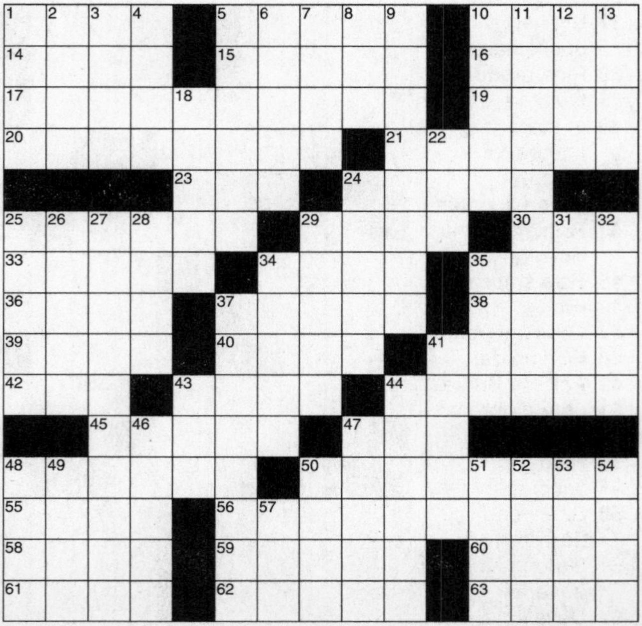

109 CAR POOL

by Randy Sowell

ACROSS
1 Eban of Israel
5 Snake sound
9 Fills film roles
14 Ring event
15 Nabisco nosh
16 National Leaguer
17 "This one's __!"
18 Apple-pie partner
20 Cong. member
21 Rummy variety
22 Bobby of hockey
23 "Harper Valley __"
24 Like the prairie
27 King, in Cannes
29 Bring up
30 John Major's predecessor
35 Liner levels
37 Sci-fi film of '82
38 It has its ups and downs
39 Incoming plane: Abbr.
40 "__ Folly" (Alaska)
43 Richard Skelton
44 Apollo objective
46 Fictional Lane
47 Works at a bar
49 Grass-roots politician
51 Achy or angry
52 __ *Tac Dough*
53 Date time
57 Author Fleming
60 Third word of "America"
62 One way to stand
63 Delta competitor
64 New York City neighborhood
67 Complain
68 House of Lords member
69 "I cannot tell __"
70 Kennel comment
71 Fine wood
72 __ the lily (overdo it)
73 Tags on

DOWN
1 Scrub a mission
2 Big mistake
3 Farmer's delight
4 Chowed down
5 More comfy, in a way
6 Golf-bag contents
7 Fixed
8 London district
9 Lunch for Bugs
10 Blonde shade
11 Cool it
12 Easy run
13 Kid's pop
19 Trip for Mom, maybe
21 Corning's concern
25 "A mouse!"
26 They may be dire
28 Unfriendly
31 __ d'oeuvres
32 Western lizard
33 Looked at
34 Steiger and Stewart
35 Clammy
36 Slangy suffix
37 Ark arrivals
41 Bring out
42 Ale relative
45 Filbert, e.g.
48 Go wrong
50 Prolonged account
51 Refused to go
54 Shower time
55 Oscar, e.g.
56 Americans, to Brits
57 "Let __" (Beatles tune)
58 Ishmael's skipper
59 Pianist Peter
61 Woodland creature
65 __ vivant
66 Yale student
67 Finance deg.

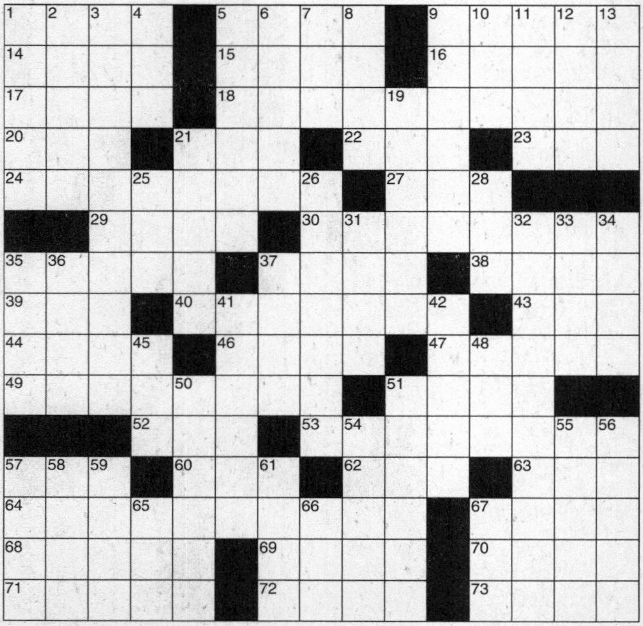

110 FEBRUARY BIRTHDAYS

by Mel Rosen

ACROSS

1 Watch the grandchildren
4 Etchers' needs
9 Walked through water
14 Excessively
15 Riveter of song
16 More frosty
17 Charged atom
18 Comedian born 2/2
20 True-blue
22 Round: Abbr.
23 Sub weapon
26 Unstressed vowel sounds
30 Not to be believed
32 Card game
34 Funnyman Murray
36 Did cobbler's work
38 Twine fiber
39 Actor Ray
41 Up to now
43 Sleuth Wolfe
44 Castle defenses
46 Student's jottings
48 Just published
49 Ran away
51 Sign of spring
53 Overly ornate
55 "__ to Watch Over Me"
58 Declare to be true
60 Taj __
61 Actor born 2/18
67 *Wheel of Fortune* purchase
68 Nostalgic tune
69 Less encumbered
70 Digital-watch type: Abbr.
71 *Revenge of the __*
72 Tex-Mex treats
73 Soapmaker's need

DOWN

1 Circus prop
2 Ten grand
3 Actor born 2/26
4 Naive
5 Bill's partner
6 Doctrine
7 Computer storage device
8 Highway rigs
9 Macbeth trio
10 Essen exclamation
11 Gaming cube
12 Election suffix
13 AMA members
19 Theater section: Abbr.
21 LAPD alert
24 Twosomes
25 Synthetic fabric
27 Farm wagon
28 Talk-show host born 2/12
29 Long look
31 Clear the windshield
33 Leisurely
34 Doorway part
35 Indifferent
37 Takes out
40 Director Preminger
42 San __, Italy
45 Mexican wraps
47 Cooks on low heat
50 Opera star
52 Teachers' org.
54 Dutch earthenware
56 Mrs. Reagan
57 Omit in pronunciation
59 __ avis (something unusual)
61 Actor Voight
62 British beverage
63 Nav. rank
64 Barnyard baby
65 IBM competitor
66 Bus. bigwig

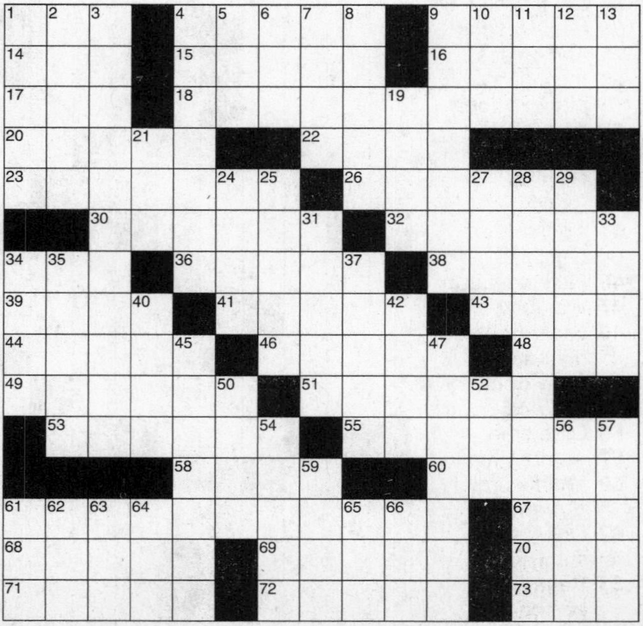

111 PAUL'S PICTURES

by Mel Rosen

ACROSS

1 Kind of excuse
5 Fix socks
9 Govt. agent
13 Comic Idle
14 Lumberjacks' competition
15 Sitarist Shankar
16 Former soccer org.
17 Late-blooming plant
18 Actor Baldwin
19 Newman/Field film of '81
22 Coral island
23 Presidential nickname
24 Out of practice
27 Droop
30 Mideast nation
34 Italian wine region
35 SAG members
37 UN workers' agcy.
38 Newman/ Cruise film of '86
41 Poetic nighttime
42 Bank (on)
43 Sotto __
44 Dickens character
46 Shoe width
47 "Phooey!"
48 Salesperson, for short
50 Galley implement
51 Newman/ Woodward film of '76
60 Travel widely
61 Plumed military hat
62 Ms. Moffo
63 Part of AFL
64 Cut off
65 Champagne bucket
66 Hankerings
67 Gives the twice-over
68 Anchorman's spot

DOWN

1 Olin of *Havana*
2 Jordanian, e.g.
3 Long for
4 Choosy, in a way
5 Vitamin amount
6 Sax range
7 Sand bar
8 __ *Rae*
9 County Kerry capital
10 Niger neighbor
11 With: Fr.
12 Delightful
14 Slightly improper
20 Thumbs-down vote
21 Bottomless pit
24 Had some standing
25 Show to a seat
26 Office skill, for short
27 Sub device
28 "A poem lovely as __"
29 __ better (top)
31 Not important
32 Single out
33 British poet Alfred
35 Hearty brew
36 Postal-service abbr.
39 Comparatively peculiar
40 Was owed a credit
45 Military papers
47 Old horse
49 Western band
50 __ about
51 Serving prop
52 Native land
53 Uniform
54 Curds' partner
55 Church area
56 Turner and Pappas
57 Some time ago
58 Till contents
59 Carefree escapade

112 STOOGE SETTING

by Fred Piscop

ACROSS

1 Simon and McCartney
6 Corn eater's throwaway
9 Language of the Yucatan
14 Postulate
15 Ms. Gardner
16 Occupied
17 Laugh scornfully
18 Kilmer of *The Doors*
19 Low-calorie
20 Poetic stooge?
23 Barnyard parent
24 It's split for soup
25 African snakes
28 "__ Entertain You"
32 "Later, dude!"
36 *The Hustler* prop
37 Arouse, as interest
38 Remote computer user's ritual
39 Magazine stooge?
42 Think-tank output
43 River in Pakistan
44 Indivisible
45 Jury member
46 Hiccup, e.g.
47 Lemon-lime concoctions
48 Mrs. Nixon
50 Cambridge sch.
52 Actor stooge?
59 Turning point
60 Bossy comment
61 Battery part
63 Acid type
64 Peanut product
65 From the __ (from square one)
66 Expand, in a way
67 Foxlike
68 Slalom curves

DOWN

1 Second ltr. addendum
2 Outstanding
3 Pre-owned
4 Feudal lords
5 Adobe ingredient
6 Vena __
7 Roundish
8 Cinderella scene
9 Pooh's creator
10 Disney staffer
11 Imported auto
12 Arthur of tennis
13 Badminton need
21 Historical souvenir
22 Go __ (rant)
25 __ off the old block
26 Leather variety
27 Martinique volcano
29 Rig out
30 __ profit (make money)
31 Blends
33 ". . . __ cigar is a smoke"
34 *Chinatown* screenwriter Robert
35 Queen __ lace
37 IOU relatives
38 Freight amts.
40 Radio plug-in
41 Scrumptious
46 Cardinal's insignia
47 Makes amends
49 Playwright Chekhov
51 Public persona
52 Guitarist Hendrix
53 Roman poet
54 Big name in cookies
55 Make muddy
56 Poly preceder
57 Spoils
58 __ out (barely beat)
59 Ben, to Hoss
62 Aurora's counterpart

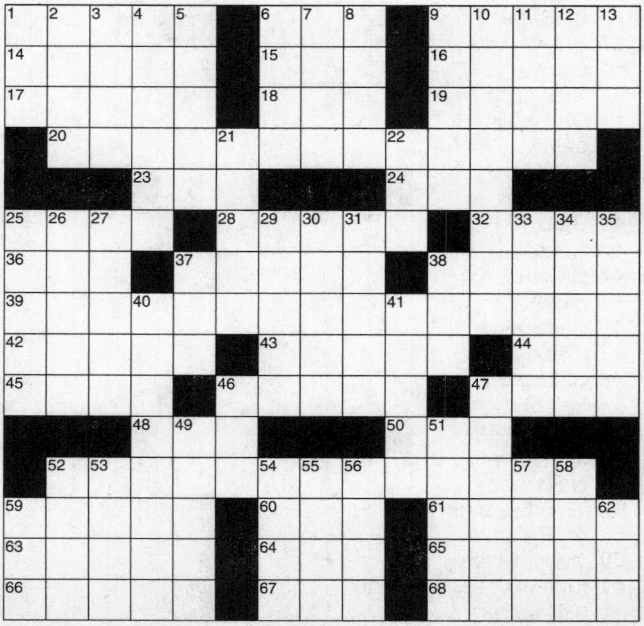

113 CAPITAL IDEA

by Richard Silvestri

ACROSS
1 Former filly
5 Likable Lee
9 Freeway entrance
13 Part of BTU
14 Actress Papas
16 ". . . baked in __"
17 Midwestern capital
20 __ *Haw*
21 Auxiliary verb
22 Nattily dressed
23 Trap material
24 Macabre
25 Copyright kin
28 "Slippery" trees
29 Barbara __ Geddes
32 Due
33 "You're __ Need to Get By"
34 Scope starter
35 Midwestern capital
38 Cover the inside of
39 Mesabi products
40 Make joyful
41 Oink spot?
42 Walkie-talkie word
43 Current 007
44 End of a CSA signature
45 Installs a lawn
46 Hitching post?
49 Turn on a pivot
50 Trifle (with)
53 Midwestern capital
56 Glee-clubber
57 Disney's "Little Mermaid"
58 *Mildred Pierce* author
59 More than half
60 Bar mem.
61 Difficult voyage

DOWN
1 Go, to the dogs?
2 Pot payment
3 Ready for picking
4 Greek letter
5 Mum
6 Packing a rod
7 Equine restraint
8 Miller who dances
9 Hoarse-voiced
10 Each, slangily
11 Little bit
12 Christmas tree?
15 Localized
18 African river
19 Head set of a sort
23 Feel the presence of
24 Immigrants' island
25 Straw votes
26 Stay for
27 Cheap-sounding
28 Bugs' nemesis
29 Sired
30 Poets' muse
31 Irish product
33 Come to terms
34 Vitamin forms
36 Short fictional work
37 Face-first fall
42 Bogus butter
43 Extra
44 Magic Kingdom neighbor
45 Winter fall
46 Steamed seafood
47 Aloha State city
48 Aardvark's entree
49 Bad mood
50 Romanov ruler
51 Steinbeck character
52 Tug hard
54 New Deal agcy.
55 Take steps

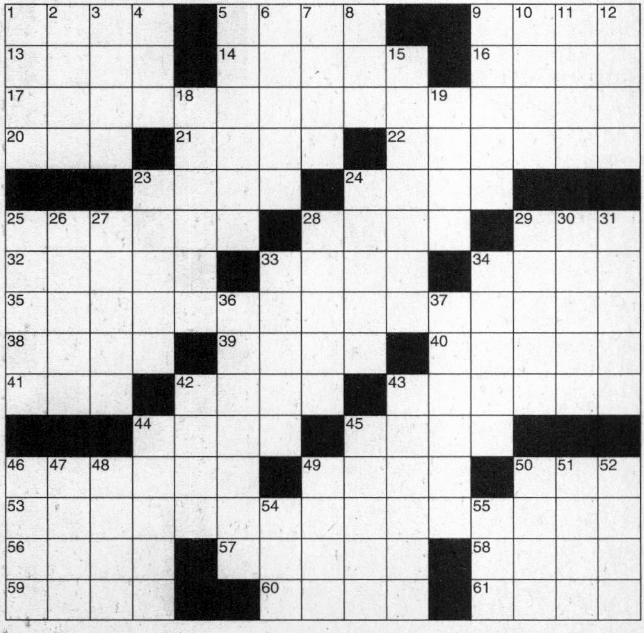

114 TALKING SENSE

by Shirley Soloway

ACROSS

1 Hemingway's nickname
5 No gentlemen
9 Boca __, FL
14 "Too bad!"
15 __ end (over)
16 Be penitent
17 Deep breath
18 Home-repair pro Bob
19 Talks up
20 Understand at last
23 Army bed
24 Implore
25 "To __ His Own"
27 Snack on
28 Least resonant
32 Sire
35 Actor Keenan
36 Smith of economics
37 Commotion
38 Some inadmissible evidence
41 Hula instrument
42 Author Uris
44 Story line
45 Rockies resort
47 Comes out for
49 Farm female
50 Small band
51 Gets even for
55 Ms. Gardner
57 Was suspicious
60 Tomato product
62 Small bottle
63 The O'Hara home
64 Make an appearance
65 TV award
66 Unlidded
67 *Mr. __ Goes to Town*
68 Lunch time
69 Comic Foxx

DOWN

1 No longer chic
2 Totally unfamiliar
3 Debra of films
4 Hardwood source
5 Word of warning
6 Slanting
7 Spanish surrealist
8 Fly in the ointment
9 Chair material
10 From __ Z
11 Improved a bit
12 Not fooled by
13 Roosting place
21 Seventies prime minister
22 Redhead's secret, maybe
26 FBI counterpart
28 Fledglings
29 *Meet Me __ Louis*
30 Benefit
31 Some govt. agents
32 Farm package
33 Heaven on earth
34 Esthetic discernment
35 Corduroy texture
39 Sort of salts
40 Went off course
43 Eur. nation
46 Glenn's title
48 Stair parts
49 Actress Keyes
51 Hertz rival
52 Juice choice
53 Golden-__ corn
54 Get up
55 Imitated
56 Housetop sight
58 On a par
59 Wheels of fortune?
61 Newsman Koppel

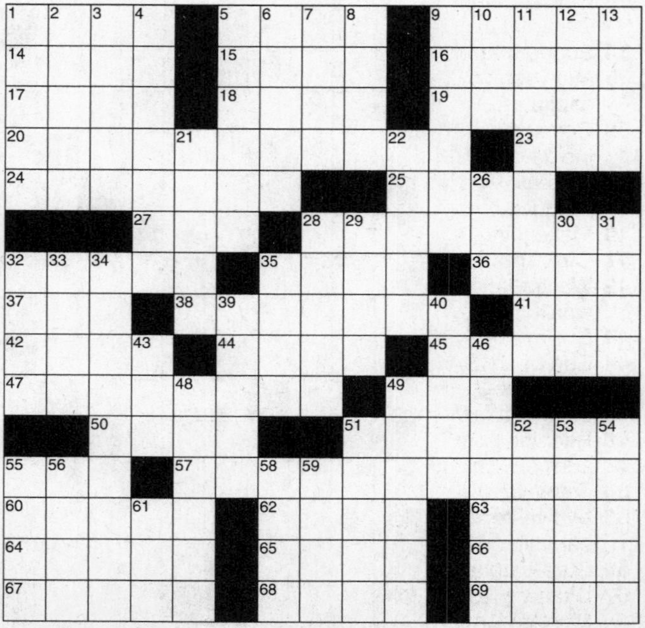

115 CARPENTRY

by Karen L. Hodge

ACROSS

1 Shish __
6 Datum, for short
10 G.P. grp.
13 Ms. Trump
14 Protagonist
15 Rude ones
17 Rock bottom
18 PC owner
19 Columnist Bombeck
20 How some fight
23 Cereal topping
26 Conductor Toscanini
27 "Are you a man __ mouse?"
28 Catchall abbr.
30 Five-star monogram
31 Home room
32 Sondheim musical
36 Canadian flier
37 Noise pollution
38 Assistant
42 American industrialist
47 Classified contents
50 Crew-team prop
51 Pro golfer Woosnam
52 Arabian Baba
53 Duplicates, in a way
55 Block deliverer of old
57 Realizer's cry
61 *Andy Griffith Show* kid
62 End-of-semester event
63 Butler in-law
67 Dried out
68 Do followers
69 Fall tools
70 Hallucinogen letters
71 Read quickly
72 Midmorning munch

DOWN

1 The family
2 __ Marie Saint
3 Acting up
4 *West Side Story* role
5 Minor peer
6 Seal up
7 *Entertainment Tonight* cohost
8 Vicinity
9 Oz transport
10 Without __ (broke)
11 Act the pirate
12 Look up to
16 Ritzy shop
21 Inauguration highlight
22 The __ Scott Decision
23 Start to bubble
24 Cartoonist Peter
25 Alliance acronym
29 Closet lining, often
30 Adoptee of the comics
33 *Strangers __ Train*
34 Carry the day
35 Dave's singing partner
39 Muslim leader
40 Oscar __ Renta
41 Green land?
43 Cheer (for)
44 Kitchen tools
45 Reagan Cabinet member
46 Popeye's tattoos
47 Parting word
48 Drive away
49 Elevator alternative
54 Suit material
56 Frome of fiction
58 Co. bigwig
59 Shangri-La resident
60 "__ the Mood for Love"
64 Alias: Abbr.
65 __ room
66 Seek to know

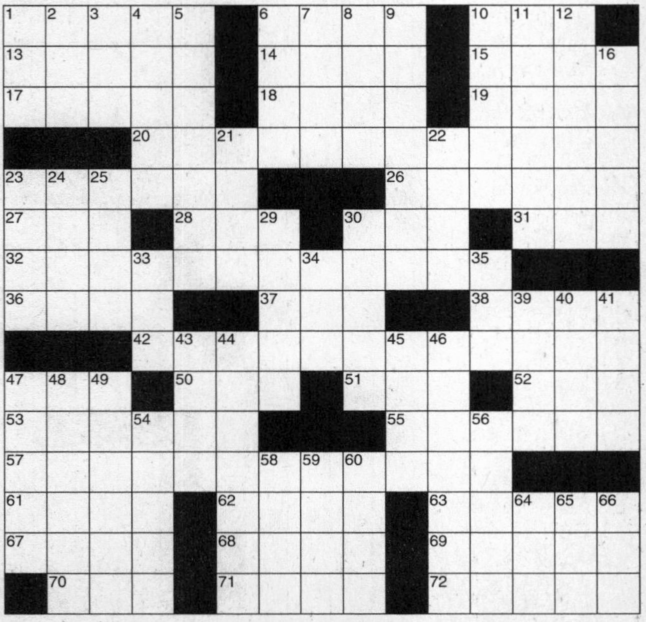

116 SONGS OF '72

by Mel Rosen

ACROSS
1 Surrealist painter
5 Oil-bearing rock
10 Cheese choice
14 Stratford's river
15 Eroded
16 Pastrami parlor
17 God: Lat.
18 Gilbert O'Sullivan '72 tune
20 __ spumante
21 Used a fax
22 Dig (into)
23 Pvt.'s superior
25 Organic compound
26 Sammy Davis, Jr. '72 tune
33 One who wanders
34 *__ to Utopia*
35 African nation
39 Water pitcher
40 Powerful sharks
41 Actor's quest
42 Something __ (unusual)
43 AT&T employee
44 Mint-family herb
45 Don McLean '72 tune
47 High country
51 Genetic material
52 Have life
53 Ray of films
56 Strait-laced
60 Harry Nilsson '72 tune
62 Rate of speed
63 Gin flavoring
64 Buenos __
65 Mortgage, e.g.
66 Longings
67 "__ not amused"
68 Some footballers

DOWN
1 Nursery word
2 Urban rtes.
3 Impolite type
4 Like crocodile tears
5 Spring, e.g.
6 Patriot Nathan
7 Like __ of bricks
8 Fast time
9 Compass dir.
10 Sidles (toward)
11 Passed out
12 Still in the game
13 Clementine's dad was one
19 Mideast port
24 Train unit
26 Genealogy diagram
27 Wolf's cry
28 Two December days
29 Window treatment
30 Oxen handler
31 New Zealand native
32 Marketing-budget items
35 Juice blend
36 Med. facility
37 Et __ (and others)
38 Proofreader's directive
40 *Mr.* __ (Teri Garr film)
44 Outlaw
45 Vocal range
46 Lindsay's writing partner
47 Worth gossiping about
48 Cast out
49 Climber's spike
50 Cookout residue
53 End in __ (require overtime)
54 Vega's constellation
55 Active person
57 Come down in buckets
58 Topped a cupcake
59 Clothing department
61 Reuther's org.

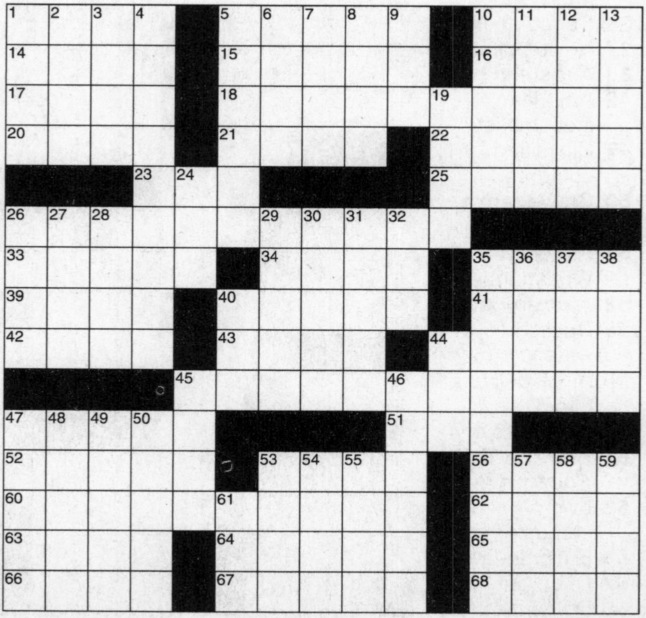

117 THE BOLD ONES

by Trip Payne

ACROSS

1 Distaff soldier
5 Hosiery shade
10 Box a bit
14 Verdi opera
15 German industrial city
16 Give a hoot
17 FBI agent
18 Gather wool
19 Not care __
20 Brecht title character
23 Not so many
25 90-degree letter
26 Johnson of *Miami Vice*
27 Pub pour
28 "La donna è mobile" is one
32 16th-century council city
34 Platter
36 Becomes beloved
39 Southern sluggers
43 Footrest
44 Vitamin unit
46 Make fit
49 Highfalutin' one
51 Moo __ gai pan
52 The P of "wpm"
53 She's "sweet as apple cider"
56 Extremely pale
58 Classic comic
63 Simpson sibling
64 Not even once
65 Dynamic prefix
68 Preceding periods
69 No longer cutting-edge
70 Iambs and anapests
71 Faxed, perhaps
72 Sportscaster's numbers
73 Take apart

DOWN

1 Shake a finger
2 Marksman's must
3 He played Batman
4 Crusoe carved one
5 *Entertainment Tonight* cohost
6 Arthur of tennis
7 Computer worker
8 Dove's goal
9 Sign up
10 Lasting aftereffect
11 5/30 event
12 Catherine's home
13 Feel contrition
21 Singing syllable
22 "Infra" opposite
23 Craze
24 Lamb's alias
29 Lessee's payment
30 Fascinated by
31 Monroe's successor
33 Invitation abbreviation
35 Hoofbeat sound
37 Statesman Abba
38 Florence's river
40 Rarely visited room
41 Just old enough to vote
42 __ gin fizz
45 Many-faced Chaney
46 Granny Smiths
47 Trace the origin of
48 Gotten out of bed
50 What ewes say
54 Fender flaws
55 Head off
57 Major mess
59 Early cartoonist
60 Nike rival
61 Riga resident
62 Infuriates
66 Beaujolais color
67 __ 60 (acceleration standard)

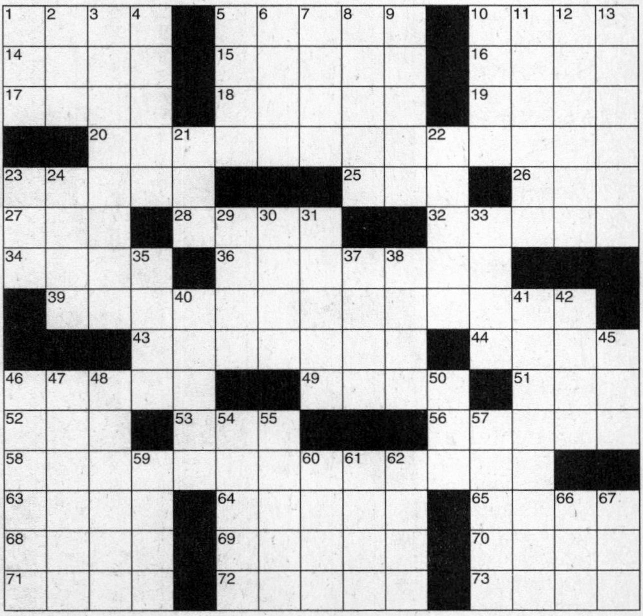

118 SMOOTH SOLVING

by Alex Vaughn

ACROSS

1 Enliven
6 Get past the goalie
11 Affectedly shy
14 Senate's colleagues
15 Today's craze
16 Actress Merkel
17 Draw a conclusion
18 Walters spot
20 Smooth
22 "Who __ kidding?"
24 Satisfied sounds
25 Former Belgrade bigwig
27 Redeems, in a way
30 Belly muscles
33 A Bobbsey twin
34 Stick back together
35 Sha Na Na personae
37 Environmental headaches
39 Garage work
42 Tabernacle tables
46 *Wheel of Fortune* buy
47 __ glance (quickly)
48 Bottomless pits
49 Take to the cleaners
51 Topmost numero
52 Ms. Gardner
53 Pennsylvania university town
59 Sylvester Stallone role
60 Corn-chip name
63 Yoko __
64 Mischa of music
65 __ *Attraction* ('87 film)
66 Intuition, plus
67 Wood tool
68 Borg or Ekberg

DOWN

1 __ Beta Kappa
2 L-o-n-g time
3 Breathing hard
4 Software buyer
5 Scope starter
6 Craftspersons
7 Caesar's dog
8 Not fooled by
9 Nothing: Fr.
10 Jazzman Hines
11 Cooking style
12 Brigadier's insignia
13 Go off-course
19 American Legion member
21 Loewe score
22 Part of ETA
23 Dogpatch's Daisy __
26 Light-switch positions
28 Plum variety
29 Board at parties
30 Onassis' nickname
31 Harp on
32 Charlie Brown's sister
35 Some MDs
36 Heathrow craft
38 Little-firm agcy.
39 Chem room
40 Unharmonized passages
41 Hotel staffer
43 High __
44 Race the motor
45 Retiree-payment org.
48 Whoever
50 Family group
51 Sort of sprawl
54 Get ready, for short
55 Grow tiresome
56 Actress Samms
57 Bake-__ (cooking contests)
58 Stick in one's __ (rankle)
59 Doakes or DiMaggio
61 Tiny bit
62 Flamenco dancer's shout

119 KNIGHT TIME

by Mel Rosen

ACROSS

1 Cold period
5 Fast planes, briefly
9 Rural structures
14 Roll-call response
15 Luau spread
16 Single-masted boat
17 Storied sword
19 Entertain
20 Beale and Bourbon: Abbr.
21 Vote in
22 Over again
23 Last name in plows
24 Deck worker
26 Inquisitive types
29 Type of birthday card
32 Maui mementos
33 U.S. artifacts
35 Storage container
36 Lerner and Loewe musical
38 "It's cold!"
39 Like a cad
41 Mailbox feature
42 Sadistic sorts
43 Thin cereals
45 Goes like lightning
46 "Get lost!"
48 Bons __ (witty remarks)
50 Free of errata
51 NFL gains
54 Cookout residue
56 Quest object
58 Mystery data
59 Gilligan's home
60 "__ Want for Christmas . . ."
61 Large group
62 Hammer hurler of myth
63 Fuse metal

DOWN

1 "__ a Lady" (Tom Jones tune)
2 Deli-counter call
3 Circle segments
4 Soup ingredient
5 Rural crossings
6 Cavalry weapon
7 Cease-fire
8 Put in order
9 Eagles' org.
10 Fact book
11 Business conference
12 Small margin of victory
13 Throw out
18 Sly expression
23 __ Moines, IA
24 Gutsy chap
25 Touched down
26 Photo holder
27 Paris' river
28 Malory character
29 Clobber
30 Place on a list
31 Pub game
33 Amo, __, amat
34 Guys
36 Cut out
37 Malt beverages
40 Liqueur flavoring
41 Bottom line
43 Comparatively cloudy
44 Called up
46 Move through water
47 Casals' instrument
48 __ 1 (speed of sound)
49 Cold capital
50 IOU
51 W.'s alma mater
52 Pickle choice
53 Lost traction
55 Vane dir.
57 Not refined

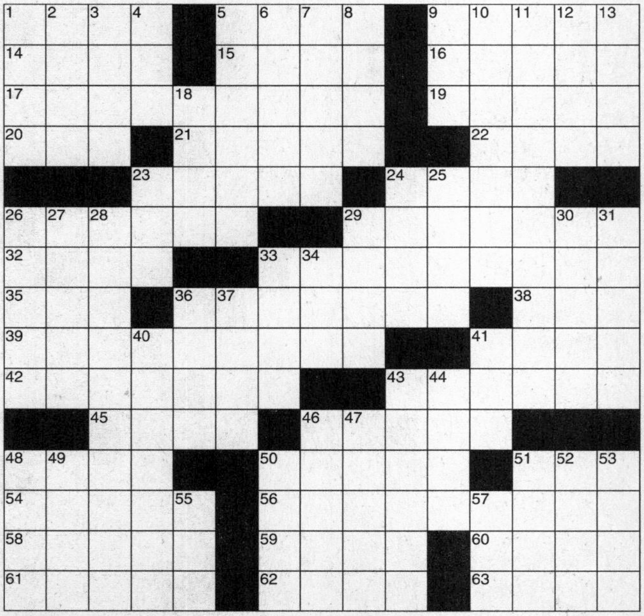

120 BRR!

by Shirley Soloway

ACROSS
1 Mardi __
5 Spheroid hairdo
9 Disaster film?
13 Latvia's capital
14 Prepares presents
16 Out-of-the-ordinary
17 Opening remark
19 In the past
20 San __, CA
21 Minimal money
22 Burn the surface of
23 Rat follower
25 Toward the dawn
27 Under-the-table cash source
31 Upright, for one
35 Barnyard sitter
36 Bombay wear
37 "If You Knew Susie" singer
38 Craving
40 Actress Berger
42 Was generous
43 Least ruddy
45 Dame __ Chaplin
47 Author Buscaglia
48 Barbecue order
49 Grows rapidly
51 Circle meas.
53 Stage pullers
54 Author Ambler
57 Pause in the action
59 Hangs ten
63 Lorre's detective
64 Excludes from participation
66 Admired one
67 Blazing
68 *Born Free* character
69 Be disposed (to)
70 Ltr. writer's courtesy
71 Forest dweller

DOWN
1 Hold tight
2 Chinese-restaurant freebie
3 Matured
4 Native-born Israelis
5 Impress a lot
6 Break
7 Garden tool
8 Broke into
9 Cake feature
10 Country path
11 Whale of a '77 film
12 Mr. Gynt
15 Sp. miss
18 Author Philip et al.
24 Pull __ one (try to cheat)
26 Health club
27 Armada members
28 Permit access to
29 Defeated one's cry
30 Curtain fabric
32 In any way
33 Innovative
34 Black-and-white snacks
37 "__ talk?": Rivers
39 Sneezing cause, maybe
41 Whistle blowers
44 Emulate Killy
46 Take down a peg
49 Blue cartoon characters
50 Gratified
52 __ Romeo (auto)
54 Send forth
55 Took the bus
56 Take __ the chin
58 *Star Wars* princess
60 Portrayal
61 Circuit device
62 Hollywood Boulevard embedment
65 Last letter

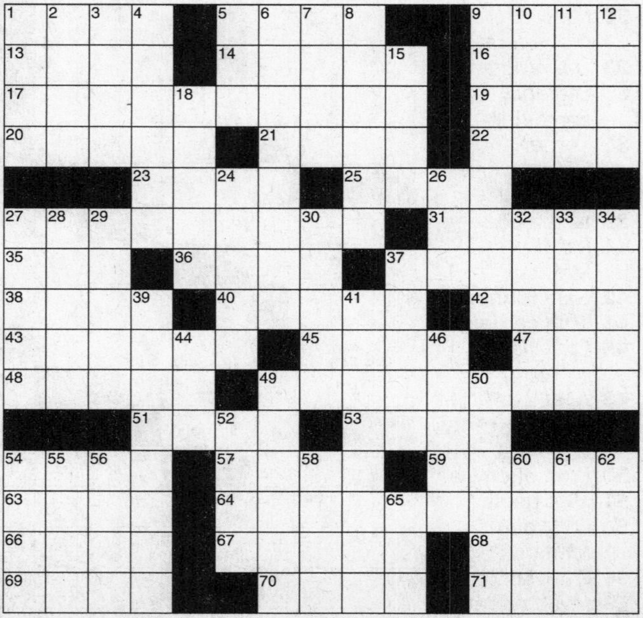

121 SPORTS HIGHLIGHTS

by Wayne R. Williams

ACROSS

1 Made logs
6 Ambience
10 Taj Mahal site
14 Luncheonette's lure
15 Like horses' hooves
16 Bread unit
17 Blood part
18 Football event
20 Huntz or Arsenio
21 Roman playwright
22 Plains Indian
24 Thurber dreamer
28 Pro golf event
30 Sci-fi author James
32 Revoke, in law
33 Comic DeLuise
34 One __ million
35 Capek play
36 Hockey event
40 Extra ltr. addendum
41 MDX divided by X
42 Road hazard
43 Used used candles
45 Make a list
48 Tennis events
50 Part of PGA
51 Full of aphorisms
52 Fanatical ones
55 Boast
58 NCAA semis teams
61 Mrs. Helmsley
62 Nasal sensation
63 Change the decor
64 Single
65 Simpson kid
66 Bk. after Amos
67 Burn, in a way

DOWN

1 Beauty-pageant accessory
2 Vicinity
3 Baseball event
4 Take after
5 Beaver project
6 Selling points
7 Enterprise crew member
8 Cowboy's accessory
9 Mideast port
10 Even if
11 Infant's syllable
12 Sushi-like
13 CIO's partner
19 Sergeant Preston's grp.
21 Rocky crag
23 Bush Sr. Cabinet member
25 Horse-racing event
26 Bowler's target
27 Leavening agents
28 Actress Strassman
29 Eighteen-year-olds
30 As well
31 UN currency agcy.
33 Commercial coloring
37 Designer Claiborne
38 Sure shot
39 Gift-tag word
44 Unisex
46 Salieri's tormentor
47 N. Atlantic nation
48 Not walked upon
49 Sea plea
51 Soft cheese
53 Hendrix's hairdo
54 Leopold's colleague
56 Till contents
57 Walk in water
58 Watch pocket
59 Ms. Lupino
60 Negative conjunction
61 Director Jean-__ Godard

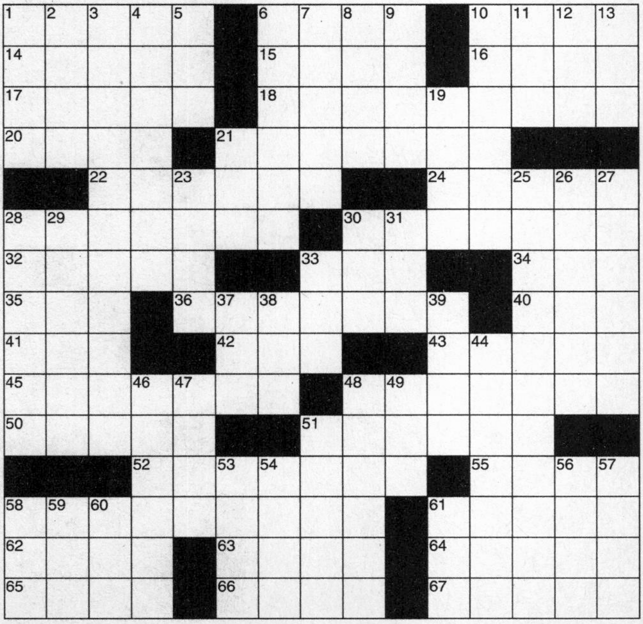

122 MEN OF LETTERS

by Trip Payne

ACROSS

1 Legume holders
5 Après-ski spot
10 Turn-of-the-century ruler
14 Devilish doings
15 Sports stadium
16 Tropical spot
17 "since feeling is first" poet
19 Author Hunter
20 Gussies up
21 Agent 86's series
23 Authoritative statement
24 Undergrad degs.
25 Prime-time hour
26 Hymn book
29 Trivial Pursuit need
32 __ Paulo, Brazil
35 XIII qvadrvpled?
36 Bearer's task
38 "The Four Quartets" poet
40 *Beasts and Super Beasts* author
41 Parthenon dedicatee
42 Curly poker?
43 Spelling meet
44 Soldier-show sponsor
45 Sissyish
48 Battleship letters
50 Deluge refuge
51 __ living (work)
56 Don't fret
59 More grainy, perhaps
60 Soprano Gluck
61 *Women in Love* author
63 Ladder-back chair part
64 Electron tube
65 "__ silly question . . . "
66 Glass square
67 Sneetches' creator
68 Fine kettle of fish

DOWN

1 Looks through the door
2 Has __ barrel
3 Unpredictable
4 Pivots
5 Rotating pieces
6 *Exodus* hero
7 Language of India
8 Absorb food
9 Magazine magnate Condé
10 "__ Kangaroo Down, Sport"
11 Philo Vance's creator
12 Controversial tree spray
13 Office expense
18 Pre-Q queue
22 Senator Thurmond
24 Worms, often
27 Novelist Wilson
28 Merman or Mertz
30 Memo heading
31 I, to Claudius
32 Jet-set jets
33 "A Shropshire Lad" poet
34 Grand __ Opry
37 Bathday place
38 Greek letter
39 Occupied
40 Use the horn
42 Ms. Retton
46 Golfer's iron
47 Datebook duration
49 Put forth
52 Mr. T's ex-group
53 Shampoo-bottle instruction
54 Bottle parts
55 Geometrician's finds
56 Grate upon
57 Actress Joyce of *Roc*
58 Interjects
59 Is beholden to
62 TV spots

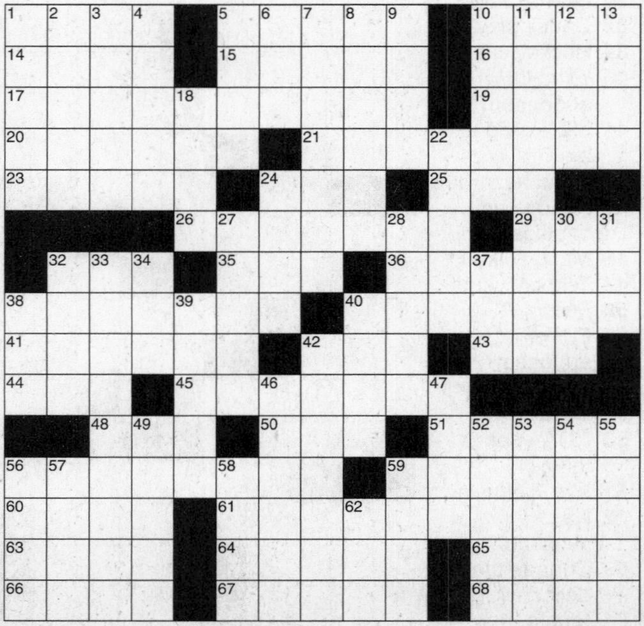

123 HARD-HITTING

by Eric Albert

ACROSS

1 It cools your head
7 Parisian pal
10 Big shot
13 City on Lake Erie
14 Blueprint
15 Dublin's loc.
16 Like a mosaic
17 Soufflé ingredient
18 Use the microwave
19 Round a rink
20 Snoop's motivation
22 LBJ son-in-law
24 Central sections
25 Poodle name
28 Unpaired
29 Pittsburgh player, for short
30 "Get a load of that!"
31 European airline
32 Request
36 On the summit
37 British playwright Joe
39 Consequently
40 In sad shape
42 Tampa clock setting: Abbr.
43 Course length
44 Have vittles
45 Recording label
46 Shed tears
47 Slyly malicious
50 Hue and cry
52 Bow material
54 Katmandu's country
58 George's brother
59 Sea swallow
60 Conventional city?
61 Handy Latin abbr.
62 Sharp taste
63 Milk holder
64 Baseball commissioner Vincent
65 Before, in palindromes
66 Walk of life

DOWN

1 Like __ (candidly)
2 Bop on the bean
3 Singer Fitzgerald
4 Ferlinghetti and Ginsberg, e.g.
5 Parting word
6 Saturn or Neptune
7 Police bulletin
8 Hawaiian isle
9 Ready to use, as a camera
10 *Arabian Nights* bigwig
11 Really steamed
12 British diarist
14 British cash
20 Closet lining
21 Mechanic's tool
23 Become mellow
25 Unwanted fat
26 Tiny speck
27 Alimentary input
29 Small chicken
33 At large
34 Mean man
35 Easy victory
38 *Sesame Street* grouch
41 County in 11 states
47 Foremost
48 It comes from the heart
49 Beatty role
50 Chile partner
51 Slightly ahead
53 Pay attention to
55 Lap dog
56 Declare
57 Behind time
60 *Pygmalion* monogram

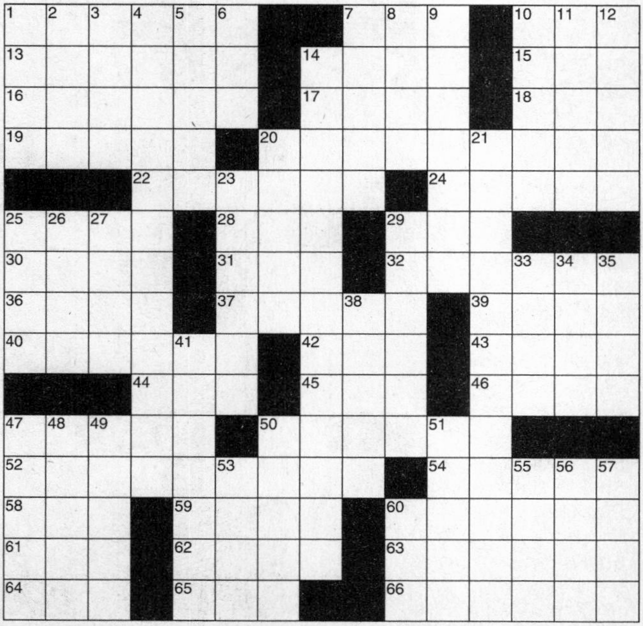

124 VERTICES

by Mel Rosen

ACROSS
1 Fill fully
5 Show amazement
9 *Person to Person* network
12 Brick worker
13 Earthly extremes
14 Move quickly
15 Short of cash
17 Chicken-king link
18 *Much __ About Nothing*
19 Bring up
20 First name in glue
22 Open-hearted
24 Drawer attachment
25 Talks too much
30 Singer Lane et al.
33 Simple Simon's yens
34 Seafood delicacy
35 Litigious one
36 Old hat
38 Brassy Horne
39 Under the weather
40 Nibble on
41 Was helpful
42 Every available means
46 "As __ going to St. Ives . . ."
47 Seltzer-making gadget
51 Fudge nut
53 Small role
55 Major rte.
56 Swear words?
57 Foundation element
60 USO visitors
61 Large antelope
62 Sahara stopovers
63 Sault __ Marie, MI
64 Makes a dress
65 Told a whopper

DOWN
1 Riyadh resident
2 __ Martin (007's auto)
3 One __ customer
4 Menu choices
5 Lots and lots
6 Skin-cream additive
7 Church bench
8 Ancient ascetics
9 Having rooms
10 Peevishness
11 Burn the outside of
12 Extinct birds
13 Worked at a trade
16 Be worthy of
21 Spanish article
23 "Good buddy"
24 Baby bouncer
26 Give rise to
27 Wildcat strike
28 First-rate
29 Audition (for)
30 Korea, China, Iran, etc.
31 Wall Street optimist
32 Eager to fight
36 __ *Gotta Have It* ('86 film)
37 Afternoon ritual
38 "Mona __"
40 Raffle tickets
41 Spray can
43 LAX client
44 Patronized a casino
45 A certain smile
48 "__ Were the Days"
49 Had the deed to
50 Bologna breads
51 Swine
52 Work in the cutting room
53 Stick in one's __ (rankle)
54 Sothern and Miller
58 Señor's "Hurrah!"
59 Skater Babilonia

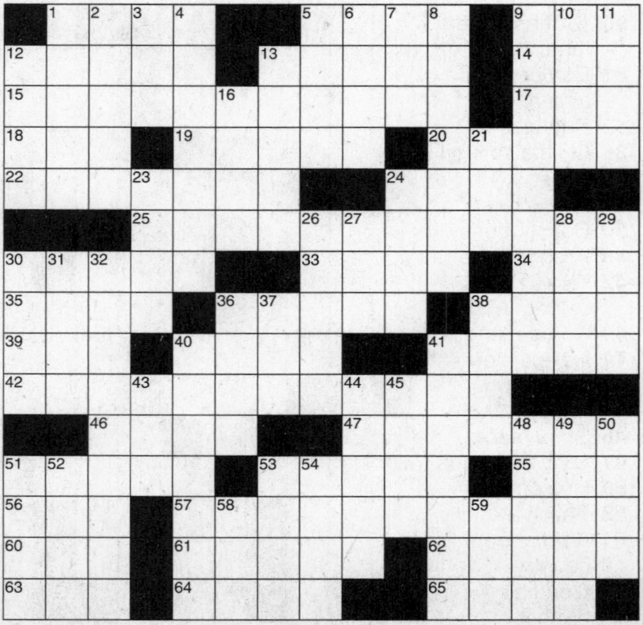

125 WEATHER REPORT

by Wayne R. Williams

ACROSS

1 Take for granted
7 Foolishly fond
11 Actress Ullmann
14 Slo-mo showing
15 *Topaz* author
16 Hole-in-one
17 *The Invisible Man* star
19 __ Tin Tin
20 Jannings or Zatopek
21 Computer command
22 Part of Cohan's signature
23 Delany and Carvey
25 *My Little Margie* star
29 Tug's offering
31 Drink for two?
32 *Scarlett* predecessor
41 Continental abbr.
42 Gallagher's vaudeville partner
43 Actor Beatty
44 Florida collegians
49 Penultimate Greek letter
50 One on the beat
51 Stroke of luck
57 Visual aid
61 Historic time
62 Midday
64 Digestive-system word form
65 Break in the action
66 Sudden noise
69 Had a snack
70 Peter the pianist
71 Filmdom's T.E. Lawrence
72 Directed
73 Prepares to drive
74 Cleared, as salary

DOWN

1 Moved in a curved path
2 Alabama town
3 Columbus' sponsor
4 Lament loudly
5 Hatterlike
6 Spud features
7 Tropical fruit
8 Prospero's servant
9 Rummy game
10 Horse's cousin
11 Slow tempo
12 More aloof
13 Malice, so to speak
18 Dustcloth
24 Scatter seeds
26 Kind of pride
27 "Understand?"
28 Fancy marble
30 "__ and Hopin' "
32 Precious stone
33 Arles assent
34 New Deal grp.
35 Calendar abbr.
36 One of the ladies
37 Sea dog
38 Rustic hotel
39 Society-page word
40 Graduate deg.
45 Velocity abbr.
46 Adherent's suffix
47 Machine tooth
48 Brandy flavor
51 Statutory
52 Seeing red
53 Opened wide
54 Habituate
55 Child's taboos
56 Vulcan, e.g.
58 Parcel out
59 Norman Vincent __
60 Had aspirations
63 Light gas
66 Explosive letters
67 __ *Haw*
68 Hwy.

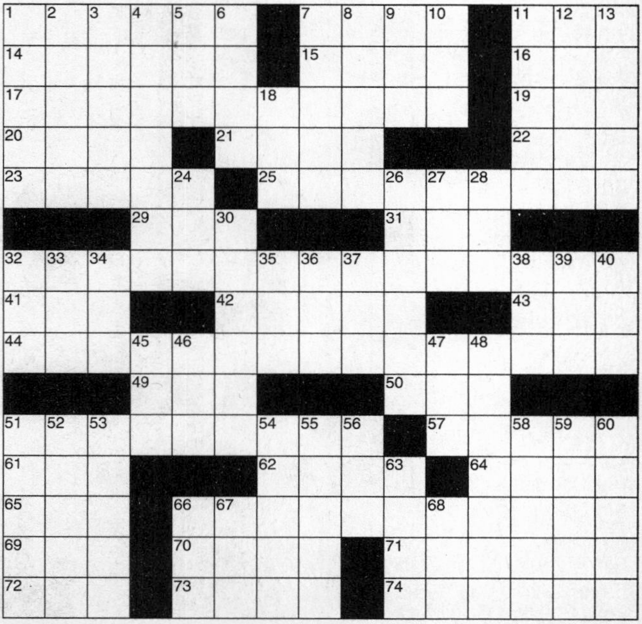

126 *BIKE RACK*

by Randolph Ross

ACROSS

1 Play parts
5 Kipling character
8 Pet-shop purchase
12 Café au __
13 __ *Kleine Nachtmusik*
14 Figurine mineral
15 Logic
16 Throw for a loop
17 Totally attentive
18 PR representative
21 Big-time operators
24 Actress Garr
25 Pseudonym
27 "Now I gotcha!"
30 __ of passage
32 Burning
33 Up-to-date
34 Make __ of the tongue
36 At this time
37 Most important
40 Draft status
42 *The Joy Luck Club* author
43 Murrow's __ *Now*
44 Stock speculators, for short
46 Economist's concerns
53 Slacks style
54 Ring out
57 Thine: Fr.
58 CAUTION: __ WORK
59 Coffee
60 Property claim
61 Writer Kingsley
62 Chop __
63 Nav. rank
64 Kent's coworker

DOWN

1 Hebrew letter
2 Kayak kin
3 "A __, a tasket . . ."
4 NFLer
5 Flew, in a way
6 Accustom (to)
7 High-IQ group
8 Ivy League school
9 Santa __, CA
10 Take to the cleaners
11 Phone no. abbr.
13 Lively qualities
15 Vane dir.
19 Episodic show
20 Norwegian royal name
22 Cheerful
23 Dr. Mead's hangout
26 Basted, perhaps
27 Fuse units
28 Biblical peak
29 French farewell
31 *Xanadu* rock group
32 Brief glimpse
35 Reeling
38 Do wrong
39 End in __ (require overtime)
41 Just awful
45 Conceptual framework
47 Chip __ (Disney cartoon pair)
48 Avoid restaurants
49 Plumlike fruits
50 Bolshevik bigwig
51 Wipe out
52 Orly bird?
54 Evening wear
55 __ de toilette
56 St. crosser

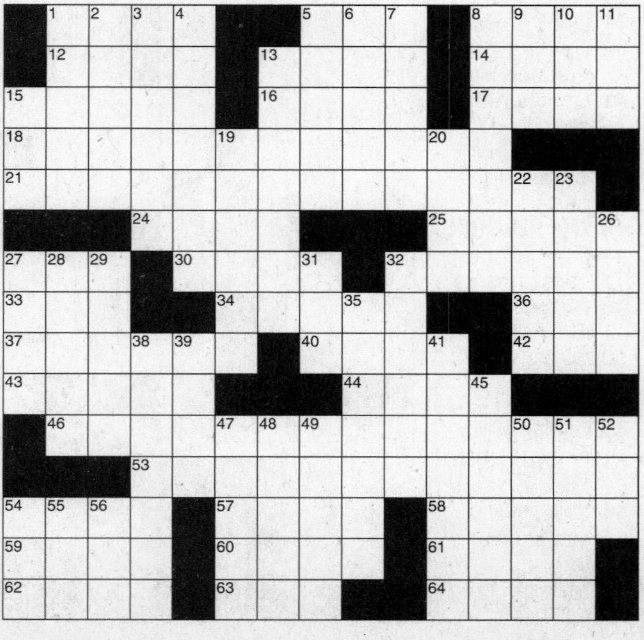

127 WORLD HUES

by Mel Rosen

ACROSS

1 Onetime inkwell sites
6 Was in front
9 At the apex
13 Immigrants' island
14 Safety feature
16 NHL team
18 Real doozy
19 Beau Bridges, to Lloyd
20 So long, in Salerno
21 Burden
23 ASAP relative
25 __ Brownell Anthony
29 *Dances With Wolves* home
31 Shake up
34 Happy state
37 "That hurts!"
38 Exotic houseplant
42 CIO's colleague
43 One at large
44 Glacier feature
47 Interstate exits
51 Terry product
52 Wine word
55 Drained of color
56 Vessel of 1492
59 Bar bill
61 Novelist Kesey
62 Some chickens
67 Plant classification
68 Blue __ Mountains
69 Samoa studier Margaret
70 Wind up
71 Commented, cattle-style

DOWN

1 Tyrannical one
2 Actress Stritch
3 Make a mistake
4 They're related
5 Heathrow sights
6 Brooklyn, NY school
7 Clapton of rock
8 Lucy's son
9 Total
10 Upsilon preceder
11 It's in the veins
12 Aft. periods
14 __ of (sweet on)
15 Take down a peg
17 Cut (off)
22 Nostradamus, for one
24 Marmalade fruits
26 Eye problem
27 "Little Things Mean __"
28 Improved's partner
30 New Haven student
32 PBS series
33 Use scissors
35 Virtuosos
36 Russian news agcy.
38 Big hairdo
39 Soloed in the sky
40 "__ the fields we go . . ."
41 Spring up
42 Behave
45 Offered at retail
46 Quite unfamiliar
48 Get along somehow
49 Frat hopeful
50 Had an inkling of
53 List abbr.
54 Corn holder
57 Clementine's shoe size
58 P __ "pneumonia"
60 Apt. unit
62 Spinning-rate abbr.
63 __ *Haw*
64 "Are you a man __ mouse?"
65 Little boy
66 South American port

128 SHIPMATES

by Randy Sowell

ACROSS
1 Le Sage's Gil __
5 Iraqi port
10 Citrus drinks
14 Ready to pick
15 Fields of expertise
16 Noel trio
17 Violin virtuoso
19 Stratford-on-__
20 Actress Mason
21 Tree-to-be
23 Latched onto
25 Police operation
26 Important
29 Slalom curve
32 Repair software
35 Product patron
36 Each
38 Stop __ dime
39 Leave one's seat
40 Of interest to Peary
41 Loretta of *M*A*S*H*
42 Radio spots
43 __ *Rides Again*
44 Yugoslav statesman
45 Somewhat suspicious
47 Look at
48 Ms. Garson
49 This: Lat.
51 Be bold
53 Amusing story
57 Theater district
61 Columbo portrayer
62 *Dallas* star
64 "Don't throw bouquets __"
65 Ice rink, e.g.
66 To be, in Paree
67 What's left
68 Socially inept
69 "__ Me" (Roger Miller tune)

DOWN
1 Hat edge
2 Actress Hartman
3 On __ with (comparable to)
4 Resort locale
5 Kind of metabolism
6 Sculptures and such
7 Gets the point
8 Seldom encountered
9 *JFK* actor
10 Charlotte __, VI
11 British rock star
12 Designer von Fürstenberg
13 Vocalize
18 Chastity Bono's mom
22 Miami's county
24 Topple from office
26 Diego Rivera work
27 Short digression
28 Southern senator
30 Sedimentlike
31 Burned, in a way
33 Bring together
34 Florida collegian
36 Big lummox
37 Hue's partner
41 Went quickly
43 Recolored
46 Annoying noise
48 Football field
50 *George M.* subject
52 Orderly grouping
53 Worship from __
54 Hoops star Thurmond
55 Ripped
56 Water pitcher
58 "I __ Song Go . . ."
59 Gull relative
60 Designer Cassini
63 Common conjunction

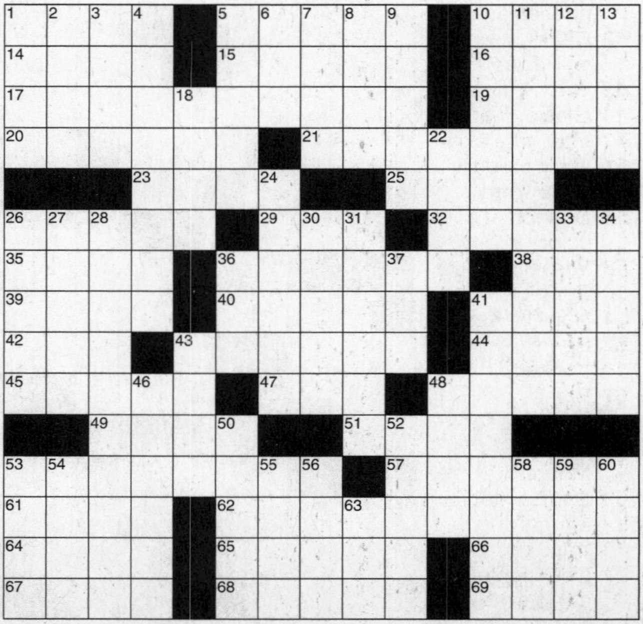

129 BAR FARE

by Bob Sefick

ACROSS

1 Deep cut
5 *Love Story* author
10 Boone portrayer Parker
14 Run in neutral
15 Hispaniola part
16 Bound
17 Bouncy standard
20 Made beloved
21 Second-place finisher
22 Wine category
23 "__ she blows!"
25 Sampled some soup
29 Any day now
30 Provide firepower to
33 Reactor part
34 Mall unit
35 Lamb comment
36 Sailor's saying
40 __ Grande
41 Has the impression
42 Mental picture
43 Way down yonder
44 Master stroke
45 Promising ones
47 Medicinal medium
48 Mauna __
49 Donkey's uncles
52 End of the instructions
57 With *The,* Salinger novel
60 Puccini piece
61 Boléro composer
62 Glance from Groucho
63 *Green Acres* structure
64 Oboelike
65 "__ we forget"

DOWN

1 Taunt
2 Mideast port
3 Snow vehicle
4 Wherever I am
5 Divvied up
6 Golden-__ corn
7 Hem in
8 Absorbed, as costs
9 __ Abner
10 Wax target
11 Sushi selection
12 Japanese drink
13 Practice boxing
18 Unadorned
19 Wood smoothers
23 Roger Rabbit and colleagues
24 Israeli dance
25 Winter warmer
26 Old Aegean region
27 *Stir Crazy* star
28 Vivacity
29 Clown's prop
30 Lodging place
31 Blue moon, vis-à-vis full moon
32 "Last of the Red Hot __" (Sophie Tucker)
34 Super buy
37 Aloof
38 Film holder
39 Baseball star Raines
45 Not at all cheap
46 Solemn word
47 Pie ingredient
48 Like highways
49 Hailing __ (urban action)
50 Lee of cakedom
51 Agitate
52 Electrically charged
53 Part with, perhaps
54 Genealogy chart
55 Seeing things
56 Boldly forward
58 "To __ is human"
59 Comedienne Charlotte

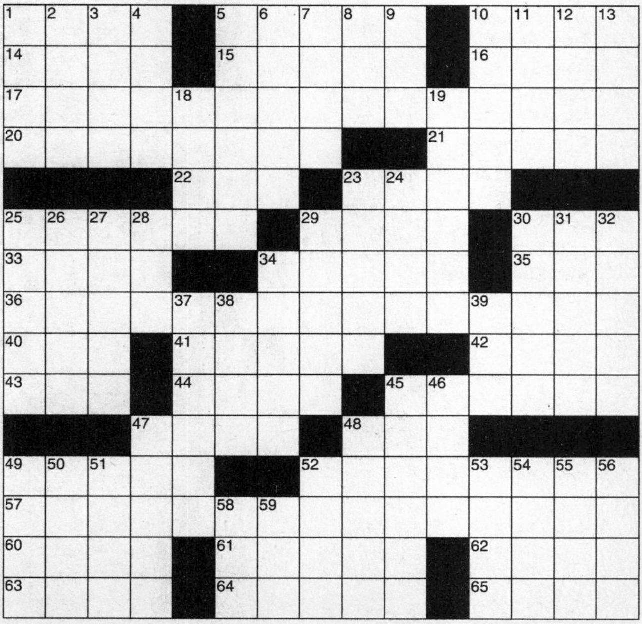

130 CAR-ICATURES

by Fred Piscop

ACROSS

1 Mardi __
5 Performs like L.L. Cool J
9 Heats and dashes
14 Carson's successor
15 Jai __
16 "__ a River"
17 __-deucy
18 Lily-pad locale
19 Courtyards
20 Sentimental journalist?
23 Pool-table covering
24 Mayo and marmalade
25 Naval officer
27 Belly muscles
28 City in Italia
31 Pro golfer __ Stewart
34 Errand person
37 Former Mideast org.
38 Burden
39 Actor's words
40 Gin flavoring
41 Siamese twin
42 Traffic cone
43 Bridle and primrose
44 Whistle blower
46 Frat symbol
47 Mild acid
49 Book section
53 Baby elephant
55 Walk-on parts?
57 Lettucelike
59 Run like heck
60 Journalist/reformer Jacob __
61 Followed a circular path
62 Hydrox rival
63 Borge, for one
64 __ around (pries)
65 High schooler
66 Jet-set jets

DOWN

1 Sand product
2 Summarize
3 Lend __ (listen)
4 Versatile veggies
5 White-water locale
6 At __ for words
7 Breathe heavily
8 LP surface
9 TV name
10 Like Dickens' Dodger
11 Rostand hero?
12 Actor Jannings
13 Government center
21 Kemo __
22 McIntosh relatives
26 Letter starter
29 Lye, chemically
30 Bauxite and galena
31 Ode writer
32 Part of A.D.
33 Former Supreme Court Justice?
34 Hodges of baseball
35 Yoko __
36 Boggy area
39 Ode-like
40 Redd Foxx's TV family
42 __ capita
43 Docking place
45 Candy flavor
46 Hydrogen atoms have one
48 Henry __ Lodge
49 Martinique volcano
50 Assumed name
51 Dirty Harry portrayer
52 Mississippi quartet?
53 Thunder sound
54 Prefix for space
56 *Utopia* author
58 NFL distances

131 NICKNAMES

by Max Hopkins

ACROSS

1 Kemo Sabe's trademark
5 High-interest activity
10 Open a bit
14 ". . . __ saw Elba"
15 Word not used in *The Godfather*
16 Big party
17 Riotous brawl
19 Makes a decision
20 Copier chemical
21 Short distance
23 Sennett staffer
24 One being used
26 Barber's need
28 Compass pt.
29 Chatter
31 Pirate's chant
34 __ *from a Mall* (Woody Allen film)
37 Up and around
38 Cremona craftsman
41 Do lunch
42 Sail holders
43 Breakfast fruit
44 Stylish
46 *Batman* butler
48 Fall guy
49 Norton's namesakes
52 Make a new chart
54 Small sum
57 Lamb's mama
59 Atmosphere
61 Get in
62 Durante's claim to fame
64 Girl of the '40s
66 Savage and Severinsen
67 Banquet host
68 Swampy ground
69 Job opening
70 Gave medicine to
71 Billion-selling cookie

DOWN

1 Army healers
2 Odors
3 Where Dole deliberated
4 David and Solomon
5 What the miffed take
6 Mediterranean isl.
7 Strange sightings
8 Barrels of laughs
9 Yak preceder
10 __ Khan
11 Big prizes
12 Vocal range
13 Scrape
18 Slangy assent
22 Some golf tourneys
25 Petered out
27 Anthem starter
30 NFL team
32 Stage success
33 Hosp. locales
34 Put away
35 Film world
36 Place
38 *I __ Camera*
39 Gibson of *Lethal Weapon*
40 Out-of-doors
45 Used an atomizer
47 Painted poorly
49 Cure-all
50 Actress Trish Van __
51 Sound system
53 PR gimmick
55 Treas. Dept. agcy.
56 Headache remedy, familiarly
57 Winds up
58 Yarn material
60 Fundamentals
63 Adjective ending
65 Little stinger

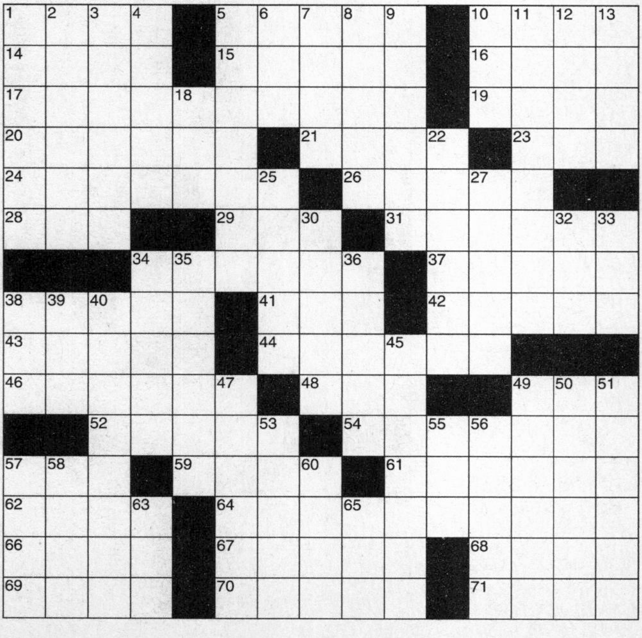

132 EXPLORERS CLUB

by Mel Rosen

ACROSS

1 Walk through water
5 Mouth off
9 Like the polo set
14 Actress Barbara
15 Dull pain
16 Oahu greeting
17 __ *Called Horse*
18 NYSE alternative
19 Stair post
20 Alaska explorer
23 Compass pt.
24 Moral standard
25 Lulu
27 Greenland explorer
33 Dowser's tool
36 Newspaper notice
37 Admit frankly
38 *Arabian Nights* character
40 War-prone
43 Office note
44 Mountain lion
45 Vast amount
46 Florida explorer
50 Operatic solo
51 Like some pitchers
56 Guys
59 Africa explorer
62 Kitchen come-on
64 __ instant (quickly)
65 Bookie quote
66 Exodus mount
67 Corsica neighbor
68 Mild-mannered
69 Villain's look
70 Method: Abbr.
71 Puts in a lawn

DOWN

1 Work at the loom
2 Let in
3 __ *of a Salesman*
4 Boredom
5 Swedish auto
6 Top of the mountain
7 Dessert choice
8 More alluring
9 Mental block
10 Grand __ Opry
11 Ticket details
12 "__ a Lady"
13 W.'s alma mater
21 Boston entree
22 Abolitionist Turner
26 Ship wood
28 Oriental sash
29 Coal container
30 Hertz competitor
31 Got up
32 Ladies' club of a sort
33 Freeway exit
34 Bread spread
35 __ *Yankees*
39 Medicos
40 Cry's partner
41 I love: Lat.
42 Eases off
44 Without adornment
47 Rich dessert
48 "Agnus __" (hymn)
49 Would like to be
52 Cyclotron fodder
53 Copland work
54 Finished
55 School furniture
56 Church service
57 "*__ go bragh!*"
58 Not a soul
60 Captures
61 Small fly
63 Ginnie __ bonds

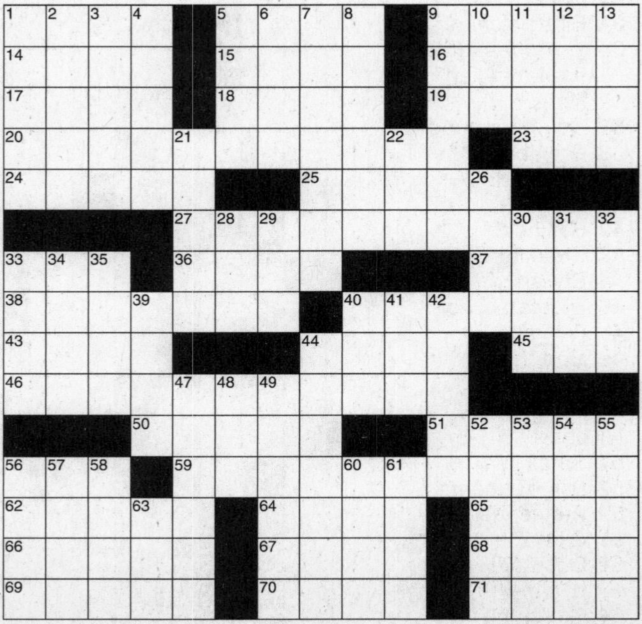

133 COUNTS

by Mel Rosen

ACROSS

1 "__ Lisa"
5 Abraham's wife
10 Cry loudly
14 Roberts of Tulsa
15 Wear gradually
16 Lebanon's locale
17 Anger, pride, etc.
20 Trifle (with)
21 Old oath
22 Balances evenly
23 Historical periods
24 Imported autos
25 Argentina steppes
28 Business transaction
29 "Telly" network
32 Cancel a mission
33 Layer of paint
34 Court statement
35 Athos and company
38 Heavy weights
39 Mars' counterpart
40 Ledger entry
41 Mos. and mos.
42 Singer Kristofferson
43 __ Berry Farm
44 Put on an act
45 Eye coverings
46 Tests metal
49 Hollywood Boulevard crosses it
50 Binet's concerns
53 Grist for De Mille
56 Essential point
57 Art stand
58 Revue piece
59 Work units
60 Indigent
61 Recipe amts.

DOWN

1 The lion's share
2 Sandwich snack
3 Dark blue
4 Potent potable
5 Marsh plants
6 Fields of expertise
7 Byway
8 Tack on
9 Companion/assistant
10 Supporting factor
11 Sale caveat
12 Bordeaux or Beaujolais
13 Glasgow gal
18 Bring to naught
19 Cry of pain
23 __-ski outfit
24 Nestlings' noses
25 Hamburger unit
26 Can't stand
27 Pre-noon times
28 Vitamin amounts
29 Declared holy
30 Toulouse topper
31 Playbill listings
33 Radium discoverer
34 Cancún cash
36 Skilled shots
37 Kind of bicycle
42 Boxing result
43 Good-hearted
44 Hard data
45 Like some paper
46 "Ma, He's Making Eyes __"
47 Omen observer
48 Hidden obstacle
49 Posy holder
50 Printer's purchases
51 Stick it in your ear
52 Atl. speedsters
54 Dogpatch's Daisy __
55 Superlative suffix

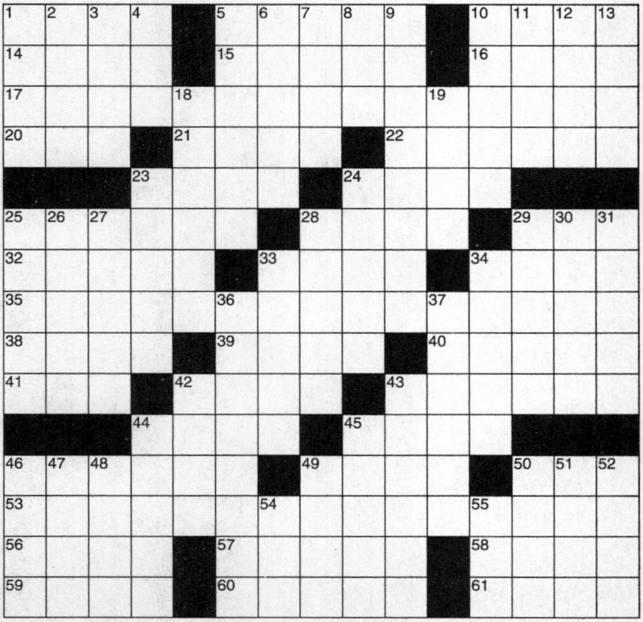

134 HARDWARE

by Richard Silvestri

ACROSS

1 Curved letters
6 Ego
10 Ring rocks
14 Monetary gain
15 Word form meaning "thought"
16 Came to earth
17 Soft hat
18 In the vicinity
19 __ *18* (Uris novel)
20 Wolfed down
21 Storm phenomenon
24 Burton's birthplace
26 "Uncle" of early TV
27 Highwayman
29 Macbeth's title
31 Whitish stone
32 Adventuresome
34 Acknowledge applause
37 Astrodome gridder
39 Moving vehicle
40 Beetle Bailey's boss
42 Actress Harris
43 Throws out
46 Hill's partner
47 Head off
48 Knocked for a loop
50 Pygmalion product
53 Turbaned seer
54 Laundress
57 Baton Rouge campus
60 ". . . __ forgive those . . ."
61 First name in whodunits
62 Turner and Louise
64 Ollie's pal
65 Latvia's capital
66 Stinker
67 Some brooders
68 Get top billing
69 Register for

DOWN

1 Mediterranean isle
2 Tallow source
3 Eccentric
4 Palindromic preposition
5 Come to terms
6 Hole in your head
7 Paradise
8 Heavy metal
9 Boxer George
10 Take a chance
11 Mr. Ness
12 Metric prefix
13 Union member?
22 Bovine bunch
23 Circus trio
25 Up to the task
27 Leeway
28 *Andy Griffith Show* kid
29 Brief treatise
30 Subtle indication
33 Assert
34 Three-sided snack
35 Make eyes at
36 Garden bane
38 Show with sketches
41 *Bonanza* brother
44 They give a hoot
45 "I never __ purple cow"
47 European capital
49 Yankee Hall-of-Famer
50 Buckle starter
51 Try a tidbit
52 Nile dam
53 Mudslinger's specialty
55 Court order
56 Ms. Korbut
58 Letter encl.
59 Computer owner
63 Electrovalent atom

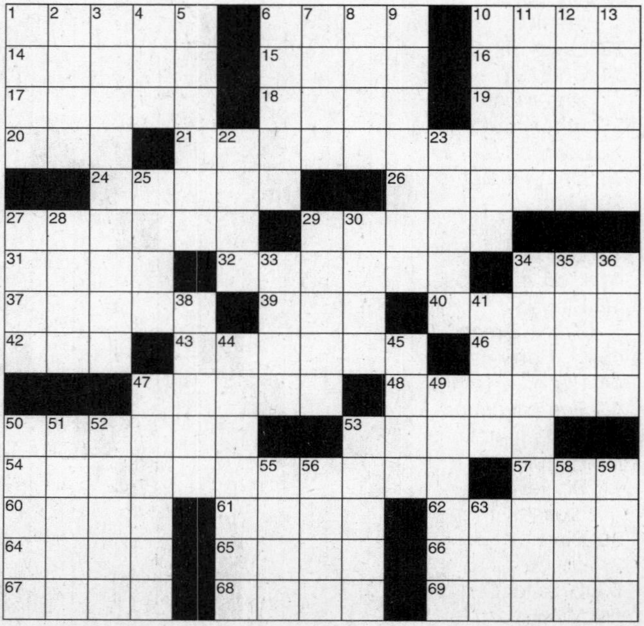

135 SHORT STORY

by Trip Payne

ACROSS

1 River in Spain
5 *M*A*S*H* star
9 Bring in crops
13 Villainous expression
14 Black and Baltic
15 Author Seton
16 Arachnid of song
19 Forest females
20 Cowardly types
21 Paramedic: Abbr.
22 Summertime cooler
23 Sidelong look
27 Soak up
29 Tommy of Broadway
31 Galley paddle
32 Prepared to drive
34 "My Way" composer
35 Hornblower of rhyme
39 Martin's nickname
40 Game-show groups
41 Not quite right
42 Plate officials
44 Attractive person
48 Name of three presidents
50 Motherly attention, briefly
51 Yoko __
52 Fast tempo
55 Guzzlers
56 Runner of rhyme
60 Roundish shape
61 Olympian Korbut
62 Prides' pads
63 Moistens
64 Be patient
65 Foil alternative

DOWN

1 Cover with earth
2 Harasses
3 Actor Alejandro et al.
4 Scepter topper
5 TV's Gomez Addams
6 Diminished by
7 Journal pages
8 Give homework
9 Mikhail's wife
10 Finish off
11 Mate's reply
12 Duffer's goal
13 Front of an LP
17 Sanford of *The Jeffersons*
18 Soccer great
22 Guitar ridge
24 Not well-to-do
25 Soap unit
26 Historic time
28 Herr von Bismarck
29 Deep winds?
30 Bone __ (study)
33 Teen heartthrob Johnny
34 Not to mention
35 "__ is but a dream"
36 Hard facts, for short
37 Like sapsuckers' bellies
38 Political group
39 Shepherd or schnauzer
42 Tangelo variety
43 Laid-back
45 Edd Byrnes role
46 All-inclusive
47 Pasadena-parade posies
49 Singer Lou
50 Pay for dinner
53 First name in scat
54 Leslie Caron musical
55 Something easy
56 "That's amazing!"
57 Second name?
58 Scarf down
59 __ de France

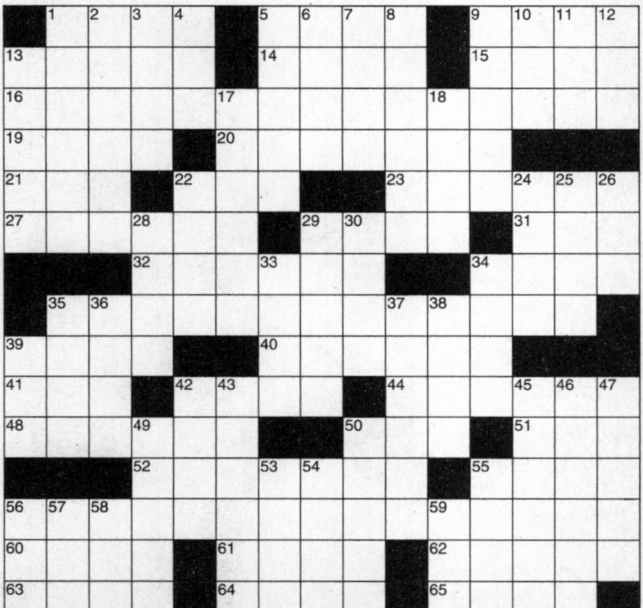

136 ELEMENTARY

by Shirley Soloway

ACROSS
1 Fur piece
5 Flexible armor
9 The Babe's sultanate
13 __ close to schedule
14 Country singer Travis
15 Othello's adversary
16 Top-rated
17 Starlike flower
18 Corner sign
19 Get things out in the open
22 Swelled head
23 How some try
24 Do the pots
26 Bank jobs
29 Newsman Vanocur
32 Drum's partner
35 Paint layer
37 Bucks
38 Onassis' nickname
39 Pet rodents
41 See the point of
42 Greene of *Bonanza*
44 Right-hand person
45 On a cruise
46 Prepares for prayer
48 Mideast desert
50 Cooks, in a way
52 Of an eye part
56 Pullman, e.g.
58 Levelheaded
61 "Woe is me!"
63 Song of joy
64 Unlikely to bite
65 Carry on
66 Falls loudly
67 Actor Sharif
68 *60 Minutes* name
69 Sudden urges
70 Mouthy Martha

DOWN
1 Prepare eggs
2 __ *Gay* (WWII plane)
3 Solitary one
4 Foot control
5 Moonshine-to-be
6 Part of A.M.
7 Mental flashes
8 Hammerstein's forte
9 Family member
10 Retrievers, for instance
11 Excited
12 "__ the morning!"
14 The daily grind
20 Antique auto
21 Goes here and there
25 Important "numero"
27 Writer Ephron
28 Vaccine discoverer
30 "Waiting for the Robert __"
31 Pro follower
32 Columbo portrayer
33 Nutritive mineral
34 Hothead
36 Oxydol competitor
39 Ice-cold
40 Great numbers
43 New beginning?
45 Rickenbacker or Wright
47 Not carefully done
49 Prior to, in poems
51 Lowland
53 Molière's milieu
54 "Be that as __ . . ."
55 Dear, in Deauville
56 Irene of *Fame*
57 King of comedy
59 Light gas
60 A little night music
62 Hog's home

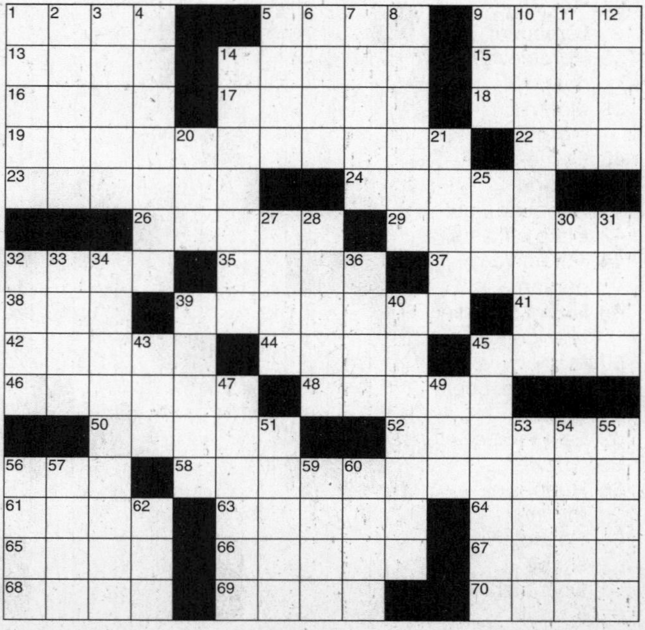

137 TAKE OFF

by Wayne R. Williams

ACROSS

1 Poker stake
5 Got up
10 African nation
14 Old codger
15 Pygmy antelope
16 Latvia's capital
17 Take off
19 Menu listing
20 Correction spots
21 Likes and dislikes
23 Actor Beatty
24 Tissue fluid
25 Wheel-alignment measure
29 Neuwirth of *Cheers*
30 McBain and McMahon
33 Symbol of achievement
34 Take off
36 Oven setting
37 Indicate indifference
38 Characterization
39 Take off
41 Serenity
42 So far
43 Lady Chaplin
44 More incensed
45 Disprove a point
47 __ Paulo, Brazil
48 Concentrating viewer
50 Heel style
55 Ms. Chanel
56 Take off
58 Places of refuge
59 Bring joy to
60 Otherwise
61 Army outpost
62 Became the father of
63 Highland loch

DOWN

1 Dull pain
2 Roulette bet
3 Frat-party attire
4 Ordinal endings
5 One flying high
6 Sampled
7 Art medium
8 Kimono sash
9 Sailor's tote
10 Crunchy
11 Take off
12 Film critic James
13 Boulder and Aswan High
18 Adjusted plugs and points
22 Hemsley sitcom
24 Diminishment
25 Hack driver
26 In the know
27 Take off
28 La __ Tar Pits (L.A. locale)
29 Mandalay's locale
31 Sweet, in Seville
32 Smile derisively
34 Protester's litany
35 __ Scott decision
37 Causes of calamity
40 Japanese metropolis
41 Director Pier __ Pasolini
44 Injured severely
46 Irregularly worn
47 Put into words
48 Strikebreaker
49 Synagogue scroll
50 Arcturus or Aldebaran
51 All tied up
52 Scope starter
53 Prepare salad
54 Washington bills
57 Yale student

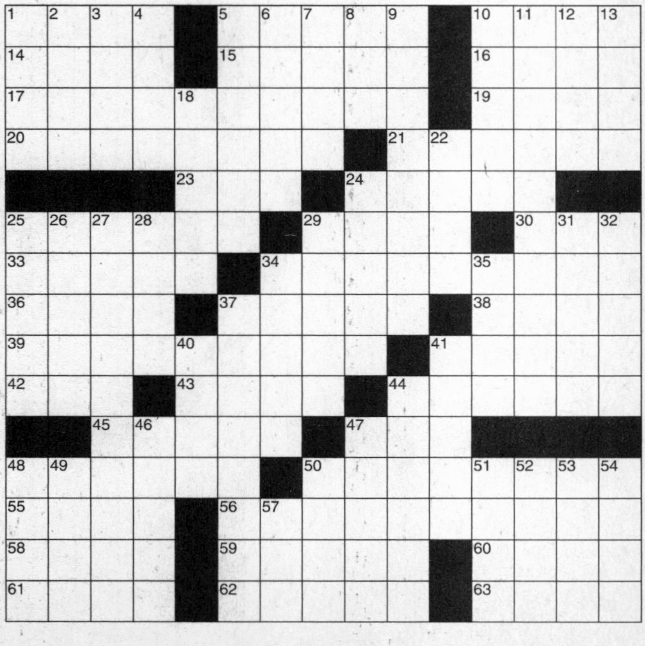

138 BASEBALL FILMS

by Mel Rosen

ACROSS

1 Recedes
5 Room's companion
10 WWII date
14 Actress Russo
15 Bowler's milieu
16 __ Lackawanna Railroad
17 Reverse, e.g.
18 Family member
19 Chance to play
20 '89 Costner film
23 Integers: Abbr.
24 Biol. or astron.
25 '76er or Celtic
28 For each
31 Open up, in a way
35 Computer "reading" method: Abbr.
36 Caught in the act
39 Syllogism word
40 '76 Matthau film
43 Natural eyewash
44 Be a sign of
45 Use the peepers
46 Put __ to (halt)
48 Marino of football
49 Comes in second
51 Humorist Shriner
53 Kind of camera, initially
54 '27 Beery film
61 Biblical stargazers
62 Loverboy
63 Tennessee's state flower
65 Ready for business
66 Having no point
67 Salad base
68 Hazard to navigation
69 Change components
70 All-in-one dish

DOWN

1 Bit of work
2 Complaint
3 __ B'rith
4 Cool and collected
5 Parade participants
6 Mixed bag
7 Hebrew letter
8 Bill-of-lading abbr.
9 Textile workers
10 Hostage, euphemistically
11 Instrument for Ringo
12 Affectations
13 Kyoto cash
21 Doone of fiction
22 Old French coin
25 Terra __
26 Yearns (for)
27 *All Creatures __ and Small*
28 Yearned for
29 Actress Verdugo
30 Took back in battle
32 Heavy metal
33 Reach accord
34 "Everything's Coming up __"
37 Say more
38 April setting: Abbr.
41 Window-shopping
42 Snoopy's sister
47 Slapstick missile
50 Planetary paths
52 Sammy Cahn creation
53 Mules and pumps
54 Batman's accessory
55 Maturing agent
56 First-class
57 Fed. agent
58 Bivouac shelter
59 In __ (stuck)
60 Fork point
61 Unruly bunch
64 Wood processor?

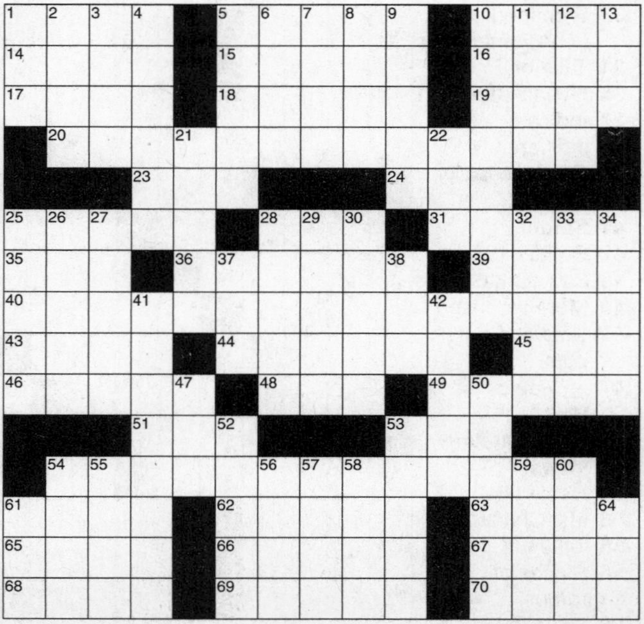

139 NO SOUR NOTES

by Mel Rosen

ACROSS

1 Sore spot
5 Hot tub
8 Boston NBAer
12 Cozy spot
13 Paid out
15 He raised Cain
16 3/4 of a dozen
17 Tall bird
18 Cathedral area
19 Grand __ Opry
20 Sammy Davis, Jr. tune
22 Judaism's Allah
24 Twosome
25 Ornamental flower
27 Turndown
31 Elementary particles
32 Cartoon creature
34 GI's hangout
35 Large amounts
36 __ with faint praise
37 Not "fer"
38 Compass dir.
39 Ports and such
40 Foil, for example
41 Fox's name
43 Not as well-done
44 Directional ending
45 Added attractions
47 Eurythmics tune
51 Former Mideast org.
54 Some shortening
55 Ease
56 Mean monster
57 Similar (to)
58 Early cataloguer
59 Miss the boat
60 Bump into
61 Ga. neighbor
62 Set-to

DOWN

1 __ Domini
2 Wrap around
3 Abba tune
4 Supplement, with "out"
5 Wild escapade
6 Yellowish pink
7 Magnani of film
8 __ *Top This?* (old game show)
9 Wax-coated cheese
10 It's enlarging Hawaii
11 Fed. agents
13 Vowel sound
14 Makes an offer
20 "__ Magic Moment"
21 Actor Howard
23 Charity
25 Library stamp
26 Seeing eye to eye
27 Hose mishaps
28 Archies tune
29 Out of the way
30 Antisocial type
32 True grit?
33 Sra., in France
36 Tyrolean skirts
37 Skin-cream additive
39 Toad feature
40 Factory manager
42 Have no obligation to
43 Some shoes
45 "She loves me" scorekeeper
46 Singer Branigan
47 Bridge coup
48 Greet the day
49 Toledo's lake
50 Sailing hazard
52 Domingo melody
53 Bank (on)
56 Switch position

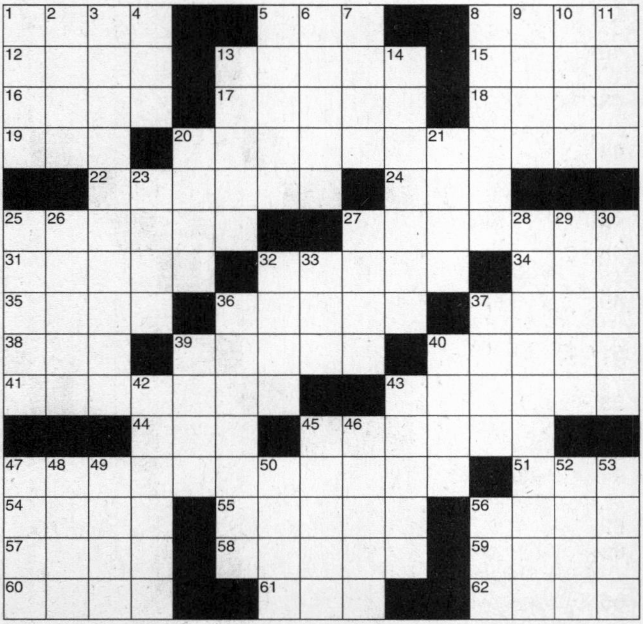

140 ALTERNATE ROUTES

by Eric Albert

ACROSS
1 Itty-bitty branch
5 Say "guilty," say
10 *Green __ and Ham*
14 Whale of a movie
15 Rent
16 Leave flat
17 Ritzy New York store
20 Be a mole
21 Hamelin menaces
22 Pull up stakes
23 Small liqueur glass
24 Guitarist Atkins
25 Utterly hopeless
28 Max of *The Beverly Hillbillies*
29 Book after Esther
32 Haunted-house sound
33 Gymnast Korbut
34 Asian desert
35 '80s police series
38 They're slippery when wet
39 Conform to
40 Rope ring
41 High's partner
42 Cut quickly
43 Lend an ear
44 Comply with
45 Makes a wager
46 Ancient
49 Sweater eater
50 Phi-psi link
53 Centrist
56 Theater award
57 Hawaiian "Hi!"
58 Bewilder with a blow
59 Look to be
60 Not at all tame
61 Lumber choppers

DOWN
1 Sleep unsoundly
2 Stole, for example
3 Revolting
4 Argon or neon
5 Easily bent
6 *Waiting for __*
7 Gulps down
8 Volcano output
9 Racetrack tie
10 Kick out
11 Ms. Lollobrigida
12 Down in the mouth
13 "That's one small __ . . ."
18 Monks' wear
19 Change course
23 Rings out
24 Sly as a fox
25 Felt pity
26 Bramble, e.g.
27 Bread spread
28 Delete an expletive
29 Go lance to lance
30 Overly large
31 American buffalo
33 Go around
34 It'll hold water
36 Poor at crooning
37 Gay and cheerful
42 Bear's advice
43 __ *Weapon* (Gibson film)
44 Computer-telephone device
45 South Africa's former PM
46 Football's __ Alonzo Stagg
47 Taunt
48 Adams or McClurg
49 *Dial __ Murder*
50 Try to influence
51 Visibility problem
52 March 15th, for one
54 ". . . Round the __ Oak Tree"
55 Nutrition stat.

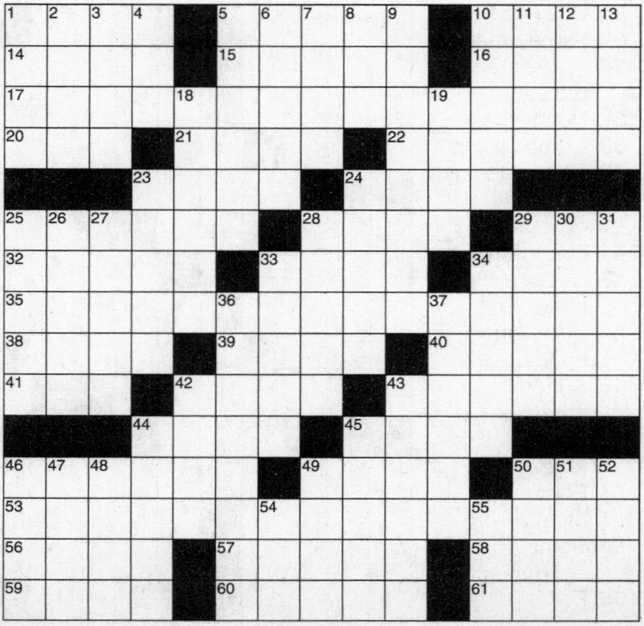

141 GOING PLACES

by Shirley Soloway

ACROSS

1 Sch. at Tempe
4 Dieter of rhyme
9 Ms. Verdon
13 Connery role
15 Author Jong
16 Hard to find
17 Yearbook inscriptions
19 Spanish I verb
20 Tip over
21 Golf gadgets
22 *Moonstruck* Oscar-winner
23 Some makeup
25 Majestic story
27 Lawyers' grp.
28 Eased
31 Church official: Abbr.
34 Repair a tear
37 Mom's brother
38 __ *American Cousin*
39 Dining-room staffers
41 Research room
42 Make a speech
44 Half a Samoan city
45 Flexed
46 Noisy celebration
48 Central mail loc.
50 Nathan Hale's alma mater
51 Office tyros
56 Pats lightly
58 Prefix for dynamics
60 Move laterally
61 Orchestral instrument
62 Geometric intersection
64 Fish-story teller
65 Omit in pronunciation
66 Market rise
67 "Shall we?" answer
68 Boca __, FL
69 Antique car

DOWN

1 Demean
2 Silly Sales
3 Loosen a knot
4 Sun. talk
5 Empty talk
6 More mature
7 Dull pain
8 Mortarboard attachment
9 "Ode on a __ Urn"
10 Launderer's concern
11 Art Deco artist
12 In the neighborhood
14 Canadian cash
18 Smooth-talking
24 Whale of films
26 In addition to
28 Sick as __
29 Lively spirit
30 Obligation
31 Othello was one
32 Free of doubt
33 Dinner-service piece
35 Catch sight of
36 Hoop group: Abbr.
39 Ameche role
40 Meditative discipline
43 Little puzzles
45 __ up on (studying)
47 Cyrus McCormick invention
49 Tower town
51 Characteristic
52 Concerto movement
53 Seer Cayce
54 *Dallas* mama
55 "__ evil . . ."
56 Well-behaved kid
57 Rose's beau
59 Singer Fitzgerald
63 Poetic night

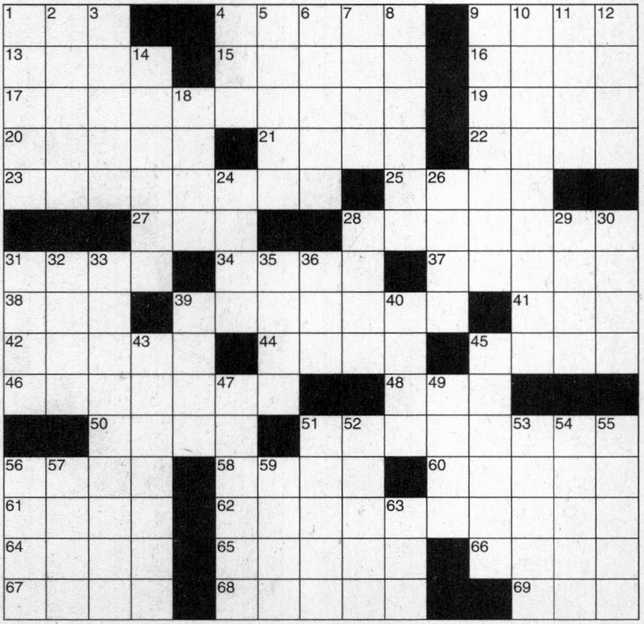

142 ENOUGH!

by Mel Rosen

ACROSS

1 Shopping prop
5 Get off, on the gridiron
11 Banned pesticide
14 Theater award
15 Spice things up
16 Seafood delicacy
17 Put a stop to
19 Pussycat's companion
20 Took the wheel
21 Force forward
23 Jaguar or Cougar
24 Appeals-court rulings
26 Goes bad
29 Knock down
30 Get together
31 Clark's colleague
32 No gentleman
35 Sprightly tune
36 Turn (to)
37 Hailing call
38 Wright wing
39 Quail quantity
40 Norwegian coin
41 Molecular variation
43 Flew like an eagle
44 Afternoon performance
46 Draw on
47 Video-game name
48 Provides comfort
52 Near the center
53 Cease
57 Resembling
58 Heavens-related
59 Nobel Peace Prize city
60 Squalid quarters
61 Prying needs
62 *Pygmalion* playwright

DOWN

1 Friday and Drummond
2 Border upon
3 Get one's goat
4 Put on the air
5 They lead you on
6 Must have
7 Unsubstantial food
8 Catalina, for one: Abbr.
9 Singer Rawls
10 Fire trucks
11 Prepare to rest
12 Wooden rod
13 Spills the beans
18 Hors d'oeuvres holders
22 Actress Farrow
24 __ decimal system
25 Kuwaiti prince
26 Hill's partner
27 Runner Zatopek
28 Close up shop
29 Take a back seat (to)
31 River structure
33 High-grade
34 __-in-the-wool
36 "The Eternal City"
37 Wyoming Indians
39 Funnel-shaped
40 Arboreal Aussie
42 *To __ With Love*
43 Bar seating
44 __ *Family* ('80s sitcom)
45 At an angle
48 Top draw
49 Pocket money
50 Scat queen
51 Pack away
54 Sugary suffix
55 VH-1 rival
56 Sooner than

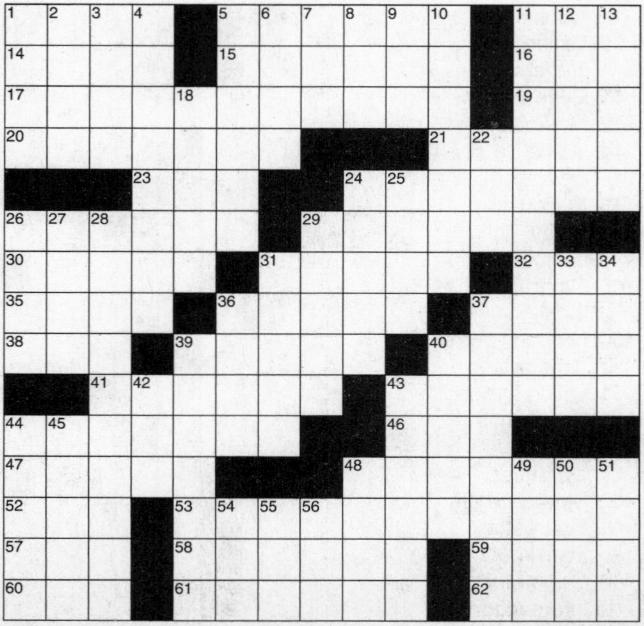

143 SMALL TALK

by Shirley Soloway

ACROSS

1 Real money
5 Become blurry
9 Dirty air
13 Racqueteer Arthur
14 By __ (barely)
16 Point out
17 Of limited duration
19 Poker payment
20 Part of TLC
21 __ Na Na
22 Rivers, to Roberto
23 Derisive look
24 Take away (from)
26 Ready to pick
28 Actress North
31 Chem rooms
34 Lee of cakedom
37 Wipe out
38 Nest-egg letters
39 '60s pop singer
41 An NCO
42 Dietary need
44 Put on the market
45 "The __ the limit!"
46 *Butterfield 8* star
48 __ mater
50 Dresses up
53 Roundish shapes
57 Powder ingredient
59 Memorable time
60 When *Dallas* was on
61 Touch against
62 Clam variety
64 Jury member
65 It divides Paris
66 Happiness
67 Actress Lanchester
68 Ship out
69 Makes a statement

DOWN

1 Throws out a line
2 Pale-colored
3 Was all aglow
4 Sheepdogs, for instance
5 Jamie or Felicia
6 "Eureka!"
7 __ *Macabre*
8 Dinnertime of film
9 Less common
10 Satellite-locating system
11 Director Preminger
12 The Bee __ (rock singers)
15 Brings up
18 Ms. Garr
24 College officials
25 "Excuse me!"
27 Greek letter
29 Catch sight of
30 Long swimmers
31 Pick-me-up
32 Oratorio piece
33 Some eyes, so to speak
35 Deli bread
36 Earth bound?
39 Walked over
40 Under the weather
43 Agamemnon's daughter
45 Nest eggs
47 Country dances
49 Last word of "I Got Rhythm"
51 Shouts out
52 *The Sons of __ Elder* (Wayne film)
54 Writer Rogers St. Johns
55 Cagney's TV partner
56 Actress Brenda
57 Finish-line prop
58 Genesis son
60 Took off
63 Country-music cable sta.

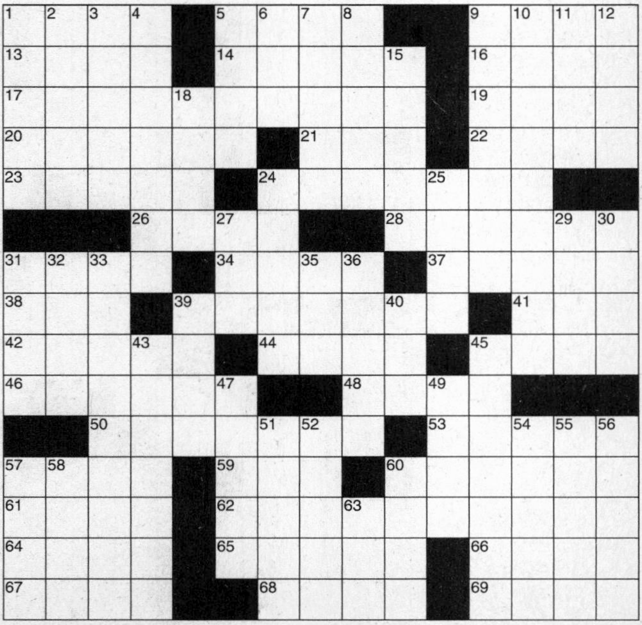

144 BEARDS

by Cynthia Lyon

ACROSS
1 Plumb crazy
5 Stroller, in Sussex
9 S.V. Benét's Farmer Stone
14 The Bard's river
15 Big fuss
16 Unanimously
17 Eatery listing
18 Bearded leader
20 Rural sts.
21 Wasn't colorfast
22 Police-blotter abbr.
23 Citric quencher
24 Cereal grain
25 Darth Vader's side
28 Trees akin to cashews
31 Has the potential to
32 Freud's concern
33 Bearded monarch
36 Up
38 Bearded cartoon character
40 Macho type
43 Bearded sibs
47 Thurman of *Henry & June*
48 Squid squirt
50 *This __ Life*
51 Percussion gourd
53 Mineo of movies
55 High range: Abbr.
56 Zilch
57 Paris hotel
59 Airborne Dracula
60 Bearded gift-bearer
63 "Dueling," to "indulge": Abbr.
65 Mr. T's former group
66 Actress Sedgwick
67 Gross
68 Madison vice president
69 "Wait __!" ("Hold on!")
70 Abound

DOWN
1 Felon's flight
2 Past the deadline
3 Judge unfit
4 Responsibility
5 Harper Valley org.
6 Actor Benson
7 Astaire's sister
8 Double agent
9 Funnyman Murray
10 Songwriters' org.
11 Bet middlers?
12 Blow up
13 Buddhist sect
19 Thought
23 Fire wood?
24 Write that you're coming
26 Yule aromas
27 Zillions of years
29 Instrument for an ángelo
30 Bluish
31 La Bohème
34 "And all __ is a tall ship . . ."
35 Doctrine
37 "One __ land . . ."
39 Electric co., e.g.
40 Render a tune
41 Flow forth
42 American Leaguer
44 Harlequin genre
45 Movie-set blooper
46 Grads.-to-be
49 Anti-drug officer
52 Wedding setting
53 Collar inserts
54 Sky's color
58 Chase of Hollywood
59 Worms, often
60 Lose firmness
61 *Little Women* girl
62 Air Force org.
64 Prom locale

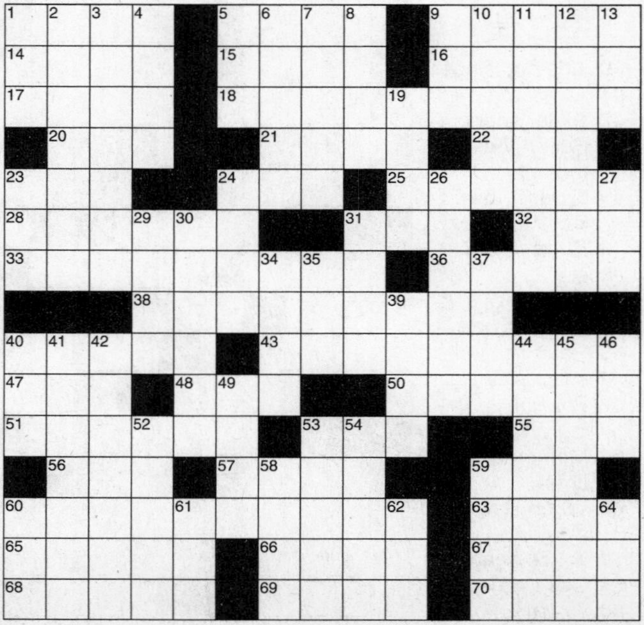

145 ALLITERATION

by Mel Rosen

ACROSS
1 Ump's call
5 Llama land
9 *Misery* star
13 Singer Guthrie
14 Church area
15 Bring to naught
16 Mr. Connery
17 Low-priority place
19 Owns
20 Love-neighbor link
21 London section
22 Some sandwiches
24 Teachers' org.
25 Roof support
27 Pre-meal drink
32 Meadows' hubby
33 *The Plains of Passage* author
34 Milan money
35 As well
36 Summer spell
39 Abolitionist Turner
40 Genesis character
42 Bridal wear
43 Fake jewelry
45 They make conclusions
47 Like baby food, often
48 Neither fish __ fowl
49 Strike a pose
50 Tenderly, in music
54 "Absolutely!"
55 Lacrosse-team complement
58 Small stitch
60 Ace in the __
61 Diner sign
62 Machu Picchu people
63 Night fliers
64 Wild plum
65 Some votes
66 Tiny fly

DOWN
1 Waistband
2 General vicinity
3 Heavy-rain result
4 Very long time
5 Stage shows
6 List-ending abbr.
7 Croupier's gadget
8 In a suave manner
9 Shorten
10 Last Stuart monarch
11 Yemen seaport
12 L'Etoile du __ (Minnesota's motto)
14 Can't stand
18 __-friendly computer
20 The way things are going
23 French season
25 Appraised
26 Without equal
27 German cars
28 Ring out
29 Hollywood's nickname
30 Hopping mad
31 Destined
33 Worry, it's said
37 Tennis effect
38 Commercial canine
41 Crowing time
44 "Chances __" (Mathis tune)
46 Old geezer
47 Yeats and Keats
49 Caged talkers
50 Joe Young's family
51 It may be square
52 Football great Graham
53 Mrs. Chaplin
56 Jazz-singing name
57 Bird house
59 Not at all friendly
60 Monopolize

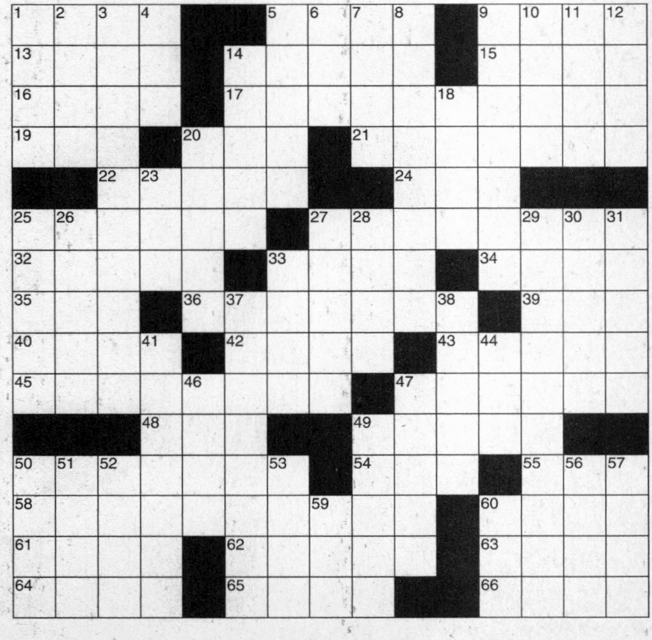

146 INSTRUMENTAL

by Shirley Soloway

ACROSS
1 South __, IN
5 Platter
9 At a distance
13 One more time
15 Roman orator
16 Where the grapes are
17 Interfered with
19 Author Ferber
20 Scenery suffix
21 Went too far
23 Kept up the criticism
26 Bandleader Brown
27 Pregrown grass
30 Reclined
31 Oxen harness
33 Circular dance
35 Absorbed with
37 Roebuck's partner
40 Responsibility
41 Operetta composer
43 Water holder
44 Circus star
46 Fully convinced
47 Breathe heavily
48 *Serpico* author
50 DC 100
52 Roll-call vote
53 Beer kin
55 "Quiet!"
58 Fashion designer
60 *Salvador* star
63 Pour __ (exert oneself)
64 Biology branch
68 Amaze
69 Software buyer
70 Sticky stuff
71 Sound-stage areas
72 Be abundant
73 Stack role

DOWN
1 Ebenezer's outburst
2 Swelled heads
3 Antidrug cop
4 Singing Shore
5 CCC plus CCCI
6 Author Fleming
7 Got to one's feet
8 Escort fleet
9 Declare
10 Waste, as time
11 Musical of "Tomorrow"
12 Hits the books
14 High land
18 Get off the track
22 Slaughter of baseball
24 Some evergreens
25 Show excitement
27 Took a photo of
28 Charlie's wife
29 Dismissed from the service
32 Hold on to
34 En route, in a way
36 Used paddles
38 M. Descartes
39 Sp. miss
42 Fame or acclaim
45 Criticizes
49 Don't participate in
51 Descend rapidly
53 Not quite right
54 Singer Lenya
56 By itself
57 "The Man Without a Country"
59 Traveler's stops
61 Medicine amount
62 Some NCOs
65 Wide-eyed remark
66 Furnish weapons to
67 "__! We Have No Bananas"

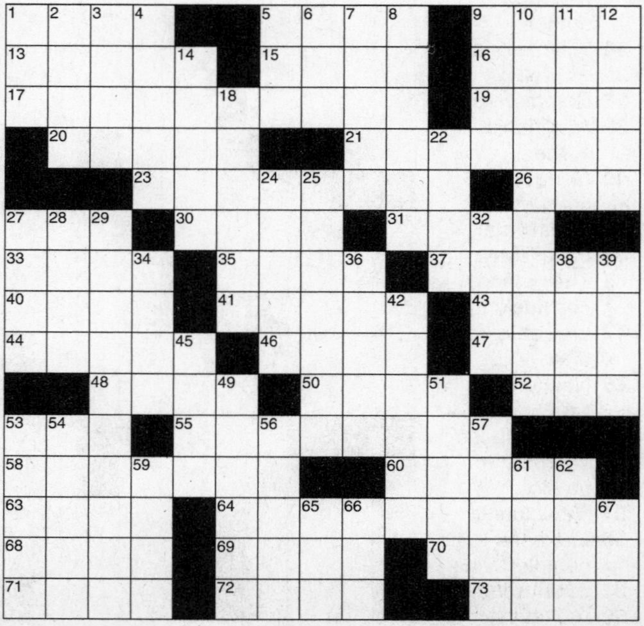

147 BIRTHDAYS THIS WEEK

by Mel Rosen

ACROSS

1 The word, at times
4 Scale a peak
9 Pa Clampett
12 "I beg your pardon!"
14 Traffic-report source
15 Opera star
16 Film critic born June 18th
18 Give off
19 Transparent act
20 Okay as food
22 Cairo waterway
24 Zilch
25 Complain in court
29 Beef cut
31 Detective Archer
34 Truth, old-style
35 Animation frames
36 As __ (therefore)
37 What the suspicious smell
38 Silently understood
39 Cuba, *por ejemplo*
40 Auction word
41 "Do __ others . . ."
42 Taj __
43 Letter carrier: Abbr.
44 Harris' __ Rabbit
45 Mideasterner
46 Mideasterner
48 Sore spot
50 Deer meat
53 Skilled worker
58 Vaccine type
59 Comedian born June 17th
61 Shredded
62 Barkin of *The Big Easy*
63 "What __ is new?"
64 Native Alaskan: Abbr.
65 Claude's cup
66 __ Monte

DOWN

1 Mr. Antony
2 "Oops!"
3 Bytes or bucks lead-in
4 Bank offering
5 Recording company
6 Chemical suffix
7 Swampland
8 Plant pro
9 Actor born June 15th
10 Demonic
11 See socially
13 *Mal de* __
15 Senior member
17 Western spread
21 32,000 ounces
23 Orestes' sister
25 Missouri river
26 Element #5
27 Actress born June 16th
28 Leather ending
30 Mixed bag
32 Showy display
33 Migratory mammal
35 Walking stick
36 Anna's adopted home
38 Airplane engine
42 Bumps into
44 Coll. degrees
45 Holy place
47 Get one's goat
49 Superheroes' wear
50 Have one's say, in a way
51 Greek Cupid
52 Novelty piano piece
54 Rink surface
55 Real-estate sign
56 Cathedral area
57 Coward of the theatre
60 High trains

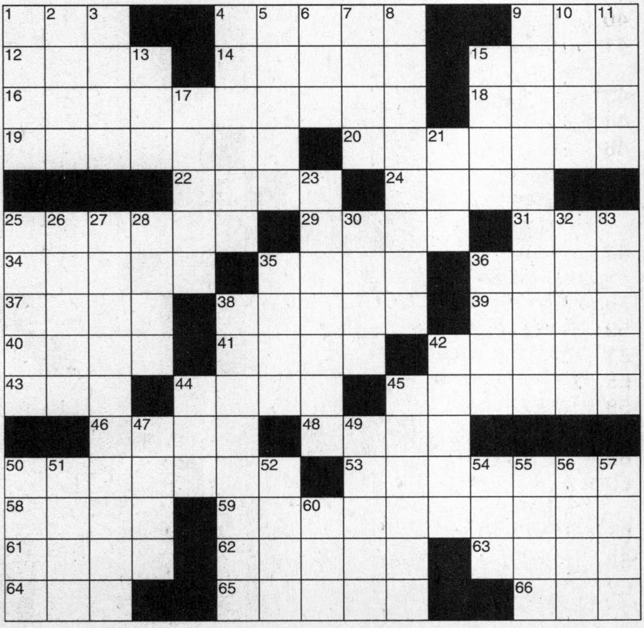

148 *ISLANDERS*

by Randy Sowell

ACROSS

1 Piano practice
6 Army leaders
11 Mature
14 War hero Murphy
15 News summary
16 *Pillow Talk* star
17 Indonesian singer?
19 Pub potable
20 __ Kleine Nachtmusik
21 *For the Boys* actor
22 "A Boy __ Sue"
24 Pooh's pal
25 Rhyme for fizz
26 "You bet!"
27 Mediterranean actor?
33 Prayer beads
36 Cruise in films
37 Feedbag fill
38 Stay clear of
39 Morning moisture
40 Kind of rate or rib
41 Architect Saarinen
42 Coach Parseghian
43 Left port
44 Indonesian crooner?
47 Short sleep
48 Collection agcy.
49 Brobdingnagian
52 Fictional flying monster
55 *Born Free* roarer
57 It often turns
58 Charlottesville sch.
59 Mediterranean actress?
62 __ Aviv
63 Make amends
64 Hole-__
65 Whichever
66 Seasons, maybe
67 Word on a nickel

DOWN

1 *60 Minutes* reporter
2 Unusual art
3 *A Bell for* __
4 Bank sight
5 Comics cry
6 Poultry part
7 Singer McEntire
8 Open up __ of worms
9 Actor Mineo
10 Small piano
11 First-family member
12 High wind
13 Looked at
18 In an unfriendly way
23 Oregon city
25 __ Krishna
26 Sweet tuber
27 Rock megastar
28 Work as __ (collaborate)
29 Cut the lawn
30 Pellets of a sort
31 "Don't look __!"
32 No longer new
33 Coral creation
34 Ham's word
35 FDR's mom
39 Actress Joanne
40 Botches the birdie?
42 Nile reptile
43 Leave the path
45 Dole's home
46 Bridal paths
49 American buffalo
50 "__ Want to Walk Without You"
51 Chromosome parts
52 Actress Lee
53 Hot spot
54 See 57 Down
55 Earth sci.
56 Washer fuzz
57 With 54 Down, *Cagney & Lacey* star
60 Call-day link
61 __ *Tac Dough*

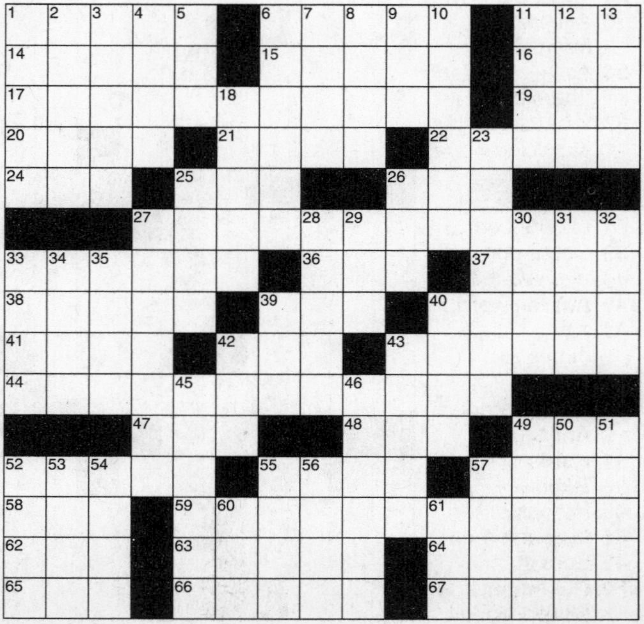

149 KID STUFF

by Trip Payne

ACROSS

1 It's often filed
5 Hold at fault
10 Some
14 Farming word form
15 Company takebacks
16 Sgt. Friday's employer
17 Burn the surface of
18 "This is only __"
19 Greek consonants
20 Kids' activity
23 Weaver sci-fi film
24 Sea shocker
25 Anderson's *High __*
27 Hwys.
28 Dutch cheese
32 G&S title character
34 Lawrence's locale
36 Actor Baldwin
37 Kids' activity
41 Ashbrook of *Twin Peaks*
42 Bulls, at times
43 Come out
46 Droops down
47 Promgoers: Abbr.
50 Outdated discs
51 College major
53 Actor Milo
55 Kids' activity
60 Right-hand person
61 Furnace fodder
62 One chip, often
63 Ship's staff
64 *Fiddler on the Roof* star
65 Hwys.
66 Turner and Danson
67 Huge number
68 Legal wrong

DOWN

1 Auto-racing org.
2 From time immemorial
3 Rafsanjani's followers
4 Greene of *Bonanza*
5 Bric-a-__
6 Riga resident
7 In __ (peeved)
8 General Dayan
9 High regard
10 Kal Kan competitor
11 Con man's specialty
12 Serial parts
13 Dict. entries
21 January, to Juan
22 Flavius' 551
26 Mythical bird
29 __ es Salaam
30 ". . . __ fat hen"
31 Cretan king
33 *Get Smart* baddies
34 Controversial tree spray
35 Taj Mahal city
37 Wiener-roast spot
38 Unbalanced
39 Canine command
40 Mr. Welles
41 Wilm.'s state
44 One-liner
45 Puts up a building
47 Japanese religion
48 Leaseholder
49 Most worldly-wise
52 Scout group
54 Maze word
56 11:00 feature
57 Hemingway's nickname
58 Plenty
59 Capri, for one
60 Make a decision

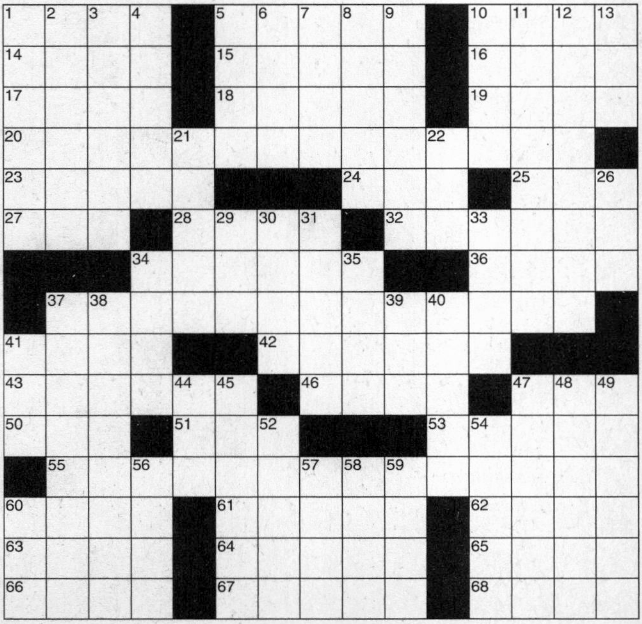

150 CAR-NATION

by Wayne R. Williams

ACROSS

1 Nightwear
8 Left undone
15 Admire a lot
16 Cane cutter
17 Silverdome home
19 *Gorillas in the Mist* director
20 Visitor from space
21 Rating unit
22 Free-for-all
24 Mini-army
28 Self-satisfied
30 Vacation spot
32 __ Baba
35 Rachins of *L.A. Law*
37 Eagle's nest
38 W.J. Bryan's home
42 Furnishings
43 Architect of St. Paul's
44 Slippery catch
45 Common mushroom
47 Like some Fr. nouns
49 Meeting: Abbr.
50 Mad. Ave. guy
53 Virginia dance
57 Moffo and Magnani
59 Desert Storm target
60 Marshal Dillon's home
65 Adds territory
66 Most creepy
67 Not at all polite
68 Power et al.

DOWN

1 __ *Delicate Condition* ('63 film)
2 Take up
3 Ruling group
4 Lets out, maybe
5 __ Marian
6 One-time connection
7 Wine word
8 Funt's request
9 More like a fine fabric
10 Rue one's run
11 Arm of the Pacific
12 Beer barrel
13 Schedule abbr.
14 Retreat
18 __ de mer
22 Comic Martin
23 First governor of Alaska
25 Mythology branch
26 Toddler's transportation
27 Big bargain
29 Native New Zealander
31 Has coming
32 Robert and Alan
33 Hamlet, to Horatio
34 Ancient Peruvians
36 Dir. opp. SSE
39 Formal flowers
40 Columnist Bombeck
41 High-fiber food
46 Stamp a stamp
48 Head-y word form
51 Henry James' __ *Miller*
52 CO clock setting
54 Ruhr Valley city
55 Wipe clean
56 Holds up
58 Waiting-room call
59 Roseanne, originally __
60 Bit of butter
61 Top ranking
62 Genetics letters
63 To date
64 Cipher code

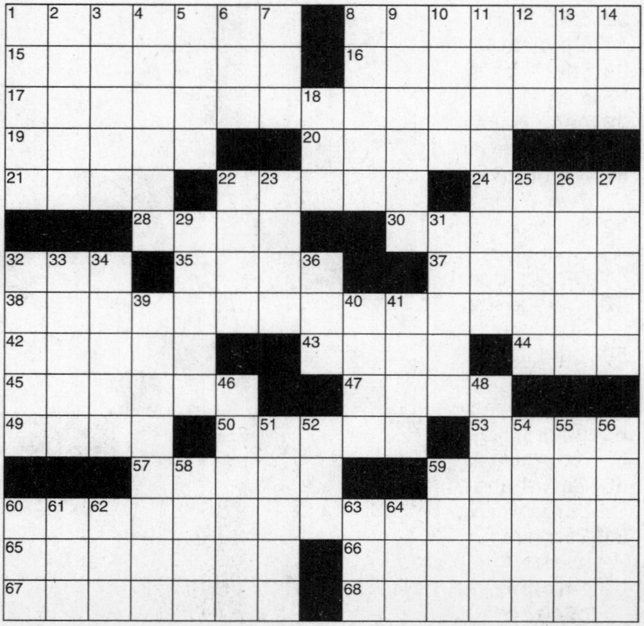

151 FIRST LADIES?

by Mel Rosen

ACROSS

1 VHS alternative
5 Hens or mares
9 Not quite closed
13 Cheer words
14 Packs down
16 Path or phone opener
17 Satan's doings
18 __ asst. (office aide)
19 "You're So __" (Simon song)
20 Comic actress
23 Ping-Pong need
24 Common Mkt. money
25 Big-beaked birds
27 Conducts (oneself)
32 Ski lift
33 Lawyers' org.
34 Reaches quick conclusions
36 __ nous
39 Civil case
41 Hogan rival
43 Revue, e.g.
44 *One Touch of* __
46 Wish granter
48 Put to work
49 Finished a cake
51 States
53 Makes minor adjustments
56 Decimal base
57 "What __ doing?"
58 *Charlie's Angels* actress
64 Skirt length
66 *Glengarry Glen Ross* playwright
67 Soil additive
68 Psyche sections
69 Nimble-legged
70 New Haven students
71 Make a bad impression
72 Building wings
73 Two-year-olds

DOWN

1 *Song of the South* title
2 Chalet overhang
3 Rarefied
4 Out like a light
5 Heights
6 "If I __ Hammer"
7 Small-screen award
8 Like some milk
9 Off-road transport, in short
10 *Shane* star
11 Martian, e.g.
12 Leases out
15 Snobbish type
21 EPA concern
22 Cartoonist Goldberg
26 Preserves, in a way
27 HBO's system
28 Bassoon's relative
29 Audrey Hepburn's singing stand-in
30 Sharp taste
31 Ten-__ bicycle
35 Sensible
37 Mrs. Kennedy
38 Woolly beasts
40 Nip's partner
42 Gives orders
45 Go after
47 TVA product
50 Stage production
52 Bobby-sock relative
53 Brought under control
54 Mental picture
55 Rocket section
59 Actor Jannings
60 Congeal
61 Grain building
62 Skip over
63 Capone's nemesis
65 -arian relative

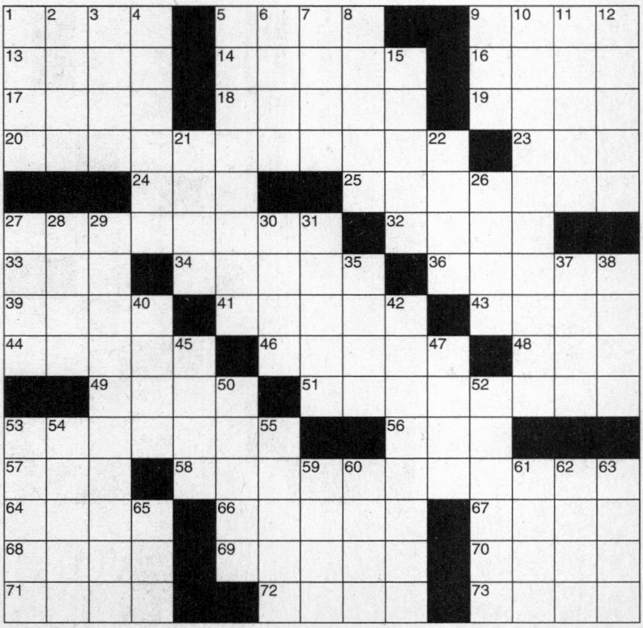

152 AMAZING PHRASING

by Wayne R. Williams

ACROSS
1 Dawber or Shriver
4 *Exodus* author
8 Removed soap
14 Southern st.
15 Window glass
16 Main course
17 Flap one's gums
18 Goodman's nickname
20 Before, poetically
21 *Xanadu* rock group
22 Narrow opening
23 Overact
25 In force
27 Make one
30 Ali technique
32 Altar words
33 Flows out
35 Greek letter
36 Beatle in the background
38 Sheet fabric
40 Soil
42 Earn after taxes
43 Eur. nation
44 Chocolate products
45 Pay stub?
46 Charity race
50 Tongue-clicking sound
51 Classic sagas
52 "I Am Woman" singer
55 Prof.'s rank
56 __ chi (martial art)
58 Anonymous John
59 Meet requirements
63 Quaint hotel
64 Excessively affected
65 Like Nash's lama
66 "Ready or __, here I come!"
67 Lyndon's running mate
68 Important times
69 Important time

DOWN
1 Check name
2 Cause anxiety
3 Be critical
4 Maintenance cost
5 Support bar
6 Do something new
7 Portion: Abbr.
8 Toss another coin
9 Ones in the know
10 Product package info.
11 __ Lanka
12 Poet's dusk
13 BA or MBA
19 Cold capital
24 Puccini opera
26 Nabokov novel
27 Entertain lavishly
28 Bergen or Buchanan
29 Cabinet features
31 Cave-dwelling fish
33 Florida attraction
34 Hour indicators
37 Permeate
39 Cop, at times
40 Giving a leg up to
41 Go wrong
43 Super Bowl team's div.
47 Outcome
48 Marquee word
49 Superfluous items
53 Philanthropist
54 Overinquisitive one
55 Old one: Ger.
57 Nautical direction
59 Six ft., at sea
60 Debt letters
61 Seles shot
62 Long scarf

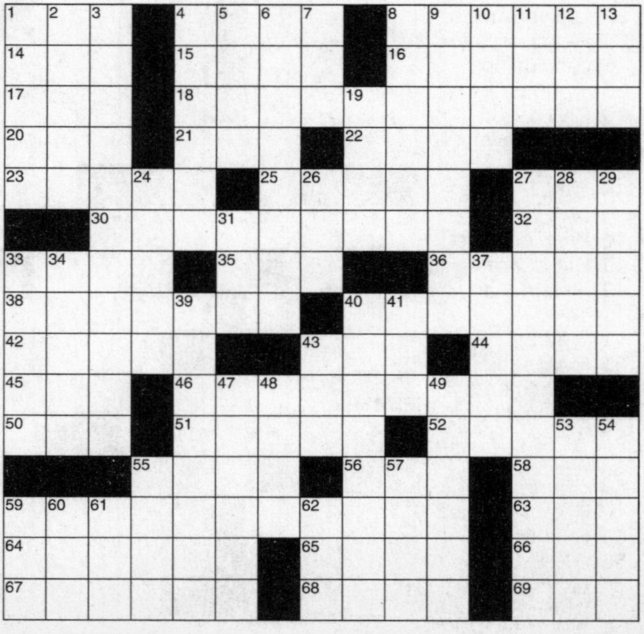

153 *CONTRASTS*

by Shirley Soloway

ACROSS

1 First vice president
6 Use a camcorder
10 *Born Free* roarer
14 Make a new wager
15 Astronaut Shepard
16 Follow behind
17 Quite clearly
20 __ distance (far away)
21 Comedienne Charlotte et al.
22 Where llamas roam
23 Musical breather
24 "__ but known!"
26 Is inconsistent
33 Bring down the house
34 Starchy side dish
35 Sticky stuff
36 Santa __, CA
37 Had hopes
40 Mr. Chaney
41 Headline of '14
42 Caviar versions
43 Laura of *Blue Velvet*
44 Total difference
49 Takes home
50 Oklahoma Indians
51 Reference book
54 Cartoonist Peter
55 *The Golden Girls* name
58 Completely
62 Make angry
63 Screenwriter James
64 Kind of kitchen
65 Milky gemstone
66 Forest growth
67 Room to maneuver

DOWN

1 Diva's solo
2 Fender bender
3 Eban of Israel
4 Blanc or Brooks
5 Takes a long look
6 Learn to like
7 "Too bad!"
8 Review poorly
9 Put a stop to
10 Kind of pride
11 __-back (relaxed)
12 Locale
13 Pub servings
18 Legal tender
19 In a clump
23 "Concord Hymn" monogram
24 Hide's partner
25 Suffix for attend
26 Rowdy to-do
27 Polynesian porch
28 Arkansas range
29 Actress Van Devere
30 Stared rudely
31 "Too-Ra-__-Loo-Ral"
32 Marie Osmond's brother
37 *Gunsmoke* star
38 "And __ goes"
39 Board inserts
43 Shingle letters
45 Nail polish
46 Rich cakes
47 __ time (never)
48 Rope loops
51 Oversized hairdo
52 Game-show prize
53 Entertainer Falana
54 Iowa city
55 Greek letter
56 Author Ambler
57 Diarist Frank
59 Scottish topper
60 Swelled head
61 Beer barrel poker?

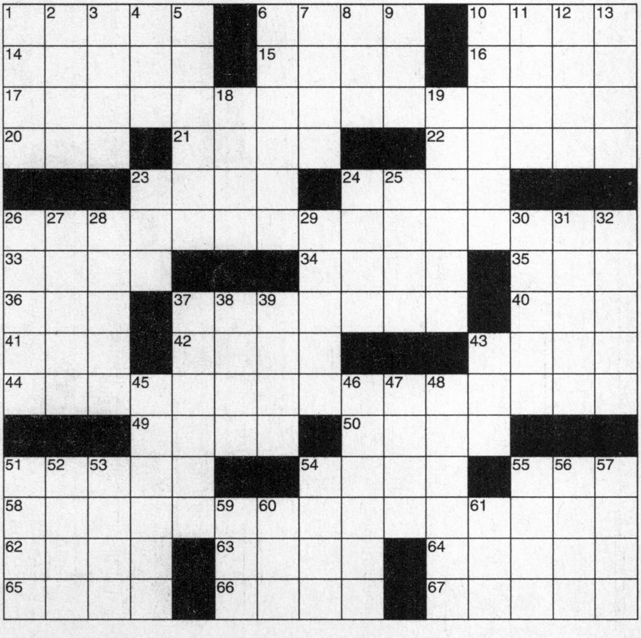

154 *NEW WORDS*

by Mel Rosen

ACROSS
1 Not fully shut
5 Track circuits
9 Evert of tennis
14 Mexican nosh
15 Give off
16 Port-au-Prince's land
17 Musical work
18 Meatless patty
20 Back of the neck
21 USNA grad
22 Put away
23 Infuriated
25 Plaster paintings
29 LAX stats
30 Little bits
31 Away from the office
32 Soda buys
34 Sidekick
35 Colorado Indian
36 Hirt and Pacino
37 Like Cajun food
40 Computer screen: Abbr.
41 Winter bug
42 Big cheeses
43 Barbecue leftovers?
45 Musical discernment
46 Reminiscent of port
47 Get ready, for short
48 The whole shootin' match
50 Signify
53 Business abbr.
54 "My __ Sal"
55 Surmounting
56 Jet-setters
60 Roll on the tarmac
61 Nick of *48 HRS.*
62 "__ a man with seven wives"
63 Ear-related
64 Lost color
65 Cut back
66 Mythical birds

DOWN
1 Make up (for)
2 Honshu's land
3 Massage method
4 Optimistic
5 Protective embankments
6 Make a change to
7 Pen pals?
8 Relig. title
9 Mail channels
10 Rabbit's cousins
11 Predetermine the outcome
12 Mineral suffix
13 Military address
19 Figaro's job
24 Huff and puff
25 Loses color
26 TV addict
27 Bizarre
28 Leaves in the manuscript
30 A little weird
32 Sidewalk eateries
33 God of Islam
34 Impressionist's work
38 Show plainly
39 Tall tale
44 Hill figure
46 On a poster, perhaps
47 Nice to deal with
49 Please, in Potsdam
50 Provide food (to)
51 Poisonous
52 Grand tales
54 Explorer Vasco da __
56 Econ. datum
57 Mauna __
58 Unsatisfactorily
59 Actor Torn

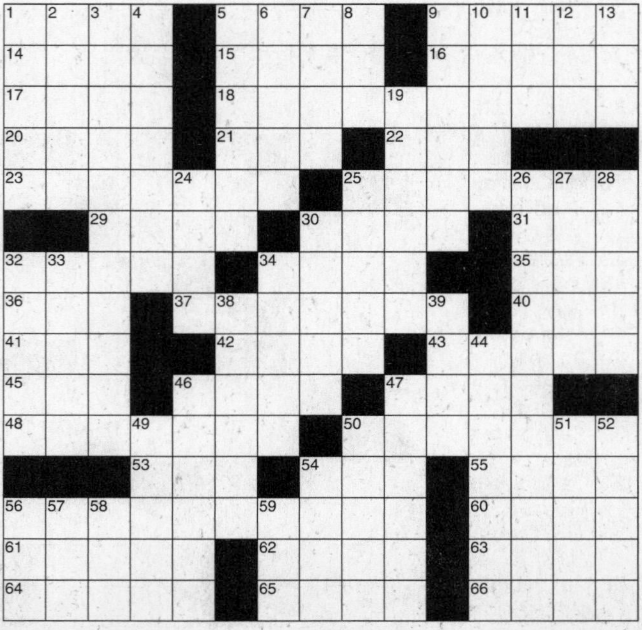

155 MUSIC LESSON

by Mel Rosen

ACROSS
1 Woolly beasts
5 __ Penh, Cambodia
10 Prefix for light
13 Newspaper section, for short
14 Residence
15 Span. ladies
16 Musical embellishments
18 Break the news
19 Kind of kick
20 Worth salvaging
22 Bradley and Sullivan
23 Light into
24 Good relations
27 "His Master's Voice" co.
28 Say "howdy" to
31 Say it isn't so
32 Paper Mate rival
33 Brawn
34 Dict. abbr.
35 Musical conclusion
37 Perjure oneself
38 Whom Simple Simon met
40 Actor Beatty
41 Ponce de __
42 Seer's deck
43 Off-rd. transportation
44 Portsider's nickname
45 Glove leathers
47 Battery size
48 Swizzle stick
50 Eccentric senior
54 Roger Rabbit, for one
55 Ultra-loud, musically
58 Jillian and Sothern
59 Receded
60 Kimono closers
61 Roll-call response
62 Bridle straps
63 After-tax amounts

DOWN
1 Therefore
2 Put on
3 Greek letters
4 It may be high
5 Window glass
6 Cable channel
7 *Wayne's World* catchword
8 Black Sea port
9 Western hills
10 Musical symbol
11 Berlin had one
12 Seagirt land
15 Cellar access
17 Nelson of old films
21 Not specific
23 Musical stresses
24 Keep up with the times
25 __ event (photo op)
26 Chord transpositions
27 Free (of)
29 *Silas Marner* author
30 Smaller than small
32 Throw out
33 1400, in old Rome
35 Supply food for
36 Calif. neighbor
39 Bewails
41 Entices teasingly
43 Kind of bacterium
44 Southeast Asian land
46 Put aside
47 Etching liquids
48 Stand pat
49 Musical sound
51 Taunt
52 Give off
53 "It's My Turn" singer
56 Slugger's stat.
57 Perfect score, often

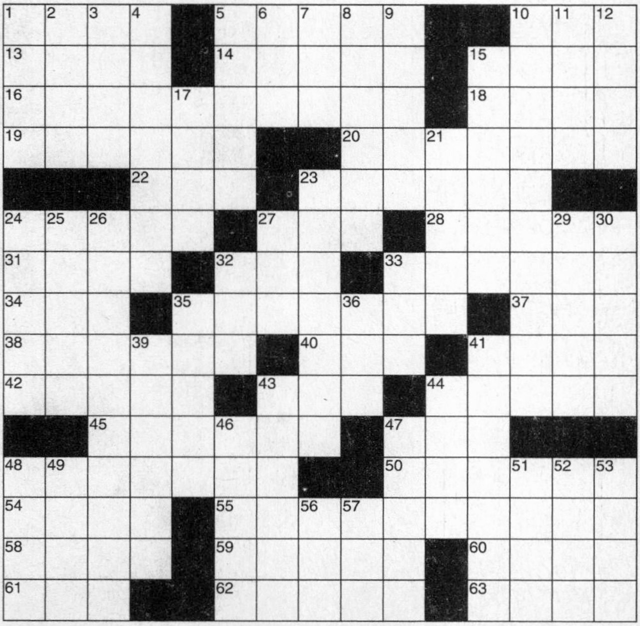

156 *SIMPLE FARE*

by Wayne R. Williams

ACROSS

1 Health haven
4 Barn baby
9 Call up
14 Floral loop
15 String-quartet member
16 Ancient Greek region
17 Simple, foodwise?
19 Put into effect
20 __ Stanley Gardner
21 Asian celebration
22 Movie parts
23 Satisfy
25 To be, in Toulouse
27 Polite word
28 Catcallers' compatriots
33 CIA forerunner
36 Pope's crown
39 Che's colleague
40 With 64 Across, simple, foodwise?
43 Noted violinmaker
44 Mural starter
45 Citrine quaff
46 Stocking style
48 Pedigree org.
50 Small fly
52 Of the nerves
56 *War of the* __
60 Out of the ordinary
62 Singer McEntire
63 Parting word
64 See 40 Across
66 Municipal
67 Hollywood's golden boy?
68 Poor grade
69 Move furtively
70 Good-guy group
71 Isr. neighbor

DOWN

1 Nod off
2 Irritation creation
3 Congregation separation
4 Eggs: Lat.
5 Climbing shrub
6 Easy gait
7 Privileged few
8 Inventor's initials
9 Something simple, foodwise?
10 Sharpen
11 __ even keel
12 Riviera resort
13 Breaks a fast
18 Some votes
22 Sellout sign
24 Something simple, foodwise?
26 Waldheim's predecessor
29 Aunt, in Alicante
30 Novelist Ferber
31 Funny Foxx
32 Roy Rogers' real name
33 Norwegian king
34 __ Valley, CA
35 Jamaican tunes
37 Japanese dog
38 __ Tin Tin
41 Ordinal ending
42 Some doters
47 USN rank
49 Street edge
51 Sort of sculpture
53 Studies
54 Historic Dublin theatre
55 Hen, for one
56 Fem. soldiers
57 Valhalla VIP
58 Bank of France?
59 *Star Wars* princess
61 Medicos
64 Vain man
65 "You __ what you eat"

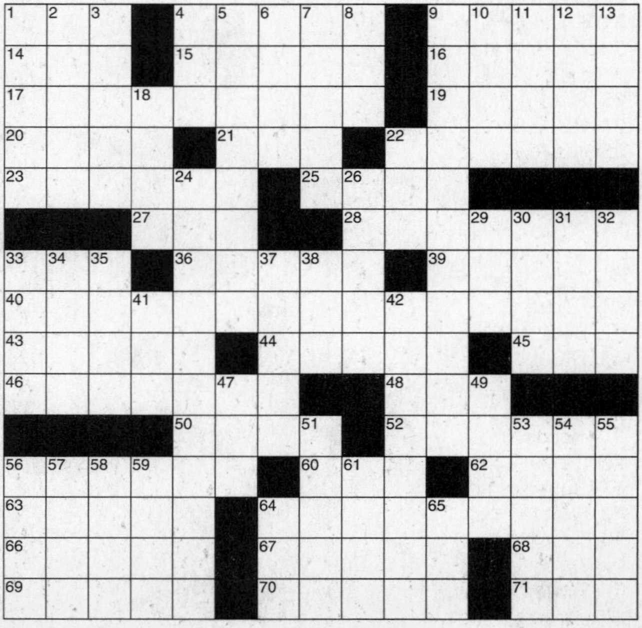

157 POWER PLAY

by Mel Rosen

ACROSS

1 Raced Mark Spitz
5 "__ Ha'i"
9 F-sharp's alias
14 __'-shanter
15 Puts to work
16 Green hue
17 Abbr. in Bartlett's
18 Clock face
19 Judge's prop
20 Powerful, in the weight room
23 Musical transition
24 Comic Philips
25 Work with acid
29 Not for
31 Do cobbling
33 West of *Batman*
36 DeLuise film of '80
39 Underwater shocker
40 Powerful, in business
44 Eur. nation
45 Stratum
46 Aware of
47 Business-page listings
49 Stable baby
52 Twelve Oaks neighbor
53 Get __ for effort
56 Hallow
59 Powerful, in a crisis
63 1492 vessel
66 Cabbagelike plant
67 Jai __
68 Quite mature
69 __ on (goads)
70 Kindergarten breaks
71 Is overfond
72 Vast amounts
73 Three, in Toledo

DOWN

1 RR terminals
2 Wish-list items
3 Love, Italian-style
4 Marital fidelity
5 Spending plan
6 Laos' locale
7 Tenant's pact
8 Mideast belief
9 Full of energy
10 Linen plants
11 Actress Ullmann
12 Rosary prayer
13 __ Aviv
21 Convent dweller
22 Scandinavian
26 Wheel-alignment term
27 Soccer-shoe feature
28 Conversation starter
30 Not certain
32 Very long time
33 Sailor's shout
34 River region
35 __ Day (tree-planting time)
37 Tankard filler
38 Surf partner
41 Sort
42 Nose-related
43 Open-minded
48 Big house
50 Preoccupy
51 Chicken __ king
54 Reeboks' rivals
55 Old truism
57 Kind of power
58 Land or sea ending
60 Bran source
61 Aquatic organism
62 Show of affection
63 Paper tablet
64 Oath words
65 Fanatic follower

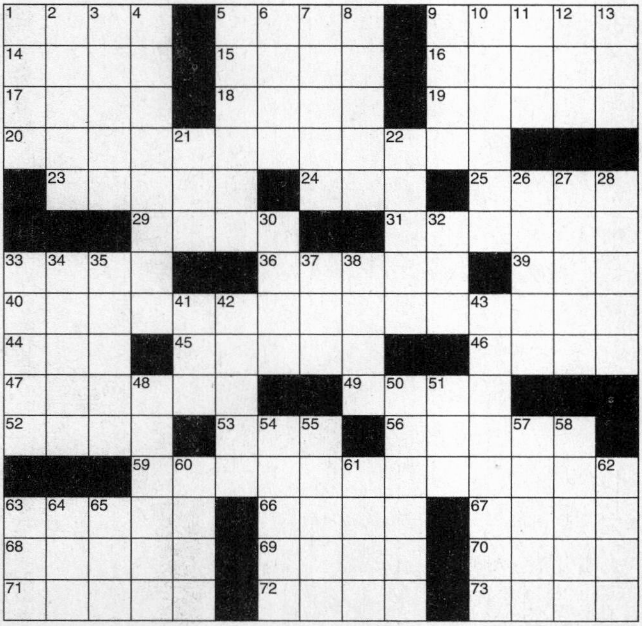

158 STATELY SOLVING

by Trip Payne

ACROSS

1 *Hill Street Blues* actress
6 Health hangout
9 4/1 victims
14 Out of the way
15 Some votes
16 Parks and Bonheur
17 What "they call the wind"
18 Capp and Capone
19 North's nickname
20 Washington's state gem
23 Maryland's state sport
24 Plant part
28 Stay in hiding
32 Cockpit person
33 Started the hand
36 Hardwood tree
37 Abba of Israel
38 Modine movie of '84
39 *To Live and Die* __
40 Free (of)
41 Actor Willie
42 Slow mover
43 Dinkins and Bradley
45 Pom or pug
46 Wisconsin's state domestic animal
50 Alaska's state fossil
55 Two-faced god
56 Tread the boards
57 24-book poem
59 "Not on __!" ("Never!")
60 Highlands refusal
61 Slow tempo
62 High-IQ group
63 Snake's sound
64 Misplaces

DOWN

1 Amateur-radio operator
2 Memo abbr.
3 Swampland
4 Revise copy
5 Corporate plane
6 Messed-up situation
7 Greek city-state
8 Good quality
9 Show disapproval of
10 Bird's-egg study
11 Chilly capital
12 Installed carpeting
13 Vane dir.
21 Charged atom
22 Lalapalooza
24 With 31 Down, Connecticut's state animal
25 Leg bone
26 "Luck Be __"
27 Calendar abbr.
29 Pearl City porch
30 Country singer K.T. __
31 See 24 Down
33 Not well-lit
34 Palindromic preposition
35 Paid notices
38 Pesto ingredient
39 Lodging place
41 Asian inland waterway
42 Lumber center
44 Aromas, in Exeter
45 Part of FCC
47 __ *Hope* (old soap)
48 Workout places
49 Actress Phoebe
50 Step through water
51 __ even keel
52 Muffin spread
53 Some containers
54 Can't stand
55 Freeway snarl
58 __ and don'ts

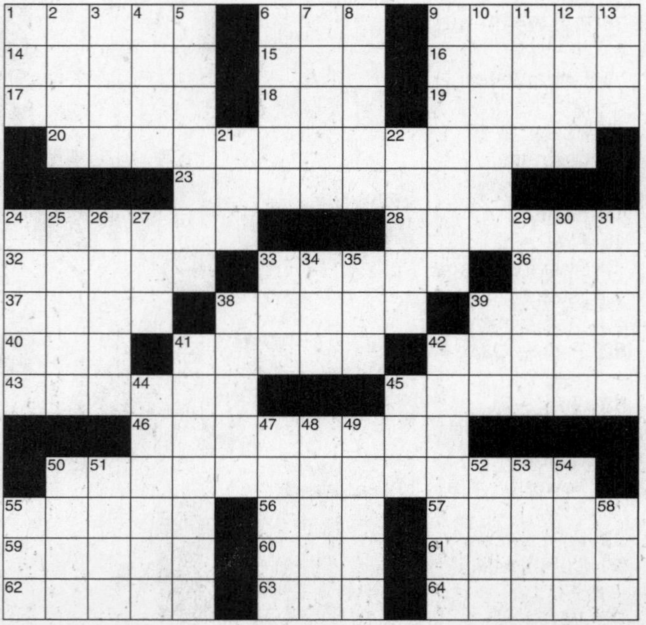

159 CULT CARTOON

by Mel Rosen

ACROSS

1 Fast-food drink
5 Proficient
9 Mr. Kadiddle-hopper
13 Wading bird
14 Grande and Bravo
15 Give up
16 Flying cartoon hero
19 Wide shoe width
20 Something funny
21 React to a pun
22 Place
23 Come up short
24 Destructive one
27 Eat well
28 Undergrad degs.
31 Make a complaint
32 Varieties
33 Bonn exclamation
34 Spy foes of 16 Across
38 Compass pt.
39 Dairy-case buys
40 Tall grass
41 Alert color
42 Feels bad about
43 Adjective for Merman
45 Rifles and revolvers
46 Appear to be
47 Maestro's stick
49 Psychic's sight
50 Work to do
53 Best friend of 16 Across
56 Territories
57 Jazz phrase
58 Castaway's home
59 Circle segments
60 Med-school subj.
61 Author Uris

DOWN

1 Become a father
2 Bassoon's kin
3 Monopoly props
4 Seek knowledge
5 More Bohemian
6 Old theater name
7 At sea
8 Atty.'s title
9 Yuletide music
10 Milan money
11 Equally balanced
12 Singer Tormé
15 Most lean and strong
17 Buffalo's lake
18 Kampala's country
22 Burt Reynolds' ex
23 Helsinki natives
24 Earth tone
25 Rope loop
26 Took a chance
27 Foolish capers
28 Diamond sacks
29 Dull pains
30 Not really legit
32 Pants parts
35 Misfortunes
36 Reunion invitees
37 Composer Khachaturian
43 Deprived (of)
44 Paper measure
45 Man of the world?
46 Bacteria fighter
47 Jefferson's VP
48 Actor Baldwin
49 Related
50 San __, CA
51 European capital
52 "I've __ had!"
53 Cote comment
54 New Deal agcy.
55 Tin Man's need

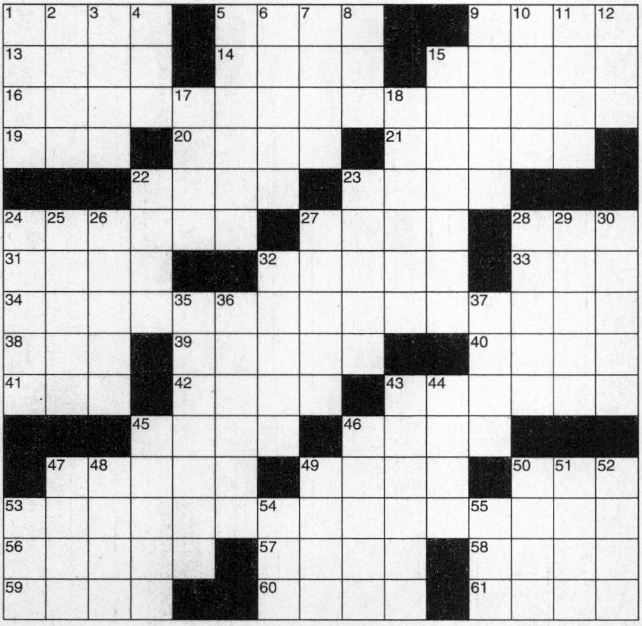

160 FRUCTIFEROUS

by Bob Lubbers

ACROSS

1 Rat-__
5 Break off
9 Uses a VCR
14 Solemn ceremony
15 *La __ aux Folles*
16 Without __ (broke)
17 Kemo __ (Tonto's pal)
18 Waikiki wiggle
19 Rent document
20 Tea variety
23 Tea holder
24 Singer Cole
25 Creeps along
27 Chew the fat
28 The __ the earth (kindly one)
30 Made a stack
33 Mrs. Roy Rogers
34 Big brass
37 Actress Meyers
38 Half a ten-spot
39 Buddhist sect
40 __ Cass Elliot
42 Peggy and Pinky
43 Nodded off
45 Marsh birds
47 Cratchit's kid
48 Heavenly lights
50 D.C. landmark
54 Bordeaux buddy
55 Clam variety
58 __ Carta
60 *Hud* Oscar winner
61 Three of a kind
62 Vermonter Allen
63 "__ each life . . ."
64 British prep school
65 Supple
66 Active one
67 Family rooms

DOWN

1 Fiery ambition?
2 Royal crown
3 Facing the pitcher
4 __ *Mutant Ninja Turtles*
5 Earl of car-painting fame
6 Brown shade
7 Give the eye
8 Highest level
9 Scout's quest
10 Old pro
11 Adolescent's "beard"
12 Come next
13 Flights have them
21 Pleased
22 NFLer or NHLer
26 Army bed
28 Puts away
29 Pub supply
30 Robin's *Mork & Mindy* costar
31 Author Levin
32 Chaplin film of '52
33 Calorie-counter's concern
35 Nectar collector
36 "__ then I wrote . . ."
38 Pink shade
41 Heretofore
43 Sour-cream concoctions
44 Skipped over
46 Repair a chair
47 "You've Got a Friend" singer
48 Veronica of *Hill Street Blues*
49 Fine fiddle
50 Rickety auto
51 Rich cake
52 Burger topping
53 Spinks and Uris
56 Oklahoma city
57 Betting setting
59 Slangy refusal

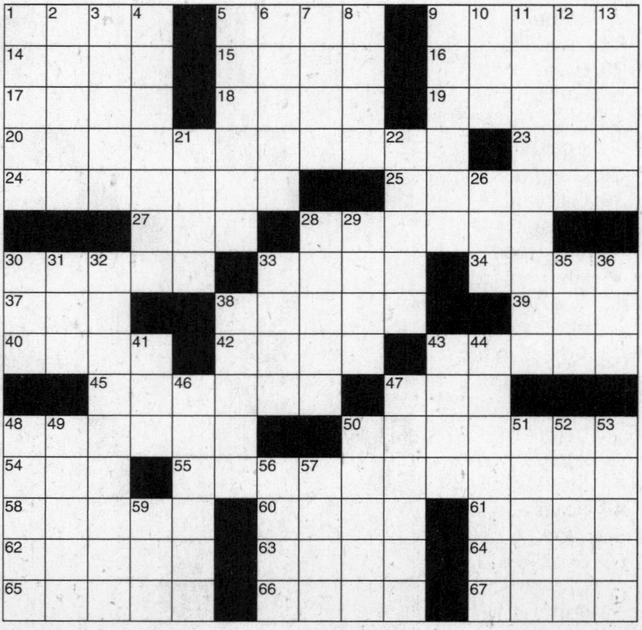

161 PRECISELY!

by Mel Rosen

ACROSS
1 Was an agent
6 Daytime TV fare
11 Three, in Turin
14 Like a washing-machine filter
15 Part of a ream
16 Free (of)
17 Precise, as to facts
19 Half of bi-
20 Day laborer
21 __ in "apple"
22 Most up-to-date
24 "What's __ for me?"
26 Take turns
27 Jazz fan
30 Paid escort
31 Cobbler's tool
32 Rose portion
34 Multi-person race
37 Teachers' grp.
38 Evans and Robertson
40 "__ Got Sixpence"
41 Practice routine
44 Ziti or rigatoni
46 Five-spot
47 __ *Off* (Burnett film)
49 Implants
51 Soda-shop order
52 Johnson of *Laugh-In*
53 Mecca pilgrim
54 Mao __-tung
55 Close loudly
59 Like Methuselah
60 Precise, as to appointments
63 __ glance (quickly)
64 Nintendo forerunner
65 Easy victories
66 Poodle size
67 Madagascar mammal
68 Flooded with water

DOWN
1 Feed the pigs
2 Maine's state tree
3 Enthusiastic about
4 Kind of pride or food
5 Use henna
6 Short and wide
7 Inning's sextet
8 River islet
9 Play intro
10 State representative
11 Precise, in painting
12 Car-wash step
13 Use a blue pencil
18 Set a trap
23 It may be tall
25 Short snooze
26 Gets one's goat
27 Poker holding
28 Vase-shaped pitcher
29 Precise, in speaking
30 Festive events
33 Patched, perhaps
35 Rarin' to go
36 Hankerings
39 Hi-fi system
42 Lounge about
43 Not exaggerated
45 Tsp. or tbsp.
48 Middle Easterner
50 Give a gift
51 Very, in music
52 Up and about
53 Castle adjunct
54 Finished, for short
56 Peru's capital
57 Audio boosters
58 Fit together
61 School of whales
62 Gun org.

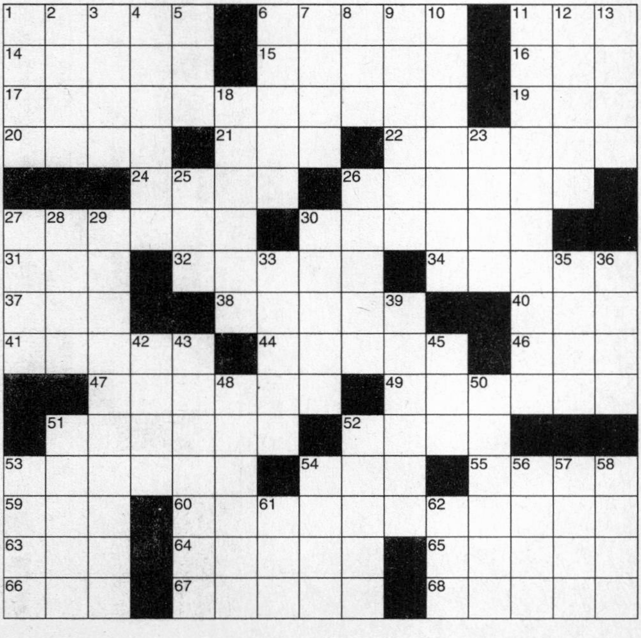

162 OUT OF THIS WORLD

by Trip Payne

ACROSS

1 Fergie's first name
6 Sudden sound
10 Lie in the sun
14 Uneven
15 MP's quest
16 Not fooled by
17 Sprang up
18 Give an assessment
19 Singer Redding
20 Aliens, supposedly
23 Second person
24 Crossed out
25 Grammarian's concern
27 Baggage handlers
30 Play a part
32 Golf prop
33 Hearty brew
34 What some play by
35 Sharp pull
36 Alien vehicles
40 *Get Smart* group
41 Drain, as energy
42 Actress Caldwell
43 Quite cold
44 Author Du Bois
45 Goulash spice
49 Gettysburg general
51 Assistance
52 The bottom line
53 Meeting with an alien
58 Household helper
59 Sharp pull
60 TV exec Arledge
61 Words of approximation
62 Cleveland's lake
63 Loudness units
64 Banned pesticides
65 Husky's burden
66 Concerning

DOWN

1 Paint coat
2 Get in
3 Showed team spirit
4 Helper: Abbr.
5 Ladder base
6 Trash boats
7 Bestow
8 Mini-missive
9 High-spiritedness
10 Ship poles
11 Picnicker's pet?
12 Brandy cocktails
13 Boxing stats
21 Outlay
22 Eccentric type
26 Squealing shout
28 Low islands
29 __ Baba
30 They go tow-to-tow: Abbr.
31 Brazilian money
34 Mentalist's claim
35 Scoff at
36 King, but not prince
37 Spanish Civil War fighter
38 Chatter
39 *Beverly Hills* __
40 Kipling novel
44 Director Craven
45 Settled on
46 Chant
47 Actor __ Ivory Wayans
48 Not moving
50 Extinct birds
51 Potts of *Designing Women*
54 "I Only Have __ for You"
55 Viscount's superior
56 Bear, to astronomers
57 *Darkness at* __
58 Stylish, for short

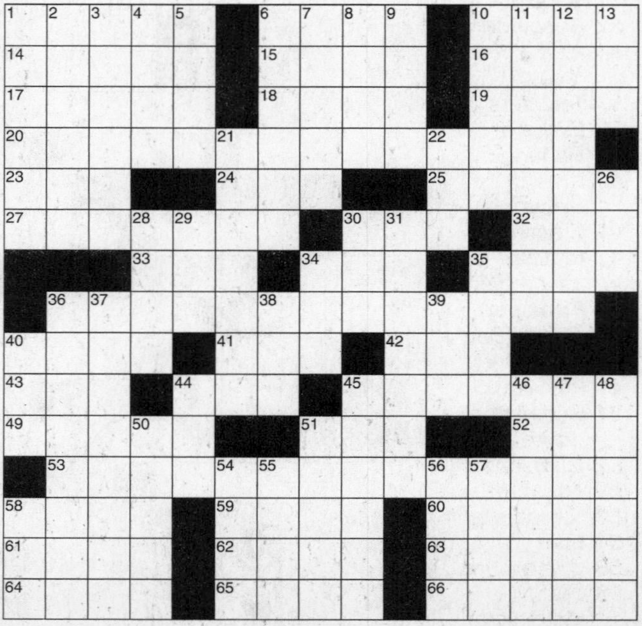

163 AMENDMENTS

by Shirley Soloway

ACROSS

1 Reach across
5 Mardi __
9 Free rides
14 Angel topper
15 Make a scene
16 Soaps actress Slezak
17 Scandinavian city
18 Sicilian spewer
19 Anglo-__
20 Transfer ownership
23 Compass pt.
24 Jay's follower
25 Top pilots
26 Funny Foxx
28 Done with
29 *Raging Bull* star
31 Anti-Dracula weapon
34 Winslow Homer painting
36 Ceramic square
37 Waker-upper
39 From Florence: Abbr.
40 Scared off
42 Bell sound
43 Alludes (to)
44 Sharp pain
46 Make over
47 Fizzy drink
48 Deli meat
51 British brew
53 Lighting accessory
56 Sired, old-style
58 Day's receipts
59 Olympian warmonger
60 __ *Gay* (WWII plane)
61 At any time
62 Nifty
63 Last-place finisher
64 Parcel (out)
65 Jane Austen novel

DOWN

1 Surprise, and then some
2 Turkish title
3 Calm down
4 Lunch time
5 Corfu's country
6 CBS anchorman
7 Christie and Karenina
8 Getz of jazz
9 Abates
10 Author Levin
11 Kind of mortgage
12 Ring decisions
13 Fully competent
21 Made a donation
22 Dorothy's Oz visit, e.g.
27 Processing veggies
28 '40s actor Dennis
29 __ *Rosenkavalier*
30 Whitish gem
31 Part of MST
32 Wedding-cake level
33 Inseparable friends
34 Having the blues
35 Plumber's connection
37 Traffic-sign shape
38 Guitarist Paul
41 Soviet symbol
42 Prefix for sack
44 Shirt feature
45 Stick (to)
47 Barrel part
48 Sultan's pride
49 First-string players
50 *Call Me Madam* inspiration
51 Second son
52 Emcee Jay
54 Gossipy tidbit
55 Country road
57 Chilean cheer

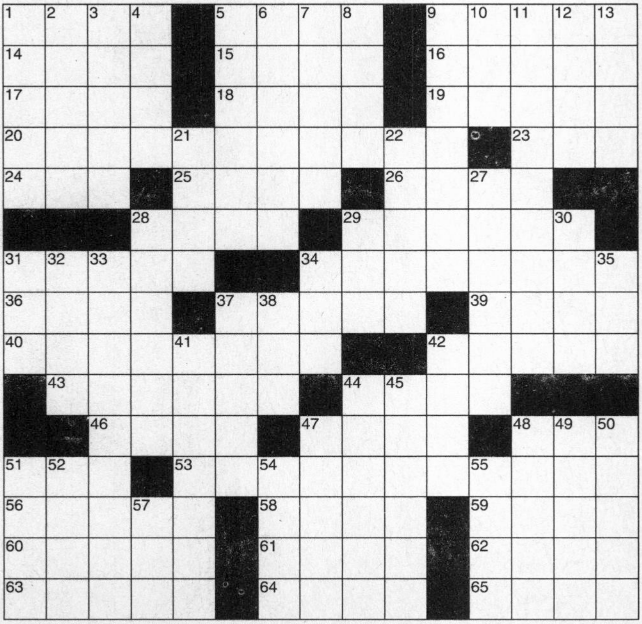

164 DO SOMETHING!

by Trip Payne

ACROSS

1 Blessed events
7 Wax-coated cheese
11 Reb general Stuart
14 Third of an inning
15 Levee kin
16 Bunyan's tool
17 Olmos movie of '87
20 Paris airport
21 True-blue
22 Brewery hot spot
23 May honoree
24 Video room
25 He went east of Eden
27 Least dangerous
29 __ Monica, CA
33 Nepal native
36 Personal quirks
38 Campy exclamation
39 Become brave enough
42 Refrain bit
43 Martin Mull's *Roseanne* role
44 Donkey's comment
45 Work a puzzle
47 Depressed sorts
49 Not on the job
51 Fleur-de-__
52 Actor Kilmer
55 Not to mention
58 Mr. Doubleday
60 Tractor-trailer
61 Take up arms
64 Mamie's man
65 Blackjack cards
66 Eerie get-together
67 Marked out
68 Congressman Gingrich
69 Attacks

DOWN

1 __ buddies (close pals)
2 Preface, for short
3 Kingdom
4 Cereal tiger
5 Paul Newman role
6 Chess result
7 Sea swirl
8 Preachy, as literature
9 Scouting leader
10 Director Brooks
11 Coffee, so to speak
12 Former spouses
13 Ernie's roommate
18 Not a soul
19 New York college
24 Spotted, as a horse
26 Distributors
27 Capote's nickname
28 Person in a pool
30 Biblical sailor
31 Forum wear
32 Several
33 "Master" NCOs
34 Man of the hour
35 Bibliography abbr.
37 Estate sharer
40 Do-it-yourself beer
41 Scale notes
46 Shop clamp
48 First-year cadet
50 Joust weapon
52 Leaf channels
53 Chevron rival
54 Irish export
55 Grand __ racing
56 Delight in
57 Pre-owned
59 Hummingbird's home
60 Chair part
62 Ziering of *Beverly Hills 90210*
63 Golfer Trevino

165 GETTING PHYSICAL

by Mel Rosen

ACROSS

1 One or the __
6 Historical period
9 Auction actions
13 Panda land
14 Wernher __ Braun
15 TV and radio
16 Carryalls
17 Catchall abbr.
18 Salad veggie
19 On the town
20 Start work, perhaps
23 Split __ (be too fussy)
25 Orchestra member
26 Onetime deliverers
28 Hee-haw
29 Airline to Tokyo
32 Bill on a cap
33 Venetian-blind part
34 Author Victor
35 Norwegian king
36 Brown shade
37 Parisian pals
38 Pasta alternative
39 Church area
40 Twofold
41 Asian ox
42 Picnic pests
43 Landlord's client
44 In the old days
45 20 percent
46 Child's song
50 Lodge member
53 Sandy's owner
54 Shout disapproval
55 Cosmic Carl
57 Adjust a lens
58 Easily deflated item
59 Piano piece
60 Student's hurdle
61 Free (of)
62 Closely packed

DOWN

1 Prefix meaning "eight"
2 Holier-than-__
3 Go to bed
4 Helmsman's dir.
5 More throaty
6 Makes level
7 Coll. army program
8 Alaska city
9 Uncle Miltie
10 Word form for "thought"
11 Platter
12 Can. province
15 Hatfield foe
21 Coffee maker
22 Ease up
24 Get __ on (rush)
26 Scrimshaw stuff
27 Eyelashes
28 Elated state
29 Make a false start
30 Quick on one's feet
31 Also-ran
33 Start to fall?
34 Visit often
36 Baccarat announcement
40 Did a bomb-squad job
42 Chips in
43 Carioca's home
44 Religion, to Karl Marx
45 Inundate
46 Sound's partner
47 Fort __, KY
48 Ancient Peruvian
49 Guru's title
51 Small boys
52 Patella's site
56 Had a bite

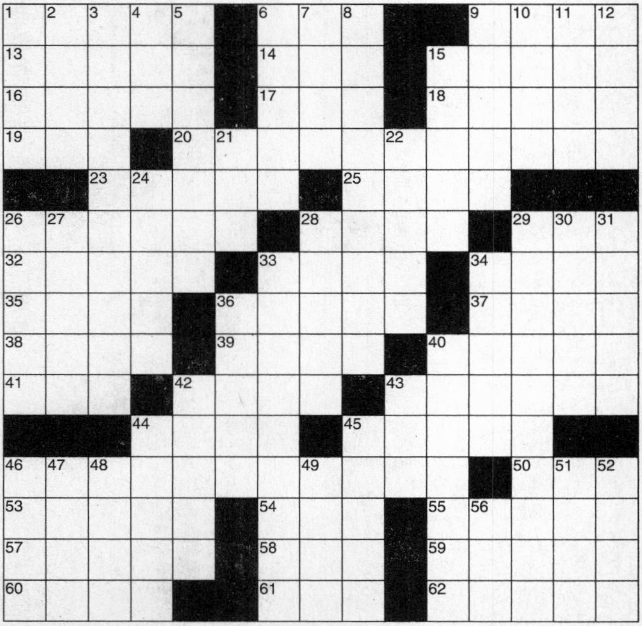

166 COUNTRY FOLKS

by Alex Vaughn

ACROSS
1 Finance degs.
5 Texas A&M rival
8 Leaves out
13 Utah resort
14 The census, e.g.
15 __ noir (red wine)
16 Betray boredom
17 Part of BTU
18 Lauder of lipsticks
19 Literature Nobelist in '21
22 Gets lost
23 FDR's dog
24 Vitamin quota: Abbr.
27 Old horse
29 Toddler swaddler
31 Witch
34 Boxer in the news
37 Plains natives
39 Easiness epitomized
40 Irene of *Fame*
41 *Life Wish* author
46 Ginza gelt
47 Seasoned veteran
48 Ms. Farrow
49 Aves. cross them
50 To be: Lat.
53 N.L. team
58 Basketball star
61 Miss something?
63 Insanity, at times
64 Painter Joan
65 Rocket brake
66 Cribbage need
67 Latch __ (get)
68 Quite pale
69 Mos. and mos.
70 Yawl pole

DOWN
1 Early Americans
2 He spoke for Daffy
3 Doing battle
4 December flier
5 Actor Franchot
6 *Cheers* character
7 Extremist
8 Out-of-doors
9 File category: Abbr.
10 Give-and-take
11 Sock part
12 Sault __ Marie, MI
14 Celestial object
20 Atlanta arena
21 *M*A*S*H* star
25 Plowman John
26 Indo-European
28 Stare open-mouthed
30 Pedigree org.
31 Orange-roof eatery, familiarly
32 Like Pisa's tower
33 Locket artisan
35 Zilch
36 Smile radiantly
38 VCR speed setting
42 Countrified affirmative
43 __ Hashanah
44 Kiddie turtle tetrad
45 Belafonte's holler
51 Over-sentimental
52 Fishing specialist
54 Keaton/Garr film of '83
55 Minneapolis suburb
56 Knave's booty
57 Stuck-up one
59 Legalese phrase
60 Chippendale quartet
61 Swimsuit part
62 Congressman Aspin

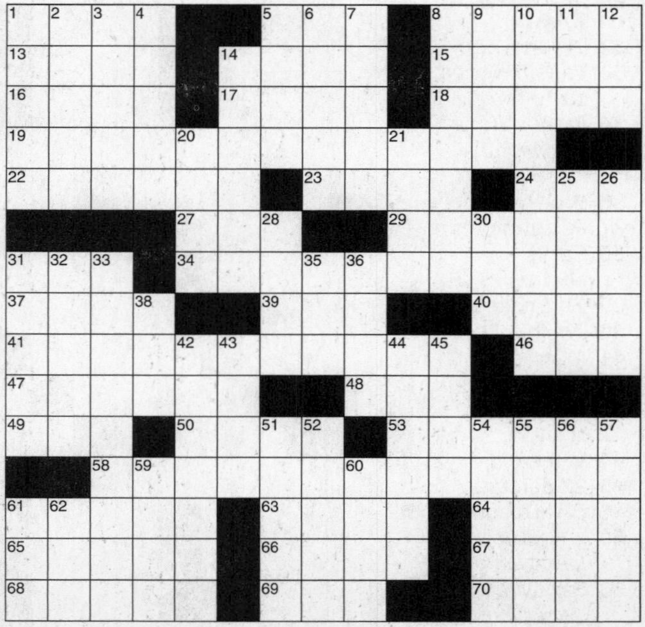

167 S-CAPADE

by Fred Piscop

ACROSS

1 Quasimodo creator
5 Pipemaker's material
8 Hiccup, e.g.
13 Right away: Abbr.
14 Raw metal
15 __ *of the Jackal*
16 THE STAR
18 Expose to the atmosphere
19 Commandment
20 Sitting room
21 Neighbor of Isr.
22 "We aim to __"
25 Cravings
26 __ Blow (average guy)
27 Hat material
29 __ spumante
32 Glum drop
34 Cronies
38 Cell, so to speak
40 Skilled worker
42 Hindu's destiny
43 __-de-camp
45 Tijuana nosh
46 Baker's need
48 "C'est la __!"
50 Prefix for space
53 Bird, often
55 Trophy shape
58 __ *17* ('53 film)
60 Alphabet inventor
62 "Could __ Magic" ('57 tune)
63 STAR'S LADY FRIEND
64 Close again
65 Tavern
66 Tehran's land
67 Charlie Chan portrayer
68 Wooden pin
69 __ out (supplements)

DOWN

1 Some fasteners
2 Loan-sharking
3 Sort of starer
4 Oil cartel
5 All-in-one
6 Speak on a soapbox
7 Mr. Jonson
8 Mets' stadium
9 STAR'S BOSS, AT TIMES
10 Allan-__
11 Squashed, maybe
12 Bristol's partner
15 Come to a point
17 Take-back, for short
23 Simile center
24 Valuable violin
26 STAR'S MALE FRIEND
28 Give a show
29 Pop a question
30 Hearst's kidnappers: Abbr.
31 Pavement material
33 Wipe out
35 UN member
36 Bub
37 __-cone (cool treat)
39 Ginnie __
41 Respecting deeply
44 "For what __ worth . . ."
47 Play backer
49 Some nest eggs: Abbr.
50 National Leaguer
51 Mrs. Mertz
52 Mrs. Gorbachev
54 Steak order
55 Lewis' partner
56 Forearm bones
57 Hammer parts
59 "I'm __ boy!" (Costello)
61 Nastase of tennis
63 Back talk

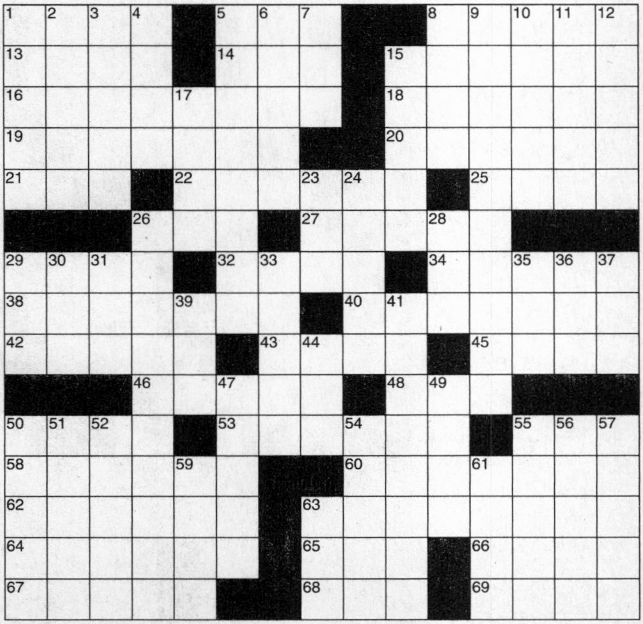

168 SPORTSMANSHIP

by Shirley Soloway

ACROSS

1 Cotton fabric
5 Yard tool
9 "So be it!"
13 Gusto
14 Preceding nights
15 St. Kitts-__ (Caribbean nation)
17 Takes chances on the rink?
20 Beret relative
21 Bordeaux et Champagne
22 Lucky charm
23 Drapery support
24 Singing sound
25 Start a swan dive?
32 Cool spot
34 Day saver
35 Piano piece
36 Helen's abductor
37 Prior to, in poetry
38 Furry fish-eater
39 Cupid's equivalent
40 Inflated psyches
41 Loud shouts
42 About to score on serve?
45 Pigpen
46 Days of yore
47 Mortar mate
51 __ cost (free)
53 Copacabana city
56 Getting close, in a race?
59 Vacancy sign
60 Beloved
61 Prince of opera
62 __ *and Lovers*
63 "__ forgive those . . ."
64 Actress Rowlands

DOWN

1 Pain in the neck
2 Chase of films
3 Polite address
4 Aardvark tidbit
5 Call home
6 Stratford's river
7 Teen dolls
8 Cleve.'s zone
9 Barbarian
10 Bistro list
11 Morally wrong
12 Riviera resort
16 Stuck in place
18 Calls forth
19 Silent screen star?
23 Salad veggie
24 Singer Brewer
25 Clairvoyant's card
26 *Zorro, __ Blade*
27 Crane's cousin
28 Never walked on
29 "__ I can help it!"
30 Cheerfulness
31 What walls may have
32 Shoot forth
33 Mata __
38 It's spotted in the zoo
40 Make an appearance
43 Cartographer's dots
44 London hub?
47 Dutch oven, e.g.
48 Genesis man
49 Normandy town
50 Afterwards
51 A long time
52 Spring event
53 Intense anger
54 Sect's symbol
55 Gumbo ingredient
57 Wyo. neighbor
58 Nautical gear

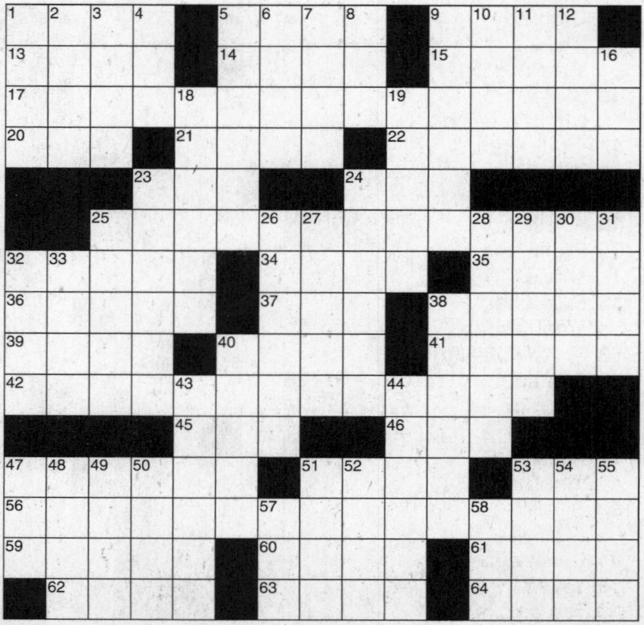

169 FRUIT SALAD

by Mel Rosen

ACROSS

1 Iceberg part
4 "Sink" or "swim"
8 Ranks high
13 Pisa dough
14 Roundish
15 Wear away
16 "What's the big __?"
17 *Doctor Zhivago* heroine
18 Mongol invader
19 Not fem.
20 Loud firecracker
22 Gibson of tennis
24 Gather in
25 Big jerk
27 Masters, for one
32 Office areas
37 Sketched out
38 Skin-cream additive
39 Sprinter's must
41 Made an unreturned serve
42 Sweeps upward
44 Harvesting machines
46 Complained
48 Fairway warning
49 Camp beds
52 Behind-the-scenes
56 "Nonsense!"
61 "Would __ to you?"
62 Told the world
63 Present time?
64 Church area
65 Crème de la crème
66 Treat meat
67 Greek letters
68 Houston's home
69 Makes a choice
70 Choose: Abbr.

DOWN

1 Kind of wave
2 "__ my case"
3 "Dandy!"
4 Pinatubo and Krakatoa
5 "Well, Did You __!" (Porter tune)
6 Less common
7 Loud sound
8 Did a letter over
9 Bedouin
10 Oz visitor
11 Dutch cheese
12 Belgrade native
13 Succotash bean
21 Teen's exclamation
23 Dumbo's wing
26 Keystone __
28 Info sources
29 Dash or relay
30 Water pitcher
31 Some footballers
32 On the toasty side
33 Mixed bag
34 Sub __ (secretly)
35 Came upon
36 Feudal worker
40 Bishops' districts
43 Withdraws (from)
45 Big leaguer
47 Big parties
50 Mexican resort
51 Provide a recap
53 Tickle pink
54 Be a match for
55 Some shirts
56 Aid in crime
57 Lose color
58 __-fixe menu
59 "__ smile be your umbrella . . ."
60 Tea table

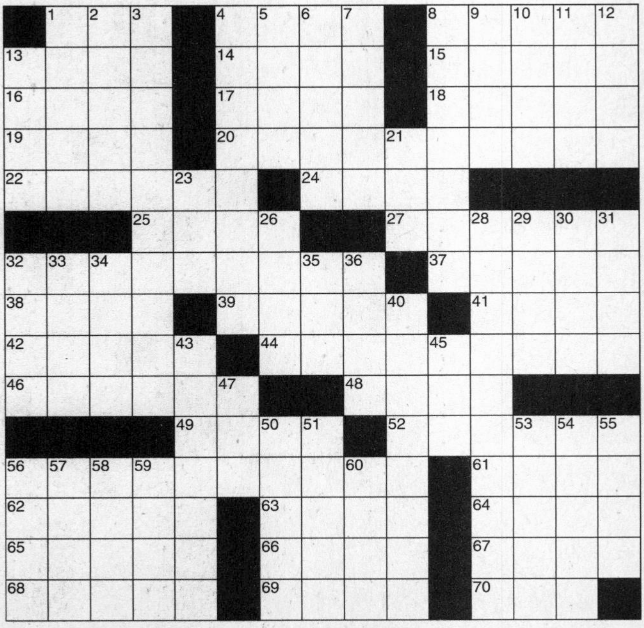

170 CHILD'S PLAY

by Eric Albert

ACROSS

1 Mensa qualifier
7 Boy Scout's reference
15 Swain
16 Open to discussion
17 Western hero
19 "__ Smile Be Your Umbrella"
20 Boffo show
21 "No __, ands, or buts!"
24 Brit's greeting
26 Lose brightness
30 Dust-jacket text
33 Frolicsome
34 Grandchild of Adam
35 Governmental system
37 Gizmo
39 Square-dance song
41 Sort of sword
43 Turn into steam
46 "Famous" cookiemaker
47 Actor Cariou
48 Artist's A-frame
49 Ancient story
50 Andrea __
52 Clothes line
53 Cranberries' place
54 PDQ relative
57 Whoopi Goldberg film of '86
65 Silk headgear
66 Wears away
67 Wearying
68 Squirrel, for one

DOWN

1 Mr. Kabibble
2 Status __
3 Inside info
4 List-ending abbr.
5 Where the rubber meets the road
6 Faithfulness
7 Old witch
8 In a mischievous manner
9 Mystery writer Marsh
10 Wipe the woodwork
11 __-relief
12 Japanese sash
13 Of long standing
14 Important
18 Nothing at all
21 Apple rival
22 Andy Capp's wife
23 Astronomer's sighting
25 Pilot's break
26 It's often felt
27 Great suffering
28 Deer's daughter
29 Superlative suffix
31 Debonair
32 French cheese
36 EMT specialty
37 Rip off
38 Spiny succulent
40 Zealous sort
41 Wool source
42 A Little Woman
44 Last letter
45 Shade source
47 Big blockage
50 "Tiny Bubbles" singer
51 One with a query
53 Slant
55 Oversized hairdo
56 Walk wearily
57 Make a note
58 Wire-service abbr.
59 Mal de __
60 Prefix for fix
61 Corroded
62 Citrus drink
63 State rep.
64 FDR's successor

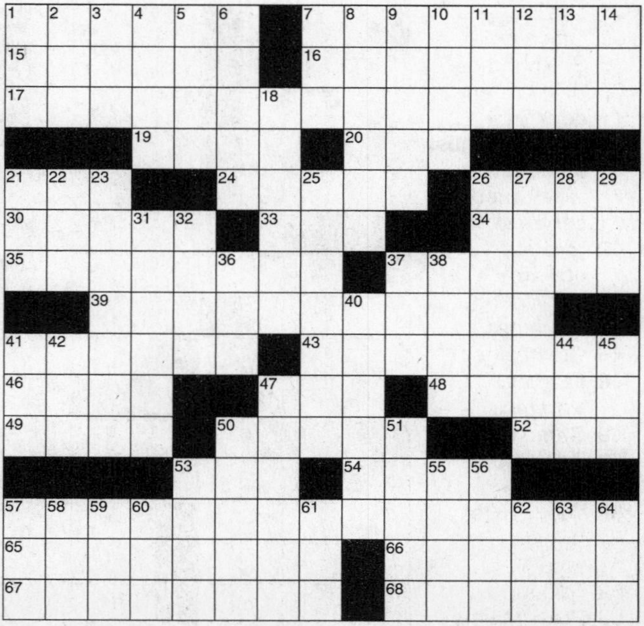

171 COMPARISONS

by Mel Rosen

ACROSS

1 Practice boxing
5 Break up
9 Work out on ice
14 Wash up
15 Bassoon relative
16 Heaps up
17 Voice of America org.
18 Wildcat
19 Showy display
20 Quick-witted
23 Plane holders
24 Datsun, nowadays
28 AP rival
29 New York stadium
31 Cable choice
32 Sagacious
36 Sounds of delight
37 Oath words
38 Sun. speech
39 Seafood delicacy
40 Bro or sis
41 Unfettered
46 "Annabel Lee" author
47 Hitchcock's __ *Window*
48 Cutesy suffix
49 Wimpole or Wall
51 Sponsors of a sort
55 Really irate
58 Have a nosh
61 Solitary
62 Tibetan monk
63 Blender setting
64 Rom. Cath. official
65 Estrada of *CHiPs*
66 Fed the kitty
67 Bean plants
68 Be worthy of

DOWN

1 Semi-melted snow
2 Turkish title
3 Bird-related
4 Debate again
5 The North Star
6 Chasm
7 Writer Jaffe
8 Schoolbook
9 Short-term sale
10 Soccer shots
11 The whole nine yards
12 1773 jetsam
13 Part of i.e.
21 "__ Doc" Duvalier
22 Over again
25 Puppeteer Lewis
26 Dislike a lot
27 __ around (snooped)
29 Scornful look
30 Israeli dance
32 Filmy strands
33 Dostoyevsky's *The __*
34 Levelheaded
35 On a cruise
41 __ out (went berserk)
42 On a pension: Abbr.
43 Volcanoes, e.g.
44 Top-notch
45 Soda maker
50 Variety-show host
51 Mean and low
52 Tara family name
53 Send money
54 Idaho river
56 Charity
57 Just fair
58 Hot tub
59 Convent resident
60 Mr. Buchwald

172 NAME-ING NAMES

by Eric Albert

ACROSS
1 Quite stylish
5 Wood-trimming tool
9 Monastery head
14 Late-night TV name
15 Make money
16 Zero people
17 Harsh, as weather
19 These times
20 BING
22 Choir offerings
23 Jimmy Carter's daughter
24 Sample soda
27 The night before
28 On edge
31 Jupiter's wife
32 Bring together
34 Civil-suit subjects
35 MING
40 Flatten
41 Up, on a map
42 State with confidence
43 Sir Newton
45 Shoot the breeze
48 Basinger of *Batman*
49 African snake
50 Delicate purple
52 RING
57 Man with a horn
59 Tropical fish
60 Basic belief
61 Stare stupidly
62 Dennis, to Mr. Wilson
63 Has in mind
64 *Born Free* character
65 Genealogy diagram

DOWN
1 Overused phrase
2 Shakespearean subject
3 What you earn
4 List-introducing punctuation
5 Peak
6 Person of action
7 Galvanization need
8 Catch, in a way
9 Champing at the bit
10 Hapless one
11 Ride the waves
12 "__ Clear Day"
13 Mystery writer Josephine
18 USN rank
21 "Peg __ Heart"
25 Excited by
26 Sit for shots
28 Lively dance
29 E.T. vehicle
30 Leading lady Loy
31 Kid around
32 Software runner
33 Gretzky's org.
34 Explosive initials
35 Hostile reaction
36 Jeans name
37 Common prayer
38 Film-noir classic
39 Mythical beast
43 Funnyman Kabibble
44 Sea creature
45 Author Grass
46 Not willing
47 Scold severely
49 Building blocks of matter
50 Gold-chained actor
51 Highly skilled
53 Familiar with
54 Honest-to-goodness
55 Nadirs
56 "My Way" singer
57 Rye partner
58 What a feller needs?

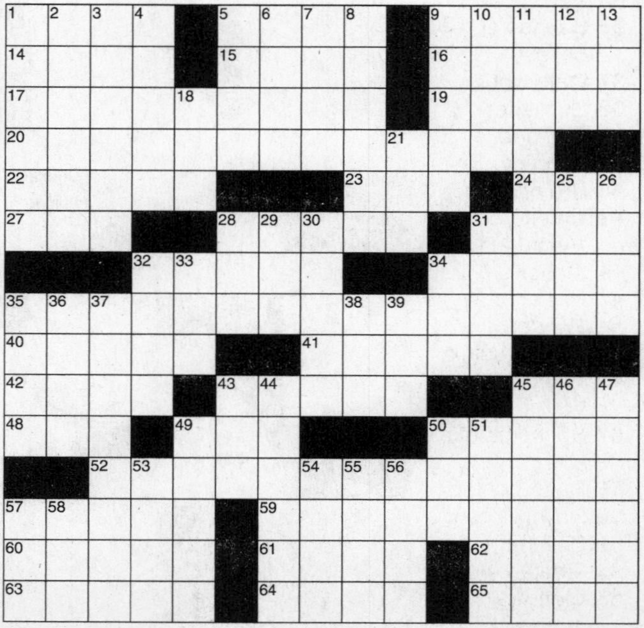

173 SACK TIME

by Bob Lubbers

ACROSS
1 Short letter
5 No longer trendy
10 Did the butterfly
14 General Idi
15 Dangerous whales
16 Mexican money
17 Doris Day film of '59
19 Mr. Preminger
20 What you wear
21 Kenyan capital
23 Parking aide
25 Steel factory
26 Pasta shapes
28 Dwarf trees
31 Like __ of bricks
32 Rat-race result
34 FDR agency
35 Seamstress Ross
37 Corn unit
38 Accurate, pitchwise
40 Outs' partners
41 __ *of Jeannie*
44 Poetic nighttimes
45 Hats, so to speak
47 So far
49 Part to play
50 Pavarotti, for one
51 Elizabeth II's house
53 Beethoven opus
57 Author Morrison
58 Ductwork material
60 Suggest strongly
61 Floor, in France
62 Shaker contents
63 Porgy's love
64 Copter part
65 Normandy town

DOWN
1 Western wine region
2 Leave out
3 Pinball problem
4 Perks up
5 General Colin's family
6 Whistler works
7 Barely enough
8 Room, to Roberto
9 Kayak builders
10 Thread holders
11 Party pooper
12 Italy's answer to 1 Down
13 Pasture plaint
18 Evangelist Roberts
22 Duz rival
24 Organic compounds
26 Dictation taker
27 Arkansas resort
28 Chew out
29 Actress Dunne
30 Simon follower
31 Just slightly
33 *Norma* __
36 Investor's concern
39 Proximity
42 Bedroom piece
43 Godzilla or Rodan
46 Shetlands, e.g.
48 Unavoidable fate
50 Pick up the tab
51 Got tiresome
52 "__ be in England . . ."
54 Rat-__
55 Hard to believe
56 Palo __, CA
57 Rickety ship
59 Self-image

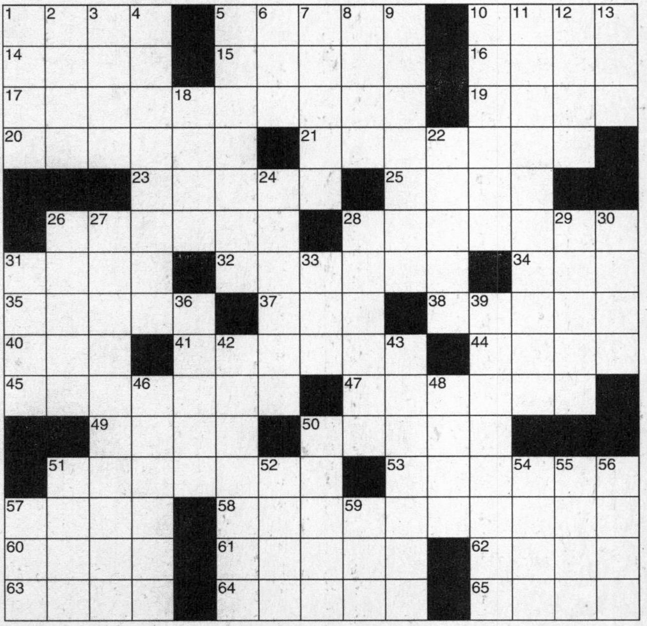

174 IT'S SHOW TIME!

by Eric Albert

ACROSS

1 Johann Sebastian __
5 Dick and Jane's dog
9 Son of Seth
13 .405 hectare
14 Knee-bone neighbor
16 Norway native
17 Jane Fonda film of '86
20 Chop down
21 Anti-flood structure
22 Senselessness
23 Beauteous group
24 Mr. Laurel
25 Sale sweetener
28 Smile broadly
29 Fast way to England
32 Eye-bending designs
33 All in
34 Concerned with
35 Pacino film of '75
38 Cools down, in a way
39 "Working or not"
40 Marry in haste
41 Bobby Orr's org.
42 Englishman, for short
43 Belmont Stakes winner in '75
44 Brought into being
45 Chicken fixin's
46 Girl, to Dundee
49 "Excuse me!"
50 Sundial's 7
53 Randy Quaid film of '78
56 *Exodus* author
57 Country singer Steve
58 Kind of vaccine
59 Nerd
60 African nation
61 Little shaver

DOWN

1 Shower alternative
2 Liniment target
3 Stagehands
4 Fabric border
5 Work hard
6 Little finger
7 Off-Broadway award
8 Soft metal
9 Like leprechauns
10 Post-WWII alliance
11 Cartel in the news
12 Energetic
15 Stir up
18 Folk-blues singer
19 Economist Smith
23 Epic poets
24 Does ushering
25 *The Thinker* sculptor
26 Noteworthy period
27 Roll with a hole
28 Are suited for
29 Snobby one
30 "His face could __ clock"
31 Copier need
33 Count of jazz
34 Bride's acquisition
36 Gridiron gain
37 Make over
42 It's east of Java
43 Karamazov brother
44 Capital of Belorussia
45 Nut case
46 Too confident
47 Take on
48 Singer Adams
49 Razor brand
50 Oft-used adverb
51 Meryl, in *Out of Africa*
52 Capri, for one
54 Swiss partner
55 Balderdash

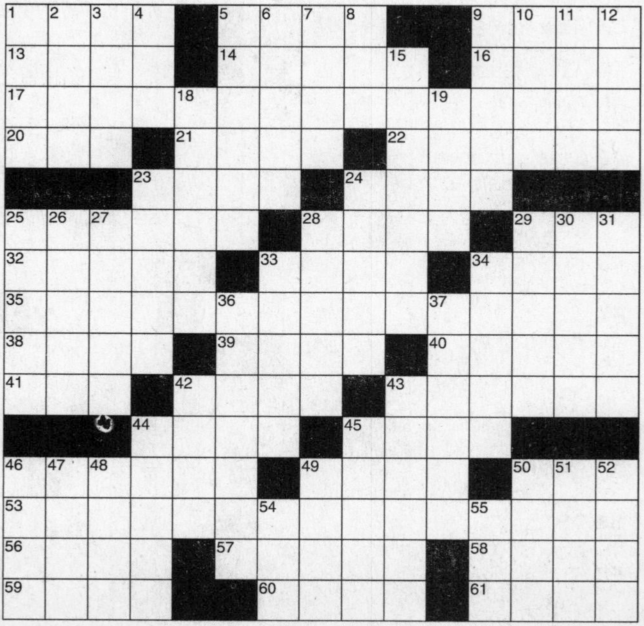

175 *GOOD SKATES*

by Randolph Ross

ACROSS

1 Actress Gardner
4 Shipboard officers
9 TV host Donahue
13 Like a wet rag
15 Some exams
16 Not well-done
17 __ above (minimally)
18 '88 Olympics skater
20 Of a lord's estate
22 Beginning
23 '68 Olympics skater
26 Actor Alejandro
27 *Exodus* role
28 Mauna __
31 Grimm villain
34 Utmost, so to speak
36 '92 Olympics skater
40 Shares secrets
41 Converse
42 It's inspiring
43 Get __ of (eliminate)
44 Suns do it
46 '84 Olympics skater
52 Crazy as __
55 Paint solvents
56 '32 Olympics skater
59 Ms. Barrett
60 "Cheerio!"
61 *Look Back in __*
62 Tree knot
63 Haywire
64 Impolite looks
65 Els' followers

DOWN

1 ". . . __ unto my feet"
2 Curriculum __ (resumé)
3 In the company of
4 Make changes to
5 "And we'll have __ good time"
6 Postpone
7 Actor Wallach
8 Sleek plane
9 Fork tine
10 Deli meats
11 "Dies __" (hymn)
12 "__ we forget"
14 Go forward
19 Sharpening
21 Whiskey type
24 Address after "yes"
25 Film role for Shirley
28 Polish political name
29 Workplace agcy.
30 Working hard
31 Ark. neighbor
32 Got taller
33 Communion, e.g.
34 Marino or McGrew
35 Air carriers
37 Albania's capital
38 Monogram part: Abbr.
39 *The Empire Strikes Back* teacher
44 Shows contempt
45 Stop for a bite
46 Savalas role
47 Kitchen appliance
48 More frosty
49 Make a hole __
50 Midmorning
51 Peter and Nicholas
52 Nick Charles' pooch
53 Sandy soil
54 Familiar with
57 *2001* computer
58 Compass pt.

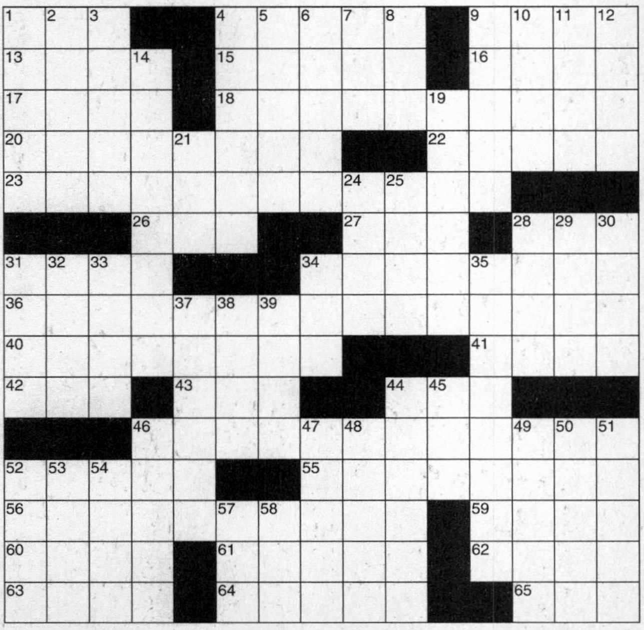

176 *SO WHAT?*

by Trip Payne

ACROSS

1 Barely open
5 Con game
9 Paper layers
14 US national flower
15 Balsa or balsam
16 Long gun
17 '77 Linda Ronstadt tune
19 Oil source
20 '84 Pointer Sisters tune
22 *Falcon Crest* star
26 Binge
27 Draft org.
28 Makes up (for)
30 Dolores __ Rio
32 Mrs. Truman
33 Cajun veggie
37 They hold water
40 '83 Lauper album
43 Kiss follow-up?
44 Piece of cake
45 Halves of quartets
47 Could possibly
49 Heavy-hitting hammer
51 Pedigree grp.
54 Snake poison
58 "__ my case"
59 '73 Carly Simon tune
62 Gourmand
63 '63 Chiffons tune
68 Skirt style
69 Midwestern tribe
70 Hertz rival
71 Gave a PG-13 to
72 Go down
73 College book

DOWN

1 Onassis, familiarly
2 Scribble (down)
3 Nincompoop
4 Musical notes
5 Wineglass part
6 Boorish and rude
7 Man with morals
8 Mr. Lansky
9 Goes forward
10 Caron movie
11 __ *Tuesday, This Must Be Belgium*
12 Arctic assistants
13 Burpee products
18 French river
21 Crossed out
22 Chemist's second home
23 Bomb tryout
24 General Dayan
25 11th-century saint
29 "Send help!"
31 Cosmetics name
34 Wins the bout
35 10-K, for one
36 Santa __ , CA
38 Bea Arthur sitcom
39 Walks heavily
41 Drooled
42 Pkg. co.
46 Matched group
48 "Without a doubt!"
50 Floor covering, for short
51 Once __ (annually)
52 Eucalyptus muncher
53 Make the grade
55 "Never!"
56 __ Culp Hobby
57 Bricklayer
60 Russo of *Lethal Weapon 3*
61 "Uh-huh . . ."
64 What *gras* means
65 "__ been had!"
66 Put the kibosh on
67 Guinness Book suffix

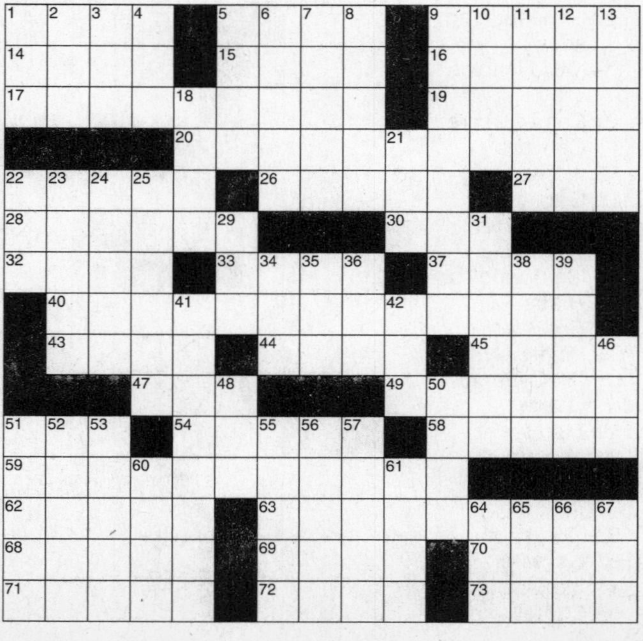

177 ORAL EXAM

by Bob Lubbers

ACROSS

1 Emerald Isle
5 "This is only __"
10 Open slightly
14 Author Vidal
15 Use pointlessly
16 Prohibition
17 Litter bit
19 Is in debt
20 Two-__ (small plane)
21 Show fear
23 Verdi work
26 Kuwaiti ruler
27 Cow quarters
30 Poem of praise
32 Pop singer Billy
35 Yale athletes
36 Mixed drink
38 In the past
39 Actress Ullmann
40 Leaf-covered
41 Josh around
42 Peggy or Pinky
43 European airline
44 Soccer great
45 Sign up
47 Dapper __
48 Peels off
49 Trumpet accessory
51 Not bogus
53 Stifle
56 Unfinished rooms
60 Serve tea
61 Just misses a putt
64 Caesarean phrase
65 Select group
66 Ms. McEntire
67 Attorney Roy
68 French painter
69 Sp. ladies

DOWN

1 Ham partners
2 Libertine
3 *My Friend* __
4 Isaac and Wayne
5 Cognizant (of)
6 Beer device
7 Mind reader's talent
8 Editor's notation
9 __ Haute, IN
10 Kind of energy
11 Very hard candy
12 Genesis son
13 Ploy
18 Agts., e.g.
22 Overdo a role
24 Stirred up
25 Nimitz's title
27 Ball girl?
28 Little green man
29 Delta's locale
31 Director May
33 Fast on one's feet
34 Junction points
36 Sailor, slangily
37 Greek letter
40 Dirty stuff
44 Talks quickly
46 Beat in a heat
48 Essential part
50 Fished, in a way
52 Fence openings
53 Chance-taking, for short
54 Lorre role
55 Make angry
57 Cake topper
58 Havana locale
59 Fitness centers
62 Pen dweller
63 RR stop

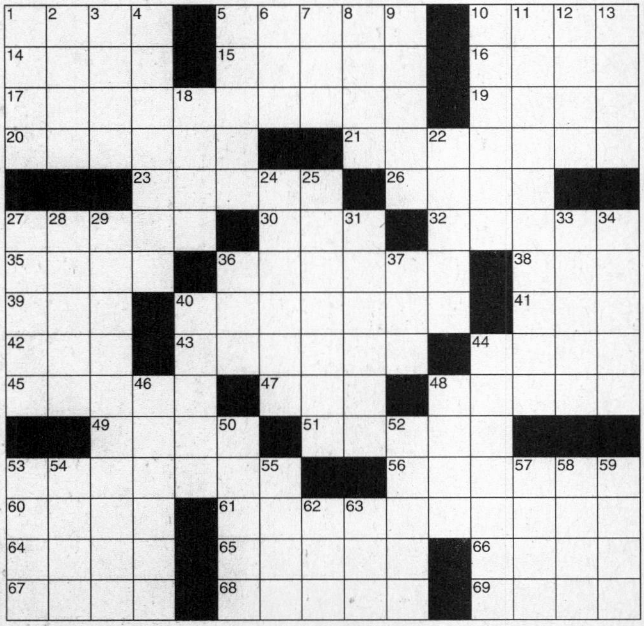

178 KID STUFF

by Eric Albert

ACROSS

1 Ralph __ Emerson
6 Lifeline locale
10 Wine barrel
14 Belted constellation
15 __ vera (shampoo ingredient)
16 Put money in
17 Kid-lit gold spinner
20 Leg joint
21 English prep school
22 Symbol of love
23 Vanquish a dragon
25 Potter's material
27 Squeezing snake
30 Make bubbles
31 Actress Dawber
34 Exclaimed in delight
35 Put something over on
36 Lucid
37 Kid-lit builders
40 Eccentric guy
41 St. Louis landmark
42 Fork parts
43 A question of method
44 Logan of Broadway
45 Sweet-smelling place
46 Dinner giver
47 Walesa, for one
48 __ von Bulow
51 Untrustworthy sort
53 Cluckers
57 Kid-lit siblings
60 Sty cry
61 Aroma
62 Copycat's phrase
63 The hunted
64 Actress Daly
65 Hurled

DOWN

1 Put in effort
2 Make __ for it
3 Jell-O flavor
4 Racetrack info
5 I, to Claudius
6 __-faced (pale)
7 Sax range
8 Tarzan's garment
9 Director Brooks
10 Deejay Kasem
11 "Diana" singer
12 Mix a martini
13 Superman's alter ego
18 Low in fat
19 Defrost
24 Mine find
26 Lounge lazily
27 Cover a hole
28 Exuberant cry
29 Lose on purpose
30 Make a mess of
31 *Common Sense* writer
32 Make mad
33 Needing cleaning
35 Mamie or Rosalynn
36 Shoe projection
38 Myanmar neighbor
39 Latin abbr.
44 "No way, __!"
45 Net star Bjorn
46 Sled dog
47 Army spiritual leader
48 Piece of pork
49 Den
50 Diarist Frank
52 Privy to
54 "__, Brute!"
55 Noble gas
56 Walk through mud
58 Unimproved land
59 Real-estate ad wd.

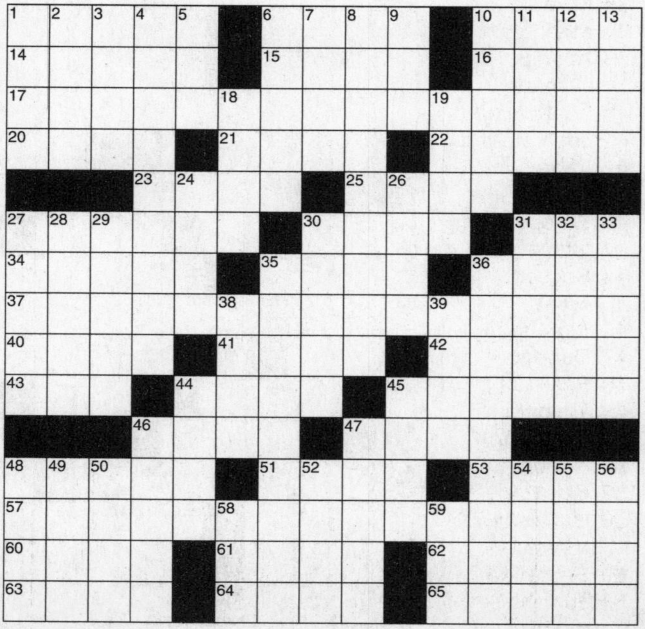

179 FIND AWAY

by Trip Payne

ACROSS
1 Mr. Selleck
4 Filibuster
9 Glove-box items
13 Gray's field: Abbr.
15 Poet Elinor
16 Kind of sax
17 Bethlehem trio
18 Sports stadium
19 Satiate
20 TV accessory
23 Start of a proverb about silence
24 Digger's tool
26 Rock singer John
27 Nicklaus' grp.
30 The other team
31 King of Norway
32 Swiss home
34 White alternative
35 Hippie's remark
38 White House nickname
41 Shopping sprees
42 Director Preminger
46 Fourbagger
48 Chariot suffix
49 Smug expression
50 Barbarian
52 Porcupine features
53 Midler top-10 tune of '90
57 Royal decree
58 *The Prince of Tides* star
59 Gobbles up
61 Comic Johnson
62 Perrier competitor
63 Organic compound
64 Have to have
65 "__ evil, hear . . ."
66 Secret stealer

DOWN
1 Scottish headgear
2 Continuously successful
3 Red shade
4 Sharp blows
5 Brit's radial
6 Actor Baldwin
7 Carpet alternative, for short
8 Relies (on)
9 Long-vowel indicator
10 Everywhere
11 Ancient astronomer
12 Sauce variety
14 Vacation period
21 Keep for oneself
22 Greek letter
23 New beginning?
25 Caustic chemical
27 Ring up
28 Measure
29 Raise the hem, maybe
32 Dernier __ (latest fashion)
33 Printer's measures
36 James __ Garfield
37 Possible award-winner
38 "What ho!"
39 Big blaze
40 Kuwait, for one
43 Soup holders
44 Lullaby locale
45 Signs off on
47 Hammed it up
49 Health resort
51 Bowling places
52 Office worker
54 Hawk's opposite
55 "Would __ to you?"
56 Ollie's pal
57 Ardent watcher
60 Foxlike

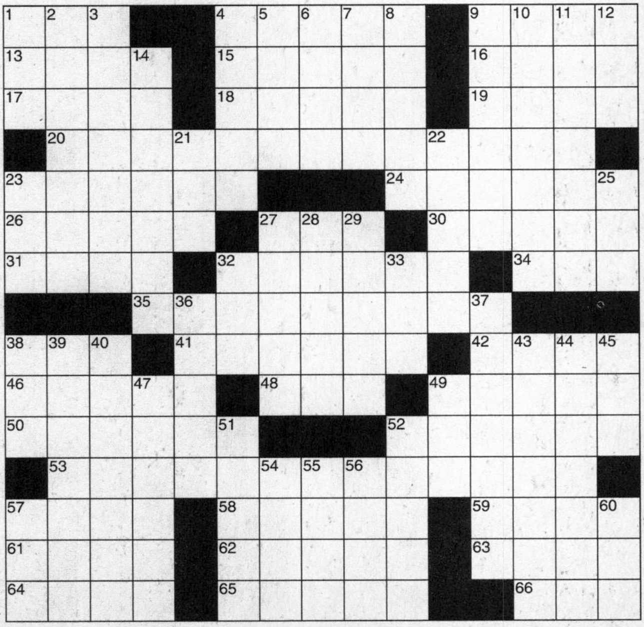

180 *FICTIONAL PHYSICIANS*

by Randolph Ross

ACROSS

1 Opera star Merrill
7 Prince Charles' sport
11 Wild blue yonder
14 Have __ many
15 Literary VIP
16 Hasten
17 MD once on ABC
19 Switch settings
20 Fruity dessert
21 Biblical twin
22 Illiterate endorser
24 Mlle. of Madrid
26 Combustible heaps
29 Recipe direction
32 *Star Trek* doctor
35 Send to cloud nine
36 Usually
37 Babysitter's banes
39 Memos
40 Scatterbrained sort
43 Gives testimony
45 MD once on NBC
47 Controversial tree spray
48 Thai or Mongol
49 Cub Scout units
53 Speedwagon maker
55 Starting
57 Mauna __
58 Oliver Stone film
60 Conan Doyle doctor
64 Pub order
65 Greek theaters
66 Chore
67 Future flower
68 Bastes or hems
69 Ear pollution

DOWN

1 Easy victories
2 TV studio sign
3 Artist's topper
4 List ender
5 No gentleman
6 Drunkard
7 Lung lining
8 Tulsa product
9 Slow pitch
10 Figurine mineral
11 Timesavers
12 Relatives
13 "You bet!"
18 *True Grit* Oscar-winner
23 Placed in a third-party account
25 *Compos mentis*
27 Chapter in history
28 '60s radical org.
30 Hercules' captive
31 Bakery buys
33 Lets up
34 Lord's land
35 Singled out
37 Mexican peninsula, for short
38 Irani money
41 Blotter initials
42 Insult, in current slang
43 "Add __ of salt . . ."
44 Dey's *L.A. Law* role
46 Forest vines
50 Lanchester et al.
51 All's opposite
52 Time, metaphorically
54 Eyes: Sp.
56 Old card game
58 Holyfield hit
59 Winter bug
61 Tribute in verse
62 Chop down
63 Pod prefix

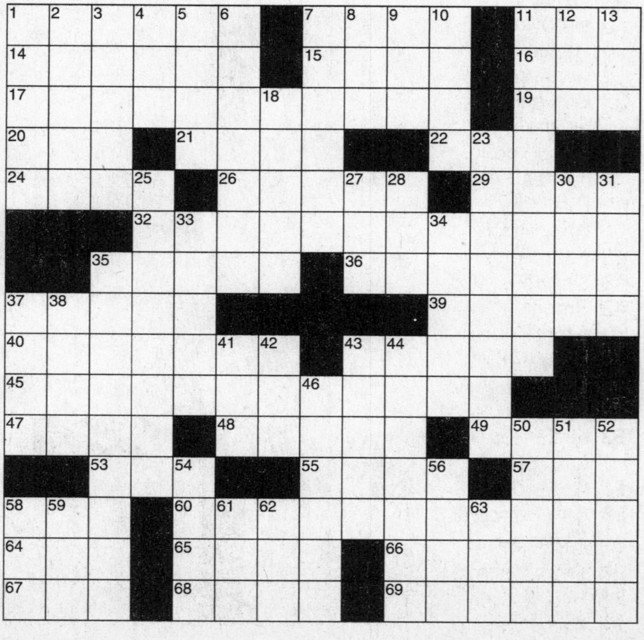

181 STRIKE IT RICH

by Shirley Soloway

ACROSS

1 Beach surface
5 Western writer on a $5 stamp
10 Acting job
14 Small band
15 Factory group
16 Water pitcher
17 Part of CPA
18 Sober-minded
19 *Bus Stop* writer
20 Get rich quick
23 Button directive
24 After six
28 Grass purchase
29 Liza's Oscar film
33 Coral or Caribbean
34 Baseball exec Al
35 School grps.
36 Get rich quick
41 Cathedral area
42 Charlie Chan portrayer
43 British brew
44 Brain part
47 Señora Perón
50 Not at all friendly
52 Female fox
54 Get rich quick
58 A real clown
61 __ Boothe Luce
62 Environmental sci.
63 Genesis site
64 Floor installer
65 "Don't look __!"
66 Heredity unit
67 Derisive look
68 Church service

DOWN

1 Philatelist's fodder
2 Jockey Eddie
3 Cut a little
4 Is overfond of
5 Corn covering
6 Opposing one
7 Mideast money
8 Hard worker
9 Salad vegetable
10 Have sovereign power
11 __ up to (admit)
12 Turkey part
13 Prior to, in poems
21 Wide tie
22 Court barrier
25 Ratio phrase
26 Well-ordered
27 Regular, e.g.
30 Hardwood
31 Flying buzzer
32 Pear variety
34 Line on a map: Abbr.
35 Not COD
36 Saintly ring
37 Currier's partner
38 100 percent
39 White House nickname
40 Scoundrel
41 Slangy refusal
44 Russian space station
45 Votes in
46 Sell
47 Track bet
48 Some poisons
49 Bracelet holders
51 Steak order
53 Construction girder
55 Moolah
56 Nut source
57 Kohl's title
58 Canine command
59 Kind of poem
60 Buddhist sect

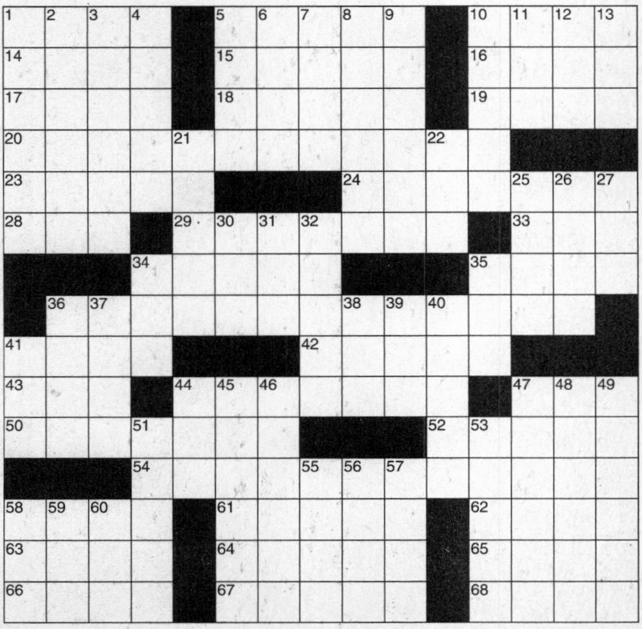

182 TODAY'S PUZZLE

by Randolph Ross

ACROSS

1 Apply (to)
8 Keep at it
15 Hillary's height
16 Replenish inventory
17 Former *Today* cohost
19 Child pleaser
20 Oklahoma Indian
21 Els' followers
22 Mel of baseball
24 Gibbon, e.g.
25 Pitcher's stats
26 See 17 Across
31 Smith of Rhodesia
32 Green land
33 Fit for farming
37 Earned, so to speak
39 Frying pan
40 Lady of Spain
41 Oil acronym
42 "__ Clear Day"
43 Former *Today* semi-regular
46 African nation
49 Popular suffix
50 Some magazine pages
51 Ms. MacGraw
52 Levee kin
54 Leb. neighbor
56 *Today* cohost
62 Command stratum
63 Veal dish
64 Causing bias
65 Still standing

DOWN

1 Urban walker: Abbr.
2 Night before
3 Soldier in gray
4 TV reporter Liz
5 Prefix for space
6 Brit's exclamation
7 Ultimate degree
8 President __
9 Architect Saarinen
10 Gad about
11 __ Lanka
12 Lazybones
13 Alabama city
14 Lock of hair
18 "__ intended"
22 "__ Ben Jonson"
23 Critic Kenneth
24 Not "fer"
25 Mideast airline
26 Chest protectors
27 Silents star
28 Error's partner
29 Like Alaska?
30 Ambler and Idle
34 *Captain* __ (Flynn film)
35 Fasting times
36 Coup d'__
38 "__ lay me down . . ."
39 Energetic
41 Like some cereals
44 Partiality
45 Opera immortal
46 Puts together
47 Word of regret
48 Easily bent
52 Sandwich shop
53 Barbell material
54 "If __ make it there . . ."
55 Gather, in chemistry
57 Use an axe
58 Big bird
59 Not refined
60 Spot for a cartographe
61 Good-for-nothing

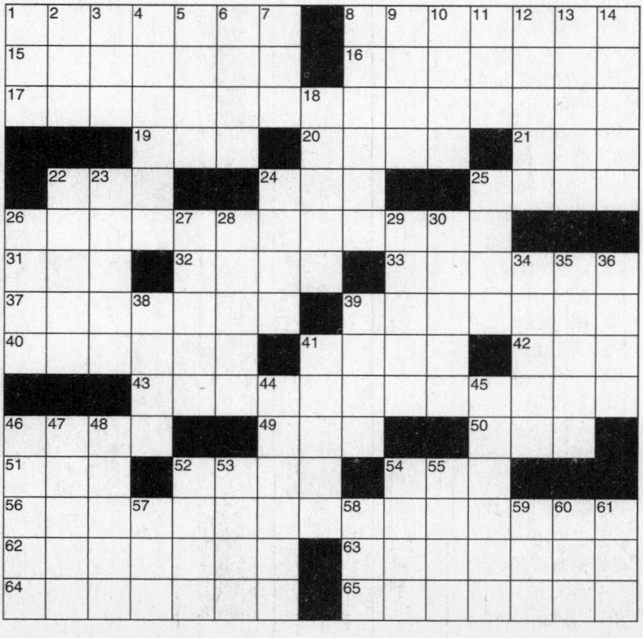

183 BODY LANGUAGE

by Bob Lubbers

ACROSS

1 Acting job
5 Greek column style
10 Aid in crime
14 On top of
15 Stew style
16 Cabbie's take
17 Sports stadium
19 USC rival
20 Capture a fish
21 Mean one
23 Church area
26 *Billboard* entry
27 Alda and King
30 Bible line: Abbr.
32 *Father Knows Best* actress
35 Stable parent
36 Western capital
38 __ Zedong
39 Nimitz's rank: Abbr.
40 Chafes
41 Sprint rival
42 Iced drink
43 La Cosa __
44 Planting ground
45 Gold bar
47 Shoe width
48 Batters' ploys
49 Oklahoma city
51 Faint
53 Back-of-book sections
56 Brook's big brother
60 Pedestal part
61 Small rodent
64 Venerable prep school
65 Divided nation
66 Thailand, once
67 *My Three __* (sitcom)
68 Take the wheel
69 Relaxed state

DOWN

1 German valley
2 Ronny Howard role
3 Run easily
4 Board a Boeing
5 "They __ Believe Me"
6 Bobby of hockey
7 __ de Janeiro
8 Doctrines
9 Atkins and Huntley
10 *__ Thing Happened on the Way . . .*
11 Board game
12 Writer Gardner
13 Run like crazy
18 Stops from squeaking
22 Midwest Indians
24 Reluctant (to)
25 Tells a story
27 Violin maker
28 Burdened
29 Ultimate battle
31 Made a new sketch
33 Not spoken
34 Works hard
36 Cable channel
37 Teachers' grp.
40 Playful trick
44 *__ at Campobello*
46 Burger topping
48 The two of them
50 Ship strata
52 Mr. de la Renta
53 Midmonth day
54 Alliance acronym
55 Took a photo of
57 Director Kazan
58 Regretful word
59 Fictional aunt
62 Anger
63 Society-page word

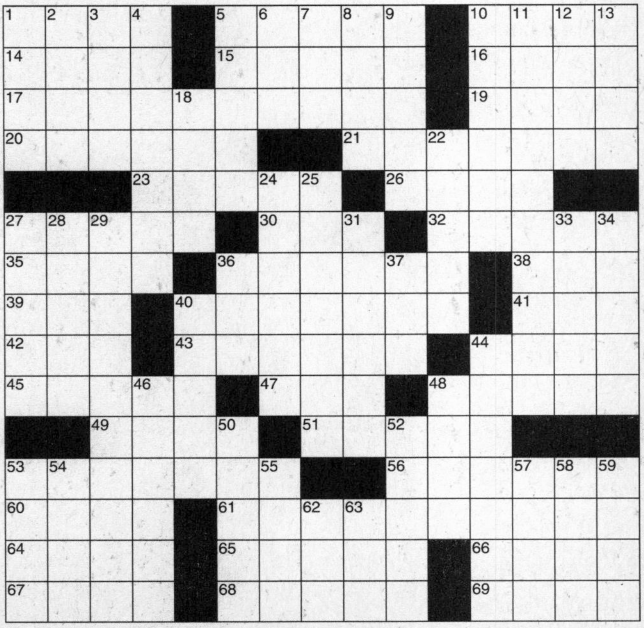

184 AGES

by Wayne R. Williams

ACROSS

1 Part of speech
5 Map collection
10 Smack hard
14 *Beetle Bailey* dog
15 Requirements
16 Lamb's pen name
17 Yuppie TV series
20 Common Market abbr.
21 Deep voices
22 Lets up
23 Northern constellation
25 Statuesque
27 Poker stakes
31 In advance
35 Milne book
39 Steno book
40 Egyptian bird
41 First course
42 British Isles republic
43 Gold container
44 Janis Ian tune of '75
46 Turkish export
48 Car choice
49 *Scarlett* setting
51 Noted virologist
55 English racecourse
58 Much loved
62 Yoko __
63 Beatles tune of '67
66 Solitary
67 Eagle's nest
68 Old Testament book
69 Drunkards
70 Editorial commands
71 Sleep symbols

DOWN

1 Widely recognized
2 Additional
3 New York city
4 Scand. land
5 Writer Seton
6 Hardy heroine
7 Most August-born folks
8 Own up to
9 Compass dir.
10 Sake
11 Wallach and Whitney
12 "Come here often?" is one
13 Merchandise labels
18 Steak cut
19 Fax ancestor
24 Crow cries
26 Tolerated
28 Winery worker
29 Time periods
30 Graf rival
32 Mayberry kid
33 Few and far between
34 First place
35 Puppy bites
36 Bassoon kin
37 Clever people
38 Computer command
42 Sicilian volcano
44 Cremona craftsman
45 Villainous
47 Makes amends
50 Selling feature
52 Rotgut
53 Become accustomed
54 Dunn and Ephron
55 Hole-making tools
56 "Skedaddle!"
57 Minimum change
59 Cable element
60 Cinema sign
61 Summers on the Somme
64 Bell and Barker
65 Shriner's topper

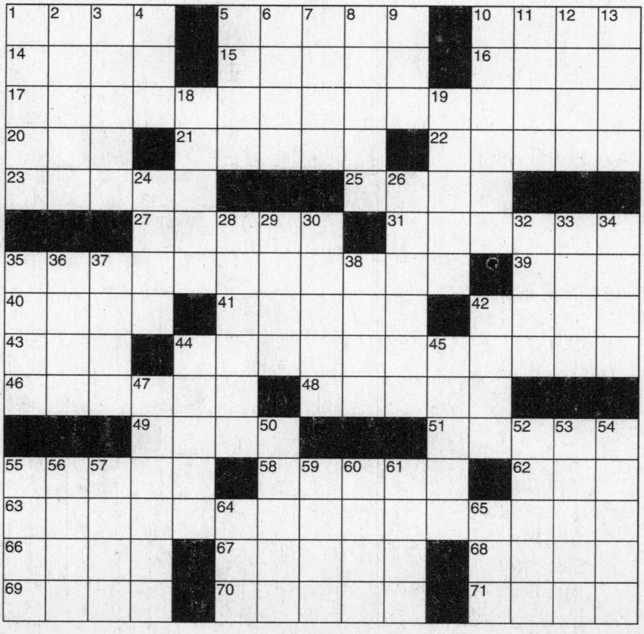

185 ON HAND

by Randolph Ross

ACROSS

1 Jocular sounds
5 Stopwatch, for instance
10 Counterfeit
13 __ *Three Lives*
14 Pull out
15 Lea lady
16 California city
18 Anchorman Rather
19 Nearly alike
20 Auto center
22 Dwelt
24 Small salamanders
25 Chipped in
28 Physique, for short
29 Rag-doll name
30 "Boola" relative
31 Jarreau and Jolson
32 Like short plays
35 Punch in the mouth
39 African native
40 UN agcy.
41 Bit of deceit
42 __ around (wander)
43 *Playboy* founder's nickname
44 Washbowl
46 Asian sea
48 Pinta was one
50 Tries to persuade
52 Young or Swit
56 "What a good boy __!"
57 Sponge cakes
59 Wine variety
60 "On __ Day"
61 Curriculum part
62 Rudolph's mother
63 Sharpens
64 Comics possum

DOWN

1 Pants supports
2 Jai __
3 Pilot's place
4 Look up to
5 Like Ivan
6 __ *on parle français*
7 Repaired
8 Moved sideways
9 Take it easy
10 Fakir's mattress
11 Anticipate
12 Fender benders
14 Fitness centers
17 Snow glider
21 Extend a subscription
23 Secret file
25 Places of refuge
26 Prefix for second
27 Hitchhike
29 In addition
31 Mr. Baba
32 Yoko __
33 One-fifth of MX
34 At that time
36 Seal a tub
37 Dutch airline
38 Forage plants
43 Teacup part
44 European capital
45 Give __ (assist)
46 Honor
47 Shakespearean teen
48 Football job
49 __ dire (jury-selection process)
51 Cabbage product
53 __' clock (midmorning)
54 Math subject
55 Legalese phrase
58 So far

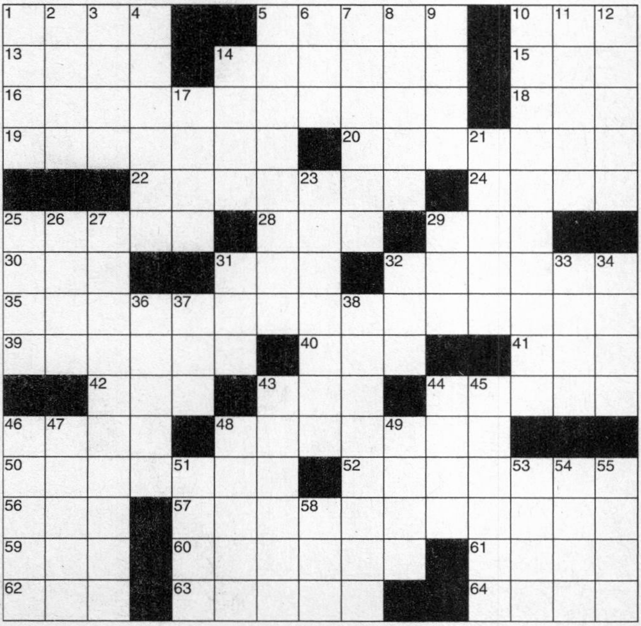

186 THE DOCTOR IS IN

by Eric Albert

ACROSS
1 Small songbird
5 Societal no-no
10 Quite luxurious
14 Give a job to
15 Squirrel snack
16 Singer Guthrie
17 Dr. Seuss book
20 Wind instrument
21 Make mad
22 Newsman Koppel
23 Hoosegow
24 Trite writings
28 Like some hair
29 Mouth piece
32 Series of steps
33 *Of __ I Sing*
34 Mediocre
35 Dr. Seuss book
38 Actress Bancroft
39 Tehran's country
40 Leered at
41 NBA coach Unseld
42 Half hitch or bowline
43 Expressionless
44 Meditate (on)
45 Sock part
46 Formal wear
49 Latin prayer
54 Dr. Seuss book
56 Words of understanding
57 Fencing swords
58 Moore of *Ghost*
59 People
60 Mean and malicious
61 Kemo __

DOWN
1 Propeller's sound
2 Teeming (with)
3 Author Ambler
4 Roman emperor
5 Two-person bike
6 Played a part
7 Physicist Niels
8 Lode load
9 Cursory cleaning
10 Ward off
11 '77 whale movie
12 Hit hard
13 Stockings
18 Conductor Toscanini
19 Deep black
23 Song of praise
24 "Fiddlesticks!"
25 Make up (for)
26 Where livestock live
27 Beer adjective
28 Golden grain
29 Bloodhound features
30 Embers, eventually
31 *Bananas* name
33 Lose on purpose
34 It's a long story
36 XIX
37 Serious and somber
42 Aga __
43 Take it slow
44 Kiss target
45 Station receiver
46 End-of-week remark
47 Roughly
48 Orange cover
49 Ripens, as cheese
50 Tags on
51 Perlman of *Cheers*
52 Poetic foot
53 French friend
55 Valedictorian's pride: Abbr.

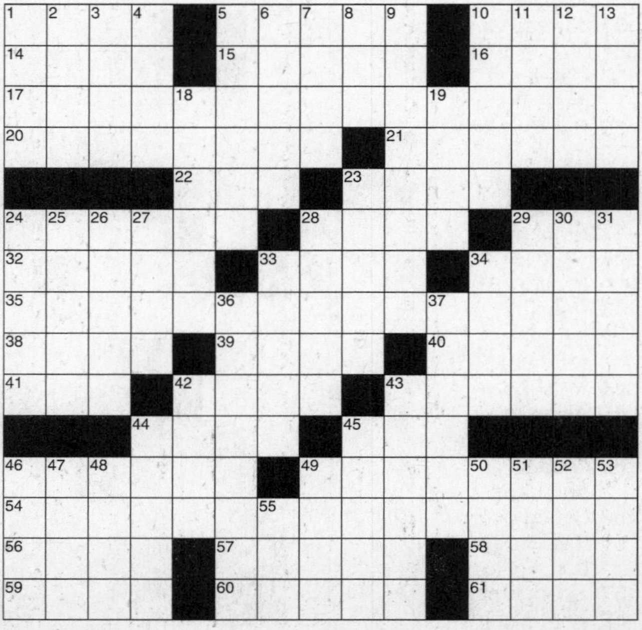

187 PLACES TO PLAY

by Wayne R. Williams

ACROSS

1 Jazzman Waller
5 Nonfilling dessert
10 Confused states
14 Vicinity
15 More frosty
16 Honolulu shindig
17 Fruit coat
18 Palmer's place
20 Country's count
22 Recording medium
23 Inventor Howe
24 Second ltr. addition
26 Open, in a way
30 Al Capp beast
32 Fur wrap
33 Gretzky's place
37 Clever person
38 Yoko __
39 Go bad
40 Miami Bch. road
42 Pasture
43 Hosp. area
44 Holyfield's place
47 More certain
50 Evasive maneuver
51 Tropical fish
52 Author LeShan
53 Barely beat
56 Filled with breezes
58 Small tree
59 Winter Olympics place
64 Past due
65 Cleveland's lake
66 Explosive, for short
67 Genesis name
68 Fetches
69 Prepare to drive
70 Family rooms

DOWN

1 Broad comedy
2 Statesman Sharon
3 Seles' place
4 Inept soldier
5 Lively dances
6 Coll. major
7 Diamond lady
8 Some jabs
9 Dangerous whale
10 Well-versed
11 __ *Miss Brooks*
12 Flivver fuel
13 Take to court
19 Musical work
21 Stadium seater
24 __ Alegre, Brazil
25 Taro product
27 Striker's place
28 Little green man
29 Price twice
31 Advice-column initials
33 Lifting device
34 When actors enter
35 Mrs. Yeltsin
36 Good-natured
41 Think alike
45 Marked a ballot
46 Became flushed
48 Wipes off
49 Metal rod
52 Singer Gorme
54 Iacocca's successor
55 Clothe oneself
57 Monthly check
58 Queue before Q
59 Canine command
60 Unrefined metal
61 Wee amount
62 Hwy.
63 S.A. nation

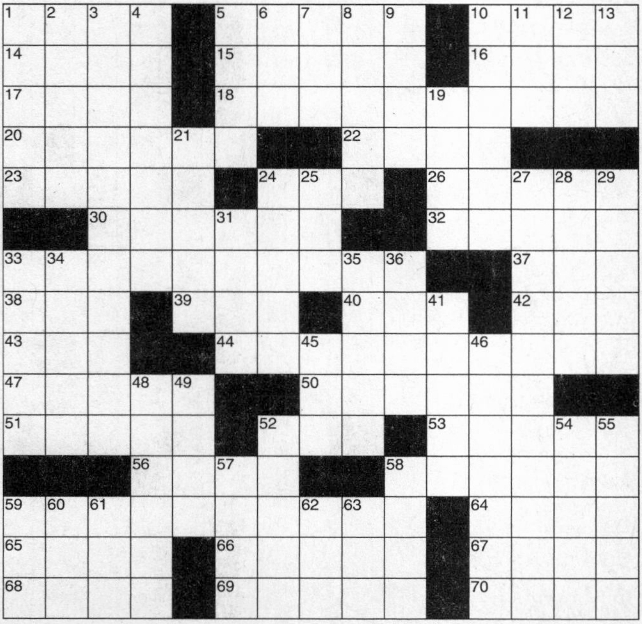

188 TWENTY QUESTIONS

by S.N.

ACROSS

1 Spill the beans
5 MacLeod of *The Love Boat*
10 Word on a fuse
14 Actress Anderson
15 Singer Cara
16 Kingly address
17 Rolaids target
18 Light beer
19 Get __ the ground floor
20 What the Mets play at Shea
22 Least usual
24 Fuss
25 Phone co.
27 Comparative suffix
28 Twelfth letter
30 Has at
33 Writer Burrows
36 Filmed a new version of
38 Ankle adornment
40 Ending for opt
41 Charles' princedom
43 First name
44 Scout's asset
46 "Be __ your school"
48 Thesaurus find: Abbr.
49 Punctilious
51 Omega's preceder
52 Mr. Wallach
54 Slinger's handful
55 Word form for "equal"
57 Sense
60 Court players
64 It's east of the Urals
65 Governor Stevenson
67 Robert De __
68 Catch some rays
69 Runner Steve
70 __ end (over)
71 Grade-school homework
72 Where things are
73 Cosby's first series

DOWN

1 Not very interesting
2 Plumb crazy
3 Charisma
4 Waited awhile
5 Arizona river
6 One of the Musketeers
7 Meatless main course
8 -esque relative
9 Pianist Peter
10 Out of the way
11 Ore veins
12 Big leaguers
13 Transmitted
21 Egg on
23 Half of DJ
26 Akron product
28 Onetime Indians
29 General Curtis __
31 Underground passage
32 Holds up
34 Overcomes
35 "Me too," in Montreal
37 100%
39 __ de cologne
42 Morning, à la Winchell
45 Grand-scale
47 Jockey's controller
50 Have thoughts
53 Pipe problems
56 Mideast region
57 Little bits
58 Jacob's twin
59 New Mexico town
61 What criticizers pick
62 Corner
63 Panasonic rival
66 A third of MDXVIII

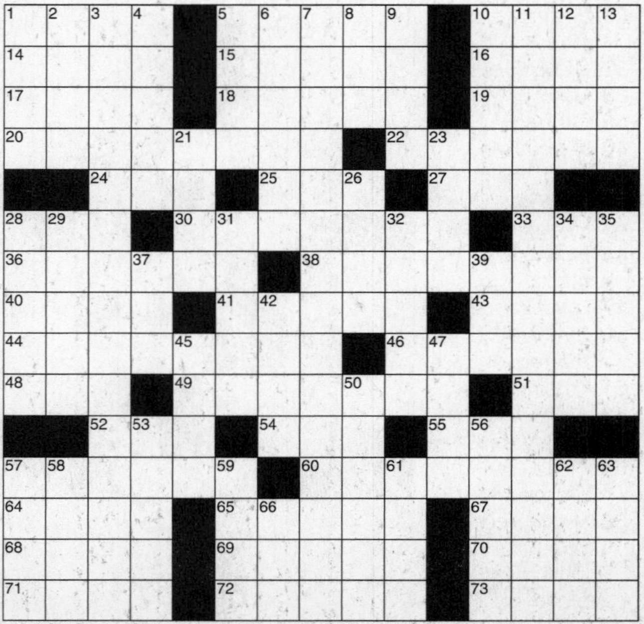

189 *CLEANUPS*

by Trip Payne

ACROSS

1 Behold, to Brutus
5 James and Kett
10 Prejudice
14 "__ I say, not . . ."
15 Precious kids
16 Mrs. Lindbergh
17 Book protector
19 Thurmond of basketball
20 Country music?
21 Makes captive
23 Act as pilot
24 Chicago's zone: Abbr.
25 Santa __, CA
26 Bring up
28 Geronimo, for one
31 Cornfield cries
34 Some cars
37 Former Mideast nation: Abbr.
38 High __ kite
39 Ratfink
40 Coffee brewer
41 __ *Misérables*
42 Quitter's word
43 Iowa city
44 Composer Gustav
46 Jamie of *M*A*S*H*
48 Franklin's nickname
49 Dietary component
51 Actress Slezak
55 Outer limit
58 Dotes on
59 Pasturelands
60 Important time for networks
62 Memo phrase
63 Gives for a time
64 Feminine ending
65 Pea holders
66 Use the delete key
67 Owner's proof

DOWN

1 Icelandic classics
2 Make a difference
3 Social position
4 Williams and Rolle
5 Gouda alternative
6 Gumshoe
7 Can hold
8 Don't exist
9 Concordes, e.g.
10 Split need
11 Where sound can't travel
12 Chip in
13 Understands
18 Burns of *Dear John*
22 Slip-up
24 *Antigone* king
27 "Swinging on __"
28 Ms. Bryant
29 Krishna preceder
30 Ocean fliers
31 Not upset
32 Taking a cruise
33 Kind of stomach
35 Put on
36 High above
39 Bloodhound's track
43 Like a one-way sign
45 Camera parts
47 Cincinnati team
49 Not so many
50 Sports palace
52 Actress Dunne
53 New Hampshire city
54 Was inquisitive
55 Gymnast's maneuver
56 Betting setting
57 Capri is one
58 Church area
61 Bradley and Begley

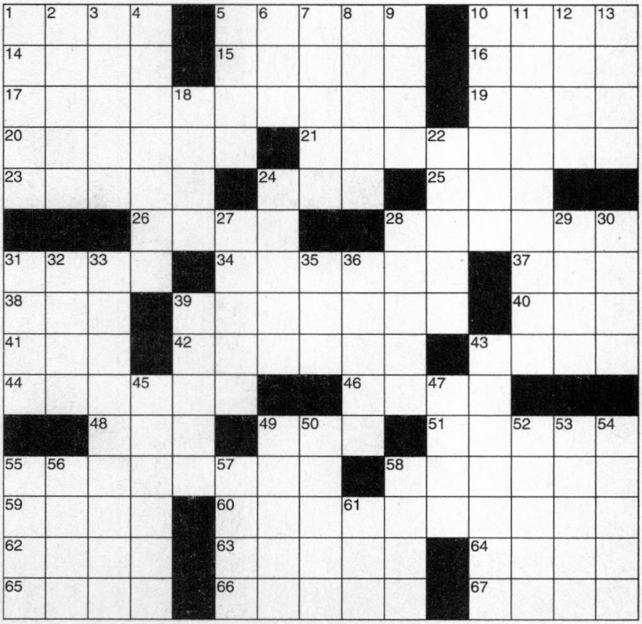

190 WALL COVERING NEEDS

by Bob Lubbers

ACROSS

1 *Casablanca* role
5 Pay out
10 Practice punching
14 Arthur of tennis
15 Rarin' to go
16 Top of the head
17 Loco
19 Enjoying the Love Boat
20 Like some steel
21 Bent a fender
23 __ *October* (fictional sub)
24 Painter/inventor
25 Sitter hirer
29 Board-game pair
30 Troop grp.
33 Likeness
34 Rope twist
35 Hockey target
36 Judy's daughter
37 Mails away
38 Rajah's spouse
39 School founded in 1440
40 Poker card
41 __ blanche
42 Leb. neighbor
43 Phobos orbits it
44 Make angry
45 Not much, so to speak
47 Josh around
48 Was generous
50 Work together
55 Elite alternative
56 Harmless loudmouth
58 Varieties
59 Way to the altar
60 Scarlett's home
61 Airplane tip
62 Equine gaits
63 Pretentious

DOWN

1 All ears
2 Cartographer's speck
3 Good buddy
4 Bush Sr. Cabinet member
5 Covert
6 Peeled off
7 Old oath
8 Pince-__ glasses
9 Ship-repair spots
10 Reaches across
11 Paper product
12 Suited to __
13 Perused
18 Swiss city
22 Poetic preposition
24 Mork's friend
25 Lots (of)
26 Friendliness
27 Arkansas athletes
28 Actor Richard
29 Eats in style
31 "*A votre* __!"
32 Green-card holder
34 Deborah and Graham
35 Alumnus
37 Take no more cards
41 West Pointer
43 Miss West
44 British bishops' hats
46 Rub out
47 Prepared to be knighted
48 Joyride
49 Hawaiian city
50 __ facto
51 Comedian Rudner
52 Seaweed product
53 Part of CD
54 Serving piece
57 Make public

191 PULLING RANK

by Eric Albert

ACROSS
1 Social blunder
6 "This can't be!"
10 Mistake-maker's cry
14 Expect
15 Way out
16 Give a hand
17 Doctor's career
20 Brontë heroine
21 List entry
22 Extend a subscription
23 Tuna holders
25 Touch against
27 State strongly
30 Trojan War hero
31 Violinist's need
34 Classic Western film
35 Computer owner
36 Clown character
37 Bob Keeshan role
40 European range
41 Weave a web
42 In unison
43 Single layer
44 Day laborer
45 Gas-range part
46 Cry
47 Eight furlongs
48 In the know
51 In the know about
53 Not at all stiff
57 Long-running soap opera
60 Hardwood trees
61 Couple
62 Knot again
63 Irritating insect
64 First name in mysteries
65 Days __ (yore)

DOWN
1 Stare openmouthed
2 Out of whack
3 County event
4 Words on a nickel
5 Greek letter
6 *Waiting for Lefty* playwright
7 Clinton's hometown
8 Marilyn's real name
9 ". . . man __ mouse?"
10 Eightsome
11 Lena of *Havana*
12 Leaders set it
13 Gush forth
18 Delicate color
19 Key point
24 General vicinity
26 Horse's home
27 Composers' org.
28 "__ We Dance?"
29 Foolish
30 Invite to stay
31 Element #5
32 Layer in the news
33 Swain
35 Not much liked
36 Sculpture variety
38 Understanding words
39 Caesar's conquest
44 Jury member
45 Storage boxes
46 Take by force
47 007 portrayer
48 Excited
49 Withdraw (from)
50 "Lonely Boy" singer
52 Mr. Donahue
54 "Tell __ the judge!"
55 Body armor
56 Said "guilty," perhaps
58 Tailless simian
59 In favor of

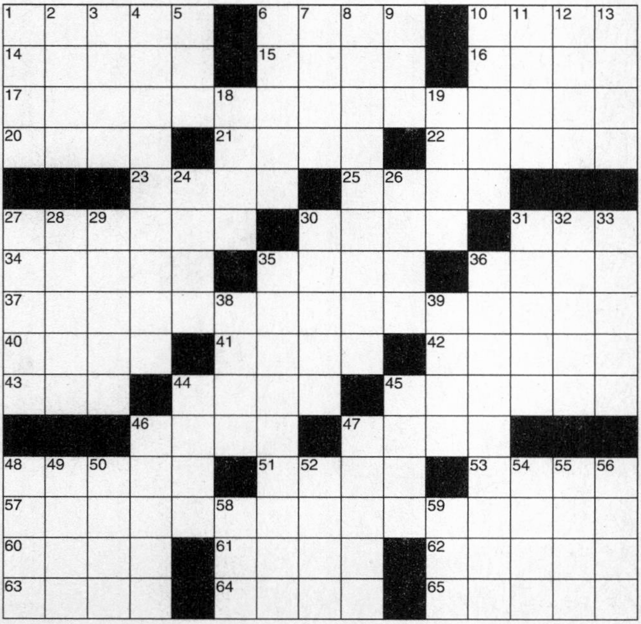

192 FLAG-WAVING

by David A. Davidson

ACROSS

1 Lip service of a sort
5 'Tis, in the past
9 Wearied
14 Add to the pot
15 Indian chief
16 Green shade
17 Ballet bend
18 Russian river
19 O-shaped roll
20 Flag-hoisting contests?
23 Storm
24 Adorn an i
25 Cry of contempt
28 Kon-Tiki Museum locale
31 Cash alternative
33 Arctic or Antarctic
37 Director Preminger
39 Boxer Max
40 "Flag Factory Robbed"?
43 Pain in the neck
44 Change course
45 Gets an apartment
46 St. Francis' home
48 Ready to pick
50 Author Buscaglia
51 Summer in Quebec
53 Pacific island
58 Flag day?
61 Set firmly
64 Adverse fate
65 Eban of Israel
66 Having knowledge
67 Science mag
68 Bridge support
69 Less outdated
70 Shoe inserts
71 Injury

DOWN

1 Key letter
2 Shore recess
3 Be frugal
4 "You look as if you've __ ghost!"
5 Swimwear
6 Toad feature
7 Open a bit
8 Bar food
9 Williams of *Poltergeist*
10 Word of regret
11 Use a backhoe
12 Garden dweller
13 Pa. neighbor
21 Squash variety
22 Tropical bean
25 Einstein
26 Artist's rep
27 Toast beginning
29 Traditional knowledge
30 Supplementary
32 Well-qualified
33 From John Paul
34 Corpulent
35 Cow catcher
36 One of the opposition
38 Actress Garr
41 Señora Perón
42 Be apprehensive about
47 Bird dog
49 Authorize
52 The __ the line
54 Bacterium type
55 Leg bone
56 Barbecue leftover
57 Get guns again
58 Kingly address
59 Circular roof
60 First-rate
61 Omelet cooker
62 Be a mortgagor
63 Got a peek at

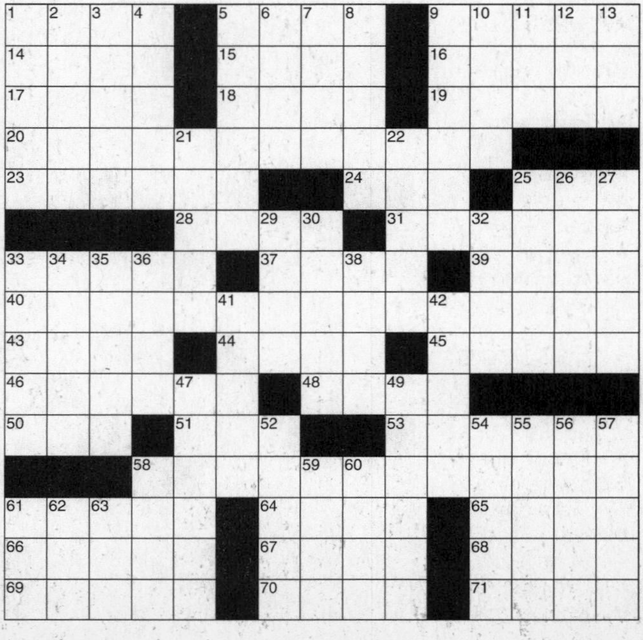

193 ZOO FILMS

by Eric Albert

ACROSS
1 __ *Having a Baby*
5 Suitor
10 Iced dessert
14 Roof edge
15 "Stormy Weather" singer
16 Ballerina Pavlova
17 Hepburn film of '68
20 Music character
21 Unbind
22 "__ the season . . ."
23 Emmy-winner Daly
24 Mature woman
28 Cuts the grass
29 *Murphy Brown* network
32 Circle the earth
33 Toll road
34 Dr. Jonas __
35 Hogan film of '86
38 Bumper-sticker word
39 Religious image
40 *M*A*S*H* extra
41 Inspire wonder
42 Sounds of censure
43 Optimally
44 Slow and dull
45 Act human?
46 Professional penman
49 Help hatch
54 Heston film of '68
56 Become a landlord
57 Locker-room garment
58 Milan money
59 __ Ono
60 Nail-board stuff
61 Entrée list

DOWN
1 Abel's brother
2 Laughing sounds
3 Mr. Knievel
4 Prefix for propelled
5 Sure winner
6 Usual practices
7 Auto-racer Luyendyk
8 Tavern or hotel
9 Yesterday's groom
10 Lake craft
11 Picnic pests
12 Anatomical hinge
13 Deserve for deeds
18 Wholly
19 Charged particles
23 Small souvenir
24 Fudge flavor
25 Quiver contents
26 Steak cut
27 *Casablanca* character
28 Director Forman
29 Core group
30 Glorify
31 Trapshooter's target
33 Overly exacting
34 Social slight
36 Data holder
37 Not so
42 Fit-tied link
43 In a mischievous manner
44 Kind of bean
45 Go into
46 Vigorously active
47 Singer Laine
48 Foul-smelling
49 "__ Only Have Love"
50 Soothing cream
51 ". . . baked in __"
52 Sea swallow
53 Birthright seller
55 Pah-pah preceder

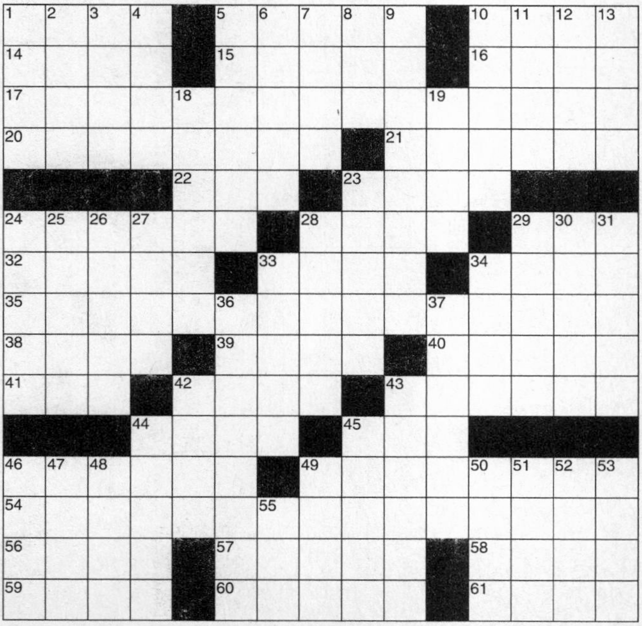

194 STAGE NAMES

by Fred Piscop

ACROSS

1 Señor's squiggle
6 __ *Richard's Almanack*
10 Sp. woman
13 Indian, for one
14 __ snuff (acceptable)
15 Recipe component
16 BERNARD SCHWARTZ
18 Order for dinner
19 Cool treat
20 More harsh
22 Taurus preceder
24 As Darth Vader would
25 Gunboat feature
28 Discoverer's cry
30 Patella locale
31 At any time
33 Extends one's enlistment
36 Peculiar
37 "Inner" word form
38 US draftees
40 Cheerleading word
41 __ as a judge
43 Small songbird
45 Prefix for nautical
46 Turmoil
48 Man with a megaphone
50 George C. Scott role
52 Mideast rulers
54 Decks out
56 South American airline
60 Gator kin
61 RICHARD STARKEY
63 Fork prong
64 Secluded valley
65 Lama land
66 __ in "solve"
67 Exercise system
68 Caravan stops

DOWN

1 Little shavers
2 Sect's symbol
3 Arsenio Hall rival
4 Preschoolers' supervision
5 Bonus piece
6 Thick soup
7 Pick
8 Elevator man
9 Player list
10 ARTHUR JEFFERSON
11 Party hearty
12 Mimic's skill
15 Gray bird
17 Puts together
21 New York's Medgar __ College
23 Visualize
25 Ring results
26 Take apart
27 AARON CHWATT
29 Egg on
32 Solemn promises
34 Trim off
35 Brake device
37 Shortstop's slip
39 Not outside the body
42 Tempt
44 Numbered hwy.
45 Old French region
47 Get-up-and-go
49 Brit noble
50 Nation's agreements
51 High-ceiling courts
53 __ Carta
55 Missile housing
57 Captures
58 Native Canadian
59 They may be liberal
62 Electron's chg.

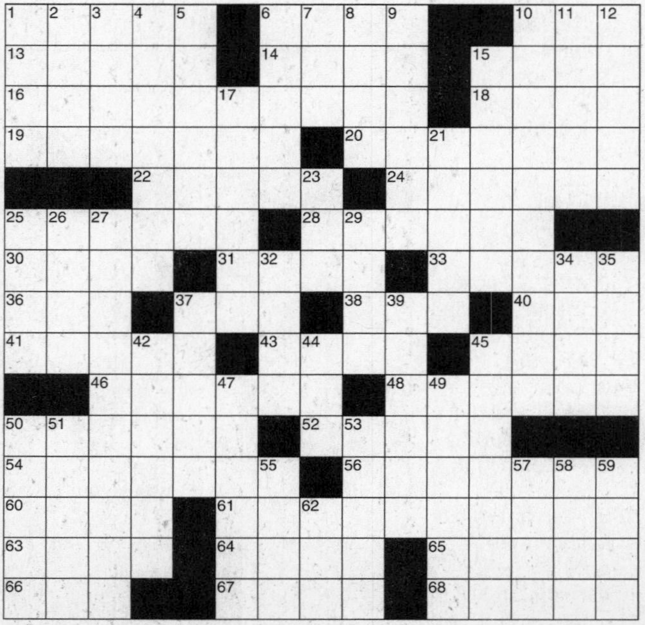

195 ALL WET

by Eric Albert

ACROSS

1 Historical period
4 Cup of coffee
8 Betrayed boredom
14 Actor Herbert
15 *Exodus* author
16 *The List of __ Messenger*
17 Rock Hudson film of '68
20 Oedipus' mother
21 Maui strings
22 Needing a massage
23 __ en scène (stage setting)
25 Diplomacy
29 Farm tool
30 Tornado, so to speak
33 Pigeon sound
34 18th President
35 Wife's mom, e.g.
37 Chinese-food ingredient
41 Family car
42 Indian corn
43 Night before
44 *La Mer* composer
47 "Tea for __"
50 Horn sound
52 Sleeveless garment
53 Impatient one's query
54 Clark's coworker
56 Color close to cranberry
59 Old-time engine
63 French mathematician
64 Owl outburst
65 Singer Damone
66 Main road
67 Poet Millay
68 Doe beau

DOWN

1 Biblical prophet
2 Art genre
3 *Cocoon* Oscar-winner
4 Sticks out
5 Smell __ (be suspicious)
6 Pauling's specialty
7 "__ was saying . . ."
8 American Leaguer
9 Ax cousin
10 Twist violently
11 Pen point
12 Corn unit
13 Heredity letters
18 Pronounce
19 Kick out
24 Panama, for one
26 Rights org.
27 Paint layer
28 Aspen machine
30 Tendency
31 Kid's card game
32 Real swank
34 Onetime sports car
36 Compass pt.
37 Sand-castle destroyer
38 Film critic James
39 Dirty Harry portrayer
40 Sibling, for short
41 Spider product
45 As Satan would
46 Kiss: Sp.
47 Be prosperous
48 Cotton killer
49 At bat next
51 Finish second
53 Drenched
55 Actor Sharif
57 "__ Fire" (Springsteen song)
58 __ bene
59 Health center
60 Paving material
61 Superlative suffix
62 Señor Guevara

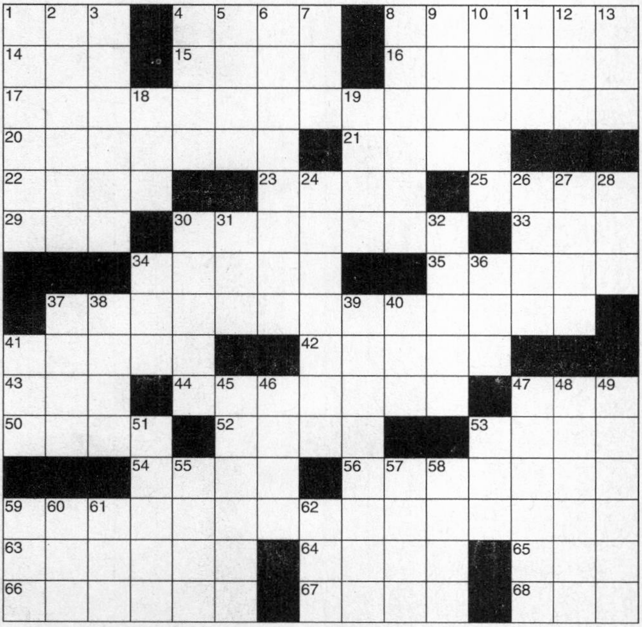

196 ALL THINGS BRIGHT

by Richard Silvestri

ACROSS
1 Midway attraction
5 Sound of fright
9 Robin Cook book
13 In a while
14 No-no
15 More than
16 Bowling, New England-style
18 Zola novel
19 Charm
20 Chow down
21 Black card
22 Echo
24 Standard charge
26 Heads the cast
28 Parking place
32 Tesh colleague
35 Facial feature
37 "Born in the __"
38 Procedure
39 Pub potation
40 Attacking with satire
45 Cleveland or Washington: Abbr.
46 Come into view
47 Hefty
49 Real bummer
51 As __ pin
55 '60s TV talker
58 __-Magnon man
60 Gets around
61 Univ. unit
62 Barge crew
64 Up to it
65 New York island
66 Where to see FDR
67 __-do-well
68 Gravity-powered vehicle
69 Ending for joke or game

DOWN
1 Indy entrant
2 Senseless
3 Ladies of Spain
4 Last
5 Big difference
6 Rose lover of fiction
7 Sub device
8 Mail-order extra
9 Anxiety
10 Sort of circular
11 Café handout
12 Riyadh resident
14 Threefold
17 Boorish fellow
23 Tied
25 Roof goo
27 Slowpoke
29 Not quite shut
30 Strong wind
31 Flock females
32 Luau lesson
33 PDQ kin
34 Gangplank
36 Critic Kenneth
41 Pushcart proprietor
42 Regatta need
43 Wise guys
44 Welcomes
45 Kinds of firecrackers
48 Was resilient
50 Cross-examine
52 Own up to
53 "Come up and __"
54 Actor Ed
55 Thom of shoedom
56 After-bath wear
57 Fashion mag
59 Make eyes at
63 Took cover

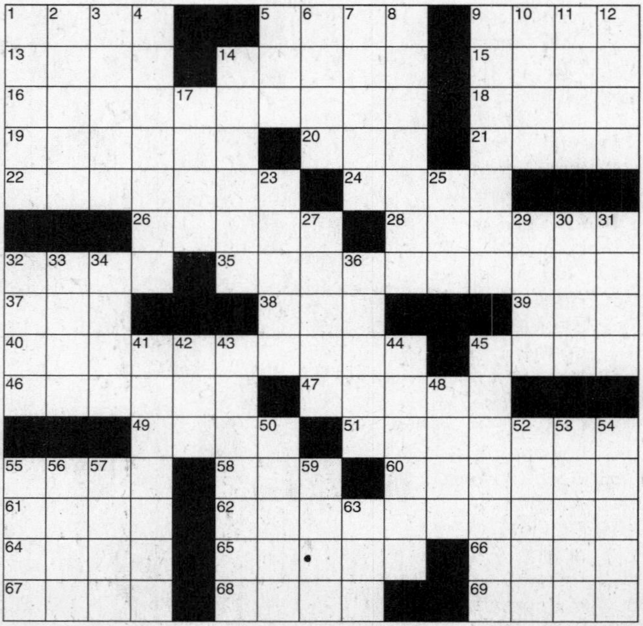

197 WEATHER-WISE

by Shirley Soloway

ACROSS

1 Five-time Wimbledon champ
5 Hurt badly
9 Small pieces
13 Lhasa's locale
14 Ms. Abzug
15 "Put a lid __!"
16 Doesn't exist
17 TV studio sign
18 Theda of silents
19 Quite appropriate
22 Dr. Casey
23 Leave behind
24 Singer Barbara
26 Beef cut
28 __ Field (old Brooklyn ballpark)
31 Breakfast order
34 Vicinity
37 Tatum or Ryan
38 "That's awesome!"
39 Act of deception
41 San Diego attraction
42 Conductor Dorati
44 Withdraw (from)
45 Constant irritant
46 Wetter, in a way
48 Hire a decorator
50 Thrust upon
53 Draws out
57 Play on words
59 Make a great impression
61 *M*A*S*H* star
63 Yes ending
64 Sea flier
65 Privy to
66 Took a crack at
67 Vex
68 Flat craft
69 Dance move
70 Editor's instruction

DOWN

1 Puppeteer Bil
2 Actor Davis
3 Christmas-song quintet
4 Gets together
5 Haberdashery department
6 Warning sound
7 Sacro follower
8 Leatherneck
9 Short haircut
10 Very easily
11 Grow weary
12 Ollie's buddy
14 Rudder operator
20 Capote's nickname
21 Big shot
25 King __ Saud
27 Ship's forepart
29 New Mexico town
30 Pigeonhole
31 Old oath
32 Heredity unit
33 Hear about
35 Ram's mate
36 Slightly open
39 Sacked out
40 Kind of jack
43 Purpose
45 Sulky ones
47 Cooks chestnuts
49 Tooth pro's deg.
51 Mini, for one
52 Very strange
54 French painter
55 Comic Kovacs
56 Refine metal
57 Matched set
58 Forearm bone
60 Horn sound
62 Ubiquitous bug

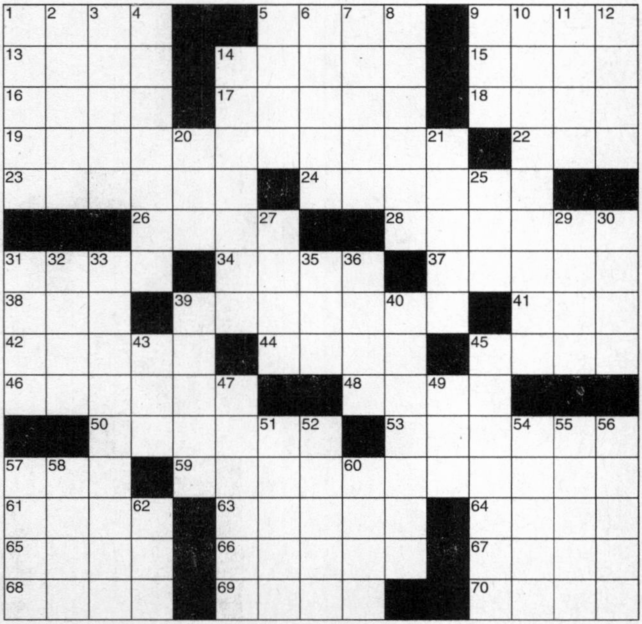

198 POLITICS AS USUAL

by Richard Silvestri

ACROSS

1 Pompous people
6 Where the Vikings landed
10 Riga resident
14 Written exercise
15 Smart guy?
16 Hodgepodge
17 Gobbled up
18 *Educating* __ ('83 film)
19 Secluded valley
20 Political PR person
22 Hard to find
23 It may be legal
24 Slots spot
26 Change chemically
29 Make happy
33 Spheres
37 Hodges of baseball
38 Something to sneeze at?
39 Collect the crops
40 Alpha's antithesis
42 Major Hoople's cry
43 Prohibit by law
45 Bern's river
46 NFL team
47 Connecting flight
48 Opposition group
50 Principal role
52 MCI rival
57 Not as much
60 Political operative
63 Grad
64 Author James
65 More than
66 Crib cry
67 "Them" or "Us"
68 Mystic writings
69 In a while
70 One of the gang
71 Oscar-night sight

DOWN

1 Bikini event
2 Physical condition
3 Become established
4 Correct a text
5 "Return to __"
6 Painter Chagall
7 Came to earth
8 Snappy comeback
9 Make quake
10 Political crony
11 Ms. Fitzgerald
12 Section of seats
13 Color variation
21 The Beaver State
25 Modernizing prefix
27 Fire preceder
28 Unsullied
30 Pond life
31 Stagecoach puller
32 Tackle's colleagues
33 Metallic rocks
34 Find a tenant
35 __ California
36 Political opportunist
38 Louisiana county
41 Gunsel's weapon
44 Fury
48 Musically slow
49 Asparagus units
51 Flooded
53 Answer a charge
54 Actress Massey
55 "When pigs fly!"
56 Lock of hair
57 Prayer-wheel user
58 Zing
59 Big-time wrestling?
61 Take it from the top
62 Homeowner's holding

199 GETTING GOOFY

by Fred Piscop

ACROSS

1 Puccini opera
6 Biblical king
11 __ Paulo, Brazil
14 Detest
15 Full of energy
16 "__ a boy!"
17 "That's All, Folks!" series
19 Meadow
20 Ponce de __
21 Conger
22 Mark again
24 Mr. Sharif
26 "__ Back to Old Virginny"
27 Max of makeup
30 Convertible, slangily
31 *The Lady* __
32 Rayburn and Kelly
33 Unexplained sighting
36 Greek H's
37 Hand-cream additives
38 Short distance
39 Shriner's topper
40 Ships' staffs
41 Absolute
42 Naval aide
44 Drearily
45 Bone-dry
47 "Purple __" (Prince tune)
48 Total (to)
49 Dinghy need
50 Info
54 __ es Salaam
55 Sunday-news insert
58 Foolish fellow
59 Poetic muse
60 Shriver of TV
61 Mao __-tung
62 __ *Seed* ('77 movie)
63 Jazz dance

DOWN

1 Hard to believe
2 Orchestra member
3 "Get lost!"
4 Implies
5 "__ you serious?"
6 Bigot, for one
7 Hebrew month
8 __ Tin Tin
9 Excess supplies
10 Just __ (punishment)
11 Pliable toy
12 *The* __ (Mr. T series)
13 American Indian
18 Planetary lap
23 To opposite
25 Stylish, so to speak
26 Bamboolike grasses
27 Feudal estate
28 Feed the kitty
29 Custer opponent
30 Take title to anew
32 Gather slowly
34 Sense
35 Grand Ole __
37 Generator part
38 Maintain one's position
40 Like some beef
41 Mentalist Geller
43 __ Claire, WI
44 Robin Williams role
45 Camp David Accords signer
46 Collect
47 Semi-synthetic fabric
49 Aware of
51 Dynamic start
52 Barbershop order
53 PDQ
56 Asian nation, for short
57 Mornings: Abbr.

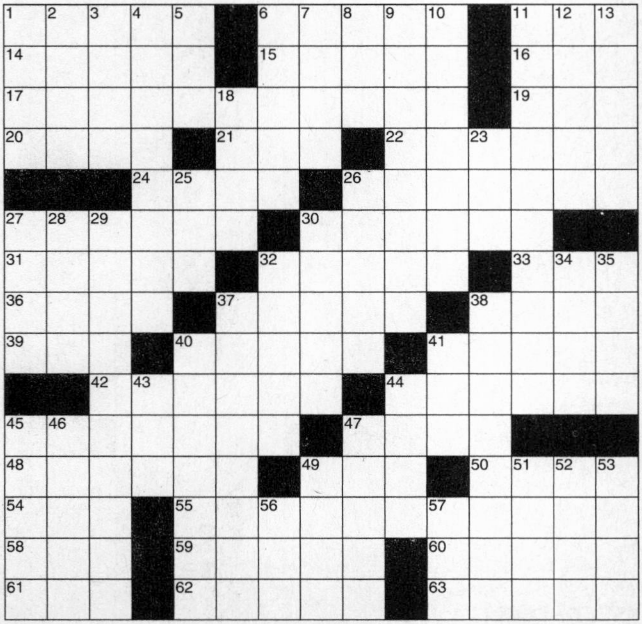

200 WATER PIX

by Alice Long

ACROSS

1 Go for a rathskeller record
5 __ as a hatter
10 Hacienda home
14 Looking up
15 __ la Paix (Paris street)
16 Polly or Mame
17 "Excuse me!"
18 More fitting
19 The Lettermen, e.g.
20 Book of pride and Joy?
22 Sham
24 Controversial tree spray
25 Feed the hogs
26 Action film of '80
33 Ham it up
34 Steno's boss
35 Hamper fill
36 "Uh-uh!"
37 Loft lava
38 Actress Zetterling
39 Airport stats.
41 Rocky peaks
42 Gather bit by bit
44 War film of '60
47 Woolly moms
48 Bridge section
49 Drawing room
52 Hold one's hand?
56 End-of-scene direction
57 Gourmand
59 *Star Trek VI* captain
60 Chorus singer
61 States
62 Iowa State address
63 Low in fat
64 Breach of judgment
65 Staple to a board

DOWN

1 Hermit by the sea
2 Jocular sounds
3 Computer owner
4 Olympics entrant
5 Ark docking site
6 Comics crew
7 Distribute
8 Wine-cooler base
9 Ghost ship
10 Unwitting tool
11 Ambiance
12 Ornery mood
13 The gamut
21 Hightail it
23 Balderdash
25 Cinderella characters
26 Clair and Auberjonois
27 Stradivari's teacher
28 Grant Wood was one
29 Commuter's home
30 Finger-pointer
31 Esau's father
32 Armor flaw
37 Otherworldly
40 Hope contemporary
42 FBI employee
43 Map-making Earth orbiter
45 Early afternoon
46 Thinly distributed
49 Ring out
50 Linchpin locale
51 Beatles' meter maid
52 Plan part
53 Wild cat
54 Sir Guinness
55 Walrus feature
58 Rock-video award

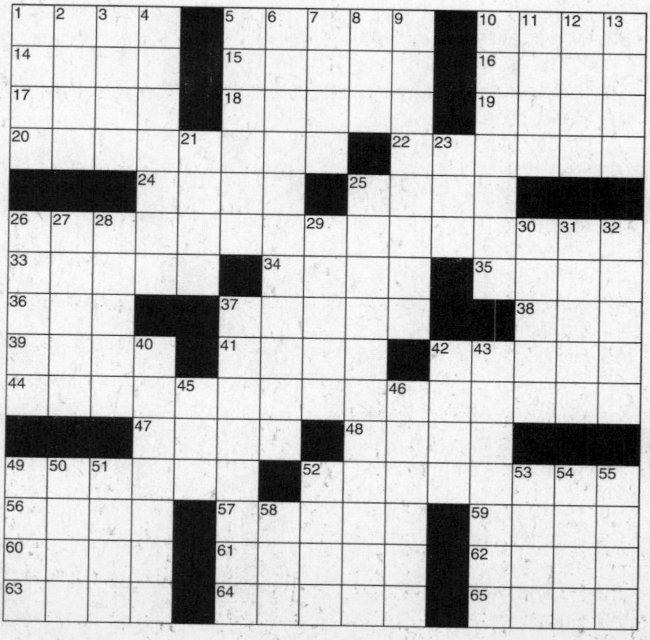

201 BOXER SHORTS

by S.N.

ACROSS
1 Hemingway's nickname
5 Petty
10 Paper package
14 "Son of __!"
15 Check receiver
16 Therefore
17 Tear apart
18 Circus emcee
20 Disapproved of
22 Cat breed
23 Wedding-song start
24 Tylenol rival
25 Trademark coined by Eastman
27 Sow's quarters
28 Track offerings
32 Like some dicts.
33 Threshold
35 When some workdays start
36 First course
38 Hosiery material
40 Hosiery shade
41 Playwright Ibsen
43 Martial art
45 Zilch
46 *Jeopardy!* contestant, often
47 One's wheels
48 Interstate stopover
50 *Coffee, __ Me?*
52 Parcel (out)
53 Lacking fullness
56 Femme fatale
59 Tourney type
61 Gallic girlfriend
62 Makes mad
63 Merman of song
64 Desideratum
65 Put together
66 Labor-history name
67 Chip in the pot

DOWN
1 Cowboy's pal
2 Screenwriter James
3 Slaphappy
4 Singer McArdle
5 Wild outburst
6 Mansion worker
7 Author Rand
8 Info gatherer
9 Wallace's running mate
10 Stifle
11 Art Deco artist
12 A long time
13 Twist's request
19 Cause for alarm
21 Pesters
24 Vacuum container
25 Buckwheat side dish
26 Tubular instruments
27 Paper layer
29 Coffee-shop worker
30 "__ Was a Lady"
31 Common sense
34 Squid's weapon
35 Abbott-Costello link
37 Sham
39 __ *Miss Brooks*
42 "__ you" (radioer's reply)
44 Sign of the future
47 Road Runner's foe
49 Canadian capital
51 To the point
52 Macho
53 Barbershop job
54 Bar-mitzvah dance
55 Felt remorseful
56 Appearance
57 "__ We Got Fun"
58 Rose or Rozelle
60 Food-preservative initials

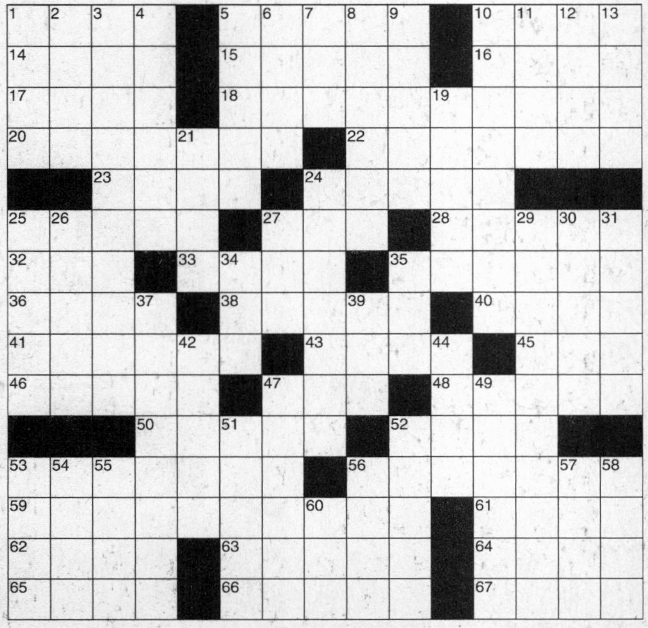

202 APT ANAGRAMS

by Eric Albert

ACROSS

1 Repeated idea
6 Unflinching
11 Refuse to commit
14 On the whole
15 Rallying cry
16 Dorm covering
17 AN ORAL EDICT anagram
19 Storage receptacle
20 Type of triangle
21 Actress Scacchi
23 Unruffled
24 Ardently enthusiastic
25 Do some damage to
29 Writer Runyon
30 Pitcher's place
31 Donut covering
33 Sponsored messages
36 Small horse
37 Mondale's nickname
38 Telegram term
39 __ Lanka
40 The sauce
41 Yerba __, CA
42 Pool-hall predator
44 Schoolwork holder
45 Church split
47 Uncovered wagon
49 Arizona city
50 Thatcher's group
55 Lyric poem
56 NAME FOR SHIP anagram
58 Was in charge of
59 Bridge phrase
60 Be a squealer
61 *D.C. Cab* actor
62 Midafternoon
63 Deuce beaters

DOWN

1 Skirt style
2 Small bills
3 Mexican munchie
4 Evils
5 Soft and limp
6 Rabbi detective
7 Eskimo carving
8 Elevator inventor
9 "Who am __ complain?"
10 Sting, e.g.
11 BEAR HIT DEN anagram
12 Juan's wife
13 Caged talker
18 Bring up
22 Pi follower
24 Heckle
25 Mischievous kids
26 Othello, for one
27 NINE THUMPS anagram
28 __ *Which Way You Can*
29 See regularly
31 Understand, in sci-fi slang
32 Claiborne of fashion
34 Sufficiently cooked
35 Sail supporter
37 Make up
38 Grab some rays
40 Average improver
41 Walk-on
43 With it
44 __ Mawr
45 Rant and rave
46 Chest material
47 Small-tree thicket
48 Get out of bed
50 Former Russian ruler
51 At a distance
52 Learning method
53 Aeneas' home
54 Strong longings
57 Dashboard letters

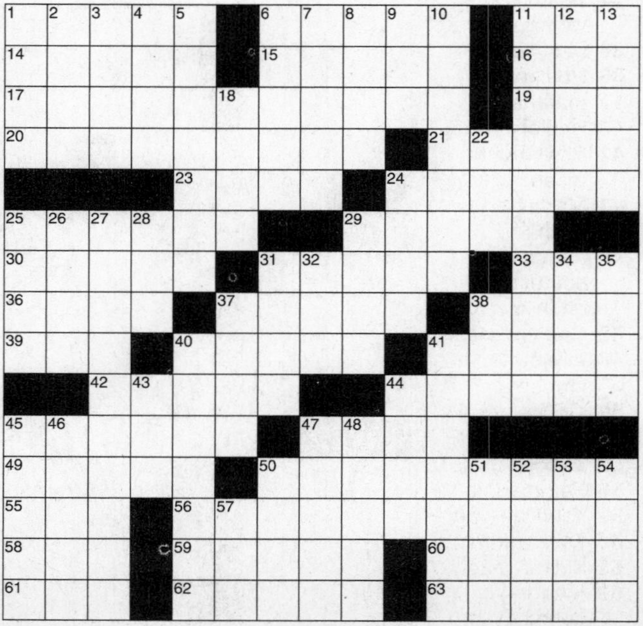

203 PLACE SETTING

by Ronnie K. Allen

ACROSS

1 Yodeler's perch
4 "__ to you!" (buck-passer's words)
9 Genghis, e.g.
13 Coral formation
15 Kid-lit rabbit
16 Local theater, for short
17 Exxon rival
18 Introduction
19 Gilligan's home
20 Impolite one
21 Like __ of bricks
22 In pursuit of
23 Ebert's former partner
25 Form of pollution
27 Employees
29 Rang out
33 Kind of boom
36 Distinctive quality
38 Cairo's water
39 "__ in Rome . . ."
40 Man-made fiber
41 Yuletide buy
42 Part of MIT
43 Court jester
44 Birdcall
45 __ City (Batman's base)
47 Highway alert
49 Civil-rights leader Medgar
51 Farm horse
55 Ms. Barton
58 Quasimodo's creator
60 Jason's ship
61 Hawaiian city
62 Active strength
63 Select
64 Author Bombeck
65 Just ridiculous
66 Tie feature
67 Leafed through
68 Customs
69 "Little piggie"

DOWN

1 Sheiks' subjects
2 Poet Jones
3 Texas river
4 African speedster
5 Legal wrong
6 *Mary Poppins* tune, with "A"
7 "__ HOOKS" (crate phrase)
8 *Miss __ Disposes* (Tey novel)
9 Metaphorical treachery
10 Possess, previously
11 Competent
12 __-do-well
14 Traveler's choices
22 Bat wood
24 Handy abbr.
26 Optimistic phrase
28 Gambling game
30 Soggy bog
31 General Robert __
32 Heartfelt
33 Quick gulp
34 Remark of dismay
35 Robin's home
37 Rock partner
40 "All __" (Sinatra tune)
44 __-Magnon man
46 Actress Gardner
48 Idolizes
50 Horned herbivore
52 Main impact
53 Northern hemisphere?
54 *North Dallas Forty* star
55 One-name singer
56 Pisa dough
57 __ mater
59 Auctioneer's last word
62 See 62 Across

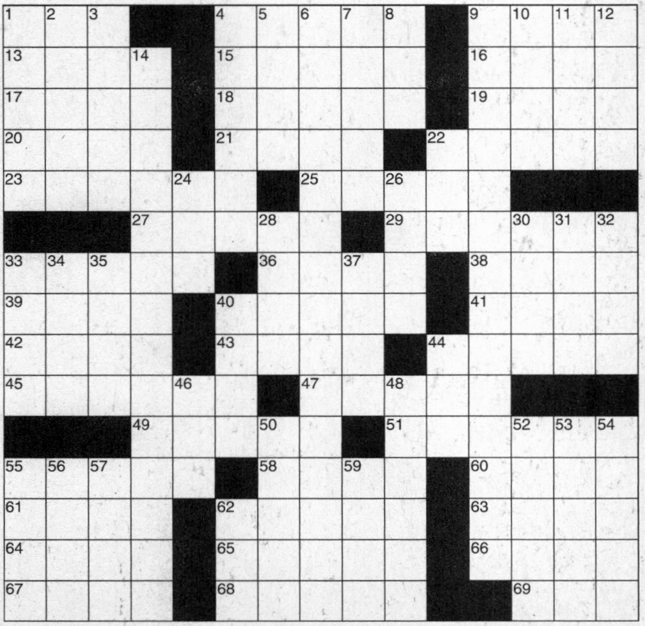

204 CARD TRICKS

by Karen Hodge

ACROSS
1 Beaver's project
4 *M*A*S*H* star
8 Tend to the turkey
13 Composer Bartók
14 Nuthatch's nose
15 Sandwich snacks
16 Rack's partner
17 One opposed
18 Ferber novel
19 Baseball star?
22 Literary class
23 Undergrad deg.
24 RR stop
27 Golfer's iron?
32 D.C. lobby
35 Mah-jongg piece
36 Teasdale et al.
37 "I've Got __ in Kalamazoo"
39 High spirits
42 Used to be
43 Less easy to find
45 Neckline shapes
47 Atl. flier
48 World-class lover?
52 Santa __, CA
53 Busy buzzer
54 Select few
58 Hammett trilogy?
63 ". . . I say, not __"
65 Burglar's take
66 NBAer, for short
67 Kind of prize
68 Poet Pound
69 Cabbage kin
70 Bops on the bean
71 Hind or hart
72 Foxy

DOWN
1 Two in a deck
2 Out of this world
3 Feudal estates
4 "I'm __ boy!"
5 Director Riefenstahl
6 Computer input
7 With hands on hips
8 After-dinner drinks
9 Dry as dust
10 Comforts
11 Wernher __ Braun
12 Superlative suffix
13 Toot one's own horn
20 Verse syllables
21 Taking a vacation
25 Ski lifts
26 Something desirable
28 Get-up-and-go
29 Actor Wallach
30 Daredevil's need
31 Long-armed entity
32 Juneau jacket
33 Once more
34 Lapel flower
38 Trip component
40 Crumpets' colleague
41 Yonder yacht
44 Scotch cocktails
46 Start walking
49 Service charge
50 Well-__ (loaded)
51 Pants
55 Ultimate standard
56 Brit's boob tube
57 Italian princely family
59 Manual: Abbr.
60 Exude
61 Fairway warning
62 Top-billed one
63 Letter openers?
64 Jack of *Barney Miller*

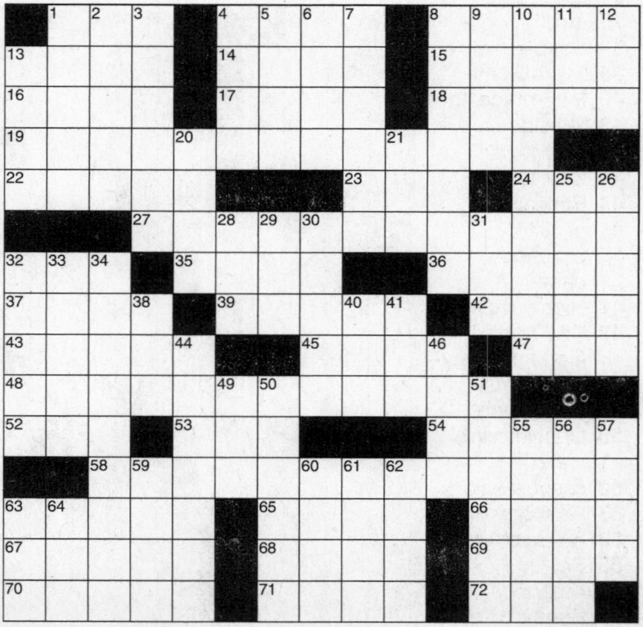

205 SPORTS FIGURES

by Trip Payne

ACROSS

1 Funny one
5 Slack-jawed
10 Does in
14 Melville novel
15 Cato, for one
16 Sing lightly
17 Tippling baseballer?
20 Ottawa's prov.
21 "__ only as directed"
22 Billy __ Williams
23 Earth-conscious org.
24 Fred Astaire's sister
26 Unadorned
27 Mah-jongg suit
28 Actress Thompson
29 Fourth Estate
31 Cat's-paw
32 They may be aquiline
34 *I Know Why the __ Bird Sings*
35 Former Soviet footballer?
39 Sheets of glass
40 Calendar page
41 Hts.
42 Put up with
44 Goofs up
48 Tell a whopper
49 Read quickly
50 High-minded
51 __ Arbor, MI
52 Plant pouch
53 Alley follower
55 RR destination
56 Serious basketballer?
60 Biblical brother
61 Love, Italian-style
62 __ *fixe*
63 Noticed
64 Toyland visitors
65 Social misfit

DOWN

1 Hot drinks
2 Donohoe of *L.A. Law*
3 Went bad
4 Happy's brother
5 Greek warmonger
6 Quayle's successor
7 "__ Blue?"
8 National Zoo beasts
9 Puts in one's diary
10 Bullring cheer
11 Pyromaniacs
12 Swatter alternative
13 Really mad
18 Cry's partner
19 __ *Haw*
25 Jousting needs
26 Wedding figure
29 Greek letter
30 Stimpy's cartoon pal
31 Prancer's sleighmate
33 Approves of
34 Director's yell
35 Indonesian islander
36 Ant's receptors
37 Sweetie pie
38 Put a stop to
39 Royal residences
42 Ancient amulet
43 City on Puget Sound
45 Occupy a spot
46 Cat, often
47 Didn't move
49 Compass pt.
50 Coll. student's pride
53 Mean one
54 Mines' lines
57 Cask of wine
58 Vest pocket
59 Word on Burgundy bottles

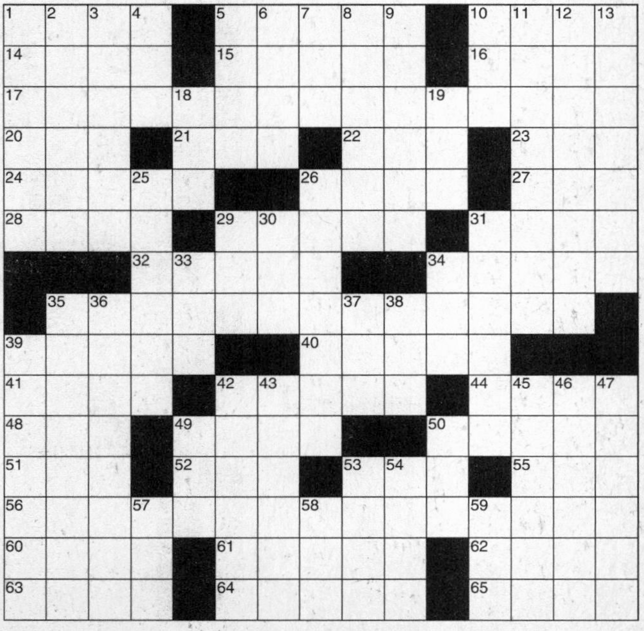

206 MEN OF LETTERS

by David Owens

ACROSS
1 Phony
5 In the center of
9 Gourmet James
14 Sprint need
15 Tough to find
16 Beer variety
17 *Joie de vivre*
18 Yoked team
19 Big family
20 Lower-case poet
23 Chihuahua cheers
24 Pastrami surroundings
25 Life of Riley
26 Togs' tags
28 Job to do
29 Actress Anderson
30 Jingle writers
33 Unsuitability
38 Bubble up
39 It may be purple
40 Break sharply
41 Tubular tobacco
43 Actor McDowall
44 Clever folks
45 Cowboy's strap
47 Cash alternative
50 "I'm __ boy!": Costello
51 H.S. subj.
54 Weak, as excuses
55 *Monkey Business* screenwriter
58 "__ ear and out . . ."
60 Arkin or Alda
61 Broadcasts
62 Present time
63 Moore of *Ghost*
64 Gin flavoring
65 Aggressive sort
66 Toward Tangier
67 Circus structure

DOWN
1 Direct
2 *Roots* author
3 Quite quickly
4 Diner's directory
5 Olfactory inputs
6 Ankle coverers
7 "Goodnight __"
8 Chinese leader
9 Sandwich order
10 "Miniver Cheevy" poet
11 Fleet-footed
12 Mutineer, e.g.
13 Cassini creation
21 Intend
22 Ski spot
27 Army or carpenter
28 Peter O'Toole portrayal
29 High-tech tools
30 *Millionaire* network
31 "Why __ Love You?"
32 Russian plane
34 "__ on your life!"
35 Grid player
36 Regrettable
37 Catch sight of
39 __ *Dragon* (Disney film)
42 Oil apparatus
43 Sally in space
46 Make money the old-fashioned way
47 Dirty Harry player
48 Asian capital
49 Surrounded by
50 Cop __
51 Your umbrella?
52 *Gigi* star
53 Mini-map
56 Green gem
57 Ultimate
59 Mountain ending

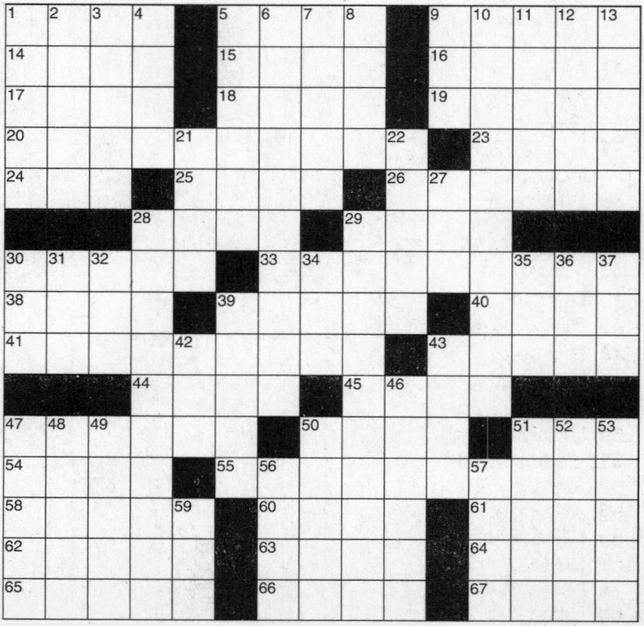

207 SCUBA SIGHTINGS

by Bob Lubbers

ACROSS

1 Barrymore or Pearson
5 Singer Vikki
9 They often overrun
14 Be concerned
15 *M*A*S*H* star
16 Bracelet locale
17 Lawn intruder
19 Come in second
20 Algiers district
21 Bandleader's "Go!"
23 Fly high
26 More sensible
28 Paint with dots
31 *"Ach du __!"*
33 Stays away from
34 Actress Barkin
36 Flamenco shout
37 Drops a fly, e.g.
38 Pick up the tab
39 Hazel, for one
40 *Wayne's World* word
41 Sp. misses
42 Took a chance
43 New Orleans school
45 Duelists' aides
47 Evil spirit
48 Love god
49 Geeks
51 Monster's nickname
56 Process ore
58 He takes a lot of interest in his work
61 Desi's daughter
62 Willing partner
63 Popular houseplant
64 Actor Werner
65 Pleasingly warm
66 Repair

DOWN

1 800, to Antony
2 "Ta-__-Boom-De-Ré"
3 Historic times
4 Friday portrayer
5 Drive-in server
6 Pie-mode link
7 Hwys.
8 Too swift to act
9 Bligh's title
10 Working, as a computer
11 *Back to the Future* prop
12 RN's specialty
13 Get the point
18 Sounds of shock
22 Geographic speck
24 Wide awake
25 Set free
27 Banks (on)
28 Cover in mystery
29 Sweater style
30 __ and outs
32 Funny Foxx
33 Mailed away
35 Medical beam
38 General course
39 *__ of La Mancha*
41 Bull, often
42 Vitamin amounts
44 Aviator Earhart
46 Fleeced
50 Bridge coup
52 Something phony
53 12/26 event
54 Tailor's tool
55 Supplemented, with "out"
56 __-mo replay
57 Greek letters
59 Sapporo sash
60 Completely

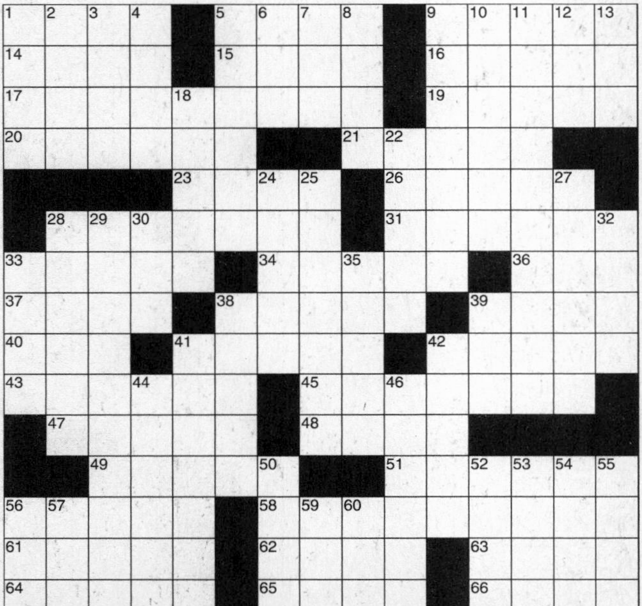

208 FARM CAMP

by Wayne R. Williams

ACROSS

1 Hankering
5 Tonsorial tool
10 Flat-bottomed boat
14 Cairo's river
15 Attu resident
16 Star stage
17 Race edges
19 Hebrew measure
20 Boom times
21 Pavarotti, e.g.
22 Unwritten promise
23 Cleaned the deck
25 Persian Gulf fed.
28 Funny Charlotte
29 State of readiness
30 One way to win
33 Junction point
34 Salon job
35 Speakers' platforms
36 Theme of the puzzle
39 Court business
42 Smeltery stack
43 Put up a fuss
47 Sincere
49 Kukla's colleague
50 Mess up
51 Possesses
52 Bring into being
53 Confess
55 Impassive one
58 Kingsley or Jonson
59 Landscape dip
60 Political issue
62 Pindar's output
63 Battery terminal
64 Latin 101 verb
65 Poetry syllables
66 Thumbs-up answers
67 Beer ingredient

DOWN

1 Monstrous
2 Fresco painter
3 Held tight
4 Contraction with two meanings
5 Scored
6 King of comedy
7 Love, to Laver
8 Win a chase
9 Civ. liberties
10 Bamboozle
11 Nation off Mozambique
12 Frighten into defeat
13 Game officials
18 Proofreading term
24 Like better
26 Confuse
27 Jacob's twin
30 __ *Alibi* (Selleck film)
31 Dramatist Fugard
32 Gardener's tool
34 Antibiotic precursor
37 Solemn vow
38 TV screen
39 Before
40 Spread throughout
41 Former convict, perhaps
44 "Heart of Dixie"
45 Word-for-word
46 Most sharp
48 Ancient Palestinian
49 Theater sec.
52 Summons to court
54 Author Nathanael
56 Southwest art colony
57 Ye __ Tea Shoppe
60 Foal feed
61 Machine part

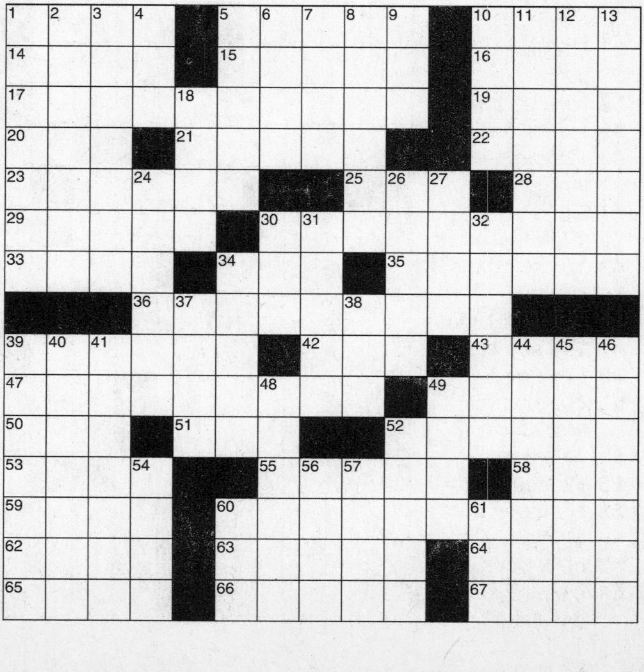

209 ON TIME

by Shirley Soloway

ACROSS

1 Wilander of tennis
5 Guns the engine
9 "Oh!"
13 Working hard
14 Shake off
15 Iowa city
16 Fast-food drink
17 Mrs. Perón
18 Shopping center
19 No time at all
22 Golf ball's position
23 Yule song
24 Casino employee
26 Latter-day
29 College major
31 Get away from
32 Copycat
33 Guided trip
36 Nothing at all
37 Go backwards
40 Suffix for press
41 __ podrida
43 Salad to sundae
44 Shirt size
46 Swallow
48 Removed the suds
49 Fast talk
51 __ good example
52 *Strangers __ Train*
53 Beef cut
59 Mayonnaise covers
61 Weather satellite
62 Aware of
63 Rat-__
64 Functional
65 Circus cat
66 Beams of light
67 Ltr. encl.
68 Author Ferber

DOWN

1 Brit's raincoats
2 On the summit
3 Cash drawer
4 Dyed furniture
5 Have a blast
6 Monumental
7 Turn down
8 Does a hatchet job on
9 Time after midnight
10 Time after midnight
11 Unearthly
12 Organic compound
14 Adjust your clock
20 Skin cosmetic
21 Actress Ruby
25 Burlesque bit
26 Casino city
27 Villainous
28 Go home
29 Dieter of rhyme
30 Fruit cover
32 Long time
34 Do lobbying
35 Oboe insert
38 Honorary title
39 Narrow openings
42 Opp.-meaning word
45 Author France
47 Precious stone
48 Singer Della
49 Of interest to Peary
50 Ms. Bryant
51 Fur piece
54 Silents actress Naldi
55 *Exodus* author
56 Oklahoma city
57 Like __ of bricks
58 Hawaiian resort coast
60 Canonized ones: Abbr.

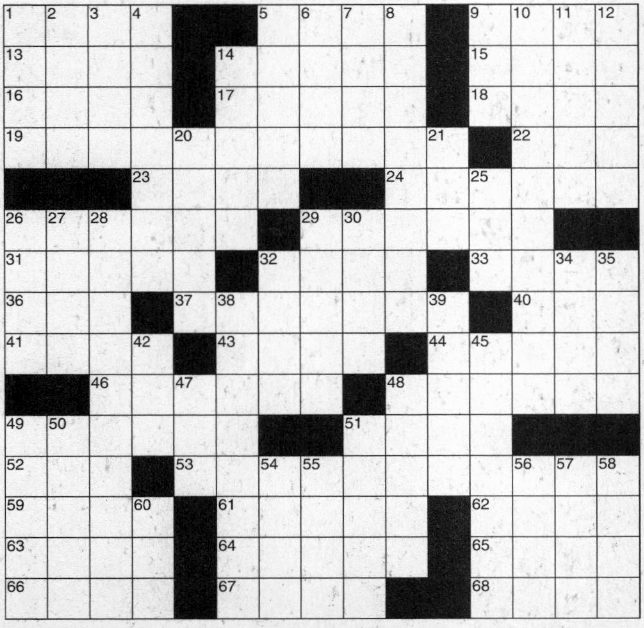

210 THEY'RE NUMBER ONE

by Trip Payne

ACROSS

1 Loft cube
5 Emergency call
8 Young haddock
13 Squashed circle
14 Lunch container?
16 Butler's concern
17 National Leaguers
18 Reunion attender
19 A clue like this has four of them
20 Wage earners
23 Language ending
24 Vane dir.
25 Batman and Penguin, e.g.
29 Star in Cygnus
31 Riveter of song
33 "I don' wanna!"
34 Zombie ingredient
36 Smoke, for short
37 Raison d'__
38 Movie-musical dancer
42 Sushi-bar selections
43 Rocky peak
44 Tire contents
45 Company quota?
46 Straightens out
48 "Horse behind bars"
52 It goes to your head
54 From A __
56 Squeal (on)
57 *The Robe* star
60 Pop-jazz singer
63 Olympic weapon
64 Hurries along
65 Kick out
66 Real bummer
67 Igor, for one: Abbr.
68 Shows the way
69 Sumac of song
70 Volstead opponents

DOWN

1 Failed badly
2 Disinclined
3 Triangular-sailed ship
4 Klensch of fashion
5 Bring forth
6 More overtly suave
7 Totally surprise
8 Dinner party
9 Unjumpable gorge
10 Zodiac animal
11 Eye, to a poet
12 Legal offs.
15 Soap-opera gimmick
21 Fix a program
22 Puzzlement
26 Excited by
27 Make worthy of
28 Yonder yacht
30 Fouls up
32 Earthy color
35 Kilo's system
37 Homonym of 44 Across
38 Back street
39 Not quite straight
40 Made a difference
41 Pie before dessert
42 H's ancestor
46 *Equal Justice* scenes
47 Steady succession
49 Black-and-blue mark
50 Least common
51 Explosive experiments
53 Like Yale walls
55 The end
58 Grand Ole __
59 Spring event
60 Author Kaufman
61 Tin Woodman's tool
62 Evian or Bath

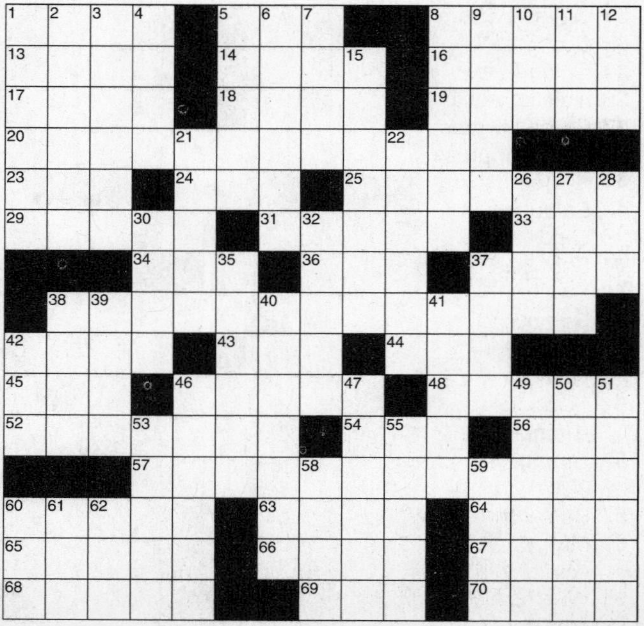

211 PRECIOUS

by Eric Albert

ACROSS

1 Quick kiss
5 Columnist Herb
9 "Nattering nabobs" veep
14 Singer Guthrie
15 Actor Alan
16 Play genre
17 Muffin ingredient
18 *Pal* __
19 Kind of kitchen
20 Stevenson character
23 Mork's planet
24 Styled like
25 Comrade
26 Parting word
27 Gomer of TV
28 Famous first baseman
31 Jokingly
34 *The Bridge of San Luis* __
35 Induce
36 Exec's protection
40 Roman poet
41 Writer Rand
42 Pulitzer poet Conrad
43 Music style
44 Sherry stopper
45 Current unit
46 Show anger
47 Justice Fortas
48 Chat
51 Marilyn Monroe, for one
55 *Ulysses* writer
56 Noted canal
57 Author Victoria
58 Ms. Moorehead
59 Morning meal
60 Leave out
61 TV Hall of fame
62 Storied septet
63 Goddess of youth

DOWN

1 Picasso or Casals
2 Inaccuracy
3 Chain sound
4 Movie monster
5 Wheedle
6 Hawaiian greeting
7 Perfect place
8 One opposed
9 Fitness expert Davis
10 Unexpected extra
11 Hoopster Archibald
12 Kuwaiti ruler
13 Pallid
21 Mansfield of movies
22 *The Man From U.N.C.L.E.* character
26 Melville hero
27 4/1 action
28 *The Winds of War* author
29 Can't stand
30 Plow pullers
31 Composer Stravinsky
32 TV science show
33 Go crazy
35 Pot item
37 Mama Judd
38 European range
39 "Ship of the desert"
44 Affectedly attractive
45 Convent head
46 Diamond plane
47 García's girlfriend
48 Folklore being
49 Extemporize
50 Margo in *All About Eve*
51 Cartoon possum
52 Vanessa's sister
53 Advocate strongly
54 "Yikes!"
55 Bread spread

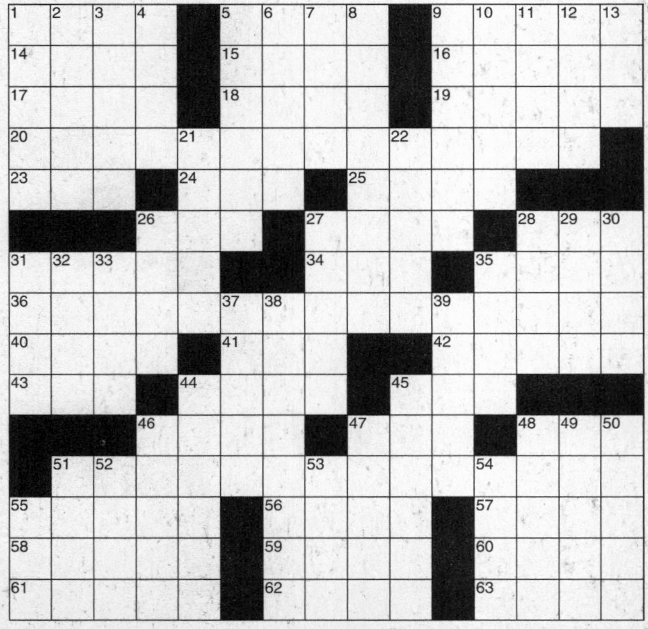

212 SISTER CITIES

by Rebecca Alexander

ACROSS
1 Luce's creation
5 Unornamented
10 Actor Mineo
13 Maturing agent
14 Sonata movements
16 Sen. Sessions' state
17 City on the Mohawk
19 Tasseled topper
20 The way things work
21 Gray work
23 Tit for __
24 Ballet bend
26 City on the Ohio
32 Band section
33 Vladimir's vetoes
34 Dine
36 "__ to differ!"
37 Words to the audience
38 Seles' org.
39 West ender
40 Fetch
41 Like krypton
42 Bulldogs' hometown
45 Clan man
46 Mixologist's milieu
47 Capital way down south
50 Capital management
54 Coffee brewer
55 Northwestern lumber town
59 In the past
60 Beethoven's Third
61 Not irregular
62 Osaka scratch
63 Interrupt dancers
64 Flower droplets

DOWN
1 Infield cover
2 Fictional aide
3 Office note
4 Putting up
5 Magic word
6 Weather fronts
7 Unspecific amount
8 Oath response
9 Postal-creed word
10 In the clear
11 Hasn't __ to stand on
12 Slothful
15 Hanks of yarn
18 Closes in on
22 Summer sign
24 Fraternity hopeful
25 Lo-cal
26 Charmer's snake
27 Don't exist
28 Refuse to budge
29 Using a chaise
30 Japanese-American
31 *Kama* __
32 Move quickly
35 Butter bit
37 Cartoonist Peter
38 Still to be marked
40 Suit well
41 Qum resident
43 FDR VP
44 Luke's mentor
47 Berth place
48 Push along
49 A party to
50 Central points
51 Church area
52 Prepare to swallow
53 Many a millennium
56 Mythical monster
57 Old French coin
58 Summer-camp apprentice: Abbr.

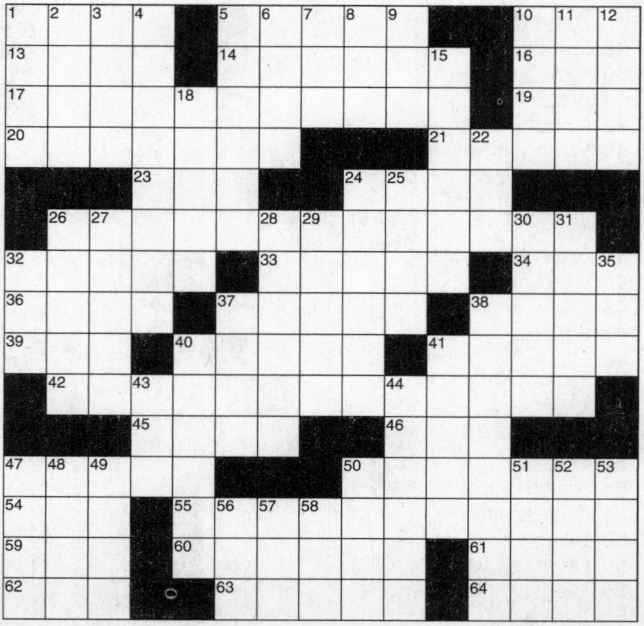

213 EASY AS PIE

by Richard Silvestri

ACROSS

1 Spruce cousin
4 All by oneself
8 Reads carefully (over)
13 *Coffee, Tea, __?*
14 Enjoy gum
15 Accustom
16 Pizza topping
18 Zoo attraction
19 Addison colleague
20 Author Seton
22 Works too hard
24 Attic
28 Hair jobs
30 1850s war site
32 Pile up
35 Pizza topping
37 Actor Ayres
38 Sports-shoe attachment
39 Explosive letters
40 Pizza topping
43 Rodeo rope
45 Flow (in)
46 Ade ingredient
48 Shut carefully
50 Corrupt
53 Belt holder
55 Be a snitch
57 Bakery emanation
61 Pizza topping
63 First-discovered asteroid
64 Alpine comeback
65 Pillage
66 Big happening
67 Homeowner's holding
68 McMahon and Sullivan

DOWN

1 Worries
2 Drive forward
3 Summer TV fare
4 Slide-show need
5 Cry of contempt
6 Singing Horne
7 Due (to)
8 Peru conqueror
9 __ in a million
10 Massage
11 Make a blunder
12 Dead or Red
13 Co-__ (urban apartments)
17 Bill Clinton's idol
21 Big boat
23 Play for time
25 *6 Rms __ Vu*
26 Sends forth
27 Freezing temperatures
29 Fishhook fastener
31 Regarding
32 Charitable donation
33 Bumps into
34 In the know
36 Looked over the joint
38 Engraved gem
41 Darjeeling export
42 Sub stabilizer
43 Of a lung division
44 Mr. France
47 Stanislavsky teaching
49 Like planetaria
51 Arose
52 *St. __ Fire*
54 Purple shade
56 Superlative suffix
57 Top-notch
58 Gun the motor
59 Bedrock deposit
60 Old boys?
62 "__ loves me . . ."

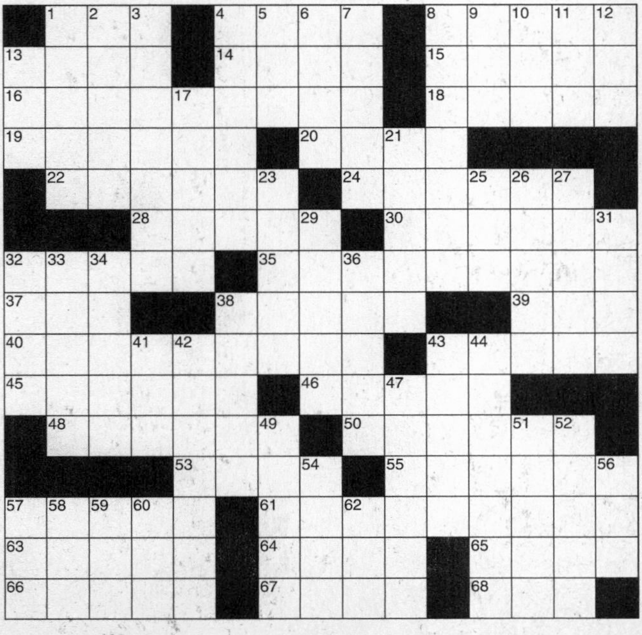

214 LETTERS FROM ATHENS

by Bill Swain

ACROSS

1 Tends the soup
6 Climbing gear
11 Ritzy rock
14 Celestial transient
15 Rock ridge
16 Pub pour
17 Relaxation waves
19 Ms. Farrow
20 Tells about
21 Hoffman Oscar film
23 Composer Jule et al.
24 Garden bloom
25 Actress Scacchi
27 Worthy of reverence
30 Short hairdo
33 Peruses
35 Get away
36 State with conviction
38 Musical combos
40 Pitcher Nolan
41 Germanic invaders
43 Conical quarters
45 Mach 2 traveler
46 Explosive mixture
48 Outcropping
50 Hooky player
52 Mariners
56 '92 World Series winner
58 Southwest sight
59 Fuss
60 Like some sleek jets
62 Author Kesey
63 John of rock
64 Pizza topping
65 Hesitater's sounds
66 Fabric workers
67 Assays, e.g.

DOWN

1 Lasting impressions
2 Apartment sign
3 Use subtlety
4 Put back pictures
5 Ancient Greek coins
6 Cheerleading yells
7 Adjective suffix
8 Lab's __ dish
9 Allen and Frome
10 Highly original
11 Atomic photons
12 Director Kazan
13 Have in mind
18 Excise
22 More simpatico
24 Most wacky
26 Sour-tasting
28 Spacewalks: Abbr.
29 Push in
30 __ California
31 Egg cell
32 Particle accelerators
34 Second-year student
37 Nostalgic clothes style
39 Vacillate
42 Rang, as a bell
44 Gray was one
47 Since last week
49 Animals
51 *Teachers* star
53 Caspar was one
54 Standing tall
55 Focal points
56 Carry off
57 German river
58 __ *souci* (carefree)
61 Rocky crag

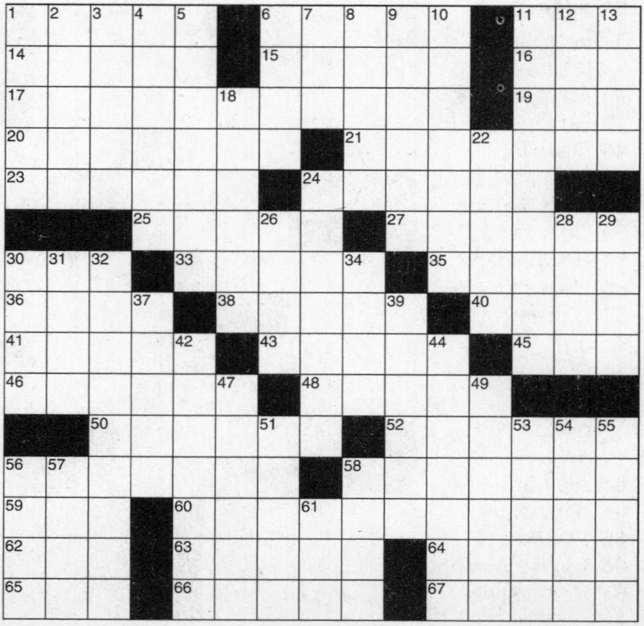

215 *BREAKFAST ORDERS*

by Randolph Ross

ACROSS

1 Reiner or Lowe
4 Last word in prayer
8 Delicious or Granny Smith
13 Major work
15 Singer Falana
16 Polynesian parties
17 Breakfast order
20 "Get lost!"
21 San Diego attraction
22 *Casablanca* character
23 European capital
26 Queue after Q
28 Breakfast order
36 Luxurious
37 Arkin or Alda
38 Win by __
39 Sculptures and such
40 Most clichéd
42 Hwy.
43 Mythology branch
45 Maryland collegian
46 __ off (angry)
47 Breakfast order
50 Cambodia's Lon __
51 Genesis locale
52 Datum
55 Cable network
58 Becker of tennis
62 Breakfast order
66 Cook's wear
67 Brainstorm
68 Filet fish
69 Othello's countrymen
70 Told tall tales
71 Danson of *Cheers*

DOWN

1 Fabled birds
2 Cartel initials
3 Perry Mason portrayer
4 100%
5 Lower the lawn
6 Brit. monarch
7 Post-WWII alliance
8 Governor Landon
9 Overly moral one
10 Name of six popes
11 Director Buñuel
12 *"¿Cómo __ usted?"*
14 Hunt
18 Run __ (go crazy)
19 Hirt's instrument
24 Castle protection
25 Some black keys
27 Sing like Ella
28 Point of view
29 *Burden of Proof* author
30 National Leaguer
31 Archaeologist's word form
32 Hit __ (affect)
33 '88 Olympics host
34 Adlai's '56 running mate
35 Run-down
40 Utah's state flower
41 Exceeded the limit
44 Summoned
46 Parts of wood joints
48 Sticky stuff
49 Country singer McEntire
52 Con game
53 "__ the mornin'!"
54 Spheroid hairdo
56 Leave port
57 *The King* __
59 Melee
60 Capri, for one
61 Tool building
63 Nav. rank
64 Poor grade
65 June honoree

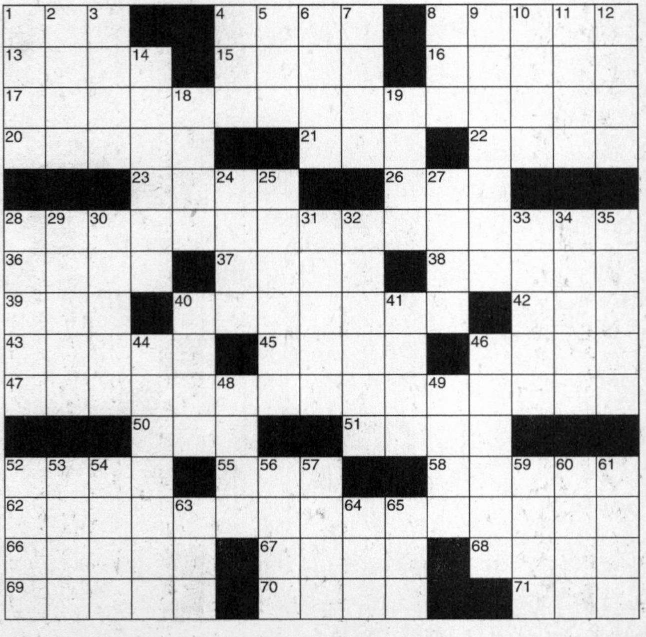

216 CLUB SONGS

by Scott Marley

ACROSS

1 Sheepish remarks
5 Art Deco artist
9 Thanksgiving celebration
14 __ cost (free)
15 Forecast word
16 Flirt
17 Song for an intergalactic golf course?
20 Was a model
21 San __, TX
22 How some order lunch
23 Mideasterner
25 Start the pot
27 Fix, as a copier
31 Purposeful trip
35 Soprano Moffo
38 Declare openly
40 Cool quarters
41 Song for an overused golf course?
44 Some kin
45 __-do-well
46 Wheel connector
47 Cow, often
49 Pipe problems
51 Half a fortnight
53 Desirable possession
57 __ Major
60 Beetle or bee
64 Inventor Whitney
65 Song for a fancy golf course?
68 Dieter's no-no
69 Telegram
70 "He's the Wiz and he lives __"
71 *Casey __ Bat*
72 Stern's opposite
73 Nix

DOWN

1 Baritone's colleagues
2 Fighting
3 Ms. Bryant
4 Henry VIII's desire
5 Leprechaun land
6 Called up
7 Buster Brown's dog
8 __ *Gay*
9 Prescription agcy.
10 Spring-basket material
11 Sax range
12 Smeltery leftovers
13 First-timer
18 Acquire
19 "__ but the brave . . ."
24 It doesn't wind up
26 Math subject
28 Golfer Stephenson
29 The Bard's river
30 Roadside inn
32 Haley of *Roots*
33 Yuletide
34 Cooked enough
35 Expressing pleasure, as a dog's tail
36 Word form for "nerve"
37 Grandma
39 "What fun!"
42 Understanding words
43 NOW cause
48 Steed's strap
50 Actress Capshaw
52 Has down cold
54 Parisian divider
55 Singer John
56 Frenzied state
57 "__-daisy!"
58 Least of the litter
59 Baseball record
61 Foul mood
62 Raison d'__
63 Sci. class
66 Five-star nickname
67 Free (of)

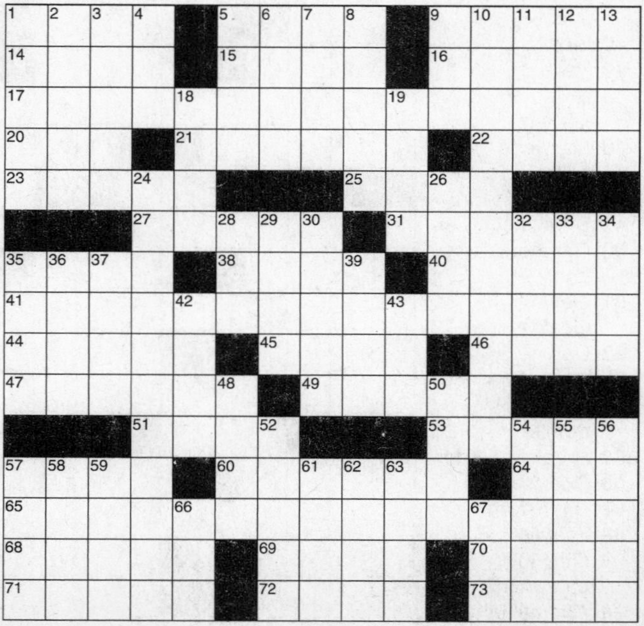

217 LAST COURSE

by Randolph Ross

ACROSS

1 High country
6 Enthusiastic
11 Fireman's tool
14 Really go for
15 Castle or Cara
16 Samovar
17 Something simple
19 Little bit
20 "__ boy!"
21 Sleeveless tops
22 Santa's stockpile
23 French king
25 __ something (scheming)
27 Favor-currying credits
33 Be situated
34 City light
35 Western range
37 __ Raton, FL
39 Juan's "one"
41 Popular cookie
42 Less fresh
45 Golden Rule word
48 OAS member
49 Neat situation
52 Medieval menial
53 Social-page word
54 Binges
57 Intermission follower
60 Scientist Sagan
64 Need to pay
65 Clever one
67 Moving vehicle
68 Richards of tennis
69 Barcelona bye-bye
70 CBS logo
71 Beasts of burden
72 Clark's foster parents

DOWN

1 Wine valley
2 Correct copy
3 Frost, for one
4 Jockey Eddie
5 Grant's foe
6 Filled (with)
7 Rainbow shapes
8 Pummel
9 Blotter mark
10 Poor grade
11 Geo or Reo
12 Diagnostic device
13 Pass catchers
18 Sheeplike
22 Kemo Sabe's pal
24 Have title to
26 Even up
27 Regional fauna and flora
28 Short summary
29 Chit
30 Listless feeling
31 Musical Mel
32 Nasty look
33 Many oz.
36 Boston Red __
38 *Suisse* sights
40 Top ranking
43 Overhead trains
44 Titles differently
46 Elixir
47 Mine find
50 Ice-cream topping
51 Puzzle out
54 Roman god
55 Not home
56 Barry or Rayburn
58 Shade source
59 Inhabitants' suffix
61 Related
62 Funny joke
63 Not as much
65 Sp. lady
66 Symbol of might

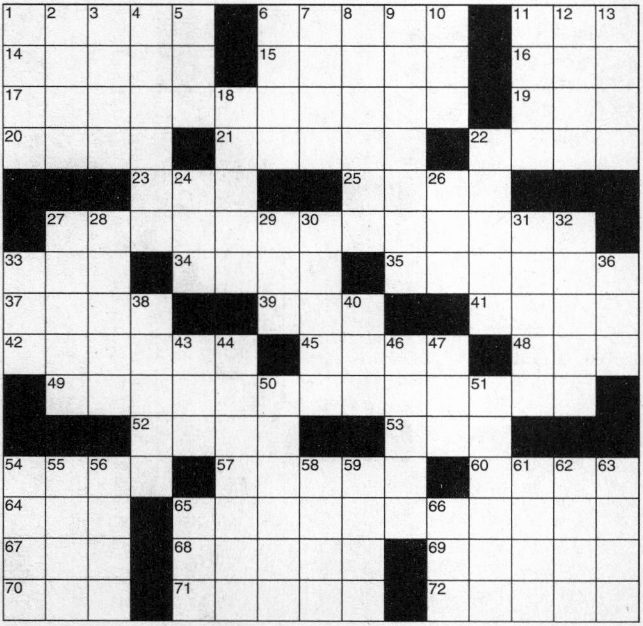

218 *SEEING RED*

by Eric Albert

ACROSS
1 Chasm
6 They have their points
10 Pronto
14 Small stream
15 Calendar row
16 Timber wolf
17 Justice, prudence, etc.
20 "__ pin, pick it up, . . ."
21 Annoy
22 Like heaven's gates
23 Carry on
25 Radio "good buddy"
26 Make stick
29 Take it easy
30 Ad-free network: Abbr.
33 Bouillabaisse base
34 Places
35 Metric weight
36 Fats Waller tune
39 Done with
40 Cafeteria carrier
41 Liking, and then some
42 Scale notes
43 Go bankrupt
44 Caustic comment
45 Look after
46 Out of control
47 A real nut
50 Relatives
51 Top with tar
55 Conan Doyle book
58 *The King and I* locale
59 Duster's target
60 Deceive
61 Thing with strings
62 Actress Jurado
63 Shell rival

DOWN
1 Basic elements
2 Scottish hillside
3 Time long past
4 Drink diluter
5 Hit the slopes
6 In the know
7 Bubbly band leader
8 *My Name Is Asher __*
9 Lam before trial
10 Sacred spot
11 Off-pitch
12 Genesis name
13 Bouquet
18 Coming soon
19 Ship hazard
24 Sore
25 Too confident
26 Can't stand
27 Booty collection
28 Sound qualities
29 Express alternative
30 Fork part
31 Count of jazz
32 Vilify
34 Of interest to tabloids
35 Big race
37 *Double Indemnity* star
38 Actor Jannings
43 Nosebag fill
44 __ oxide ointment
45 Beat badly
46 Fine and filmy
47 Redeem
48 Kubla Khan's continent
49 Rigel is one
50 Speed unit
52 Emcee Trebek
53 Kill a bill
54 School founded in 1440
56 Keogh cousin
57 British brew

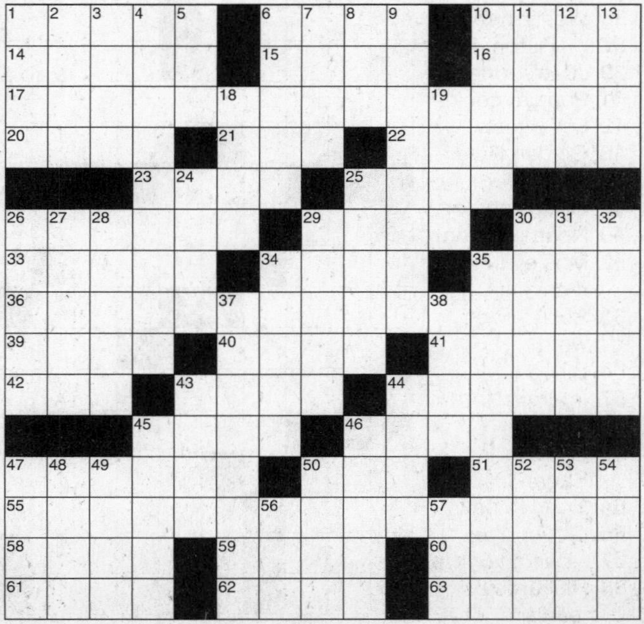

219 METALLURGY

by Shirley Soloway

ACROSS

1 Gymnast's maneuver
6 "It's __-win situation!"
9 The basics
13 Dress style
14 Sprightly tune
16 W.C. Fields' "Phooey!"
17 Fortune hunter
19 Jutland resident
20 Singer Adams
21 Elephant keeper
23 Sault __ Marie, MI
24 Puppy bite
26 Office tool
28 Ingenue, e.g.
32 Rope feature
33 __-mo replay
34 New York city
36 Composer Carmichael
39 Of Swiss peaks
41 Coach Parseghian
42 How actors enter
43 Family members
44 High-tech beam
46 Gold meas.
47 Ireland's alias
49 Bring under control
51 Makes a __ difference
54 Explorer Johnson
55 Stadium shout
56 Wiped off
59 Knocks sharply
63 Agenda element
65 Tarpon, for one
67 Sign of sorrow
68 Author Wiesel
69 Murphy of WWII
70 Leftovers
71 Blooming time: Abbr.
72 *Cagney & Lacey* star

DOWN

1 Cook's herb
2 Tramp along
3 Leslie Caron role
4 Start a paragraph
5 Turner of CNN
6 Seaweed
7 Close by, in poems
8 Butter substitutes
9 Total up
10 The nitty-gritty
11 Poem part
12 Rodeo mount
15 18-wheeler
18 Drive forward
22 Petty tyrants
25 Raymond Burr role
27 Any time now
28 __ breve (music marking)
29 American snake
30 Ball balancer
31 Mrs. Brady
33 Maple product
35 *Atlantis* org.
37 Courage
38 "May I help you?"
40 British nobleman
45 Wear away
48 Ancient Scandinavian
50 "Cheerful Little __"
51 Put on paper
52 Made of grain
53 Lays an egg
57 Vocal gaffe
58 At any time
60 Assistant
61 Greek letters
62 Ewes and mares
64 First Lady's title
66 Duster's need

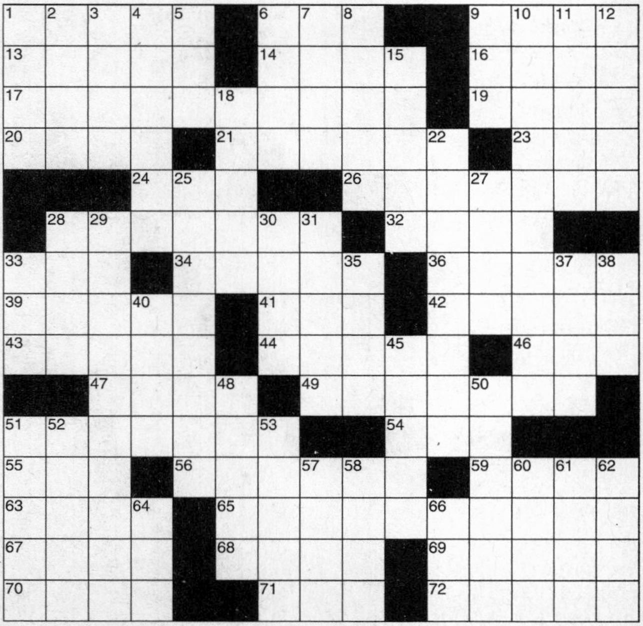

220 BON VOYAGE

by Alfio Micci

ACROSS

1 Musical finale
5 Inclined paths
10 Carnegie or Evans
14 Eager
15 *Silas Marner* author
16 Lupino and Tarbell
17 Ultimatum phrase
20 __ Miss
21 Calculator key
22 Make clear
23 Prefix for graph
24 Algerian port
25 Punjab capital
28 Small pianos
31 How others see us
32 Word on a penny
33 Point at the target
35 War god
36 In the center of
38 Comic Rudner
39 Dug in
40 Israeli statesman
41 Kind of eclipse
42 Thoroughly soak
44 Kitchen closet
45 Smell __ (be suspicious)
46 Math course
47 Wheel inventor
50 One of these days
51 Supplement, with "out"
54 Classic sitcom
57 Comic Johnson
58 Sheer fabric
59 Warble
60 Yule song
61 Went astray
62 Choir voice

DOWN

1 Roman VIP
2 Track shape
3 Netherlands sight
4 Summer quaff
5 Fix the roof
6 By oneself
7 Bog
8 Campaigning one
9 At the helm
10 Just heavenly
11 Mideast gulf
12 Not of the clergy
13 Spanish direction
18 French river
19 __-garde
23 Apparel
24 Dentist's request
25 Green bean
26 Violin maker
27 Ladies' room
28 Tea partner
29 Spoil
30 Shankar's instrument
34 "A grand old name"
36 Harsh-talking
37 Sloop pole
38 Ladder part
40 Macabre
41 "Mule Train" singer
43 Comics Captain
44 Looked into
46 Peter O'__
47 Iberian dessert
48 Architect Saarinen
49 Size up
50 Recipe verb
51 Hardly angelic
52 Town near Cleveland
53 Thus
55 Rocky peak
56 Cool __ cucumber

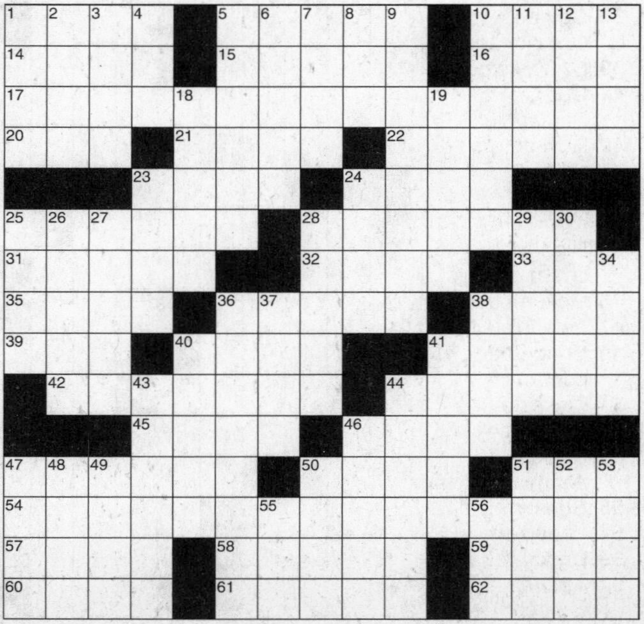

221 CRAZY

by Bob Lubbers

ACROSS

1 Truck maker: Abbr.
4 Toy-truck maker
9 Bit of gossip
14 __ de Cologne
15 Diamond miscue
16 __ nous (confidentially)
17 Wall St.'s home
18 Train pullers
20 Director's shoots
22 Scope starter
23 Long-__ (anteater-like)
26 Washes well
30 Public speaker
32 Put in fizz
34 English channel?
36 Hair cutter
38 Hair shop
39 Feels poorly
41 Kids' blocks
43 K-P filler
44 Impassive
46 "Forget it!"
48 *Oui* or *da*
49 Battle zone
51 Sound effect, for short
53 Biased
55 News stories
58 Vigoda and Burrows
60 Red as __
61 Almond accessories
67 Ecology org.
68 Pigtail, e.g.
69 Wild cat
70 Move sideways
71 Christie and Karenina
72 First vice president
73 Mag. bosses

DOWN

1 Fellows
2 Yucatan culture
3 German export
4 '60s satellite
5 Spanish gold
6 AEC successor
7 Former Surgeon General
8 Weapons: Fr.
9 Hits the hay
10 Mono- kin
11 VH-1 cousin
12 Crude copper
13 Musical notes
19 Killer whale
21 Lisbon's loc.
24 Latin abbr.
25 Jury complement
27 Range dividing Europe and Asia
28 Some summer air
29 Hard stuff
31 Radioer's response
33 Genesis name
34 Sport fish
35 Small snacks
37 Fido's friend
40 Construction area
42 Golfer Ballesteros
45 No heroes
47 Meals
50 Singer McEntire
52 Director Reiner
54 Crosby record label
56 Lukewarm
57 Half the deer
59 Lose traction
61 Shaq's league
62 Tea brewer
63 Brown shade
64 Spy grp.
65 Miss Gabor
66 Sleep phenom.

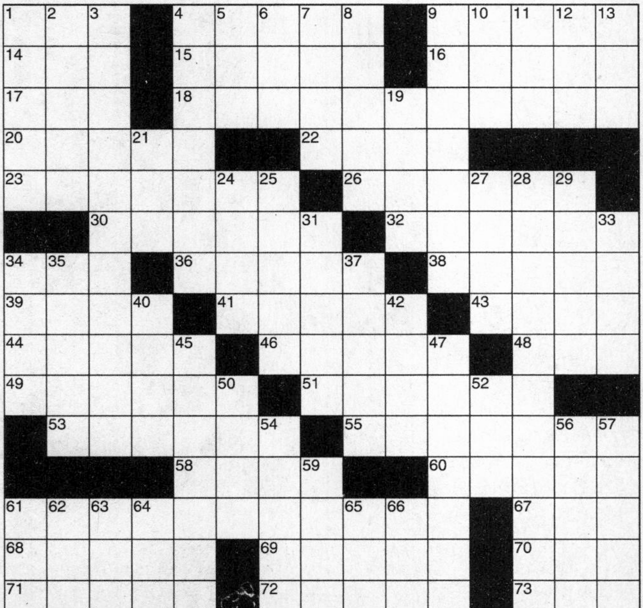

222 SOMETHING FOR ALL

by Eric Albert

ACROSS
1 Dennis the Menace's dog
5 Glance through
9 Sibilant sound
14 Kind of vaccine
15 Broad-based
16 *Cheers* role
17 TOM
20 Start the pot
21 Wet dirt
22 His, to Henri
23 Family member
24 Wild guess
26 Bishop of Rome
27 Restore to health
28 Water pipe
29 Actor Farr
30 Printing measures
31 Small eatery
32 Remnant
33 DICK
35 Singer Vic
38 Buddhist monk
39 Israeli airport
42 Dizzying designs
43 Help with the dishes
44 Kind of admiral
45 Hard and unyielding
46 Joke
47 Full of filth
48 Remain quiet
49 Anchor Rather
50 Contribute to a cause
51 HARRY
55 Sports site
56 Kampuchea's continent
57 Let loose
58 No longer bothered by
59 *What's My Line?* host
60 Donkey dinner

DOWN
1 Cartland offering
2 Heavy metal
3 Breaks stride
4 Clip
5 Give tit for tat
6 Modeling buy
7 Common vow
8 Broadway's Oakley
9 Mideast victim
10 Go Fish alternative
11 Annoying
12 Get up late
13 Hick
18 Subtle suggestion
19 Soaking spot
24 Not out
25 Father's Day gift
26 Errand doer
28 Buddy, in Britain
29 Indonesian island
31 Bit of change
32 *Newsweek* rival
33 Quad building
34 Use a VCR
35 Sirius
36 Independent of experience
37 Headwaiter
39 Smiley's creator
40 Hardwood source
41 Unmoved
43 "FOR SALE: Refrigerator, like new, $140 or best offer. Call 555-7826 evenings"
44 Head for the hills
46 Funnyman Murray
47 Cut the lawn
49 Unwilling to listen
50 6/6/44
52 LP center?
53 Stiff __ board
54 Zilch

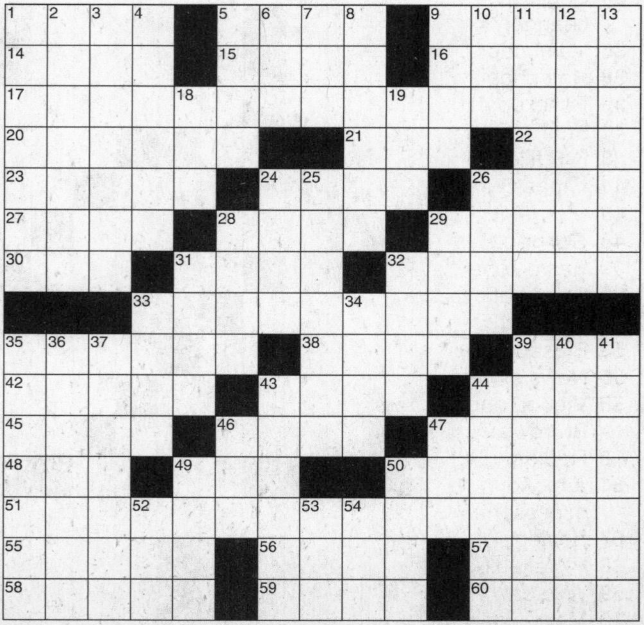

223 FIGHTING WORDS

by Shirley Soloway

ACROSS

1 Soup holders
5 Rams and roosters
10 Saudi native
14 Support in crime
15 Have __ (participate)
16 Angler's device
17 Negri of silents
18 Gold bar
19 Diminutive suffix
20 Hold back
23 Have a bite
24 Ecology agcy.
25 Santa __, CA
28 Comet part
31 Screenplay
36 Ballad subject
38 "What's __ for me?"
40 Wild West show
41 Well-positioned
44 Respectful refusal
45 Fashion mag
46 Relaxation
47 High regard
49 Make an engraving
51 Showed the way
52 "Unforgettable" name
54 Put-it-together buy
56 Act unethically
65 Neighborhood
66 Ritzy headpiece
67 Spiny houseplant
68 Broadway bestowal
69 Actress Burstyn
70 Get up
71 Last vestiges
72 Removed from copy
73 Caught in the act

DOWN

1 Abner's creator
2 Mideast name
3 Singer Carter
4 No longer fresh
5 Keep up
6 British composer
7 Captains' diaries
8 Wed in haste
9 Installations
10 Sir Guinness
11 Old Testament book
12 Comic Johnson
13 Honey bunch
21 Sort of cereal
22 Mother-of-pearl
25 Skirt style
26 Forbidden things
27 Sea shout
29 *Bus Stop* playwright
30 Sock material
32 Garden growth
33 Made in heaven
34 "__ porridge hot . . ."
35 Dragged around
37 Pennsylvania city
39 Pinball woe
42 Dunne or Castle
43 Crew member
48 Soda-shop order
50 Make tracks
53 Cotton fabric
55 Ski lifts
56 Despise
57 Heavy metal
58 Take care of
59 Hudson and Baffin
60 Financial street
61 Fruit producer
62 Author Wiesel
63 Come in second
64 SAT taker

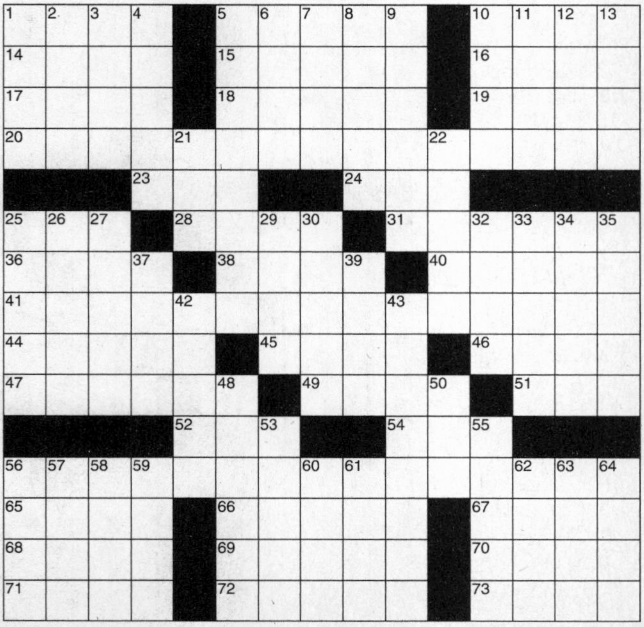

224 SPREAD IT AROUND

by Carol Fenter

ACROSS

1 A summer place
5 Start for breadth
10 Week-ending cheer
14 Actor Sharif
15 Marsh bird
16 "Rule, Britannia" writer
17 Spread it around
19 Trim back
20 Wild donkey
21 Removed varnish
23 Rogers and Clark
25 Loosen
26 Frome of fiction
29 Luxury, so to speak
31 Pear type
34 Gift-card word
35 Work on a soundtrack
36 Writer Horatio et al.
37 Daily grind
38 Auto options
40 Bigger than med.
41 Fine fur
43 Praiseful poem
44 Big family
45 Pitcher's place
46 School org.
47 Nancy Reagan's advice
48 Mall tenant
50 Young lady
52 Garden chore
55 Explains
59 Lendl of tennis
60 Spread it around
62 President in '76
63 Sully
64 Unlikely story
65 Some 49ers
66 Robert and Alan
67 Writer Gardner

DOWN

1 "It's Impossible" singer
2 To __ (unanimously)
3 Ancient Mexican
4 Theater freebie
5 Tudor name
6 __ Khan
7 Spring bulb
8 Take it easy
9 Violinist Isaac
10 Using a keyboard
11 Spread it around
12 Memo phrase
13 Cater to
18 Light gas
22 Type like *this*: Abbr.
24 Speak indistinctly
26 Mr. Zimbalist
27 Cape Cod town
28 Spread it around
30 Monastery head
32 Stadium instrument
33 __ HOOKS
35 Trivial Pursuit need
36 Historical time
38 Choice words
39 Hoss' brother
42 Has in mind
44 Girl Scout rank
46 Foreign correspondent?
47 Farm structure
49 Gaucho's rope
51 S&L items
52 Kate, to Petruchio
53 Name that may ring a bell
54 Electric-power network
56 Open slightly
57 Slow down, in mus.
58 Hook's henchman
61 Once __ blue moon

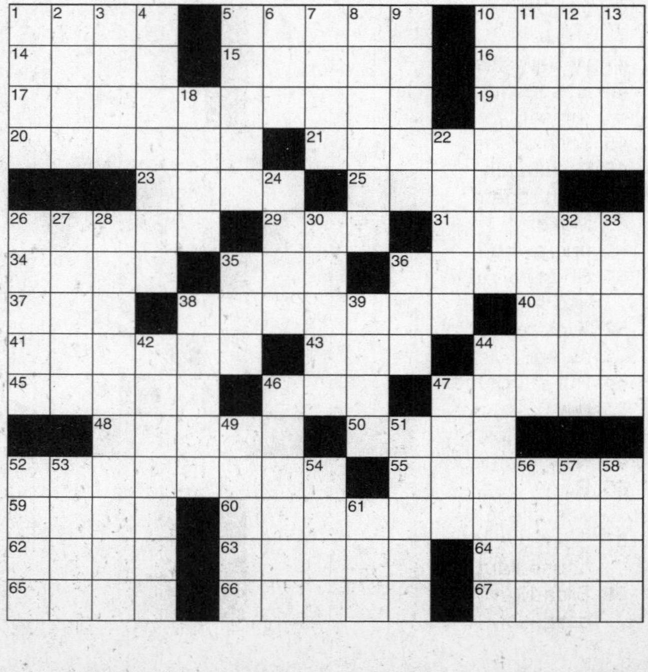

225 AT THE RODEO

by Shirley Soloway

ACROSS

1 Practice boxing
5 Country singer Davis
8 Not refined
13 Ashen
14 British noble
15 Mighty strange
16 "__ Mommy Kissing . . ."
17 Aleutian island
18 Frankie or Cleo
19 Tell lies
22 Tire town
23 Fully grown
27 Be conversant
31 Religious believer
34 Chess castle
35 National Leaguers
36 Right-angle shape
37 Serial starter
38 Comic Louis
39 Soften up
41 Rat-__
42 Standish stand-in
44 Acting haughty
47 *Mad* genre
48 "Thereby hangs __"
51 Gamble recklessly
56 Heavy metal
59 Tibia, for one
60 Before an audience
61 Room group
62 Withstand
63 __ out a living
64 Griffith and Rooney
65 ID of a sort
66 Soviet news agency

DOWN

1 Barbecue need
2 Turkish title
3 Happy as __
4 Does over
5 SAT section
6 Johnson of *Laugh-In*
7 One of the suits
8 Storage area
9 House agent
10 Onassis' nickname
11 Transgression
12 Get the point
14 "His wife could __ lean"
20 Refuses to
21 Actress Miyoshi
24 Turn over
25 Change color
26 German city
28 Intense anger
29 Synagogue scroll
30 Too __ handle
31 Floor models
32 Actress Verdugo
33 __ ease (stressed)
37 Called for
40 Parched
42 Fictional terrier
43 Info sheet
45 Spring flowers
46 Less common
49 '50s space dog
50 Arctic aides
52 Flows back
53 Antagonists
54 __ even keel
55 Not as much
56 "Be Prepared" org.
57 Dash off
58 Lend a hand

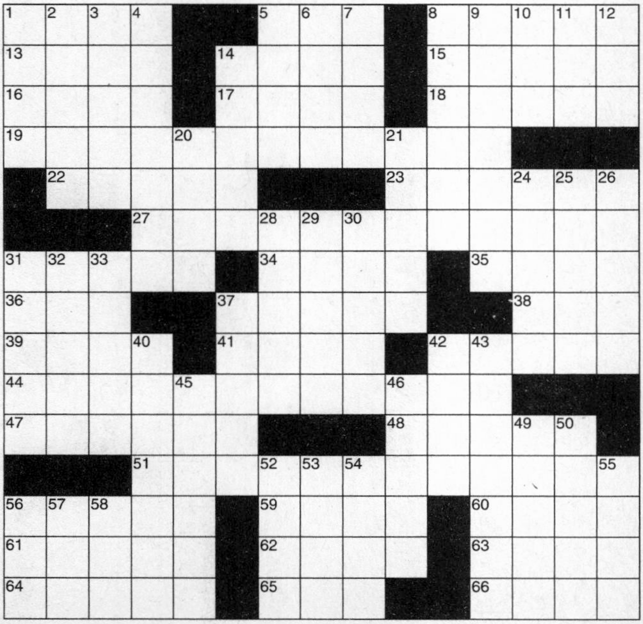

226 ON THE MOVE

by Trip Payne

ACROSS
1 Post Office buy
6 Women's mag
10 Beer ingredient
14 Singer Osmond
15 "Pants on fire" preceder
16 Nobelist Wiesel
17 Indian, for one
18 Oratorio solo
19 Tide cause
20 __ long way (last)
21 Move quickly
24 *Idée* __
25 Encircles
26 Move slowly
31 Actor Fernando
32 "Waiting for the Robert __"
33 Barracks bed
36 Riyadh resident
37 Prepares a package
39 "__ Don't Preach" (Madonna tune)
40 Hoosegow
41 Really exhausted
42 Taken in
43 Move quickly
46 Safe place
48 Diamond stats
49 Move slowly
52 List-ending abbr.
55 Ore source
56 Zimbabwe, once: Abbr.
57 Midwest metropolis
59 Cheers for toreros
60 Nary a thing
61 Wandering one
62 Hair line?
63 Exceeded 55
64 Nectarous

DOWN
1 Urban problem
2 Crunchy snack
3 General vicinity
4 Ms. Farrow
5 Solvers' tools
6 Works too hard
7 Emerald Isle
8 Cougar's home
9 HBO puppets
10 *Cats* song
11 Orally
12 NFL team
13 Take care of
22 Gas' word form
23 Make mad
24 Exerciser's concern
26 Show offense, perhaps
27 Word in many Bugs Bunny titles
28 "__ Old Cowhand"
29 Wasteland
30 Heidi's hangout?
33 Roman statesman
34 Available to the public
35 Sharp flavor
37 *Shane* and *Silverado*
38 Bleachers cry
39 Bosom buddies
41 *Night Court* character
42 Masthead names
43 Least civil
44 Ate away
45 __ Dhabi
46 String-quartet member
47 Poisonous reptile
49 Unpopular play
50 "Just __, skip and a jump away"
51 Doggie munchie
52 Roof feature
53 Quaker pronoun
54 Golfer's vehicle
58 Cut lawns

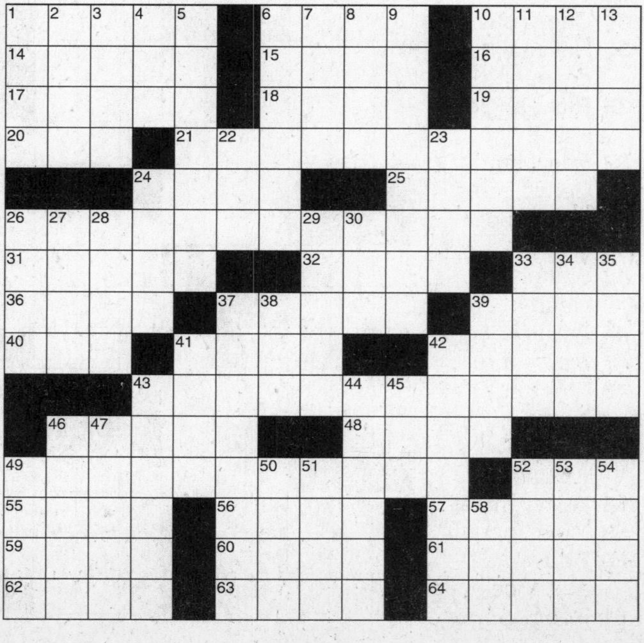

227 LAUGHING MATTER

by Richard Silvestri

ACROSS
1 Beyond repair
5 Big chunk
9 Number-picking game
14 Mountain lion
15 Tra trailer
16 G-man Ness
17 River to the Caspian
18 Cookie king Wally
19 Well-versed
20 Comedy classic of '31
23 Isolate
24 I, to Claudius
25 Columnist Bombeck
28 Like Macbeth
33 Dam site in Egypt
37 Love, in Latin
39 Actress Rowlands
40 Stars of 20 Across and 57 Across
43 Bog
44 Gets a move on
45 Comic actor Jack
46 Taking that into account
48 Colorful horse
50 Junk mail
52 Starter's gun
57 Comedy classic of '30
62 It takes a licking
63 Came to earth
64 __ *Christie*
65 Man-made waterway
66 College department
67 Harbor sound
68 Without rhyme or reason
69 Fluctuate
70 Tolkien creatures

DOWN
1 Sea foam
2 Superior neighbor
3 Muscat resident
4 Schmoozes
5 David, to Goliath
6 Moussaka ingredient
7 Baseball family name
8 Low man at the opera
9 Horseshoes score
10 Merrie __ England
11 Connections
12 A-one
13 Giant Hall-of-Famer
21 Actress Verdugo
22 Musical lead-in
26 Ankle-length
27 Color of caution
29 Turkish title
30 Nerd
31 Letters at Calvary
32 Detective work
33 "Don't throw bouquets __"
34 Thug's knife
35 *The Way We* __
36 Word of approval
38 Approximately
41 Valerie Harper role
42 Popular mixer
47 Those polled
49 Lack of concern
51 Shuts with a bang
53 Glide on the ice
54 Mortise mate
55 Ripley ending
56 Atty.-to-be's exams
57 __ impasse
58 Grandma
59 African-born supermodel
60 Hammer type
61 Ms. Moreno
62 Bot. or bio.

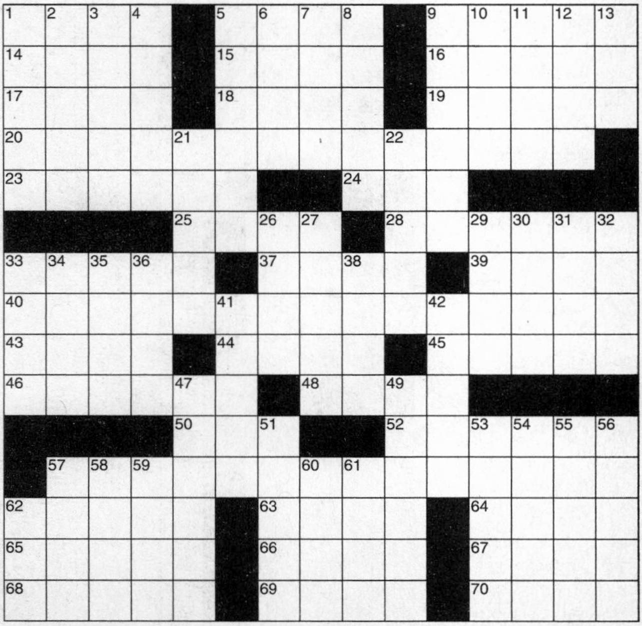

228 KERN TUNES

by Scott Marley

ACROSS

1 Coup __
6 Dressing-room door symbol
10 Summertime sweets
14 Sky blue
15 Gondolier gear
16 __ E. Coyote
17 Soda size
18 "How sweet __!"
19 Chief Norse god
20 1928 Kern tune
22 Clears
23 Add'l phone
24 Shade source
26 Berth place
30 Band aid?
32 Inc., in England
33 Pressure
34 Denver's height, more or less
36 Passover piece
40 Garage-sale words
41 Discount drastically
43 "High" time
44 *Divine Comedy* poet
46 High-flying toy
47 Old fool
48 Broad-antlered deer
50 Candlelit
51 Fire man?
52 *Gypsy* wardrobe
56 Like Lucia di Lammermoor
58 Newspaper page
59 1928 Kern tune
65 Casserole ingredient
66 Serve food
67 Out of the way
68 It may take a deuce
69 Unfounded
70 Canine canines
71 Pants inhabitants
72 Koppel and Kennedy
73 Bird sound

DOWN

1 *Cagney & Lacey* star
2 Singer Pinza
3 '84 Peace Nobelist
4 Geometry problem
5 __ Haute, IN
6 What can't be undone, metaphorically
7 Kansas canine
8 Kicking partner
9 Act as a distributor
10 1934 Kern tune
11 Fruit product
12 Cream of the crop
13 Sight or smell
21 Course completers
25 TV production company
26 Campus region
27 __ Major (constellation)
28 Not "fer"
29 1933 Kern tune
31 Tartan pattern
35 Pre-repair data
37 Decorate, as leather
38 Move rapidly
39 Aware of
42 Model of virility
45 Actor Wallach
49 __-all (smart aleck)
52 "I __ Right to Sing the Blues"
53 Reject disdainfully
54 Doctrine
55 Forest clearing
57 Unwelcome wind
60 Not sharp
61 *Vidi*
62 It intersects Hollywood
63 __ out (defeat narrowly)
64 Take a break

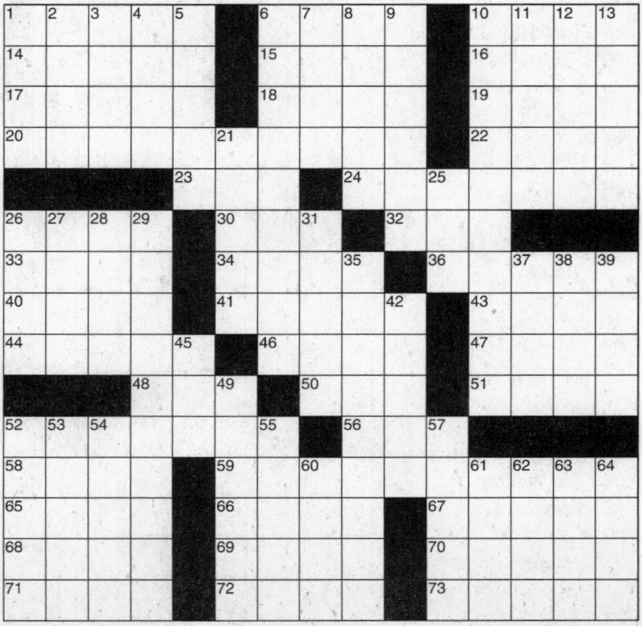

229 *NATURE WALK*

by Bob Lubbers

ACROSS

1 Volcano output
5 Stay away from
9 Go bad
14 Take on
15 __ Nostra
16 Therefore
17 Verbal sigh
18 Supremes leader
19 Bandleader Shaw
20 Get going
23 That girl
24 Fortas and Lincoln
25 Fudd et al.
27 Supermarket saver
30 Big to-do
32 Purina rival
33 Raison d'__
35 Scout group
38 On Soc. Sec.
39 Pencil ends
41 Naval rank: Abbr.
42 Pale
44 Narrow street
45 Related (to)
46 Make possible
48 Brought a smile to
50 City near Seattle
52 "Shoo!"
53 Basic education?
54 Past one's prime
60 On __ (spreeing)
62 Lettuce piece
63 Oil of __
64 Feudal lord
65 *Venus de* __
66 Dough does it
67 Popped the question
68 Unique person
69 Tennis segments

DOWN

1 Persian ruler
2 "Hi __, Hi Lo"
3 Smell __ (be leery)
4 WWII secret police
5 Projectionist, e.g.
6 Derisive cries
7 Former UN member
8 *Discovery* org.
9 Onions' kin
10 __ capita
11 In ruins
12 More frosty
13 Lustful looks
21 Cable network
22 Cash ending
26 Damage
27 Irene of *Fame*
28 Cheers for the matador
29 In big trouble
30 Bears, to Brutus
31 Hammer end
34 Like some tales
36 Mayberry boy
37 Duck's home
39 Infatuated
40 Try to grab
43 Rock producer Brian
45 Mailer and Michener
47 German region: Abbr.
49 Ginnie __
50 Singing syllables
51 *"Ars Gratia* __*"*
52 No longer fresh
55 Kid in *Blondie*
56 Mount's strap
57 Mr. Nastase
58 Remain active
59 Cleaning solutions
61 Mature

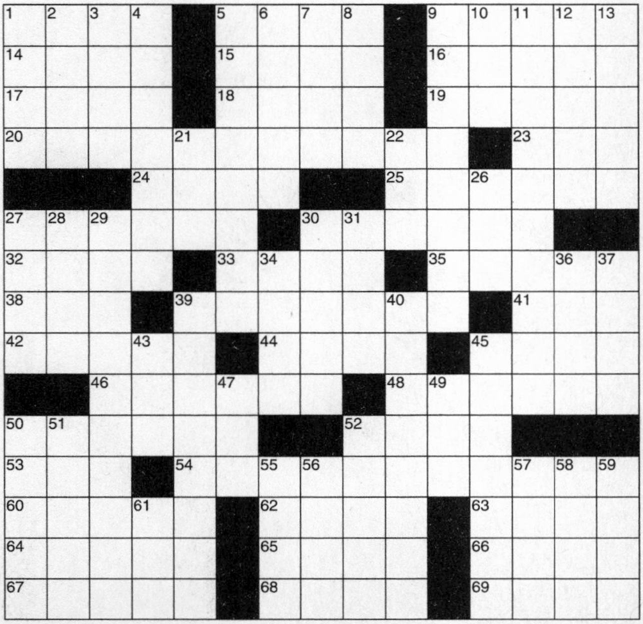

230 MALE CALL

by Eric Albert

ACROSS
1 Cement a deal
6 Athlete's bane
10 Eject
14 Available for rental
15 Corn country
16 Early zookeeper
17 Western film of '70
20 Out of shape
21 Singer Tillis
22 Grocery store
23 The least bit
25 Red wine
26 Adds decorations
29 Best buddy
30 Remain quiet
33 Mata Hari portrayer
34 Kaput
35 Batman's creator
36 Whodunit film of '36
39 Got hold of
40 City on the Brazos
41 Turns unfriendly
42 Poetic contraction
43 *Dallas* patriarch
44 Setting
45 Provide support for
46 Nursery color
47 On the move
50 Dazzling expert
51 Product showing
55 Adventure film of '32
58 Ronny Howard role
59 Blow your horn
60 Three-line verse
61 Pain in the neck
62 Undulate
63 Kills time

DOWN
1 Wild guess
2 Habitat
3 Defender Dershowitz
4 Veteran infielder
5 List shortener
6 Beef cut
7 Lounge about
8 Fear + wonder
9 Disparage
10 Quick swig
11 Political patronage
12 Life of Riley
13 Make keener
18 Cookie tycoon
19 Do damage to
24 __ about
25 Glossy, e.g.
26 Playing marble
27 *Mississippi Burning* star
28 Dramatist Joe
29 "Your king is threatened"
30 Mead subject
31 Combined
32 Feeling the strain
34 Crude cabin
35 Impress mightily
37 Conversation contribution?
38 Religious image
43 Indonesian island
44 Judy's daughter
45 *L'Arlésienne* composer
46 Dutiful respect
47 Surmounting
48 Horn, for one
49 Baseball great Speaker
50 Steed stopper
52 Actor Jannings
53 Put together
54 Difficult duty
56 Drag behind
57 Frat letter

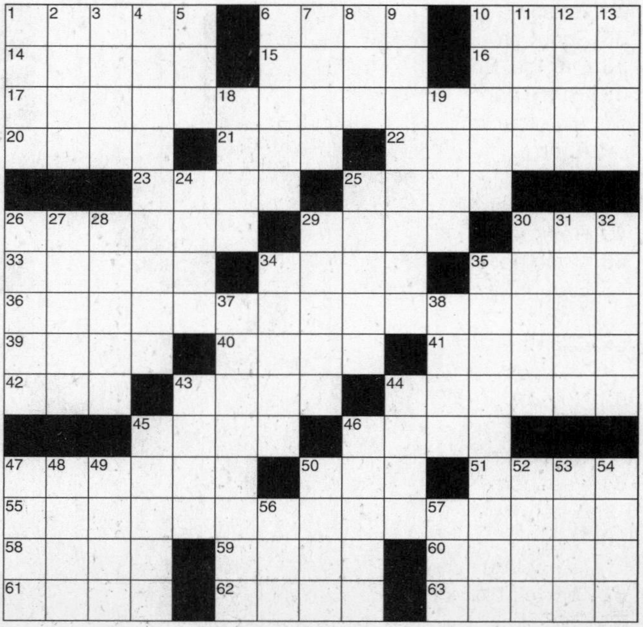

231 ELECTION DAY

by Trip Payne

ACROSS

1 Tiny coin
5 Bird call
10 Russian range
14 Egyptian goddess
15 Pay tribute to
16 Zilch
17 Election-day sights
20 Take a look at
21 "__ helpless . . ."
22 Sound-effects specialty
23 English architect
24 Pavlov's signal
25 Makes furious
28 __ and void
29 Wanted-poster abbr.
32 Parisian aunt
33 Wooded valley
34 Give __ (care)
35 Election-day mail-ins
38 The __ Seasons
39 Early automaker
40 Kate's roommate
41 Lex Luthor, to Superman
42 Supercomputer company
43 Women's scarves
44 Pretentious
45 Made a landing
46 Crybaby's sound
49 Don __ (legendary lover)
50 Get the point
53 Election-day focus
56 Hold as an opinion
57 __ Hawkins Day
58 Theater sign
59 Smart-mouth's talk
60 Gives off
61 Unit of force

DOWN

1 Casino cubes
2 Englishman's "Golly!"
3 Street performer
4 Psychic ability
5 Doorbell sounds
6 Golfer Ben
7 Bed-and-breakfast spots
8 Pilfer
9 *Fawlty Towers* actress Scales
10 *Wait __ Dark*
11 Down under leapers
12 Novelist Tyler
13 Not as much
18 Lindbergh and Yeager
19 Road charge
23 Restaurant freebie
24 Onion plants
25 Walking stick
26 It's a no-no
27 Come afterward
28 Indigent
29 On __ (hot)
30 Couric of *Today*
31 Church areas
33 Gap in time
34 Ration out
36 Famous race-winner
37 Hispanic
42 Gator's kin
43 Works like a horse
44 Throat-clearing sounds
45 Taxpayer's fear
46 Flowers-to-be
47 Draft status
48 Keats creations
49 *Return of the __*
50 Alluring
51 Actress Moran
52 Italian clan
54 Hoover or Grand Coulee
55 Senator Kennedy

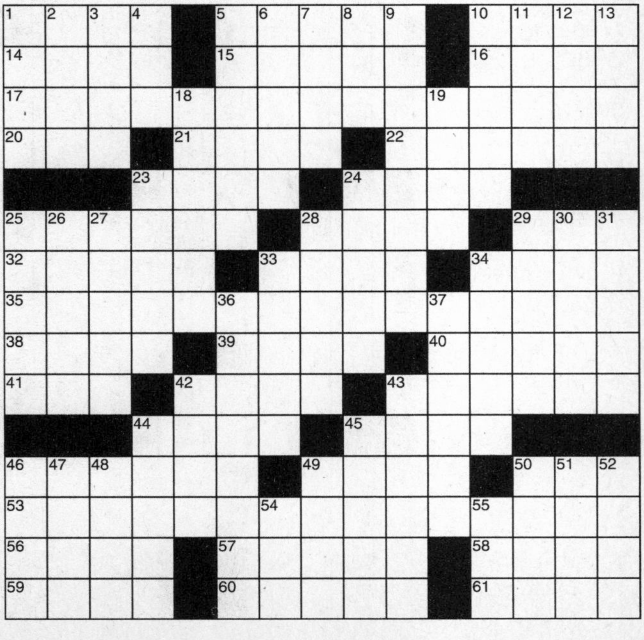

232 *IN PLACE*

by Shirley Soloway

ACROSS
1 Singer Patti
5 Realty sign
9 *Bonanza* brother
13 *The Good Earth* wife
14 Inventor Howe
16 Fruit center
17 Nonclerical
18 Cup, in Caen
19 *The __ McCoys*
20 Happy as a lark
23 Newsman Rather
24 Prosecutors: Abbr.
25 Indy participant
28 Ave. crossers
31 Envelope requirement
35 Notable period
36 Overly decorative
39 Brainstorm
40 Nebraska natives
43 Software buyer
44 Submerged
45 Engineers' univ.
46 Sting operation
48 __ Vegas
49 Graff of *Mr. Belvedere*
51 Little one
53 Ghostly sound
54 Where to seal a deal
63 Additional
64 Shakespearean sprite
65 "__ a Little Prayer" ('67 tune)
66 At all times
67 Sign a new lease
68 Trunk item
69 Anti votes
70 Smaller amount
71 Makes an inquiry

DOWN
1 Royal sport
2 Actor Ladd
3 Trot or gallop
4 Send a secret message
5 Author Anya
6 Norwegian monarch
7 Shopping aid
8 Take off
9 Puzzle type
10 Hard worker
11 Asian sea
12 Canasta objective
15 Plant start
21 Word of mouth
22 Used to be
25 Fictional uncle
26 Get up
27 West Point student
28 Slowpoke
29 Florida city
30 Escalator alternative
32 "There Is Nothin' Like __"
33 __ blue (police)
34 Glue
37 Silly Skelton
38 Prior to, in poetry
41 One's own way
42 Turn of phrase
47 "The Raven" author
50 Nabokov novel
52 Ski lift
53 Fastens securely
54 Seer's sign
55 PBS science show
56 Low card
57 Hurler Hershiser
58 Floor covering
59 Casual shirts
60 Wife of Osiris
61 Vice agent
62 Spud buds

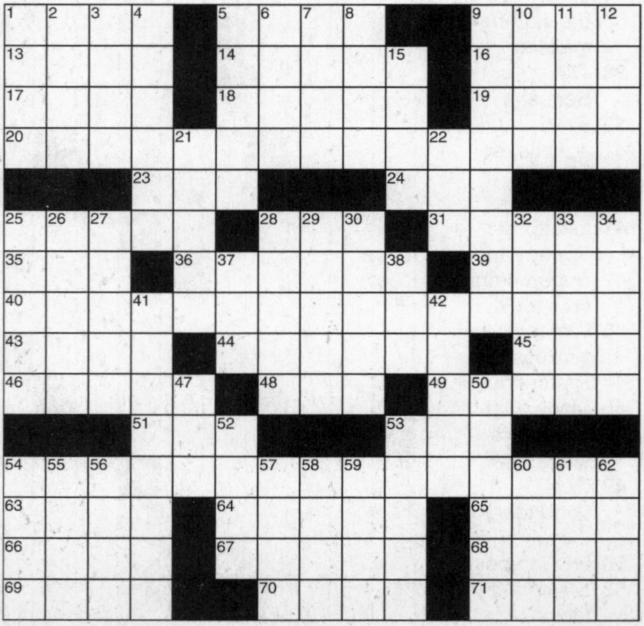

233 SPACE VEHICLES

by Bob Lubbers

ACROSS

1 Apropos of
5 Dunderhead
9 Florida city
14 Machine parts
15 Garfield's pal
16 Sandwich cookies
17 Tyrone Power film of '57
20 Pacific current
21 Rocky hills
22 Part of DA
23 Raison d'__
25 Stuck-up one
27 __ as a wet hen
30 Popular pasta sauce
32 Haifa's locale
36 Bordeaux bye-bye
38 Pesky insect
40 __ de Pascua (Easter Island)
41 Charlton Heston film of '68
44 Actress Olin
45 Single quantity
46 "__ You Glad You're You"
47 Puts up
49 Scottish caps
51 Technical advisory org.
52 Clock sound
54 Actress Charlotte et al.
56 Peter Jennings' network
59 Stick around
61 Noisy to-do
65 George Sanders film of '42, with *The*
68 Of interest to Peary
69 Challenge
70 Carter of Broadway
71 Word with grand or band
72 Sp. ladies
73 Greenish blue

DOWN

1 Entr'__ (musical interlude)
2 Witty Mort
3 Eliot Ness' colleagues
4 Actor Davis
5 Mexican state
6 Actress Lupino
7 Cartoonist Caniff
8 Acapulco pocket money
9 Sculpted trunks
10 Onassis' nickname
11 Flattop of a sort
12 Keats or Byron
13 Off. helper
18 Not for real
19 Word form for "bird"
24 Urge into trouble
26 Pipe wood
27 Sappy tree
28 Harmonica virtuoso Larry
29 Keaton of *Interiors*
31 Not qualified
33 Colorado ski resort
34 Ms. Verdugo
35 Endures
37 Make into law
39 Perfume ingredient
42 Florentine fellow
43 Relax
48 In the area of
50 Groucho, Harpo, and Chico
53 Notorious pirate et al.
55 Bloodhound motivator
56 Fuse word
57 Overshoe
58 Soft-drink flavor
60 Russian despot
62 __-jerk reaction
63 West Coast campus: Abbr.
64 Put on the market
66 A Bobbsey twin
67 Author Levin

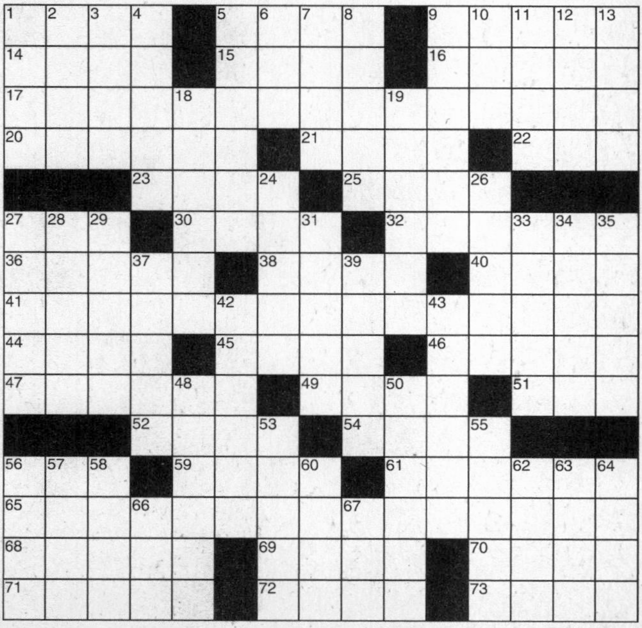

234 WHAT'S COOKIN'?

by Harvey Estes

ACROSS
1 Obligation
5 Clock sound
9 Russian czar
13 At any time
14 German sub
16 Risqué
17 Dean Martin specialties
20 Trainee
21 Earth
22 Make a knot
23 *"Vaya con __"*
25 Soft drink
27 Ex-soldiers' org.
30 Nights before Christmas
32 Arrow part
35 Hipbones
37 Directional suffix
38 Sharon of Israel
40 Higher priorities
44 Patriot Allen
45 "The Gold Bug" author
46 Fiery fiddler?
47 Mixes
49 Rug style
51 __ Jose, CA
52 Alaskan seaport
54 Baltic tributary
56 Common article
59 Mythical mom of twins
61 Prepares pork chops
65 Become quite annoyed
68 Teheran's country
69 Reveal
70 "For Pete's __!"
71 Fedora fabric
72 Come down to earth
73 Looked at

DOWN
1 Liter leader
2 Neck and neck
3 Sash, e.g.
4 Cornered, in a way
5 Breakfast pastry
6 __-Wan Kenobi
7 Canvas beds
8 Ring wins
9 Lyricist Gershwin
10 Far-flung
11 Play start
12 AMEX rival
15 Some combos
18 Soft, white cheese
19 Dated
24 Medieval menial
26 Moses' brother
27 Bad __ (uneasy feeling)
28 Flies like a canary
29 England's Isle of __
31 Small cuts
33 Drums' companions
34 __ cotta
36 One more time
39 French city
41 Sign up
42 London area
43 Tennis accessory
48 Sniff the air
50 Microbe
53 Ford flop
55 Shortstop Pee Wee
56 End-of-week initials
57 Roll-call response
58 List ender
60 "__ boy!"
62 Queen for __
63 British nobleman
64 Rushed
66 Industrious insect
67 Years on end

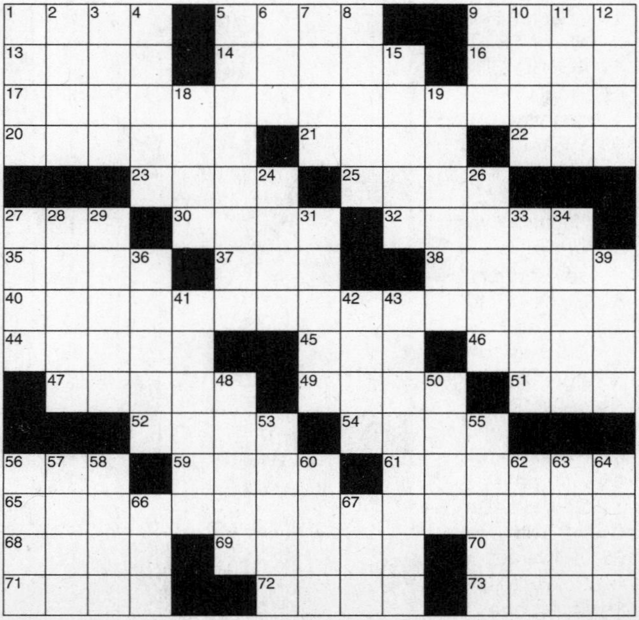

235 AUTO PARTS

by Mary E. Brindamour

ACROSS
1 Table accessory
5 Barcelona residences
10 Dull sound
14 Region
15 Alpha's opposite
16 Like magic
17 Bug barrier
19 Blow one's top
20 Jockey seat
21 Slowed down
23 Dryer fuzz
25 Adds up
26 Desirable quality
29 Some are personal
31 52, to Caesar
32 House members: Abbr.
33 Master hand
34 Tropical fruits
37 Tax specialist: Abbr.
38 Prolonged sufferings
40 Deli buy
41 Hard and fast
43 Chip off the old block
44 Major ending
45 Word form for "outside"
46 Cozy room
47 Out-of-date
48 *Remington* __ ('80s TV show)
50 Sling mud
52 Immature
54 Director Hitchcock
58 Steakhouse word
59 Engine energizers
61 Tarzan's pals
62 Rich cake
63 First person
64 Army meal
65 Be at the wheel
66 Hosiery purchase

DOWN
1 Statutes
2 Soprano's showcase
3 Patch up
4 Canoe power?
5 Comic Myron
6 "What a good boy __!"
7 Fortune-teller
8 Shoelace parts
9 __ say (regrettably)
10 Tract of land
11 Interstate illuminators
12 Persuades earnestly
13 Colored Easter eggs
18 Narrow opening
22 Cartographer's book
24 Pedro's snack
26 Curved lines
27 Labor Day mo.
28 Trunk contents
30 Closely packed
33 PR man
34 Game pieces
35 Feedbag filler
36 *Hook* pirate
38 Did something
39 Charged atoms
42 Defrosted
44 Cap feature
46 Absolute ruler
47 Papermaking material
48 Square or circle
49 Shopping agendas
51 Los Angeles cager
52 Pull an all-nighter
53 Jackrabbit, for one
55 Boorish
56 Mild oath
57 Mil. awards
60 Highway: Abbr.

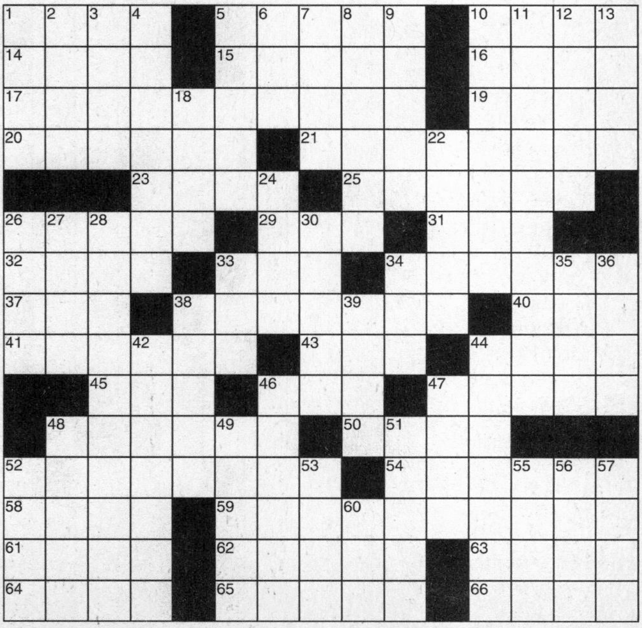

236 FAMILY BUSINESS

by Shirley Soloway

ACROSS

1 Outer edges
5 Formal agreement
9 Prohibit by law
14 Ear-related
15 __ breve
16 *I Was __ War Bride*
17 Small food markets
20 Elementary-school book
21 Affirmative answer
22 Brewery kiln
23 Shelley specialty
25 Large tub
27 Cowgirl Evans
30 Women's group
36 General Bradley
37 Cool spot
38 Take off
39 Washer cycle
41 That girl
42 Stable unit
44 "The Lady __ Tramp"
45 Watch faces
47 Pitcher Hershiser
48 Easy job
51 Barber and Buttons
52 Motorists' org.
53 Fill the hold
55 Slight fight
58 Psyche sections
61 Church leader
65 In a scolding way
68 Cake topping
69 Detective's discovery
70 Jeff Bridges film of '82
71 *"La Plume de Ma __"*
72 Legal wrongdoing
73 The unelected?

DOWN

1 Frisky frolic
2 *Ripley's Believe __ Not*
3 Chevalier song
4 Runs quickly
5 San Diego team
6 Heidi's home
7 Surfeit
8 Use the VCR
9 Have a snack
10 Like marble
11 Fictional plantation
12 Corrida cries
13 Pain in the neck
18 Word form for "recent"
19 Set aside
24 Little accident
26 Olympian warmonger
27 Kind of column
28 Pennsylvania sect
29 Pearl City patio
31 Shore find
32 Of the anklebone
33 Chicago airport
34 Lubricated
35 Small valleys
40 Norse verse collection
43 Attacked viciously
46 "I Am . . . __" (Neil Diamond tune)
49 Potential
50 Kotto of *Alien*
54 Actress Joanne
55 Skirt feature
56 Type of type
57 Similar
59 Air vent
60 Normandy battle site
62 Light tan
63 Coin depository
64 Hamilton's bills
66 Get mellow
67 Mongrel

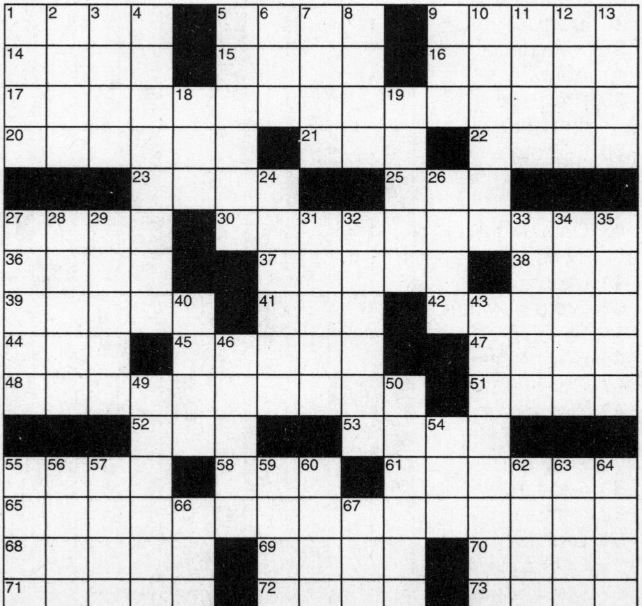

237 NUMISMATICS

by Shirley Soloway

ACROSS
1 Pulls a fast one
5 Sharp blow
9 Fountain fizzes
14 Attention-getter
15 Scarlett's estate
16 West Indian nation
17 New Testament sages
18 Former African dictator
19 Knight wear
20 Lots of money, with "a"
23 Nav. rank
24 Hard-hearted
25 Use for support
27 Actor Byrnes
29 Summer fruits
32 Brimless hat
36 Nurse's __ (hospital worker)
39 Tony-winner Judith
40 Be adjacent to
41 Prepared a press
42 Ernest's pal
43 Word with trench or house
44 Country dance
45 Fuses metal
46 Singer Brewer
48 Lawyers' org.
50 Groups of three
53 They get squirreled away
58 Farm tool
60 Cable channel
62 Cook's coverup
64 Frees (of)
65 Theater award
66 *The Picture of Dorian Gray* author
67 Forearm bone
68 Trick
69 __ up (nervous)
70 Close forcefully
71 Spin suffix

DOWN
1 Vacation sites
2 Illinois airport
3 Mideast desert
4 Strike down
5 Remained
6 Light source
7 Sharon of Israel
8 Velvety fabric
9 Sleuth Michael
10 Kayak propeller
11 Paperback book
12 Like __ of bricks
13 Gentlemen
21 Shady character?
22 Christened
26 Martini additive
28 Hamlet, for one
30 Picked-on student
31 Thesaurus entries: Abbr.
32 Diplomacy
33 Woodwind instrument
34 Certain periodical
35 Make a remark
37 34th president, to pals
38 Oscar __ Renta
41 Teheran native
45 Texas town
47 Fell from grace
49 Evergreen
51 Shades of beige
52 Abundant ability
54 Aromas
55 Prove false
56 Disturbing sound
57 Look down one's nose
58 Bird of prey
59 Mayberry boy
61 __ May Oliver
63 "__ to Joy"

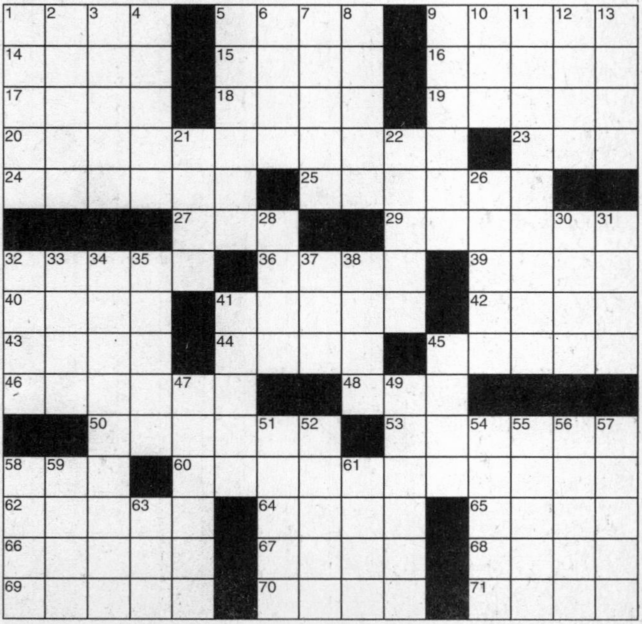

238 BABY TALK

by Bob Lubbers

ACROSS

1 Rope fiber
5 Sawyer of ABC News
10 Prayer finale
14 Insist on
15 Andean Indian
16 *I Remember* __
17 Report from the field
19 Analogous
20 Helps develop
21 Chemical compounds
23 "__ the fields we go . . ."
24 Fundamental
25 Back a motion
29 Fills road cracks
30 Old crone
33 Scottish families
34 Construct
35 Shopper's paradise
36 One of the Aleutians
37 Handled clumsily
38 Aware of
39 Novelist Macdonald
40 Country hotels
41 Theater sections
42 SASE, e.g.
43 Quite a few
44 Kenny of country
45 Sorrel steeds
47 Cambridge univ.
48 Leisurely, to Liszt
50 They're crackers
55 Pie à la __
56 Capital of Arkansas
58 Small burrower
59 Like some triangles
60 Tennis great Arthur
61 Mine finds
62 Trig functions
63 Broadway offering

DOWN

1 David's instrument
2 "If __ I Would Leave You"
3 Post-it message
4 High-school formal
5 Passed the butter?
6 Draw a conclusion
7 The Four __ ('50s group)
8 Dundee denial
9 Won over
10 Fancy fiddle
11 Break a buck
12 Kuwaiti ruler
13 Merriman and Grey
18 *The Simpsons,* for instance
22 Cobra's comment
24 Makes muffins
25 Fill with fright
26 Singer __ John
27 Children's game
28 Burden
29 Yellowish-brown
31 Shorten the sleeves
32 Lipstick type
34 Nobelist Thomas et al.
35 Electronic synthesizer
37 Automatic uprights
41 Singer Lenya
43 Actress Zetterling
44 Moon valleys
46 Curved moldings
47 Dull finish
48 Bullets, for short
49 Entryway
50 Shake up
51 Keogh alternatives
52 Snack
53 Sound effect
54 Swerve sharply
57 Here, in Havre

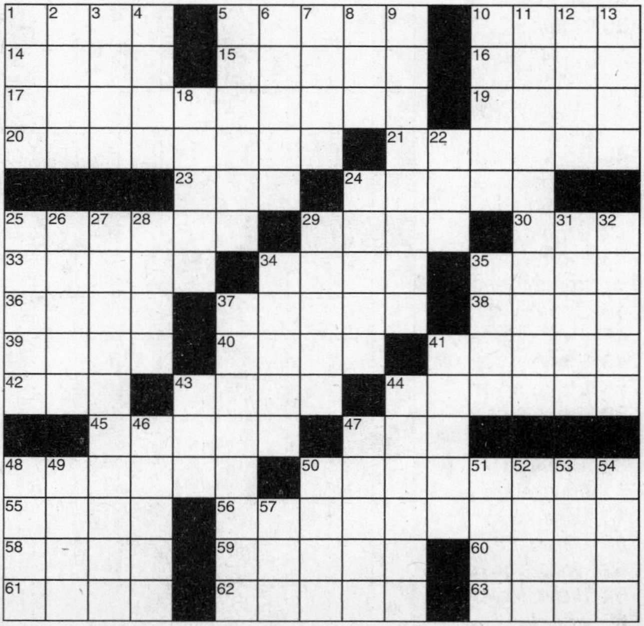

239 TABLE TALK

by Shirley Soloway

ACROSS

1 Treats leather
5 Irritated
10 Arkin or West
14 Busy as __
15 Minneapolis suburb
16 100 centesimi
17 Astonished
19 "Now it's clear!"
20 Jesse James, for one
21 Buckwheat dish
23 "From __ 60 in 8.2 seconds"
24 Becomes unusable
27 Kitchen addition?
28 Nosy types
30 Newsman Rather
33 __ Romeo (auto)
36 Mrs. David Copperfield
37 Deep black
39 Mrs. Helmsley
41 Small piece
42 In for __ awakening
43 Challenged
44 Part of MIT
46 Rat-__
47 Noah's craft
48 Most humid
51 Café au __
53 Break suddenly
54 Coal container
57 Spotted steed
58 Containing sodium
60 Skillful
61 Printer's apparatus
65 Italian wine region
66 More sickly
67 Nonpayment take-back, for short
68 Office kingpin
69 __ *Irish Rose*
70 Garfunkel and Fleming

DOWN

1 Forbidden
2 Approximately
3 Recently involved with
4 Hawk
5 California giant
6 Altar words
7 Actress Ullmann
8 Chemical ending
9 More shaded
10 "He's making __ . . ."
11 Dispensed freely
12 Region
13 West of Hollywood
18 Make a buck
22 Confused
25 Poorly fitting, in a way
26 Leaps up
28 Logical
29 Has dinner at home
31 *A Man __ Woman*
32 Raisa's refusal
33 Alan of *Betsy's Wedding*
34 TV producer Norman
35 Warehouse vehicles
38 Spoiled kid
40 Own up to
45 Advertising lures
49 Perfect place
50 Sandwich meat
52 Pros' foes
54 Tour de France participant
55 Clumsy
56 Franco and Peter
57 Tijuana currency
59 *Doctor Zhivago* character
60 Apply lightly
62 Legal deg.
63 "The Greatest"
64 Shirt style

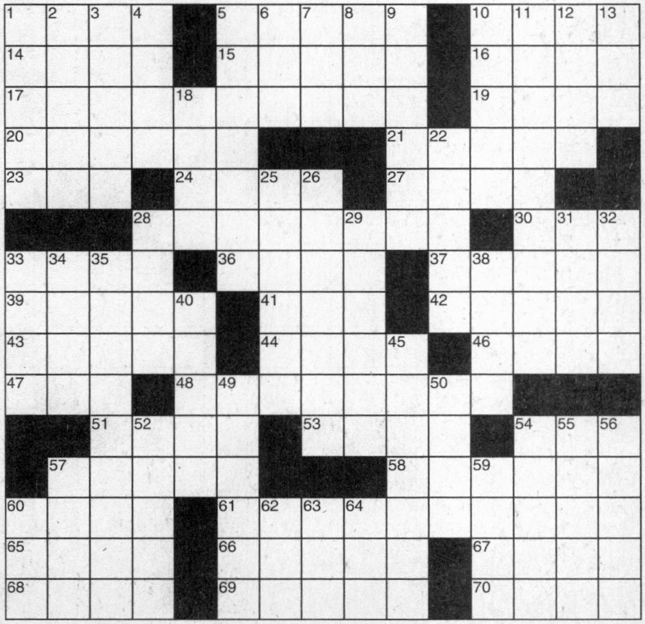

240 BASEBALL ROOKIES

by Peter Gordon

ACROSS
1 Kind of heating
6 Man-mouse link
9 Divulged, as facts
14 Eat away at
15 Lowe of *Wayne's World*
16 In the know
17 Legitimate
18 Sailor, in slang
19 Dens
20 Miami baseball team
23 Long time period
24 In demand
25 Show up
29 Rotisserie part
31 Jim Bakker's org.
34 Sociologist Hite
35 Ready for business
36 New York City area
37 Denver baseball team
40 Norse god
41 Prepare a meal
42 Wash cycle
43 *Tic __ Dough*
44 Earn a living
45 Focus
46 Above, to Keats
47 Constricting snake
48 20 Across and 37 Across, e.g.
56 Land measures
57 Madison Avenue output
58 Dark
59 Be generous
60 Manager Durocher
61 TV honcho Arledge
62 True-blue
63 Clinton's instrument
64 Senator Kefauver

DOWN
1 Egotist's concern
2 Pitcher Hershiser
3 Trademark design
4 Jewish month
5 Late-inning pitcher
6 Choir instrument
7 *Make __ for Daddy*
8 Swedish rock group
9 Candidate list
10 Expect
11 Picnic bane
12 Botches up
13 __ Moines, IA
21 Unknown John
22 Large horned animal
25 Tie type
26 Valerie Harper sitcom
27 Archaeologist's find
28 Heavy metal
29 Ghost or goblin
30 Bonus
31 Heart of the matter
32 "__ Boots Are Made for Walkin'"
33 Ne'er-do-well
35 Disagreeable smell
36 Membrane
38 Future oak
39 Man or monkey
44 Sneaky sort
45 Pro's antithesis
46 Verdi production
47 Fenway Park club, for short
48 Reverberation
49 Medical photo
50 Bando and Maglie
51 Mental image
52 Genesis name
53 Scads
54 Ore store
55 Canonized *Mlles.*
56 Marlee Matlin medium: Abbr.

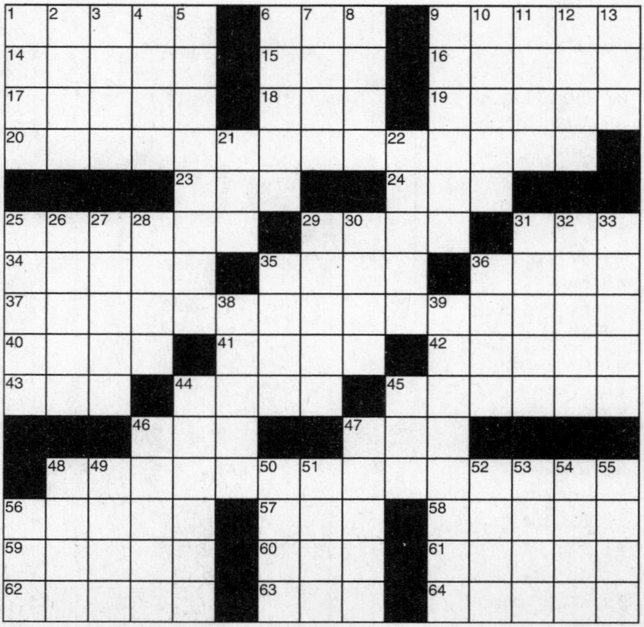

241 WHAT-KNOT

by Bob Lubbers

ACROSS

1 Karate kin
5 Agt.'s take
8 Tijuana treats
13 PDQ, politely
14 Hand-cream additive
15 Helmsman's term
16 Opinion taker
18 *Odyssey* siren
19 Tusked sea mammals
21 Cocktail cheese
22 Sodium solutions
25 Public-__ television
27 Thinks
28 Fairy-tale youngster
30 Jessica of *Cape Fear*
31 Movie director Alexander
32 Little fellow
35 High cards
36 Scrumptious
37 Chan's assent
38 Gettysburg soldier
39 Crowd maker?
40 Singer Springsteen
41 Far and wide
43 Formal living room
44 Holy
46 Volcanic rocks
47 *Kon* __
48 Pain reliever
51 Sports palace
53 First-__ (game starters)
57 Brink
58 Tiny amounts
59 Actor Estrada
60 Road curves
61 Draft agcy.
62 Say it isn't so

DOWN

1 Jelly container
2 Troop troupe: Abbr.
3 Drink like a sparrow
4 First nights
5 Blizzard fleet
6 Fizzy favorite
7 Spill the beans
8 Tic-__-toe
9 For each
10 UN founding father
11 Aquarium denizens
12 Sunflower supports
14 __-ski party
17 Calcutta queen
20 Hall of Famer Koufax
22 Kind of calculator
23 Quickly
24 Defensive players
26 Jefferson Davis' dom.
28 Watered the lawn, e.g.
29 Jocular Johnson
31 Malden or Marx
33 Fashionable neckwear
34 Active ones
36 Bara of the silents
37 Put in order
39 Father's Day gift
40 "__ Street Blues"
42 Surrey trim
43 Bastille locale
44 Barrel part
45 Buenos __
46 Condor and canary
49 Fast fliers
50 School grps.
52 DDE opponent
54 Before, in verse
55 __ Tin Tin
56 The wild blue yonder

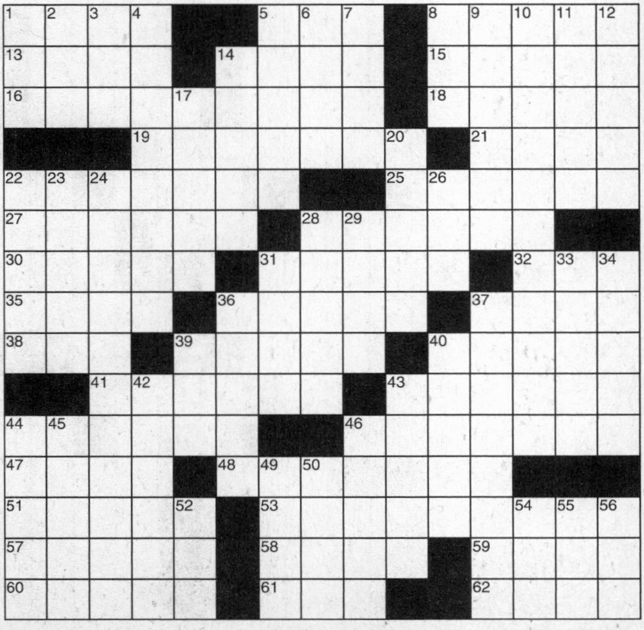

242 SHOCKING SUBJECTS

by Eric Albert

ACROSS

1 Block bit
5 Stress-free
9 Easy __
14 In the pink
15 Mayberry boy
16 Mike of *Wayne's World*
17 Where most people live
18 Actress Perlman
19 Puts up
20 WWII partisans
23 Tie the knot
24 Lawyer's letters
25 Ice-T's music
28 Chess maneuver
32 Root beer alternative
33 Flowery necklace
34 Bounding main
35 Asian tongue
36 Ping-__
37 Diplomatic official
41 Feels ill
42 Mouth piece?
43 Fat-eschewer of rhyme
44 No longer working: Abbr.
45 Ball callers
46 Fourth-rate
47 Numeric prefix
48 Parisian possessive
49 *Peggy __ Got Married*
50 Pitch woo
57 Hindu ascetic
59 "If __ a Hammer"
60 Kind of history
61 Like Nero Wolfe
62 Form loops
63 38 Regular, e.g.
64 Pizzeria patron
65 MacLachlan of *Twin Peaks*
66 Mist

DOWN

1 Light talk
2 Mess-hall meal
3 Tennis player Nastase
4 Still-life subject
5 It's a cinch
6 Plant pest
7 Bears false witness
8 Diner fare
9 Blake of *Gunsmoke*
10 In __ (meshing well)
11 *M* man
12 Make mad
13 Start start?
21 *Dallas* family name
22 "__ Me" (Sinatra tune)
26 Virgil's hero
27 Foul spot
28 Kid's racer
29 Needing massage more
30 Means of support
31 Forbids
32 Gives a hand
36 Organ piece
38 Glue guy
39 Oil-level indicator
40 Grate stuff
45 Shylock, e.g.
46 Hug affectionately
49 Slow mover
51 Belgian river
52 Crow's-nest cry
53 Elegant
54 Pavarotti piece
55 Make fun of
56 Swiss artist Paul
57 Hostile force
58 Perry Mason's org.

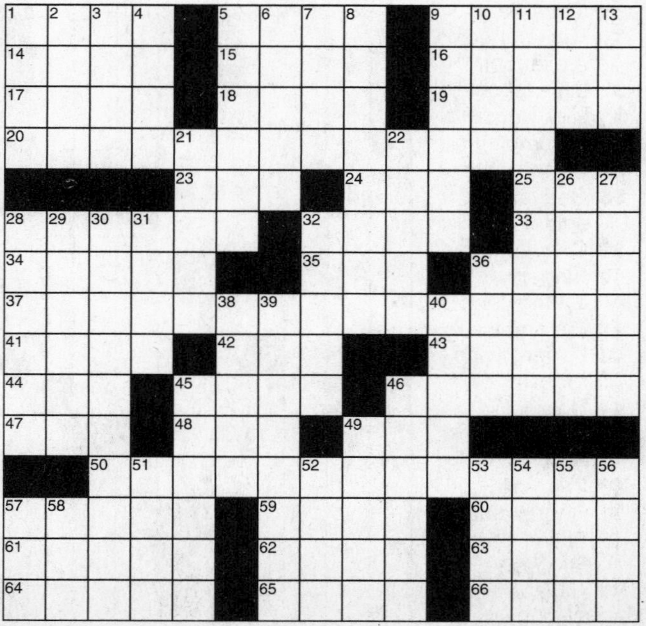

243 HURRY UP!

by Shirley Soloway

ACROSS

1 __ *la Douce*
5 Paid performers
9 Actress __ Jessica Parker
14 Genuine
15 Steakhouse word
16 Spread joy
17 British composer Thomas
18 At any time
19 Government takebacks
20 Mercury
23 __ and outs
24 Twangy
25 Large antelope
27 *Empty* __
30 Work forces
33 Famous feline
37 Century segment
39 Novelist Zola
40 Pulls apart
41 Jazz instruments
43 Gray or Moran
44 Upright
46 Monthly expenditure
47 Adjusts a clock
48 Takes the wheel
50 Dried out
52 Window covering
54 Wed in haste
58 __ and don'ts
60 Con artists
64 *Some Like* __
66 Got hold of
67 Thicke or Alda
68 Shoulder scarf
69 Border
70 __ *Can* (Davis, Jr. book)
71 Managed somehow
72 Down the __ (in the future)
73 Trickle slowly

DOWN

1 Desert Storm locale
2 Summer TV show
3 Excessive enthusiasm
4 Actor Baldwin et al.
5 Elvis and Priscilla
6 Sitarist Shankar
7 Dodger Hershiser
8 Dish out dinner
9 Notched like a saw
10 Bar order
11 Occurring swiftly
12 Like __ of bricks
13 Musician Myra
21 Topeka's st.
22 Overhead trains
26 Prospective parents' concerns
28 Scorch
29 Levies a tariff
31 Dart about
32 Capitol VIPs
33 Aphrodite's son
34 __ filter (dryer feature)
35 Hot-rodder's store
36 *Lou Grant* star
38 Monsieur Clair
42 Moved like lightning
45 Sketched an outline
49 Dieter's resort
51 Pipe type
53 Chemical compound
55 Rubber-stamps
56 Martinique volcano
57 Use the pencil end
58 Kind of brake
59 Producer Preminger
61 Big fuss
62 Roman garment
63 Small bit
65 Bilbao bravo

244 LILAC TIME

by Eric Albert

ACROSS
1 Mandlikova of tennis
5 Polychrome parrot
10 Piece of truth
14 Trojan War hero
15 Make self-conscious
16 Felipe, Jesus, or Matty
17 Crooks in a '51 film
20 Boil in oil?
21 "Zip-__-Doo-Dah"
22 Roughhouse
23 Piece for two
24 *Pretty Woman* man
25 Quit office
28 Vane silhouette
29 Tom or tabby
32 'umble Heep
33 Living-room piece
34 Cotton quantity
35 Having royal blood
38 Piece of one's mind?
39 Approach
40 Peer-group member?
41 Director Russell
42 Tribal division
43 Molar hole
44 Virtuous
45 Italian river
46 Conductor Toscanini
49 Tangle up
50 *JAG* network
53 Shy one
56 Ring out
57 Sociologist Durkheim
58 On guard
59 Alike in amount
60 Gave a score to
61 Bobcat

DOWN
1 One, to two
2 Open a bit
3 Dark blue
4 Tin Man's tool
5 Drive crazy
6 Red as __
7 International help org.
8 Hard wood
9 Breaking wave
10 F, on some tests
11 Donations to the poor
12 Under control
13 Subway, in Suffolk
18 Zilch
19 Move furtively
23 Paul Anka song
24 Errand runner
25 Cube man
26 Cause to decay
27 Wailing warning
28 *Yankee Doodle Dandy* subject
29 __ pants (casual slacks)
30 Mete out
31 Smaller than small
33 Place
34 Crowd cry
36 Witness
37 African border river
42 Husky vegetable?
43 Hungered after
44 Artful deception
45 Sharp corner
46 Venomous vipers
47 Mrs. Danny DeVito
48 London streetcar
49 Fit of anger
50 Terra cotta
51 Switzerland's capital
52 Charon's river
54 "Baby __ Want You" ('71 tune)
55 He gives a hoot

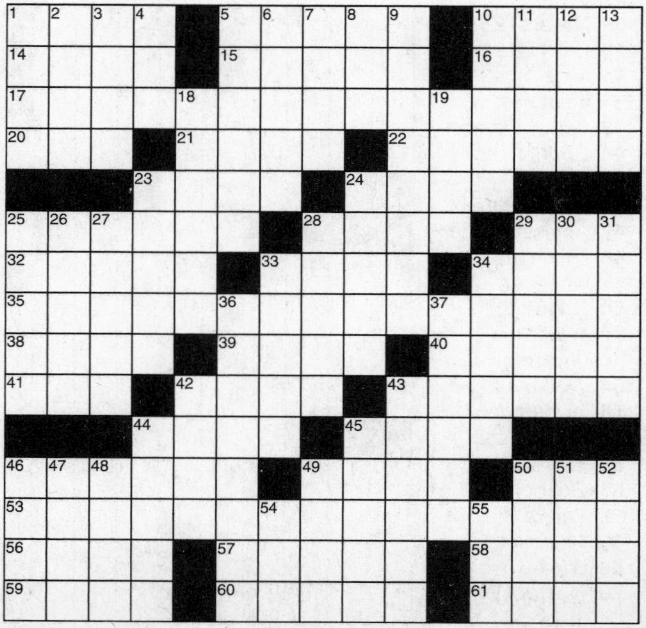

245 ACROSS AND DOWN

by Trip Payne

ACROSS

1 Yuppie car
4 Are able to, to Shakespeare
9 Go a few rounds with
12 Actress Bernhardt
14 Make merry
15 Zombie's punch?
16 Like some cases
18 Frozen dessert
19 Noun suffix
20 Matador's foe
21 Funk pianist
23 Amahl's creator
25 Jeff Bridges' brother
26 Good and bad times
31 Casey Kasem countdown
34 Little carpenter
35 Family card game
36 Popular theater name
37 FedEx rival
38 Poem division
40 *"Sprechen __ Deutsch?"*
41 Columbus sch.
42 __ cream pie
43 Spread out
47 "Last one __ rotten egg!"
48 Rubs the wrong way?
52 Anytown, USA locale
55 Poi party
56 Strike sharply
57 Mensa measurements
58 Tolstoy novel
61 Total cost
62 Tut's turf
63 "Grody __ max!"
64 Profs.' aides
65 Marsh flora
66 Leaky-tire sound

DOWN

1 Danny of *Not Necessarily the News*
2 Chesspiece
3 "And after that?"
4 Actor Hardwicke
5 Not to mention
6 Slangy negative
7 Notetaker, often
8 Group of four
9 Vivacity
10 "Hey, that smarts!"
11 Comic-book hero group
12 "__ told"
13 Church area
17 "__ a million years!"
22 Stick out
24 __ von Bismarck
25 Prohibits
27 Not working
28 Search for
29 Fascinated by
30 High time
31 Brit's baloney
32 Garfield's canine pal
33 Jury member
37 Milk grader, for short
38 Leads astray
39 All confused
41 Acting, perhaps
42 Misbehave
44 One, to Wagner
45 Response
46 Regular hangouts
49 Mild oaths
50 Every one
51 *Graf* __
52 Driving hazard
53 Blue hue
54 Beliefs
55 Sgt. Friday's outfit
59 Bread or booze
60 Dawn goddess

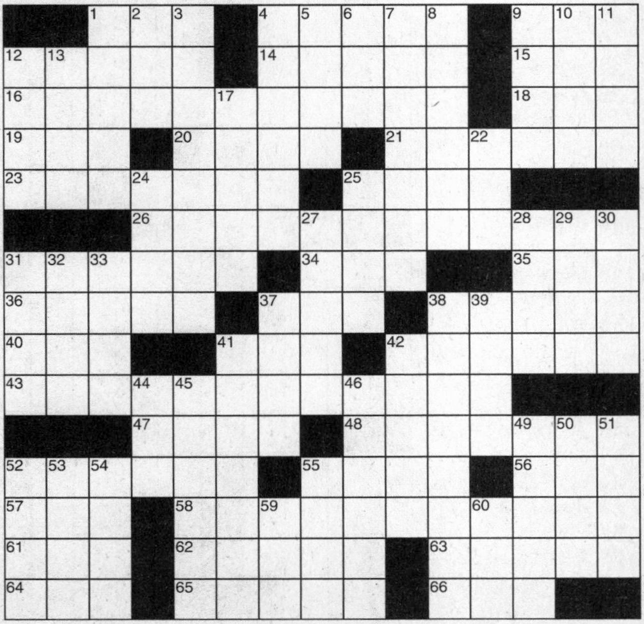

246 *SOMETHING FISHY*

by Shirley Soloway

ACROSS

1 Doll's word
5 *Butterfield 8* author
10 Cookie keeper
13 Brutus' birds
14 Showed again
15 Window glass
16 Misleading clue
18 Makes believe
19 Musical chord
20 Boat trip
21 Comic sketch
22 Flower segment
24 Sofas and stools
26 __ *Gay*
29 Skiing areas
32 West Coast cops, for short
35 Fixes the outcome
37 Quiver item
38 Mr. Baba
39 Ore processor
41 Santa __, CA
42 Stage star Theodore
44 Vincent Lopez theme
45 __-bitsy
46 Shorthand specialists
48 Have __ (argue)
50 Meat and veggie combos
52 Soap opera, for one
56 __ in (victimize)
58 Andy Taylor's son
61 Zoo attraction
62 Finished
63 Patti Page song
65 *Serpico* author Peter
66 Metrical foot
67 Cooking fat
68 Caribou kin
69 Get up
70 Leicester lodgings

DOWN

1 Shopping centers
2 Ward off
3 Radio and TV
4 Humiliated
5 Bobby of hockey
6 Towel inscription
7 Sills solo
8 Sari sporters
9 Ulterior motives
10 Lean-cuisine eater
11 Opposed to
12 Take five
15 Religious leader
17 *East of* __
23 Comedian Crosby
25 Controversial tree spray
27 Mortgage, e.g.
28 Shining brightly
30 Ages
31 Move in the breeze
32 Research rooms
33 Touched down
34 Western mountain
36 Normandy town
39 __ gin fizz
40 Be all __ (listen)
43 Becomes a participant
45 Haifa native
47 Descends swiftly
49 Johnny of *Edward Scissorhands*
51 Tomato-throwing sound
53 Peruvian Indian
54 Decorate
55 Alan and Cheryl
56 "The Eternal City"
57 Like Humpty Dumpty
59 Notion
60 Coll. major
64 Compound-sentence connector

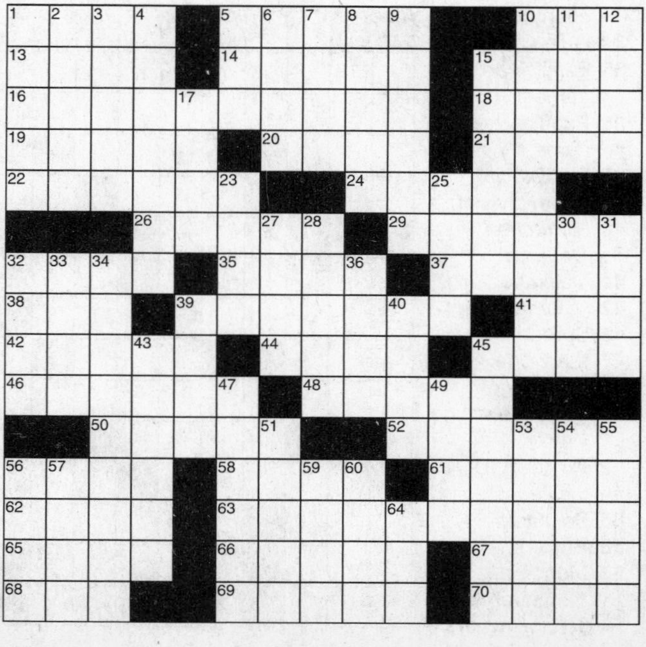

247 DOG DAY

by Shirley Soloway

ACROSS

1 *Diary of __ Housewife*
5 Theater turkey
9 Curved
14 Photogravure process, for short
15 "The __ of the Ancient Mariner"
16 Actress Dern
17 Canine pedigrees?
19 Italian bread?
20 __-Barbera cartoons
21 Place in one's care
23 Mrs. Perón
24 *My Three __*
26 Form a concept
29 Gets a new tenant
31 US native
32 Outfits
35 Inc., in England
36 Canine documentaries?
40 Tempe coll.
42 Sound system
43 Golden raisin
47 Shop machine
51 Jai-alai ball
52 Superstar
54 __ carte
55 Aerosol gas
57 He keeps lions in line
59 Catch container
61 Canine devotion?
63 Cancel
64 Ratio words
65 Change for a five
66 Grating sounds
67 Adventure story
68 Left the premises

DOWN

1 Private eye Lew
2 California desert
3 Musically untraditional
4 Quilt filling
5 Part of TGIF
6 Napkin fabric
7 Seer's signs
8 Nuisance
9 Refer (to)
10 Hair-__ (scary story)
11 Canine appendages?
12 Century 21 rival
13 Prosecutors: Abbr.
18 Stretchable thread
22 Edge
25 Word form for "bone"
27 Explosive initials
28 Actor Byrnes
30 Big head
31 Tennis great Arthur
33 __ Major
34 Oregon hrs.
36 Terrier enclosures?
37 Approximately
38 Lots
39 Heavy weight
40 Cleo's attacker
41 Lyon of *Lolita*
44 Ripped to shreds
45 Coral islands
46 Short snooze
48 Singer Vic
49 Dice throw
50 Most unusual
52 Occupied
53 Store divs.
56 Buy __ in a poke
58 In the hold
59 Sedan or coupe
60 Heredity letters
62 Saucepan

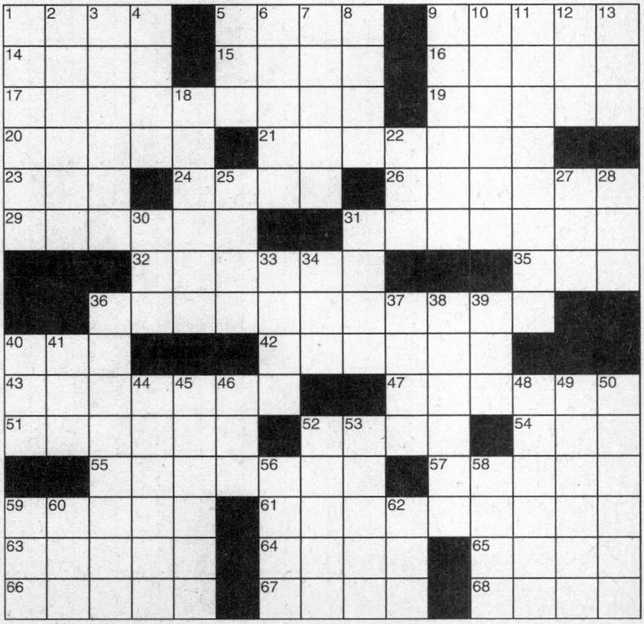

248 LANGUAGE CLASS

by Bob Lubbers

ACROSS

1 Psyched up
5 Come to light
10 Type of map
14 Actress Velez
15 Mortise's mate
16 "__ Lama Ding Dong"
17 Shirt feature
19 "Put __ writing"
20 Cherry-topped treat
21 Siege activity
23 Liqueur flavoring
25 Bank offering
26 Convalescent's need
29 Canadian currency
32 Reunion attendee
33 Least
36 Lode load
37 Less caloric, in ads
38 Part of USNA
39 Cosmetics company
40 Bomber grp.
41 Snow __ (shovel alternative)
44 Sleeveless garment
45 On land
47 Worships
49 Govt. agt.
50 Step
51 Like mom and dad
54 Cellist Pablo
58 Rod attachment
59 Tablecloth material
61 *"Dies __"*
62 Desi's daughter
63 "The __ Love" ('87 tune)
64 Feminist Lucretia
65 Bergen dummy
66 Tree house?

DOWN

1 Politician Landon et al.
2 Spiritual guide
3 Unlocked
4 Cannes cop
5 Godlessness
6 __ room (family hangout)
7 Temporarily unavailable
8 Like a plush toy
9 Hugs, in a way
10 Basic
11 Valentino, for one
12 Ugandan dictator
13 Sharp taste
18 Walking stick
22 Tooth part
24 Office worker
26 Hobbyist's wood
27 Inventor Howe
28 Split bill
30 Gertrude Stein phrase
31 Landlord's take
34 Damp and cold
35 Three-time Wimbledon winner
39 Loathing
41 Fiber source
42 Soup legumes
43 Arrived at
46 Brunch basic
48 Perfume bottle
50 Pizza piece
51 Stiffly formal
52 Space starter
53 __ for one's money
55 Ms. Bancroft
56 Wine dregs
57 Grumpy mood
60 *To __ With Love*

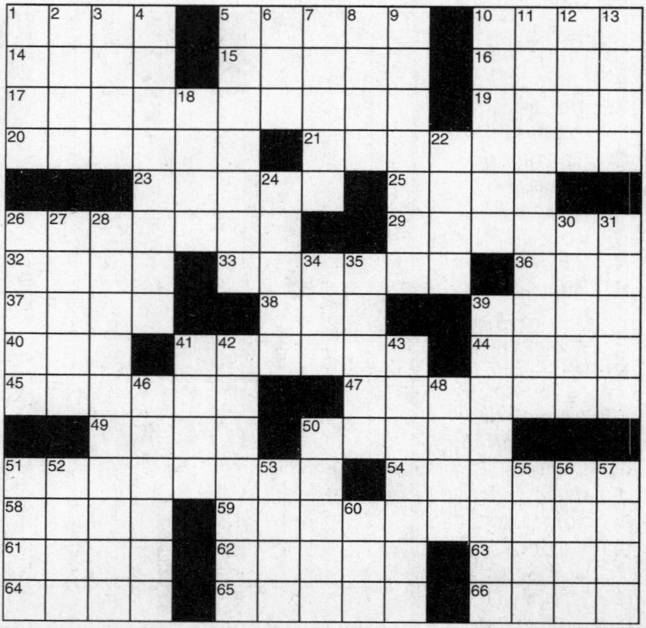

249 *SOLID STATE*

by Shirley Soloway

ACROSS

1 Fitness farms
5 Pitchfork part
10 Daily drama
14 Come to the rescue
15 Solitary soul
16 Little pie
17 King of the Huns
18 Entertain
19 Kett of comics
20 Long, cold look
23 Trig functions
24 Played for time
28 Coronet
32 *Superman* star
33 Inc., British-style
36 European sable
39 Exist
40 Easily duped
41 Explosive letters
42 Teen scene
46 Ave. crossers
47 Cuddly Australian
48 Singer Presley
50 Indulge oneself
53 Household job
57 Like Andy Devine
61 Quiet sort
64 *West Side Story* song
65 Wine valley
66 Verdi opera
67 Prepares for the press
68 Jack of *Rio Lobo*
69 Nasty
70 Actress Taylor
71 Declares

DOWN

1 Rug types
2 Lab dish
3 Edgar __ Poe
4 Small piano
5 Kind of map
6 European capital
7 Burden
8 Heron homes
9 Terrific
10 Pittsburgh player
11 Cereal grain
12 Museum display
13 School org.
21 Egyptian goddess
22 __ avis
25 Baltic natives
26 Happening
27 Car scars
29 __ time (never)
30 Equine shade
31 "Have __ day!"
33 Escapades
34 Scout unit
35 Stick-on
37 Daredevil Knievel
38 TV tycoon Griffin
43 Jack of *The Odd Couple*
44 Singer Vikki
45 Half a Latin song
49 Radiates
51 More courageous
52 Stay away from
54 Florida city
55 Clear a loan
56 Dutch exports
58 "__ go bragh!"
59 Lo-cal, in ads
60 Bouquet holder
61 Machine part
62 Tell a fib
63 Nabokov novel

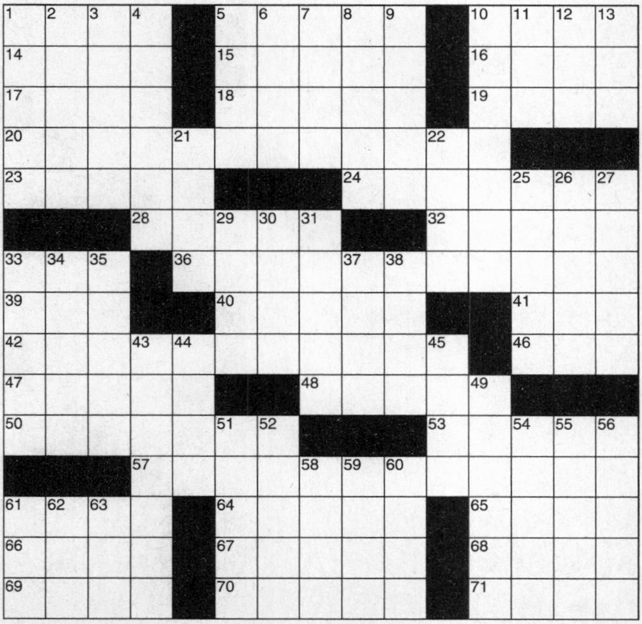

250 HEAD GAMES

by Dean Niles

ACROSS

1 United group
5 Sow chow
9 Oral
14 Bowling alley
15 Feel concern
16 Make merry
17 Enlightening experience
19 Loose-limbed
20 Actor Wallach
21 Bring to ruin
22 Fiddle around
23 Hang down
25 Just out
26 Attacked
29 Dusting cloth
32 Think the world of
35 Rope in
36 Run-of-the-mill
37 Dryer deposit
38 Puts on
39 Throw out a line
40 Butterfly kin
41 Sheep shed
42 Terra __ (clay)
43 Blonde shade
44 Speak boastfully, in a way
46 Pass over
48 Cracked dish?
52 Mortise mates
54 Ray of light
56 Chopping tool
57 Wed in haste
58 Kept in reserve
60 Selling point
61 Soft cheese
62 Social misfit
63 Thin-voiced
64 Gave rise to
65 Pretentiously highbrow

DOWN

1 Run in the wash
2 Derek and the Dominos song
3 __ a million (rare)
4 Corporate VIP
5 Play parts
6 Real estate
7 Layered cookie
8 According to
9 Made much of
10 Fails to mention
11 Ruthless
12 Tennis great Arthur
13 Wolfish expression
18 Life sign
22 Makes ready
24 Singer Brooks
25 Burned brightly
27 In
28 More than mad
30 Helper: Abbr.
31 "I __ Name" (Croce tune)
32 __ mater
33 God, in Guadalajara
34 To a tee
36 Range of view
38 Jillions
42 Punctuation mark
44 XC
45 Wandered
47 Cantered easily
49 L.A. hoopster
50 Put into use
51 Kennedy or Roosevelt
52 Pull apart
53 Otherwise
54 Roseanne, née __
55 A Great Lake
58 Tides do it
59 Genetic info

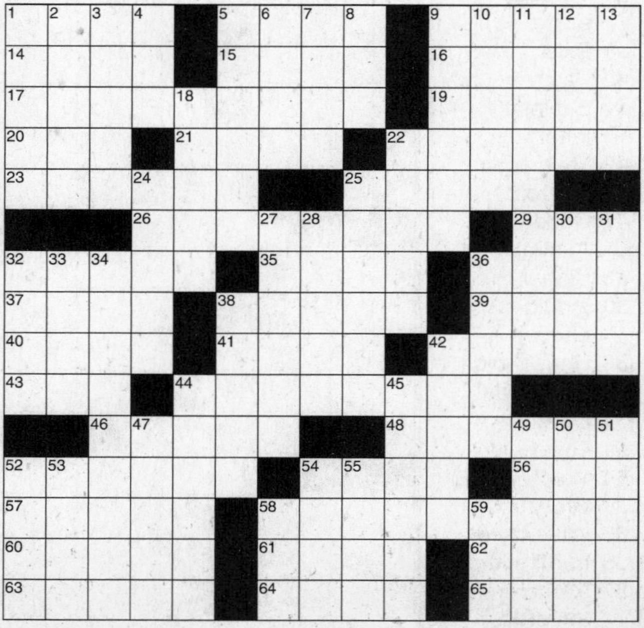

251 FIGURE IT OUT

by Eric Albert

ACROSS

1 Baseball gloves
6 Small bay
11 Traveler's need
14 Pinhead
15 Grown-up, legally
16 Altar vow
17 The best
19 *Platoon* setting
20 *The Big Chill* director
21 "And I Love __"
22 Foul person?
23 Sneaky
24 Taped sports event?
27 Mix a salad
29 Violinist Perlman
31 Central point
34 Everyman Doe
37 Epsilon follower
38 Five clubs, e.g.
39 Cry of pity
40 Pleasure cruiser
42 Bread spread
43 Computer problem
45 Quiz choice
46 Cozy retreat
47 Conductor Kostelanetz
48 Author/critic Susan
50 Take care of
52 Beaver's dad
53 Flow back
56 Tai __ (martial art)
58 Snaky swimmer
60 Open acknowledgment
62 Dress border
63 Famed watershed
66 It's all the rage
67 Residence
68 Burn a bit
69 *King of Queens* network
70 Onetime Hollywood Square
71 Moved sideways

DOWN

1 Small weasels
2 Without a flaw
3 Slightly sloshed
4 Recounted
5 Actor Whitman
6 Red letters?
7 Patriots' org.
8 Strip of wood
9 Plumed bird
10 Run away
11 Super-small
12 First person
13 Regal magnificence
18 Stylish
25 Con men
26 Admit an error
28 "Toodle-oo!"
29 Guarantee
30 Hawaiian honcho
32 Puts to work
33 Ammo
34 It's south of Borneo
35 Ken of *thirtysomething*
36 Dickens novel
41 Group of four
44 Dakar's nation
49 Counsel
51 Bat Masterson's hat
53 *Dallas* surname
54 Lawman's symbol
55 Feel sympathy
56 Elegant
57 Parsley or peppermint
59 Boxer Spinks
61 Roman poet
64 Append
65 Casual shirt

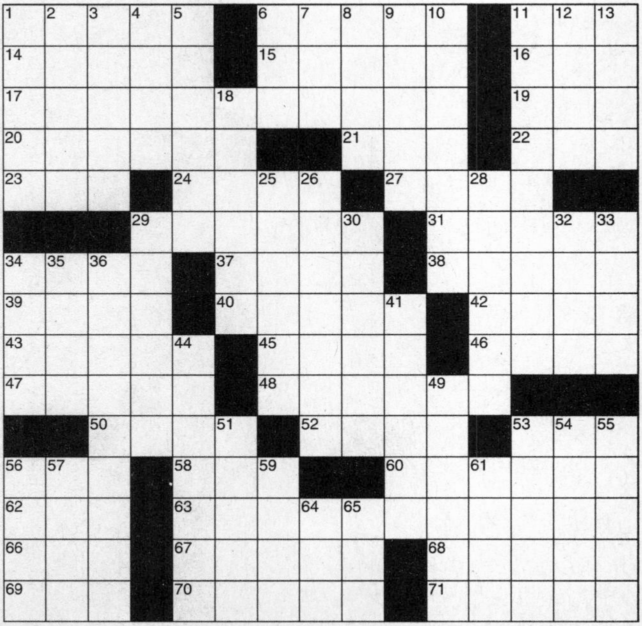

252 HEAVE-HO

by Fred Piscop

ACROSS

1 Thunder sound
5 Pleasure craft
10 Explode
14 Mata __
15 Be off
16 Ms. Lenska
17 Emulate Perry White
18 Aquatic mammal
19 Mo. expense
20 Undergo chemical change
22 Small carpets
24 Fit
26 Porker's pad
27 Brigitte's brother
29 Six-line stanza
34 Ajax alternative
37 Comics villain Luthor
38 Break one's back
39 Petri-dish filler
40 Decree
43 Turner et al.
44 Lifts a barbell
46 "Rub-a-dub-dub" craft
47 Loch __
48 "__ Fideles"
50 Comedian Arnold
52 Feeling poorly
54 Glacial effect
58 Lightning bugs
63 Push
64 Shaquille of the courts
65 Armor type
67 Change for a five
68 Wipe out a diskette
69 First name in daredeviltry
70 Pale color
71 Fathers
72 Eastern European
73 Back talk

DOWN

1 Dijon darling
2 Full
3 *Norma* numbers
4 Farm tools
5 __-mo
6 Used a stencil
7 "Dang!" e.g.
8 Excess production
9 Ross and Margot
10 __ Rabbit (Harris character)
11 Humdinger
12 Designer Cassini
13 Female mil. personnel
21 Paving material
23 YYY
25 Soccer great
28 Walks out
30 Schoolboys' shooters
31 Appropriate
32 Holiday preceders
33 __ *of the D'Urbervilles*
34 Lower California
35 Matured
36 Bring to light
41 Cloyingly prettier
42 Ski lift
45 Puts an end to
49 Building wing
51 Denials
53 Drink garnishes
55 Ancient Greek colony
56 Pizzeria equipment
57 Tree houses?
58 Adversaries
59 Calvary inscription
60 Parent
61 Peace of mind
62 Icicle locale
66 Law deg.

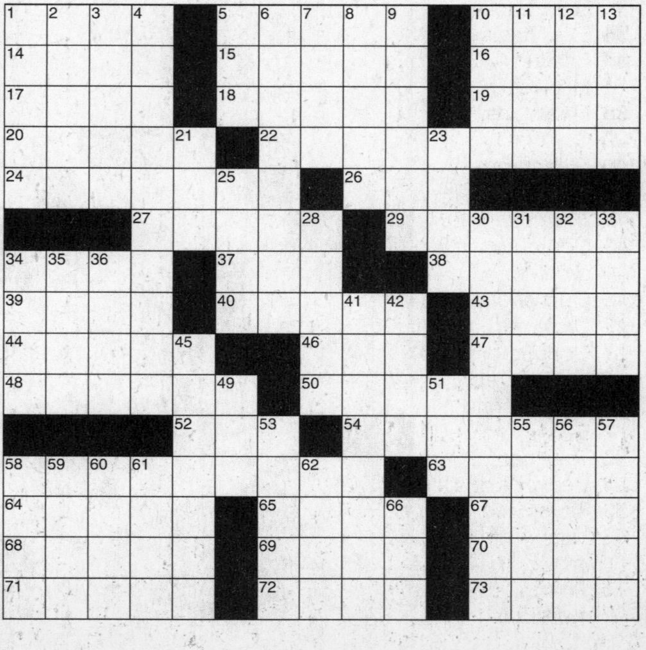

253 *PACK TALK*

by Shirley Soloway

ACROSS

1 Slightly moist
5 Prepares to fire
9 Extreme
14 McClurg or Adams
15 Sudden thought
16 City on the Seine
17 Mattress platform
19 Confused
20 Caesar's foe
21 Predetermine
23 Slangy affirmative
24 Health resort
26 Fuel container
27 Roasted treat
30 Badminton stroke
33 Just fair
36 Reverberation
37 Upper crust
39 Hebrew month
40 Back areas
42 "What's __ for me?"
43 Sways
45 Greenish blue
46 "Untouchable" Eliot
47 Genesis vessel
48 Social worker's duties
51 Family group
53 Naval off.
54 Bandleader Calloway
57 Made arrangements
60 Graceland, e.g.
62 Audibly
63 Table game
65 Tropical fish
66 Writer Stoker
67 Strip of wood
68 Taj __
69 Big rig
70 Respond rudely to

DOWN

1 Pat Boone's daughter
2 Love madly
3 Snafu
4 Pain in the neck
5 Pilot's concern
6 Dictator Amin
7 Repair a rip
8 Spice-rack item
9 To the north
10 Livy's language
11 Telephone channel
12 Chinese staple
13 Make an inquiry
18 Shove
22 Letters after R
25 Fancy neckwear
27 Bottle stop
28 *My __ Sons*
29 Cash-register key
31 Singer Redding
32 Wagers
33 Poet Teasdale
34 Cologne characteristic
35 Coarse fabric
38 "The Swedish Nightingale"
41 "All __" (Brenda Lee song)
44 Public disgrace
49 Tapper Miller
50 Exec. aide
52 Designer Ashley
54 __ lily
55 Book of maps
56 Borscht ingredients
57 Court action
58 Dwindles
59 Throw down the gauntlet
61 Dick Tracy's lady
62 Fast money source: Abbr.
64 Actress Rita

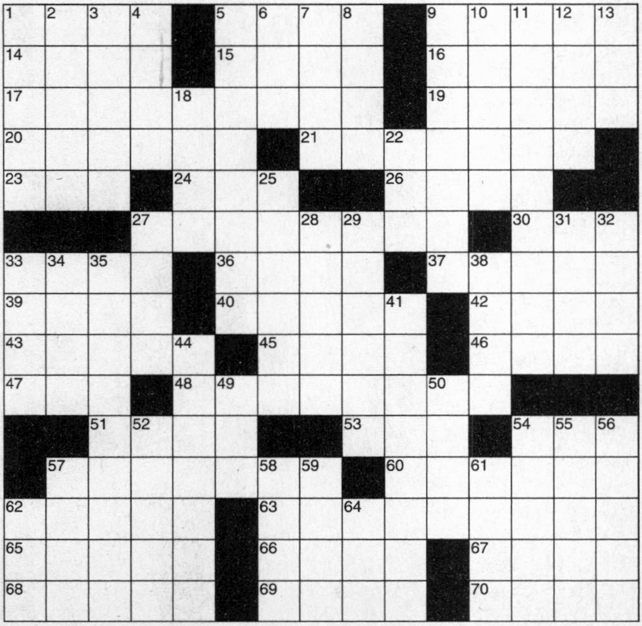

254 AD DICTION

by Trip Payne

ACROSS
1 __ Vanilli
6 Lingerie item
9 Cafeteria selections
14 Zodiac sign
15 __ room (den)
16 Foreword or overture
17 One way to advertise
20 Dash lengths
21 Less speedy
22 Concerning
23 Kansas city
24 __ *That Jazz*
26 One way to advertise
32 Milk measures
33 Bauxite and galena
34 Treasure-hunt need
36 Ruin
37 Challenging one
39 Holyfield's defeater
40 Famed architect
41 Moore of *A Few Good Men*
42 Joan of Arc site
43 One way to advertise
47 "__ was saying . . ."
48 Polly or Esther
49 First name
52 Call __ (remember)
55 __ double take
58 One way to advertise
61 Says for sure
62 + or &
63 Actress Anouk
64 It gives you a rise
65 Auto acronym
66 Computer fans

DOWN
1 Full-grown filly
2 Where Shiraz is
3 Mason-jar toppers
4 Ring around the collar?
5 Marine crustaceans
6 NBC newsman
7 Two after do
8 Highest point
9 Douglas tree
10 Ready for summoning
11 Inventor Elisha
12 "Phooey!"
13 One-man show
18 Aspen's st.
19 Delete key's ancestor
23 Fascinated by
25 CD predecessors
26 Reds and whites
27 Calcutta's country
28 Column style
29 Fury
30 Love affair
31 Deviated
32 Baby basset
35 Cross product
37 Statesman Clinton
38 "__ Blue?"
39 Gravy vessel
41 Shingle letters
42 Short poem
44 Title assigners
45 Bob or beehive
46 A lot of rot
49 *Queen for __*
50 Seedy joint
51 General vicinity
53 General Bradley
54 Pride of lions?
55 Tiny coin
56 Unique person
57 Long periods
59 Chicago's zone: Abbr.
60 "Deck the Halls" word

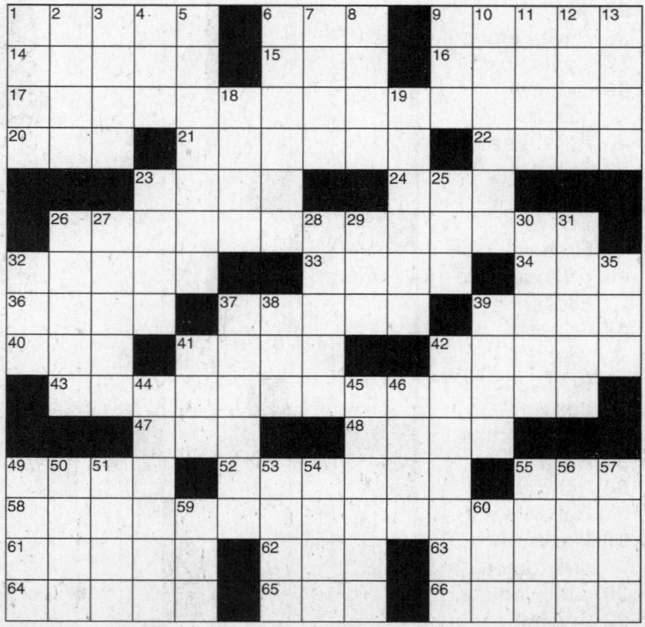

255 *FILM FORECAST*

by Eric Albert

ACROSS
1 Twist in wood
5 Do the decks
9 Spanish seaport
14 Composer Stravinsky
15 Tiny amount
16 Pure, fresh air
17 Speak without words
18 Nursery furniture
19 Cleanse
20 Eastwood movie of '71
23 Strong craving
24 Pub potable
25 __ *Grit*
26 Some jump for it
27 Overshoe
28 Turkish topper
31 Love, in Lyon
34 Pairs
35 Be an omen of
36 Kelly movie of '52
39 Misfortunes
40 Foot feature
41 Have as a goal
42 The blue yonder
43 The one and the other
44 Madness?
45 Chevalier song
46 Farm worker
47 Tabloid subject
50 Poitier movie of '61, with *A*
54 Knight fight
55 Advantage
56 Kind of kick
57 Dweller in Dogpatch
58 Noticed
59 *Othello* villain
60 Subway
61 Common condiment
62 Cut out coupons

DOWN
1 Popeye's pal
2 Sprightly
3 Type type
4 Hunted animal
5 Palermo is its capital
6 Inferior
7 Go __ (fight)
8 Fairy's purchase?
9 Duck responsibility
10 Light blue
11 Quad building
12 *Bus Stop* playwright
13 Our omega
21 New Zealand native
22 First-class person?
26 Earthenware vessels
27 *The Brady* __
28 Bubbles
29 Rework words
30 Founder of Stoicism
31 "Functioning or not"
32 Cookies' accompaniment
33 As recently as
34 Filth
35 Cheeseboard choice
37 Country singer Judd
38 Your home
43 Small restaurant
44 Firmly fixed
45 Dough nut?
46 Heavenly being
47 Customary
48 Mold and mildew
49 Doing best
50 After-bath wear
51 Cousin's mother
52 Light-bulb lighter?
53 Homeric specialty
54 Bread spread

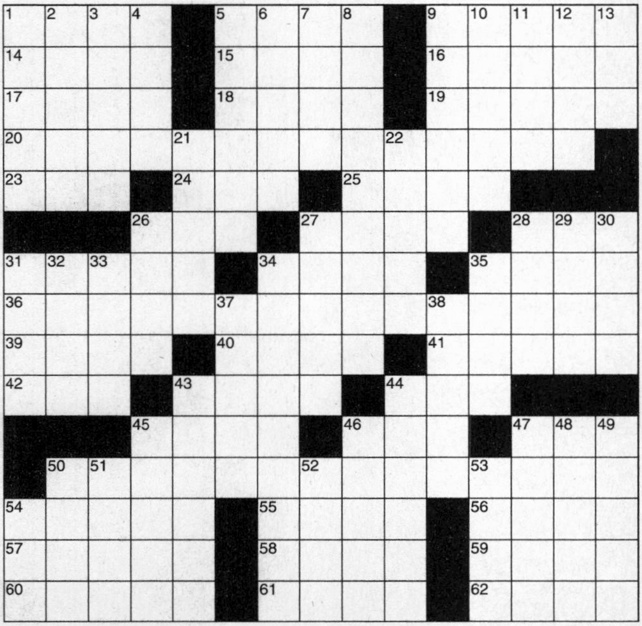

256 *ECHOIC ADDRESSES*

by Bob Lubbers

ACROSS

1 Tacks on
5 Statesman Eban et al.
10 CLIV + XLVII
13 IHOP rival
14 Knots
15 Supply with weapons
16 Zoo performer
17 Deft
18 Pom's perch
19 Last Frontier city
21 Location
22 World-weary
24 Wrote graffiti
26 Suffix with profit
27 Opens to view
31 "That's __" (Dean Martin song)
32 Anti-colonist?
34 Arafat's grp.
35 L.A. suburb
39 Vietnamese holiday
40 Blow up
42 Sellers or Fonda
45 *King Lear* daughter
46 AAA offering
47 Supervise
49 Sitcom afterlife
51 Lion lairs
52 Eastern capital
56 Officeholders
57 *Remington* __
58 Agree (with)
61 Western Indian
62 Scotto or Tebaldi
63 Element
64 Edit. submissions
65 Song opener
66 Omelet ingredients

DOWN

1 Joyful sounds
2 Buck's mate
3 Indonesian capital
4 Arias, e.g.
5 *Three Men __ Baby*
6 Conifer covering
7 Studio lamps
8 Similar
9 Heathrow arr.
10 Gingham alternative
11 Volcano feature
12 Block
14 Moo goo __ pan
20 Lincoln and Douglas, e.g.
21 Polynesian islander
22 Actress Arthur
23 Camera part
25 Medieval sport
28 Rat-__
29 Sleep phenom
30 Wear away
33 Comes in
34 Pocket bread
36 Photog's orig.
37 __-on (wild behavior)
38 Westernmost Aleutian
41 Sundown, to Shelley
42 Speaker's platform
43 Occurrences
44 Tightens up
45 Give way
48 Gobbled up
50 Happen next
53 Yogi or Smokey
54 Choir member
55 Teachers' org.
57 __ Lanka
59 Excavate
60 UFO crew

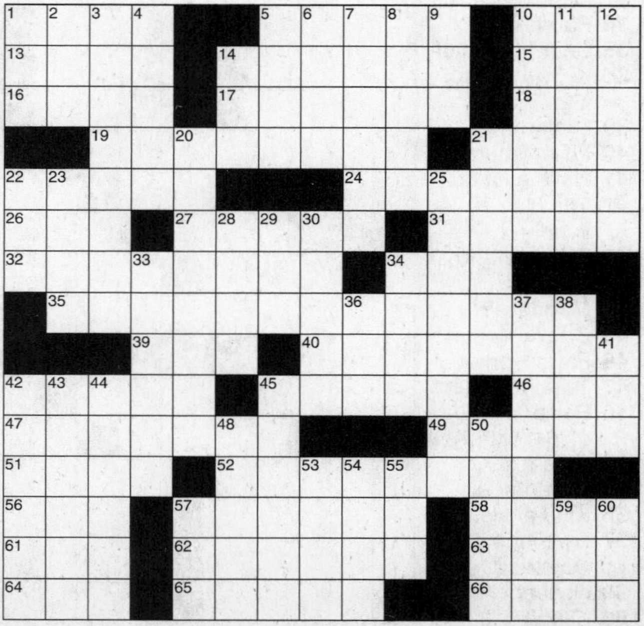

257 *IN THE MAIL*

by Shirley Soloway

ACROSS

1 Tater
5 Irene of *Fame*
9 Starts fishing
14 Rocker Turner
15 Cassini of fashion
16 "__ of Old Smokey"
17 Hertz competitor
18 Director Wertmuller
19 *A Bell for* __
20 Precisely
23 Ran into
24 *Remington* __
25 Assembles
27 Deep breath
29 Becomes rigid
32 The Cumberland __
35 Actress Durbin
38 Politico Bob
39 Wed impulsively
41 __ de Janeiro
42 Mickey or Mighty
43 Passable
44 Blake of *Gunsmoke*
46 Highlander's hat
47 Aquarium denizens
49 Long periods
51 "__ go again!"
54 Write in the margins
58 Actress Lupino
60 Union member, e.g.
62 Jai alai basket
64 __ were (so to speak)
65 Poet Khayyám
66 Join up
67 Sampras of tennis
68 Mexican money
69 Office worker
70 Winter vehicle
71 Crystal gazer

DOWN

1 Sports data
2 Turn on an axis
3 Bring together
4 Short races
5 Prof's place
6 "I cannot tell __"
7 Landlords' income
8 Striped stone
9 Rough
10 *Sanford* __ *Son*
11 Eradicates
12 Musical quality
13 Catch sight of
21 Leave out
22 James or Place
26 Take apart
28 Injure
30 *Born Free* lioness
31 Appear to be
32 Adventure story
33 Healing plant
34 ASAP
36 Dancer Peeples
37 *And Then There Were* __
40 Skin opening
42 Feudal estate
44 On a cruise
45 Made a contribution
48 Jockey Eddie
50 Razor sharpeners
52 Envelops
53 Defunct car
55 Actress Anouk
56 Poke fun at
57 Bad move
58 Frozen desserts
59 Car scar
61 Refer to
63 Perfect rating

258 DOUBLY QUIET

by Shirley Soloway

ACROSS

1 Church officer
6 Pleased
10 Mil. female
13 Singer Branigan
14 Almost there
15 "__ Were a Rich Man"
16 Some knots
18 Turf
19 Actor Carney
20 "__-porridge hot . . ."
21 Resort lake
23 Highways and byways
24 Pastoral poem
25 Hebrew month
27 Up __ (yet)
29 Kind of communication
33 Venomous viper
36 Singing Mama
37 Sews a toe
38 Tennis star Arthur
39 Adjectival suffix
40 Couture event
42 *America's Most Wanted* host
44 "__ sow, so shall . . ."
45 Former New York senator Al D'__
47 Premiere performance
50 Assail
51 Price twice
52 Used to be
55 Crank's comment
56 Little or no attention
59 Mine find
60 Actress Anouk
61 __ firma
62 Paving material
63 Unassuming
64 String toys

DOWN

1 Martinelli or Lanchester
2 Comedian Bert
3 Performance for two
4 Before, poetically
5 Good relationship
6 Tumbler
7 Solitary
8 Make an inquiry
9 Preordain
10 On the fence
11 "__ Such As I" ('59 song)
12 Castro of Cuba
14 Niger's neighbor
17 Cousteau's workplace
22 Big fuss
23 Knocks sharply
25 Discovery shouts
26 Kitchen appliance
27 Singer Tennille
28 Approximately
29 Anat., e.g.
30 Harem rooms
31 Dress accessory
32 Prince Charles' title: Abbr.
34 Oxford or brogan
35 Church bench
38 Helper: Abbr.
40 Ocean wreckage
41 Mischievous
43 Had a bite
45 Monastery head
46 Stiller's partner
47 John or Bo
48 Novel ending
49 __-relief
51 European capital
52 Lean and sinewy
53 Curly coif
54 Depots: Abbr.
57 Rush off
58 Vintage car

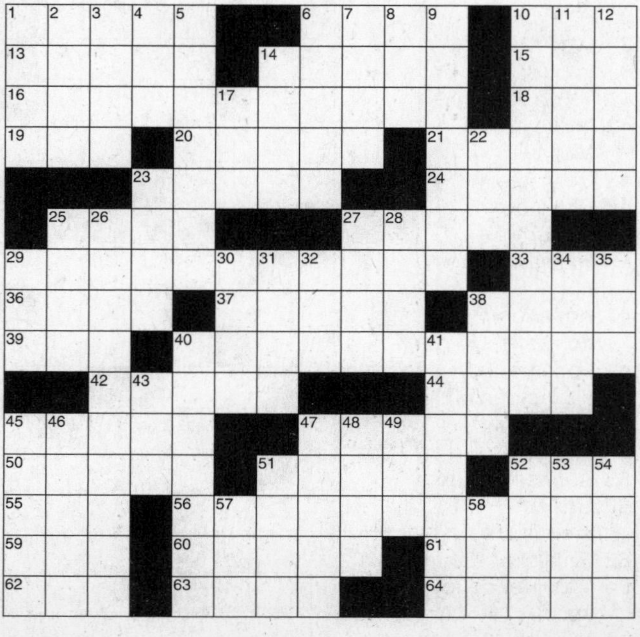

259 *ZILCH*

by Eric Albert

ACROSS

1 Require a rubdown
5 Grate stuff
10 Shopper's paradise
14 Donkey's cry
15 Canary's cry
16 Bassoon relative
17 '60s phrase
20 Lamb's kin
21 In the bag
22 Surrounded by
23 James of *Brian's Song*
24 Soft cheese
25 Descend upon
28 Asks for alms
29 Janitor's item
32 Valerie Harper sitcom
33 Bill of fare
34 Of sound mind
35 *Fin de siècle* epithet
38 Archer or Jackson
39 Birdhouse visitor
40 Elevator tunes
41 Oxford omega
42 Funnyman Sahl
43 Actress Tyson
44 Racer's gauge
45 Stocking material
46 Glacial period
49 Singer of Hollywood
50 "The Greatest"
53 Hanks/Gleason drama
56 Chanel of fashion
57 Indian language
58 Crazed
59 Tennis ace Arthur
60 "The final frontier"
61 Slow

DOWN

1 Fit for the job
2 Emulate a rooster
3 __ *Gun Will Travel*
4 Spud bud
5 Bona fide
6 Fleeced
7 Roll-call response
8 Sushi selection
9 *Thunderball* prop
10 The reel thing
11 Undercover?
12 *The Daily Planet*'s Lane
13 Latvian
18 Biblical prophet
19 Brest buddies
23 Bum
24 Dahomey, today
25 Ball's costar
26 1953 western
27 Talkies' attraction
28 Stephen Vincent __
29 Indian ears
30 Ryan or Tatum
31 Kid-brotherish
33 42 Down gift
34 Puzzled
36 Conversation contribution?
37 Actor Estevez
42 Star followers
43 Hem in
44 Resort lake
45 Type of boom
46 Pizarro victim
47 Speaks softly
48 Engrave
49 Kind of bean
50 Bullets and bombs
51 Take a peek
52 Totally black
54 Breach
55 Put on the __ (make famous)

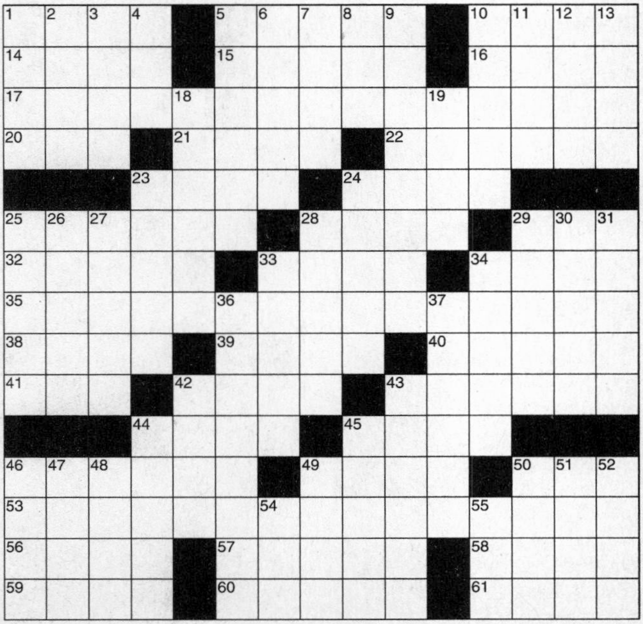

260 MORE ZILCH

by Fred Piscop

ACROSS

1 ABC rival
4 "__ Breaky Heart"
8 Group of lions
13 Secular
14 Tried-and-__
15 *Bolero* composer
16 Egyptian cross
17 Mrs. Chaplin
18 Basketballer Shaquille
19 They may be whispered in your ear
22 *Amateur Hour* host
23 Society-column word
24 *People* __ *Funny*
25 North Pole worker
27 Mess specialist
31 __ Domingo
34 Zorba or Jimmy
36 Drivers' org.
37 Claims to public land
40 "The Boy King"
41 Mules and moccasins
42 Telegraphy code
43 Window frame
45 Olden times, in olden times
46 Workweek start: Abbr.
47 Superlative suffix
49 Beach footwear
53 *Song of the South* tune
56 Israeli seaport
58 Hoss' brother
59 Actress Anderson
60 Doubleday or Yokum
61 __ *18* (Uris novel)
62 St. Louis sight
63 Bolivian city
64 Hammer part
65 "I told you so!"

DOWN

1 "__ talk?": Joan Rivers
2 Did the Tour de France
3 Plans
4 Right away
5 Shepherd's staff
6 Peck partner
7 "She Loves You" word
8 Lying flat
9 Kitchen appliances
10 Currier's partner
11 Narc's org.
12 Building addition
13 Wear well
20 Seer's cards
21 Have a hunch
25 Slipped up
26 Minus
28 Cowardly Lion portrayer
29 Feedbag filler
30 Foundation
31 JFK landers
32 Blue hue
33 Bonkers
34 An earth sci.
35 Japanese robe
38 Eta follower
39 Venetian traffic
44 Young cow
46 Lunatic
48 Trunk item
49 '60s activist Bobby
50 Idolize
51 Jousting weapon
52 __ Tzu (Tibetan dog)
53 Brass component
54 Clammy
55 Singer Adams
56 Owns
57 __ Dhabi

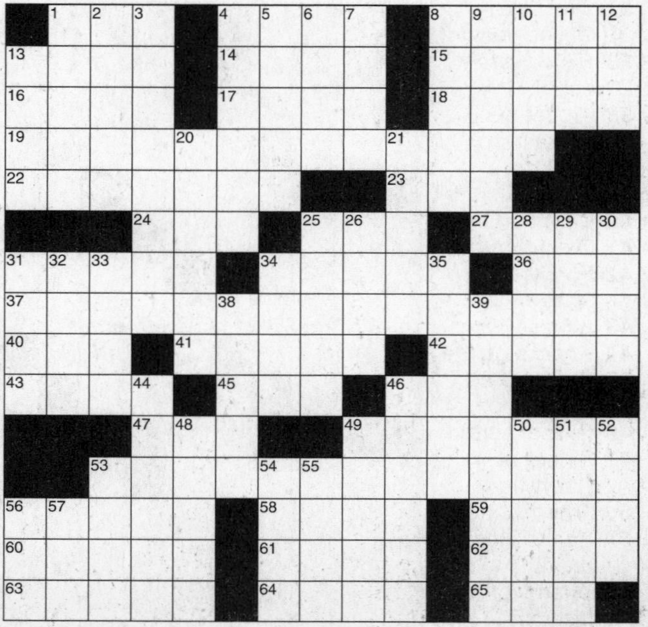

261 *ELEMENTARY*

by Dean Niles

ACROSS

1 Jr.-year exam
5 Wove a web
9 Dawn goddess
12 French girlfriend
13 Domingo, for one
15 __ *Ado About Nothing*
17 Lady's man?
18 Lift up
19 Meany
20 __ foo yung
21 Fertility symbol
23 Combine
25 Kind of punch
26 Three in one
28 Macadamized
30 Big name in applesauce
31 Fresco, for one
32 Pugilists' org.
35 Greek vowels
36 Quebec city
37 Columnist Herb
38 Hide-hair link
39 Tropical fish
40 Filled to the gills
41 Greets, in a way
42 Defensive back
43 Sock style
46 Passover meal
47 Fourth of July item
50 Actress Farrow
53 "__ a Name" (Croce tune)
54 Hailing from Honshu
55 Practical jokes
56 Overdo the sentiment
57 "Whole __ Love" ('70 song)
58 Fox follower?
59 Letter additions: Abbr.
60 Service charges
61 Creole veggie

DOWN

1 Colorless
2 Urban blight
3 Invisible instrument
4 Senator Kennedy
5 Attack from above
6 Pole star?
7 Moon __ Zappa
8 Snack
9 Chewed the scenery
10 Must
11 Tighten with a tool
14 Elimination
16 Submarine sandwich
21 One, in Wiesbaden
22 Scott Turow book
24 Sundae topping
26 Govt. agents
27 Printing process
28 Catty remarks?
29 Region
31 Speck of dust
32 Stationery feature
33 Borscht ingredient
34 Actor Garcia
36 More than a couple
37 __ au lait
39 Lauder powder
40 Iran's Bani-__
41 Artistic family
42 Regarded to be
43 Not give __ (be indifferent)
44 Construct haphazardly
45 Before deductions
46 Emulate Kristi
48 From
49 Make a footnote
51 Composer Stravinsky
52 Movie terrier
55 Former Pontiac model

262 FOUR GO

by Shirley Soloway

ACROSS
1 October birthstone
5 Strike ignorer
9 Lord or Lady
14 Capital of Peru
15 Hercules' love
16 *The Woman* __ ('84 film)
17 Superman's sweetie
18 Wordy Webster
19 Changes the text
20 DINGO
23 Filming session
24 Bud's buddy
25 Step on the __ (hurry)
28 LINGO
32 Rock band's need
35 Slightly moist
36 Jocular Johnson
37 Campus digs
39 Watery fluid
42 Critic Rex
43 Pavarotti piece
44 ". . . baked in __"
46 Shingle letters
47 BINGO
52 Catch sight of
53 *Norma* __
54 "To __ human . . ."
57 RINGO
62 Silvery fish
64 *Doctor Zhivago* character
65 Concerned with
66 Singer Della
67 Egg-shaped
68 High time?
69 Strongboxes
70 Puts in stitches
71 Sicilian spewer

DOWN
1 __ podrida
2 Reverent
3 Pennsylvania sect
4 *The* __ *the Mohicans*
5 Frank and Nancy
6 Self-possessed
7 Jai __
8 On __ of (representing)
9 Unavailable
10 __-European
11 Set off
12 Give permission
13 Asner and Wynn
21 Crucifix
22 Calculator figs.
26 Made believe
27 Lean-tos
29 Married *Mlle.*
30 Talk-show host Winfrey
31 Corn portion
32 Proverb
33 Tropical eel
34 Top-quality meat
38 West of Hollywood
40 "__ Lazy River"
41 Iron and calcium
45 Light tan
48 Speaks one's piece
49 Dieter's no-no
50 Stringed instruments
51 Winter weasel
55 __ *Rappaport*
56 Novelist Anya
58 "What __ can I say?"
59 Icicle site
60 Sketch
61 Gossipy Barrett
62 S.A.T. takers
63 "Cry __ River"

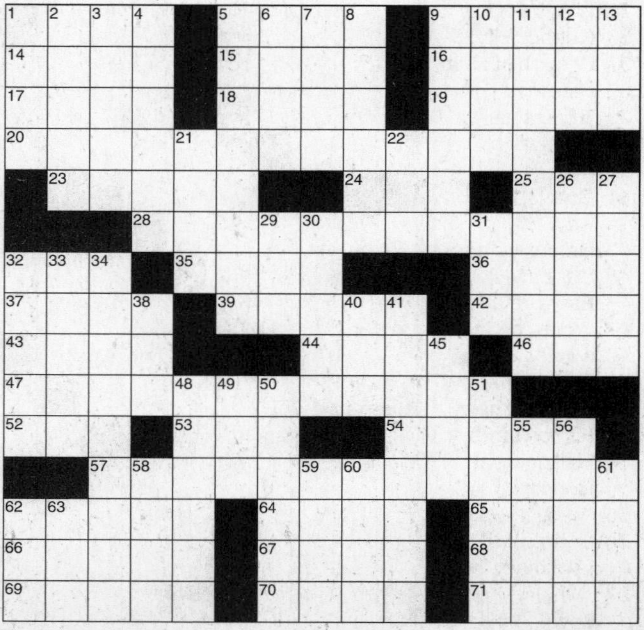

263 TIMELY PHRASES

by Eric Albert

ACROSS

1 Dismal dwelling
6 ’60s dance
10 Exercise aftermath
14 Mrs. Kramden
15 Greek liqueur
16 Egg on
17 Dotage
20 Currently popular
21 __ *Man Flint*
22 Too sentimental
23 Desert refuge
26 Slog along
27 Soul singer Gaye
29 Horn honk
30 *Judging Amy* network
33 White as a sheet
34 *Scarlett* setting
35 Not give __ (be indifferent)
36 Coveted shape
39 Wild revelry
40 Drama award
41 Grayish tan
42 New beginning?
43 Banned insulators: Abbr.
44 Made a muscle
45 Puttering
46 Singer Lenya
47 Houston team
50 Binge
51 __ Lanka
54 Thriller of ’73 (with *The*)
58 Short swims
59 Viscount’s superior
60 Pull a fast one
61 __ gin fizz
62 Freshwater fish
63 Bashful colleague

DOWN

1 Leftover dish
2 Butter substitute
3 Quasimodo’s creator
4 Author Umberto
5 Spy novelist Deighton
6 Adjust a camera
7 German valley
8 Israeli weapon
9 Gilding metal
10 Plant pest
11 Cut short
12 Earring shape
13 Circular current
18 Rub out
19 Quit, as a course
24 Comic Schreiber
25 Vocalize
26 In itself
27 Ed Mc__
28 Stick out like __ thumb
29 Foundation
30 *Pacific Princess*, for one
31 Freight boat
32 Risk a ticket
34 Striped cat
35 Bond or Smart
37 March style
38 “Yeah, sure”
43 Vanishing sound
44 West African country
45 Everyday language
46 Big dipper
47 Appends
48 Leave port
49 Secretary’s error
50 Pull sharply
52 Pilaf ingredient
53 Dark as night
55 “Bali __”
56 Inc., in England
57 Favoring

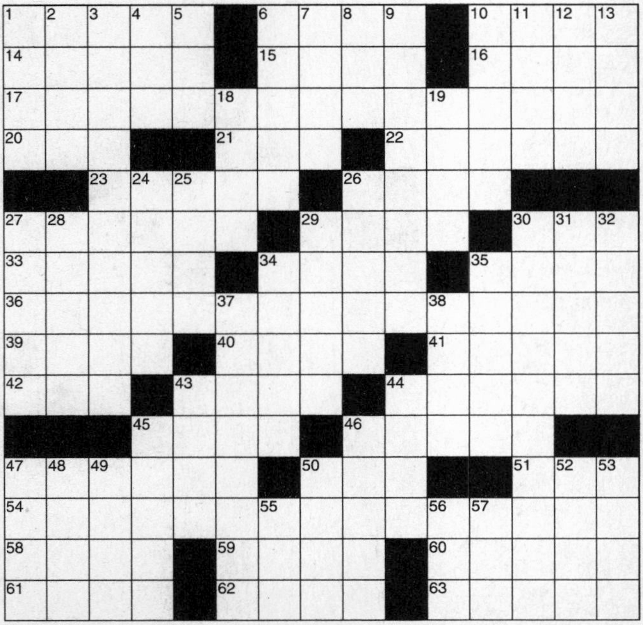

264 BOX SCORE

by Dean Niles

ACROSS

1 Author Kingsley
5 How-to part
9 Find fault
13 "__ you be my neighbor?"
14 Actress O'Neal
16 Exploits
17 *Against All __*
18 Basketball venue
19 Without
20 Hawaiian garland
21 Satisfies
23 Lee of *The Fall Guy*
25 Gobbled up
26 Pecs' partners
27 Drop out
32 Bandleader Artie
35 __ *Shelter* (Rolling Stones film)
36 "The loneliest number"
37 Outdoes
41 Baba beginning
42 Adult insect
43 Some necklines
44 Digestive gland
46 Doctor's charge
48 Augsburg article
49 Painted or drew
52 Non-mechanical failures
57 Quick punch
59 Colorful fish
60 Swarms
61 He may be up to Paar
62 Sun. magazine section
63 Camp David visitor
64 Septi- successor
65 Hill dwellers
66 Coloratura Lily
67 Hold back

DOWN

1 Army offender
2 Computer accessory
3 *A Passage to __*
4 Ave. crossers
5 One way up
6 Little pies
7 Soissons seasons
8 Soccer kick
9 Said "Dang!"
10 Relative of PDQ
11 Casino city
12 "Hey, you!"
15 Gandhi honorific
21 Prefix for "goblin"
22 Early anesthetic
24 Gripping movie?
27 Eccentric
28 "__ Excited" (Pointer Sisters song)
29 Libertine
30 Novelist Rice
31 Takes the plunge
32 Sp. ladies
33 A shake in the grass?
34 Indigo plant
35 Snarl
38 Split apart
39 Turkish inns
40 Hot spot
45 Baking potatoes
46 Guinness specialties
47 Some dashes
49 Miller's Willy
50 Kick out
51 Beatrice's beau
52 Israeli dance
53 "Once __ a time . . ."
54 Actor Dillon
55 Harvest the crop
56 Try again
58 Explosive sound
61 __ Alamos, NM

265 AT THE OFFICE

by Mary E. Brindamour

ACROSS
1 Rosemary or thyme
5 Fancy cravat
10 Chits
14 Screenwriter James
15 Trouser material
16 Slow-witted
17 Secretary's machine
19 Sicilian volcano
20 Antipollution grp.
21 Up-front
22 Blind as __
23 Fashions
25 Bruins' sch.
27 Fiery felony
30 Grapple, down South
33 Archbishop of Canterbury's headdress
36 Like a lion
38 Actress Novak
39 Got by, with "out"
40 Uses a stopwatch
41 Trucker's rig
42 Toothpaste type
43 *For __ Sake* ('74 film)
44 Cook for a crowd?
45 Letter sign-off
47 Begin
49 Jack of *The Tonight Show*
50 Playground fixture
54 Diamond Head's island
56 Sergeant's order
60 Lawyers' org.
61 Army offender
62 Accountant's tool
64 Camper's shelter
65 Hot coal
66 Earsplitting
67 Observes
68 Shovel's kin
69 Industrious insects

DOWN
1 Despises
2 Tut's territory
3 Settle a debt
4 Opie's aunt
5 Puzzle heading
6 Leg part
7 Summon to court
8 Dollar bills
9 Plagues
10 Standards of excellence
11 Messenger's pickup point
12 Forearm bone
13 Strip of wood
18 __ *the Boys Are*
24 Cooking fat
26 Scoundrel
28 Leave out
29 Tom, Dick and Harry
31 Life Savers flavor
32 Kuwaiti ruler
33 Byte beginning
34 Turner and Pappas
35 Receptionist's device
37 Heron's home
40 Patios' kin
41 Satisfy completely
43 Tiny green veggie
44 Angler's basket
46 Strongboxes
48 State confidently
51 Suppressed
52 More or less
53 City divisions
54 Feedbag filler
55 Bide-__ Home
57 Pat down
58 Exile isle
59 Made a hole in one
63 Pie __ mode

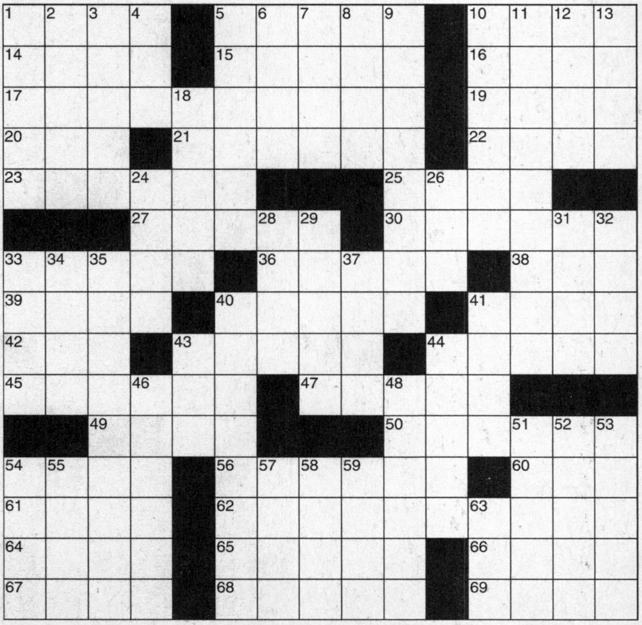

266 FEATHERED FRIENDS

by Fred Piscop

ACROSS

1 Daddies
6 Musical finales
11 __ *My Children*
14 Raise a fuss
15 Saint Theresa's home
16 Caviar
17 Former Globetrotters star
20 Rage
21 Grazing land
22 El __, TX
23 Make a racket
27 Number one
29 Galley feature
30 Illinois city
33 "We __ the World"
34 Ref. books
37 Research awards
39 *Roots* character
43 "I __ tell a lie"
44 Unsuspecting
46 Caesar's tongue: Abbr.
49 Gymnast Mary Lou
51 Actress Arthur
52 Disinclined
54 Seer's sign
57 Stuff to the gills
58 Nicklaus' org.
61 Sonny and Cher, once
62 English naval hero
68 Dockworkers' grp.
69 John or John Q.
70 Lamb output
71 Man of Steel monogram
72 Ethyl acetate, for one
73 Way to go

DOWN

1 Actress Dawber
2 Rickenbacker, e.g.
3 "Harper Valley __"
4 Taxpayer's fear
5 Curling, for one
6 "Silent" president
7 Track shape
8 __ Straits (rock group)
9 Caustic
10 Mr. Mineo
11 Warship fleet
12 Less restrictive
13 Poe poem
18 "Read 'em and __"
19 MPG testers
23 Fish dish
24 Secular
25 St. Louis sight
26 University honcho
28 Actress Shirley
31 *Believe It* __
32 Auto style
35 Personal quirk
36 Traumatizes
38 Mexicali Mrs.
40 Gridder's gear
41 Scoff at
42 Level
45 Gobble up goodies
46 Timmy's pooch
47 Is of use
48 Aquarium denizens
50 Dozes off
53 Third man in the ring
55 More boorish
56 Trunk
59 Pesky insect
60 Pinnacle
63 Silly Charlotte
64 Neighbor of Syr.
65 Tempe sch.
66 Krazy __
67 Potato bud

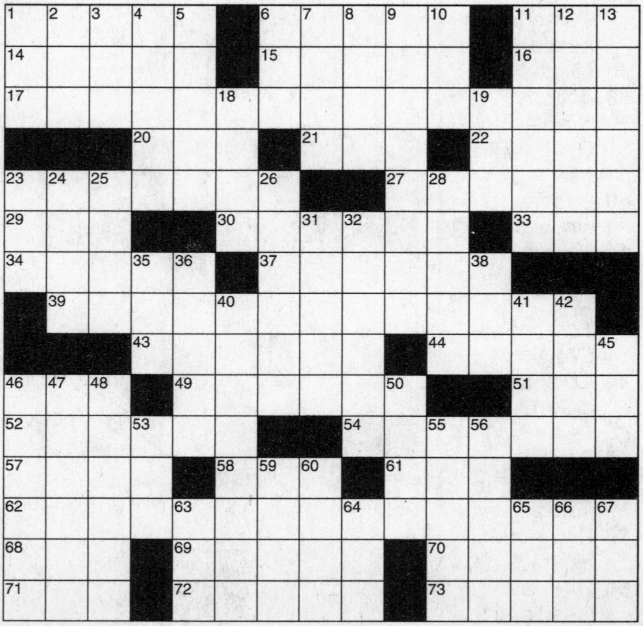

267 KEEP IT SIMPLE

by Shirley Soloway

ACROSS
1 Shoestring
5 Perlman and Howard
9 Once again
13 Actor Richard
14 Make happy
16 Singer Falana
17 Indian tourist town
18 Tropical tubers
19 Whirl around
20 "Nothing to it!"
23 *The Hunt for __ October*
24 Sporting dog
25 Portable fuel
27 Art Deco designer
29 Bow material
32 Nourish
35 Dutch cheese
38 __ lily
39 Actress Gardner
40 Envelope info
42 Med. test
43 Frisbees, e.g.
45 Pull sharply
46 Famous fellow?
47 Most cunning
49 Conn of *Benson*
51 Ancient
54 Befitting a baron
58 Bandleader Brown
60 "Nothing to it!"
62 Pearl Buck heroine
64 Fred Astaire's sister
65 Falls behind
66 French clergyman
67 Spartan slave
68 Tom Joad, for one
69 Piece of information
70 Transatlantic planes
71 Waters down

DOWN
1 Bounds
2 Playing marble
3 Insertion symbol
4 Legislated
5 Answered testily
6 Norwegian monarch
7 Drug busters
8 Summer ermine
9 Pacino and Smith
10 "Nothing to it!"
11 Nobelist Wiesel
12 Magician's prop
15 Sandy ridge
21 Always, to Byron
22 Idle and Clapton
26 Hoopsters' org.
28 Whirlpool
30 Dairy-case purchase
31 Henpecks
32 Temporary trends
33 Depraved
34 "Nothing to it!"
36 Coach Parseghian
37 Darn a rip
40 Strong point
41 Frying pans
44 Beer barrel
46 Vent output
48 Synagogue scroll
50 Fawn's mother
52 Gold deposits
53 Sword fights
55 Daddy duck
56 On the up and up
57 Affirmative responses
58 Lie around
59 Island off Italy
61 Soak up moisture
63 Fish catcher

268 SEA IT NOW

by Bob Lubbers

ACROSS

1 Aircraft abbr.
5 Dole (out)
9 Searches for treasure
14 "Whatever __ Wants"
15 *Scarlett* setting
16 "It's the end of __"
17 Figurine material
19 Mexican "monsters"
20 Make a patriotic display
22 '60s radical grp.
23 Slender
24 Out of order
26 Movie openers
29 Darned again
31 Singer Adams
32 Blue hue
34 Coral communes
37 Maiden-name indicator
38 Sound films
40 Islet, on a globe
41 No-no
43 Connery or Penn
44 LXVII x VI
45 Moon valleys
47 Ionospheric high spot
49 Gets a whiff of
51 Fly high
52 Split __ soup
53 Ice-cream flavor
59 L.A. dunker
61 Like some votes
62 *Die Fledermaus* maid
63 See red
64 Gossipy Barrett
65 Sharply to the point
66 Tracy's Trueheart
67 Govt. agents

DOWN

1 Deli side dish
2 *Welcome __* ('77 film)
3 Patron saint of Norway
4 Singer Patti
5 CA volcano
6 Consumed
7 Not kosher
8 James __ Jones
9 Some bargainers
10 Cycle starter
11 *Naughty Marietta* star
12 Play the market
13 Fresh
18 Suit to __
21 Pecs' partners
25 Must pay
26 __ caterpillar
27 Concept
28 Tennis shoot-off
29 Leaf gatherers
30 Director Kazan
33 "What __ is new?"
35 Pâté de __ gras
36 Tend the sauce
38 Like an 800 number
39 Puts into effect
42 Vinegar's partner
44 Garage alternative
46 Shreveport coll.
48 Café au __
49 *Killer Tomatoes* sound
50 Gettysburg victor
51 Appears to be
54 Dexterous
55 Sticky stuff
56 High-school formal
57 Bowling alley
58 *Joie de vivre*
60 Overhead rails

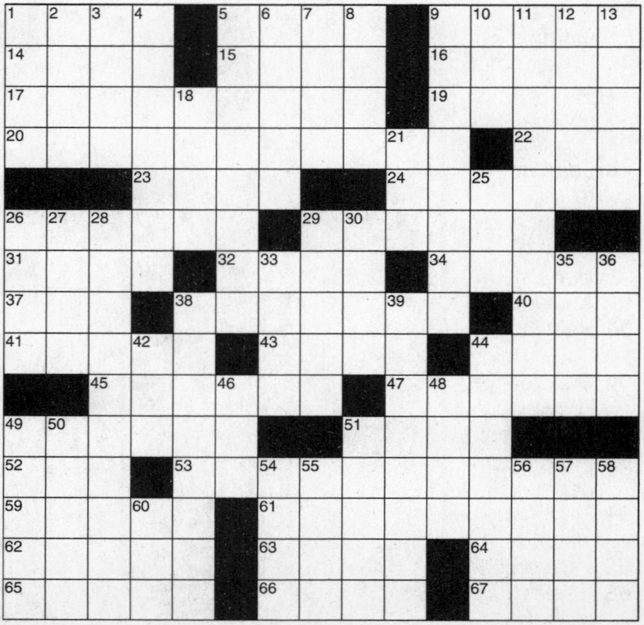

269 *TRINITY QUARTET*

by William A. Hendricks

ACROSS

1 "Hell __ no fury . . ."
5 Dundee denizen
9 "Ma! (He's Making Eyes __)"
13 Tennist Arthur
14 Canine, e.g.
15 National League stadium
16 Wiry
17 Port-au-Prince's land
18 Hound and hamster
19 Cravat
20 Soft-ball brand
21 Din
23 They're spotted in the wild
25 Ike's opponent
26 Ocean sound
27 Stash
28 Frost bite?
31 Tony
33 Early explorer
34 Savanna antelope
35 Macho man
36 Optics item
38 An NCO
39 Dairy spheroid
40 Fringe benefit
41 Thrills
43 Sinbad's bird
44 Not as much
45 Chihuahua child
46 How to pack fish
48 Utah performing clan
51 Lifework
53 Castor, to Pollux
54 Piece of advice
55 Circular sections
56 University of Maine town
58 Jocular Johnson
59 Total defeat
60 Part of NOW
61 *Educating* __ ('83 film)
62 Call the shots
63 __-do-well
64 Weirdo

DOWN

1 Must
2 Savory jelly
3 Indoor attraction
4 "Wait a minute!"
5 Flies like an eagle
6 Hair style
7 Giant with 511 homers
8 Depth
9 Adoption org.
10 "Tom Dooley" singers
11 Apportion, with "out"
12 __ *of Eden*
14 Horse racing coup
20 Wordy Webster
22 Obi-Wan portrayer
24 Latch
25 What snobs put on
27 Skater Carol
29 *Picnic* playwright
30 Places
31 *Mask* star
32 Science-fiction award
37 Pretense
38 __'War (racehorse)
40 Ballet bend
42 Delineate
47 Bird houses
48 Title holder
49 Likewise
50 Pipe up
51 Auto part, for short
52 Slangy suffix
53 Big book
57 Richard the unidentified
58 Joan Van __

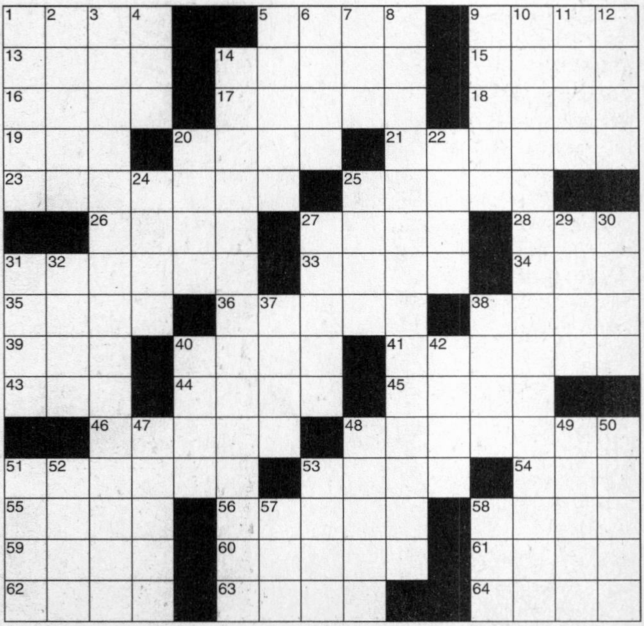

270 THAT TEARS IT

by Trip Payne

ACROSS

1 Miller rival
6 __ *Trek*
10 Former Irani ruler
14 More competent
15 Spelunking spot
16 Chaplin prop
17 Heavenly woman
18 Slaughter of baseball
19 Author Haley
20 Droopy tree
23 Be decisive
24 Use a straw
25 Colorful ring
29 "Oh, phooey!"
31 Spending maximum
34 Sentimental journalist
36 Lowly worker
38 Reggae singer Peter
39 Goes out on one's own
41 Flamenco cries
42 Inspirations
44 Scolded loudly
46 Form of ID
47 The hunted
49 Danger warnings
50 Crumpet accompaniment
51 Indefinite pronoun
52 Hit '92 film
59 Piltdown Man, for one
60 Head set?
61 Acid in proteins
63 Opera highlight
64 Fizz flavoring
65 For the __ (currently)
66 Stylist's stock
67 Loose-fitting dress
68 In a difficult position

DOWN

1 "You sicken me!"
2 Take __ (acknowledge applause)
3 In the dumps
4 Saharan
5 Libya's largest city
6 __ *of a Woman*
7 Sharp taste
8 Solemnly proclaim
9 Hold off
10 Resell tickets
11 Sign of sanctity
12 From the top
13 Witch's curse
21 "Not me, thanks"
22 Speech problem
25 Some wines
26 Crucifixes
27 Actor Buddy
28 Work-safety grp.
29 Kind of race
30 In __ (lined up)
31 Plum or melon
32 Attu resident
33 Aphids and gnats
35 Director Hooper
37 Took the bus
40 Streetspeak
43 On __ (riskily)
45 Posh
48 Least typical
50 Big Bend's location
51 Square one
52 Zipped along
53 It comes down hard
54 Connecticut campus
55 Driving need
56 Love personified
57 Go for the gold
58 Depend end
59 Old crone
62 Multi-vol. ref. work

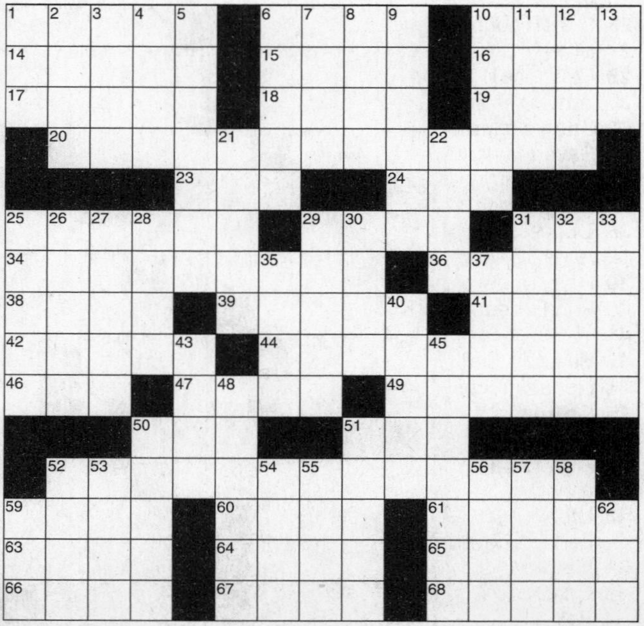

271 HARD PUZZLE

by Norma Steinberg

ACROSS

1 Bough
5 Toyland visitors
10 Bowling-equipment maker
13 M
14 Hem and haw
15 Festive
17 Salisbury attraction
19 Diver Louganis
20 Oriental tower
21 American Uncle
22 "Oh, sure!"
23 Stowe girl
25 James Dean persona
27 Advisory body
31 Leave in the lurch
34 Jeremy of *Damage*
35 Overused
38 Mean mongrel
39 Part of RSVP
40 Billy Joel's instrument
41 White-faced
42 Aruba or Atlantis: Abbr.
43 Gem surface
44 Benefits
45 Fragrant trees
47 Josephine's title
49 Prepares for publishing
51 Sugarloaf Mountain city
52 *God's Little* __
54 Sounds of recognition
56 Western desert
61 Little fellows
62 Popular hymn
64 Level
65 Diarist Nin
66 Sort of school
67 Mrs., in Marseilles
68 __ hand (help)
69 *Five __ Pieces*

DOWN

1 Speak like Daffy Duck
2 Minimal amount
3 __ synthesizer
4 Sonny or Chastity
5 Act
6 "__ Maria"
7 Makes illegal
8 Mortimer's master
9 __ be (appeared)
10 Texas A&M students
11 Bakery treat
12 Attorney Bailey
16 FBI man
18 Paradises
24 *Toys in the* __
26 Hum bug?
27 Kind of pride
28 Went up
29 Colorado power source
30 Part of SBLI
32 Calls the shots
33 Lock of hair
36 *Norma* __
37 Word form for "between"
40 Idyllic
41 __ excellence
43 Calendar abbr.
44 Takeoff
46 "__ *Fideles*"
48 Tropical tree
50 Gleamed
52 Sitcom alien
53 Serenity
55 Read hastily
57 Mock
58 Taj Mahal town
59 Neckline shapes
60 Notice
63 Baby goat

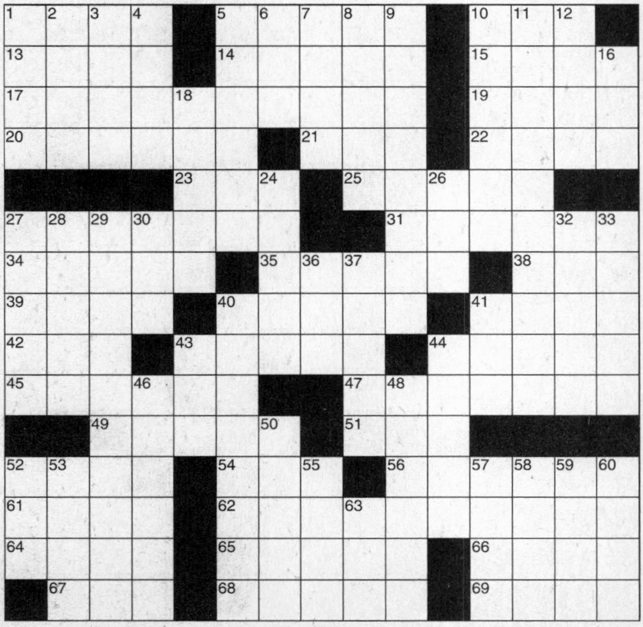

272 *MUSICAL SOUNDS*

by Fred Piscop

ACROSS

1 Von __ (*The Sound of Music* surname)
6 Flaccid
10 Limber with language
14 Courtyards
15 Sneaking suspicion
16 Descartes or Clair
17 DO
20 Cuts prices
21 Worries
22 President pro __
23 __ Spumante
24 Bans
27 Teen socialite
29 Compass points
33 Hunk of gunk
34 Alluring ad
36 Barroom spigot
37 RE
40 Gas-pump abbr.
41 Horse operas
42 Birdbath organism
43 Hägar's pooch
45 Attorney's deg.
46 Part owner?
47 "__ does it!"
49 Japanese sash
50 Sharp
53 It's often direct
57 MI
60 __-Lackawanna Railroad
61 Venetian-blind part
62 Ms. Rogers St. Johns
63 Undermines
64 Dagwood's neighbor
65 Mess around

DOWN

1 Highlands headgear
2 1 and 66: Abbr.
3 Asian inland sea
4 Philippine erupter
5 Free tickets
6 *One __ to Live*
7 Day to beware?
8 Tex-__ cuisine
9 Duelists' units
10 *Ars __ artis*
11 Microscope part
12 Actress Swenson
13 Sugar source
18 Resistance unit
19 Bigots
23 Totally ridiculous
24 Aspen apparatus
25 Standish's stand-in
26 Witty pianist
27 Skillfully
28 Steen stand
30 Wading bird
31 It requires two
32 Opera prop
34 *Prelude __ Kiss*
35 Printer's measures
38 Starchy staple
39 Mexican estate
44 Gets more mileage from
46 Overseas
48 It may be common
49 Hockey great Bobby
50 Does Little work?
51 *Buona __, Mrs. Campbell*
52 Junket
53 Silent sort
54 Capable of
55 Playwright Coward
56 Rock group Jethro __
58 *__ That Jazz*
59 Negative vote

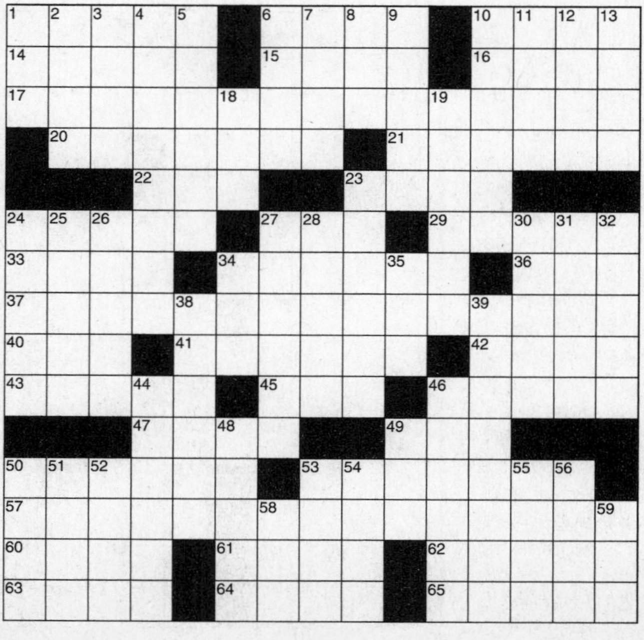

273 FABRICATIONS

by Shirley Soloway

ACROSS

1 "You __ mouthful!"
6 WWII females
10 Open a bit
14 Pilgrim John
15 Beige
16 Blood components
17 Daydream
19 Actor Kristofferson
20 Vendor
21 Duel tool
23 Easy mark
24 __ Baba
25 Clear the slate
27 Bracketed word
30 Composers' org.
33 Fit for a king
36 Hubbubs
38 "I could __ horse!"
39 Error
40 Religious ceremony
41 Loses one's footing
43 Tower town
44 Small amounts
46 "Since __ You Baby" ('56 tune)
47 Ginger cookie
48 Struck down
49 Corny goddess?
51 Ames and Asner
52 Jazz musician Red
54 Moon craft
56 Lab animal
58 Beer choice
60 Foliage
64 Old-time oath
66 Wild duck
68 Imported cheese
69 Over
70 Bad-tempered
71 Peddler's goal
72 Amphibious vehicles: Abbr.
73 Bread spreads

DOWN

1 Carpentry tools
2 Soothing plant
3 Superstar
4 Perry's secretary
5 Actress Lansbury
6 Rainy
7 Painful sensation
8 Party decoration
9 More certain
10 Inquire
11 Eastern conifer
12 *Tosca* tune
13 Grating sound
18 Gets up
22 British nobleman
26 Daily dramas
27 Delhi wraps
28 Set phrase
29 Little rabbit
31 Multicolored felines
32 *One Day at* __
34 Syrian leader
35 By __ and bounds (rapidly)
37 "From __ shining . . ."
42 __ *Dallas*
45 Belgrade native
50 Is responsible for
53 Oral
55 Silent star Normand
56 Confederate soldiers
57 Indian city
59 Sheepshank, for one
61 Bouquet holder
62 Word form for "outer"
63 "The __ the limit!"
65 Poor grade
67 D.C. second bananas

274 PULLING RANK

by Matt Gaffney

ACROSS

1 Practice boxing
5 "__ 'em, Rover!"
8 Decorates cupcakes
12 Buenos __
14 Comic Philips
15 Break to smithereens
16 Landowner's sign
19 Peace, in Panama
20 Actress Zetterling
21 There's no charge for it
22 007's school
24 Apprentice
26 "__ Fine Day" ('63 tune)
27 Jeans material
29 Crystallize, as an idea
30 Yalies
31 Andrews and Carvey
33 Lend a hand
35 "Woe is me!"
36 Tory leader, once
39 Big bash
42 OR's locale
43 Have a hunch
46 Lincoln and Vigoda
47 Massage
49 Holds as an opinion
51 Spare part?
52 Pitched a tent
55 Heartfelt
56 Mobile home?
58 Mauna __
60 Lanka lead-in
61 NBC owner
64 __ *Gay*
65 Pipe cleaner?
66 Mediterranean island
67 Dispatched
68 "Absolutely!"
69 "What __ for Love" (*A Chorus Line* tune)

DOWN

1 Weakened
2 Copied illegally
3 Painted Desert locale
4 Priest's title: Abbr.
5 "__ is believing"
6 Mischief-maker
7 __ Otis Skinner
8 "__ a man with . . ."
9 Actor O'Connor
10 Latvia neighbor
11 Introvert's quality
13 Our uncle
15 Gyrated
17 Skater Babilonia
18 "__ the fields . . ."
23 Sapporo spies
25 Joins forces
28 __ Zedong
30 Was the breadwinner
32 "Quiet!"
34 Record players
37 As a rule
38 Brit. ref. work
39 Auto shops
40 Texas city
41 Mideast land
44 Gets steamed
45 Certain retirees
48 Lovely ladies
50 Seasoned
52 *Fame* name
53 Cardiologists' org.
54 Buck's mate
57 Sash or cummerbund
59 Part of IRA
62 CBS symbol
63 Angle starter

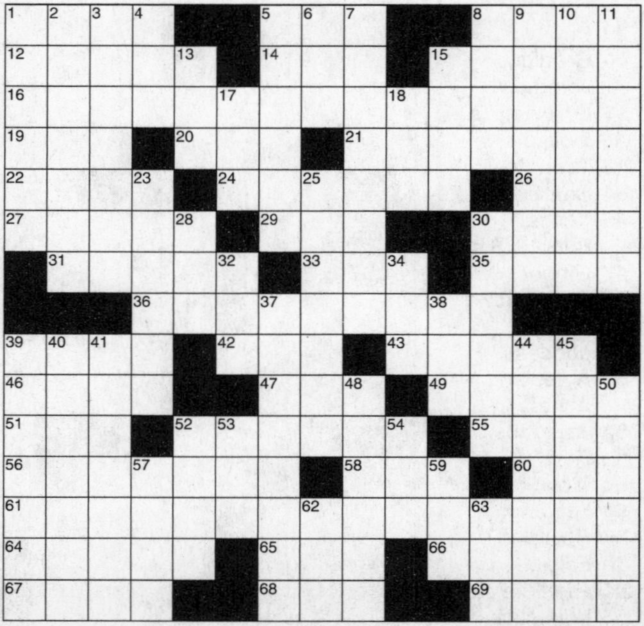

275 *JUST DESSERTS*

by Norma Steinberg

ACROSS

1 Actress Irene
6 Impertinence
10 Cathedral seating
14 Mrs. Ralph Kramden
15 Teheran's country
16 Swear
17 Michelangelo masterpiece
18 Ms. Lollobrigida
19 Krupa or Kelly
20 See 13 Down
21 Dessert
24 Beef cuts
26 Pot top
27 Ariel of Israel
29 Expression of disgust
33 *Pretty* __
34 Swamp whooper
35 Actor Holbrook
37 MP's quarry
38 Static problem
39 Prefix for "hit" or "bucks"
40 Glove leather
41 Impertinence
42 Use skillfully
43 Liquidate
45 Went after
46 Yves' "yes"
47 "The City of Trees"
48 Dessert
53 Truck part
56 Awestruck
57 Feathered scarves
58 Exchange
60 "Second Hand __"
61 Science magazine
62 Compare
63 Gave rise to
64 Affirmative votes
65 Happening

DOWN

1 Theater producer Joseph
2 "It's a Sin to Tell __"
3 Dessert
4 Put-on
5 Zoo favorite
6 Leo, Libra, etc.
7 Cal. neighbor
8 Sensible
9 Going "Grrr!"
10 Thai tower
11 Even once
12 Refuses to
13 With 20 Across, Popeye's kid
22 Bed-and-breakfast establishment
23 Use a stopwatch
25 Spoken
27 Love letters?
28 "__ that possible?"
29 Anguish
30 __ and file
31 Dessert
32 Top Scout
34 *Roman à* __
36 Actress Cheryl
38 Robed singer
39 Sara and Farrow
41 Whodunit board game
42 Bobby's prop
44 Emulated Paul Bunyan
45 *Beverly Hills* __
47 Foundation
48 What you wear
49 Frankenstein's flunky
50 Snoop, with "about"
51 A few
52 Grandma
54 Mideast gulf
55 Crooked
59 *6 Rms,* __ *Vu*

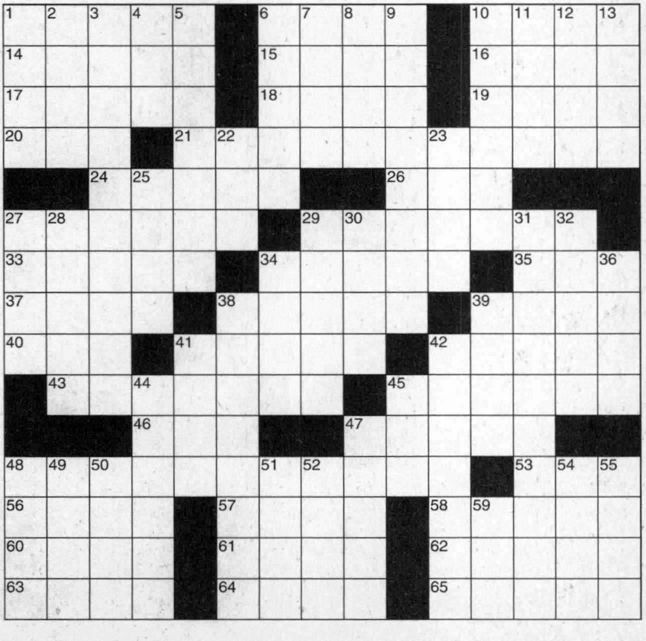

276 ON THE ALLEYS

by Fred Piscop

ACROSS

1 Ruin a reputation
6 Pinafore opening?
9 Dunks for apples
13 *Cheers* waitress
14 Actress Nina
15 Frenzied
16 Valuable violin
17 Overhaul
18 Tear down
19 Kindled
20 Proverb start
23 Ancient Greek
25 Regretted
26 __ and outs
27 Calls the balls
28 Astern
31 Jets or Mets
34 __ Gigio
36 Hawkins or Thompson
38 Start conducting
41 Actress Ekberg
42 Head of France?
43 Iowa city
44 Groovy, these days
45 Crucifix
47 Atomic energy grp.
49 Iron fishhook
50 Keds product
54 Go Dutch
58 Bristol brew
59 Egyptian port
60 Jack rabbit, e.g.
61 Defense Secretary under Clinton
63 Metric weight
64 MIT grad
65 Confidence
66 ". . . a __'clock scholar"
67 Begley and Marinaro
68 Senator Kefauver

DOWN

1 La __ (opera house)
2 Ike's lady
3 Clio's sister
4 Model Carol
5 Shriveled grape
6 Gardener, at times
7 Dylan of *The Practice*
8 Grew quickly
9 Exposed
10 General Bradley
11 TV clown
12 Timetable, for short
14 Tarkenton of football
21 Ersatz emerald
22 *Steppenwolf* author
24 Stopping point
27 Increased
28 Actor West
29 Just great
30 Koppel and Kennedy
31 Russian ruler
32 Sicilian volcano
33 Saharan
35 Beyond control
37 Manila hemp
39 Jeweler's measure
40 Eastern dye
46 ". . . __ I sing"
48 Money back
49 Doodad
50 Pun add-on
51 Ruined
52 Beethoven's *"Für __"*
53 Picks up a videotape
54 Certain NCO
55 Immaculate
56 Director David
57 Energy units
62 S.A.T. takers

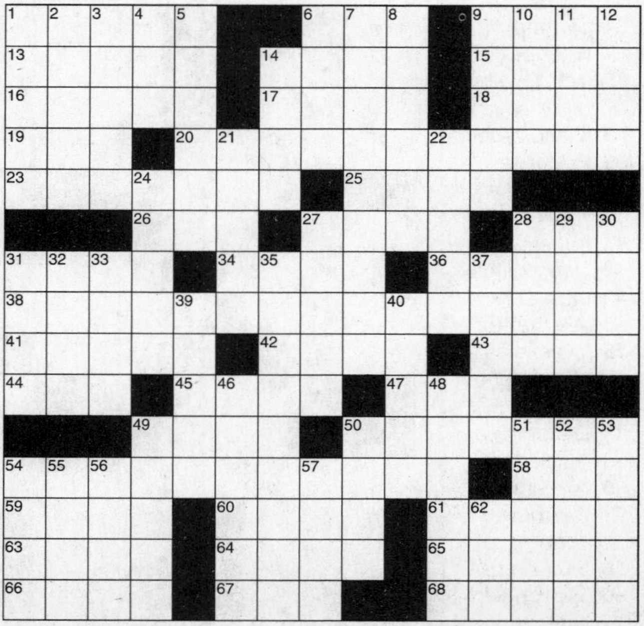

277 UP A TREE

by Shirley Soloway

ACROSS

1 Musical disk
5 Brazilian state
10 Food wrap
14 Hebrew month
15 Inventor Howe
16 Atmosphere
17 Gossipy Barrett
18 Model Cheryl
19 Sunflower support
20 Expanded one's business
23 "Just __ of Those Things"
24 Bambi's mom
25 More malicious
27 Joins up
30 Richard of *The Real McCoys*
32 Actress Thompson
33 Foy or Fisher
35 Tennist Monica
38 H.H. Munro's pseudonym
40 Assistants
42 Lose freshness
43 Take for __ (deceive)
45 Surrendered
47 Farrow of *Radio Days*
48 More orderly
50 Car's safety feature
52 *The Marriage of __*
54 Jack of *Barney Miller*
55 MTV music
56 Peruse
63 Highly excited
65 Irish county
66 Swiss artist Paul
67 Bovine bellows
68 April in Paris
69 Balin and Claire
70 Singer James
71 Word of mouth
72 Head set?

DOWN

1 Apparel
2 What the nose knows
3 Grandmother
4 Rio __
5 D.C. suburb
6 "I cannot tell __"
7 Rushed off
8 *Othello* villain
9 Take for granted
10 Musical notes
11 In a difficult situation
12 "Goodnight __"
13 Less plausible
21 Fruit center
22 Some perfect scores
26 Once again
27 Actress Lanchester
28 In the vicinity
29 Becoming established
30 Apple drink
31 Woodwind instrument
34 Casino cubes
36 Director Kazan
37 Bambi's dad
39 Thought
41 Shore find
44 British nobleman
46 Couturier Christian
49 Shoe tip
51 Raw recruit
52 Chassis
53 Gold bar
57 Thomas __ Edison
58 Jamie of *M*A*S*H*
59 The Kingston __
60 Forearm bone
61 Equipment
62 Musician Myra
64 Fed. support agency

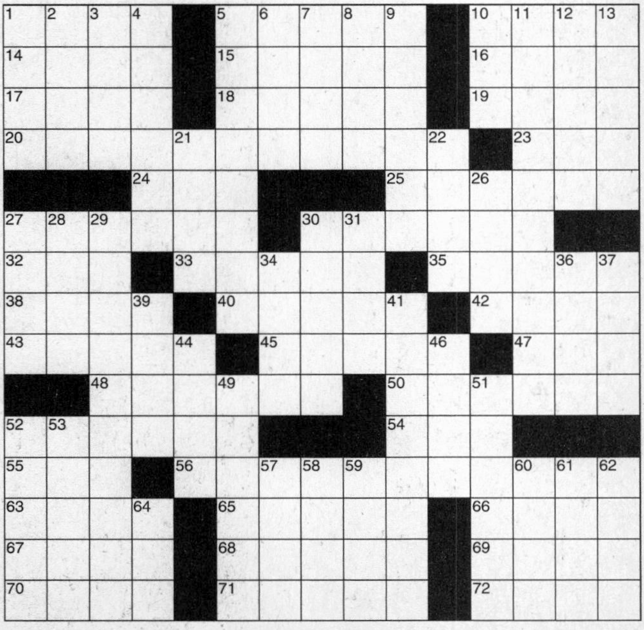

278 GLOVE BOXES

by Mary E. Brindamour

ACROSS
1 Boston or Bangkok
5 Ulan __
10 Scottish family
14 Dept. of Labor div.
15 Omit, in speech
16 Hit the ceiling
17 Grad
18 Gentlemanly gestures
20 Pro __ (for now)
21 Renown
22 Impossible to miss
23 Shout of approval
25 *Jane* __
27 Mountain-related
29 Rolls along
33 Action word
34 Abrasion
36 Rock-band's need
37 Start the day
39 __ Vegas
40 Spokes, e.g.
42 *Sanford and* __
43 Teacher, at times
46 Talbot or Waggoner
47 Small songbird
49 Tower builder
51 Goals
52 Maui neighbor
53 Makes a buck
56 Ailing
57 Pro-gun grp.
60 Jewelry item
63 Like kids at Christmas
64 Major ending
65 *Kate &* __
66 Animal skin
67 Bread and booze
68 Job openings
69 Trams transport them

DOWN
1 Paint layer
2 Gilligan's home
3 Unique impression
4 Sweet potato
5 Acts properly
6 Texas landmark
7 Fork prong
8 Unconventional
9 Legal matter
10 Longed for
11 Erie or Ontario
12 Stress, perhaps
13 Oriole's home
19 "Little Jack __"
21 Devotee
24 Umbrella parts
25 Clear the slate
26 Slangy assent
27 "Stop, sailor!"
28 *"Vive* __*!"*
29 Line of work
30 Small sponge cake
31 Novelist Zola
32 Sales pitch
35 *A Touch of* __('73 film)
38 I specialist?
41 __ Romeo (auto)
44 Daiquiri ingredient
45 Gets to
48 Parsonages
50 Printer's purchase
52 Permissible
53 Ornate pitcher
54 Pretentious
55 Religious ceremony
56 WWII battle site
58 Actor's goal
59 FBI men
61 Used to be
62 The whole enchilada
63 Mil. address

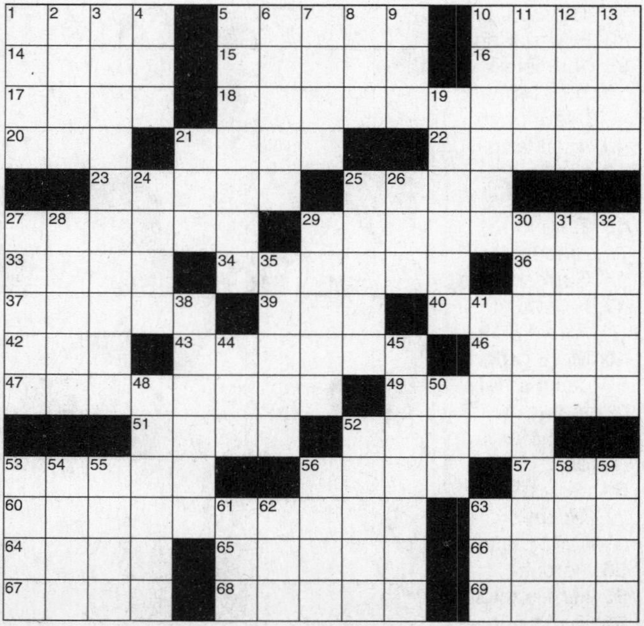

279 TOO MUCH NOISE

by Alex Vaughn

ACROSS

1 Corn holder
4 Certain Slav
8 He takes things easily
14 Get a move on
15 Vicinity
16 Supply of wine
17 Furry TV alien
18 Dines at eve
19 Emulate Earhart
20 Extreme urgency
23 Mound
24 __ the line (obeyed)
25 Estrada or Satie
28 Radiant
30 AMA members
33 Yoko __
34 Le Duc __ (Vietnamese statesman)
36 Landed
37 Gave the green light
38 It followed WWII
41 Bonfire residue
43 Lo-cal
44 Hose on a ball field
45 Wildebeest
46 For each
47 Honeybee's foothold, maybe
51 Stately shaders
53 Wife of Osiris
57 Om study course?
58 Cosmological explanation
62 Kitchen implement
64 Shielded, at sea
65 Golfer's aid
66 Big lizard
67 Highway marker
68 Woman treated as an object?
69 Opinionated list
70 Former Surgeon General
71 Gridiron units: Abbr.

DOWN

1 Mambo relative
2 Offshore platform
3 Happen to
4 Cummerbund
5 Let out the lava
6 Printer's proof
7 Musical Count
8 '80s Chrysler product
9 Stubbs or Strauss
10 Not just anyone
11 Ping-Pong place
12 "I tawt I taw a puddy __"
13 Lode load
21 Arboreal idler
22 Strange to say
26 Squid's squirt
27 Sent down for the count
29 Whipper-snapper
31 Soul-food order
32 Crouch
35 Theater award
36 Tad's dad
38 The go-ahead
39 Swanky lobbies
40 Daisy type
41 Get mellower
42 NBC comedy showcase
48 Like some smiles
49 "It's a deal!"
50 Thicknesses
52 __ the captain's table
54 Carrot stick or candy bar
55 Nanook's nook
56 Pool person
59 Actor Hackman
60 Fiber source
61 Nasty Uriah
62 Harness part
63 Past

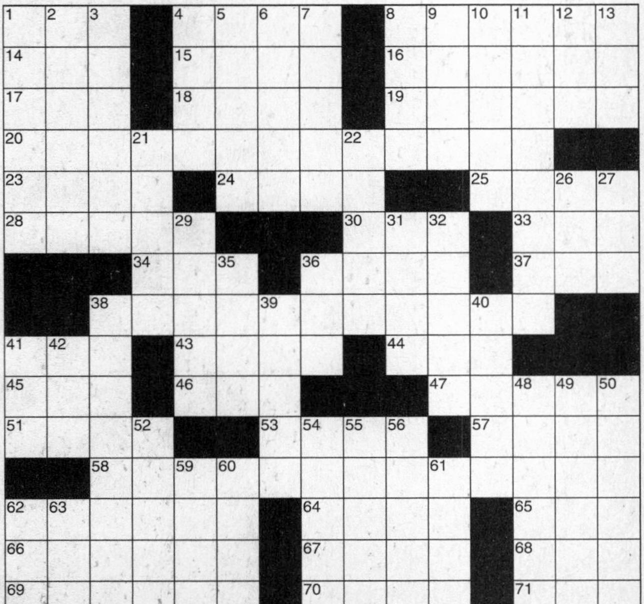

280 NATIONALISM

by Randolph Ross

ACROSS

1 Prepare vegetables
6 Compass dir.
9 Calendar abbr.
12 Delphic VIP
14 Ark architect
15 Cato's eggs
16 Warsaw angler?
18 Casserole cover
19 Asian holiday
20 Scandinavian with his back up?
22 Language suffix
23 WY setting
24 *Peyton* __
25 Ridge
27 Conduct a meeting
31 Vital statistics
32 Graf's game
34 Acidity
36 Prague publication?
38 Slowness to anger
41 Refines metal
45 Bravo and Grande
46 Strikebreaker
48 Unrestrained
49 Slipped up
51 Service div.
53 Damage
54 Stockholmer's courage?
58 Author LeShan
59 Chinese principle
60 Bangkok kin?
63 Tulsa coll.
64 *The Art of Love* author
65 Sidesteps
66 Speedy flier
67 Understand
68 Sociologist Hite

DOWN

1 Most lenient
2 Italian seaport
3 Oriental
4 Essen expletive
5 Half of MMCII
6 Goes to court?
7 Ramón's room
8 Have a puppy
9 Fall scenery
10 Brings to light
11 Evil
13 Calls it a day
14 PBS relative
17 Ancient barbarian
21 Offensive football position
23 Corn color
26 Cut into
28 Actor Milo
29 Badminton stroke
30 Pairs
33 D.C. 100
35 Type style
37 New Deal agcy.
38 Magic words
39 Sky battles
40 Removed, as pages
42 Summer cooler
43 Sycophant
44 Spandau street
47 Singer Ives
50 Clarify, in a way
52 Eye problem
55 Possess
56 Send out
57 Lend a hand
61 Watching machines?
62 Multipurpose exclamation

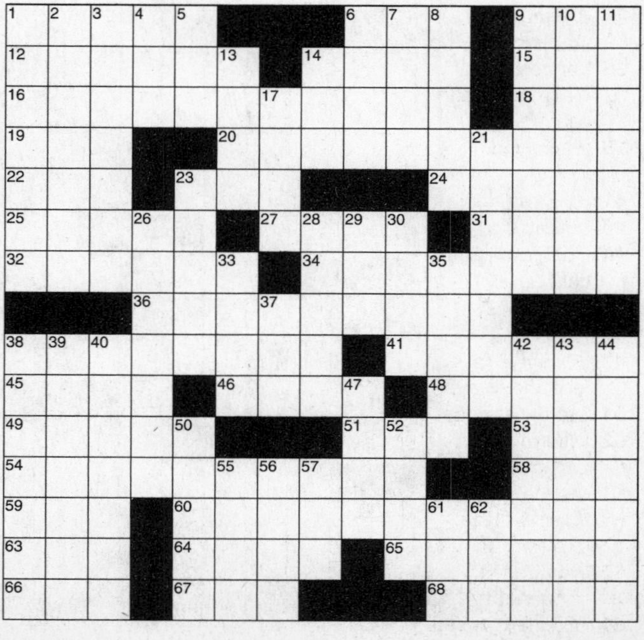

281 *IN THE CARDS*

by Shirley Soloway

ACROSS

1 Cotton bundle
5 Health clubs
9 Woodworking tool
14 Whiff
15 Soft-drink choice
16 Allen or Frome
17 __ ' War (racehorse)
18 Stir up
19 Silvery fish
20 Battle positions
23 Castilian cheer
24 Before, to Byron
25 More amusing
27 Emulate Hines
32 Author Bagnold
33 "Where Do __?" (*Hair* tune)
34 Atlantis or Long
36 Actor Sharif
39 Accepted
41 Gone by
42 Kind of drum
43 Pitcher Hershiser
44 *Tarzan, the* __
46 __ manner of speaking
47 Barbecue favorite
49 Taped
51 Gets the better of
54 *Exodus* hero
55 __ carte
56 Bar order
62 Ruffled trim
64 Busy as __
65 Barcelona bull
66 Perfect
67 Study all night
68 Pizazz
69 Tree houses?
70 Actress Jurado
71 Great dog

DOWN

1 Dismal failure
2 Hebrew month
3 Actress Anderson
4 Wore away
5 Room dividers
6 Winnie-the-__
7 Catch in __ (unmask)
8 Dieter's dish
9 Textbook division
10 Sun. banker?
11 Bette Davis film
12 Berry of *Boomerang*
13 Computer key
21 Midwest product
22 __ Scott Decision
26 Pride papa
27 Former Yugoslavian leader
28 Ice-cream ingredient
29 Inscrutable expressions
30 Applaud
31 Champing at the bit
35 Alaskan seaport
37 English composer Thomas
38 Enjoy a novel
40 Author Wiesel
42 Stallion sound
44 Italian wine region
45 *Police* __ ('84 film)
48 Deli rolls
50 Caused a commotion
51 "Mack the Knife" singer
52 Dodge
53 Light bite
57 "Cadabra" preceder
58 Orderly
59 Vincent Lopez theme
60 Pakistan neighbor
61 Ice-cream holder
63 Tam or turban

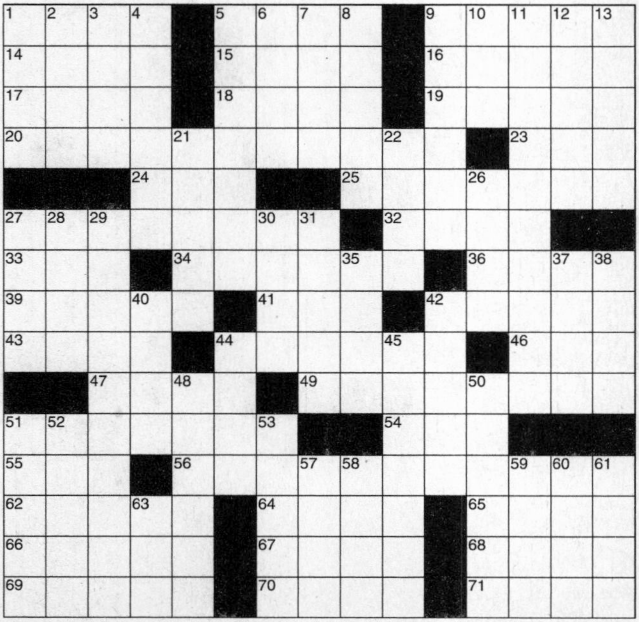

282 WINNING PAIRS

by Carol Fenter

ACROSS

1 October implement
5 Stuffy
10 "Doorman, call me __"
14 "Peek-__!"
15 Puccini opera
16 Musical conclusion
17 Winning pair in '64
20 Leatherworker's item
21 Deck member
22 Streisand song
23 Campus female
24 Took a rest
25 Goes bad
28 Ruination
29 Parisian pie
30 Postcard message
31 Greek cheese
35 Winning pair in '56
38 Walked
39 *The Defiant* __
40 "Untouchable" Ness
41 Trudge
42 __ cry (slogan)
43 Inserts more film
47 Soap setting?
48 International agcy.
49 Elaborate party
50 Cry of discovery
53 Winning pair in '44
56 *Et* __ (list ender)
57 Top-drawer
58 Forced to go
59 Wash
60 More mature
61 Wraps up

DOWN

1 Punjabi prince
2 Take __ (acknowledge applause)
3 Onetime German chancellor Helmut
4 Forever and a day
5 Salts away
6 __ down (softened)
7 Pale
8 Hosp. area
9 Laundry worker
10 Nose noise
11 Esprit de __
12 An Astaire
13 Howled like a wolf
18 Hot
19 Le Moko or Le Pew
23 Quoted an authority
24 Evaluates a movie
25 Galley notation
26 Couple
27 Approximately
28 Like a cowpoke's legs
30 Taboos
31 Foul matter
32 Way out
33 *Home Improvement* prop
34 Kick in
36 Extend an engagement
37 Tidier
41 Trot or canter
42 Pancake starter
43 Urban's opposite
44 __ *Gay*
45 7th-century pope
46 Actor Davis
47 Actress Davis
49 Wacky Wilson
50 Sunday shout
51 Ranch worker
52 Hill dwellers
54 Yalie
55 Take advantage of

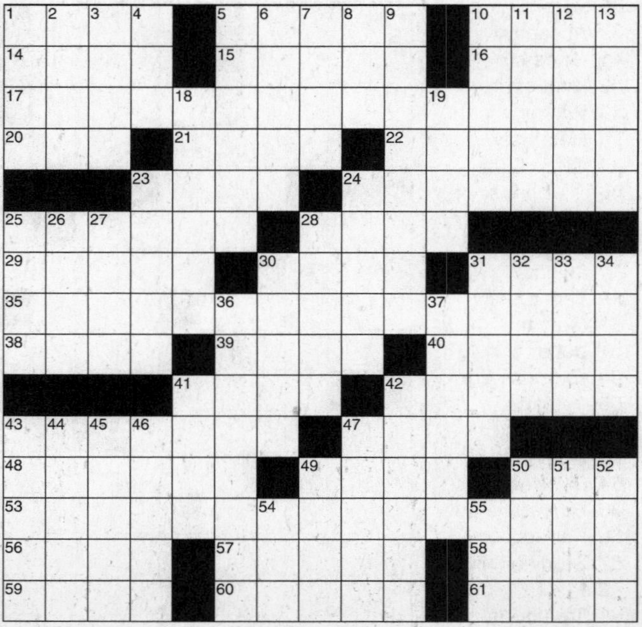

283 CULINARY COMBOS

by Bob Lubbers

ACROSS
1 Lettuce variety
5 *Vogue* competitor
9 Less
14 Actor Jannings
15 Fashion name
16 By oneself
17 Competent
18 Asta's mistress
19 Canterbury headdress
20 Little girl's makeup
23 Saw serrations
24 Visualized
25 B&O and NY Central
28 Asp gasp?
29 She-bear, in Seville
32 Vendor
34 Put on a pedestal
37 Mrs. Chaplin
38 Everyday dinner
42 Jocular Johnson
43 Persian potentates
44 Short snooze
46 Kitchen meas.
47 Author Levin
50 Language suffix
51 Mad as a hatter
54 Less plausible
56 Common condiments
60 Copycat's cry
62 Taleteller
63 As a __ (usually)
64 Happening
65 Ore source
66 Eye part
67 Walks through water
68 Ginger cookie
69 Gave temporarily

DOWN
1 Burden bearers
2 Permeates
3 Ship sections
4 Act sheepishly?
5 Best of films
6 Jungle king
7 Some nobles
8 Remove graphite
9 Feast or __
10 DeMille specialty
11 Napoleonic defeat site
12 "To __ is human . . ."
13 Hwy.
21 Valerie Harper sitcom
22 Coins of Spain
26 Russo of *Lethal Weapon 3*
27 Mexican *Mmes.*
30 Solar occurrence
31 *M*A*S*H* man
33 Oodles
34 "__ o'clock scholar"
35 Fitting
36 Legal wrong
38 Medieval weapon
39 Historical periods
40 Swore (to)
41 Tell target
45 Portions out
47 Tainted
48 Retrieve a trout
49 Clap in cuffs
52 Rings up
53 Burger topper
55 Taxing time?
57 Top-notch
58 Doll's word
59 Make ready
60 Kitten's comment
61 __ Marie Saint

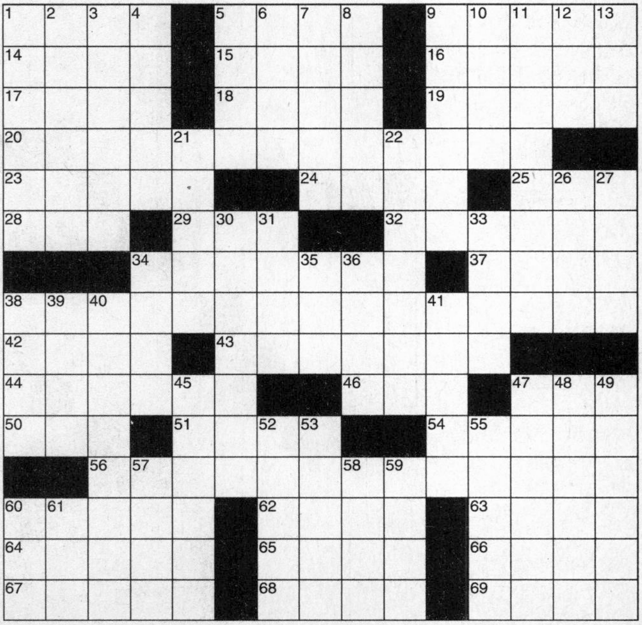

284 WATER LOG

by Dean Niles

ACROSS
1 Holey roll
6 Choir member
10 Actor Auberjonois
14 Toughen up
15 NASA destination
16 *Tosca* tune
17 Book of maps
18 1961 invasion site
20 Grid judge
21 Cast off
23 Restive
24 Animal trail
26 Olympic runner Lewis
28 Pacino's profession
30 Wedding dance
34 Weight allowances
35 Takes off
36 Baseball stat
37 Wedding-cake layer
38 Paper measures
39 Lowdown
40 Lyricist Gershwin
41 Accordingly
42 Journalist Joseph
43 Clever retort
45 Playful
46 Traditional knowledge
47 Renaissance fiddle
48 Texas __ University
51 California city
52 *Norma* __
55 Linda Ronstadt song
58 Tenth-graders
60 Wagers
61 Viet __
62 Colosseum contest
63 Take a breather
64 TV's Downs
65 Fall tools

DOWN
1 Put up with
2 Pay to play
3 Warm current
4 Distinct period
5 Textbook topics
6 Light color?
7 Fill up
8 Plaything
9 Yoko __
10 With total absorption
11 __ the Red
12 Imminent
13 No sweat
19 Pink-slips
22 Take everything
25 Docking place
26 Weather condition
27 Pub orders
28 Top level
29 Mubarak's city
30 "Woe is me!"
31 Mary Steenburgen film
32 "You can't judge __ . . ."
33 Unsteady
35 Yard barrier
38 __ *Window*
39 Ballet bend
41 Nuclear weapon
42 Go-between
44 Firstborn
45 Invited to dinner
47 Unrefined
48 Short form, for short
49 Sheltered, at sea
50 "Phooey!"
51 Stretched out
53 Actress Baxter
54 Guesses: Abbr.
56 Essen expletive
57 "__ don't say!"
59 Gabor sister

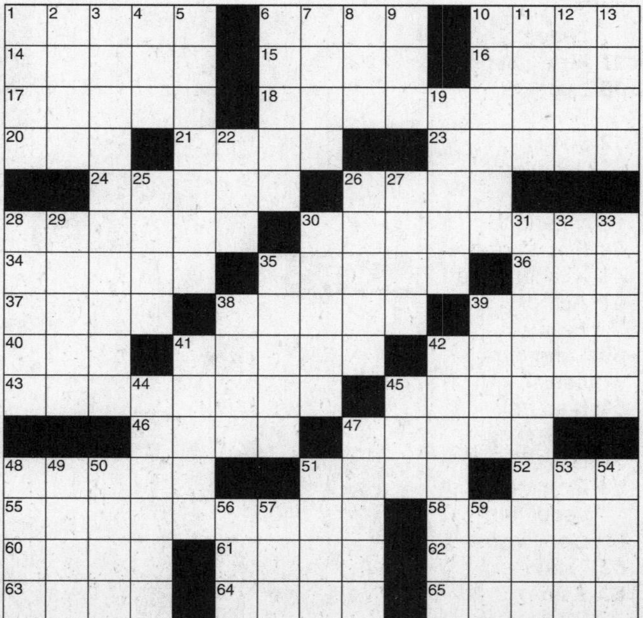

285 SWAP MEET

by Trip Payne

ACROSS

1 Inner personality
6 Loft cube
10 __ carotene
14 Secondary
15 Colorado tribe
16 Burly Burl
17 Pupil from abroad
20 Face lifts?
21 It can be common
22 UN branch
25 *Wheel of Fortune* buy
26 Clever repartee
27 __ on the chin
29 Prudish person
31 Former jrs.
32 Versatile batter
35 On the briny
36 Bunyan's whacker
37 Gymnast Korbut
41 Job-training places
46 Squeal
49 Russian river
50 First stage
51 Steamy
53 Meditative words
54 Scone partner
55 Decide about
56 Actress Tomei
59 Reason for travel
64 Scrabble piece
65 Poi base
66 Absurd
67 Cong. meeting
68 School on the Thames
69 Ephron and Dunn

DOWN

1 Soul, in Soissons
2 Prohibit
3 Stateside Ltd.
4 __ scale (hardness index)
5 Old Semitic language
6 Troop tooter
7 To __ (just so)
8 Not as much
9 Guinness Book ending
10 Delaware Democrat
11 Contests
12 More nervous
13 Autumn bloomers
18 Baseball climax, usually
19 Grammarian's concern
22 __ *Wonderful Life*
23 Statutes
24 Joad, for one
26 Small amount
28 *"L'__, c'est moi"*
29 TV-display speck
30 Hwys.
33 "If I __ hammer . . ."
34 Carrot or radish
38 Out of sight?
39 Untamed joy
40 *The Thin Man* terrier
42 Regretting
43 Lob path
44 Crystal or Carlin
45 Jordan's onetime king
46 Does a double take
47 Jughead's pal
48 Thoroughly destroys
52 Vocal sounds
53 Bean or Welles
56 Castle ditch
57 Bushy do
58 Part of A.D.
60 Bastille Day season
61 Canal zone?
62 Genetic material
63 "You bet!"

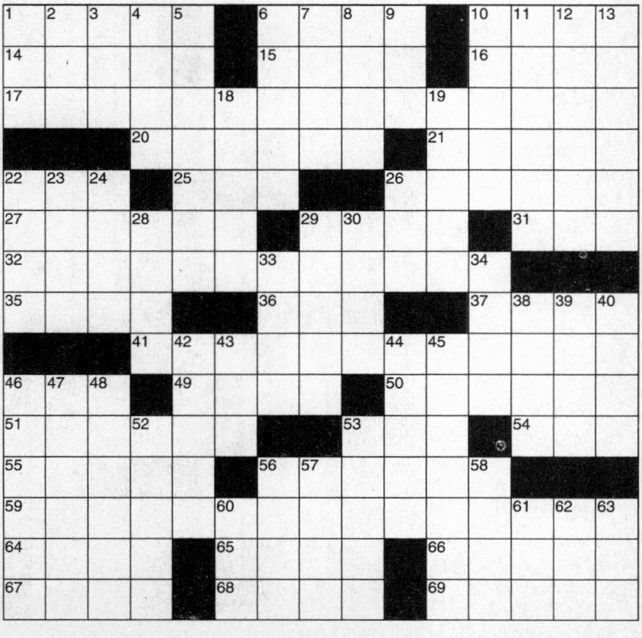

286 GRID PLAY

by Matt Gaffney

ACROSS
1 Shed, in Shrewsbury
6 French bread?
11 That woman
14 Potts or Oakley
15 Edmonton athlete
16 Sleeve contents?
17 Part of the NFL
20 In the style of
21 Architect I.M.
22 Switzerland's capital
23 Comic DeLuise
24 Thesaurus man
28 *My Life as* __ ('85 film)
29 States emphatically
32 Couch
33 Alaskan seaport
34 Soldier's awards
36 Wonka's creator
38 Part of CBS
39 3 points in football
42 Slightly spoiled
45 Request
46 Head and Wharton
50 Train track
52 Painter Chagall
54 Jacobi of *I, Claudius*
55 __ way (not at all)
56 Legal catchall
58 Woodsman's tool
59 Missouri range
61 Physique, for short
63 Dershowitz specialty
64 Football placement
69 SASE, e.g.
70 Jazzman Chick
71 Bravery
72 "I told you so!"
73 Garden tools
74 Reads quickly

DOWN
1 Paving material
2 Carpenters tune
3 Not indicated
4 Ignited
5 Univ. of Maryland player
6 Page numbers
7 Free (of)
8 "The Greatest"
9 Calif. neighbor
10 Baby furniture
11 Beehive and bob
12 Election issue
13 Goes back on a promise
18 __ Lingus
19 Penn or Young
25 Actress Paulette
26 HS math course
27 Western lake
30 *Luftwaffe* opp.
31 Lose one's footing
35 Alabama city
37 Actress Cheryl
40 Fit and trim
41 Stretch the truth
42 Baltimore players
43 Aficionado's periodical
44 MBA major
47 Sung syllables
48 Geometric figure
49 Spits
51 Folk tail?
53 Snake charmer's crew
57 Louis, *par exemple*
60 Dinkins' predecessor
62 Auto offs.
65 Egg __ yong
66 Promgoers: Abbr.
67 Average grade
68 Ringo's raincoat

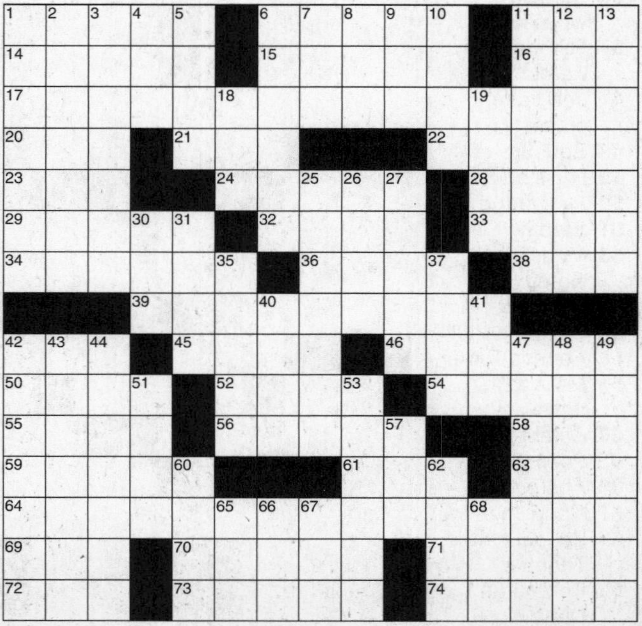

287 UP-TO-THE-MINUTE

by Shirley Soloway

ACROSS

1 Bedtime story
5 "__ It Romantic?"
9 Let up
14 "In the twinkling __ eye"
15 Scorch
16 *Concentration* feature
17 "And __ goes"
18 *"¿Cómo __ usted?"*
19 Thrill
20 It's news
23 Firm, pasta-wise
24 Greek letter
25 Traveler's guide
28 Up-to-date fashion
31 La __ Opera House
35 AAA way
36 Monogram pt.
37 Hawaiian island
38 Oriental sauce
39 Moccasin or mamba
40 Shortly
41 Poke fun at
42 A real knockout
43 Contemporary furnishings
47 Get the message
48 Shoe width
49 Opening
54 Avant-garde movies
56 Yucatán yummies
59 "I'm __ girl now!"
60 Danson and Kennedy
61 Striped stone
62 Carson's successor
63 Concerning
64 Head tops
65 Shakespearean actor Edmund
66 Noted loch

DOWN

1 Puccini opera
2 In a tangle
3 Scottish landowner
4 __ nous
5 __ *Letter to My Love*
6 Sonnet part
7 Hoopster Thurmond
8 Poor imitation
9 Sports stadiums
10 Swig
11 Belli org.
12 "The Boy King"
13 Compass pt.
21 Chou __
22 Diminutive suffix
25 Sociable starling
26 Similar
27 Newsman Jennings
29 Wear away
30 Subtle shade
31 Closes noisily
32 Light boat
33 Battery part
34 Stroller's spot
38 Stroller's spot
39 Printer's stroke
41 Was acquainted with
44 __ Pieces (candy)
45 California town
46 Idaho neighbor
50 Be part of the crowd
51 Actress Graff
52 Naval offs.
53 Road curves
54 Postcard message
55 Busy as __
56 Keyboard stroke
57 __ Khan
58 Felix, e.g.

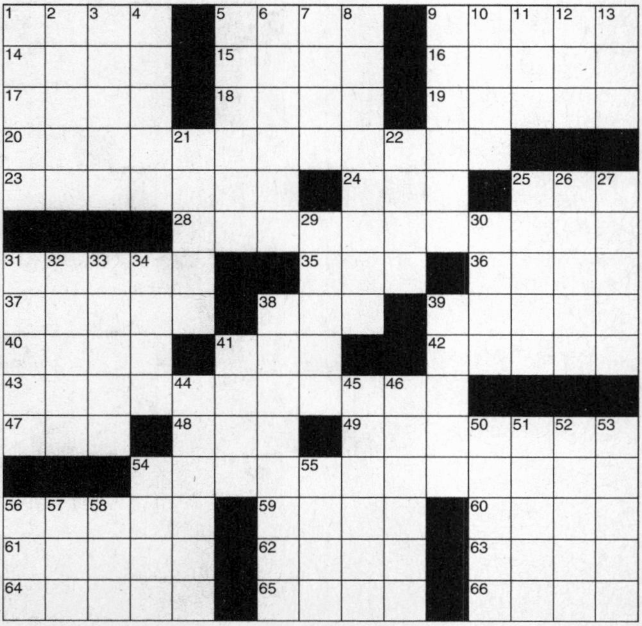

288 BODY LANGUAGE

by Harvey Estes

ACROSS

1 Old pro
4 Urban eyesore
8 UAW stronghold
12 Sweater muncher
14 Cash for Carlos
16 Worship
17 Arctic sight
18 Like some combat
20 Made threats
22 Unit of energy
23 Maiden-name indicator
24 __ *Rosenkavalier*
25 Short notice
27 Like some smiles
31 More prized
35 Baja bye-bye
36 Metallic fabric
38 Ice-cream holder
39 Waist band
40 __ metabolism
41 Leg joint
42 Duel tool
43 Brezhnev's dom.
44 Sunflower supports
45 Handbag parts
47 Like most agreements
49 Some secretaries
51 Catch a crook
52 Classified info
55 Chowed down
56 "__ two to tango"
60 Like some meetings
63 Bat habitat
64 Dash
65 Actress Laurie
66 Swiss artist Paul
67 Amusing sorts
68 Beatty flick
69 Final point

DOWN

1 Radio type
2 __ slaw
3 007's school
4 Area of influence
5 Starring role
6 Service div.
7 Reproduction
8 Speedometer abbr.
9 Persia, today
10 Walking stick
11 Jekyll's bad side
13 Like some competitions
15 Apple pastry
19 Fairy-tale monster
21 Corporate VIPs
25 Bright metal ornaments
26 Like some victories
27 Gently maneuvers
28 Learn the ropes
29 Step part
30 "Woe is me!"
32 Singer Blakley
33 Foe
34 Shortstop Pee Wee
37 New Testament figure
40 Inge drama
44 "Hurry!" in a hospital
46 Marsh matter
48 Records in a ledger
50 Fermented milk
52 __ *Good Men* (Cruise film)
53 Surrealist Salvador
54 "Beat it!"
56 Finished the cake
57 Leafy vegetable
58 Level
59 Plant-to-be
61 Pulver's rank: Abbr.
62 Mimic

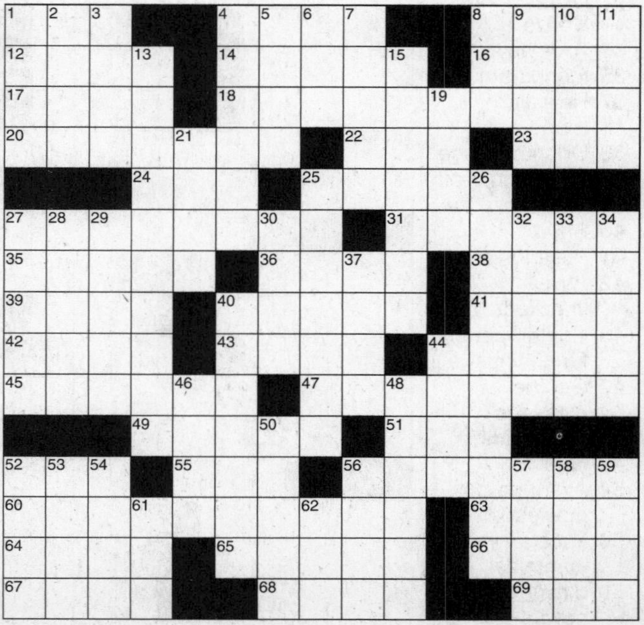

289 AIM OF THE GAME

by Mary E. Brindamour

ACROSS

1 Charitable donation
5 Police raid
9 Emulate a bloodhound
14 Chimney dirt
15 Way off
16 Peter of *Casablanca*
17 Golfer's aim
19 In front
20 Come in
21 Filler/driller
23 Landlords' income
26 Even so
27 *Lou Grant* star
30 __ as a board
34 Cartwright or Matlock
35 Timeless, to Tennyson
37 Islamic prince
38 Malaise, with "the"
40 Place
41 Teheran native
42 Director Kazan
43 Felt sorry for
45 "Holy cow!"
46 Mean coward
48 Jimmy and Rosalynn
50 *TV Guide* abbr.
51 Late bloomer
52 Decked out
55 Supermarket path
59 Nectarine or kumquat
60 Olympian's aim
63 Clear the windshield
64 Sting like __
65 St. Louis footballers
66 Echelons
67 Rep. rivals
68 __-Ball (arcade game)

DOWN

1 Tennis great Arthur
2 Diving bird
3 Shed feathers
4 Takes the reins
5 Forbid
6 Flying saucer
7 __ *of Iwo Jima*
8 Genealogy chart
9 Blackboards
10 Pitcher's aim
11 Gets one's back up
12 College club
13 Nourished
18 Papas and Dunne
22 NASDAQ rival
24 After taxes
25 Fearful
27 Flowed back
28 Perry's secretary
29 Diarist Nin
30 Playful pranks
31 Icon
32 Better quality
33 Burger partner
36 Tire track
39 Gretzky's aim
41 __ *of Jeannie*
43 Implore
44 Dig in
47 Winds down
49 Wine tasters, e.g.
51 Hacienda material
52 __ rug
53 Devastate
54 Mild oath
56 Pierre's st.
57 Metallic material
58 "So what __ is new?"
59 HST predecessor
61 Apollo craft
62 __ Moines, IA

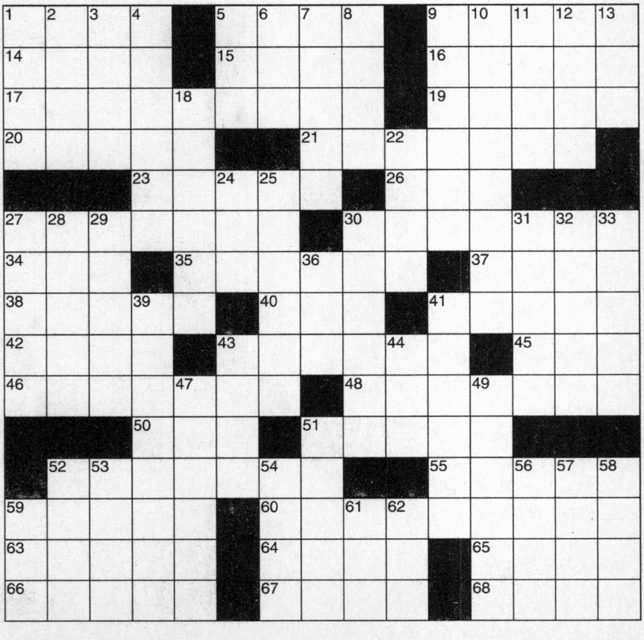

290 PLAYING 'ROUND

by Harvey Estes

ACROSS

1 Japanese wrestling
5 Gouda alternative
9 African country
13 How-to part
14 Marry on the run
15 Comedian Foxx
16 Press down
17 Indifferent
18 Ransom Eli __
19 Play basketball
22 Noticed
23 Northern seabird
24 '60s singer
27 Mardi Gras follower
29 Star Wars abbr.
32 Borders on
33 Conservative skirt
34 Holstein's home
35 Where clowns play
38 Billions of years
39 __-deucy
40 Solemn music
41 AMA members
42 Congregational comeback
43 Not quite
44 PD alert
45 Pub drinks
46 Wordplay game show
53 Prejudice
54 *Dallas* matriarch
55 White stone
56 Natural hairdo
57 Brings up
58 Comic Crosby
59 Profound
60 Unit of loudness
61 Pass catchers

DOWN

1 Former JFK landers
2 Hatch's home
3 Office note
4 They attract
5 Vocalist John
6 Condemn
7 ". . . baked in __"
8 Skilled technician
9 Shepherd's staff
10 Beatles movie
11 Slaps on
12 Driller's deg.
14 German city
20 Needle
21 End of an inning
24 Destined
25 Strongly dislike
26 Allen's partner
27 Flax fabric
28 Uptight
29 Orthopedic prefix
30 Pharmacopoeia
31 Map in a map
33 Mickey's kin
34 Sermon ingredient?
36 Wanderers
37 Gentleman of leisure?
42 Orang, e.g.
43 Medicinal plants
44 Moral man?
45 Blazing
46 Chaucer's __ of Bath
47 "__ Krishna!"
48 Butter substitute
49 Spanish dessert
50 Familiar with
51 Biblical ointment
52 Shade trees
53 Spoiled

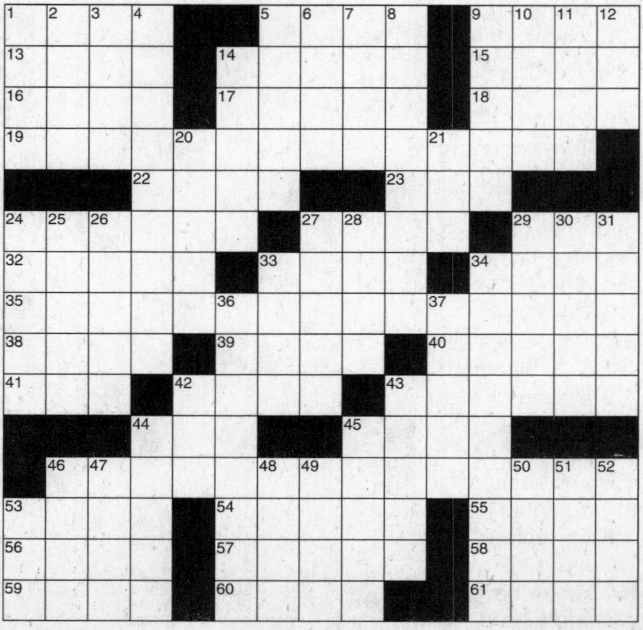

291 *HAVE A FLING*

by Eric Albert

ACROSS

1 Polite request
5 Camera-lens setting
10 Forest male
14 *East of* __
15 San Antonio landmark
16 "Gosh!"
17 Help prepare dinner
19 Riding stick
20 Green club
21 Devout
22 Fancy fronts
25 Take a bad turn
26 Introduction
27 Promotion, plus
29 Selling point
30 Furniture wood
31 Pear-shaped fruit
34 Goes bad
35 Stupefied
36 __ qua non
37 Antipollution grp.
38 Defraud
39 Bobby of tennis
40 Bladed tool
42 Sizzling
43 Borgnine role
45 *No, No,* __
46 Kipling's Kim
47 Dress parts
49 Fizzy drink
50 Camp out
54 God of love
55 Just right
56 Great Lake
57 Evergreen trees
58 Poor
59 Hemingway's nickname

DOWN

1 Ran into
2 Big scene
3 "Okay!"
4 Extremely
5 "__ your seat belts"
6 Venetian-blind parts
7 Narrative
8 Poet Khayyám
9 Engine enclosure
10 Get-together
11 Take a dive
12 Love, in Lyon
13 Natalie Wood musical
18 Check the books
21 Bishop of Rome
22 Breakdown beacon
23 Famous fabulist
24 Block the sun
25 It's often panned
27 Eye color
28 Serving customers
30 Labyrinth
32 Metal bar
33 *Beau* __
35 Cote creature
36 Dodge
38 Soft drink
39 Oscar de la __
41 Bug
42 Without caution
43 Amble
44 Tedious task
45 Battery type
47 Of great extent
48 Suit to __
50 Wrestling win
51 Period
52 Bit of a bite
53 Coffee alternative

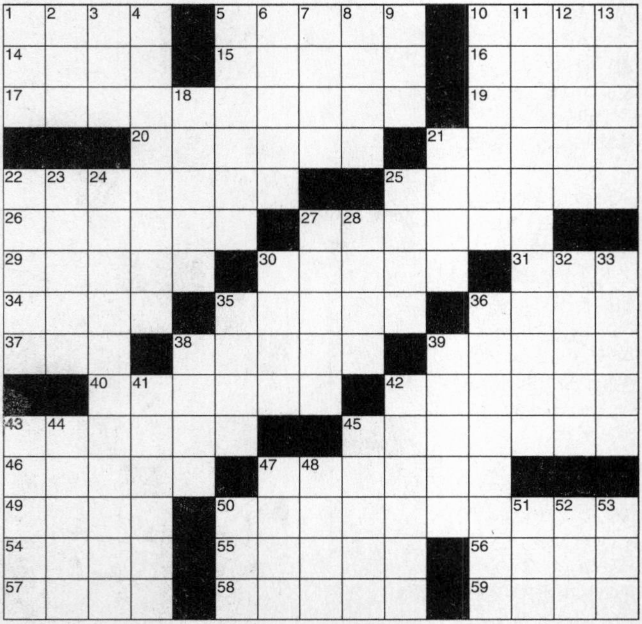

292 TERRAINIANS

by Randolph Ross

ACROSS
1 Director Sergio
6 Keats or Pindar
11 Commotion
14 "A House __ a Home"
15 Tony of tennis
16 Dublin dance
17 Milton Caniff character
19 100%
20 Afternoon delight?
21 Fabulous birds
22 Channel-swimmer Gertrude
24 Highly original
26 Fill the hold
27 He knew how to win friends and influence people
32 Roll with a hole
35 Falsifies
36 Unspecified amount
37 Nest eggs
38 Exchange
40 Hot stuff
41 Tot's time-out
42 Dates regularly
43 Ached (for)
44 "Gentle on My Mind" singer
48 *Alice's Restaurant* character
49 Sweet girl of song
53 Sign of neglect
56 Citrus cover
57 Watched junior
58 *A Chorus Line* number
59 Margaret Hamilton role
62 Caustic substance
63 Aromatic seed
64 *Año* opener
65 Switchboard abbr.
66 Olympic skater Carol
67 Locations

DOWN
1 Shopping aids
2 First name in cosmetics
3 Wee hr.
4 Fall mo.
5 Perpetual
6 Delphic VIP
7 Adams and Ameche
8 Slick
9 Pump stuffer
10 Sinews
11 Slightly open
12 Pickling herb
13 Check out, in a way
18 Barbecue fuel
23 Flock female
25 Bad day for Caesar
26 Uttered
28 Envelope closer
29 Profit
30 Memo words
31 Observed
32 Cherry choice
33 Russian sea
34 Rubberneck
38 Aquatic shade
39 San __, Italy
40 Pump gas
42 Shrill sound
43 Oaths
45 Slangy negative
46 Scottish youngsters
47 __ St. Vincent Millay
50 Cay
51 Mother-of-pearl
52 Group morality
53 Nat or Natalie
54 Black stone
55 Borscht veggie
56 Journalist Jacob
60 Lexington sch.
61 Verse starter

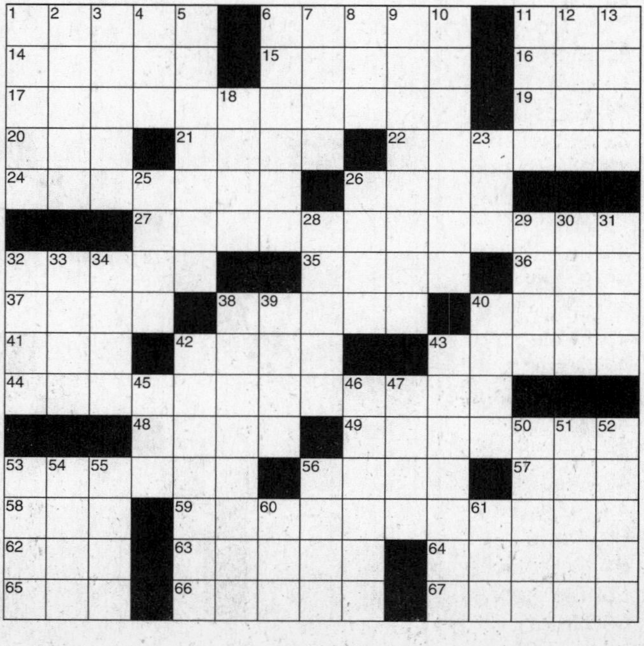

293 SPOTLESS

by Shirley Soloway

ACROSS
1 __ lazuli
6 Unruly youngster
10 Gentle __ lamb
13 Smart __ (wise guy)
14 Architect Saarinen
15 *"__ bien!"*
16 Dump the unnecessary
19 Chemical ending
20 Revealed
21 Kunta __ (*Roots* role)
22 Singer Shannon
23 Gets closer to
25 Search thoroughly
30 Eyelets
31 Send out
32 Mineo and Maglie
36 Egg-shaped
37 Steer clear of
38 Suit to __
39 Wallet bills
40 Actor Wilder
41 Mideast coin
42 Disposed of quickly
44 Compensation
48 *Birth __ Nation*
49 Assumed name
50 Land measure
52 Actress Lupino
55 Walk away from
59 RSVP cards, e.g.
60 Choir member
61 Perry's secretary
62 Aves.
63 Drop heavily
64 Nasty smile

DOWN
1 Metallic fabric
2 Arkin or Alda
3 Chinese pooch
4 Winter hazard
5 Fleming and Witt
6 Classroom clanger
7 Woodwind
8 Coach Parseghian
9 "This weighs a __!"
10 Israeli statesman Moshe
11 Take care of
12 Colorado resort
15 Castor or Pollux
17 Carbonated cooler
18 Go out of control
22 Sword fights
23 Tour leaders
24 Poker stake
25 Took a picture
26 Grotto
27 Pearl Buck heroine
28 Makes merry
29 Muscat native
32 "You __ mouthful!"
33 __ time (never)
34 Book page
35 Medieval worker
37 Swelled heads
41 Stands up for
42 Mexican money
43 Israeli dance
44 Less experienced
45 African antelope
46 Computer accessories
47 Team screams
50 Concerning
51 Karate blow
52 Tropical spot
53 Clinton opponent
54 At a distance
56 Short snooze
57 Building wing
58 TV room

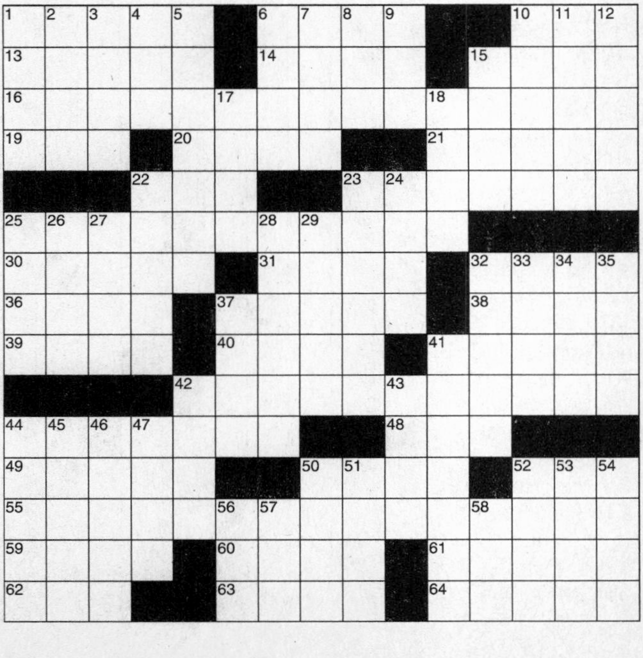

294 FAMILY REUNION

by Carol Fenter

ACROSS

1 Asian desert
5 Autumn fruits
10 Exec. degrees
14 "__ the Mood for Love"
15 Strong point
16 Give a yes-__ answer
17 Man with a scythe
19 New Rochelle college
20 __ water (stays afloat)
21 Menacing
23 Borscht veggie
25 Up in the world?
26 Oat or wheat
29 Find the sum
31 Wails
34 Utter defeat
35 Broad st.
36 Search, with "out"
37 Plant part
38 Looked for oil
40 Regret
41 Prepares to frame
43 Midmorning
44 Find fault
45 Troy's last king
46 Dracula's alter ego
47 Choir members
48 Brazier bit
50 Utah's state flower
52 Fruit cocktails
55 State for casinos
59 Russian range
60 Storyteller of the South
62 Renown
63 Turn of phrase
64 Pool triangle
65 Ran away
66 Fresh
67 Fr. holy women

DOWN

1 Present
2 First name in tents
3 Light snack
4 Occupy
5 Describe grammatically
6 NY hours
7 Sale sign
8 Jog one's memory
9 Office worker
10 Not as dry
11 Reagan film of '38
12 Novelist Tyler
13 Fly high
18 Paradise
22 Really annoyed
24 "Rikki-Tikki-__"
26 Hold on to
27 Oarsman
28 Rosalind Russell role
30 Actress Burke
32 Medical prefix
33 Dance moves
35 Dadaism founder
36 Bog
38 Disney pachyderm
39 "Why don't we?"
42 Toured a smorgasbord
44 St. Pat's plants
46 Singer Lee
47 Worry, for one
49 Needle cases
51 Foe
52 Sleeve end
53 Kind of exam
54 Biol. and chem.
56 *Amo, amas,* __
57 Mussolini moniker
58 Requests
61 __ Angeles, CA

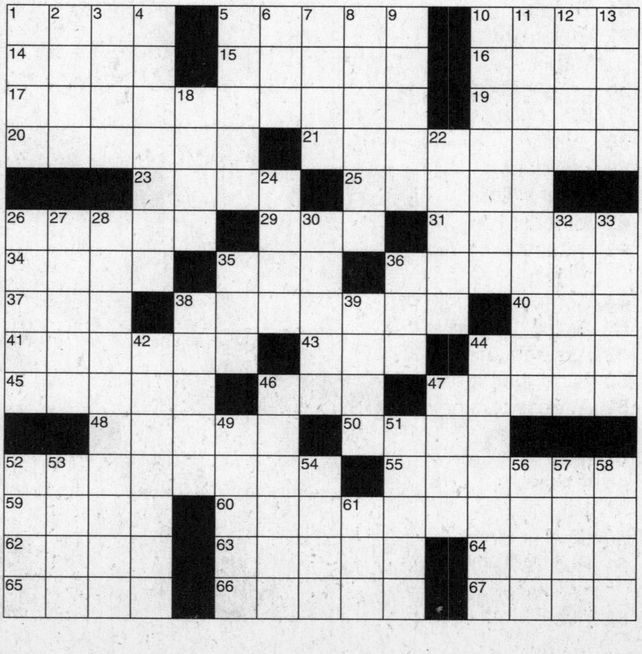

295 ON THE RISE

by Shirley Soloway

ACROSS

1 La __ Opera House
6 Actor DeLuise
9 Game-show prize
13 Immigration island
14 Emmy-winner Imogene
15 Mrs. Charlie Chaplin
16 Have high aspirations
19 Silly talk
20 Shoe part
21 Explosive initials
22 __ *of Eden*
24 Lemon skin
26 Not yet decided
30 Killer whale
34 Griddle
35 Thesaurus wds.
36 Sleep stopper
37 Throb
39 Chef's meas.
41 Maui patio
42 Actress Verdugo
43 Jai __
45 Negative prefix
46 Computer info
47 Extremely happy
50 Graph starter
52 Singer Simone
53 Make a request
56 Insertion marks
58 Bad bottom line
62 "Money is no object!"
65 Sleuth Wolfe
66 Long time periods
67 Of service
68 Boat movers
69 Genetic letters
70 Be buddies

DOWN

1 Slav
2 Singer Laine
3 "Too bad!"
4 Rock coating
5 Bonfire remains
6 Actress Diana
7 Sea animals
8 Composer Gustav
9 Cruise of *The Firm*
10 Cheer (for)
11 Aware of
12 Breathe rapidly
14 At peace
17 Suspicious
18 Shoe-box letters
23 Off the track
25 "Whatever __ Wants"
26 Raised the stakes
27 Abdul or Prentiss
28 Narrow passage
29 Size up
31 The Amazing __ (magician)
32 Diet guru Jenny
33 Pennsylvania sect
36 Set straight
38 Break suddenly
40 Foundation blocks
44 Liqueur flavoring
47 Ragged
48 Cartoonist Gary
49 Rock salt
51 Antiaircraft-gun sound
53 __ time (never)
54 NY ballpark
55 Actress Deborah
57 Sicilian spewer
59 Leave out
60 Grain holder
61 British weapon
63 Sea plea
64 Drag along

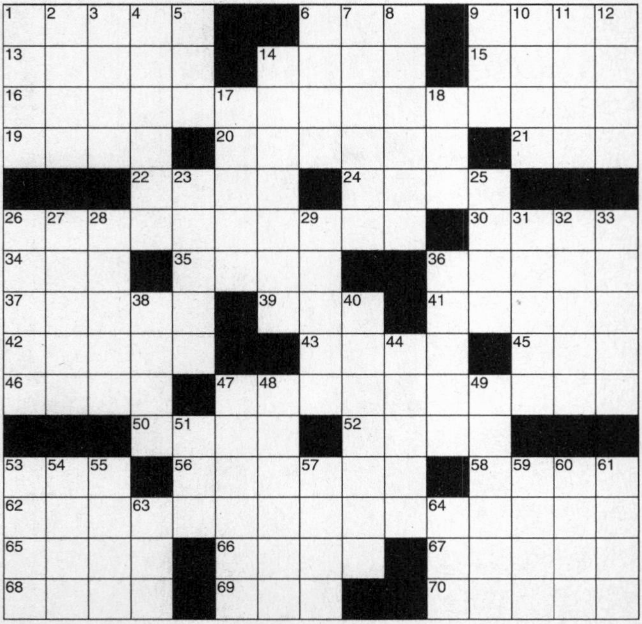

296 *BODY FOOD*

by Bob Lubbers

ACROSS
1 Moreno or Coolidge
5 *Brian's Song* star
9 Leading man?
14 Actor West
15 Girls' club: Abbr.
16 Stone marker
17 Barbecue side dish
19 Vulgar
20 "__ the barrel . . ."
22 Actress McClurg
23 Heavenly bodies
26 Brunch order
28 Wobble
29 Stand for
31 *Les __-Unis*
32 "Nevermore" bird
33 Useful article
36 Roman emperor
37 Trencherman
38 Male deer
39 Table scrap
40 Pronounce
41 Flier's floater
42 Plains Indians
44 Vestiges
45 Jungle jaunt
47 Least friendly
48 Real lulus
49 Albany or Augusta
52 Boise's locale
54 Bump on a spud
58 *The Color Purple* character
59 Hurler Hershiser
60 Stocking stuffers?
61 Toting a gun
62 Legis. period
63 Ginger cookie

DOWN
1 *Norma __*
2 Mrs. Eddie Cantor
3 Paving material
4 Little cupid
5 Pedal pusher
6 MP quarries
7 Word form for "height"
8 Ork talk
9 L.A. coll.
10 Wall or Wimpole
11 Salad foundation
12 Beast of Borden
13 Adjust a timer
18 Links alerts
21 Cosmetic purchase
23 Office worker
24 Flying Pan
25 Exotic veggie
27 Calendar abbr.
29 Goes with
30 "If __ I Would Leave You"
32 Pro __ (proportionately)
34 Can't stand
35 Discharge
37 Moral standard
38 Onion relatives
40 Former Mideast nation: Abbr.
41 Eastern European
43 #5 iron
44 Destroys the Dodge
45 Star in Virgo
46 Assistance, in court
47 Makes a footnote
50 Mil. addresses
51 Skin opening
53 Brit. lexicon
55 Years on end
56 Affirmative vote
57 Sixth sense

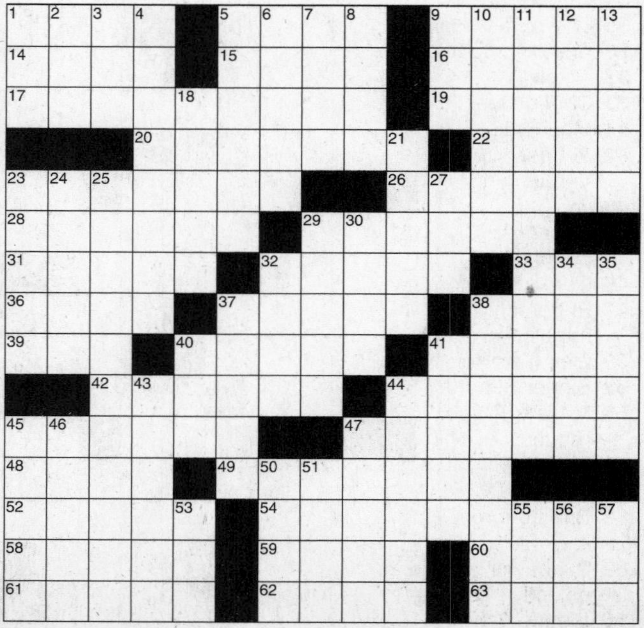

297 WORDS OF A FEATHER

by Harvey Estes

ACROSS
1 Smart talk
5 Plant pest
10 Dove sounds
14 Horse's gait
15 Spot for sports
16 Head line?
17 Reverberation
18 One way to quit
20 Race like the wind
22 Farrow and Sara
23 One of two baseball teams
24 Tells fibs
26 Busy as __
28 Latin
32 Where the Ark parked?
36 Dizzy
37 Turner and Cole
39 Singer Lesley
40 Foundry refuse
41 Light boat
42 Alan of *Shane*
43 French bean?
44 Daffy has one
45 Fix the lawn
46 On the beach
48 Wall hanging
50 Shipshape
52 Bluish-white element
53 High card
56 Level
58 Keeps the home fires burning
62 Back down
65 Textbook heading
66 Ike's ex
67 Rocket slower
68 Garr of *Tootsie*
69 Made tracks
70 Car metal
71 Oracle

DOWN
1 Do a slow burn
2 Curved structure
3 London district
4 Squealer
5 German city
6 Paid player
7 Pilot's place
8 Calcutta's country
9 Computer's collection
10 EMT course
11 Mighty trees
12 Sandwich cookie
13 Underworld river
19 __-friendly
21 Thailand, formerly
25 Six-Day War site
27 Estimable young men
28 *"¡__ la vista!"*
29 Dots in the ocean
30 Path in the grass
31 Art able
33 Dean Martin specialty
34 Passion
35 Bear in a crib
38 Yellow gem
41 Ward and Wally
45 Monthly expense
47 Stink
49 Small gun
51 Article of faith
53 Pretends
54 Cookie nugget
55 __ *kleine Nachtmusik*
57 Postcard message
59 Leg joint
60 Green land
61 Use a teaspoon
63 Scoundrel
64 Noun suffix

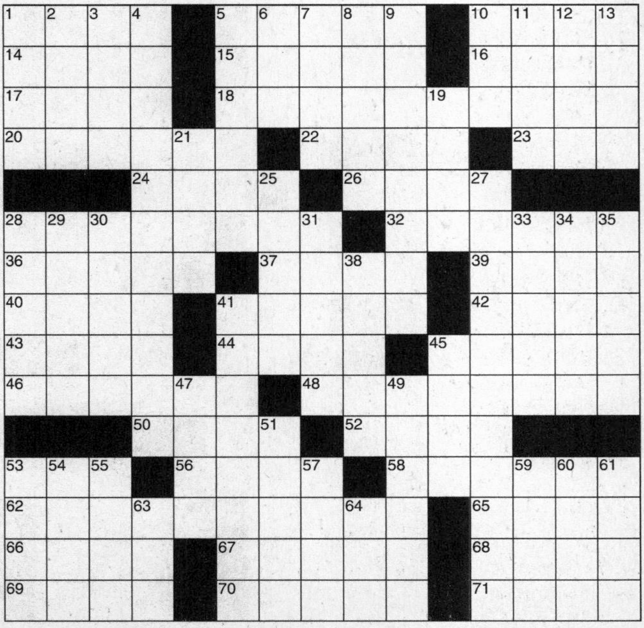

298 CHINA SYNDROME

by Trip Payne

ACROSS
1 __ *the Horrible*
6 Entreated
10 Toot one's own horn
14 Absurd
15 Hamlet or Macbeth
16 Artemis' mother
17 Ziti or rigatoni
18 Make eyes at
19 Word form for "within"
20 Vanity tags, e.g.
23 __ Baba
25 Porkpie or pillbox
26 Clear videotapes
27 Toupees
29 NASA ship
33 Inc. kin
34 Cultural character
36 Gaucho's rope
38 "The Great Pretender" group
42 Swell place?
43 Stallone role
46 Cul-de-__
49 Like zombies
52 It may be posted
53 Very loud
55 Uninformed response
57 Serling or Steiger
58 Gossips
63 Analogy words
64 Prepare a present
65 He took two tablets
68 Command to Fido
69 Bee or Em
70 *Peter Grimes*, for one
71 Soviet news agency
72 Implores
73 Gold or copper

DOWN
1 Cool
2 Literary collection
3 Boyer film of '44
4 Pro foe
5 Arrive at
6 On the double
7 Fireplace fuel
8 *Vogue* rival
9 Profound
10 Become teary
11 Traveler's car
12 Bear out
13 Moved to action
21 Canal zone?
22 I, for one
23 Emotion at Stonehenge
24 Ignited
28 Manhattan area
30 Stick one's neck out
31 Baby beaver
32 Do lunch
35 Anchored
37 Riyadh resident
39 Cross product
40 Young man
41 Fashionable group
44 Life story
45 Time-honored
46 Nasty sort
47 Record label
48 Sportscaster Bob
50 Skilled people
51 Big flop
54 Mariners' cries
56 Unauthorized TV greeting
59 Deck cleaner
60 Test choice
61 Install a door
62 Catch a calf
66 Prime time?
67 Actor Mineo

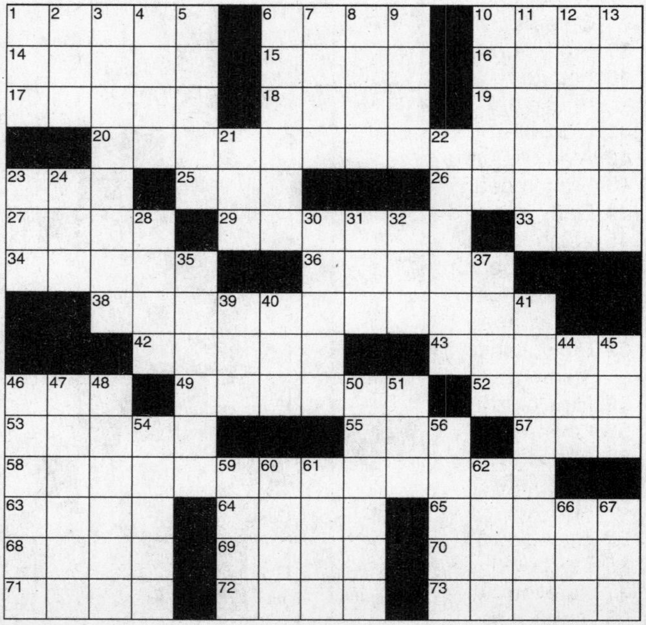

299 BEACH DAY

by Shirley Soloway

ACROSS
1 Foundation
6 Eastern European
10 Trade
14 Let up
15 Junior dress size
16 Hindu queen
17 Jason's wife
18 __'acte
19 Elevator inventor
20 Halt an advance
23 Frat letter
24 Cook, in a way
25 Marine leader?
27 Haul away
30 *Kidnapped* monogram
31 Eyes flirtatiously
32 Meager
34 Lifted, as spirits
37 Lay a sidewalk
38 Keep out
39 Relocate
40 Make payment
43 Response
45 Depends (on)
46 In favor of
47 __ "King" Cole
48 "__ to the Church on Time"
49 Word form for "outer"
51 Pastoral god
52 Participate actively
58 Assns.
60 French river
61 Janis of *Silk Stockings*
62 Not fooled by
63 Nobelist Wiesel
64 Shining brightly
65 Cracker brand
66 Wooded valley
67 *Bambi* extras

DOWN
1 Impact sounds
2 Foster a felon
3 Marquis de __
4 Units
5 Ushers and hostesses
6 Mean looks
7 Dryer fuzz
8 Counter to
9 *Marcus Welby, M.D.* actress
10 Sign of success
11 Dilutes
12 Singer Bryant
13 Italian tower town
21 Patriot Nathan
22 __ May Clampett
26 Rains hard
27 Baker's amts.
28 Colorful fish
29 On the same __ (in accord)
31 __ *Town*
33 Lease again
34 Halloween decoration
35 Eye part
36 Saucy
38 Kramden's vehicle
41 Ewe's youngster
42 Like the Cyclops
43 St. Louis landmark
44 Memo book
46 Shorebird
48 French menu word
50 Inedible orange
51 Winnie-the-__
53 Capri, e.g.
54 Simon or Diamond
55 Sly trick
56 Composer Stravinsky
57 Kitten cries
59 Jack of *Barney Miller*

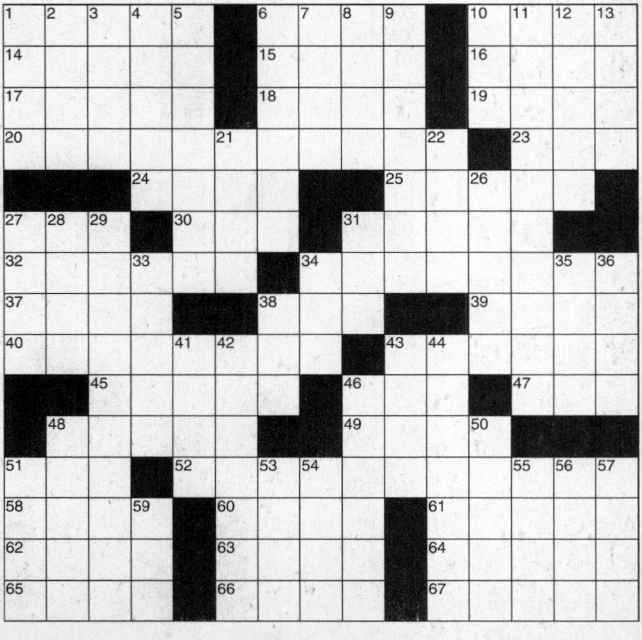

300 TRILOGY

by Dean Niles

ACROSS
1 Lauder powder
5 Dance, to Deneuve
8 Spill the beans
12 Staying power
13 Russian river
15 __ Music (British group)
16 Pay the penalty
17 Let go
18 "That's clear!"
19 Two-pair beater
22 Cousteau's workplace
23 Bear down
24 Defeats
28 __ were (so to speak)
29 Part of PST
31 Twice XXVI
32 VIP
35 Sky light?
36 Singer Eartha
37 Soap-opera staple
40 Off-the-wall
41 *Seven Days in* __
42 Teatime treats
43 Inventor Whitney
44 Actor Alastair
45 Marsh matter
46 Windblown soil
48 Propelled a raft
50 African snake
53 Club sandwich
56 New York stadium
59 Musical finale
60 Curie or Osmond
61 Rip
62 Egyptian goddess
63 Subtle sarcasm
64 Cheer (up)
65 Pipe fitter's union?
66 Walking stick

DOWN
1 Religious donation
2 Greek marketplace
3 Solitary
4 Enters furtively
5 Sideboard supper
6 Costa Rican Nobelist
7 Buttercup variety
8 __ *of Frankenstein*
9 __ Alamos, NM
10 Bunyan's tool
11 "Toodle-oo!"
12 Large tubs
14 Luau neckwear
20 Japanese art
21 Brokaw's employer
25 Adjust the car wheels
26 Ring championship
27 Locations
28 Off-center
30 Liqueur flavoring
32 Watch part
33 Author Calvino
34 Bottled spirit
35 Pigpen
36 Tie the __ (marry)
38 It may hold you up
39 Theoretical
44 Lith., formerly
45 Tickle pink
47 Very simple
49 Any Elvis recording
50 Ohio city
51 Notre Dame's river
52 Sitting duck
54 "__ *on parle français*"
55 Actress Williams
56 "The racer's edge"
57 __ *Haw*
58 Lend an __ (listen)

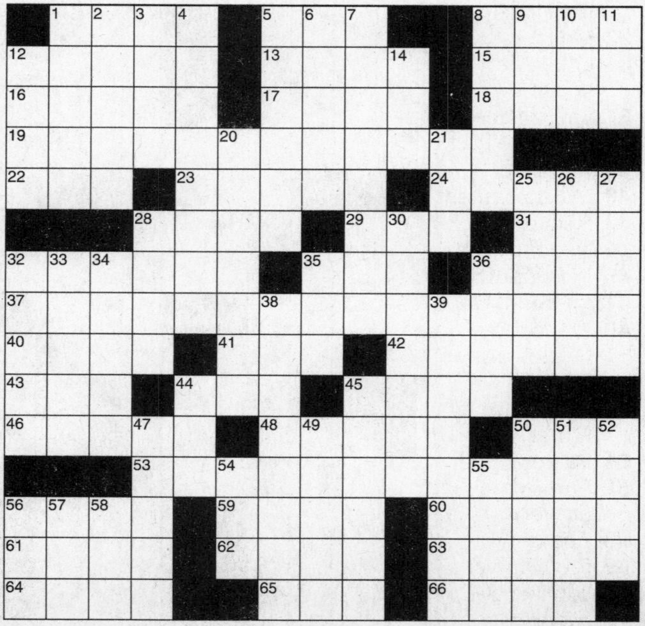

301 ANY WHICH WAY

by Mary E. Brindamour

ACROSS

1 Closed
5 Canonized Mlles.
9 Interrogative pronoun
12 Uses a VCR
14 Lo-cal
15 Camp food
16 Drained of color
17 Emphasize
19 Hedge sculpture
21 "__ With a Kiss"
22 Ease
23 Got a D
24 Tiny critter
26 Author Sinclair
27 Belfry resident
28 Paul of *Crocodile Dundee*
30 __ wave (tsunami)
34 Bit of gossip
36 Factions
38 Caesar's costar
39 Column style
41 Tide types
43 Ironic
44 More cunning
46 Makes amends
48 South Americans
50 Comedian Arnold
51 Convincing
52 Wine mavens
54 Weed-covered
56 Nebraska city
58 Writes
59 Roman poet
60 Hazardous gas
61 Pitcher's stat.
62 Droops
63 Gingrich of Georgia

DOWN

1 RR stop
2 Biblical verb
3 Pad furniture
4 Plains abode
5 Drink noisily
6 Littler than little
7 Airport abbr.
8 Teeter-totter
9 During the time that
10 Sharpened
11 Was in debt
13 Informant
15 Revered work
18 Convene again
20 Sedans
23 Word form for "five"
24 Footnote abbr.
25 Western alliance
26 Shoe salesman, at times
29 Kelly and Hackman
31 Reduce in importance
32 Land measure
33 Puts down
35 Gentlemen
37 Run-ins
40 Hold on
42 Machine part
45 Prelims
47 Kind of band
48 Sweetheart
49 Booster rocket
50 Smooths
51 Deal (with)
52 Baby branch
53 Put on display
55 Cicero's eggs
57 Picnic pest

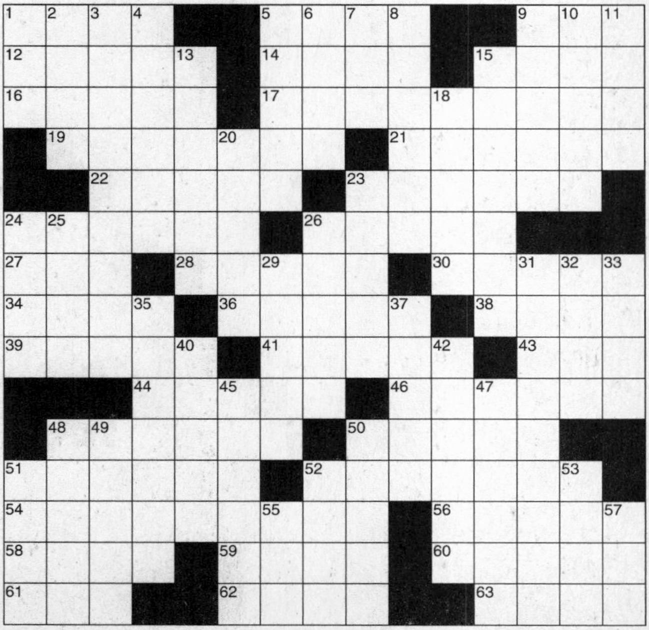

302 TRIPLE FEATURE

by Eric Albert

ACROSS
1 Unclear
5 Hot lunch
10 Con game
14 Drama award
15 Great destruction
16 Saint's circle
17 Ignore
20 Barbie's boyfriend
21 *Gentlemen Prefer Blondes* author
22 Small part
23 Actor Arnaz
24 Give a name to
25 Smitten
28 Point of departure
29 Radio regulator: Abbr.
32 Memorable ship
33 Unadulterated
34 2-D extent
35 Scold
38 "If __ I Would Leave You"
39 Of enormous extent
40 Huey, Dewey, and __
41 Writer Deighton
42 Sword handle
43 Like a puppy
44 Ship's tiller
45 Singer Patti
46 Harmony
49 Hunger pain
50 Nightwear
53 Defy
56 Être
57 Obliterate
58 Poet Alexander
59 Out
60 Tools with teeth
61 Once more

DOWN
1 Pawn
2 Ready, willing, and __
3 Jerusalem, figuratively
4 Affirmative answer
5 Opt for
6 Capital of Vietnam
7 Composer Charles
8 __ Alamos, NM
9 Cold drink
10 Unfilled pie
11 Barrel
12 Voice range
13 LEM locale
18 Huddle count
19 New Haven campus
23 Giving person
24 Jeweler's measure
25 Constrain
26 Like a babe in the woods
27 Bedclothes, e.g.
28 Invitee
29 Impostor
30 Beany's buddy
31 Sweet and crumby
33 Sacred song
34 Home
36 Bad guy
37 Nancy's pal
42 Oregano, for one
43 French port
44 Cozy and comfortable
45 Like Nehru jackets
46 "__ girl!"
47 Medium-sized dog
48 Castro's country
49 High point
50 Laborer
51 Wisecrack
52 Fret and fume
54 Gun-lobby grp.
55 Whirlpool bath

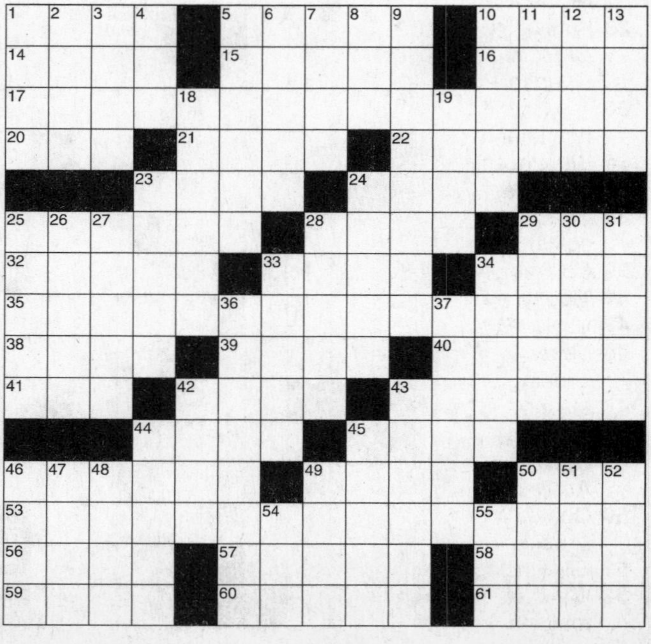

303 SHOOTING STARS

by Janie Lyons

ACROSS
1 Freshwater fish
5 Shame
10 Burn slightly
14 Felipe of baseball
15 Italian bowling
16 Nevada city
17 *Butch Cassidy and the Sundance Kid* star
19 Word form for "within"
20 Car-radio feature
21 Captivated
23 Helper: Abbr.
25 Middle
26 Printer's directions
29 Irving or Carter
31 Tips a hat
34 Story
35 Arafat's org.
36 Previously
37 "The Greatest"
38 Helium holder
40 Society column word
41 Poet William
43 Atty.'s degree
44 Pierre's st.
45 Tree bumps
46 Deli bread
47 Hardwood trees
48 __ as a goose
50 Aroma
52 Aetna rival
55 Senator Muskie
59 Harvest
60 *High Noon* star
62 Noun suffix
63 Cop __ (bargain, maybe)
64 Mrs. Nick Charles
65 Danish physicist
66 Oozing
67 Winter forecast

DOWN
1 *Li'l Abner* cartoonist
2 Winglike
3 Don Juan
4 Throb
5 Helps a hood
6 Violinist's need
7 Highest point
8 Meager
9 Siva worshiper
10 __ the crop (finest)
11 *The Tin Star* star
12 Poker stake
13 Crucifix
18 Noted loch
22 German seaport
24 Lofty
26 Pile up
27 Claw
28 *The Magnificent Seven* star
30 Actress Ringwald
32 Anomaly
33 Searches for
35 Golf goal
36 Hope or Newhart
38 Intoxicate
39 Bread spread
42 Flourish
44 Sunday talks
46 Record again
47 Hubbub
49 Adventure stories
51 Corrode
52 Jordanian, for one
53 *Tonight Show* host
54 __ Stanley Gardner
56 Well-informed
57 Pianist Peter
58 Sketch
61 Slangy assent

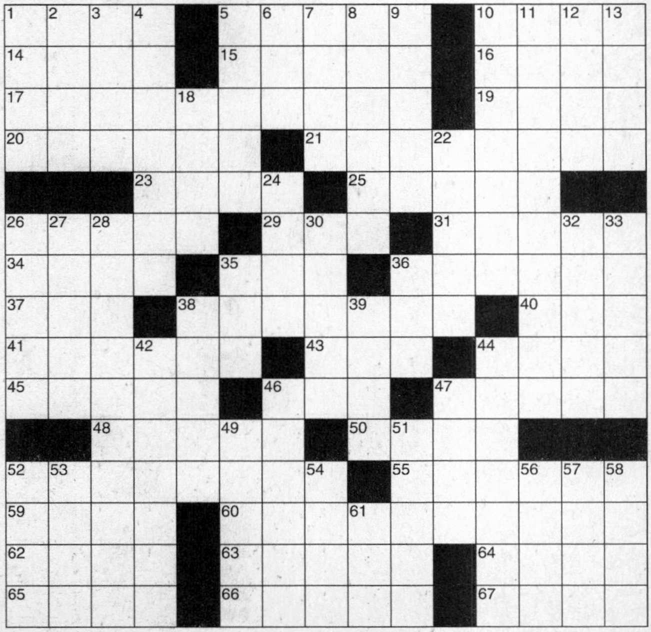

304 *MATTERS OF TASTE*

by Dean Niles

ACROSS

1 Dull
5 Bogged down
10 "Waterloo" group
14 Leak slowly
15 Rub out
16 Wedding-cake level
17 Disdain for the unobtainable
19 List entry
20 EMT procedure
21 Gave temporarily
22 Insignificant
24 Serengeti sillies?
26 Please, in Potsdam
27 Serious cinema
30 Gun an engine
33 It makes waste
36 *Picnic* playwright
37 Brooks and Gibson
38 Part of QED
39 Burn
40 Yardstick org.
41 Comrade
42 Tom Joad, for one
43 Appendix neighbor
44 Little child
45 Deviating
47 Aviator Post
49 Calf
53 More economical
55 Headliner
57 1300 hours
58 Courtly instrument
59 Widespread craving
62 Sign of the future
63 Rockies range
64 Floundering
65 Peel an orange
66 Roman parent
67 Balkan

DOWN

1 Painter Hieronymus
2 Daft
3 Blue hue
4 __ *Alibi* ('89 movie)
5 Slightest
6 Isfahan's country
7 Engrossed
8 Journal ending
9 Very unpopular
10 Leaning
11 Furthest extremity
12 Bar order
13 Troops
18 Annoying light
23 Dined
25 Cooper hero Bumppo
26 Morning musician
28 *The Iceman Cometh* character
29 Studio sign
31 Otherwise
32 Engine option
33 Solar output
34 Singer Guthrie
35 Taffy type
37 Devilfish
39 Regains control
43 Motionless
45 Bristol brew
46 Personification
48 Actress Worth
50 On the prowl
51 Computer key
52 Fix up
53 Hog food
54 Mountain lion
55 Transmitted
56 Head: Fr.
60 Mil. stat.
61 US alliance

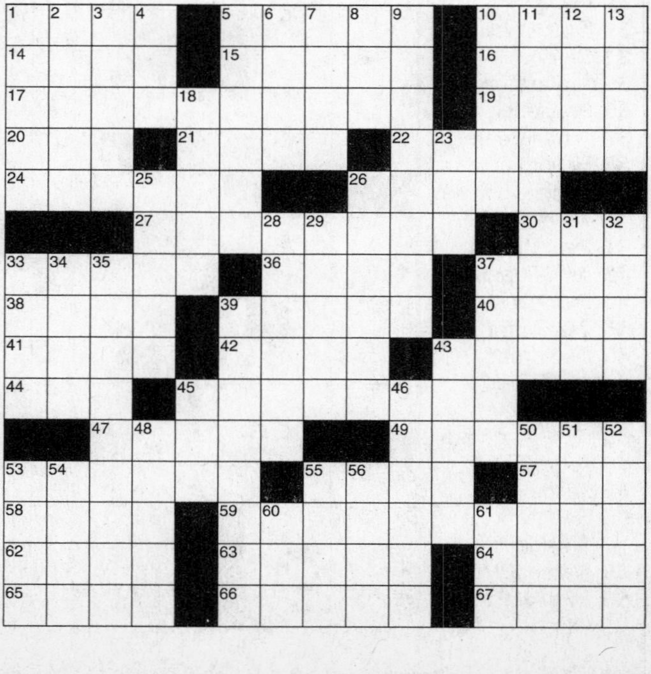

305 COUPLES

by Shirley Soloway

ACROSS
1 Birthday figures
5 Talks wildly
10 "__ boy!"
14 Burrowing rodent
15 Similar
16 Clean the deck
17 Poker hand
19 Become winded
20 Step
21 Hummingbird's home
22 Picnic pests
23 Out of kilter
25 Spew forth
27 Serves the soup
30 __ David (religious symbol)
32 Greek love god
33 Border on
36 Whines
38 R-V center
39 Car coloration
41 Shoe width
42 Rome's river
44 Neck part
45 Soho streetcar
46 Screenwriter May
48 '92 Wimbledon winner
50 Therefore
51 Hunt or Hayes
53 Env. notation
55 Designer Cassini
57 Carpenter's items
61 French silk
62 Simon and Garfunkel, e.g.
64 Diminutive dogs
65 "Untouchable" Ness
66 *Desire Under the __*
67 Editor's word
68 Office worker
69 Taken-back auto

DOWN
1 Electrical units
2 Capricorn symbol
3 Director Kazan
4 Ongoing dramas
5 Brit. fliers
6 Thicke and Young
7 Bad habits
8 Gets by, with "out"
9 Six-line verse
10 Rogers' partner
11 Kuala Lumpur skyscraper pair
12 Fruit pastry
13 Vigoda and Burrows
18 *Coffee, Tea, __?*
24 "__ Mommy Kissing Santa Claus"
26 Fictional aunt
27 For fear that
28 Bandleader Shaw
29 Holiday pay rate
30 Corner sign
31 Dog lovers?
34 Skeleton part
35 Actress Hagen
37 Big rig
39 Math subject
40 Actress Patricia
43 Purposeful
45 Scarlet bird
47 Rope loops
49 British actor Leo
51 Skater Sonja
52 Encourage vigorously
53 Vipers
54 Horn-blower's sound
56 Cheerful song
58 Run in neutral
59 Sugar serving
60 Mediocre
63 "How was __ know?"

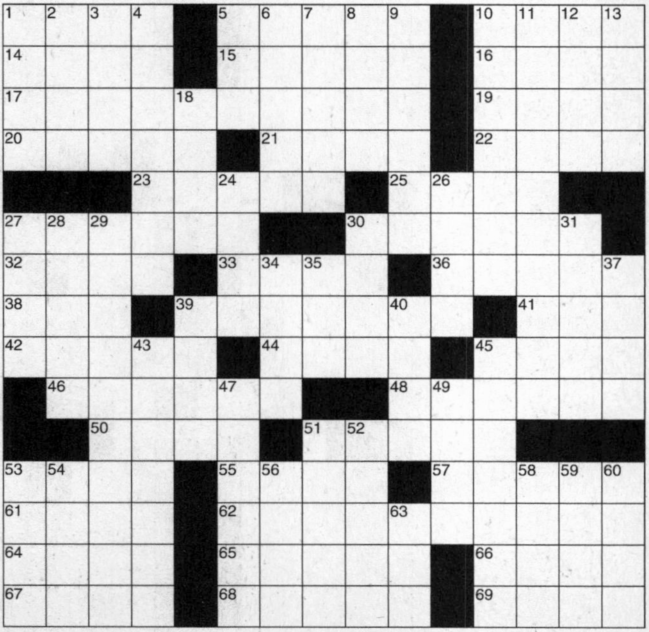

306 COURSE WORK

by Nancy Salomon

ACROSS

1 Toe woe
5 Fundamental
10 Duel tool
14 Peek-__
15 Luncheonette lure
16 Pop
17 Pest-control devices
19 Tend the sauce
20 Shortstop Reese
21 Back-pedals
23 *Born Free* lioness
25 Tilted
26 Roman garments
29 Faux __
31 Disdain
34 Ache
35 Buck and bull
36 Coins
37 Chowed down
38 Terrestrial
40 "In what way?"
41 Lofty goals
43 Rogers or Clark
44 Cherry stones
45 Tunes
46 Hilarious Hope
47 Slightly stewed
48 Nimble
50 Just for the fun __
52 Add to
55 Summaries
59 Wear out
60 Battle of 1775
62 Dollar bills
63 Do-__ situation (crisis)
64 Buffalo waterfront
65 Famed loch
66 Musical pauses
67 Turned blue?

DOWN

1 Summer place
2 Woodwind
3 Libertine
4 "Piece of cake!"
5 Last name in motels?
6 Part of ETA
7 Fly high
8 Forces
9 Social class
10 Lifeblood
11 TV snack
12 Prepare for publication
13 Head set?
18 Slippery swimmers
22 Grating
24 Copycat
26 Bangkok natives
27 Exceed
28 Gabor sitcom
30 Houston ballplayer
32 Uproars
33 Full of the latest
35 Owns
36 Like a fox
38 Beast of Borden
39 Freight-car hopper
42 Start a fight
44 Threw a strike
46 "How Can I __?" ('67 tune)
47 Row
49 Sweat and slave
51 Releases
52 Pour __ (strive)
53 Workday start
54 Pass catchers
56 Well-ventilated
57 Ballet bend
58 Toboggan
61 Hobby-shop buy

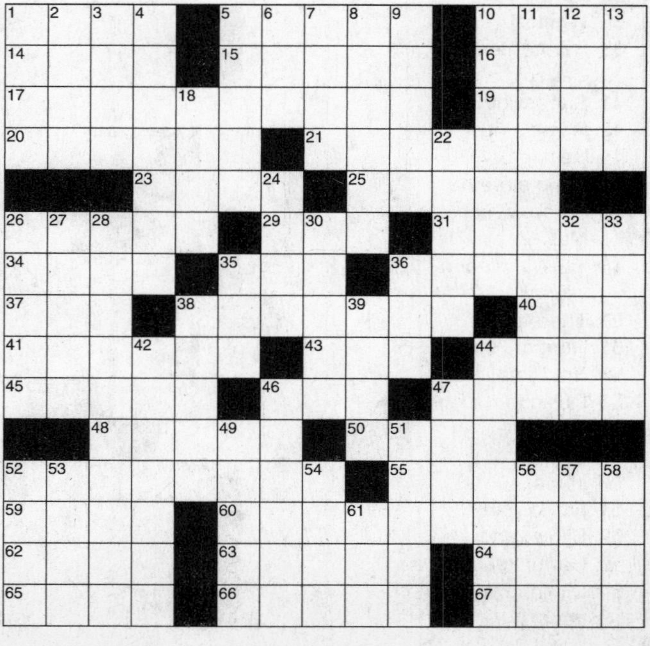

307 WHAT'S COOKING?

by Shirley Soloway

ACROSS

1 "Too bad!"
5 *Butterfield 8* author
10 Freshwater fish
14 Marquis de __
15 Boca __, FL
16 Mata __
17 Become calm
19 Gymnast Korbut
20 "For want of __ . . ."
21 Mornings: Abbr.
22 High-pitched flutes
23 Mouth pros
25 Restrain
26 Have a bite
27 Prohibited
30 Pinky or Peggy
33 "My lips are __"
36 Creole veggie
37 Shade trees
39 Make corrections
40 Century segment
41 Singer Lane
42 Waistline
44 Two-bagger: Abbr.
45 Marched up Main
47 Wynn and Asner
49 Had a mortgage
50 Kept harassing
55 Court session
57 A long way off
58 __ *Gay*
59 Shopping center
60 Lost one's temper
62 Daredevil Knievel
63 Tears down
64 Geom. shape
65 Sparks and Beatty
66 Prayer endings
67 Sciences' partner

DOWN

1 Syrian leader
2 Singer Frankie
3 Jingle guy
4 Hebrew, e.g.
5 Hockey great Bobby
6 Attacked
7 Particles
8 Moves a canoe
9 Actress Jillian
10 Church vocalist
11 Poorly planned
12 Give encouragement
13 Diagonal
18 Inventor Howe
22 Mink or beaver
24 Irritated
25 Fussed over
27 Ward (off)
28 Dreary
29 British nobleman
30 Spring
31 Exile isle
32 In a state of confusion
34 In the thick of
35 Went first
38 Beach barriers
43 Sidled
46 Dover's home: Abbr.
48 Hacienda housewife
50 Pool-table fabric
51 Songwriter Harold
52 Fido's friend
53 Put in office
54 Pub game
55 Nitti nabbers
56 Boffo review
57 Shaving cream
60 Swimsuit top
61 Road curve

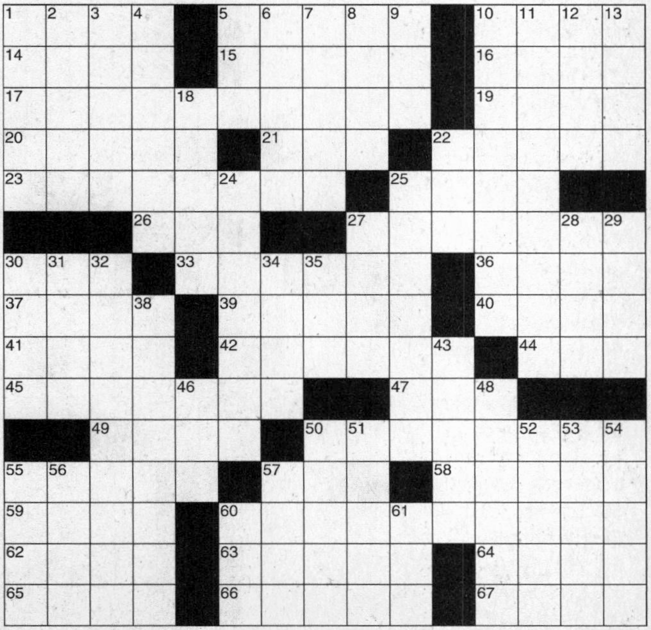

308 NUMBERS GAME

by Harvey Estes

ACROSS

1 Basics
5 Word used in dating
10 Spoken
14 Former Senate leader
15 Intense hatred
16 Red in the middle
17 Slot machines
20 Youth org.
21 Bunch together
22 Light brown
23 Range of hearing
25 Gum ingredient
28 "Absolutely!" in Baja
29 "O'er" opposite
32 Cranny companion
33 Fleur-de-__
35 Oz coward
37 Hot-shot pilot
38 Opinion
42 Wrath
43 With respect to
44 Matter for future generations?
45 Noun suffix
47 Noncom, for short
49 Row
53 Soup pot
55 Mickey's Florida home
57 Before, in verse
58 Put a match to
60 Ran for cover
61 Picnic contest
65 Scottish isle
66 Name on a plane
67 Choir member
68 Classroom furniture
69 Inserted a gusset
70 Army eatery

DOWN

1 Desert bricks
2 Teensy tree
3 Frees from blame
4 Neptune's domain
5 Practical smarts
6 Have a notion
7 Gets free (of)
8 Baby bears
9 GP grp.
10 Install a minister
11 April apparel
12 Carney or Linkletter
13 __ *Misérables*
18 Stadium shout
19 To the __ degree
24 Farm building
25 Dunce
26 __ Lomond
27 Just manage, with "out"
30 Change
31 "__ the season . . ."
34 Here, in Le Havre
36 Persona __ grata
38 Family framework
39 Zane Grey works
40 New Deal org.
41 Pro __ (proportionately)
42 Squid's squirt
46 *Silver* __ ('76 film)
48 Stare at
50 Take a breath
51 Royal decrees
52 Cowboy competitions
54 Martial arts master
56 Inc., in England
58 Late-night name
59 Frankenstein's assistant
61 Dosage schedule: Abbr.
62 Weeding tool
63 Chicken piece
64 Zodiac symbol

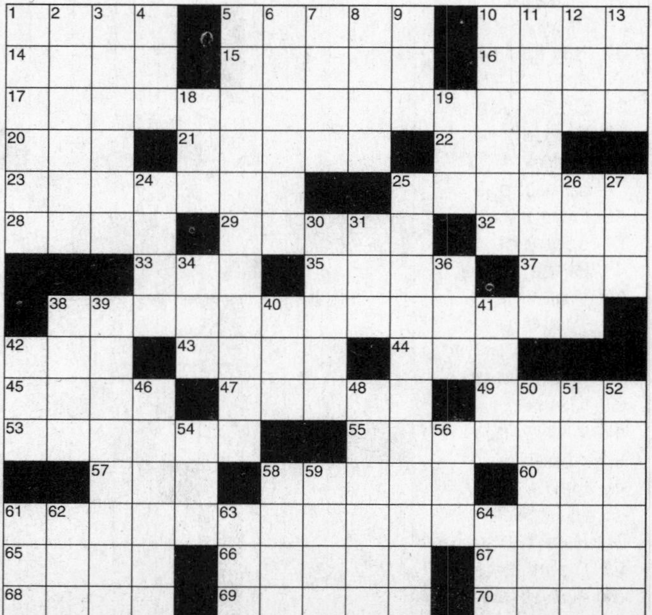

309 FAMILIAR TRIO

by Dean Niles

ACROSS
1 Mike problem
5 Stoneworker
10 Not quite closed
14 Failure
15 Low joint
16 Hold sway
17 Prerecord
18 Nasty
19 Some agents
20 C-__ (cable channel)
21 Drill sergeant's shout
22 __ down (shut up)
23 Be
25 Showy shrub
28 Copied perfectly
30 Richard of *Pretty Woman*
31 Sugar qty.
34 Cowboy country
35 Hostess Perle
36 Tango quorum
37 Omelet ingredients
38 Emcee Hall
39 "__ a Lady" ('71 tune)
40 Wine word
41 __ Island (Brooklyn resort area)
42 Touches
43 Choral syllable
44 Gardener, at times
45 Forecaster
46 Sonoran snooze
48 One of the musical B's
49 Sun screen
51 __ Mahal
53 Reagan Cabinet member
56 Go over a manuscript
57 France's longest river
59 Professor 'iggins
60 Helen's mother
61 Impassive
62 Read quickly
63 __ *of Our Lives*
64 Mr. Chips portrayer
65 Camper's shelter

DOWN
1 Salamanders
2 Show approval
3 Early TV cowboy
4 Job slots
5 Prepared potatoes
6 Singer Murray
7 Some traits do this
8 __ Maid (card game)
9 Society-page word
10 Bandleader Shaw
11 Consent avidly
12 On the sheltered side
13 Pull apart
22 Urgent appeal
24 Kind of neckline
26 Full of pep
27 Pretentious
28 Wave top
29 Bar order
32 Bulge
33 Sheriff's band
35 French Impressionist
38 Cattle calls
39 Naval footlocker
41 *Silkwood* star
42 __ Angelico
45 Beg to differ
47 Tiny bits
49 Prairie, in Pretoria
50 Notion
52 *Aida* selection
54 Teheran's country
55 Peer __
57 Psychedelic letters
58 Word form for "ear"

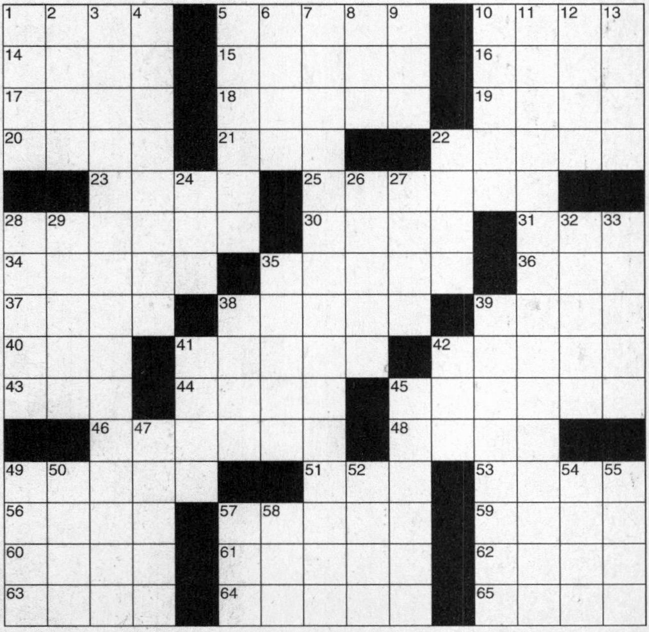

310 *BEACH PARTIES*

by Trip Payne

ACROSS

1 Star in Orion
6 Squint (at)
10 *Sesame Street* subject
14 Love a lot
15 Gen. Robt. __
16 Heap
17 Chopin's favorite novelist
19 Ken of *thirtysomething*
20 Weaken
21 It's a small matter
22 Voting sheet
24 School grps.
25 With merriment
26 Labor leader Gompers
29 Stout spots
32 Dumbstruck
33 Metric weights
34 Dovecote sound
35 Pisa dough
36 __ the Barbarian
37 Blackbird
38 Caribou kin
39 Jeans alternative
40 Put a halt to
41 French ladies
43 Cautioned
44 Florida city
45 Chaplin prop
46 Eye part
48 *Casablanca* role
49 Brown shade
52 *Diary of __ Housewife*
53 Smooch-throwing TV hostess
56 Jennifer on *WKRP*
57 "Oh, fiddle-faddle!"
58 Bulova rival
59 Pie á la __
60 Baseballer Cabell
61 Alamogordo event

DOWN

1 Old clothes
2 Birth of a notion?
3 Sticky stuff
4 Foul up
5 Heir
6 Chihuahua cash
7 Western star Jack
8 Sundown, to Shelley
9 Snoopy's foe
10 Artemis' twin
11 "Caribbean Queen" singer
12 Advertising award
13 Faxed or telexed
18 List ender
23 Superciliousness
24 Insect stage
25 Big bashes
26 Hawthorne's hometown
27 Well-coordinated
28 Former US poet laureate
29 Ties up
30 Code name?
31 Did some cobbling
33 Seoul site
36 Buddy
37 Only
39 Showed up
40 Rummy variety
42 __ Dinmont terrier
43 Do the laundry
45 Social stratum
46 Self-possessed
47 *Typee* sequel
48 Fascinated by
49 Big book
50 Bellicose deity
51 Waiting-room cry
54 Scottish John
55 Song that sells

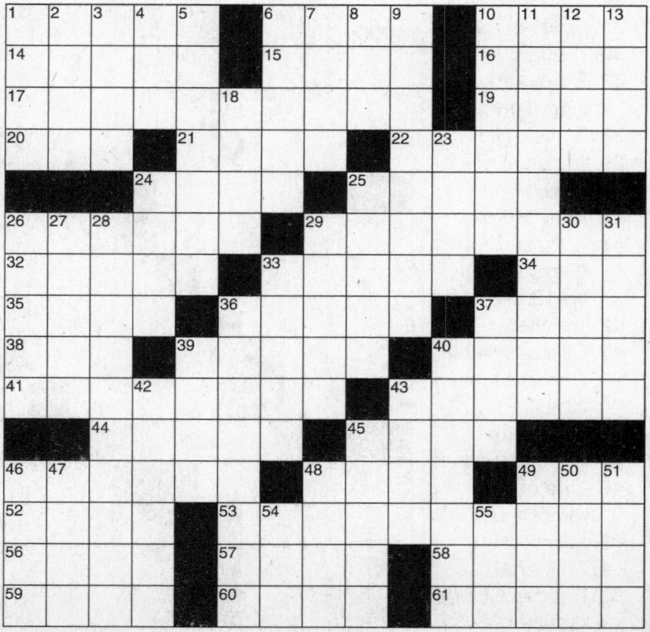

311 MOVIE MARATHON

by Shirley Soloway

ACROSS

1 Adam of *Batman*
5 Prepares to shoot
9 Mr. Brinker
13 Psychedelic musical
14 Legal paper
15 Repetitive behavior
16 Land measure
17 Top-quality
18 Actress Verdugo
19 '86 Fonda film
22 Sugary suffix
23 Tach meas.
24 Intelligent
27 Fluffy neckpiece
29 Tobacco dryer
33 Charged particle
34 Menace
37 __ consequence (unimportant)
38 '75 Pacino film
41 Popular cookie
42 Idle
43 Mine find
44 Actress Carter
45 Cat or canary
46 Politician picker
48 Greek consonant
50 Mongrel
51 '50 Widmark film
60 Warbucks' waif
61 Diva's performance
62 Israeli dance
63 Daring act
64 Tailor's tools
65 Participating
66 The biggest Cartwright
67 Fencing weapon
68 Unpleasantly damp

DOWN

1 Start of a query
2 Apiece
3 Kingly address
4 Aftershock
5 Having knowledge (of)
6 Heavy metal
7 Short skirt
8 British gun
9 Heavenly sight
10 Help a hood
11 Baseball team
12 Head the cast
15 Pile high
20 Caesar's port
21 School records
24 Lebanese city
25 Actress Demi
26 Jockey Cordero
27 Suit
28 In the know
30 In progress
31 Nap noisily
32 Copier need
35 Nearsightedness
36 Fancy appetizer
39 Marineland attractions
40 Variety show
47 Tropical flower
49 Printer's notation
50 Go after
51 Poet Ogden
52 Division word
53 Wildebeests
54 Back of the neck
55 Faucet fault
56 Fork point
57 New Rochelle college
58 '82 Jeff Bridges film
59 Pull sharply

312 SKULL SESSION

by Bob Lubbers

ACROSS

1 Ameche role
5 Socialist Eugene
9 Actor Buddy
14 Bread spread
15 Dynamic start
16 Bingo alternative
17 Foothold
19 Navigation system
20 One after another
21 Cover story?
23 Inlets
26 "I Let __ Go out of My Heart" ('38 tune)
28 Make Mickey move
31 __ *Howser, M.D.*
33 Sikorsky and Stravinsky
34 Devoured
36 Prohibit
37 Sunburn soother
38 Fills to the gills
39 Deflect, with "off"
40 Actor Beatty
41 Send payment
42 Mild oaths
43 Seasoned
45 Ideas
47 French river
48 Pesky insect
49 Drink noisily
51 Maximum
56 Sand bar
58 Former Texas arena
61 Dracula's title
62 __ En-lai
63 Bumbler
64 "High __" ('59 song)
65 Spud buds
66 Falls behind

DOWN

1 Boyish cuts
2 "Waiting for the Robert __"
3 Producer Norman
4 Places
5 Showy flower
6 Foot width
7 Lingerie item
8 Bar supply
9 Sci-fi writer Harlan
10 Small error
11 Skinny veggie
12 Airport abbr.
13 __ sequitur
18 Injures
22 Fills the hold
24 Hannibal Smith and company
25 Usher's activity
27 Jets' rivals
28 Shining brightly
29 Lunch favorite
30 Fury
32 Extremities
33 Fleming and McShane
35 Rockies range
38 Exodus commemoration
39 To and __
41 Final tallies
42 "Same here!"
44 New Orleans campus
46 Zodiac sign
50 Gallop or trot
52 1650, to Tiberius
53 Oop's girlfriend
54 Polluted air
55 Knight and Turner
56 Tchrs.' workplace
57 Owl's cry
59 Bashful
60 Sock part

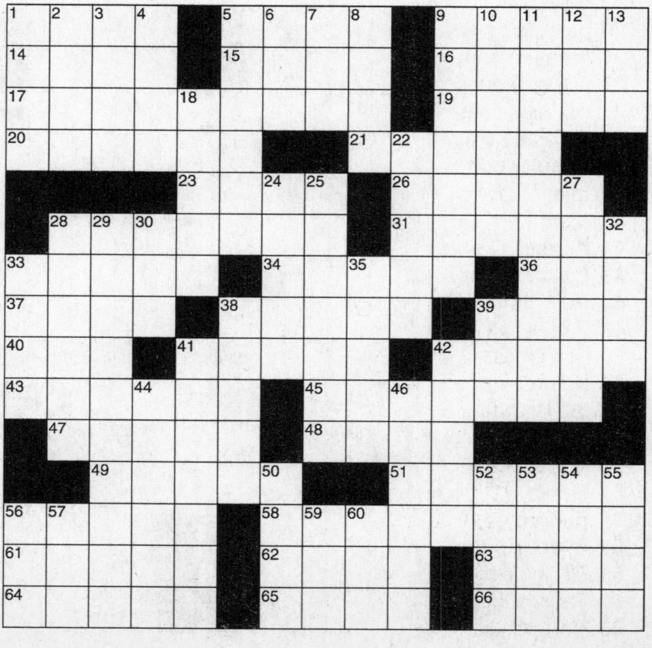

313 ALL SMILES

by Shirley Soloway

ACROSS

1 Notice
5 "I've Got __ in Kalamazoo"
9 Taj Mahal town
13 Siamese
14 Flag holders
16 Israeli airline
17 Birth, e.g.
19 Author Sheehy
20 Pencil end
21 In an impassive way
23 Aspin or Paul
24 __ standstill
26 Whiskey type
27 Gumdrop brand
29 __ rule (usually)
32 Rampur royalty
35 __ Tin Tin
36 Daisy Mae's man
38 "__ Rhythm"
39 Revises a text
42 Inactive
43 Assertion
45 Service charge
46 College degs.
47 Make a mistake
48 Choral group
52 Thoughts
54 Ocean vessel: Abbr.
55 Mythical bird
58 Auto-racer Mario
61 Performer Pia
63 Scott of *Charles in Charge*
64 Loud guffaw
66 Stopping places
67 One who watches
68 Mr. Laurel
69 One-liners
70 Transatlantic planes
71 Coop critters

DOWN

1 Lucy's landlady
2 Be generous
3 The Mamas and the __
4 Puppy sounds
5 Opening
6 State VIP
7 Bristol brews
8 Soup ingredient
9 Sponsorship
10 Seeks votes
11 Support on the stairs
12 Comrade-in-arms
15 Pack away
18 Slangy assent
22 Hartman or Bonet
25 Battery contents
27 Feline musical
28 Butter spreader
30 Ward of *Sisters*
31 Greek war god
32 Come up in the world
33 Thickening agent
34 Teenage pastime
37 Lettuce choice
40 Gumshoes
41 Carbonated drinks
44 Architectural detail
49 Wood strips
50 Bars legally
51 Russian range
53 Metal waste
55 Highway
56 Church instrument
57 Lyricist Sammy et al.
58 __ *Hand for the Little Lady*
59 *Peter Pan* pooch
60 Eye part
62 Short race
65 Congeal

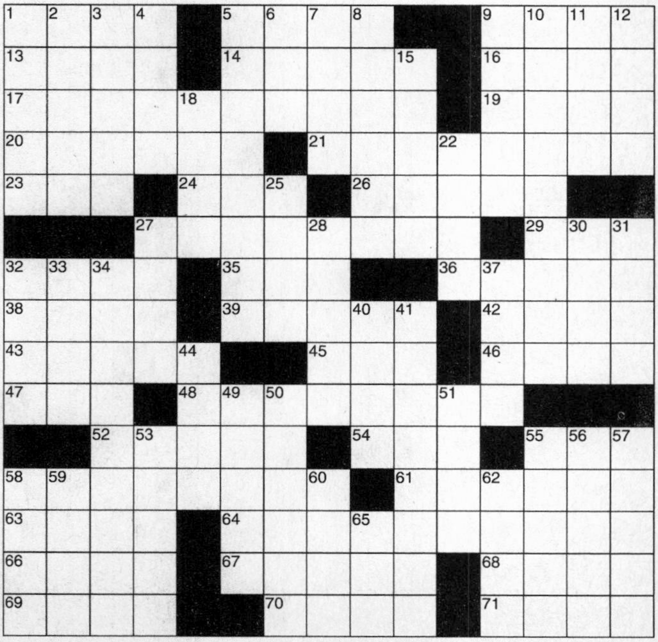

314 COLORFUL FOOD STORIES

by Dean Niles

ACROSS

1 Pizazz
6 Trombone accessory
10 For fear that
14 Light weight
15 In __ (stuck)
16 Curtain-raiser
17 Seuss tale
20 Put in stitches
21 Dehydrates
22 Solo
23 Photog.'s item
24 Behind schedule
26 Dervish
29 Plain to see
31 __ kwon do
34 Healing plant
35 In accord
36 Verbal noun
38 Anthony Burgess book, with *A*
41 Offer shelter to
42 Collection
43 Harness part
44 Timid
45 Cantaloupe or casaba
47 Ancient Persians
48 Soft drink
49 Melody
50 Oriental
53 *Jaws* menace
56 Soft touch
59 '68 Beatles movie
62 First name in daredeviltry
63 Sign on
64 *Divine Comedy* poet
65 Alluring
66 Holler
67 Furry fish-eater

DOWN

1 Beclouds
2 Entice
3 Once again
4 The __ Capades
5 Hand over
6 Biblical trio
7 Coax
8 Scuffle vigorously
9 Frat letter
10 Serve the minestrone
11 Reverberation
12 Ollie's other half
13 Use a stopwatch
18 Work unit
19 Talk and talk
23 Family member
25 Tech talk
26 The truth
27 God of Islam
28 Eccentric
29 Lennon's lady
30 Left-hand page
31 Brought into pitch
32 Actress Dickinson
33 Happy places
35 Possessed
37 Less available
39 Kurosawa costume
40 Barbie's beau
46 Timmy's pet
47 G&S character
48 "Long Tall __" ('56 tune)
49 Supply with weapons
50 Some votes
51 Golfer Ballesteros
52 Holly shrub
54 Throw forcefully
55 Cain's victim
56 Add some color
57 Poker stake
58 Jury member
60 Youngster's query
61 Inform (on)

315 IN HIS POCKET

by Mary Brindamour

ACROSS

1 Movie terrier
5 Guru
10 Not quite closed
14 Sudden idea
15 __ of Troy
16 Colorless
17 Elastic device
19 Computer symbol
20 Pub potable
21 Sneezer's need
22 Got by, with "out"
23 WWII general
25 Peanuts or popcorn
27 Signed an agreement
30 Prevailing tendencies
33 French Impressionist
36 Light beer
38 Debtor's letters
39 Greek love god
40 Philanthropist
41 Canadian prov.
42 Building wing
43 Polite refusal
44 Borscht ingredient
45 Braves the bully
47 Electrical inventor
49 Orchestra section
51 Compassionate ones
55 Jai __
57 NHL player
60 Mauna __
61 Officeholders
62 Staples alternatives
64 Ready, willing, and __
65 Crème de la crème
66 March 15th, e.g.
67 Mrs. Dick Tracy
68 Derby and dash
69 Extremely

DOWN

1 "That's __!" ("All done!")
2 Miami coach Don
3 Lama land
4 Diplomatic off.
5 Grow smaller
6 Spider's snares
7 "Woe is me!"
8 Waiter's handouts
9 Typesetter, at times
10 For each
11 Whittling tool
12 Lotion additive
13 Tear apart
18 Short jackets
24 Acapulco aunts
26 O'Hare abbr.
28 Yale students
29 Ship's crane
31 Blockhead
32 Soapy water
33 Feat
34 __ Stanley Gardner
35 Tee toppers
37 Richard of *Pretty Woman*
40 Blabbermouth
41 At hand
43 Teachers' org.
44 Mont __ (French peak)
46 Eye parts
48 Intimidates
50 La __ Opera House
52 Skip over
53 Cowboy, at times
54 Impertinent
55 Get __ on the back
56 Earring locale
58 *The Aeneid*, for one
59 Apportion, with "out"
63 Actress Ullmann

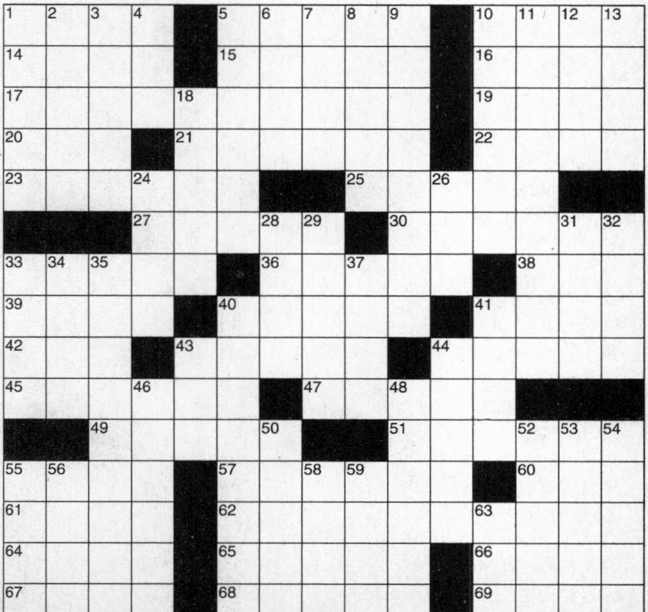

316 ASTRONOMICAL

by Fred Piscop

ACROSS

1 Stowe sight
6 Boxcar rider
10 Shed
14 Quinn of *Reckless*
15 Daredevil Knievel
16 Butter substitute
17 Ecumenical Council site
18 "__ 'em and weep!"
19 Gulf state
20 Birds' prey
22 __ Scotia
23 Coffeemaker
24 Mortarboard ornament
26 Bold
30 Sportscaster Musburger
32 Singer Lenya
33 Tater topper
37 Tony Musante series
38 Whipped-cream servings
39 Forearm bone
40 Put in the autoclave
42 Offspring
43 Foul liquid
44 Turnstile fodder
45 Drives back
48 Moray
49 Fitzgerald of jazz
50 Shades
57 Carson predecessor
58 On the briny
59 Adorable one
60 Ear-related
61 __ *Poets Society*
62 Major happening
63 Clockmaker Thomas
64 Goofs up
65 Coolidge's veep

DOWN

1 Stuff to the gills
2 Cremona cash
3 European river
4 Huff and puff
5 Bubble over
6 Wading bird
7 Above
8 "__ me up, Scotty!"
9 Seniors
10 '87 Cher film
11 Actor Edward James __
12 Corporal's time off
13 Having musical qualities
21 Twisted
25 Mandela's grp.
26 Diner orders
27 Plant part
28 "Ma! (He's Making Eyes __)"
29 Ed McMahon show
30 Hooch
31 Cartoonist Goldberg
33 Slender
34 Nobelist Wiesel
35 Shortly
36 Picks a crew
38 Ballet slide
41 "Well, __ be!"
42 Consoled
44 __ Aviv
45 Seized autos
46 Thrill
47 *S'il vous* __
48 "Zounds!"
51 __-friendly
52 Around the corner
53 Fiji's capital
54 Fret
55 "__ *kleine Nachtmusik*"
56 Collections

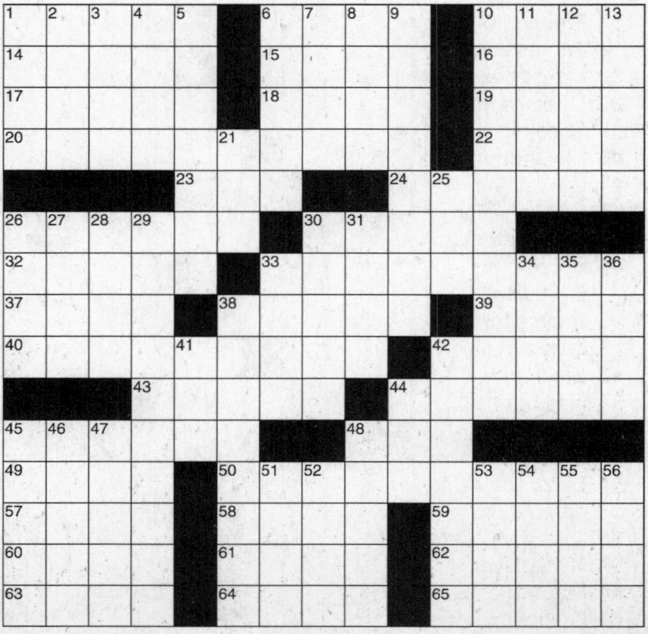

317 *CARTOON COUPLES*

by Fred Piscop

ACROSS

1 Shortstop Pee Wee
6 Iowa city
10 Comic Sahl
14 Magna __
15 Church section
16 Region
17 Specialized lingo
18 Genealogy diagram
19 *Jurassic Park* beast, for short
20 Cartoon couple
23 Wave top
24 Slugger Ralph
25 Confront boldly
28 To __ (without exception)
30 Ice-cream flavor: Abbr.
31 Lively dance
33 Climbing plant
36 Cartoon couple
40 Ecology org.
41 Hostess Perle
42 Western sch.
43 Window frame
44 Actress Rolle
46 Valuable violin
49 More sensible
51 Cartoon couple
56 Fall
57 __ *Three Lives*
58 Taxi device
60 Fill with cargo
61 Give a hoot
62 Bring together
63 *For Your* __ *Only*
64 Famous pirate
65 Landing area

DOWN

1 Communications co.
2 Lawman Wyatt
3 As a result
4 Hand-operated valve
5 Diner patrons
6 Feeds the kitty
7 French Revolution name
8 Level
9 Bird food
10 Actress Marlee
11 Senator Hatch
12 Superman portrayer
13 Congress, e.g.
21 "Are we there __?"
22 Giraffe relative
25 Pinnacle
26 Cookie nugget
27 Caesar's partner
28 *M*A*S*H* star
29 Family member
31 Nasty cut
32 Aardvark morsel
33 Ruler marking
34 Disgusting
35 Fiscal span
37 High-tech memo
38 __-man (toady)
39 Vitamin or mineral
43 Ear bone
44 Conclusion
45 Irish poet Heaney
46 Confuse
47 Tropical eel
48 Battery terminal
49 Memorable Mortimer
50 Threw in
52 Clark or Cavett
53 Jai __
54 Recipe instruction
55 Himalayan legend
59 Agent, for short

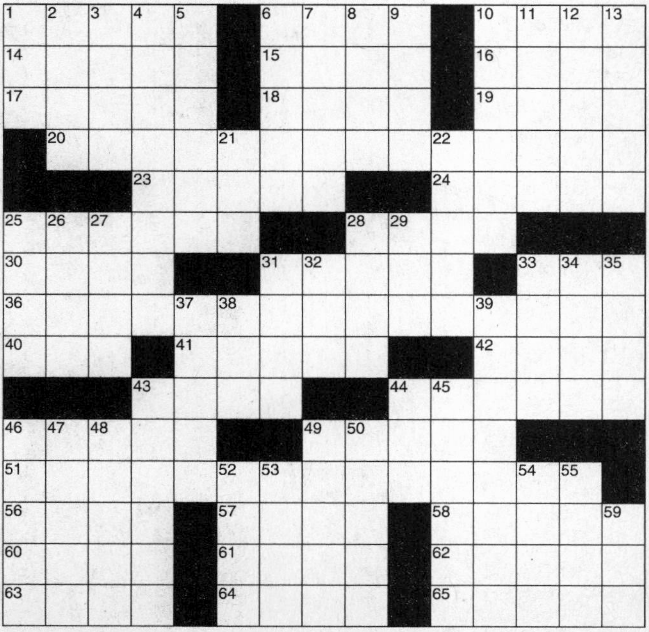

318 ROUND AND ROUND

by Shirley Soloway

ACROSS
1 Heated tubs
5 Knightly titles
9 Lassoed
14 Verb tense
15 Take a tumble
16 La Scala performance
17 Tennis great Arthur
18 Barrett or Jaffe
19 Significant others
20 Negotiate
23 Breadthless?
24 Big rig
25 Hit the slopes
28 Dos Passos trilogy
30 Harness up
32 Wide awake
36 Middle weight?
39 Ward of *Sisters*
40 Pulls apart
41 Take __ (snooze)
42 Maytag function
44 Spiner of *Star Trek: The Next Generation*
45 Gets up
46 Cardiologists' org.
48 Vane dir.
49 Paint layer
52 African antelopes
57 Ideal perspective
59 Go to pot
62 Prego rival
63 Antitoxins
64 Foot bones
65 Desire deified
66 Touch up articles
67 Confused
68 "¿Cómo __ usted?"
69 Actress Daly

DOWN
1 Generate
2 Turkish title
3 *My Name Is __ Lev*
4 Take the reins
5 Soda sippers
6 Golf club
7 Lemon peels
8 Detective Sam
9 Lettuce variety
10 Iridescent birthstone
11 Favorite
12 Prior to, in poetry
13 Trial VIPs
21 Oaf
22 Mideast rulers
25 Book part
26 Designer Donna
27 Maladroit
29 "Just __!" ("Hold on!")
31 Play the lead
32 City on the Nile
33 Absorb
34 Borden bovine
35 Cheerleader shouts
37 Good buddy
38 Vicinity
40 Emmy-winner Cicely
43 Patron saint of music
44 Cotton bundle
47 Mythical menace
50 Go along (with)
51 Peter and Alexander
53 Valuable property
54 Wanting
55 "Mack the Knife" singer
56 Give an opinion
57 Upswing
58 "__ Rhythm"
59 RR depot
60 Bit of butter
61 Hosp. areas

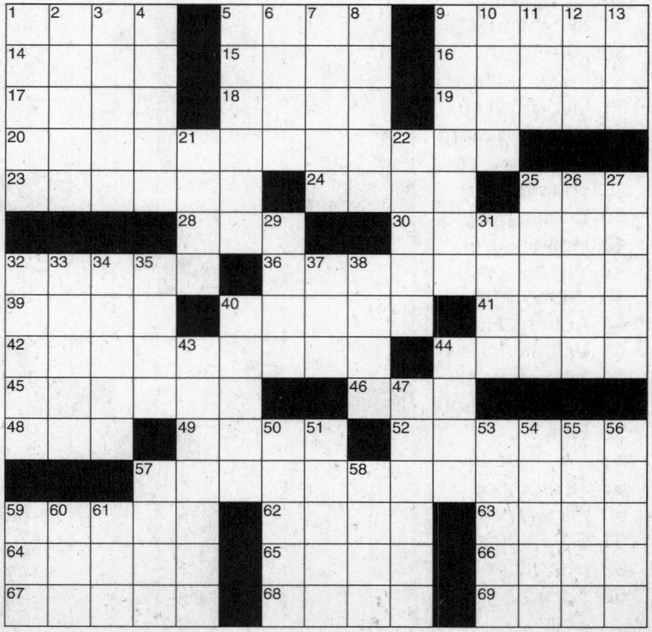

319 *LEND A HAND*

by Trip Payne

ACROSS
1 Nile slitherers
5 Lease charge
9 Razor sharpener
14 Actor's goal
15 Singer Adams
16 Billy Joel's instrument
17 Astronaut Shepard
18 Impressionist Carvey
19 Drive forward
20 *Cheers* nickname
23 Finish the cupcakes
24 Victory symbol
25 Snuggle
29 Suit fabric
31 Identical
34 Wreak havoc on
35 Work unit
37 *Reine*'s husband
38 Woodwind instrument
39 Schoolyard retort
43 *Elephant Boy* actor
44 Baden-Baden, for one
45 Mauna ___
46 Related
47 Foots the bill
49 "I give up!"
53 Tease a bit
55 Silly Putty container
57 Swiss river
58 '65 Beach Boys tune
62 Comic Myron
65 Corporate symbol
66 Writing tablets
67 Expect
68 All over again
69 Fencer's choice
70 Italian sauce
71 Ripped
72 Unpopular kid

DOWN
1 A Musketeer
2 Comfort
3 Team member
4 Put in the mail
5 Change colors again
6 *Daniel Boone* actor
7 1492 vessel
8 Greenish blue
9 Backbone
10 This typeface
11 Knock sharply
12 *A Chorus Line* number
13 Campaigner, for short
21 Olympics official Brundage
22 *Anna Christie* playwright
26 "Oom-pah" instrument
27 Jungle king
28 Chemical suffix
30 Post-sneeze remark
32 Deck out
33 Cry from the pasture
36 Mahalia's music
39 Rice wine
40 Drama award
41 "___ Lazy River"
42 Moolah
43 ___ Luis Obispo, CA
48 Folk singer Pete
50 Party snack
51 Roofer's need
52 Rubbed out
54 Slowly, to Solti
56 No longer a child
59 Land map
60 Uni- relative
61 Unlocked
62 Mortarboard
63 Must pay
64 Possesses

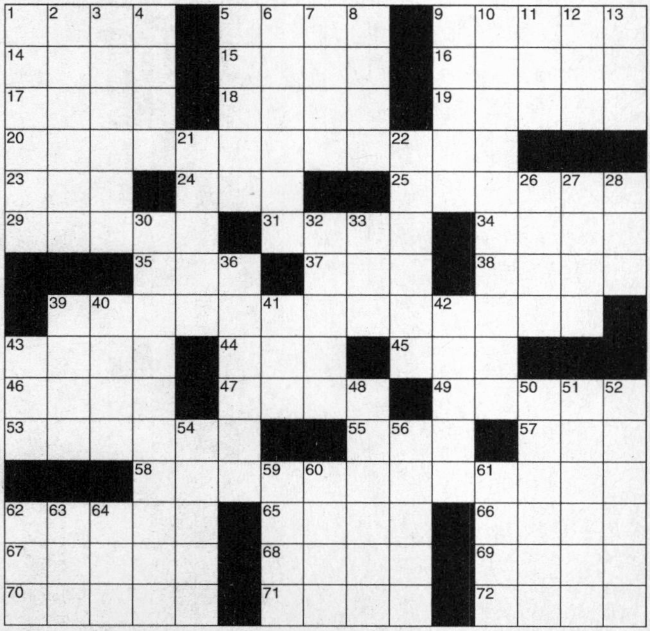

320 SLOW DOWN

by Dean Niles

ACROSS

1 Sot's sound
7 Dog doc
10 Baltimore player
11 Main character
12 Comic Conway
15 Seeing someone
16 Part of A.D.
17 Record label
18 __ *Man Answers* ('62 film)
19 Corporate raider's payoff
21 Timber tool
23 Lions' pride
24 First name in daredeviltry
25 Hamelin hero
27 Go-getters
28 Dad's lad
29 Wordsworth works
30 Coyote cry
31 Pulver's rank: Abbr.
32 Green garnish
34 List abbr.
37 African snakes
39 Steak state
40 Greek letter
41 Whoop it up
43 Tough and shrewd
45 Mesopotamian deity
46 Chelsea's former cat
47 Coll. sports org.
48 French Canadian
50 Hardwood
51 Network in *Network*
52 Mountain pool
53 Where to spend a drachma
56 Scarf down
57 Rugged rock
58 *Seinfeld*, for one
59 "Hold it!"
60 "A-Tisket A-__"

DOWN

1 Coal scuttle
2 One of the Gershwins
3 Legal recourse
4 Arranged a do
5 Arm bone
6 Wooden pin
7 Thin coating
8 Sea birds
9 Fudd, for one
11 Track activity
12 Vacation convenience
13 Less friendly
14 Shopping places
19 Staring one
20 Kitty's comment
21 Church recess
22 The Belmonts' leader
23 He had the touch
26 Seed source
27 Senior member
30 Cattle groups
33 Carefree excursions
35 __ *Team* (Mr. T series)
36 Musical conclusion
38 Wild guess
41 Irritate
42 Caribbean island
43 Cry of joy
44 Beginnings
46 Frighten
49 Engrave a design
50 Opera offering
53 Canadian levy: Abbr.
54 Runner Sebastian
55 CPR expert

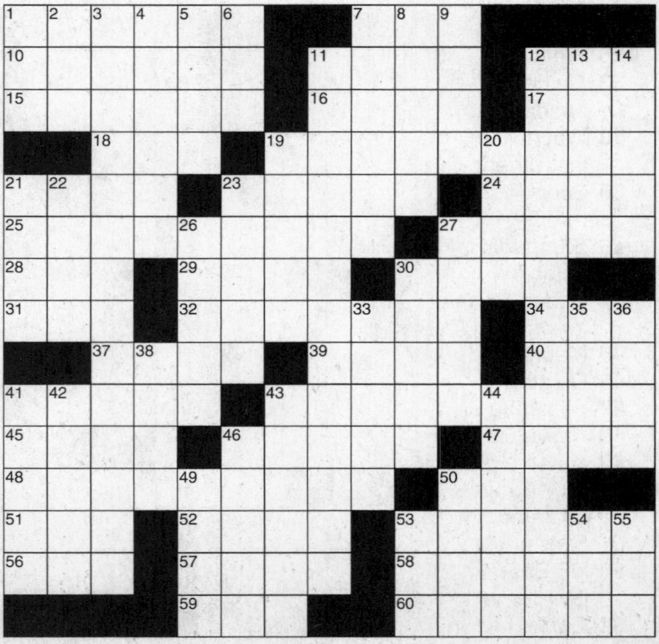

321 NEATLY DONE

by Randolph Ross

ACROSS

1 __ seed (deteriorate)
5 __ *& Moe* (Gleason film)
9 Give forth
13 Actor Mischa
14 __ *Now* (Murrow TV show)
16 Congenial
17 Stain remover
19 Aware of
20 Throw forcefully
21 Abates
23 Cause a riot
26 Values
27 Late, in La Paz
28 Part of SBLI
29 Licentious
31 Andy's friend
32 Mornings: Abbr.
33 Cash in
35 Sass
36 Has hopes
38 Inventor Whitney
39 Next to hit
41 Family member
42 Peak
43 Spiritual leader
44 Fast plane
45 Seven, in Seville
46 Junior's custodian
48 Repaired a road
49 Parlor furniture
51 Feels off
52 "__ the Rainbow"
53 Tanners
58 Swampland
59 Roman river
60 Sweet sandwich
61 Actress Lanchester
62 "So long!"
63 Like some buildup

DOWN

1 Wander (about)
2 __ *Town* (Wilder play)
3 Mystery writer Josephine
4 Prom flowers
5 Grenoble's river
6 Enthusiasm
7 Eastern discipline
8 Gives way
9 Shipwrecked, perhaps
10 Naval vessel
11 Religious symbol
12 Perfect scores, at times
15 Oak or elm
18 Early guitar
22 Silly Soupy
23 Author Calvino
24 Identifying
25 Rural aircraft
26 Knowledgeable one
28 Troublesome tyke
30 Strike out
32 Invite
33 Buttons or Barber
34 Made cocktails
36 Sharp
37 Snitch
40 African country
42 Aviation display
44 Georgetown educator
45 Common seasoning
47 Try out
48 Ornate headwear
49 "__ Enchanted Evening"
50 Satanic
51 Cooperate with criminals
54 Jordan's org.
55 Southpaw stat.
56 Reviewer Reed
57 Oriental sauce

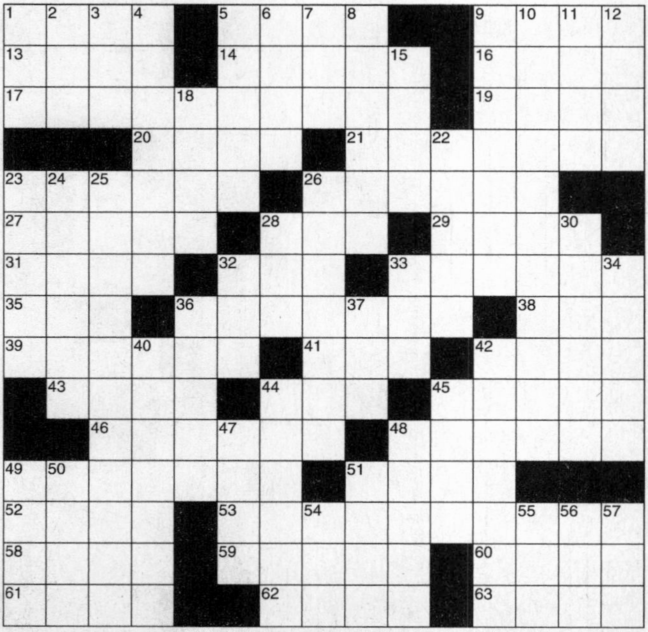

322 *CUTESY*

by Matt Gaffney

ACROSS

1 To be: Lat.
5 Nest egg, for short
8 Mensa stats
11 Pesky bug
13 Southwestern sight
15 Slashes the budget
17 Managed to include
19 Employ
20 Bilko and Kovacs
21 Wilander of tennis
23 Zuider __
24 Emulate Cicero
26 Little troublemakers
28 Jumping-peg game
31 Old Testament book
32 Eastern discipline
33 Burden
35 Plops down
37 Chores
40 Warm up the oven
42 Love the attention
44 __ up (evaluates)
45 Cable channel
47 Pianist Peter
48 Approximately
50 Medical suffix
52 Tell (on)
53 '87 Danny DeVito film
55 More adventurous
57 Eyebrow shape
58 Con
60 Saudi __
64 Short play
66 Evening out
68 Falls below the horizon
69 Family member
70 Compel
71 Hair coloring
72 Summer quencher
73 Dietitians' amts.

DOWN

1 Facility
2 Roman initials
3 Cold-shoulder
4 Rural refrain?
5 __ *Mine* (George Harrison book)
6 Beef or lamb
7 It's east of the Urals
8 I, in Innsbruck
9 Game-show host
10 Throat germ
12 Tractor name
14 On edge
16 Understands
18 Eva's sister
22 *Ivanhoe* man
25 Hackneyed
27 Another time
28 Beer ingredient
29 Calvary inscription
30 Former Philippine capital
34 Colonel Potter, to friends
36 They may be deviated
38 Turkish river
39 Primer pooch
41 Road curves
43 Beast
46 Doctor Freud
49 "Christmas comes but __ year . . ."
51 Letter stroke
53 Russian news agency
54 Annoyed
56 Stubble scraper
59 Blue hue
61 Finch, e.g.
62 Peruvian Indian
63 "Rock of __"
65 Poetic monogram
67 Devoured

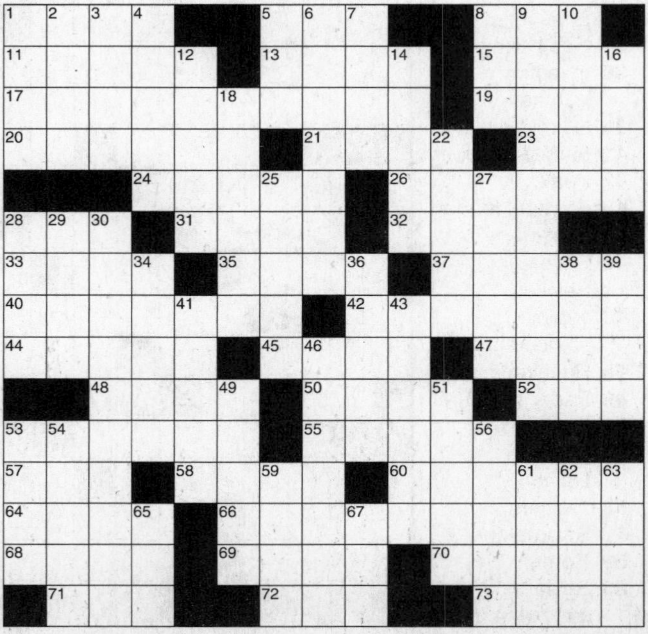

323 VOCALIZING

by Fred Piscop

ACROSS

1 US Airways competitor
4 Catlike animal
9 *M*A*S*H* character
14 Mil. unit
15 Not so congenial
16 Make reparation
17 Get mellower
18 Newscast image
20 Get together
22 Revives
23 Kett of the comics
24 *Sophie's Choice* author
26 Bumpkin
29 Fix a flat
33 Clothing
36 Arafat's grp.
38 __ Claire, WI
39 Musical message
43 Hosp. area
44 "Inka Dinka __"
45 Saps
46 __ *Is Born*
49 Tugboat or gravy boat
51 Least suntanned
53 Anthem starter
57 Unwelcome guest
60 Chosen child
63 Dental deadener
65 Supply with weapons
66 Roast host
67 Some tournaments
68 Compete
69 Willing one
70 Bronco show
71 Evening, in poetry

DOWN

1 Identify a caller
2 "Ain't __ Fun?"
3 007, e.g.
4 Give as an example
5 "Not if __ help it!"
6 Most disgusting
7 "A mouse!"
8 Tot's transport
9 Ames Brothers tune of '50
10 Daughter of Zeus
11 "Easy __ it!"
12 Med. student's course
13 Make over
19 Neither's partner
21 Flier to Rio
25 Treads softly
27 Geller the spoonbender
28 Transmit
30 Actress Garr
31 James of *Brian's Song*
32 Sings with closed lips
33 India's continent
34 Spasms
35 Hardware item
37 Early automaker
40 State's head
41 ". . . __ I saw Elba"
42 Lively dance
47 Orbit point
48 Bacon serving
50 Put on a play
52 Hawaiian souvenir
54 Barrel part
55 Raptor's nest
56 Mideast land
57 "__ a Song Go . . ."
58 Cass, for one
59 Hockey need
61 "Great" dog
62 __ buco
64 Main mail place: Abbr.

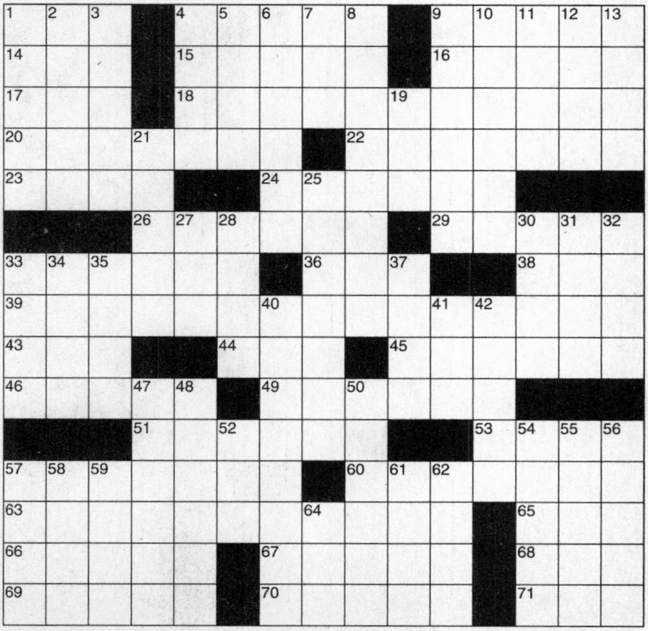

324 DAIRY CASE

by Shirley Soloway

ACROSS

1 Uncooked
4 *Little Women* character
8 Stands behind
13 Western actor Jack
15 Fencing weapon
16 Lofty spaces
17 Top-notch
18 Pharmacy bottle
19 Very small
20 Open-textured fabric
23 Classifieds
24 Drapery ornament
25 Rivulet
27 "__ go bragh!"
29 Takes on
32 Impact sound
35 Twist
38 Actor Russell
39 Boxing bigwig
40 Bookworm, maybe
43 Disgusted expression
44 Resort place
46 Actress Braga
47 In favor of
48 Subway coins
51 Younger Guthrie
53 Free
56 Seasonal songs
60 Coolidge, for short
62 Seeking favor
64 Texas landmark
66 Israeli dance
67 Olympian Korbut
68 Skinflint
69 Scandinavian king
70 Likely MTV viewer
71 Nuisances
72 Try out
73 Med. personnel

DOWN

1 Show one's feelings
2 Oahu greeting
3 Decreases
4 Cutting on a slant
5 Grand work
6 Marsh ducks
7 Spartan slave
8 Used the tub
9 Had a bite
10 Used-car descriptor
11 Good-natured
12 Articulates
14 Reagan appointee
21 Suit fabric
22 __-la-la
26 Response from space
28 Henpecks
30 Peter, Paul, and Mary, e.g.
31 Occupational suffix
32 Angler's worms
33 In addition
34 Translucent tableware
36 Greek consonant
37 Actress Olin
41 Copters and fighters
42 __ Lama
45 Always, to Keats
49 Gomer Pyle portrayer
50 Letters after R
52 "Ready __, here I come!"
54 *Some Like __*
55 Swiped
57 Eyed excessively
58 German weapon
59 Extends across
60 Army outpost
61 "I cannot tell __"
63 Memorable times
65 Encountered

325 LISTENING IN

by Shirley Soloway

ACROSS

1 Out of control
5 Cooking odor
10 Russian ruler
14 On the ocean
15 Very cold
16 Lhasa __
17 Close by
19 Art __
20 Not so hot
21 Daredevil Knievel
22 NASA affirmative
23 Wine valley
25 Sharp answers
28 Curved line
31 __ *Pass* (Uris novel)
33 Mr. Kabibble
34 *On __ Pond* ('81 film)
36 Wartime signal
40 Duel tool
41 Bit of bread
43 __ *Camera* ('55 film)
44 Come back
46 Father goose?
48 Down Under jumper
49 Physician of antiquity
51 Retirees' org.
52 Letting up
55 Objectives
57 __-relief
58 French river
60 Very fancy headgear
64 *A Farewell to __*
66 Oxymoronic display
68 Boxing event
69 First name in cosmetics
70 Unlikely to attack
71 Griffith or Rooney
72 Strict
73 Sp. ladies

DOWN

1 Desire
2 "Oh!"
3 Ballet move
4 Singer Bobby
5 Rep.
6 Use the microwave
7 Norwegian monarch
8 Ores, e.g.
9 Shake up
10 Smidgen
11 Leads the way
12 Wide neckwear
13 Corner chess pieces
18 "There Is Nothin' Like __"
24 __-nez
26 Start of a pencil game
27 K.T. of country music
28 Worry, perhaps
29 Use a lariat
30 Totally confusing
32 Gene Tierney thriller
35 Station
37 U.S. Grant's rank
38 Iowa college town
39 __ avis
42 Most tattered
45 Luau dish
47 ". . . __ all a good night"
50 Unwelcome admirer?
52 Addis __
53 Nobleman
54 Short messages
56 Prepares flour
59 Fill to the gills
61 Unlatched, maybe
62 Capital of *Italia*
63 Yes votes
65 Hog home
67 D.C. figure

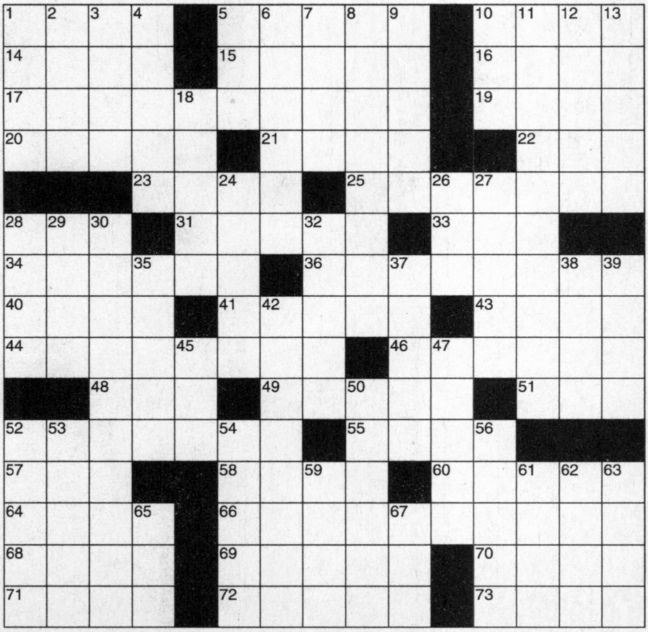

326 GO-GETTERS

by David Owens

ACROSS

1 Nickname for Hemingway
5 Lhasa __
9 One at __ (singly)
14 Declare
15 Jungle home
16 Horse papas
17 How go-getters go
20 *Our Miss Brooks* star
21 Spirited session?
22 Popeye's girl
23 Cots on wheels
24 They may be split
28 Sting
30 Swamp
32 Seer's asset
33 __ facto
37 What go-getters do
40 Eye problem
41 Detective story pioneer
42 Ceremony
43 Stir up
45 Trunk
46 Shore specialty
50 Kimono cummerbund
52 Bays
53 Blackens
58 What go-getters have, with "a"
60 Lilting syllables
61 Egotist's obsession
62 Commedia dell'__
63 Parisian legislature
64 __-European
65 Misplace

DOWN

1 Wan
2 Tel __
3 Moplike pooch
4 Region
5 "Luck Be __" ('50 tune)
6 Den wood
7 Autograph
8 Poetic eye
9 State
10 Big fellow
11 Actress Dunne
12 Clemency
13 Snaky shapes
18 Concerto __ (musical form)
19 Coup leader
23 Deep cut
24 Rock-band equipment
25 Recommend
26 Air France destination
27 Gander or cob
29 Rhythm
31 Postulate
33 "Tell __ the judge!"
34 Rain hard
35 Aerobics centers
36 Scandinavian city
38 Frog kin
39 Protests that went nowhere?
43 Phrasal conjunction
44 Germanic gnome
46 Winnows
47 Acclimate
48 Comic __ Sherman
49 *The Most Happy __*
51 Smashing, á la *Variety*
53 Paradise
54 Slanted type: Abbr.
55 Goose egg
56 Gobbles up
57 Hook's henchman
59 "Unaccustomed __ am . . ."

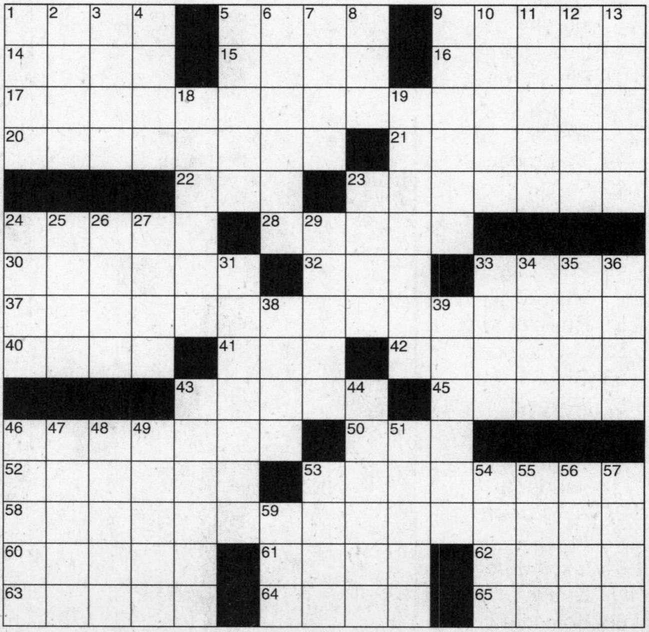

327 CATTY

by Shirley Soloway

ACROSS

1 Actress Virna
5 Belief
10 Garage item
14 Ken of *thirtysomething*
15 Daily delivery
16 Author Ferber
17 Auto maker
18 Sharon of Israel
19 Citric sips
20 Crusader symbol
23 I-beam material
24 Show pique
27 Performed diligently
31 Exploding stars
33 Tiny speck
36 Mohair producers
39 Eye area
41 More mirthful
42 Insect eggs
43 Tightly-curled fur
46 Caustic substance
47 Went awry
48 '50s Ford
50 Opera performers
53 Thompson or Hawkins
57 Chang and Eng
61 Singer Adams
64 Director Lean
65 Solidifies
66 Letterman rival
67 Graff of *Mr. Belvedere*
68 Folklore heavy
69 Fall faller
70 Sportscaster Merlin
71 Lunchtime

DOWN

1 Weavers' needs
2 __ ease (uncomfortable)
3 Edge along
4 Shoe part
5 IRS men
6 Uncommon
7 De Mille specialty
8 Horned animals
9 Synthetic fabric
10 Kitchen measure
11 Unusual
12 *A Chorus Line* number
13 *Viva __ Vegas*
21 Fitzgerald of jazz
22 Vocalized
25 Be of use
26 Shabby
28 Actress Swenson
29 Actor Richard
30 Holmes' creator
32 To be: Lat.
33 Con
34 In the open
35 __ Haute, IN
37 Peruse
38 Arsenal supplies
40 Have __ (understand)
44 __ *Do!* (Mary Martin musical)
45 Top-of-the-line
49 Sofa style
51 Dashboard feature
52 Little
54 San __, CA
55 Prelim
56 German city
58 Arden and namesakes
59 __ qua non
60 Genesis locale
61 Building wing
62 Poor grade
63 __ way (sort of)

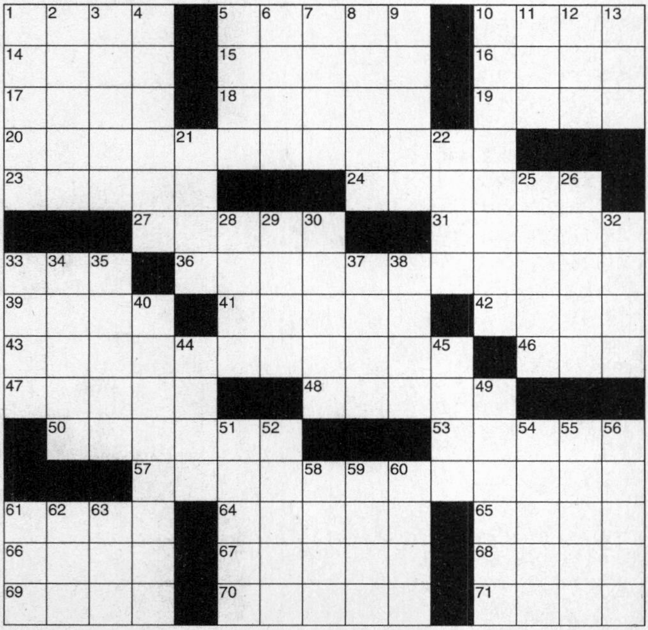

328 *LARGE-SCALE*

by Shirley Soloway

ACROSS
1 Bible book
5 Avant-___
10 Last word in church
14 "___ Be Cruel" ('56 tune)
15 UFO pilot
16 Willing
17 Diva rendition
18 Sire
19 Theater sign
20 Visible to the naked eye
23 ___ *a Wonderful Life*
24 Nasty smile
25 Summer TV shows
27 Visored hat
30 Reprimands
33 Likens
38 Archie's wife
39 Czech river
40 Big box
43 Art Deco designer
44 Cancellations
46 Came to a halt
48 Financial recipient
51 Dover's st.
52 Firefly, for one
54 Actress Emma
59 Texas coll.
61 Ethnically diverse
64 Mexican snack
66 Actor Reginald
67 ___ avis
68 "Diana" singer
69 Rub out
70 "___ the Mood for Love"
71 Chivalrous deed
72 Methods: Abbr.
73 Forgo the fettuccine

DOWN
1 Photographer Ansel
2 Erin of *Happy Days*
3 In reserve
4 Gaze intently
5 Chews the fat
6 Actor Guinness
7 Austerity
8 More profound
9 Whole
10 Make cheddar better
11 Full-length garment
12 Send out
13 Fishing devices
21 Largest dolphin
22 Sugar shape
26 Artistic subjects
28 Rainbow shape
29 For each
31 Diminutive suffix
32 Lean-to
33 Viet ___
34 Nasal appraisal
35 Big money
36 Disposed
37 In a blue mood
41 Slugger Williams
42 Compass letters
45 Sunflower support
47 *Casablanca* character
49 Classical pieces
50 Queen of mystery
53 Lab burners
55 Pungent
56 Orange Bowl's home
57 Donny's sister
58 Lean
59 Bambi's father
60 Horse hair
62 *Meet Me ___ Louis*
63 Deli breads
65 Cereal grain

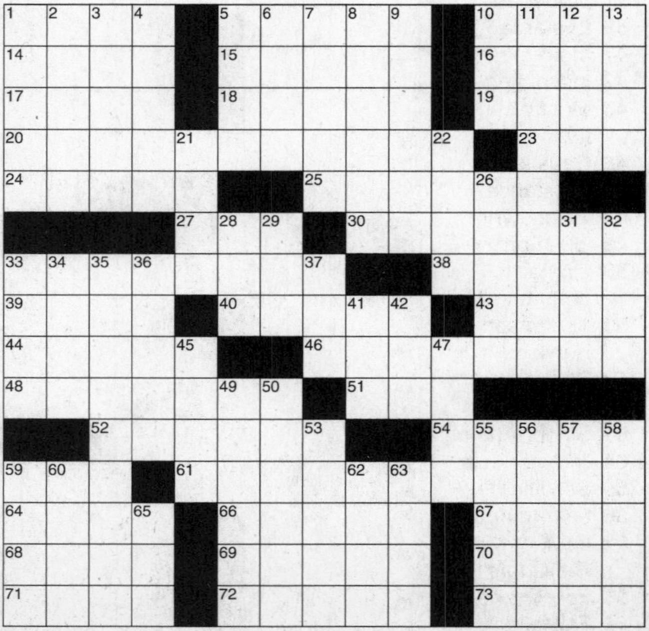

329 ENVELOPE, PLEASE

by Randolph Ross

ACROSS

1 Bates or King
5 Johnny's successor
8 He ran against Bill and George
12 Shade of green
13 Lennon's wife
14 Jacob's wife et al.
15 Envelope info
18 Before, to Byron
19 A Bobbsey twin
20 Examines the books
21 Former US territory
22 Silent okay
23 Patina
27 Invitees
31 Envelope info
33 *Exodus* protagonist
34 Dundee denial
35 Anger
36 Envelope info
43 Finish behind
44 Neatens (up)
45 Southern constellation
46 "What Kind of Fool __?"
47 Lay __ (disprove)
50 Motel freebie
51 Bread spread
54 Envelope handlers
57 Sends
58 Diamond __
59 Traffic-light color
60 Sentence part: Abbr.
61 Pinky or Peggy
62 Fabricated

DOWN

1 Orchard spray
2 Ade flavor
3 "__ Maria"
4 Newborn
5 Bennett or Blondell
6 Plus
7 Jedi instructor
8 Occupant
9 Kiln
10 Mother and daughter
11 Compass pt.
12 Washington bill
14 Ushered, perhaps
16 Muslim ascetic
17 Ladder steps
21 Small amount
23 Cabinet item
24 Forgets
25 *Hook* pooch
26 Flying pests
28 Grab
29 Garr and Copley
30 Dance movement
31 Salt, to a chemist
32 Serious
37 Two-__ (tot)
38 Emphasis
39 Breakfast bread
40 __ against time
41 M, C, or I
42 Half of MCCII
47 Autocratic ruler
48 Mayberry boy
49 Lofty
50 Dot in the sea
51 Be in harmony
52 Served well
53 Sea, to Seurat
54 Strike caller
55 First head of the UN
56 Old Dominion campus: Abbr.

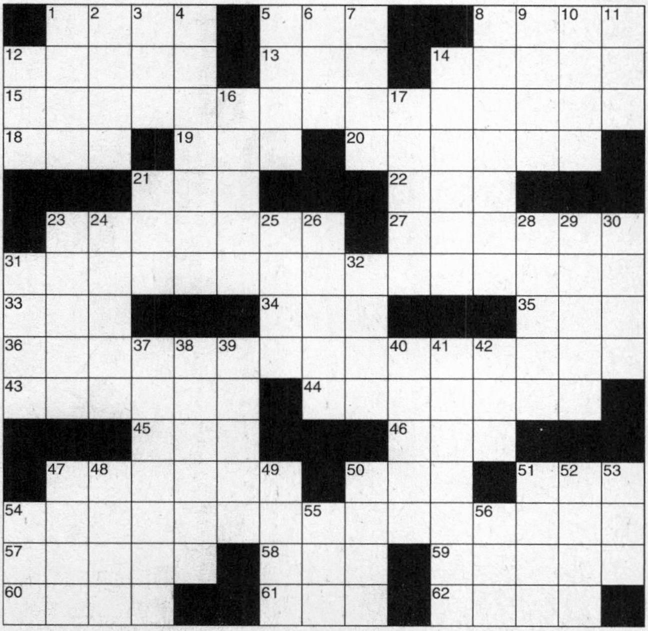

330 *PLAY BALL!*

by Harvey Estes

ACROSS

1 Fizzy drink
5 Inclined planes
10 __ *Man Flint*
13 Ring results
14 Napoleon's fate
15 Western Indians
17 Work units
18 Snake poison
19 Prepares leather
20 Pol. contributor
21 Dairy container
23 Sorrowful word
25 Neither fish __ fowl
26 Gas ratings
29 Imitator
33 Cabdrivers
34 Hammers and saws
36 Long follower
37 Arthur of tennis
38 Make tapestries
39 Approve
40 Hwy.
41 *Being* __ (Sellers film)
42 Fancy flapjack
43 Spray-can contents
45 Brushed off
47 Lass' counterpart
48 Bear in the stars
49 Blades on snow
55 Explosive: Abbr.
58 Inventor Elias
59 Lacks
60 Do a slow burn
61 Nights before
62 Public persona
63 Art __ ('20s style)
64 Superlative suffix
65 Carried around
66 Ticks off

DOWN

1 __ on it (hurry)
2 Pod veggie
3 Pound employee
4 Pack animal
5 Correct errors, e.g.
6 Ice skater's move
7 Wrap fur
8 Drop noisily
9 Florida collegian
10 Strong protest
11 Idaho neighbor
12 Descartes of math
16 Ukraine, formerly: Abbr.
21 "__ inhumanity to . . ."
22 Spinning toys
24 Blue spot on a map
26 Scarlett's maiden name
27 Social stratum
28 Foundry output
29 Sheltered places
30 Baker's material
31 With dropped jaw
32 Played cat and mouse
35 Canoe propeller
38 Novel genre
39 Heavenly bodies
41 Russian ruler
42 Scoundrels
44 Firstborn
46 Cared for
49 __ *Stoops to Conquer*
50 Tennis term
51 Lambs' moms
52 Verne character
53 In apple-pie order
54 Barely defeat
56 Bottle part
57 Ark complement
60 "Star Wars" defense program: Abbr.

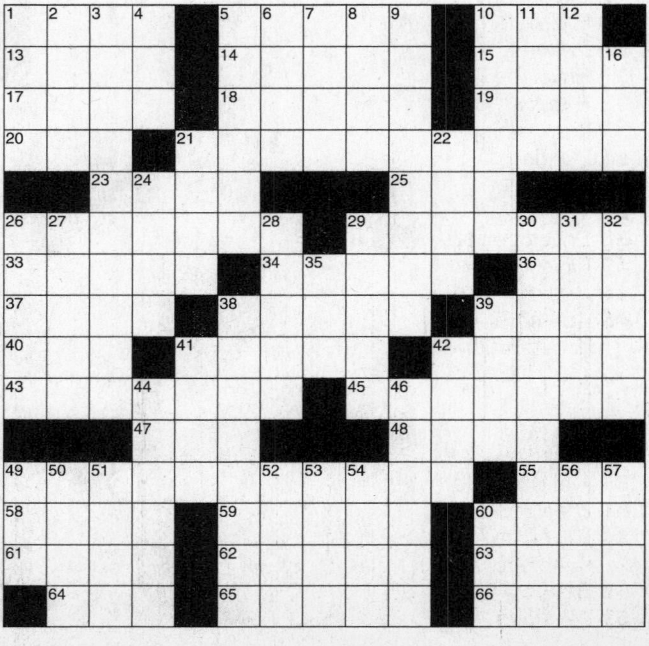

331 BODY PAINTING

by Fred Piscop

ACROSS

1 Piece of candy
5 SASE, for one
9 Tower of __
14 __ *Man* (Estevez film)
15 Spanish surrealist
16 Tabletop decoration
17 Give __ (care)
18 Music genre
19 __ *und Drang*
20 Military decoration
23 Language suffix
24 Cause by necessity
25 Egyptian amulet
27 CO clock setting
29 Blob
32 Liver, for one
36 Bar mitzvah dance
39 New York college
40 Phone line
41 Norton's workplace
42 __ War (1899-1902)
43 Having color
44 __-Lease Act
45 ". . . I __ my way"
46 "__ by Starlight"
48 Hockey great Bobby
50 __ a pin
53 Some navels
58 The __ Four (Beatles)
60 Coward
62 Mount the soapbox
64 Goalie's success
65 Dresden denial
66 Kitchen gadget
67 Radio message-ender
68 Aware of
69 *It __ a Thief*
70 Waterman's wares
71 "A friend in __ . . ."

DOWN

1 Window embellishment
2 Nick-at-Nite offering
3 Dizzying designs
4 *Where's __?* ('70 film)
5 '50s Fords
6 Lye, chemically
7 Crossword listings
8 Pale lavender
9 Small café
10 Picnic pest
11 Aristocrat
12 Wall features?
13 Old __, CT
21 Outline in detail
22 *M*A*S*H* role
26 Suspect's explanation
28 Quaker pronoun
30 "Dedicated to the __ Love"
31 Thespian's gig
32 Protest singer Phil
33 Beat decisively
34 Legal tender
35 Mix up
37 Have title to
38 Make over
41 Nominee listing
45 Beat decisively
47 Hens, e.g.
49 Galleon crew
51 Journalist Joseph
52 Drudge
54 Mortise mate
55 Actress Graff
56 Top-class
57 Church council
58 Army outpost
59 Opera solo
61 Pizzeria need
63 Placekicker's prop

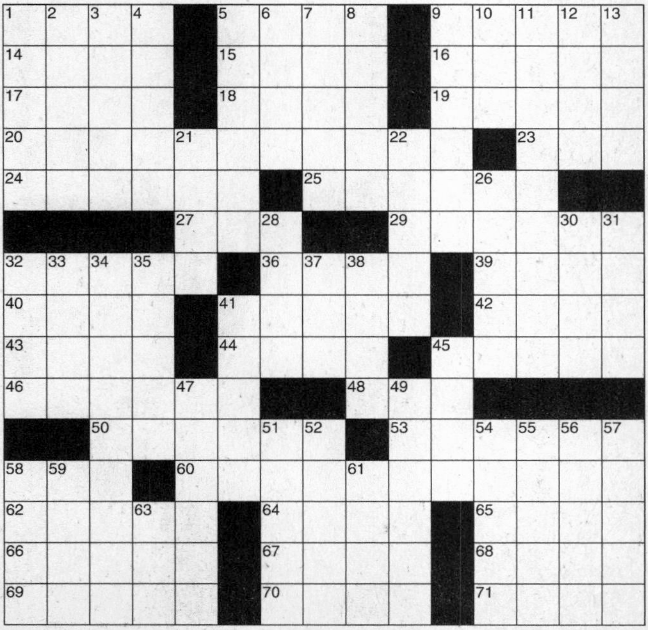

332 LOVE AND KISSES

by Shirley Soloway

ACROSS

1 School org.
4 Western height
8 Faux __
11 Word of woe
12 Asia's __ Sea
13 In any way
16 Mattress partner
18 Sitcom actress Roker
19 Book issue
20 Women warriors
22 __-mo replay
23 Heavy metal
24 Butter bit
25 Forbid
28 Not fooled by
30 Have a snack
32 "He's making __ and checking . . ."
34 Very annoying
38 Alluring
39 Actor Bean
40 Poker stake
41 Absolve from blame
43 Political ploy
44 Leningrad's river
45 Sailor's patron
47 __ Na Na
48 Lwyr.
50 Roman roadway
52 Mel of baseball
54 Church section
56 Lure
60 Go __ (deteriorate)
61 Sporting dogs
63 Singer Cara
64 Not active
65 Apple center
66 Pregrown grass
67 __-do-well
68 Naval off.

DOWN

1 Trudge
2 Car for hire
3 Office aides: Abbr.
4 Leave stranded
5 Ireland's nickname
6 __ Jose, CA
7 Pond growth
8 Logical contradiction
9 From __ (completely)
10 Jazz instruments
11 "Honest" nickname
14 Director Wertmuller
15 "__ we forget"
17 Boeing captain
21 Massenet opera
23 Popular seafood
25 Infield corner
26 Emcee Trebek
27 Watergate focus
29 Synagogue scroll
31 *The King and I* setting
33 "Auld Lang __"
35 Christmas carol
36 Mormons' mecca
37 Antitoxins
39 Make a speech
42 Forced to vacate
43 __ voce
46 __ superior (nuns' boss)
48 Play's start
49 Thunder god
51 Spritelike
53 Cessation of hostilities
55 Forbidden act
56 Wheel connector
57 After a while
58 Superiors of 68 Across: Abbr.
59 Mao __-tung
62 Keats creation

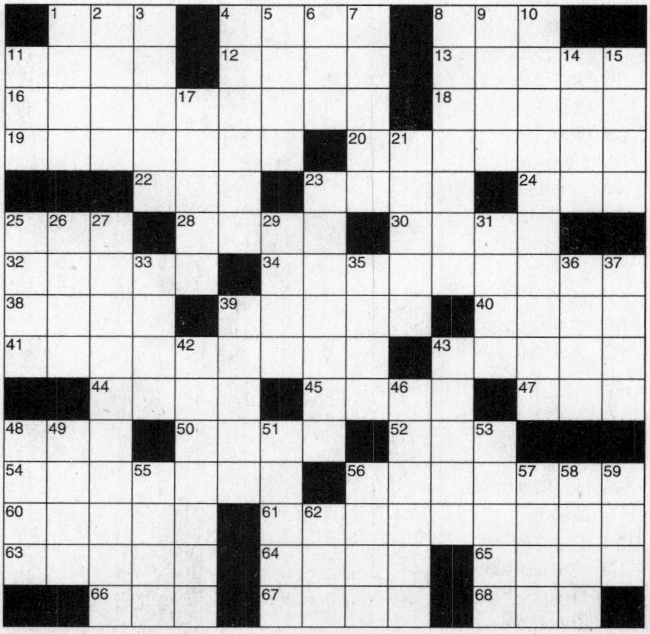

333 ALL BUSINESS

by A.J. Santora

ACROSS

1 Lhasa __
5 "Phooey!"
8 Hair styles
13 Mythical birds
14 Tony-winner Merkel
15 Get in
16 Business-acquisition specialist
19 Company's tactic against 16 Across
20 Shooter ammo
21 Irritate
22 Bar crawler
23 Reproduce
25 Actor Voight
26 After expenses
28 __ polloi
29 Goes after apples
30 Prefix for physics
34 Building addition
35 Ogle
36 EMT technique
38 Selfish sort
39 "The __ Were"
41 Legal attachment
42 Plug's place
43 Psychic power
45 Little devil
46 Script direction
47 Mimic
49 Thompson of *Howards End*
51 Five-centime piece
52 Prey for 16 Across
57 Exec's insurance against 16 Across
58 Fabled Chicagoan
59 Adams or Ameche
60 Spanish 101 verb
61 Ruses
62 Chang's brother
63 Pentagram

DOWN

1 Compass drawings
2 Express contempt
3 In a gutsy way
4 Sea bird
5 Puppeteer Tillstrom
6 Microorganism
7 Women's weapons
8 Russian river
9 Men of the cloth
10 __ harm (was innocuous)
11 Runner Steve
12 Rev.'s recital
15 "Get Happy" composer
17 __ deal (initiate business)
18 Fish with a charge
23 Eat properly
24 Alley Oop's gal
25 Bliss
27 Have coming
29 Honey bunch
31 *Teahouse of __ Moon*
32 Thoroughfare
33 Monster
36 Ferber novel
37 Vitality
40 Work time for many
41 Citrus cooler
44 Garden flower
46 "__ a jolly good fellow"
47 Reef + lagoon
48 Word form for "old"
50 Sports award
51 Anatomical pouch
53 Users: Suff.
54 Sharp flavor
55 Singer James
56 Lacerate
57 House party: Abbr.

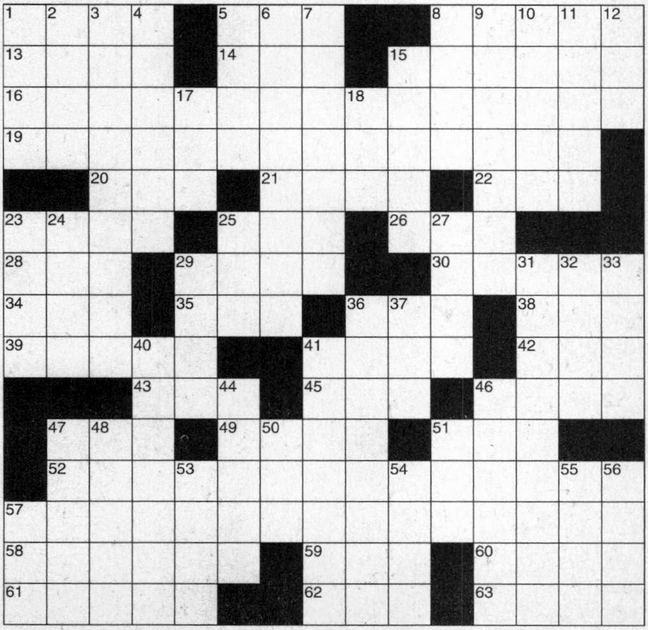

334 LENGTHWISE

by Shirley Soloway

ACROSS

1 Ship's dock
5 In flames
10 Demeanor
14 Concerning
15 Carnival features
16 __-European (prototypical language)
17 Boy Scout beginner
19 Chem. and bio.
20 Sharon of Israel
21 Actress Lanchester
22 "__ went thataway!"
23 Riddle, e.g.
25 Melt
27 Marvin or Grant
28 Search for
31 Meadow males
34 Sincere
37 Happy
38 __ Baba
39 Fast cars
41 Atlas page
42 Taco topping
44 Prerecord
45 Capri, for one
46 Assumption
48 Dancer Miller
50 Pepper's partner
51 Wipes off
54 Makes believe
56 Alda of *M*A*S*H*
59 Stacked up
61 Winnie the __
62 Railroad boss
64 Sound of mind
65 Spread joy
66 Carryall
67 Bullfight bravos
68 Writer Runyon
69 Alps surface

DOWN

1 Pocket bread
2 Not moving
3 Comic Kovacs
4 Distributes again
5 Airport info: Abbr.
6 Drummer's companion
7 Role model
8 Early autos
9 Large homestead
10 Faux pas
11 Little crawlers
12 Singer Adams
13 Prone to snoop
18 Otherwise
24 Architect Saarinen
26 Alters pants
28 Hog food
29 Russian range
30 Use a keyboard
31 Scraping sound
32 Winglike
33 Major step
35 Diminutive ending
36 Coach Parseghian
39 Solid rain
40 Costly
43 Breaks to bits
45 Won't budge
47 Remained
49 Wine valley
51 Put an __ (stop)
52 Rock singer __ John
53 Take care of
54 Lhasa __ (dog)
55 Heat source
57 "Ooh __!"
58 Composer Khachaturian
60 Made a sketch
63 Half the honeymooners

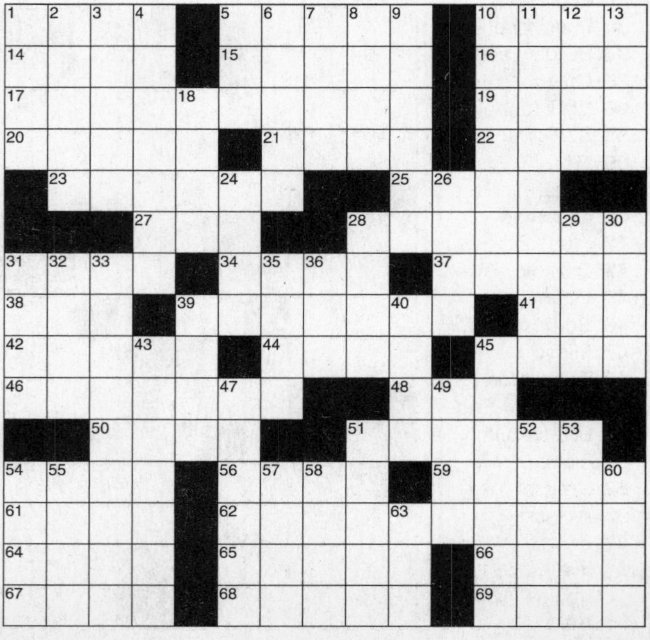

335 FAMILY TREE

by Eric Albert

ACROSS
1 Fast-food favorite
7 Shipmate of Jason
15 Shrewd-minded
16 Musical chestnut
17 English essayist
19 Betelgeuse, e.g.
20 Half of dos
21 Tiny circle
24 Thesaurus name
26 Sleeve fold
30 Not cool
33 Pooh pal's signature
34 Unimportant
35 In coastal Maine
37 Diverse
38 Famous sharpshooter
40 Chore
42 King David, for one
45 Feminist Friedan
46 Distress signal
47 __ Barbara, CA
48 Foundation
49 In a lather
51 Swindle
52 A ways away
53 Geezer
56 *Evening Shade* actress
64 Short piano piece
65 Split
66 Filament element
67 Tomboy

DOWN
1 Cave flier
2 Adjective ending
3 Racing-car initials
4 "__ the word!"
5 Rat-__
6 Señor Chavez
7 Inspire wonder in
8 Actress Welch
9 Sow sound
10 Buckeye State
11 Nantes negative
12 Bow line?
13 Manipulate
14 Mystery writer Josephine
18 Nod off
21 Defective bomb
22 Yoko __
23 Stymies
25 Degenerate
26 The pix biz
27 Eternal
28 Pro
29 Cook bacon
31 Natural-born
32 Candy cost, once
34 Cogitates
36 Help out
37 Jamaican music
39 In itself
40 Flow back
41 Stephen of *The Crying Game*
43 Pigpen
44 Phone bug
46 Undisturbed
49 Nun's wear
50 Fish unofficially
52 Thomas Waller
54 Skagerrak seaport
55 He and she
56 W. Va. setting
57 "Skip to My __"
58 Hostelry
59 Move at a sharp angle
60 Brown shade
61 Stripling
62 *All About* __
63 Strong longing

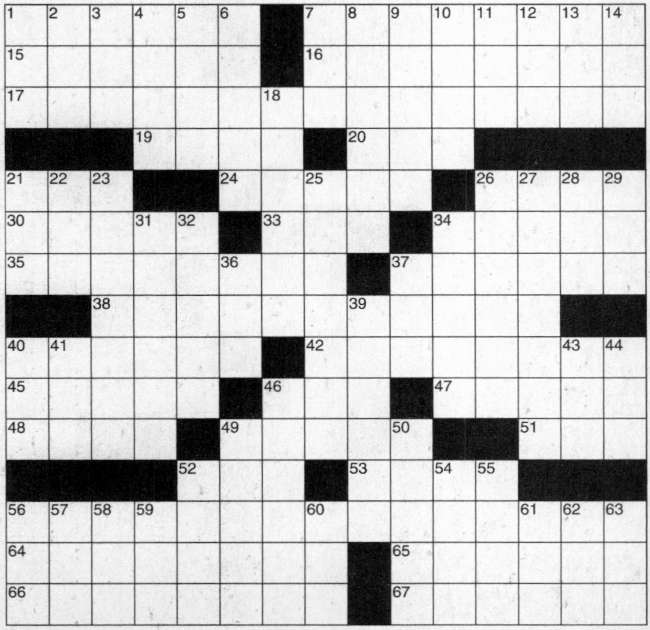

336 OUT WITH THE OLD

by Shirley Soloway

ACROSS
1 Purchase price
5 Egg-shaped
10 Movie terrier
14 Opera solo
15 __ apparent reason
16 Sgts., for example
17 Balers' tools
19 Get bigger
20 Perfectly
21 Fill up
23 Upperclassman: Abbr.
24 Reading and B&O
26 Low down
27 Like some stomachs
30 Four-poster, for instance
33 Add up to
36 Shoshoneans
37 Dover __ (fish)
38 "__ to the wise . . ."
39 Review badly
40 Got up
41 Not so much
42 Composer Porter
43 Croissant creator
44 Asner and Wynn
45 Small carpet
47 Poet Teasdale
49 Bro's sibling
50 Impersonate
53 Out-and-out
56 Starts a tennis point
58 French composer
59 Dinner entree
62 Author Hunter
63 Ghostlike
64 Tiny creature
65 Boggs of baseball
66 Golfer Sam
67 Otherwise

DOWN
1 Marvel and America: Abbr.
2 Mythical hunter
3 Shankar's instrument
4 Social asset
5 Proposes
6 "Hinky Dinky Parlay __"
7 Bobby of hockey
8 Prepares the presses
9 Square-dance call
10 Ms. Dickinson
11 Clippings holder
12 Horn sound
13 ". . . have mercy on such __"
18 Miami paper
22 __ *Little Indians*
25 Dazed state
27 Traffic jammers
28 Author Calvino
29 Extends a subscription
31 Actress Sommer
32 Forest forager
33 Anecdote
34 Had a debt
35 Dinner preparation step
37 Pirate's haul
40 One who mistreats
42 "__ Are" (Mathis tune)
45 Singer's syllable
46 Took a chance
48 Repent
50 Make use of
51 Annoyances
52 Lauder of lipstick
53 Used a bubble pipe
54 Volcanic flow
55 Afterwards
57 Capital of Italy
60 Noun suffix
61 FBI's counterpart

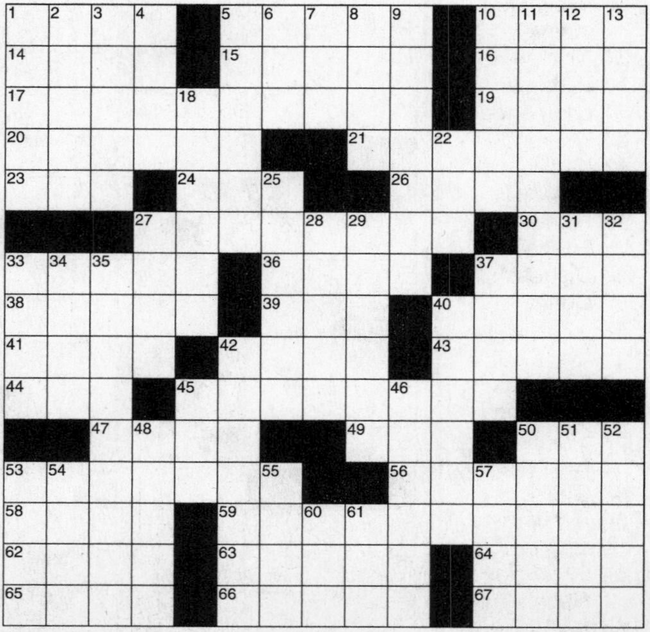

337 PHASES OF THE MOON

by Dean Niles

ACROSS

1 Bide one's time
5 Eng. honor
8 Lawn growth
13 __ *of Green Gables*
14 __ and crafts
16 Hair-care activity
17 Harplike instrument
18 __ as a button
19 Reference list
20 Porky features
23 Three __ match
24 Southern sch.
25 Spills the beans
30 Pie piece
32 Turnstile opening
34 All __ (listening)
35 Literary collection
37 Nigerian town
38 Conclusions
39 Fanatical group
43 Cartel: Abbr.
44 Mork's home
45 Many mos.
46 "Somebody bet __ bay"
47 Role for Stack
49 With an __ (in consideration of)
53 Wifely
55 Preserve, as fruit
57 Geometry proof letters
58 Debussy piece
61 __ the Hutt (*Star Wars* series villain)
65 Sports org.
66 Whence sunrise is seen
67 Outsider
68 *Edward Scissorhands* star
69 Rescind a correction
70 Give rise to
71 Ready to go
72 Antitoxins

DOWN

1 Luxuriate
2 "__ Can Whistle"
3 Progress
4 High-schooler
5 *Miracle on 34th Street* store
6 Caesar's addressee
7 Caesar's question
8 Ground grain
9 __ Tin Tin
10 Here __ now
11 Point farthest from NNW
12 Dr. Ruth topic
15 Placed in the mail
21 Actress Verdugo
22 Mel's Diner, e.g.
26 Very small
27 "Auld __ Syne"
28 Earth: Ger.
29 Draft grp.
31 Male goose
33 Last __ (final at-bat)
36 Like some modern music
39 Bobcat
40 Negate
41 Limerick location
42 Cara of *Fame*
43 Old French coin
48 Difficult situation
50 Draw a parallel
51 More wound up
52 Folk-blues singer
54 "__ Get Started"
56 Adjust to conditions
59 Readies champagne
60 Negative suffix
61 Boxer's motion
62 Dark malt
63 Tom Hanks film
64 Stinging insect

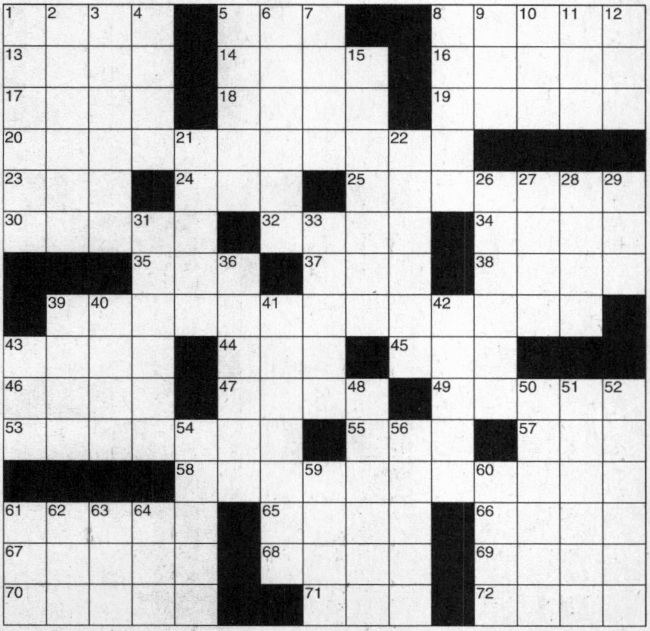

338 *SPEAK UP!*

by Shirley Soloway

ACROSS
1 Adored one
5 Heavenly instrument
9 *Leave __ Beaver*
13 Neck part
14 Screenwriter James
15 Love, in Lille
16 Claire and Balin
17 Rickey requirement
18 Boxing arenas
19 Speak the truth
22 Map close-up
23 Stephen of *The Crying Game*
24 Suction tube
27 More briny
31 "__ Blue?"
32 Proportions
36 Singer Fitzgerald
37 Chatter on and on
40 Richard of films
41 Swamp creatures, for short
42 Insect egg
43 Pours a second cup, perhaps
45 Jane and Edmund
47 Casual shirt
48 War horse
51 Say something nice
57 *The Lady __*
58 Temperate
59 He loved Irish Rose
60 Sky lights?
61 "Ye __ Gift Shoppe"
62 Take a nap
63 May celebrants
64 Wintertime vehicle
65 Changes colors

DOWN
1 "What's __ for me?"
2 Victor Borge was one
3 Milky gemstone
4 Actor __ Howard
5 Brings to a stop
6 Nimble
7 Send in payment
8 Take a look
9 Did a takeoff on
10 Singer Tennille
11 Pulls hard
12 Hosp. areas
15 Sharon of Israel
20 Opening bars
21 Mistake remover
24 Latin dad
25 Reflection
26 Rice style
27 London neighborhood
28 Massey of the movies
29 Pixieish
30 River transports
33 Fisherman
34 Afternoon socials
35 Novel ending?
38 Sweater makers
39 Made a request
44 Yorkshire city
46 Playwright Albee
48 Ability
49 The squiggle in "señor"
50 Came to a close
51 "Do __ others . . ."
52 Mine car
53 Noted cookie maker
54 Follow orders
55 Get up
56 P.D. investigators
57 Doctrine

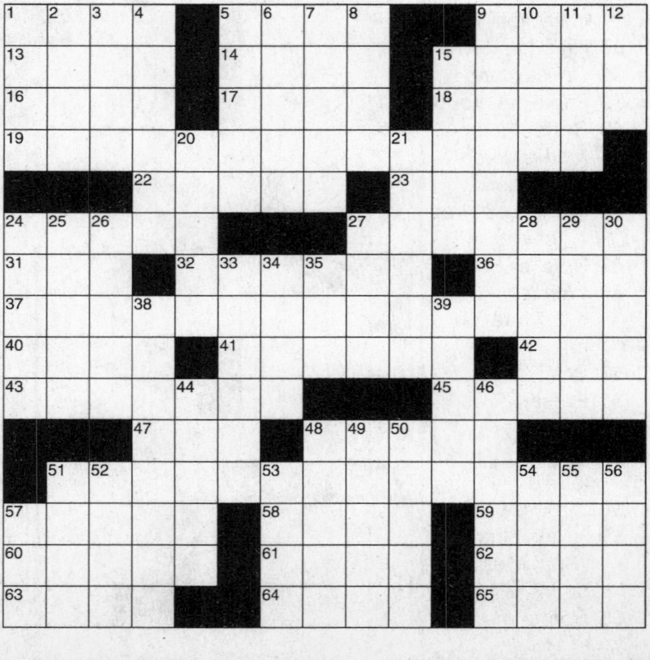

339 LITTLE CIRCLES

by Wayne R. Williams

ACROSS

1 Night-sky sight
5 Jacob's brother
9 Not suitable
14 Sky bear
15 __ best friend
16 Showy flower
17 Halfway into a flight
20 Regulations
21 Menu item
22 Comparative ending
23 Protuberance
24 Wheels around
28 Gregory Hines specialty
29 River projects
33 Small, brownish antelope
34 Shaped like a rainbow
36 Night flyer
37 Historical-movie requirement
40 Traveler's stop
41 Static
42 Composer Erik
43 Relative of "great" and "keen"
45 TV hardware
46 Bit of food
47 Alternative to a saber
49 Name a knight
50 Not noticed
53 Maladies
58 Computer-printer technology
60 Bay window
61 Pennsylvania port
62 South American nation
63 Reddish-brown quartzes
64 Neckline shapes
65 Air pollution

DOWN

1 Has dinner
2 Horse's pace
3 The largest continent
4 Declaim violently
5 Overacts
6 Morley of *60 Minutes*
7 Jillian and Beattie
8 GI entertainers
9 Overturn
10 Caught fish, in a way
11 Bridge quorum
12 Concerning
13 Newcastle's river
18 School fee
19 Examine a case again
23 Mother-of-pearl
24 Arrive unexpectedly
25 Goddess of peace
26 Actress __ Lisi
27 Kimono sash
28 Reliance
30 Borders on
31 Scientist Curie
32 Drum or wool material
34 Burning
35 Fail to heed
38 Museum guide
39 Old sailor
44 Came down in buckets
46 Rumples
48 Rings out
49 Southern anthem
50 Japanese vegetables
51 Writer Ephron
52 Be up and about
53 Ominous
54 Poisonous snakes
55 Part of a pipe
56 Architect Saarinen
57 Self-satisfied
59 Gun the motor

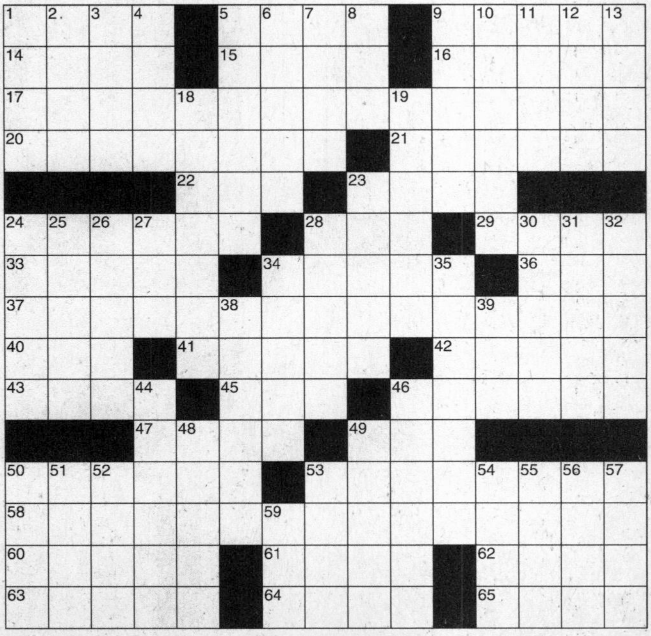

340 GIVE UP?

by Shirley Soloway

ACROSS

1 Attired
5 Mary's pet
9 Entertainers
14 Conceal
15 Iris layer
16 Kukla's pal
17 Up above
18 Price
19 Actress Davis
20 SURRENDER
23 Have a feeling about
24 Wine region of Italy
25 Boulevard liners
28 Rooftop structure
33 Swelled head
36 Counts calories
39 __ Romeo (car)
40 SURRENDERS
44 Actor Richard
45 Firm
46 Dads of Jrs.
47 Make a choice
50 Forget to include
52 Sound like a snake
55 Characteristic
59 SURRENDER
65 More or less
66 Cleo's river
67 TV handyman
68 Washer cycle
69 Church area
70 Roman road
71 Runs into
72 Have a strong odor
73 Respond rudely

DOWN

1 Converses casually
2 Graceful
3 Add embellishment
4 Put out of power
5 Lynda Bird's sister
6 Stratford's river
7 Hostess Perle
8 Washups
9 Render immobile
10 Butter alternative
11 Did in
12 Utensil point
13 Circus star
21 Attaches permanently
22 Greek vowel
26 Farrow of *Zelig*
27 Takes up a hem
29 Brit. flyers
30 Troubles
31 Distant, to Donne
32 Falls behind
33 Farm females
34 Redcoat general
35 Egg-shaped
37 However, for short
38 Grain housing
41 Chemical suffix
42 Comic Conway
43 Archie's mate
48 Skydivers' needs
49 Gratuity
51 Country singer Randy
53 Submarine system
54 Take potshots at
56 O'Day or Baker
57 Runs without moving
58 Ivan and Peter
59 Cause damage to
60 Theater award
61 Solitary
62 Homemaker's nemesis
63 "What __ is new?"
64 Look for

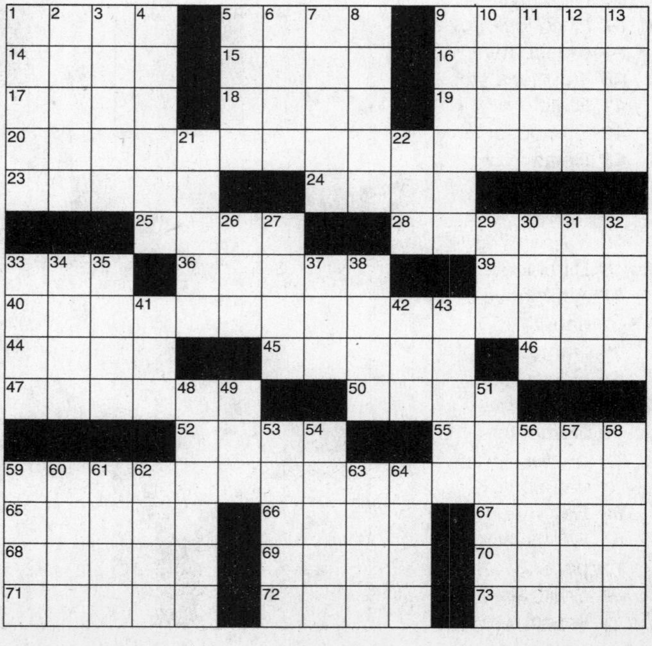

341 LONG TIME

by Wayne R. Williams

ACROSS

1 Fill too tightly
5 *M*A*S*H* star
9 Tint
14 Protagonist
15 Dates
16 Atelier item
17 Long time
20 Track official
21 Hatcher of *Lois & Clark*
22 Park art
25 Flairs
30 Strike sharply
32 "The Raven" lady
33 Existed
36 Saudis, e.g.
38 Khatami's land
39 Long time
43 Gold patch
44 Prefix for "sun"
45 Compass dir.
46 Puts up
49 Blockheads
51 Relatives of roads
53 Boat building area
57 Carpenter's need
59 French brother
60 Long time
66 Garden area
67 Hurries
68 Pennsylvania port
69 Rider's straps
70 Woodcutters
71 Mtg.

DOWN

1 Confabs
2 Send payment
3 Lure of the kitchen
4 Some Impressionist paintings
5 Volcanic dust
6 August sign
7 Quick and skillful
8 Selling feature
9 Doddering
10 Possessed
11 Simile center
12 Susan of *L.A. Law*
13 Loop trains
18 Author Capote
19 Russian river
23 Ireland
24 Hidden supply
26 Novelist Bagnold
27 Ephron and others
28 TV dinner holders
29 Significance
31 Dropped back
33 Hand signals
34 Paying attention
35 More crafty
37 Met show-stoppers
40 Fairy-tale opener
41 Small brook
42 Let know
47 Domingo and Pavarotti, e.g.
48 Laurel or Getz
50 Spending frenzies
52 Indian sect members
54 "__ the World"
55 *Mrs. __ Goes to Paris*
56 Affirmative comments
58 *Star Wars* princess
60 A ways away
61 Mine find
62 Diamond stat
63 Put on
64 Evergreen tree
65 Draft letters

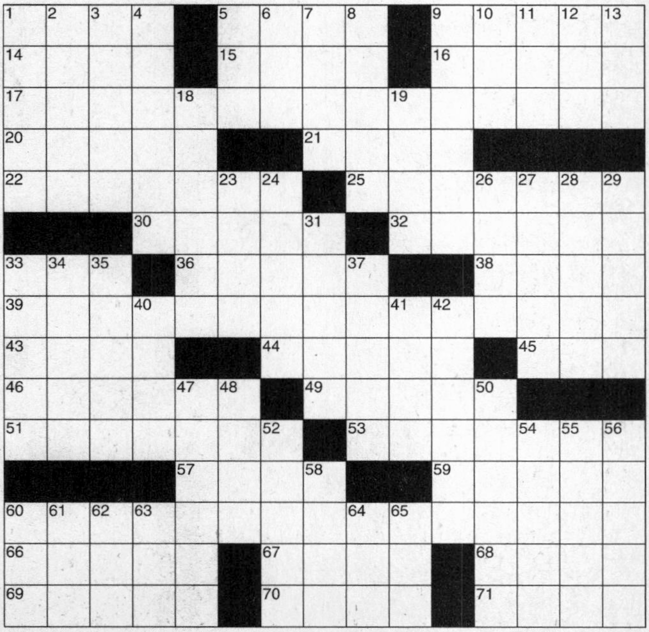

342 *WORKING IT OUT*

by Shirley Soloway

ACROSS

1 Only
5 Figure-skater Thomas
9 The Devil
14 Related
15 *The Good Earth* character
16 Novelist Zola
17 Sail support
18 Shuttle org.
19 Pee Wee of baseball
20 Somehow
23 Agree
24 Trimmed of fat
25 P.I.
27 __ *Rides Again*
32 Make changes to
36 Put on board
39 Opera highlight
40 Somehow
43 Ireland's alias
44 And others: Abbr.
45 Carries on
46 Stretching muscle
48 Lamb's mom
50 Rugged rock
53 "__ Fideles"
58 Somehow
63 Weekly pay
64 Underground growth
65 Mandlikova of tennis
66 __ a minute (fast)
67 Tommy of Broadway
68 Manages, with "out"
69 Baseballer Staub
70 Impersonated
71 Learning method

DOWN

1 Latin dance
2 Rubber-stamps
3 Shopping aids
4 __ nous (confidentially)
5 Contribute
6 Israeli airline
7 Kind of metabolism
8 Senseless
9 Cool and calm
10 From the US
11 Stadium row
12 In addition
13 __-do-well
21 Opening bars of music
22 Mommy's mate
26 Coagulate
28 Roosevelt matriarch
29 Disney film of '82
30 Hilarious performance
31 Beasts of burden
32 Support
33 Stringed instrument of yore
34 Lacking substance
35 Many centuries
37 ". . . man __ mouse?"
38 Talented
41 Tralee's county
42 Belief
47 Dramatist Sean
49 Had a yen for
51 The main artery
52 Aggregation
54 Anesthetic
55 Military headwear
56 Doctrine
57 Rub out
58 Man __ (racehorse)
59 __, *the Killer Whale* ('66 film)
60 Sponsorship
61 Shoe part
62 Tiptop

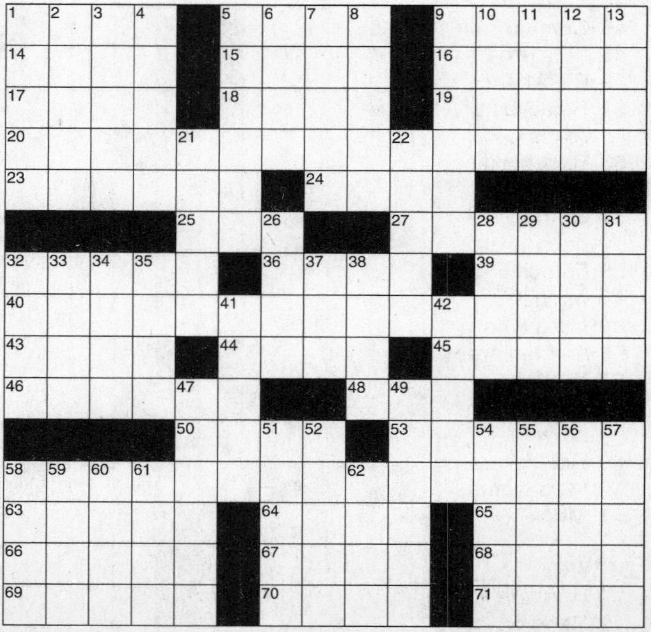

343 CREATURE FEATURE

by Cathy Millhauser

ACROSS

1 Door post
5 Polite address
10 Do one's part?
14 *Siegfried* solo
15 Mrs. Kramden
16 Milky gem
17 Sugar source
18 Wallace family's *The Book of __*
19 Inclination to anger
20 What the over-the-hill man had?
23 Sneaker need
24 Least well
25 Mock
28 "Super!"
30 Elvis' middle name
31 Kid's sandwich leftover
32 AWOL pursuers
35 What the man who jumped to conclusions had?
39 "For shame!"
40 Less than a man?
41 The Sundance Kid's girlfriend
42 Spherical hairstyles
43 One of Santa's team
45 Routine-bound
48 Florence's river
49 What the propmaster for *The Sting* had?
54 They're inflatable
55 Usage expert Newman
56 Losers of '45
58 "Rule Britannia" composer
59 British novelist Charles
60 Scout quarters
61 Overlook
62 Makes an appointment
63 Nervous

DOWN

1 Fast punch
2 Realm
3 Appearance
4 At war
5 "With __ toward none . . ."
6 Skirt shape
7 Meal choice
8 *Othello* opener
9 Superlatively sloppy
10 Blue shade
11 Put one's two cents in
12 Fountain orders
13 Hallow'd
21 Blue
22 *The Bell Jar* author
25 Cuckoo
26 Fouls up
27 Chess castle
28 Looks like Carroll's cat
29 Stratagem
31 "Ah" follower
32 Closet undesirable
33 Top of the head
34 Film rater's unit
36 Jestingly
37 Our hemisphere
38 Echo
42 Springs
43 Bagpipe sounds
44 Author Beattie
45 Car-suspension piece
46 Valentino's girlfriend
47 Ages
48 Stomach
50 Mother of invention?
51 Did the crawl
52 Marked a ballot
53 High-pitched sound
57 Hog's home

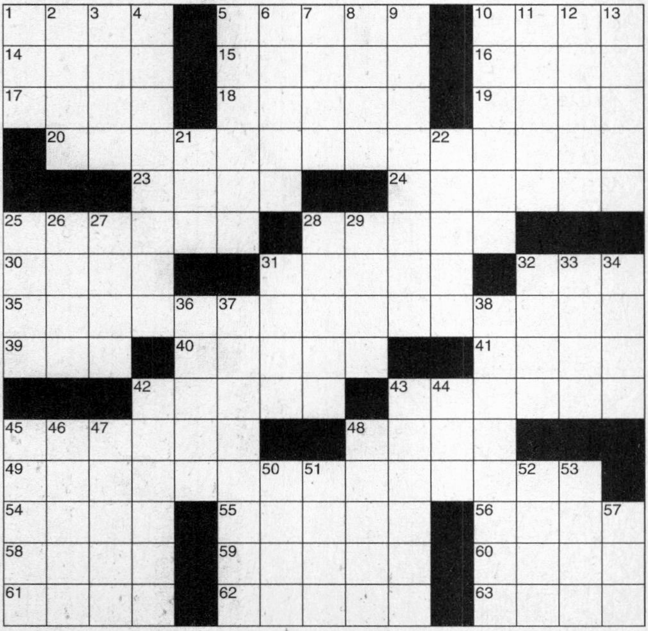

344 EURO MENU

by Carol Blumenstein

ACROSS

1 Tranquil
5 Knight's mount
10 __ up (support)
14 Culture medium
15 Rex Stout detective
16 Lanyard
17 Dinner veggies
20 In the dumps
21 Vigorous
22 Most despicable
23 Computer monitors: Abbr.
24 Rat (on)
25 Zodiacal bull
28 Out of __ (antiquated)
29 Fourth mo.
32 Felonious flames
33 Recipe word
34 Bassoon kin
35 Dark dessert
38 Spider's octet
39 A son of Zeus
40 Like most new movies
41 Ending for Japan or Siam
42 Iowa city
43 Sovereigns
44 Slipped
45 Mountain lion
46 Matches up
49 __ mater
50 Spanish article
53 Dinner starter
56 Peel
57 Go in
58 __ *Karenina*
59 *Against All* __ ('84 film)
60 Titles to property
61 Favorites

DOWN

1 Taxis
2 Site of the Taj Mahal
3 Praise
4 Title for a married woman
5 Exercise attire
6 *For Whom the Bell* __
7 Otherwise
8 Failing grades
9 Uses up
10 Sneak about
11 Cad
12 Makes a choice
13 Nuisance
18 Reduced
19 Word with play or model
23 Kin to gators
24 Appropriates
25 Put off
26 City on the Rhône
27 Custom
28 Acts riskily
29 Wane
30 Fireplace tool
31 Tall grasses
33 Not interested
34 City near Gainesville
36 Starved
37 Author Capote
42 Baldwin of *The Getaway*
43 Tabloid tidbits
44 Dispatches
45 Practiced (a trade)
46 '60s hairstyle
47 Grillwork
48 Rip
49 Poker stake
50 The __ Ranger
51 Family member
52 Health farms
54 __-armed bandit
55 Patsy

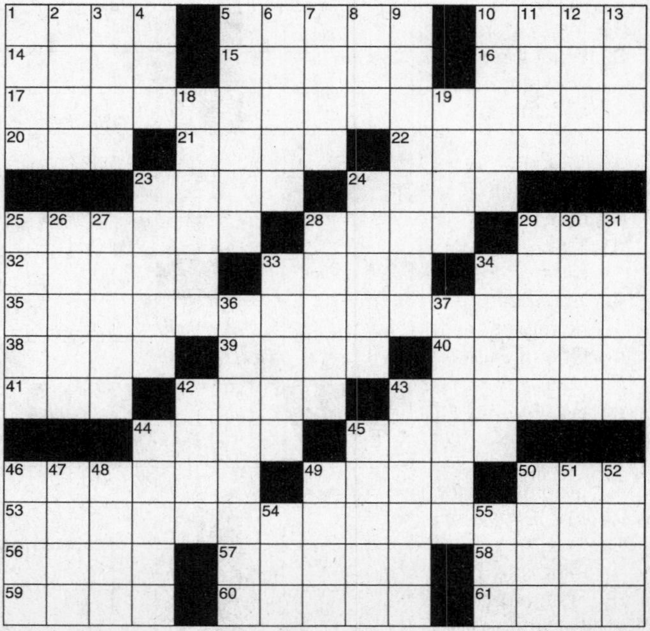

345 *WAYS TO GO*

by Robert H. Wolfe

ACROSS

1 Israeli port
6 *Bonanza* role
10 *The World According to* __
14 Visibly happy
15 Caron film of '53
16 On __ with (equivalent to)
17 Laissez __
18 Nudge a little
19 Nutmeg relative
20 High range
22 Go __ (fall apart)
24 Take time off
26 Jodie and Stephen
27 Light-dimming device
31 Percent ending
32 Negotiations
33 Carried
35 *Birth of a Nation* grp.
38 Perry's penner
39 Go __ (deteriorate)
40 Port, for one
41 Workout place
42 Pounce on prey
43 See-through
44 Nectar collector
45 Potluck dinner item
47 Expected
51 Old phone feature
52 "Go __!" (oath)
54 Covers a cutlet
58 The good earth
59 Sinful
61 Pang
62 Christian Science founder
63 Take a train
64 Spoiler
65 Thumbs-ups
66 Snow rider
67 __ on (incited)

DOWN

1 Sword handle
2 Gelatin ingredient
3 Mr. Nastase
4 Go __ (risk all)
5 Not impressed
6 Swiss height
7 Scuttlebutt
8 Unconcerned
9 Linear center
10 Reproductive cell
11 Swiftly
12 Souped-up auto
13 Conference questioners
21 D.C. clock setting
23 Key, for instance
25 Unmentionable
27 US 76 and CA 101, e.g.
28 A Marx instrument
29 "A-Tisket, A-Tasket" singer
30 *Fiddler on the Roof* star
34 Caught cattle
35 Chicken __
36 Baby bouncer
37 Lancaster's love in *From Here to Eternity*
39 Stamp collector's tool
40 Go __ (plunge in)
42 __ precedent
43 Do the unexpected
44 Budd and Bigelow
46 Don't play it straight
47 Cruising
48 Arlo's dad
49 Stand
50 New Jersey iceman
53 Faction
55 Cut __ (dance)
56 Medicinal amount
57 Tournament ranking
60 Guided

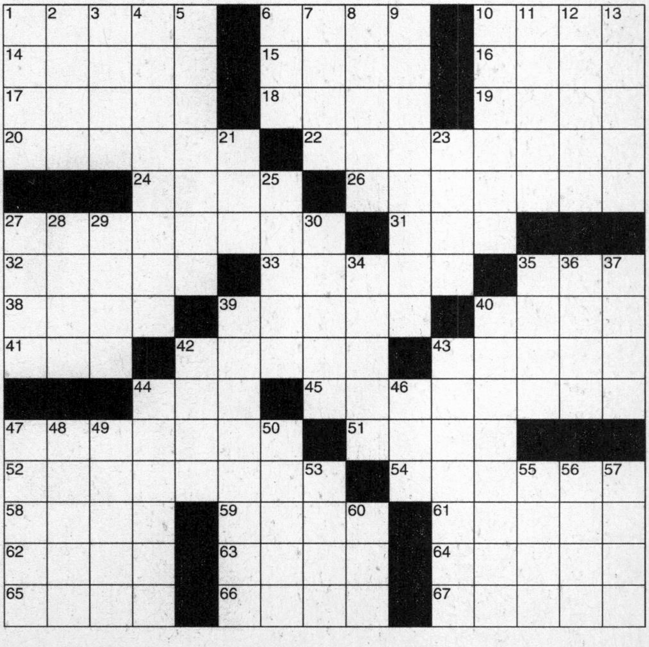

346 DRINK UP!

by Wayne R. Williams

ACROSS
1 Pepsi rival
5 "Home on the __"
10 Chair part
14 Norse god
15 Sacred images
16 Source of poi
17 Foundry form
18 "Night and Day" composer
20 Actress Dahl
22 Prehistoric
23 Flightless bird
24 Five-spot
26 Lab burners
27 Incur resentment
30 RN's specialty
31 Mr. Antony
32 Cellular substance: Abbr.
33 Director Eric
37 Dwight's nickname
38 Escape from prison
40 Actor Wallach
41 Tall buildings
43 Seabird
44 Hebrew letter
45 Ignited
46 Nevada attraction
48 Used a lariat
51 Writer Rand
52 Broadcast
53 Frozen regions
55 Horse's home
58 Snitch
61 "I've __ had!"
62 Nautical adverb
63 Fiction book
64 Allow to use
65 Orange-red mineral
66 Dirt path
67 Time periods

DOWN
1 Deep sleep
2 Aroma
3 Homer-hitter Harmon
4 Localized
5 Popular side dish
6 Fuss
7 Lon of Cambodia
8 Gather gradually
9 Sports cable network
10 Actress Elaine
11 Turn toward midnight
12 Show place
13 Law-school course
19 Spotted wildcat
21 Fanatic
24 Boggy grounds
25 In an angry way
27 Give off
28 Type of shark
29 Guardianship
30 Tree part
34 German composer
35 Novelist Kazan
36 Fruit covering
38 Wedding-related
39 Algerian seaport
42 Voted in
44 Friendly
47 Snack on
48 Moreno et al.
49 Central Florida city
50 An apostle
51 John Jacob __
54 Closely confined
55 Vend
56 Melodious Horne
57 Finishes up
59 Gardner of *Mogambo*
60 Maui garland

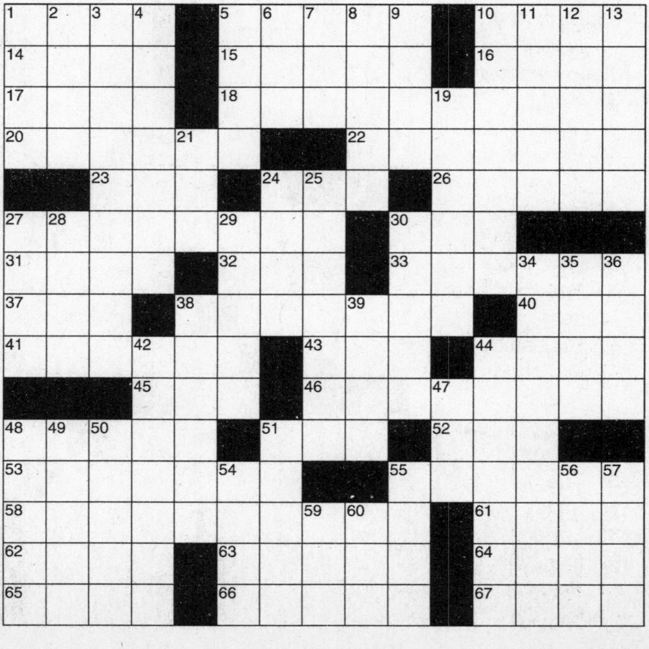

347 SCREEN SCORCHERS

by Frank Gordon

ACROSS

1 Demean
6 Cleverness
9 Forgoes food
14 Grand Prix entrant
15 Wedding words
16 Say
17 Kate's TV housemate
18 Just out
19 Writer Ephron et al.
20 Mel Brooks film
23 Misplace
24 Houston hitter
25 Indy 500 tally
27 Aliens: Abbr.
28 Weasel's sound?
29 Penn. neighbor
31 Me, to Maurice
32 Papas' partners
34 "__ a Grecian Urn"
36 '74 disaster film, with *The*
41 Egg shapes
42 Govt. security
43 Obtain
44 Printer's measures
47 Sot's affliction
48 DDE's command
51 Paris landmark
53 Santa __
55 "Put __ on it!"
56 Best Picture of '81
59 Stallone role
60 Rainy
61 Greek letters
62 Office-communication system
63 Corn portion
64 College women
65 Al __ (pasta specification)
66 Kind of martini
67 Bewildered

DOWN

1 Fit for farming
2 Voter's paper
3 In __ by itself (unique)
4 Impound
5 ". . . __ saw Elba"
6 Bird or plane measure
7 That is: Lat.
8 Facing
9 Endow
10 South Pacific feature
11 Party decoration
12 Recipe measure
13 Last year's jrs.
21 Singer Judd
22 Unknown John
26 Word form for "Chinese"
28 Analyze a sentence
30 Yuppie apartments
32 Actor Gibson
33 Cpl.'s superior
35 Billy __ Williams
36 Roman garb
37 Surmounted
38 Night worker
39 Business activity
40 Untrue
45 AT&T rival
46 Put on the brakes
48 Exclusive groups
49 Angry speech
50 Black Sea port
52 Nun's wear
54 On __ (rampaging)
55 "The game is __!"
57 Function
58 Pay-stub abbr.
59 Carpet color

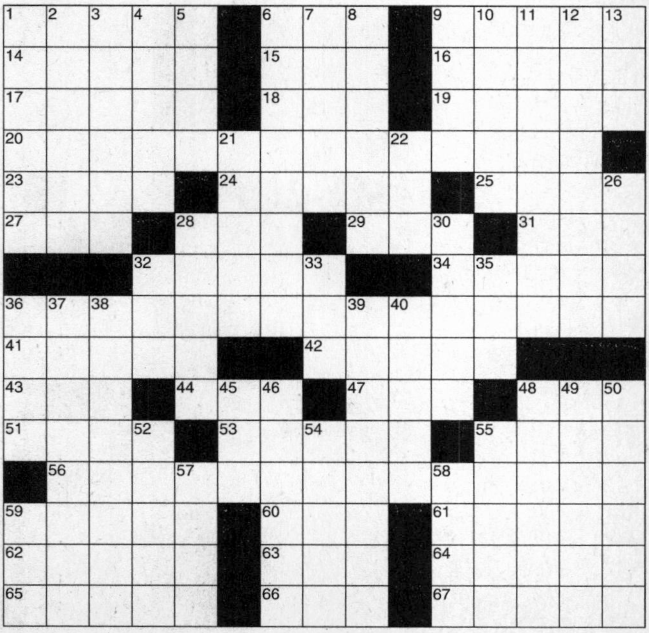

348 SHELL GAME

by Shirley Soloway

ACROSS
1 Fastener
6 Bit of dew
10 Fizzy fluid
14 Less tinted
15 Intense anger
16 Adam Arkin's dad
17 Too big
18 Prophetic sign
19 Minor damage
20 Decorative border
23 Is under the weather
24 Everyone
25 Western mount
29 Patella
33 Neutral shade
36 Actress Gabor
37 Catfish catchers
38 Coop critter
39 Yemeni port
40 __ jiffy
41 Cropped pants
45 Child protection
47 Nice and warm
48 Tapper Miller
49 Diplomacy
51 Nighttime working hours
57 Folk follower
58 Estrada of TV
59 Actress Patricia et al.
61 Always
62 Ready to eat
63 Fortuneteller's card
64 Ms. Trueheart
65 Require
66 Make a speech

DOWN
1 USN rank
2 Chem. rooms
3 Guinness or Baldwin
4 Western sight
5 Bishop, e.g.
6 Salivate
7 Inclines
8 Curved molding
9 Necklace dangler
10 Riding seat
11 Cassini of design
12 Borge, e.g.
13 Picnic pest
21 Fabricator
22 Gen. Robert __
25 Kind of boom
26 Laughing mammal
27 "Swinging on __"
28 Aves.' kin
29 Good-natured
30 Yields
31 Turn away
32 Spring bloomer
34 "Huh?"
35 Garment bottom
39 Muslim ruler
41 100-yr. periods
42 Outdoor-party light
43 Annoying sensation
44 Penetrated
46 Duel tools
49 Worthless talk
50 Made a request
51 Be enamored of
52 Mine finds
53 Great Lake
54 Feeling of dread
55 Fictional estate
56 Narrow opening
57 Permit
60 Fr. holy woman

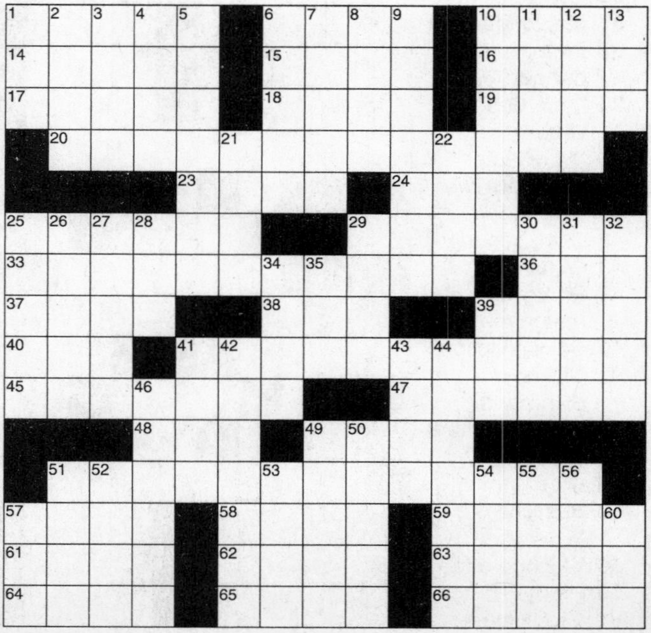

349 TRUNK SPACE

by A.J. Santora

ACROSS
1 Drivel
4 Just fair
8 Electricity
13 Airline to Tokyo
14 Lab burner
15 Bower
16 Ancient harp
18 Composer Satie
19 Dolphins' home
20 Mrs. Trump, once
23 Pitcher Darling
24 A thousand G's
25 Delhi wrap
26 On the whole
29 Some GI's
34 Chicago airport
35 Pea coats?
37 Jannings of *The Blue Angel*
38 Passé
39 Slangy suffix
40 Hersey bell town
41 Buffalo's lake
42 Ifs follower
43 Knight weapon
44 Roof type
46 Fishing boats
47 Actor Max
49 Hosp. staffers
50 Caveman Alley __
53 Hughes aircraft
58 Fork partner
60 Burden
61 Dog's bane
62 Kremlin name, once
63 Formal letter opening
64 Fond du __, WI
65 Vigilant
66 Rooney or Williams
67 Olive-tree relative

DOWN
1 Tropical tree
2 Writer Seton
3 Young salmon
4 Attractive
5 Other: Sp.
6 Small cuts
7 AL team
8 Overcrowds
9 Sch. in the smallest state
10 Steel beam
11 Singer Perry
12 Ireland
17 New Haven sights
21 Felt poorly
22 Cupid
26 Computer adjunct
27 Colleen Maureen
28 Participated
30 __ Lebanon
31 Muscat man
32 Pie choice
33 Blackthorns
35 *Bonanza* ranch
36 Ancient
40 "I'll String __ With You"
42 "I don't give __!"
45 Missing
46 Stylish
48 Argument
50 N. Mex. neighbor
51 Like Nash's lama
52 Yearn
54 Cheese lump
55 __ podrida
56 Briny septet
57 Apiece
59 Douglas __

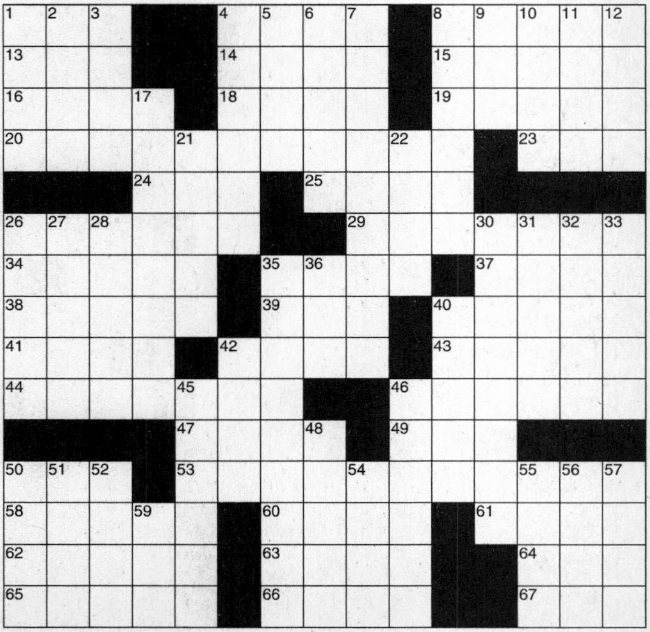

350 TWO FIRSTS

by Janie Lyons

ACROSS

1 Roseanne's former surname
5 Israeli native
10 Carpenter's tool
14 Mayberry moppet
15 Felt poorly
16 Appear
17 Hip '50s comic
19 Over with
20 Trial
21 Extra copies
23 Developed
25 Bad weather
26 Street noise
29 Donkey's uncle
31 Stiller's wife/partner
34 Nicholas, e.g.
35 Part of TGIF
36 Spanish city
37 __ Khan
38 *Wheel of Fortune*, basically
40 Scot's topper
41 Suppose, to Jed Clampett
43 Bobbysoxer's dance
44 Location
45 Old-time anesthetic
46 Civil War initials
47 Chinese cuisine
48 Negate
50 Political coalition
52 Treed
55 Foot components
59 Competent
60 *Family Affair* actor
62 Carol
63 In awe
64 Sea avian
65 Harper or Trueheart
66 Stockings stuff
67 *The Naked and the* __

DOWN

1 Western tie
2 Little or Frye
3 Melon leftover
4 Bridge botcher
5 Dark marten
6 Broadcast
7 Indistinct image
8 School break
9 Proficient
10 Had hopes
11 Ex-partner of Jerry Lewis
12 Pizazz
13 Ambulance personnel: Abbr.
18 Knitter's need
22 Type of type
24 Alert
26 Ogler's look
27 Map speck
28 R&B singer
30 Nostalgic sounds
32 Lasso
33 Commercial developers?
35 Ceiling device
36 Atlas page
38 Songstress Lena
39 Old kingdom
42 Dog sitters
44 Hit the top
46 Priests and bishops
47 Goose talk
49 Municipal
51 Napery
52 Defeatist's word
53 A woodwind
54 Watch part
56 Engage
57 Italian volcano
58 Backyard structure
61 GI's mail abbr.

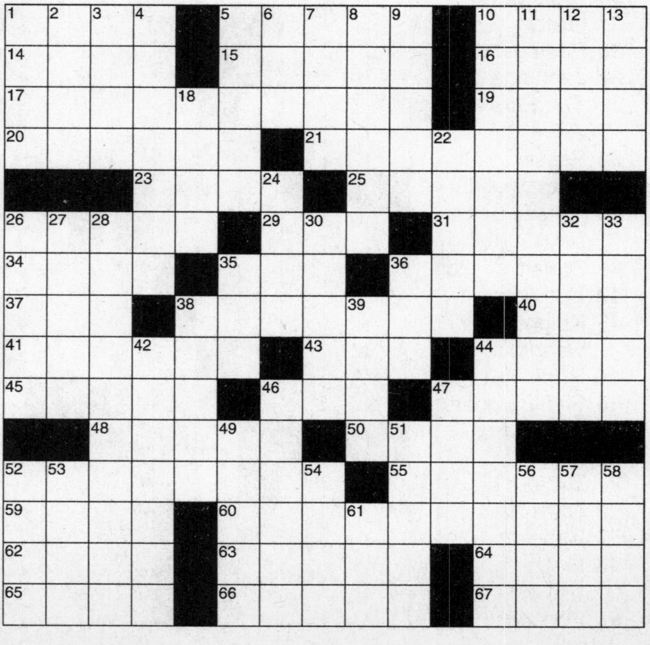

351 INTERNATIONAL GAMES

by Fred Piscop

ACROSS

1 Polite forms of address
6 Cleanser brand
10 Ninnies
14 Cat's-eye relative
15 Paper quantity
16 Prima donna's tune
17 Board game
20 He can put you to sleep
21 New hire, perhaps
22 Singer James
24 Tire features
25 Rio Grande city
29 European coal region
31 Petri-dish stuff
32 Salt, chemically
34 Inventor Howe
39 High-risk game
42 Divs.
43 Wedding-cake part
44 Seward Peninsula city
45 Former Big Apple paper, for short
47 Made reparation
49 *Being and Nothingness* author
53 Sicilian spewer
55 Alexandra, for one
57 Two continents, collectively
62 Strength game
64 Jump
65 __-Contra hearings
66 Quickly, old-style
67 Messes up
68 Seeing things?
69 Rover

DOWN

1 Some Apples
2 Turkish title
3 Not "fer"
4 Obey
5 Appeared to be
6 Commentator Musburger
7 NRC predecessor
8 Bangkok coin
9 Sworn secrecy: It.
10 Comic actor Jack
11 Field of endeavor
12 Shot off
13 Envelope encls.
18 ". . . Muffet __ tuffet . . ."
19 Library cubicle
23 Attribute
25 Cooking fat
26 Fit of chills
27 File type
28 Prefix for while
30 Houseplant
33 Opposed
35 Letterman rival
36 *Blame __ Rio* ('84 film)
37 "Look __!" ("Pay attention!")
38 Tree-to-be
40 Adriatic peninsula
41 Planet discovered in 1781
46 Michael of *The Third Man*
48 Kilt design
49 Subway entrance
50 Grant portrayer
51 Nehi drinker
52 Loses footing
54 Most high-schoolers
56 Off-course
58 Fido fare
59 *The King and I* locale
60 Peruvian of yore
61 Made mellow
63 __ Dawn Chong

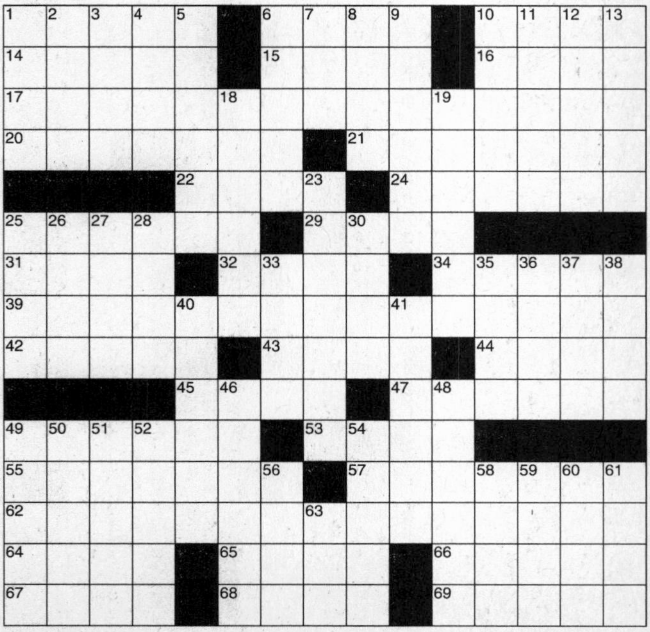

352 PLAYTIME

by Shirley Soloway

ACROSS

1 Jeanne d'__
4 Air attacks
9 Citrus drinks
13 Stinging remark
15 Cook's coverup
16 Ali __
17 Concluded
18 Hidden character flaw
20 Jason's wife
22 Peter or Franco
23 Election winners
24 Loses control
28 Kingly address
29 Bag handles
33 Start of a Latin dance
36 Burdened beasts
39 Potpourri
40 Avoid
44 Brainstorm
45 Beauty establishment
46 However, for short
47 Feathered talker
50 Run off
52 Be cooperative
58 Ecological org.
61 Love, in León
62 __ firma
63 "Get lost!"
67 April forecast
68 Clinton's veep
69 Soviet ruler
70 Normandy town
71 Walk heavily
72 Sidled
73 Inventor Whitney

DOWN

1 Manhattan Project result
2 *Bolero* composer
3 Statement of belief
4 Brit. pilots
5 Imitate
6 Actress Dunne
7 Is overfond
8 Responds derisively
9 Easy as __
10 Spanish surrealist
11 Abba of Israel
12 Utters
14 Makes tea
19 A third of a yard
21 From China
25 Approximately
26 Makes a home
27 Ship's front
30 Landed
31 Solidity
32 London neighborhood
33 Computer element
34 "If I __ Hammer"
35 State as fact
37 The Fabulous '50s, e.g.
38 Germ fighter
41 Crime fighter Wyatt
42 Univ. part
43 Genuflected
48 Oil of __
49 Mexican food
51 Water holders
53 Harnessed
54 Take along
55 Angry
56 Singing style
57 Vietnam's capital
58 Quiche ingredients
59 Mosconi's game
60 '60s hairdo
64 Chicken part
65 Make a knot
66 Finale

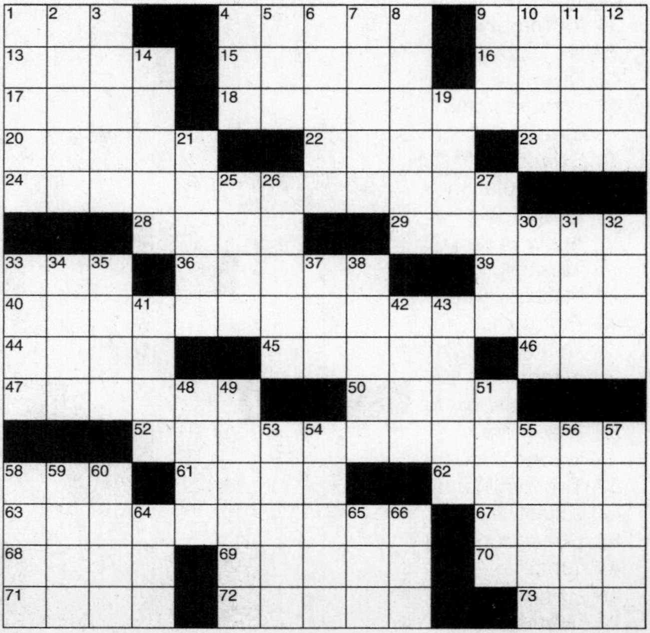

353 FEATHER REPORT

by A.J. Santora

ACROSS

1 Shocked
7 Palindromic name
10 Grassy field
13 Comic Wil
14 Fort __, NJ
15 Co. name add-on
16 Walter Lantz character
19 Rubbing liq.
20 Bk. writer
21 Prefix for dynamics
22 __-do-well
24 "Poetry Man" singer
28 '90s music form
30 Phone sound
31 De-bunk?
33 "__ Fly Now" (*Rocky* theme)
35 Poor grade
38 Grisham bestseller
41 Dawn goddess
42 Court orders
43 Escapades
44 Many eras
45 Superlative suffix
46 DeVito role
52 Basics
55 First-class
56 Namedropper
58 Anger
59 Padres' mascot
64 Part of TNT
65 Caustic solution
66 Most breezy
67 Asner and Ames
68 Moon vehicle, for short
69 Accentuate

DOWN

1 __ *in the Head* (Sinatra film)
2 Supermarket stuff
3 Secreted
4 Writer Seton
5 Gain a monopoly
6 Faithfulness
7 Combine numbers
8 Fall a bit
9 Chopper's tool
10 Compare
11 January in Juarez
12 __ to pick (argumentation)
13 Aquatic bird
17 Exulter's cry
18 In any __ (regardless)
23 Grate
25 Lab burners
26 Cold-war capital
27 Permit
29 Small fry
31 Munched on
32 Greek letter
33 Readying for inspection
34 World Series mo.
35 Motorized cycles
36 "A mouse!"
37 Gee preceders
39 Writer __ Hubbard
40 Tabula __ (clean slate)
44 Impersonated
46 Sample food
47 Stash away
48 Singer Skinnay
49 Service grp.
50 Peru natives
51 Like some Nolan Ryan performances
53 Culinary garnish
54 Mailed
57 Whirring sound
60 Not well
61 CBS logo
62 Treasure
63 Co., in Quebec

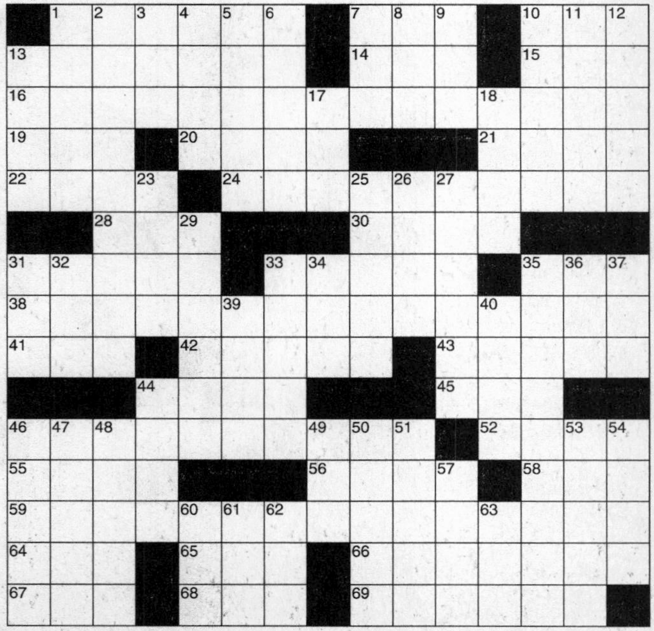

354 MOVIE PEOPLE

by Robert H. Wolfe

ACROSS

1 Humor response
5 Mass ending
9 "I've __ up to here!"
14 Pizzeria need
15 Great review
16 Martini extra
17 Margarita extra
18 George Peppard film of '66
20 Where the money goes
21 __ Antonio, TX
22 Concurrence
23 Plums' kin
25 Cotton thread
27 Plummet
29 "New" prefix
30 Collude in crime
34 Sign of a hit
36 Cosmetic
38 Football coach Don
39 Actress Del Rio
41 Hair dressings
43 Ease
44 Political football
46 __ Plaines, IL
47 Deciding factors
48 Compass pt.
49 Ribald
51 Knight workers
53 African capital
56 They should be respected
60 Tailor of song
62 A lot
63 Eastwood film of '71
65 Jean Stein bestseller
66 Steamed
67 Eye drop
68 Chances
69 Starchy veggie
70 Author Ferber
71 Wall St. org.

DOWN

1 Runs the show
2 Benefit
3 Streisand film of '69
4 Bullwinkle feature
5 They may be liberal
6 Taj __
7 Dark hours
8 Neighbor of 34 Down
9 Blackjacker's opponent
10 Pub potions
11 Thin coin
12 The typical Russian
13 Student's burden
19 Composer Schifrin
24 Rueful
26 Flows in slowly
28 "Annabel Lee" creator
30 "Gotcha!"
31 Lemmon/Matthau film of '81
32 Gen. Robt. __
33 Former Soviet news agency
34 Mt. Rushmore's home
35 Part
37 Taking advantage of
38 Fingerpainter's stroke
40 US alliance
42 __ *Town*
45 Gets mad
48 "Adam had 'em" poet
50 Entrained
51 Snoop
52 Transparent wrap
54 H_2SO_4 and HCl
55 Plural pronoun
56 Computer command
57 One coin in the fountain?
58 "Godfrey Daniels!"
59 Feminine suffix
61 Role for Raquel
64 Eroded

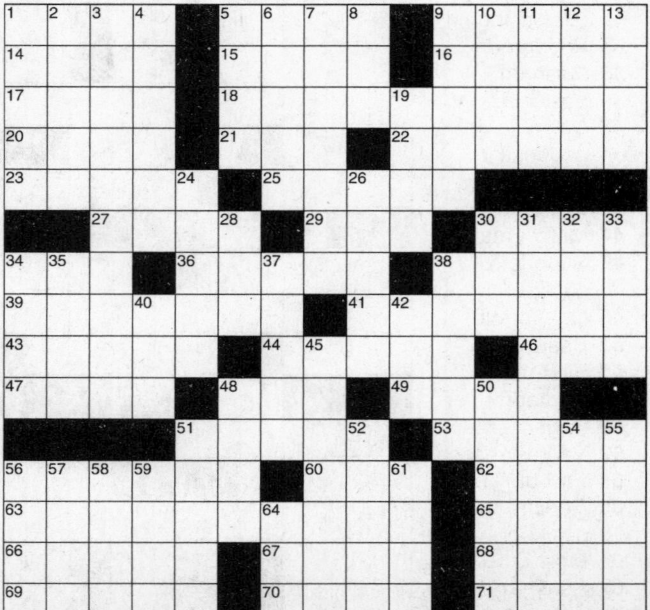

355 MONSTERMEISTERS

by Wayne R. Williams

ACROSS

1 "Non più andrai," e.g.
5 Brown furs
11 "Gotcha!"
14 Remain undecided
15 Folkloric cave dwellers
16 San Francisco hill
17 Author of "The Colour out of Space"
19 Collar
20 Worldwide workers' grp.
21 __ Downs (racetrack)
22 Alluring
23 Peace-loving
25 Broadway figure
28 Superlatively sugary
31 Price ceilings
34 Tuneful Travis
35 Polar region
36 USMC rank
39 Imperial Russian Ballet, today
41 Time remembered
42 Almighty, in Hebrew text
45 White Sea bay
48 Disarm a bull
49 Having a hissing sound
53 Gentle push
55 Flowering shrub
56 Deck officer: Abbr.
58 Buy new weapons
61 Rower's need
62 Nest-egg $$$
63 Author of *Watchers*
66 Greek cross
67 Toxic gas
68 On the briny
69 Pipe shape
70 Planting device
71 Actor Rip

DOWN

1 Garden pests
2 Do a farm job again
3 Smitten
4 Botheration
5 Author of *Cujo*
6 Trajectories
7 One of five in NYC
8 Camel kin
9 Mischievous creature
10 Mach topper
11 Author of *The Mummy*
12 Sham
13 Actress Dalton
18 Hearth goddess
22 Vague amount
24 Comparative ending
26 *The Hellbound Heart* author
27 Muscle spasm
29 "Star Wars" abbr.
30 New guys
32 Old salt
33 Healing waters
36 Frenzied
37 Fruity quaff
38 Author of *Shadows*
40 Sailors' spy grp.
43 Part of speech
44 Difficult, for a Cockney
46 Gadget
47 So. state
50 King in *The Tempest*
51 More cool
52 Jungle hunk
54 Wipe clean
56 Take the bait
57 Preacher Roberts
59 Author Bagnold
60 "Rule Britannia" composer
63 German article
64 Afore
65 Feedbag morsel

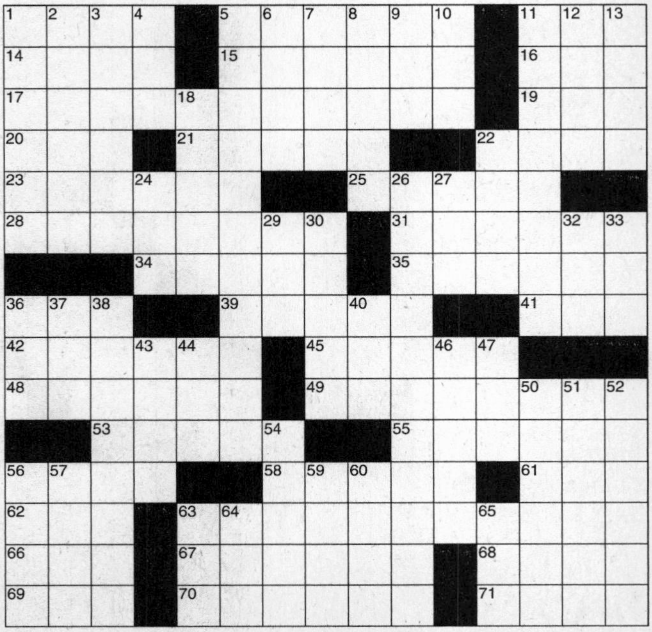

356 FLAG DAY

by Dean Niles

ACROSS
1 Whole bunch
5 Disney deer
10 Squabble
14 Tiny bit
15 Verdi selections
16 Tan-lotion ingredient
17 Lei land
18 Wash cycle
19 Elvis __ Presley
20 Nabokov novel
21 Diversion
23 Author Silverstein
25 Certain curves
26 Guiding light
29 Kerrigan's footwear
32 Bring toward fruition
33 The pokey
34 Rocker Reed
37 Office work
41 Whole bunch
42 Straw in the wind
43 Protection
44 PC operating system
46 The President, sometimes
47 Westminster __
50 *The __ of the Story* (Paul Harvey book)
51 Show prize
55 Maybe, maybe not
59 Michael or Susannah
60 "__-porridge hot"
61 Father
62 Rice drink
63 Composer Erik
64 Baking place
65 Gang ending
66 Different
67 Fishermen's needs

DOWN
1 Fool
2 Monetary advance
3 Needle case
4 Wooden wall lining
5 Unproductive
6 Spirit of *The Tempest*
7 Obey
8 Wild party
9 "Uh-huh"
10 Few and far between
11 The City of Light
12 Have __ to pick (complain)
13 Strong flavors
22 Not active: Abbr.
24 Work on the edge
26 Cry loudly
27 Cavern effect
28 Go __ (contend)
29 Markdowns
30 See 64 Across
31 __ carte
33 Kenyatta of Kenya
34 Corporate identifier
35 Emmy's cousin
36 Gorbachev's realm, once
38 Food fish
39 Charlotte and kin
40 Cast away
44 More compliant
45 Isr. neighbor
46 Surface appearance
47 Bottomless pit
48 Puff up
49 Delta of TV
50 Riveter of WWII
52 __ facto
53 Totally exhausted
54 Shower site
56 Lincoln's bill
57 Stew
58 Urges

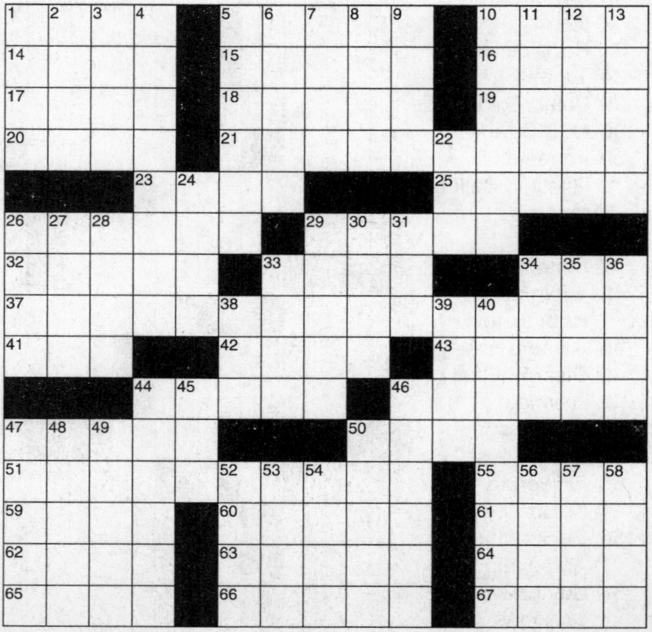

357 SIT ON IT

by Shirley Soloway

ACROSS
1 Actress Ullmann
4 Former Surgeon General
8 Pitching ace Warren
13 Part to play
14 PBS science series
15 ". . . after they've seen __"
16 Object of devotion
17 "The __ Love"
18 Opening bars
19 Court order
22 Miles or Ferguson
23 Largest continent
24 __-mo replay
27 __ about
29 Ed of mystery
31 Ticked off
34 Evening working hours
37 In its present condition
39 Bud's sidekick
40 *Pretty Woman* star
41 Meeting conductor
46 Matched pieces
47 Actor Michael
48 Russian despot
50 Miner's discovery
51 Sonja Henie's birthplace
54 Move furtively
57 Informers
60 Outpouring
63 Pertaining to lyric poetry
64 Mr. Kringle
65 Famous fur merchant
66 Put on the market
67 Comical Kett
68 Nerds
69 Perry's penner
70 German article

DOWN
1 Sources of 50 Across
2 Massey of films
3 Fastening material
4 Smarts
5 Mrs. Chaplin
6 __ barrel (helpless)
7 Twosomes
8 Popeye's power source
9 Hyperventilate
10 Sculpture, for one
11 That girl
12 Prefix for "new"
13 Barbequed bone
20 Fictional Brinker
21 Points at the target
24 Cash keepers
25 Liquid measure, in London
26 Beginning
28 Exasperate
30 Tom Hanks film
31 Very large in scope
32 *My Name Is __ Lev*
33 Ms. Keaton
35 Negative conjunction
36 Surge of wind
38 Transgression
42 Some mob members
43 Mexican money
44 Small bone
45 Da __, Vietnam
49 Smelled bad
52 Untied
53 More mature
55 Main artery
56 Makes a muffler
57 Corner sign
58 Caplet, e.g.
59 Entitlement org.
60 Observed
61 Greek letter
62 24-hr. banking aid

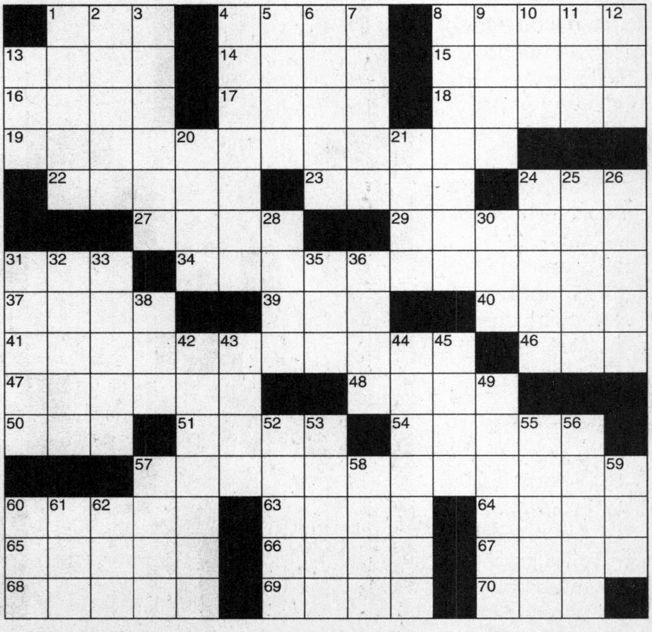

358 DUTCH TREAT

by Bob Lubbers

ACROSS
1 Floral oil
6 Big bash
10 Ore source
14 Cook onions
15 In the sack
16 Over again
17 Metric weights, for short
18 Former Netherlands inlet
20 Pointless
22 Church officers
23 African antelope
25 Taj Mahal site
27 Sent a wire
28 Gave
33 Grounded bird
34 Novelist Anya
36 Went by burro
37 Physically fit
39 Incites anger
41 Cereal holder
42 Elapse
43 Anglers' awakeners
45 Modern recording syst.
46 Hearts of the matter
49 Dancing Chita
51 Courtroom recitation
52 Makes powdery
53 Flight segments
57 Editor's marks
58 Things to tilt at
61 __ *Majesty's Secret Service* ('69 film)
64 Pedestal percher
65 Verne's captain
66 __ ear and out the other
67 Kelly or Hackman
68 Has
69 Wanting

DOWN
1 "__ not what your country . . ."
2 Mai __ (cocktail)
3 Spring sprouters
4 Keyless
5 Used-car deals
6 Stare
7 __ Dhabi
8 Aloha gift
9 Poisonous snakes
10 Animal fat
11 11, in France
12 Forest forager
13 Maa belles?
19 Aqaba port
21 Consumer advocate Ralph
23 Glacial epoch
24 Ballroom dances
25 Do away with
26 *The Maids* playwright
29 Sphere
30 Wynken and Blynken's boat
31 __ *Scissorhands*
32 River features
35 Shangri-La setting
38 Center of a hurricane
40 Lint-grabbing material
44 Steak cut
47 Comedian Crosby
48 Bettors' mecca
50 River to the Loire
53 Canteen mouthful
54 Neap or spring
55 Unknown auth.
56 Sit in neutral
57 Mil. decorations
59 *Ben-Hur* author Wallace
60 K-O link
62 Wind up
63 *The Bridge of San Luis __*

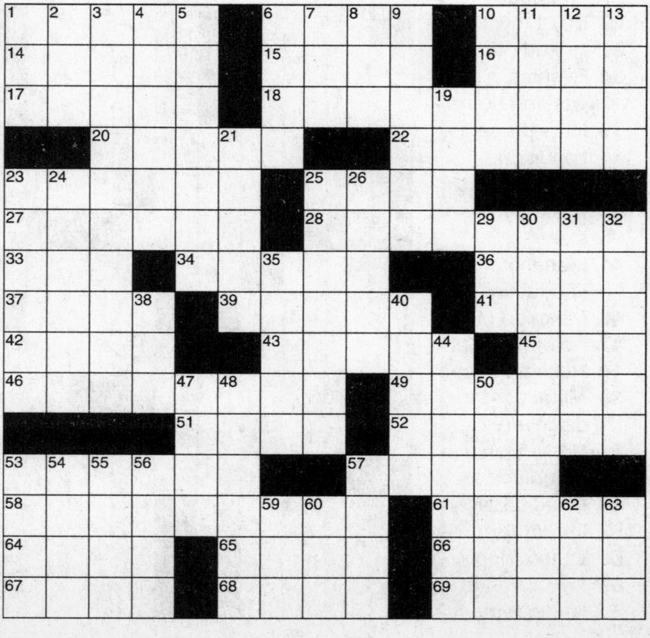

359 *BLOW ME DOWN!*

by Fred Piscop

ACROSS

1 Slider, e.g.
6 Thom of shoedom
10 Designer Picone
14 Courtyards
15 Florence's river
16 Italian island resort
17 Coney Island coaster
19 School founded in 1440
20 Gram or decimal starter
21 Word form for "ear"
22 Wash basin
24 Vietnamese seaport
27 Retail transactions
28 Comic Chuck
31 Take five
33 In favor of
34 Conical abodes
37 "__ the ramparts . . ."
40 Boxer in a Dylan song
44 Last letter
45 Miniature mint
46 Drivers' org.
47 Former member of the UN
49 Mortar mate
51 Chief Justice, 1941-46
54 Most prudent
57 Marquee word
59 Martial-arts legend Bruce
60 The Beatles' "__ Love Her"
64 Way out
65 Chicago Bears great
68 "Have a __ day!"
69 Fed. agent
70 Composer Ned
71 Change for a five
72 Yemeni capital
73 Covered with white stuff

DOWN

1 Bike lane
2 Spillane's __ *Jury*
3 Dinosaur, for short
4 Noisy insect
5 "That ain't __!"
6 Island nation
7 Emulate Bing
8 Abby's twin
9 Mr. Coward
10 Otis invention
11 Like some statistics
12 Sun-dried brick
13 Verboten items
18 Hooks up
23 Silly person
25 Opposed to
26 Say "hi" to
28 Tach abbr.
29 Santa __, CA
30 Apple throwaway
32 Prison-wall jumpers
35 Noah's passengers
36 Business letter abbr.
38 Coup d'__
39 Not imaginary
41 Brings together again
42 Holes-in-one
43 Comic Charlotte
48 Prepare the table
50 Leave later
51 Office worker
52 Antidote target
53 In reserve
55 Edgar __ Poe
56 Actress Davis
58 *Green __ and Ham*
61 Cruel ruler
62 Took a card
63 *God __ Co-Pilot*
66 G.P. grp.
67 __ Gratia Artis

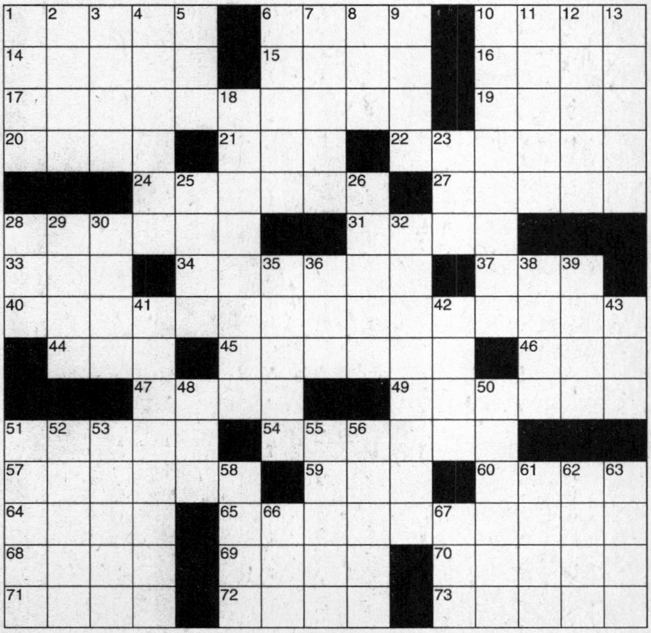

360 COLORFUL STATIONERY

by Harvey Estes

ACROSS

1 Church area
5 *Cabaret* singer
9 G-sharp's alias
14 Beethoven's birthplace
15 Eye part
16 Sister's girl
17 Bachelor's pride
19 Bride's follower
20 Sea life
21 Compass dir.
22 Goes on one's way
23 Denver clock setting: Abbr.
25 Rub a blade on stone
27 Circus swings
32 Boo-boo list
36 "__ Master's Voice"
37 Phone-book section
39 Follower of John
41 *Cheers* role
42 Beseech
43 Government reports
48 Poetic preposition
49 Shawl for a señor
50 Most cobra-infested
52 Truth stretcher
54 Racket
55 Produces 34 Down
58 __ in apple
61 "Last of the Red Hot __" (Sophie Tucker)
65 Sneeze sound
66 Schematic
68 Correct
69 Cosby show
70 *Beetle Bailey* barker
71 "Walk Away __"
72 Measure of medicine
73 Produce 34 Down

DOWN

1 Eban of Israel
2 Roper report
3 Fly in the ointment
4 Pitch a tent
5 Ad __ (wing it)
6 Wedge or niblick
7 National park in Utah
8 Out of whack
9 Belgian city
10 Tinderbox
11 Tilt
12 Etching liquid
13 Perfect diving scores
18 Author Ken
24 __-kung (Chinese city)
26 Use an ax
27 Goes soft
28 Nouveau __
29 Up and about
30 *Born Free* name
31 Hits open-handed
33 See eye to eye
34 Eye drops?
35 So far
38 Portentous sign
40 He's had a Rocky career
44 Part of a serial
45 Soup ingredient
46 Totally awesome
47 Cut corners
51 Straight
53 Like a mad dog
55 Boxer Max
56 Highest point
57 "__ in Rome . . ."
59 Too
60 Has an evening meal
62 Bit
63 Penny, often
64 Word on an octagon
67 Needle hole

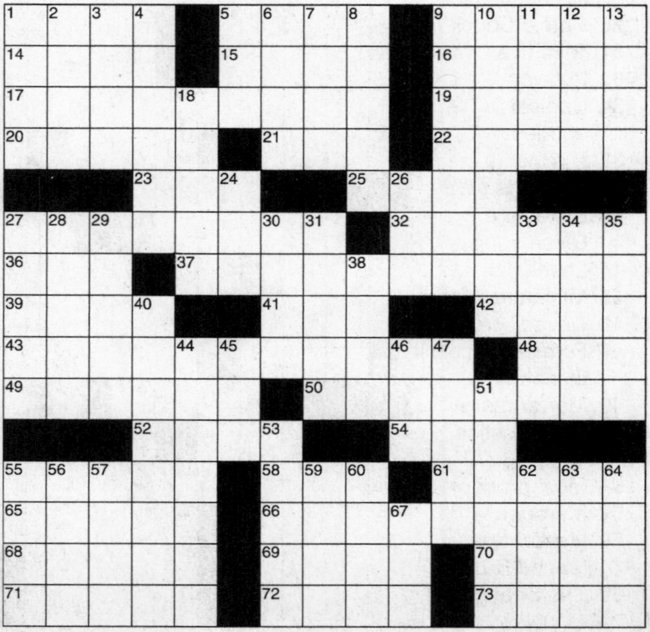

361 HIGH STEPPIN'

by Shirley Soloway

ACROSS

1 Mold
6 FDR's pet
10 Kuwait native
14 Kid around with
15 Eddie or Richard
16 Ward of *Sisters*
17 Together (with)
18 Broadway light
19 Look over
20 Evades the issue
23 Takes one's leave
24 Finery
25 Pet tenders
29 Sandy substance
31 Possessing talent
32 Fire residue
33 Cereal grain
36 One isn't enough
41 Compass pt.
42 Roundish
43 Frozen desserts
44 Actress Meg
45 Without purpose
48 French farewell
51 As well
52 Completing easily
59 "Thanks __!"
60 Challenge
61 Courtyards
62 Nevada city
63 Concluded
64 Get to work
65 Actress Cannon
66 Majors and Marvin
67 Flies alone

DOWN

1 Mild argument
2 Luau entertainment
3 Surmounting
4 Toad abode
5 Hire
6 Real-estate markers
7 Tommie and James
8 Cambodia's neighbor
9 "Getting to Know You" singer
10 Classify
11 Happen again
12 __-Dale
13 Toss back and forth
21 Partner of neither
22 Singer Bonnie
25 Destiny
26 Abba of Israel
27 Actress Sommer
28 Poor grade
29 Obtained
30 Aussie jumper
32 Impresario Hurok
33 Fairy tale opener
34 Stone, Bronze, and Iron
35 Pitch
37 Soviet spaceship
38 Hydroelectric agcy.
39 Pale-faced
40 Feel under the weather
44 Gymnast Mary Lou
45 Makes changes to
46 __ Kabibble
47 Swampy place
48 Oscar or Tony
49 Chicago mayor Richard
50 Massey of the movies
51 Match up
53 Adored one
54 Church area
55 Director Preminger
56 Russian range
57 Copter relative
58 Head warmers

362 CAMERA READY

by Dean Niles

ACROSS

1 Open one's big mouth
5 __ at (deride)
10 Biblical sufferer
13 Lord over
14 "Horrible" comics character
15 One of Hamlet's options
16 In a short time
17 Jane Curtin role
18 Hold back
19 38 Across' Oscar winner
22 1953 Alan Ladd western
23 Con job
24 Biological group
28 Not too swift
32 Letter writer's addenda: Abbr.
35 Russian range
37 Let up
38 Hollywood heavyweight
42 TV comic Bob
43 Church recess
44 Ruby or Sandra
45 Like some novels
47 Historic Crimean city
50 Slapstick projectiles
52 Intentional conflagration
56 Film directed by 38 Across
61 '60s musical
62 Relocation specialist
63 Celtic language
64 Chops down
65 Nitrogen compound
66 Root cause
67 Between, to Browning
68 Central points
69 Retton's scores

DOWN

1 Copper-zinc alloy
2 Out to __ (inattentive)
3 Islands hello
4 Actress Annette
5 Herring kin
6 Use the phone
7 Give the eye
8 County occasions
9 Painting on plaster
10 Louis and Frazier
11 Newspaper notice
12 Painter Shahn
15 Airplane stabilizer
20 Maiden-name preceder
21 Tag
25 *Sister Act* extra
26 Sky bear
27 Mawkish
29 Took advantage of
30 Desiccated
31 Boundary
32 "Hey, you!"
33 __-crossed (ill-fated)
34 __ Genesis (Nintendo rival)
36 Actress Hartman
39 Evening service
40 Moral value
41 Slippery one
46 Naval petty officer
48 Greek cross
49 Put a stop to
51 Replay effect
53 Wild time
54 Merlin or Ole
55 Craves
56 Hirsch sitcom
57 Sped
58 *Metamorphoses* poet
59 M. Descartes
60 CEO, often
61 Overdoer of a sort

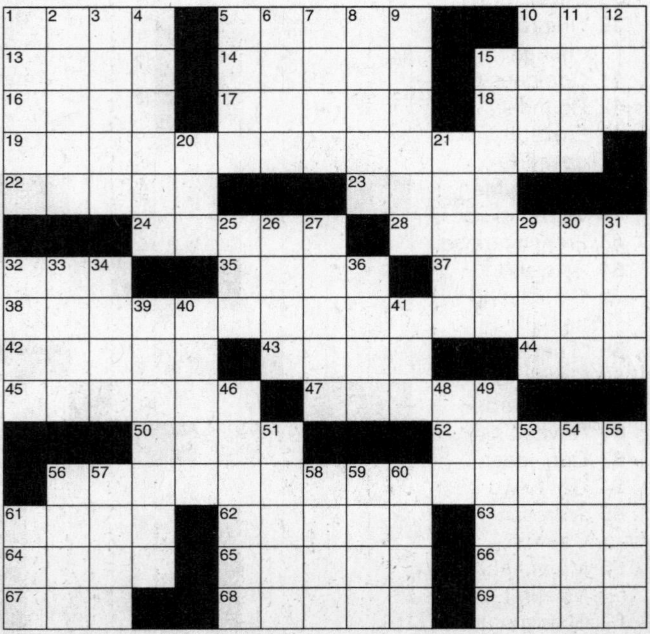

363 *OINK SPOTS*

by Robert Herrig

ACROSS
1 Anna's adopted land
5 "Big" burger
8 Plummeted
12 Small land mass
13 Nasty habits
15 Surface size
16 Market patron of rhyme
19 Calendar column heading
20 Nuptial site
21 Knack
24 Tart-tasting
25 Family MDs
28 Italian instrument
30 Rogue
32 Strauss of jeans
33 Plumber's joints
36 Standish's stand-in
37 Ozarkian grunters
40 Better fit
41 Shirley Temple's first husband
42 Senior member
44 Sentra maker
46 In accordance with truth
48 Expert
49 __ + tissue = makeshift kazoo
52 Rope loops
53 *Zoo Story* playwright
54 Econ. calculation
55 Storied homebuilders
62 Rock musical
63 Result
64 Daredevil Knievel
65 Fire man?
66 Spud sprout
67 Depend

DOWN
1 Command to Beethoven
2 Sort of a suffix?
3 "The Greatest"
4 Entrances
5 Cambridge coll.
6 Take the role of
7 Casals' instrument
8 Cloudless
9 Little bit of work
10 Hose filler
11 Install carpeting
13 Port authority?
14 Delivery extra
17 Actress Anderson
18 Avoided one
21 "My mama done __ me . . ."
22 Bitterly harsh
23 Ravel work
25 Kitchen wonders
26 Before the auction
27 Junior, for one
29 Goya patron
31 Heavy shoe
34 Fall behind
35 Lasting impression
38 Clairvoyant
39 Santa's alias
40 Trivia collection
43 Gov. Pataki's territory
45 __ *House* (Clavell epic)
47 Vanished
50 Potsdam possessive
51 Ms. Ross
53 Pertaining to planes
55 Article
56 Falstaff's pal
57 Periphery
58 Follower of 19 Across
59 I have shrunk?
60 Toothpaste type
61 Arch

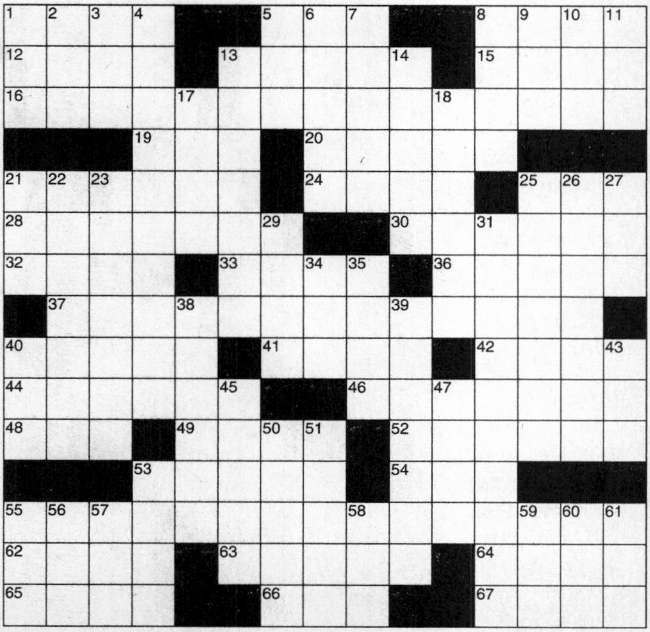

364 AYE-AYE

by Shirley Soloway

ACROSS
1 Nonsense
5 Skiers' transport
9 Asian desert
13 Art Deco artist
14 Former Attorney General Janet
15 Bodybuilder, perhaps
16 All over
17 Singer Anita
18 Prayer endings
19 Winter Olympics event
22 Aves.
23 Alias initials
24 Coffeemaker
25 Midwest Native Americans
31 Sign up
34 Dorothy's pet
35 __ Abner
36 Egg on
37 Animator Barbera's partner
39 Logical
40 Supply with weapons
41 __ Alto, CA
42 Stitch over again
43 Capital of Campania
47 Court divider
48 Short snooze
49 Skater Babilonia
52 Maui, for one
57 Turner and namesakes
58 Wise __ owl
59 __ time (never)
60 Pack away
61 Shade of green
62 Accessory for Salome
63 Take care of
64 Rude reply
65 Mars, to the Greeks

DOWN
1 Wampum units
2 "Ready __!"
3 Hearty entrees
4 Chopped down
5 Russian wagon
6 State of wild confusion
7 Job for a psych.
8 Rogers and Clark
9 Astrological sign
10 Portent
11 Loud sound
12 Election winners
15 Coiffure
20 Signal a cab
21 __ Kinte (*Roots* role)
25 Hip
26 "Let __ be said . . ."
27 Charged particle
28 Word of woe
29 Mid-evening
30 Did in
31 Actor Richard
32 Asta's mistress
33 Incline
37 Caribbean nation
38 Ring champ
39 Baltic or Bering
41 Make happy
42 Tears
44 Ahead
45 Historical records
46 Frankie and Cleo
49 Spud
50 Warbucks' charge
51 Role models
52 Abhor
53 In a while
54 Fleming and Paisley
55 Europe's neighbor
56 Volcanic flow
57 Mil. vehicle

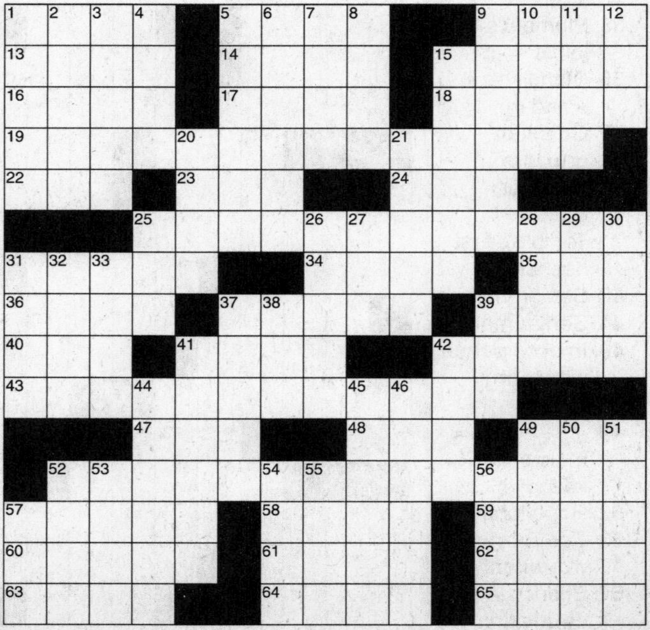

365 ON THE DIAL

by Sally R. Stein

ACROSS

1 Tree branch
5 Showed fear
10 "Okey-__!"
14 Where Laos is
15 "__ a stinker?"
16 Andy's pal
17 Misfortunes
18 Sports data
19 Runners of song
20 Superman's dressing room
23 Bearing
24 Coffee vessel
25 Goes along
28 Compass point, in Paris
30 Mail-order regulators: Abbr.
33 Breakfast food
34 Bull or Bullwinkle
35 Seatless state, initially
36 Wheeler-dealer
40 Tune from *A Chorus Line*
41 Claude of *Casablanca*
42 Be overfond
43 QB's scores
44 Mean monster
45 Bowler's prize
47 Abby's sister
48 Burn a bit
49 Digital exercise book?
56 Mardi __
57 Jeweled headband
58 Party cheese
59 Greek liqueur
60 Tube preceder
61 Singular
62 Road Runner's syllable
63 Slide downhill
64 Water jug

DOWN

1 Café au __
2 South Seas site
3 Steel factory
4 Last place, figuratively
5 Military bands?
6 Discover, as an idea
7 __ uproar
8 Minimizing suffix
9 Pay out
10 Pythias' pal
11 Forget to include
12 Former mayor of New York
13 180 degrees from WNW
21 Missile for Soupy Sales
22 Waiter's request
25 Monastery man
26 Monotony
27 Goes ape
28 Not a soul
29 Klutz's remark
30 Lens setting
31 Promise to marry
32 Nutty professor Irwin __
34 Former Israeli prime minister
37 Literary twist
38 Rife with charisma
39 Darn cute
45 Ruin someone's plans
46 Culpability
47 Old-time storyteller
48 Apple trash
49 Multiple-choice answer
50 Morning weather
51 Floor covering, for short
52 Turner around Hollywood
53 Shoot up
54 __ *kleine Nachtmusik*
55 Future examiner
56 Sea dog

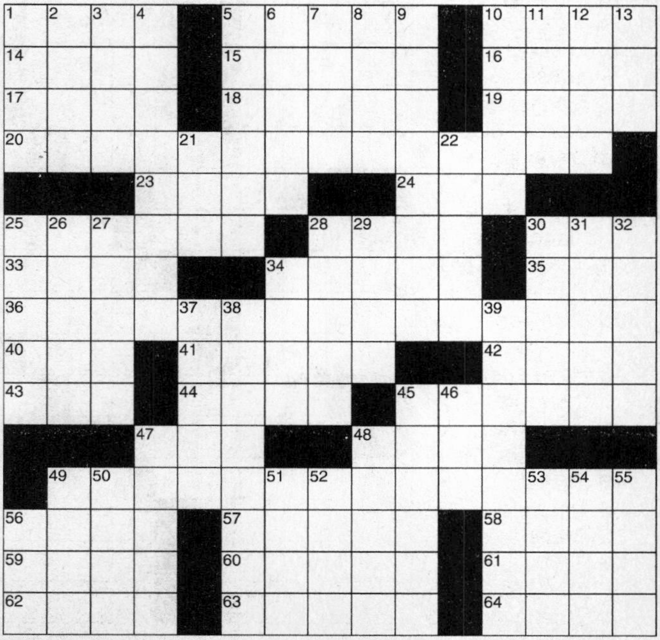

366 TAKE THE PLUNGE

by Shirley Soloway

ACROSS
1 Bread unit
5 Lord's mate
9 John or Don
14 Swedish pop group
15 The Emerald Isle
16 Rocker David
17 Christmas carol
18 Fusses
19 1984 Kentucky Derby winner
20 The farmer's milieu
21 Short snooze
22 Submerged, as a doughnut
23 Lyric poem
25 Car part
27 Had a yen for
30 Surpass
31 Sanctuary
32 Lockhart of *Lassie*
33 Ski-lift feature
37 Baker's aide
38 Dove shelters
39 Sharpen
40 Peter of the piano
41 Wedding words
42 Hammer parts
43 "__ I can help it!"
45 Have second thoughts
46 Wigwams
48 Corn serving
49 Partial
50 Doctrine
52 Brewer's oven
56 Adjust
57 *The African Queen* writer
58 Arm bone
59 __ Rogers St. Johns
60 Herring
61 Lunchtime for some
62 Feudal workers
63 Give it __
64 Names, as a knight

DOWN
1 Touch down
2 Woodwind instrument
3 Cain's brother
4 Be excessively eager
5 Stood (against)
6 Verdi work
7 Disappears
8 Word of agreement
9 Ridiculous
10 Completely
11 Up and about
12 Bannister or Ryun
13 Burpee offering
22 Sees socially
24 Lion's lair
26 Melodies
27 Beard locale
28 Competition
29 State with conviction
32 Foster of *Maverick*
34 Certain South African
35 Bancroft or Boleyn
36 Musical pause
38 Referred to
42 Soup veggie
44 6 Down and others
45 Cure
46 Spanish mark
47 Refrige-raider
49 Sheep sounds
51 Seal in the juices
53 Baseball manager Felipe
54 Snooty one
55 Takes the sun
57 Cool __ cucumber

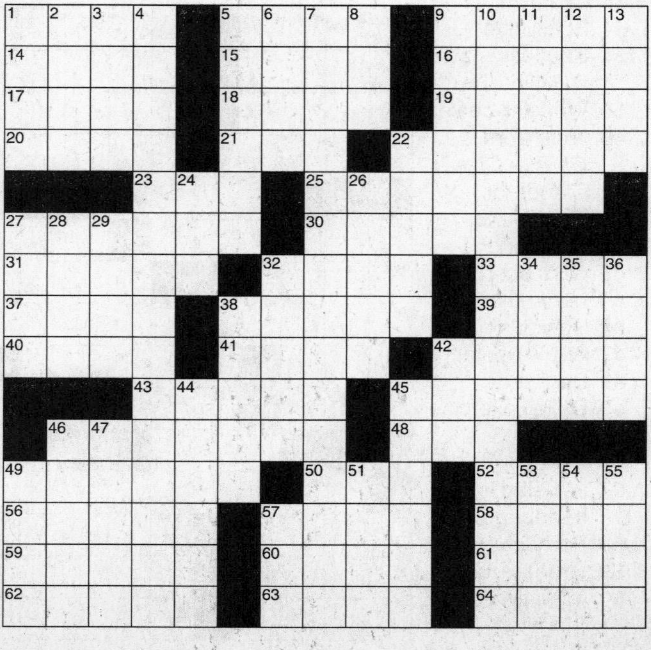

367 YOUR HIT PARADE

by Bob Lubbers

ACROSS
1 Aunts: Sp.
5 Entice
9 After-shower wraps
14 Author Rice
15 Vicinity
16 Parriers' needs
17 Needle
19 Snitches (on)
20 Captivate
21 Holy one
23 Not as much
26 West Point freshmen
29 "Who's on first?" asker
33 Draw a new line
34 Tense, slangily
35 Had a pain
37 Crow call
38 Very dry
39 Polynesian carvings
40 __ terrier
41 Luau dip
42 Wove a chair seat
43 1040 submitter
44 Evelyn of *The Wolf Man*
46 Longing ones
48 Country singer Jim
49 Perry's creator
50 Tag, bridge, etc.
52 __ de corps
57 Word form for "red"
59 Joke ending
62 Greek physician
63 Estrada or Satie
64 Shoppe descriptor
65 Libyan gulf
66 Eugene V. __
67 Unskilled laborer

DOWN
1 Recording medium
2 Privy to
3 Singer Paul
4 Appear to be
5 Partner of Hardy
6 Coffee maker
7 Stephen of *Angie*
8 Diner sign
9 Redid the bathroom, perhaps
10 First game of a series
11 Clasp of a sort
12 Wriggly fish
13 Draft grp.
18 Former House Speaker
22 After: Fr.
24 Done in
25 Kind of salmon
27 Ionospheric region
28 Underground ducts
29 One of the Magi
30 Nine-__ (emergency number)
31 Succeed
32 Mao __-tung
36 Escapee, maybe
39 Cup, in Calais
40 Envy or sloth, e.g.
42 Amati's hometown
43 Sassy
45 Tax cheat, perhaps
47 Smart __ (wise guys)
51 Went too fast
53 Drip sound
54 Steam up
55 __-European
56 College freshman, usually
57 Football linemen: Abbr.
58 "Bali __"
60 Ending for press
61 Penpoint

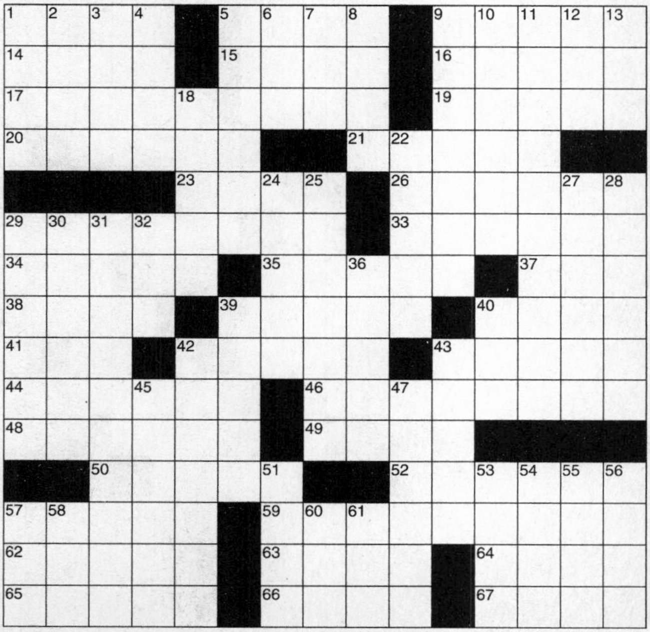

368 *INITIAL REACTION*

by Ray Smith

ACROSS

1 *I Remember* __
5 Toddlers
10 Does sums
14 Desertlike
15 "__ of robins"
16 Dull sound
17 Short sprint
18 Tobacco manufacturer
20 Never-captured hijacker
22 Turner and Cantrell
23 Not van. or straw.
24 Tendon
25 Campaign '64 letters
28 Pre-cable need
30 Cincinnati baseballer
33 Commands
35 Make a hole
36 Toy-block brand
37 Costume jewelry
38 Pepper or York: Abbr.
39 Dance that "takes two"
40 Perón and Gabor
41 Actor's prompt
42 Relief
43 Our sun
44 Stogie
46 USNA grad
47 Wight and Capri
49 Learning method
51 Put in a chip
52 Former Giants quarterback
56 Tire magnate
58 Signal (a cab)
59 Hurler Hershiser
60 Fruit for cider or sauce
61 Miss Fitzgerald
62 Put to sleep?
63 *The Sun Also* __
64 Curb

DOWN

1 Road-safety org.
2 Saudi, for one
3 Catchall abbr.
4 Kind of committee
5 Florida game fish
6 Inoculate
7 Deborah or Jean
8 Language suffix
9 Teasing, as hair
10 Make up (for)
11 *Sons and Lovers* author
12 Lemons
13 '60s campus grp.
19 *Peter Pan* dog
21 Busy airport
24 Testy state
25 Easy strides
26 Theater cheer
27 Holden Caulfield's creator
29 Gardening tool
31 Prod
32 Portals
34 ALF et al.
36 Fond du __, WI
38 Brings to court
39 __-frutti ice cream
41 Aged yellow cheese
42 Comforts
44 Role for Liz
45 Seer
48 Fur wrap
50 Anesthetic
51 Bushy hairdo
52 Kennel sounds
53 Yarn
54 "__ Marlene" (WWI song)
55 Enthusiasm
56 Newhart or Cousy
57 Troy, NY, coll.

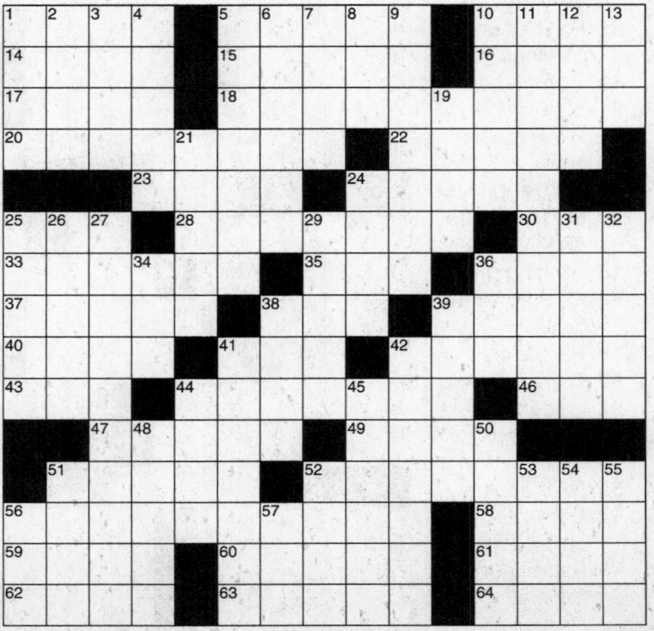

369 DISNEY WORLD

by S.N.

ACROSS
1 Impassive
6 G.P.'s grp.
9 Big shot
14 *Your Show of Shows* host
16 Political event
17 Disney's first sound cartoon: 1928
19 The "white" in Great White Way
20 Curved letter
21 Variety show VIPs
24 Joplin creation
25 Deep black
26 Mid.
29 This __ (choice words)
31 Beat walker
32 Kingston, e.g.
33 Ricochet
34 Temporary
36 Best Song Oscar recipient: 1947
38 Marginalia
39 "Ditto!"
41 Donna or Robert
42 Shaving-cream type
43 Dressy hat
44 Fed. collectors
45 Driller's deg.
46 Noticed
47 Ward healers?
48 Large lake
49 Epithet for Earl Hines
51 With *The*, TV series: 1955-59
58 Foul-smelling
59 Rake over the coals
60 Drudges
61 Penultimate letter
62 Like knives

DOWN
1 Draft org.
2 __ for tat
3 Shelley opus
4 "__ See Clearly Now"
5 Film-crew member
6 "With __ in My Heart"
7 Lea sounds
8 Illustration
9 Watch place for many
10 Haarlem painter
11 Plumber's piece
12 Yalie
13 Soap ingredient
15 PT's opposite number
18 "__ more, my lady . . ."
21 Summer shoe, for short
22 More wacko
23 Walks broadly
25 Steinbeck family
26 Disney, vis-á-vis 17 Across
27 Small-time
28 Decay
30 Trusted
31 Angler's need
32 __ over (saw through difficulty)
34 French noodles?
35 *West Side Story* tune
37 __ *Afternoon* (Pacino film)
38 __ Lanka
40 W. Hemisphere alliance
43 Dom DeLuise movie of '80
45 Exploits
46 Pasta topping
48 Wiener covering
49 Arch
50 Sulfuric or carbolic
51 Work by Mercator
52 Cola cooler
53 __-Magnon
54 Kittenish remark
55 Fall behind
56 Western Indian
57 Murphy, for one

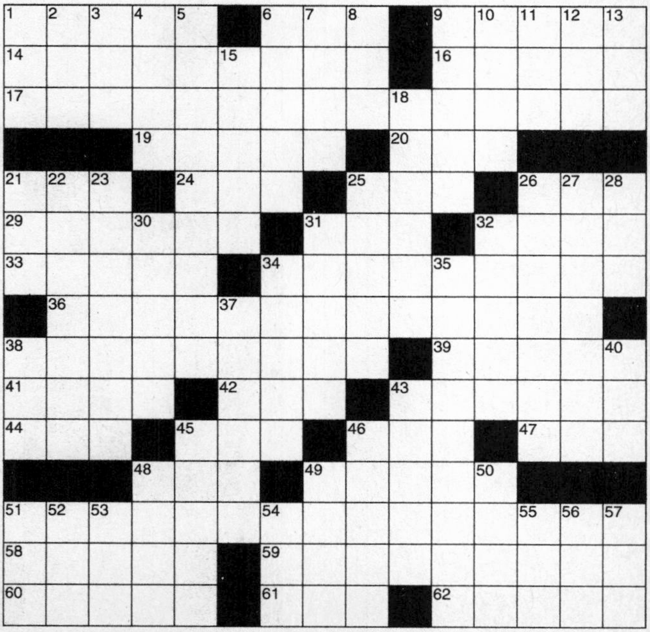

370 WILD WEST

by Deborah Martin

ACROSS

1 Quite bright
6 Commercial creator
11 Wager
14 Thespian
15 Idaho's capital
16 Midwest Indian
17 Western desperado
19 Government agcy.
20 "Michael, Row Your Boat __"
21 From a distance
22 Gregorian singers
25 Heathens
27 Glove insert
28 Spot for a boutonniere
29 Coffeepot
30 Ozzie and Harriet
34 __ *Yeller*
37 Three: Pref.
38 Superimpose
39 Spelling contest
40 Give the __ (ogle)
41 Madmen
42 "__ Got a Crush on You"
43 Forebodings
45 Toboggan
46 Hears (of)
48 Peter and Paul
52 Vessels
53 Topnotch
54 Nev. neighbor
55 He rode with Jesse James
60 Compass dir.
61 Solo
62 Frightening
63 Susan of *L.A. Law*
64 Preclude
65 Marsh plant

DOWN

1 Day of rest: Abbr.
2 Sprint competitor
3 Part of NATO
4 *Chanson de __*
5 Assignation
6 Loathe
7 Movers and shakers
8 Newsman Wallace
9 "__ was saying . . ."
10 Actor Beatty
11 Wild West Show organizer
12 __ *Frome*
13 Rips
18 Useful article
21 Ripen
22 Skydiver's need, for short
23 Ike's predecessor
24 Western markswoman
25 Lose control
26 Church areas
28 Singer Falana
30 "__ allowed" (ladies only)
31 Cowgirl Dale
32 Camera part
33 __ Lanka
35 River embankment
36 Property titles
44 *The Ghost and __ Muir*
45 Point of view
46 Spiked, as punch
47 Wipe out
48 Stadium
49 He treats
50 Meter preceder
51 Children's-book pseudonym
53 Clump
55 Scoundrel
56 Bullfight cheer
57 Wander
58 Unit of work
59 Deli bread

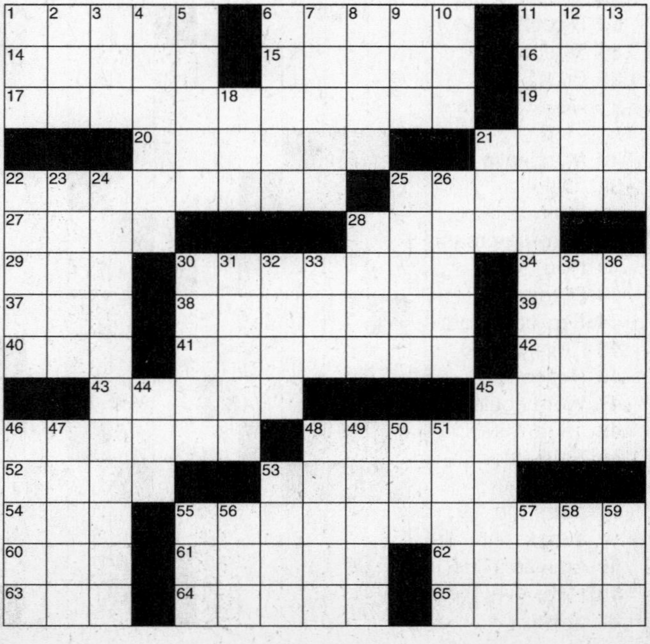

371 WASH DAY

by Dean Niles

ACROSS

1 Some saxes
6 Futures exchange, for short
10 Word of relief
14 Deception
15 Unexciting
16 Past the deadline
17 Certain line segments
18 He loved an Irish Rose
19 Pilaster
20 __ kind (unique)
22 Ornamental flower
24 One's salary, to an accountant
26 Vitamin stats.
27 Tied up
29 __ Cruces, NM
30 Voice origin
34 __ Kabibble
35 "For shame!"
36 Plead
37 Poet's eternity
38 "Agnus __"
39 Salt's response
40 Oscar-winning composer Francis __
41 Span. lady
42 Work unit
43 Mil. branch
44 Bustle
45 Green climber
46 Top type
48 Gold source
49 Grant and Madigan
50 Litigate against
51 North African
53 Send along
57 Most definite
60 Desire
61 It's easy
63 Climbing vine
64 Former Atlanta arena
65 Author Godwin
66 Stevedore, e.g.
67 Dick and Jane's dog
68 __ account
69 More wily

DOWN

1 Frizzy top
2 Director David
3 Blondie song
4 Spicy, in a way
5 Unyielding
6 Grad. degree
7 Pushes aside
8 Train track
9 Sidelines yellers
10 2-D
11 It's given in marriage
12 Suffix for kitchen
13 Put on
21 Encouraging words
23 Slow tempo
25 Of a hard wood
27 Basinlike fixture
28 Those who partake
31 Song of '65
32 Brash
33 Medical photos
35 Ford model
36 Racket
47 "__ Romantic?"
48 Garner
49 Auto appendage
52 Chicago cagers
53 Pairs
54 Slanting surface
55 __ Domini
56 __ uproar
58 Snicker-__
59 Region: Abbr.
62 Arafat grp.

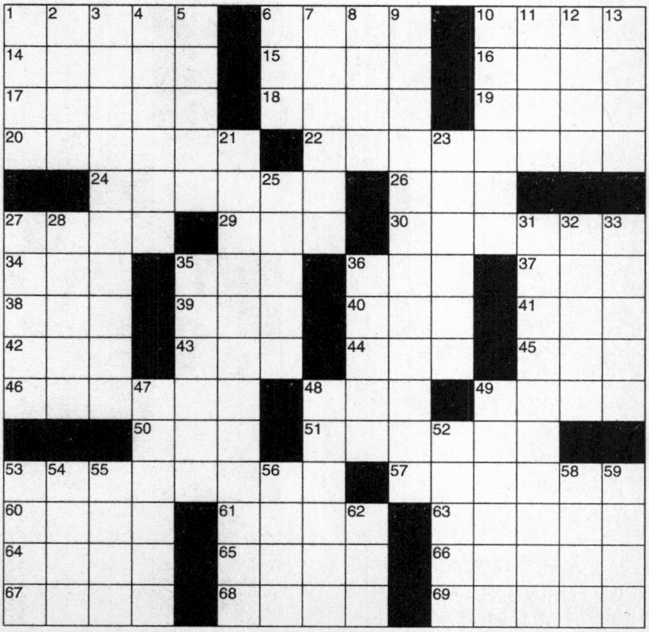

372 BE A DEER

by Shirley Soloway

ACROSS
1 Rum cakes
6 Lettuce relative
10 A long way off
14 Make happy
15 Nutritional need
16 Pasternak heroine
17 "He's somebody __ problem . . ." (L. Hart lyric)
18 "Bye!"
19 Do the backstroke
20 Shift blame
23 Short snooze
24 "When I Take My Sugar __"
25 British weapons
27 Smart
30 Madrid missus
33 Crack pilot
36 Jamie of *M*A*S*H*
38 At no time
39 Linden or Holbrook
40 "Get lost!"
42 N.Y. zone in August
43 Leg joint
45 Simplicity
46 Rogers or Clark
47 Command
49 John __ Garner
52 Cowboy flick
54 Things to be done
57 Comedian Erwin
59 Prenuptial get-togethers
63 Salad fish
65 "__ Clock Jump"
66 Capable
67 Remnants
68 Wimpy one
69 Fur-bearing swimmer
70 Intertwine
71 Gets the point
72 Jury members

DOWN
1 Electronic sound
2 __ sea (confused)
3 Opera singer
4 Bikini events
5 Six-line verse
6 Franklin's flyer
7 Part of UAR
8 Water lily
9 Passes, as a bill
10 Hirt and Pacino
11 Dotes on
12 Diva's solo
13 Incline
21 Israeli metropolis
22 New Hampshire city
26 Map dir.
28 Identify
29 React to a bad joke
31 Make over
32 Affected
33 Moby Dick captain
34 Sugar source
35 Norwegian canines
37 Madame __ (Signoret film)
40 Sleeveless jackets
41 "I __ Letter to My Love"
44 Actress Thompson
48 Wyoming range
50 Drive-in employee
51 House and grounds
53 Hindu queen
55 Kunta __ of *Roots*
56 Passover dinner
57 Flower holder
58 Melody
60 Richard of *Primal Fear*
61 Pea containers
62 Damascus citizens: Abbr.
64 Cigar end

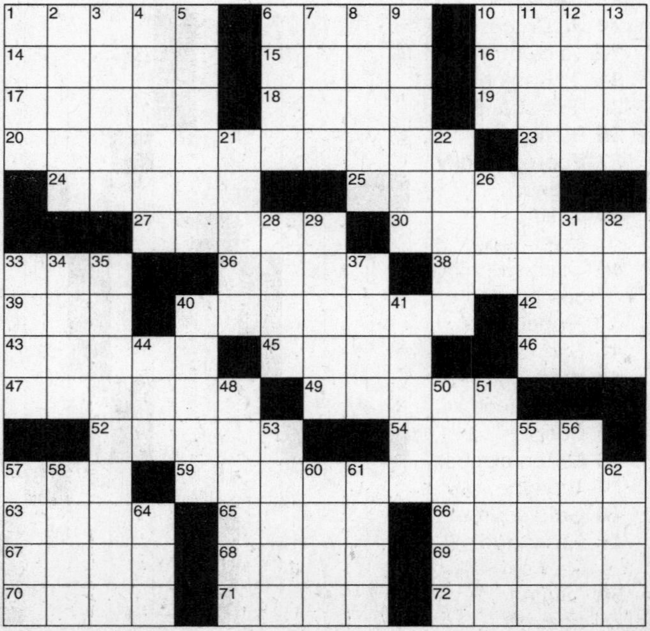

373 SHIP SHAPE

by Richard Silvestri

ACROSS

1 Gangplank, e.g.
5 Lazarus and Thompson
10 Expended
14 Brainstorm
15 Press-release addressees
16 Hang around
17 Censorship of a sort
19 Possess
20 Lode stuff
21 Let down
23 Doing an impression
26 Echo, for short
27 Home shopping network?
28 Multi-faced one of film
30 Distribute
33 Yukon, for one: Abbr.
34 Banish
36 Tire filler
37 Try a contest
39 Moose kin
40 Start a set
42 I.D. info
43 Less difficult
46 "Et tu" time
47 Consolidates
49 Pinkerton's logo
50 Five from New Jersey
51 Gave a bash
53 Impolite looks
55 Plunderers
57 Terse prez
58 Be next to
59 Violin virtuoso
65 Teddy's mom
66 Closely compacted
67 Surface extent
68 Enthusiastic
69 Berlin's "The Song Is __"
70 Coddle

DOWN

1 Barbecued bit
2 Hoo-ha
3 Sound of a Siamese
4 Digs for a beatnik
5 Stepped forth
6 "A __ bagatelle!"
7 Half of MMMII
8 Bridal path
9 Russian Tea Room server
10 Theater group
11 Rooming-house VIP
12 Roof edge
13 Prepared Easter eggs
18 *The Ghost of Frankenstein* name
22 Nathanael and Rebecca
23 Get even for
24 Prime-rib neighbor
25 About
26 Made a response
27 First-stringers
29 Two-finger signs
31 Holds one's attention
32 Hank of hair
35 __-doke
38 Teammate of Campanella
41 __ *kleine Nachtmusik*
44 Riding a horse
45 Tightened the shoestrings
48 Acquired
52 German city
54 High rails
55 Good clean fun
56 Reed instrument
57 Job for Mason
60 &
61 Boxtop piece
62 Diamond stat.
63 Gray soldier
64 Negative vote

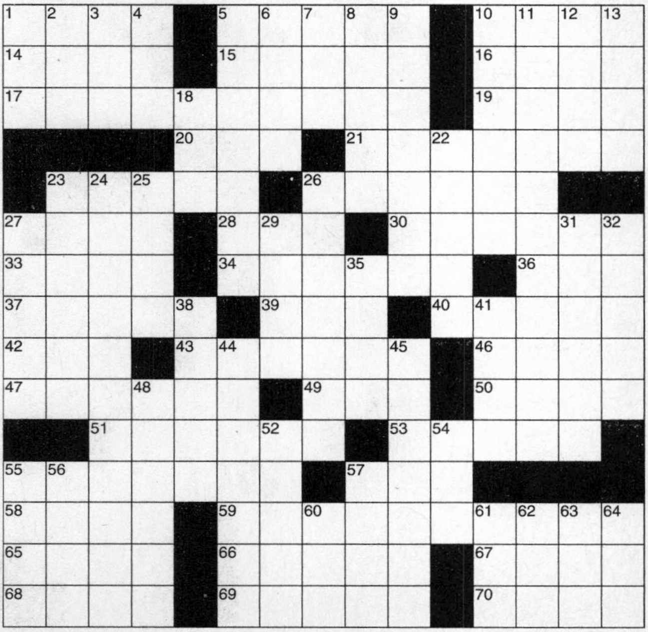

374 BODY WORK

by Shirley Soloway

ACROSS

1 Cadabra preceder
5 Suffix for special or final
8 Imitation
12 Runs in neutral
13 Not pro
14 Architect Saarinen
15 Harmonica
17 Treats leather
18 Vicinity
19 Laundry additive
21 On the __ (exactly)
22 Progression
24 Not moving
26 Cleo or Frankie
29 Go bad
31 Brit. fliers
34 Tall grasses
36 Reno or Leigh
38 Jean of *Arsenic and Old Lace*
40 Muslim title
41 Final Greek letter
42 XLIX sqvared?
43 ". . . emblem of the __ love"
45 Yanks' Boston rivals
46 "__ evil . . ."
48 Equestrian's controls
50 Unclear
52 Like some modern music
56 Coach Parseghian
58 Exertion
61 FDR's dog
62 Scrabble piece
64 Stevie Wonder oldie
66 Musical composition
67 Eight: Pref.
68 Change for a ten
69 Chick's sound
70 Charlotte of TV
71 Astute

DOWN

1 Worship
2 Sadder
3 Not wholesale
4 Cigar residue
5 Swenson of *Benson*
6 Night-sky sights
7 Dyes: Poet.
8 Tennis match unit
9 Front-page screamers
10 Florence's river
11 Largest amount
12 "__ corny as Kansas . . ."
13 Museum offering
16 Davis of *Evening Shade*
20 Swinging nightspot
23 Jewelry items
25 Sandy soil
27 Actress Patricia
28 Writer __ Rice Burroughs
30 Kids' block brand
31 St. Louis footballer
32 Navy VIPs
33 Apparent worth
35 Rational
37 April 15 concern
39 Brainstorm
44 Sawyer or Ladd
47 Looking to obtain
49 Easy mark
51 Writer Jong
53 Uninformed
54 Of the Tyrol
55 Gaelic girl
56 Over
57 Ready to eat
59 Poker entry fee
60 "__ to Rio" (Peter Allen song)
63 Clairvoyant's talent: Abbr.
65 Former D.C. stadium

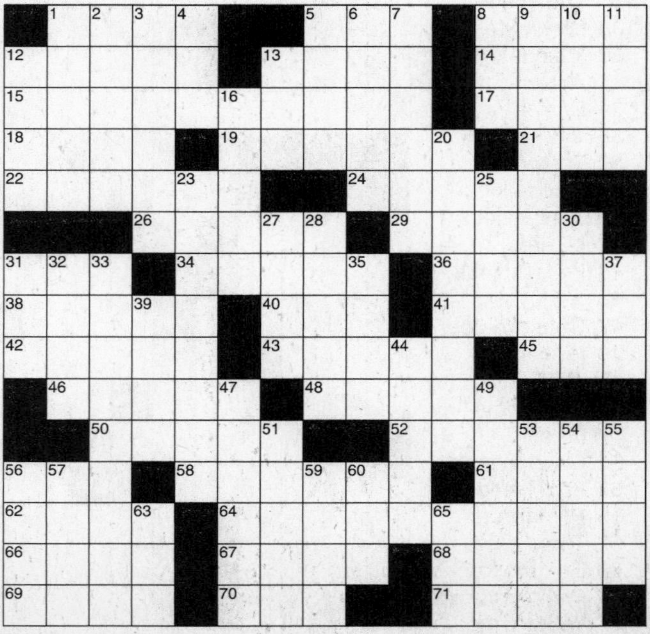

375 KNOCKING ABOUT

by Dean Niles

ACROSS
1 Popular '70s hairdo
5 Comics Viking
10 Unappetizing stuff
14 High wind
15 Last of a series
16 Casino city
17 Rowdy group
20 Sectors
21 Perfect grade
22 Civil War monogram
25 Debussy's sea
26 Highest
30 Washington's Kennedy __
32 Dad's boys
33 Colorado Native American
34 __ Thompson (Maugham character)
35 Ike's ex
36 Footnote phrase
37 Group members
40 Hem in
41 Clears
42 Best man's offering
44 Poet's contraction
45 Poet's tributes
46 Grass variety
47 Stuck
49 Sleeve filler
50 Ecol. org.
51 "__ Day Will Come"
52 Hardly right
54 Group's forte
61 Rani's garment
62 City near Gainesville
63 Pennsylvania port
64 Paired
65 Gallo products
66 Old horses

DOWN
1 Preston or Pepper: Abbr.
2 "Gotcha!"
3 Dark malt
4 Jazzman Stan
5 Little Jack __
6 Turkish title
7 The Bee __
8 Cabinet lawyers: Abbr.
9 Clear-thinking
10 Bride's mate
11 Without a __ to stand on
12 Impersonal pronoun
13 Batt. terminal
18 Family prep. course
19 Klutz's cry
22 Dosage amts.
23 More sleazy
24 Pyrenees nation
26 Theater honors
27 Beat Andretti, e.g.
28 Waits for Santa, perhaps
29 __ Aviv
31 Even-steven
32 Some sediments
35 Cornered
36 Love god
38 Surf phenomenon
39 Music marking
40 Procured
43 Pekoe or Earl Grey, e.g.
45 Magnum __ (masterpiece)
46 Uproar
48 Visit unexpectedly
49 Foot-leg link
52 See 60 Down
53 Govt. agents
54 JFK arrival
55 __ *& Order*
56 Jackie's second
57 Here, in Toulouse
58 Distinct period
59 Use a shovel
60 With 52 Down, Sammy Davis, Jr., autobiography

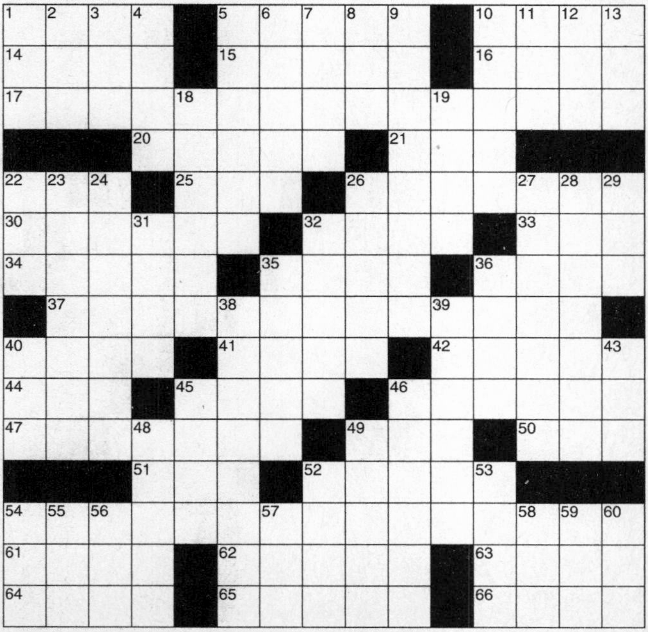

376 *OFFICEWORK*

by Dean Niles

ACROSS

1 Beer ingredient
5 Dieter's concern
10 Ax stroke
14 Mr. Nastase
15 "Live Free __" (NH motto)
16 Musical sample
17 Pigeonhole
19 Actor James
20 Bain or Hilton
21 Wood strip
23 Like the desert
24 European capital
26 Get ready to play golf
28 Doesn't get it, in a sense
32 More reckless
35 French friend
36 Winter precipitation
37 Mrs. Helmsley
38 Penny
40 Bore a hole
43 Close-fitting
44 __ the Horrible (comics Viking)
46 Fruit-filled desserts
48 Poetic preposition
49 Sign up
51 Gung-ho
53 Pixies
55 Valhalla resident
56 Ump kin
58 Special-interest orgs.
60 Prescribes
64 Allies' opponent
66 Ad creator
68 Thurber's *The __ Animal*
69 Labor group
70 Coup d'__
71 Church outcry
72 Sean and Arthur
73 Koran chapter

DOWN

1 Var. topics
2 Sax type
3 Legal claim
4 Overwhelming fear
5 Forest
6 Actor Carney
7 Pastoral poem
8 Nurse, as a drink
9 Fluctuate
10 Atlanta health agcy.
11 Walkman part
12 Mr. Sharif
13 Small horse
18 Relieves
22 Mend
25 Stink
27 Exploits for gain
28 Papier-__
29 Words of clarification
30 One way to march
31 Filch
33 Accustom
34 Vented one's spleen
39 End piece
41 Oilcloth, in Britain
42 Disappointments
45 Invitation letters
47 Bake eggs
50 China piece
52 Lingerie
54 British biscuit
56 "__ Lama Ding Dong"
57 Midterm, e.g.
59 Whirl around
61 "__, *Brute?*"
62 Bring up
63 Mlle. in Madrid
65 E.M. Kennedy's title
67 At that place

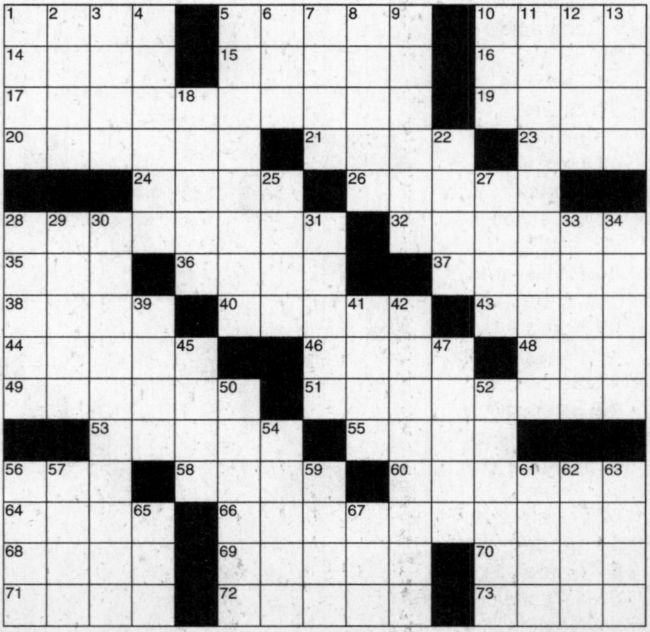

377 COLOR TELEVISION

by Harvey Estes

ACROSS
1 Life sketch
4 Jazz phrase
8 Bullets, for short
12 Sea birds
13 Walk __ (be elated)
15 Tail end
16 Gemini org.
17 "Be quiet!"
18 Is human?
19 '60s crime show
22 Show host
23 Word of cheer?
24 Gymnast Comaneci
26 Inform
27 Weed chopper
29 Words of surprise
31 Travelers' stop
32 "It" game
33 San Diego attraction
34 Editor's direction
35 '70s police show
39 Heart of the matter
40 Conclusion
41 Fall mo.
42 Singer Shannon
43 Salt Lake City setting: Abbr.
44 "Either he goes __ go!"
45 Friend of de Gaulle
48 Some circus performers
50 Actor Charleston
52 Agnew's nattering one
54 '80s sitcom
57 Puff-of-smoke sound
58 Pakistan neighbor
59 Allie's ally
60 Catch sight of
61 Takes it easy
62 Garden spot
63 Culp/Cosby program
64 Red mark
65 Beatty of *Deliverance*

DOWN
1 Hindu deity
2 Bug
3 Orange type
4 Got up
5 Not out there
6 Beasts in the flora
7 End of the line
8 The MCI Center, for one
9 Burgess of *Rocky*
10 Strict disciplinarian
11 Hosp. theaters
12 Computer key
14 Greek letter
20 Betty Ford Clinic work
21 Workers in 11 Down
25 Picnic pest
28 Stares at
30 Integrity
32 Singer Ritter
33 Last letter in London
34 An NCO
35 Where Tarzan swings
36 '50s toy
37 Up to this point
38 Cake cover
39 S&L concerns
43 Food-flavor enhancer: Abbr.
44 Big name in drama
45 Rub raw
46 Shed feathers
47 *Hedda Gabler* writer
49 Grove of baseball
51 Discombobulate
53 Conrad of verse
55 Black gold
56 Cartoonist Thomas
57 Pressure meas.

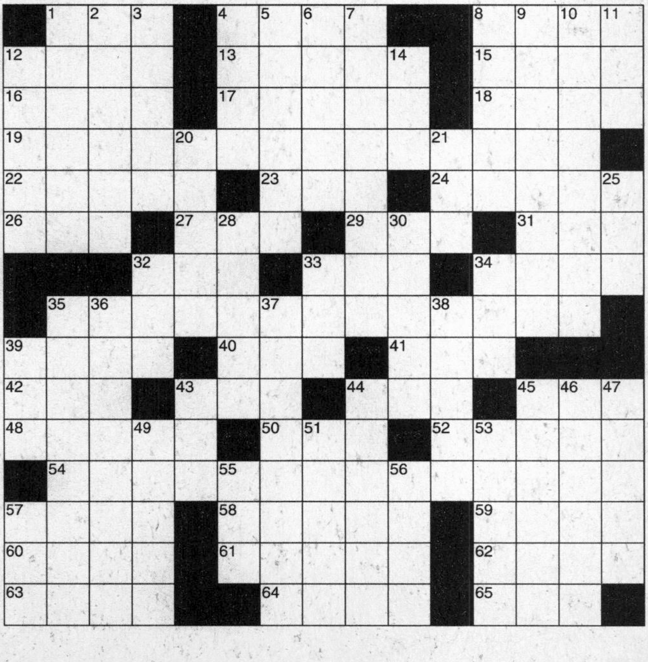

378 STORMY WEATHER

by Shirley Soloway

ACROSS
1 Offer a chair to
5 __ Major (Great Bear)
9 Greek letters
14 Wheel support
15 Tailor's line
16 Repent
17 Sounds from a comedy club
20 Land or sea follower
21 Nile snake
22 Consume
23 Robert Mitchum miniseries
28 Durango direction
29 Slangy denial
30 Health resort
33 Spring beauty
36 Taken-back purchases
40 Hi and bye?
44 Calm, as fears
45 The Elephant Boy
46 Mystery writer Josephine
47 Scottish denial
49 Concerned with
52 Summer night sights
58 __ capita
59 Pull a scam
60 __ *Grows in Brooklyn*
62 Car make
67 Belief
68 Broadway light
69 "__ Old Cowhand"
70 Bob of *Full House*
71 Sp. miss
72 Oscar __ Renta

DOWN
1 Droops
2 Precise
3 God of Islam
4 Indian tent
5 GI aid org.
6 Ring ump
7 Dinner course
8 Gather together
9 Groceries holder
10 Archaic verb ending
11 "When I Take My Sugar __"
12 Lend __ (listen)
13 Spanish artist
18 Plies a needle
19 Atop
24 "Put __ writing"
25 School outcasts
26 Cab cost
27 Sound of relief
30 __ Na Na
31 Buddy
32 Feel sick
34 __ *Man Answers* ('62 film)
35 Polio pioneer
37 Housecat, e.g.
38 Bullring cheer
39 Wily
41 Singer k.d. __
42 Indian nanny
43 Ladder step
48 Engrave
50 Ski lift
51 Offer more money
52 Martin Arrowsmith's wife
53 Not perf., as clothing
54 Verbs' subjects
55 __ *Sanctum*
56 Soot
57 Ecological adjective
58 Promoted pvts.
61 Author Ferber
63 '50s pres.
64 Little one
65 Period
66 Queen of Spain

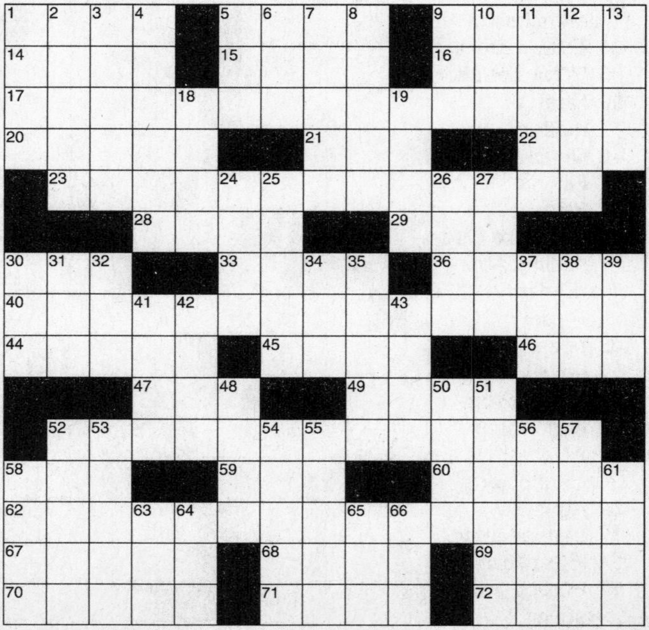

379 YANKEE DOODLES

by Richard Silvestri

ACROSS

1 Echelon
5 Jefferson's belief
10 Big chunk
14 "This one's __!"
15 "Moldy" tune
16 Flag holder
17 Yankee Hall-of-Famer
19 Serenader's instrument
20 What enemies have lost?
21 Ring around the collar?
22 Dr. Frankenstein's assistant
23 In a snit
25 Outstanding
27 Corporate cow
29 Restraint
32 Stephen and William of Hollywood
35 Darth __
37 Fink
38 *Xanadu* group
39 Western scenery
40 "__ Got a Crush on You"
41 Silly Putty container
42 A bit more normal
43 Racing sleds
45 Hem maker
47 Take hold
49 "__ Ha'i"
50 $$$
54 Mass conclusion
56 Architectural deg.
59 Sun circler
60 High in alcohol
61 Yankee Hall-of-Famer
63 Zoning unit
64 San Antonio landmark
65 Differently
66 Minimal wampum
67 David's weapon
68 Report-card woes

DOWN

1 Burgs
2 __ water (trouble-bound)
3 Author Zola
4 Hauled again
5 Senior members
6 Subordinate Claus?
7 Admiree
8 Kingly address
9 Gets both sides together
10 First-aid item
11 Yankee Hall-of-Famer
12 Sort of sax
13 "The amber nectar"
18 What Pandora released
24 Specified
26 "__ the ramparts . . ."
28 Unburdens
30 Icicle locale
31 AAA selections
32 Exemplar of redness
33 Ms. Korbut
34 Yankee Hall-of-Famer
36 Challenged
39 Mexican music makers
42 The sun's name
43 Actress Palmer
44 Took sneakers off
46 Splashed down
48 Numero uno
51 Spat's spot
52 Singer Della
53 Eye infections
54 Gregory Peck's *Moby Dick* role
55 Anti-mugger weapon
57 Pervade
58 Jai __
62 K-O interior

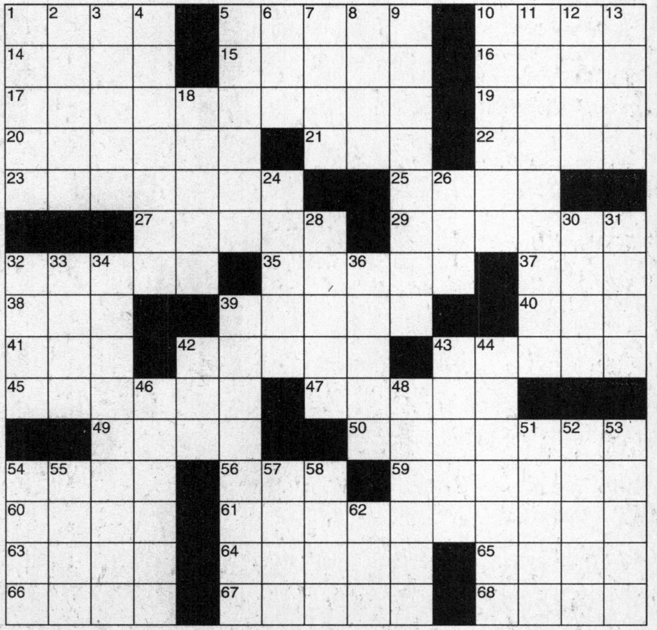

380 *IN PURSUIT*

by Shirley Soloway

ACROSS
1 Days gone by
5 Arizona river
9 Scent sensors
14 Man __ (racehorse)
15 Eden resident
16 Patriot Allen
17 Thompson of *Family*
18 Gaucho's weapon
19 Video-game name
20 Pathfinder
23 "Spring forward" time: Abbr.
24 Small sofa
25 First month, in Madrid
27 Approximately
30 Fishes with a net
33 Squelched
37 Landing place
39 Wading bird
40 "Holy cow!"
41 French director Louis
42 Classify
43 Tim of *Frank's Place*
44 Unit
45 Male and female
46 Composer Harold et al.
48 Lady of Spain
50 Welcome
52 Blake or Plummer
57 Lawyers' org.
59 List of accomplishments
62 Word before larceny or point
64 Burn
65 Yuletide buy
66 Eydie's mate
67 Casino game
68 Racetrack shape
69 Let up
70 Goulash
71 Baking apple

DOWN
1 Sends by mail
2 Cognizant
3 Mubarak's predecessor
4 Characteristic
5 Tongue wagger
6 Object of worship
7 Singing sounds
8 Stun
9 More reachable
10 Hall-of-Famer Mel
11 Spar solo
12 Corn servings
13 Foul mood
21 Writer Uris
22 __ nous (confidentially)
26 Lift up
28 Mild disagreement
29 Lubricated
31 Money in Milan
32 Overseas planes
33 Medical fluids
34 Teen follower
35 Football-party sites
36 More unusual
38 Seaman's saint
41 Penny-pincher
45 Identical
47 Retained after expenses
49 Not wide
51 Fasteners
53 Thespian
54 Vibes player Red
55 Sleep experience
56 Fred Astaire's sister
57 Church space
58 Letter after alpha
60 Newsman Huntley
61 Role for Welles
63 "__ Got Sixpence"

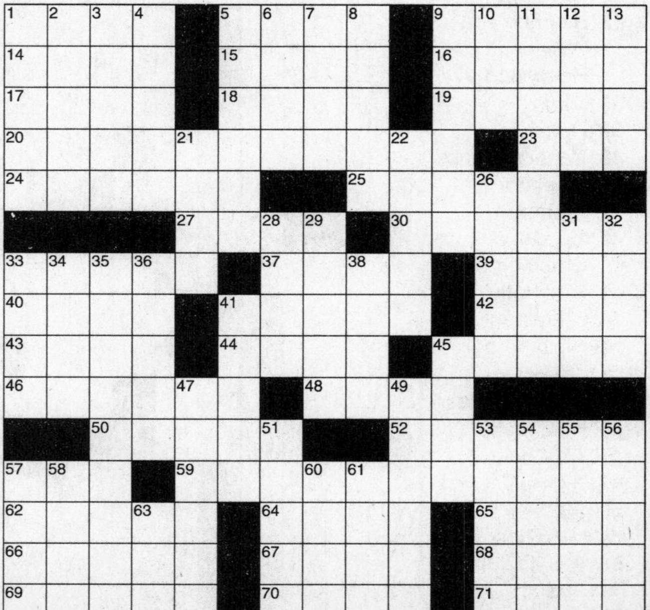

381 AS EASY AS . . .

by Fred Piscop

ACROSS
1 Castle protection
5 Chinchilla, e.g.
8 Country singer Charley
13 Chan's comment
14 Norwegian monarch
16 Sieved potatoes
17 ABC
20 Short vocal solo
21 Diplomats' quest
22 Kind of 26 Across
23 Had on
24 Prompter's lead-in
26 Fisherman
31 Former Sinclair competitor
35 Vaughn role
37 Duffer's shot
38 PIE
41 Lama land
42 Author Ephron
43 Sufficiently cooked
44 Lucky charm
46 Brewer's need
48 Actress Skye
50 Errand runner
55 Write scores
59 Bring in
60 1-2-3
62 Nine-headed serpent
63 Pâté de __ gras
64 Defeat
65 Lamb product
66 Draft agcy.
67 Sp. women

DOWN
1 Goya subjects
2 Chicago airport
3 Computer-code abbr.
4 Straphanger's purchase
5 Recliner part
6 Forearm bone
7 Spitfire fliers
8 Make-believe
9 Shine's partner
10 Computer-screen symbol
11 Fender bender
12 Leading __ (vanguard)
15 Pooch's name
18 Editor's mark
19 Actress Miles
23 Mat word
25 Beef cut
27 Tickled pink
28 Suction starter
29 Friedman's subj.
30 Actor Auberjonois
31 "*¿Cómo __ usted?*"
32 Singer Whitman
33 Star of India
34 German auto
36 Gumbo veggie
39 Big name in pianos
40 Game fish
45 Frat-party wear
47 Blue shade
49 Soft ball
51 Amorphous masses
52 Cut obliquely
53 California city
54 Fits together
55 Tennis great Arthur
56 Rogers and Acuff
57 Backwoods P.O. routes
58 Razor brand
59 Slugger's stats.
61 Dawn goddess

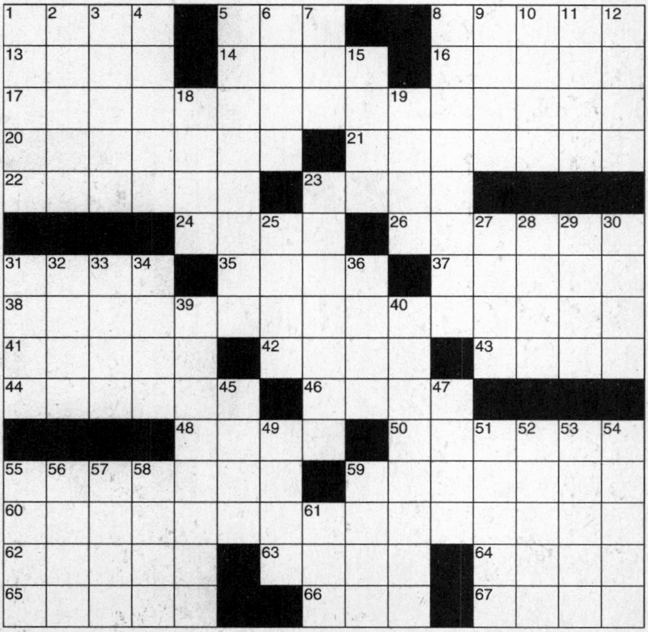

382 WISE WORDS

by Ann Seidel

ACROSS

1 Latin abbr.
5 Delhi's land
10 Strip of concrete
14 Actress Turner
15 Broadway lights
16 Lay concrete
17 Crafts' partner
18 Inspiration
20 Band leader
22 Motionless
23 Have debts
24 Carried
27 Words from experience
31 __ *Dog* (Terhune tale)
35 Embellish
36 "__ a man with seven wives"
37 K-6 school, for short
38 Auto
39 Brought the meeting to order
42 "Egg" word form
43 Recognized
45 El __, TX
46 Encounter
48 Jerk's offering
49 Corner that's less than 90 degrees
51 Throat problem
53 Steelers' org.
54 Artistic judgment
57 Of ancient Mexicans
61 What insiders bet with
65 __ mater
66 French girlfriend
67 Morning sound
68 Dines
69 Rock and __
70 Lake craft
71 "For __ jolly good fellow"

DOWN

1 Veteran actor Jack
2 O'Haras' residence
3 Pay to play
4 Cowboy, often
5 Not acquired
6 Evil emperor
7 "__ make myself clear?"
8 Gerund suffix
9 Cigar residue
10 "Do not fold, __, or mutilate"
11 Put on cargo
12 Swear
13 Patrol area
19 Overtime situation
21 Plucked sound
24 Proctor's call
25 Spotted wildcat
26 Head: Fr.
27 Baseball bases
28 *A Bell for* ___
29 Pierced, in a way
30 Lively, in music
32 "Take Me __"
33 Flavor eggs
34 Nitrogen compound
40 On __ with (equal to)
41 Kind of beer
44 Squanderer
47 Let loose
50 Digestive protein
52 Vietnamese New Year
54 Nicholas or Alexander
55 Bombs and bullets
56 Glide along
57 Dynamic beginning
58 Inkling
59 Fuse units
60 Gemini org.
62 PC alternative
63 Pay or scram ending
64 A Bobbsey

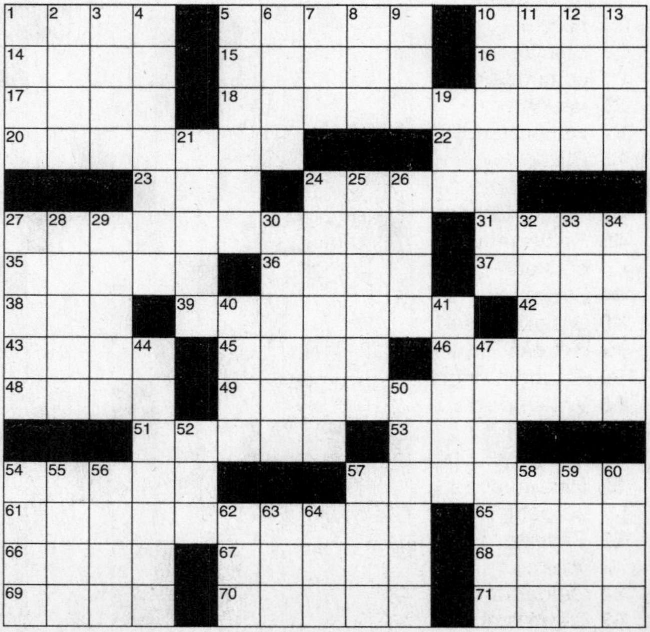

383 ASSUME THE POSITION

by Dean Niles

ACROSS
1 Photo holder
6 Bric-a-__
10 High-school equiv.
13 Famous frontiersman
14 Luxury car
15 Certain Semite
17 Actor Kathy or Alan
18 P __ "pneumatic"
19 Garrison of tennis
20 CPR giver
21 Adverse reactions
24 Earth tone
26 Shop tools
27 Argentine plain
29 Amidst
31 Rope fiber
32 Stylish
33 Goes down
37 Actor Erwin
38 Devotion
41 *You __ There*
42 Cook's portions: Abbr.
44 Talk wildly
45 Footnote abbr.
47 Slammer
49 Three-wheelers
50 F to F, e.g.
53 Encrusted
54 Back-row cry
57 CD-__ (computer device)
60 Oklahoma city
61 Comet part
62 Muscat resident
64 Slender bristle
65 Russian designer
66 Communion piece
67 Fashion monogram
68 Performs
69 Crook's "soup"

DOWN
1 Singer Lane
2 Sand, silt and clay
3 "Cheers!"
4 French article
5 Military eatery
6 Razor filler
7 __ to the occasion
8 Girlfriend: Fr.
9 Be at loggerheads
10 Newspaper name
11 Author Segal
12 *Inferno* poet
16 Mingus' instrument
22 Tax agcy.
23 Modern communications machine
25 Numbers cruncher: Abbr.
27 "Hey, you!"
28 River islands
29 __-you note
30 Shrivel
32 Greenish blue
34 1991 Ron Howard film
35 Creamy cheese
36 Puts in place
39 Got one's bearings
40 Site of Cornwallis' surrender
43 Big stink
46 Boston cream __
48 56, in old Rome
49 Catch some rays
50 Poet's tributes
51 __ Island, NY
52 Gibes
53 Nat and Natalie
55 Betting game
56 Religious ceremony
58 Unique fellow
59 Spanish painter
63 A month in Montmartre

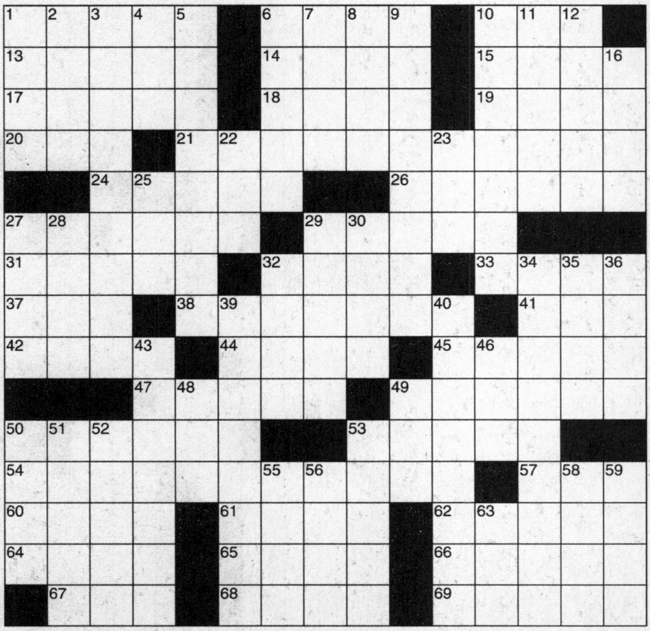

384 BEASTLY

by Eileen Lexau

ACROSS

1 Showed up
5 Ravine
10 '60s hair style
14 Tel __
15 Separated
16 City map
17 Supreme Court number
18 Naive ones
19 Left, on a ship
20 Snoozed a bit
22 Mystery board game
23 "This is only __"
24 Off one's nut
26 Gridders' org.
28 Composer Rorem
29 Bandleader Brown
32 Rock-band tour assistant
34 Soup cracker
37 Track event
38 Doesn't have much food
41 __ mater
42 Put up
43 Peggy Fleming, e.g.
45 Berry or Kercheval
46 Prevent
49 Kazakhstan, once: Abbr.
50 Soap ingredients
53 Not a soul
55 Convent room
57 Fortunate ones
60 Palo __, CA
61 Was wearing
62 Look leeringly at
63 Courage
64 In a __ (excited)
65 Civil disturbance
66 Symphony woodwind
67 High-strung
68 Mtg.

DOWN

1 High-kicking dance
2 Navigate the air
3 Manufactured coins
4 Ties the score
5 Irving character
6 "__ and Away" (5th Dimension song)
7 Tag
8 Statement of belief
9 Elevs.
10 Not theoretical: Abbr.
11 Flatfish
12 Exalted
13 Baseball great Mel
21 Map book
22 Bill's partner
25 Produce
27 Allow
30 Mystery writer Queen
31 Cooking direction
33 Amongst
34 RBI, e.g.
35 "I Like __"
36 Place for a tie
38 Fraternal group
39 Almond-flavored liqueur
40 Rochester's boss
41 Burro
44 Building extension
46 __-woogie
47 North Americans, to Latinos
48 Bowling-alley buttons
51 Fill with happiness
52 North African nation
54 Smells
56 Come in second
58 Barracks beds
59 Leg joint
60 "Long __ and Far Away"
61 FDR's third veep

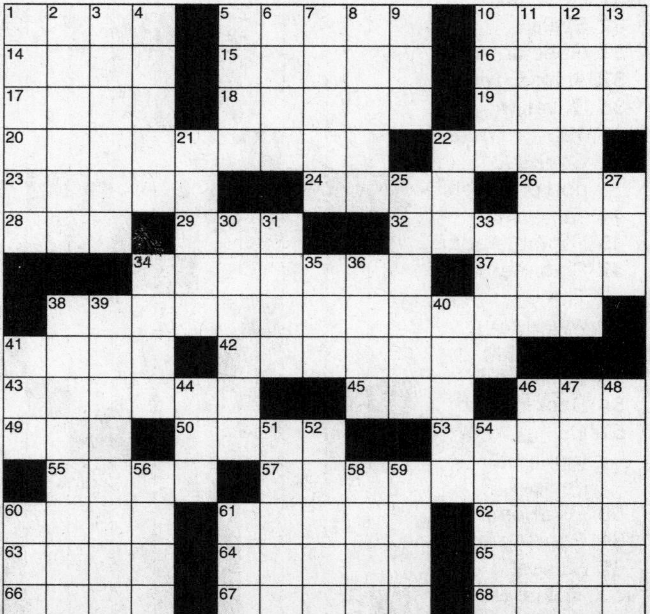

385 *WATERLOGGED*

by Shirley Soloway

ACROSS

1 The Charles' pet
5 Words before "happens" or "were"
9 "__ the night before . . ."
13 Turns to the right
14 Warwick and Westheimer
16 In this spot
17 Experiencing bad trouble
19 "I cannot tell __"
20 Wise goddess
21 Lubricated again
23 Enter, as a crowd
26 Crafty
27 Unworkable item
30 Part in a play
31 Tide type
33 Run off to wed
35 Memorable times
37 MacMurray or Allen
40 "__ Laurie" (Scottish air)
41 CPA's forte
42 Every 24 hours
43 Echelon
44 Throw out a line
45 Corbin on *L.A. Law*
46 1994, e.g.
48 Sty cry
50 Automotive fuel
51 Recede
53 Hustler's hangout
56 Disney production
58 Doing nothing
62 Clarinet cousin
63 Holds off
66 Writer Uris
67 As of
68 Point out
69 Wapitis
70 Retains after expenses
71 Pay attention to

DOWN

1 Water in Juárez
2 Labor Day mo.
3 Hebrew letter
4 Fire remains
5 Jockey Eddie
6 Big __, CA
7 Resident suffix
8 Unit of heat
9 East Asian
10 Fountainhead
11 Sharon of Israel
12 Run-down
15 Bolts of wool
18 Menu item
22 Single
24 Actress Verdugo
25 Pressurized container
27 Costly
28 Arm bone
29 Free-for-all
32 At a distance
34 Food fish
36 Up and about
38 Kazan of Hollywood
39 Changes color
42 Half of ND
44 Thieves
47 Mil. address
49 Looped ropes
51 School: Fr.
52 Biblical city
54 __ a million
55 Bandleader Miller
57 Change for a twenty
59 Theater award
60 Fill up
61 Spotted
64 Compass pt.
65 Interest amt.

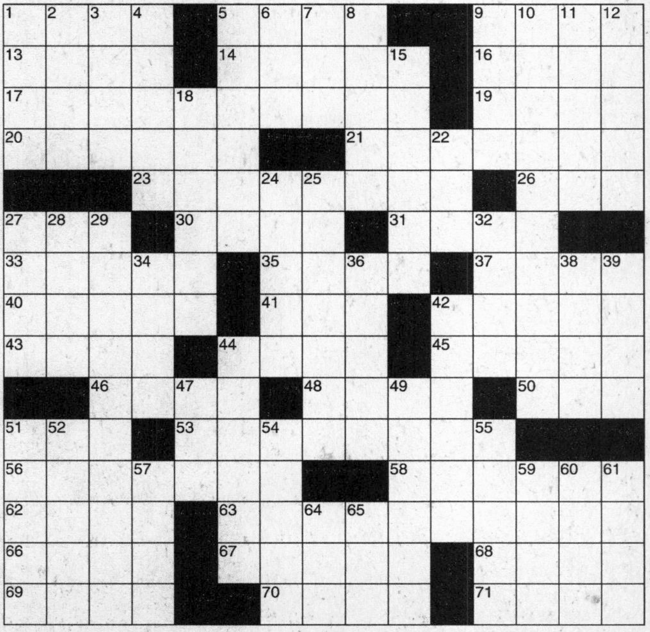

386 BB'S

by Fred Piscop

ACROSS

1 Sharp ache
5 Circuit
10 __ Eban
14 Like two peas in __
15 Island nation
16 Do another hitch
17 *Mikrokosmos* composer
19 Fourth planet
20 Unvoiced
21 Beginning stage
23 __ Na Na
24 Genesis album of 1981
26 Pole-vaulter Sergei
29 Road sign
30 *The Woman* __ (Wilder film)
33 "__ live and breathe!"
34 Sweet wine
37 Power, in combinations
38 __-de-sac
39 "Open sesame" speaker
41 Tempe sch.
42 Newsman Marvin
44 Egyptian talisman
45 Well-used pencil
46 As __ a fox
48 CPR expert
49 Fills to the gills
51 Fictional Starr
53 Go for apples, perhaps
54 '50s pitcher Ralph
56 Popular dolls
60 Knowledge
61 Baseball star
64 LL.B. holder
65 '60s tune, e.g.
66 Godunov was one
67 Lads
68 More meanspirited
69 Some turkeys

DOWN

1 Sunscreen ingredient
2 *Planet of the* __
3 __ contendere
4 Solidarity city
5 Appliance name
6 Trade center
7 Diner offering
8 Skater Midori
9 __ powder (run off)
10 Uniform accessory
11 Long-time coach at 24 Down
12 __ the hatchet
13 Lhasa __
18 Grand __ Island (vacation spot)
22 Sprint rival
24 Dixie state
25 He married Bacall
26 Supports
27 "The __" (regular's bar order)
28 Player of small parts?
29 Prepared apples, perhaps
31 Follow
32 Smears paint
35 Pacino et al.
36 Lawyers' org.
40 Suck up
43 Rubble and Fife
47 Dry, as wine
50 Comic Bud
52 Natterer, to Agnew
53 Anacin rival
54 Spill the beans
55 __-Rooter
56 Soft cheese
57 __ many words
58 Dutch cheese
59 Baltic states, once: Abbr.
62 In the manner of
63 Ave. crossers

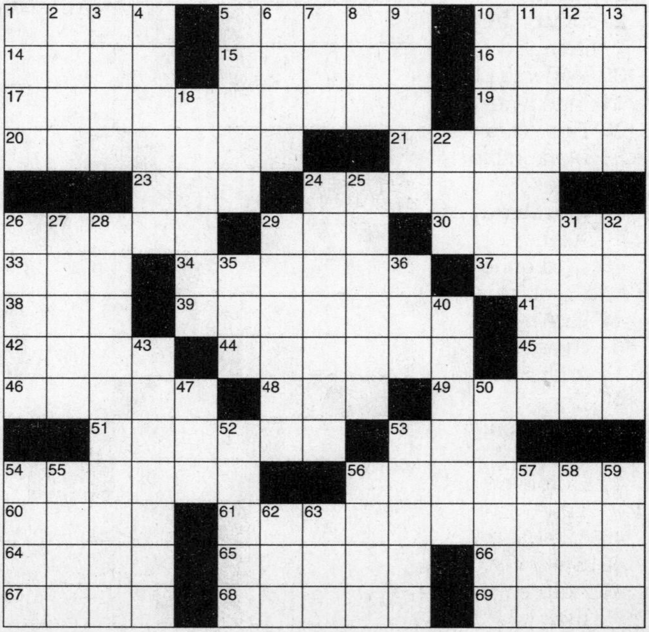

387 DELIVERANCE

by Ann Seidel

ACROSS

1 Cellist __ Ma
5 "__ Nice Clambake" (*Carousel* tune)
10 Use the molars
14 Repute
15 Bagel relative
16 Sign of sanctity
17 Overwhelming victory
18 Wears
19 Moslem honorific
20 Ens' preceders
21 Old mail system
23 Tennis star Chris
25 Young bird of prey
26 Talk-show groups
28 Singer Taylor __
30 Gide or Previn
31 Painter Claude
32 Shade source
35 Meek one
36 Hankered
37 French girlfriend
38 Sault __ Marie, Ontario
39 Big, noisy bird
40 Spring up
41 Chores
42 Carve in stone
43 Costello's foil
46 Windowpane adhesive
47 Gridiron tactic
50 Non-commercial notice: Abbr.
53 Birch or beech
54 Buenos __, Argentina
55 Weaving machine
56 Angler's aid
57 Bullwinkle, for one
58 __ of Wight
59 Tabulates
60 Back-of-the-book reference
61 English prep school

DOWN

1 The old days
2 Baseball's Blue Moon
3 Sam Cooke song
4 Food scrap
5 Loathes
6 Cheerful
7 Like pie, perhaps?
8 Skin moisturizer
9 Sharp-sighted
10 Use Visa
11 Actress Veronica
12 "Für __"
13 Least desirable
21 Soccer great
22 Breathe hard
24 Action word
26 Bosom friends
27 Med. school subject
28 Portuguese titles
29 From the top
31 Singer Jagger
32 Miss Manners predecessor
33 Talk like Daffy Duck
34 __ *the Press*
36 Deli beef
37 In __ (stuck)
39 __ Hari
40 Stops procrastinating
41 Shower linen
42 English region
43 Entertainers' union
44 Yawning
45 Animal category
46 Bel __ cheese
48 "Runaround Sue" singer
49 Urge on
51 Napoleon or Han
52 Prayer finish
55 Untruth

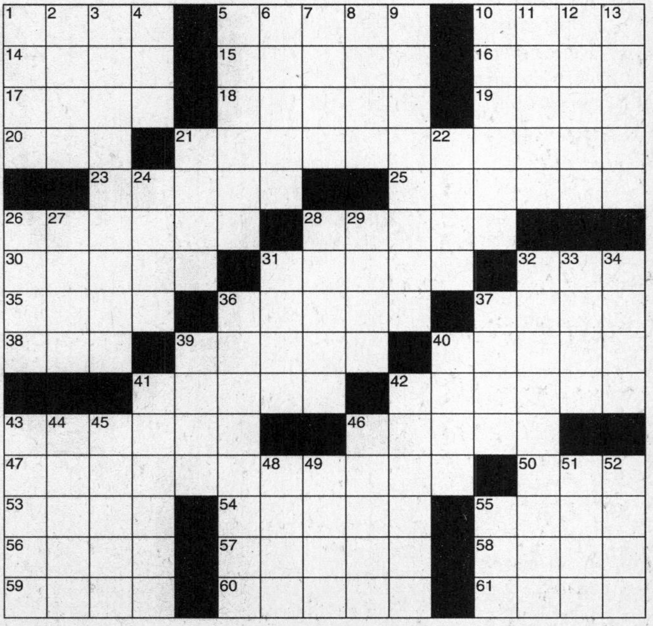

388 *FOUR-BAGGER*

by Ann Seidel

ACROSS

1 Rhyme scheme
5 Lively
9 Actress Jaclyn
14 Late singer/ politico Sonny
15 Hint
16 Sierra Nevada lake
17 "Do __ others . . ."
18 Actress Lenska
19 Lasso
20 Traveler's bags
22 Born first
23 Forgo
24 Booby __
26 *Joie de vivre*
29 __ out (exposes)
33 Hunger hankerings
37 Nuclear-warhead acronym
39 Arm bone
40 Baseball manager Felipe
41 Irate
42 Corp. bigshots
43 Aquatic bird
44 Wallet fillers
45 Enjoys gum
46 Sparse
48 Not faked
50 Abominable Snowman
52 Bahamas seaport
57 Bring about
60 Student bags
63 Open a bottle
64 Window ledge
65 Yawn inducer
66 *La __ Vita*
67 Actress Adams
68 __ about (approximately)
69 Plumber's tool
70 Catches forty winks
71 Sawbucks

DOWN

1 Treat badly
2 Employee's reward
3 Prank
4 Phone enclosure
5 Sloppy John Hancock
6 Definite asset
7 Hold sway
8 Bread necessity
9 Small river
10 Postal bag
11 "If __ a Hammer"
12 Carry around
13 Listen to
21 Mediocre grades
25 Invitation letters
27 Prayer conclusion
28 Saltpeter part
30 Swiss modernist
31 "Ah, Wilderness were Paradise __!"
32 Give lip to
33 Butter squares
34 Actor Baldwin
35 Nick Charles' mate
36 Burlap bag
38 Artful dodge
41 Pitcher __ Wilhelm
45 Show approval
47 Indian dwelling
49 Places for some bracelets
51 Norwegian dramatist
53 Wooden shoe
54 British biscuit
55 Buckeye State city
56 Manipulative people
57 Cows masticate them
58 Soon
59 Home of the Bruins
61 Verdi opera
62 Paper fastener

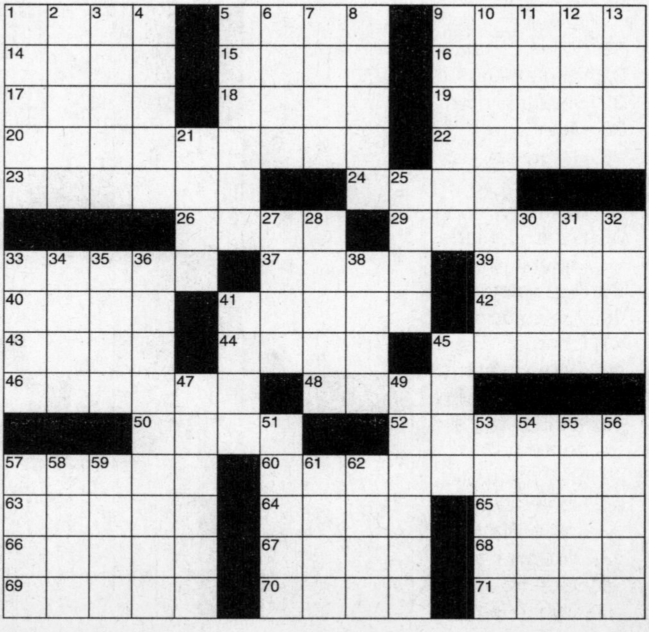

389 WONDERFUL

by Norma Steinberg

ACROSS

1 Coke and Pepsi, e.g.
6 "Yay, maestro!"
11 Actor Mineo
14 Scene of the action
15 Caesar or Brutus
16 Opposite of sing.
17 Majestic ending
19 Shade tree
20 Run in neutral
21 Convene
22 *NYPD Blue* character
23 Actress Lansbury
26 Dress fabric
28 Pavement material
29 Implant
33 Farrow or Sara
34 "Little piggie"
35 South Sea island
36 D-sharp alias
39 "__ corny as Kansas . . ."
41 Inventor Howe
43 Put away alphabetically
44 Referred to
46 Burt's ex
47 Sermon subject
48 Patriotic org.
49 Nos. for athletes
51 Holyfield feat: Abbr.
52 Happy faces
55 Posse member, e.g.
57 "*Mazel __!*"
58 Sea plea
60 Impoverished
61 Yalie
62 Food source
67 Total (up)
68 Employment
69 "High Noon" singer
70 Caustic liquid
71 Sharp pains
72 *Riders to the Sea* playwright

DOWN

1 Droop
2 Hockey great
3 Antidrug org.
4 __ *Get Your Gun*
5 Equestrian gear
6 Cheese-store choice
7 Howard or Reagan
8 *Amo, __, amat*
9 Legally binding
10 Former
11 Neurologists and OB-GYNs
12 Apportion
13 Like bad gravy
18 Afire, in a restaurant
23 Storage room
24 Wynonna's mother
25 Rocky Mountain watershed
27 Get one's goat
30 Spheres
31 Prufrock's creator
32 Dors or Sands
37 Share and share __
38 Choir voice
40 Close an envelope
42 *Roseanne* or *Coach*
45 Put on the Ritz
50 Sand bars
52 Unbelievable bargain
53 Like old bread, perhaps
54 The March King
56 Display
59 Straddle
60 Corporate exec.
63 Omelet ingredient
64 Family reunion attendees
65 School subj.
66 Casual shirt

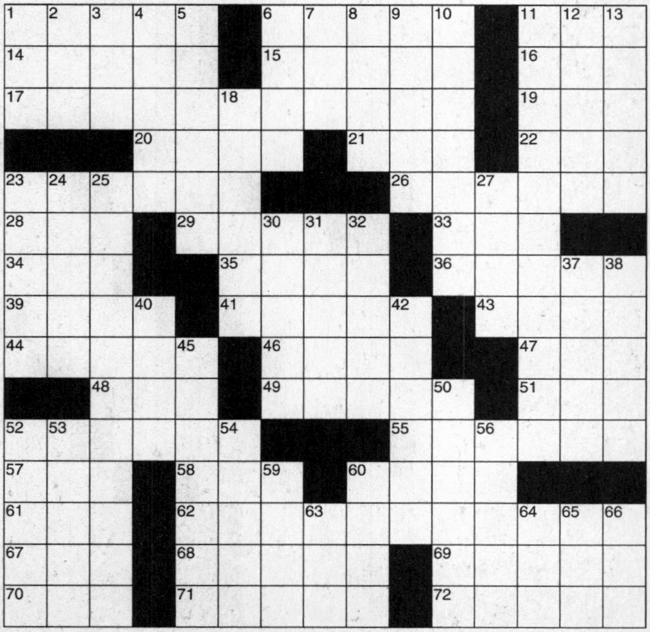

390 *GHOULISH TIMES*

by Dean Niles

ACROSS

1 Cry like a baby
5 Mrs. Gorbachev
10 Pops
14 Sore spot
15 Boo-boo
16 Drama award
17 Rock group
19 Step to the __
20 El Salvador neighbor
21 *The Most Happy* __
22 Stimpy's pal
23 __ in (get closer)
25 *Hair* star
31 Defeated overwhelmingly
33 Did a garden chore
34 Lah-di-__
35 Poker contribution
36 Coal enclosure
37 *The Thin Man* woman
38 Favorite
39 Window ledge
41 James Bond's nemesis
43 Deceptive remark
46 Get up
47 Hippie home
48 Jazz form
51 Work periods
56 Gabor and Perón
57 Date arrangement
59 Belgrade resident
60 Car pedal
61 Where the gold is
62 Do in
63 Bottomless pit
64 Astronaut Shepard

DOWN

1 Speed-of-sound name
2 Sound reflection
3 "Where or __"
4 Starring role
5 Certain tire
6 Downright
7 Rainbow
8 Part of ASPCA
9 Early vessel
10 Money
11 Cain's brother
12 "Don't touch that __!"
13 Antitoxins
18 Blender result
21 Crease
23 __ National Park, Utah
24 Spanish cheer
25 __-frutti
26 Blvd., e.g.
27 In a __ (later)
28 Embellish
29 The red planet
30 Former Irani leader
31 Transported
32 Unique fellow
36 Down in the dumps
37 Modernist
39 Jump over
40 Mensa measures
41 Hides away
42 The thick of things
44 Bing or David
45 Little bits
48 Armstrong or Myerson
49 Daredevil Knievel
50 Actress Theda
51 Stick around
52 __ *la Douce*
53 Trompe l'__ (visual deception)
54 Granny
55 Submachine gun
57 Trade-name abbr.
58 City, informally

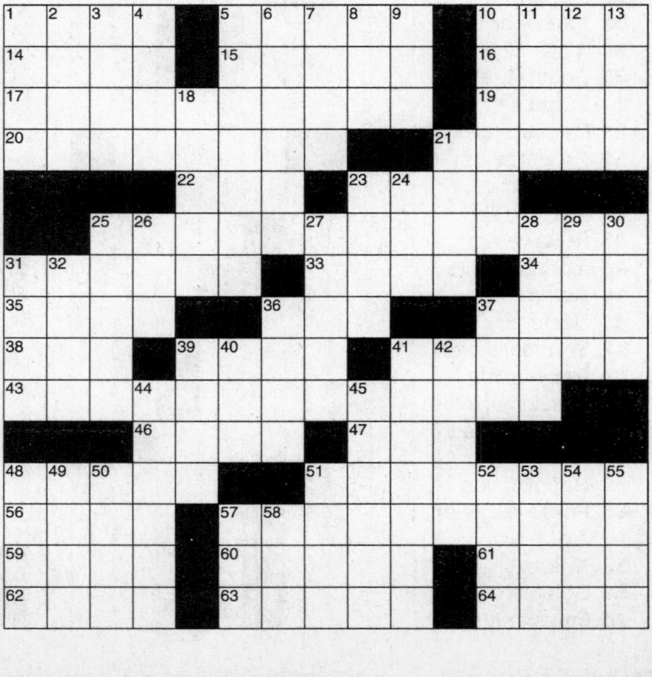

391 WEAR AM I?

by Norma Steinberg

ACROSS

1 Collins or Donahue
5 "My Way" singer
9 Endow with godhood
14 Author Jaffe
15 Appear to be
16 Additional
17 "__ Around" (Beach Boys song)
18 Montreal baseballer
19 Buffalo kin
20 North Carolina area
23 Way in
24 Conflicts
28 Literary selection
32 __ de France
33 Started the PC
37 Leather with a nap
39 "Natural" hairdo
40 Shatter
43 Plant stand?
44 Falls in drops
46 Reason for overtime
48 Sense of self
49 Symphony conductor
52 Thickly
54 In __ (neither here nor there)
59 Prodigies' opposites
63 George Burns prop
66 Weaving machine
67 __-a-brac
68 Up
69 Early Peruvian
70 *M*A*S*H* star
71 Gas-powered bike
72 Way out
73 Bambi, e.g.

DOWN

1 Cost
2 *__'s Heroes*
3 Bumbling
4 "See ya!"
5 On a cruise
6 Barber's cry
7 Retained
8 One-celled animal
9 Campaign events
10 Be
11 *__ Always Fair Weather* ('55 film)
12 To and __
13 PBS' *__ Can Cook*
21 Exaggeration
22 Scott Joplin creation
25 Try to deceive
26 __ statesman
27 "Come up and __ sometime"
29 Help-wanted notices
30 Total
31 Shoe coverings
33 Revealed
34 *Coming __ in Samoa*
35 Celestial hunter
36 Heavy weight
38 Western sch.
41 Pose
42 That girl
45 Bedaubed
47 Perform alone
50 High, in music
51 Place for shadow
53 Quench
55 Phrase from a Michael Jackson tune
56 Singer Haggard
57 Newlywed
58 Felix's roommate
60 Cher's surname, once
61 In __ parentis
62 General Bradley
63 Projection on a wheel
64 __ Jima
65 Wide divergence

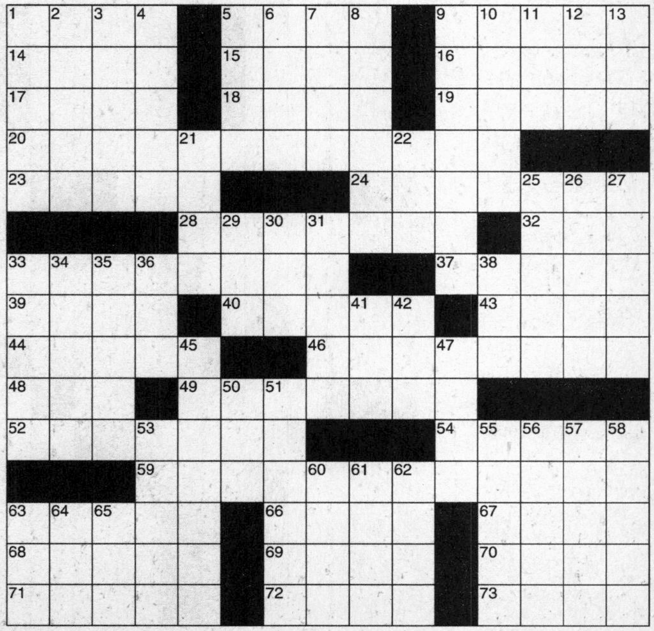

392 *INCENDIARY*

by Shirley Soloway

ACROSS
1 Saudi citizen
5 Tortoiselike
9 Own up
14 Libertine
15 Mandlikova of tennis
16 Weepy
17 "Bye-bye!"
18 In a while
19 Weasel relative
20 Misleading device
23 Navy VIP
24 Art Deco name
25 Hurries off
27 South American rodent
30 Tumult
32 Woke up
33 Food store, for short
34 Western alliance
37 British title
38 Hot under the collar
41 Berry or Kercheval
42 Author of *The Nazarene*
44 Crimson and cerise
45 Perfect
47 Employers
49 With an even hand
50 Composer Mahler
52 __ *Misbehavin'*
53 Soldiers' org.
54 July 4 noisemaker
60 City dept.
62 Astringent
63 Mata __
64 Parisian wild cat
65 Distribute, with "out"
66 Ardor
67 1987 world champion figure skater
68 Jury member
69 Writing place

DOWN
1 Cultural pursuits
2 Wander about
3 Roadster
4 Lab vessels
5 California peak
6 Galahad's weapon
7 __ about (approximately)
8 Diminish
9 Like some modern music
10 P.I.
11 Dolly Levi, e.g.
12 Dunne or Papas
13 Novices
21 Eastern Indians
22 Comedian Murphy
26 __ Jose, CA
27 Space agcy.
28 Writer Leon
29 Heartsick ballads
30 Necklace units
31 Shade trees
33 Forest forager
35 Blue-green
36 "My One and __"
39 Fountain of Rome
40 Singer Ross
43 Big success
46 Jilted
48 Ceiling support beam
49 More solid
50 Zest
51 United competitor, formerly
52 Keen
55 Incline
56 Gen. Robert __
57 Leafy green
58 Distinctive periods
59 Ice arena
61 Dudgeon

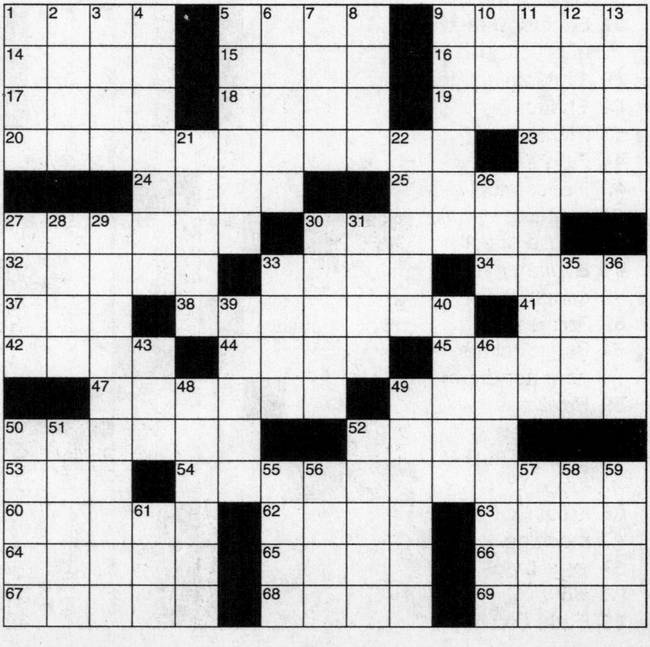

393 *BOARING*

by Dean Niles

ACROSS

1 Shop shaper
6 Roseanne's surname, once
10 Music-score notation
14 Collection
15 Sheriff Andy's son
16 Tortoise competitor
17 Lowlife
18 Alight
19 __-de-camp
20 Part of M.I.T.
21 Senate bill of a sort
23 Skulks
25 Pick, with "for"
26 Good __ Policy
30 "__ was saying . . ."
33 Forest clearing
36 Chess piece
37 Nerve
38 Split apart
39 Fish-eating eagle
40 Fable ender
41 In the course of
42 Floral vessel
43 Chicago airport
44 "Certainly!"
45 Decisive defeat
47 Funding source in D.C.
48 Christmas quaff
52 Uninformed buy
58 Had on
59 Pure black
60 __ *bene*
61 Blend
62 To be, to Babette
63 Potter's need
64 Escapee
65 __ and die
66 Cellist Ma
67 Mix up

DOWN

1 Endures
2 Senator Specter
3 In a __ (quickly)
4 Clumsy
5 Take a gander at
6 Western tie
7 On __ with (equal to)
8 Skating floor
9 Women's magazine
10 Map
11 Hideaway
12 "*Das Lied von der* __" (Mahler work)
13 Experience
21 Tire-pressure inits.
22 Tax mo.
24 Supercool
27 *The* __ *Gatsby*
28 Flicka, for one
29 Goof
30 Heavenly glow
31 Headliner
32 Man or Capri
33 Overcast
34 Whitewash component
35 Hertz competitor
37 Run riot
40 Synthesizer eponym
42 Motel sign
45 Pallid
46 Spike or Bruce
47 TV-screen element
49 Famous
50 Bay window
51 Comedy or tragedy, e.g.
52 Yeats or Keats
53 Absorbed by
54 Stabilizer, for short
55 Mallet sport
56 Buckwheat's affirmative
57 Flatten in the ring
61 Rural grp.

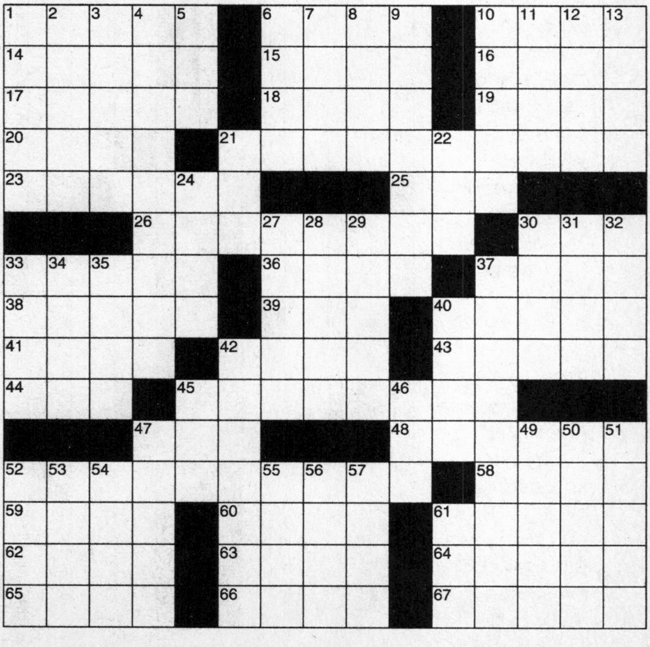

394 BRILLIANCY

by Shirley Soloway

ACROSS
1 Shoots out
6 Worry
10 First-grade lesson
14 Yankee Yogi
15 Take out, to an ed.
16 Perry's creator
17 Loss of creative talent
19 100 dinars
20 Return addressee
21 West or Clarke
22 Folklore meanie
23 Love god
25 Hoards
27 Break of day
30 Corrida shout
32 Pigeonhole
33 Touched down
34 Egyptian cotton
36 Martini additive
39 __ Vegas
40 Cosmetic-pencil target
42 Female deer
43 Lying still
45 Tim of *WKRP*
46 Spill the beans
47 Coin . . .
49 . . . and its color
50 Ingests
51 Positive
54 Ward of *Sisters*
56 Actor Sharif
57 Puppy bite
59 Ferguson and Miles
63 *Of __ and Men*
64 Wise investors
66 Chase of films
67 River in Spain
68 Corn concoctions
69 "__ la vie!"
70 Told a tall tale
71 Little fish

DOWN
1 Recedes
2 Like a pittance
3 Where to spend 19 Across
4 Neptune's staff
5 More logical
6 Four-term pres.
7 Paper pack
8 Inventor Howe
9 Principles
10 Pressurized can
11 Inspired thought
12 County in Ireland
13 Monica of tennis
18 Sagging
24 More wily
26 In the ship's hold
27 Spanish surrealist
28 Greenspan or Shepard
29 Sarcastic remarks
31 Burning particle
35 First zodiac sign
37 Electrical unit
38 Morays
40 Sicilian hot spot
41 Most unusual
44 Fall back
46 Specialized restaurant
48 Christmas tree enhancement
51 Humorous
52 Author Zola
53 Rain clouds
55 Nightstand items
58 Remove a covering
60 Jackson or Meara
61 Command to Rover
62 Meth.
65 Serling of suspense

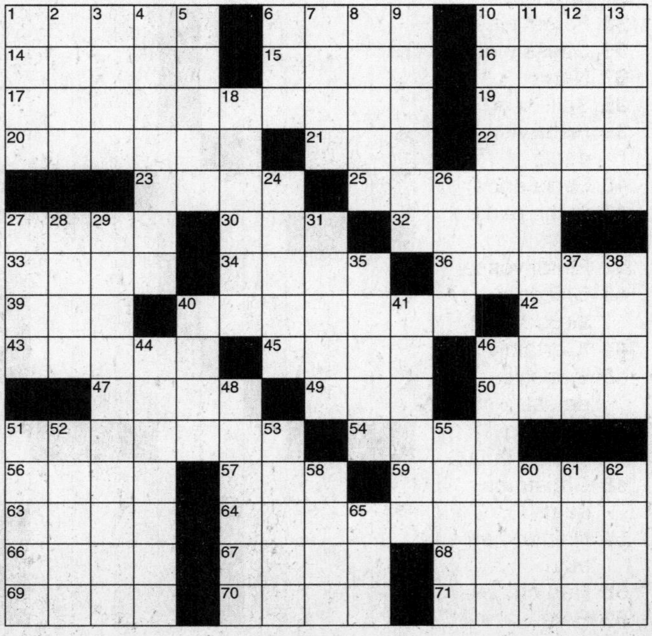

395 APT NAMES

by Norma Steinberg

ACROSS
1 Church service
5 Hayworth or Coolidge
9 Economic indicator: Abbr.
12 "So long, Pierre"
14 Japanese fare
15 __ *Bravo* (John Wayne film)
16 He's a Hollywood bigwig
18 Years: Fr.
19 Maine town
20 Sing like Ella
21 Forum garments
24 Nicks or Wonder
26 *Greed* and *Intolerance*, e.g.
28 Yangtze boat
31 Desertlike
32 Diner sign
35 Chelsea, to Roger
36 Washroom: Abbr.
37 Hawaii components
39 Fish eggs
40 Skilled
42 Buffalo's water
43 Condor or finch
44 Flotsam and jetsam
46 Clientele
48 Allergic reactions
51 Byways
52 Stick around
54 Kicks out
56 Follower of Attila
57 She's got great hands
62 Where to see *Spin City*
63 Clarinetist Shaw
64 Poet Dickinson
65 "Gotcha!"
66 Strong __ ox
67 Mayberry moppet

DOWN
1 Leader met by Nixon
2 Public notices
3 [Not my mistake]
4 Bering __
5 Ladder steps
6 *Once __ Enough* (Susann novel)
7 "__ a Small Hotel"
8 Tire filler
9 She'll be patient
10 Columbus' smallest ship
11 Hitching __
13 Of the city
14 Sermon subject
17 Spends foolishly
20 __ Valley, CA
21 Temper tantrum
22 She's a peacemaker
23 HS diploma alternative
25 Moving vehicles
26 Pre-entrée course
27 Vendition
29 Squirrel food
30 Requisites
33 Roofing material
34 Trim the bangs, e.g.
37 "How sweet __!"
38 Absence
41 Speak to God
43 Swimsuit part
45 Clippers
47 ". . . __ the Wizard"
49 Webber/Rice opus
50 Stay-put protest
52 Pahlavi's title
53 Oompah horn
55 Fidel's co-revolutionary
57 Fed. airport monitor
58 __, *amas*, *amat*
59 Pitcher part
60 Actor Wallach
61 Bar or bakery order

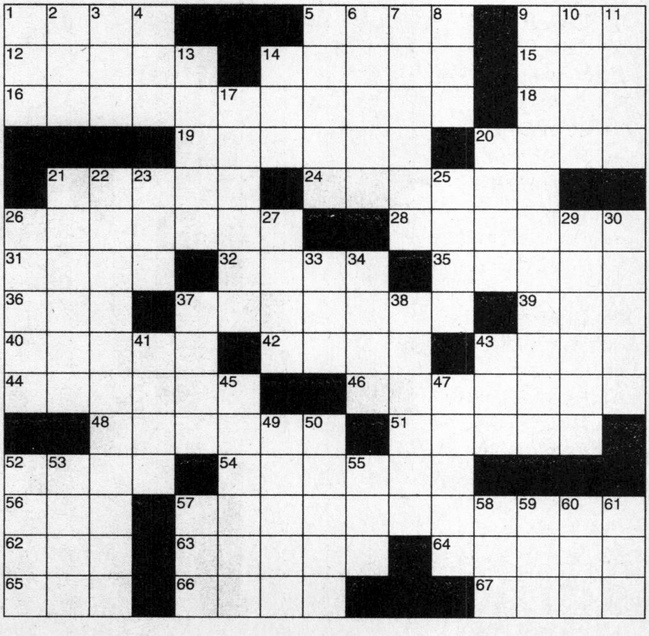

396 BREAKFAST TIME

by Lee Weaver

ACROSS

1 They play for pay
5 Large aquatic mammal
10 Singe
14 *Charley's* __
15 Music hall
16 Angel topper
17 Breakfast fare
19 Muslim religious leader
20 Stadia
21 Cravat holder
23 Conks out
25 Beer mug
26 Appalling
29 Hibachi residue
31 Fix the sound track again
34 Instrument for a Marx brother
35 Grande or Bravo
36 Spanish coin
37 __ *Ventura: Pet Detective*
38 Diminishes
40 Sloe __ fizz
41 Acted like a dictator
43 "Here Comes the __" (Beatles tune)
44 Stare at
45 Pelvic joint
46 __ diem
47 Melts together
48 A Little Rascal
51 Very dry, as champagne
53 Area for Old MacDonald
55 Quiver contents
59 With 64 Across, John Wayne film
60 Breakfast fare
62 Sponsorship
63 Official proclamation
64 See 59 Across
65 Learning method
66 Errata
67 "I'm all __"

DOWN

1 Sobriquet for Hemingway
2 Regretful one
3 In the past
4 __ and be counted
5 Mountie's mount
6 Altar response
7 Pepper with pebbles
8 Spit and __
9 Beginning
10 Hot peppers
11 Breakfast fare
12 "Too bad!"
13 Frolic boisterously
18 Carpenter's need
22 Goddess of grain
24 Spoke
26 Moby Dick seeker
27 Texas city
28 Breakfast fare
30 Toper
32 Practical
33 Bêtes noires
35 Eric the __
36 Bill-signing need
38 Answer an invitation
39 Sidewalk's edge
42 Like Anna's King
44 Abominable act
46 Send-up
47 Roll up, as a flag
48 Later than
49 Slow and majestic, in music
50 Aspect
52 River floaters
54 Faucet problem
56 Gumbo ingredient
57 River dam
58 De Gaulle arrivals
61 Sgt., e.g.

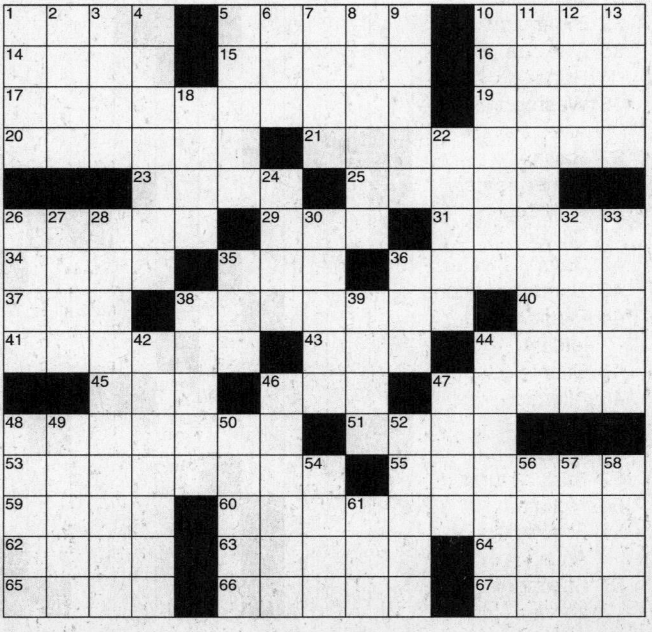

397 OVER YOUR HEAD

by Fred Piscop

ACROSS

1 Violet variety
6 Indy 500 entrant
11 Hole-punching gadget
14 Teddy Roosevelt's daughter
15 Athens marketplace
16 Cedar Rapids college
17 Mars phenomenon
19 __ *Sharkey* (Rickles sitcom)
20 Appear
21 Skating place
22 It's a wrap
24 Sole-related
27 Deserve
28 Dash competitor
31 Take advantage of
32 Track figure
34 Sam of *Jurassic Park*
36 More despicable, perhaps
39 Racetrack event
43 Dreamy state
44 Hall of Famer Banks
45 Modify text
46 Opening Day mo.
48 CIA precursor
49 DeVito series
52 Most lemonlike
55 1936 Olympics star
57 Actress Swenson
58 Dynamic start
62 Poor review
63 Leo G. Carroll role
66 In favor of
67 Starts the pot
68 Source of annoyance
69 Sun Yat-__
70 Irascible
71 Lock of hair

DOWN

1 Soft foods
2 __ vera
3 Aswan Dam site
4 Rascal
5 Law or saw ender
6 Wisconsin city
7 Ten-percenter
8 Crested parrot
9 Bullpen ace's stat
10 Hard knocks
11 Ghana's capital
12 Tom of *The Dukes of Hazzard*
13 Sierra __
18 Tax-deferred accts.
23 More pretentious
25 Put to sleep
26 Red horse
28 "__ how!"
29 Impolite look
30 Lawn chemical
33 Milkers' handfuls
35 "__ Bloom"
36 Popular June gift
37 Mr. Rubik
38 Slugger's stats
40 Eye part
41 Followers of Josip Broz
42 "Permission granted!"
46 Merchant ship
47 Bog material
49 Baseball card company
50 Cognizant
51 Noble gas
53 Not dealt with
54 Slender candle
56 Command to Socks
59 Fencer's weapon
60 Guns the engine
61 Galena et al.
64 Singleton
65 Make a choice

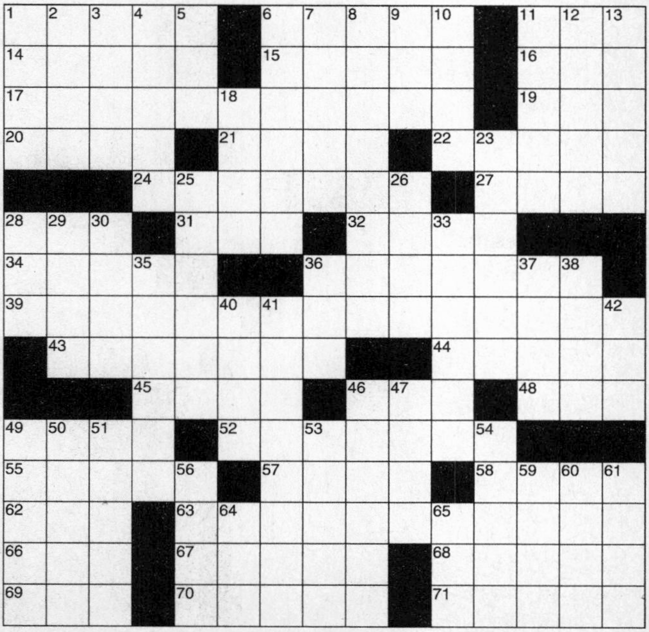

398 *OKAY*

by Shirley Soloway

ACROSS

1 Trunk item
6 Took off
10 Dick and Jane's dog
14 Attacks
15 Rajah's wife
16 Forum wear
17 Coarse-leafed vegetables
19 Manages, with "out"
20 Monty Hall offering
21 Individual
22 Goes along
24 ___-of-mouth
26 Sidelong glances
27 African desert
30 Baseball's ___ Fame
32 Tactics
33 Circle of light
34 Vocalized
37 Response from space
38 Japanese island
41 Mil. officer
42 Footfall
44 Prepares the press
45 Actress Garbo
47 Leaveners
49 Did farm work
50 Mimics
51 Shopping aid
52 The Bunkers' daughter
53 Ventilate
54 Levin and Gershwin
58 Gardening tool
59 Swimming motion
62 Singer Ed
63 Money in Milan
64 Varnish ingredient
65 Young men
66 Heavenly spot
67 Birth cert., e.g.

DOWN

1 Roe source
2 Trim, as expenses
3 The Charles' terrier
4 Train line
5 List-ending abbr.
6 Palm branch
7 Ontario or Michigan
8 Map dir.
9 Refuse, as testimony
10 Sound systems
11 Expressionless
12 S-shaped moldings
13 Soviet news agency
18 Circle dance
23 Solidify
25 Approximately
27 Dieters' retreats
28 Greatly
29 Alley Cat step
30 *Philadelphia* Oscar-winner
31 Word of woe
33 Suggestion
35 Short message
36 Happy
39 Ready for smooching
40 Matures
43 Noblewoman
46 No longer working
48 Hero of *Exodus*
49 Knightly addresses
50 Memorable mission
51 Compare
52 Snatch
53 Land measure
55 Billy or Pete
56 Related
57 Dispatched
60 Lend a hand
61 Prefix for angle or color

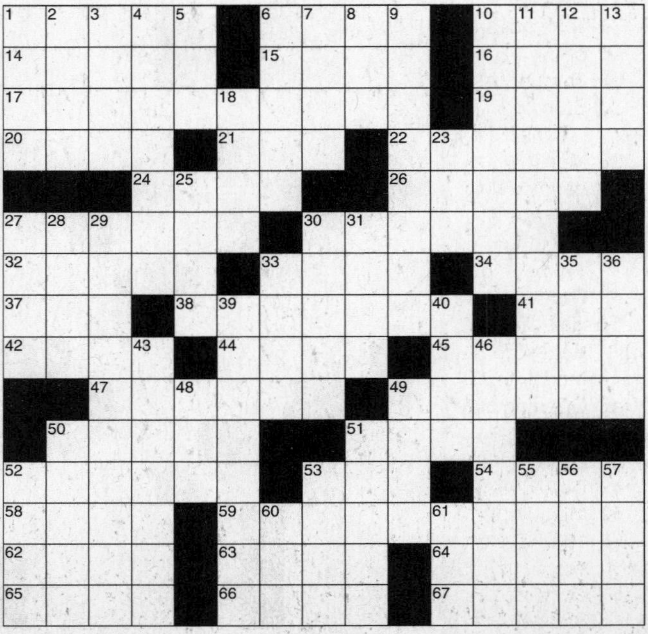

399 GO WITH THE FLOW

by Frank Gordon

ACROSS

1 Jazz singer Vaughan
6 Result of a conking
10 Angry
13 Inflationary __
15 Jacob's twin
16 Indefinite pronoun
17 Colonial silversmith
18 Puma's pad
19 Rap sheet abbr.
20 Dakar's country
22 Bee's quest
24 CD-__ (computer adjunct)
25 Inferior
27 Word with sell or shell
29 In a tizzy
30 Rub-__
34 Train unit
35 Naval rank: Abbr.
36 *Raising* __ ('87 film)
38 "I'd like to propose __"
40 Lineup at Lillehammer
41 Horse-race measures
43 Bolger or Charles
44 Coll. basketball event
45 "*¿Cómo* __ *usted?*"
46 __ salts
48 Singer Lovett
49 Recite magic words
51 Wail
52 Horner's milieu
55 JFK or O'Hare
58 Gold, to Gomez
59 Stink
61 Ceylonese teas
63 *Krazy* __
64 Billy Budd's captain
65 Completely
66 Overhead trains
67 __ out (just got by)
68 Symbol

DOWN

1 Azerbaijan, once: Abbr.
2 Large primates
3 Reds' stadium, formerly
4 "We __ amused"
5 Seraglio
6 Starr et al.
7 Cable network
8 Having prevalent attitudes
9 Blender setting
10 Medieval defense
11 Pop singer Paul
12 Letter opener
14 Drumstick
21 Kal Kan rival
23 Fad
26 Vast expanse
27 Grocer's need
28 Author Joyce Carol __
29 In a tough spot
31 Free-for-all
32 Up to
33 Moisten meat
35 Winter time in Chi.
37 Garden climber
39 Once more
42 Bath or Bad Ems
43 French roast
47 Twisted and turned
48 Seek advice from
50 Brass
51 All in
52 Pepsi rival
53 Spoken
54 Decays
56 Troy, NY, coll.
57 Head overseas?
60 Poetic preposition
62 "That's a joke, __"

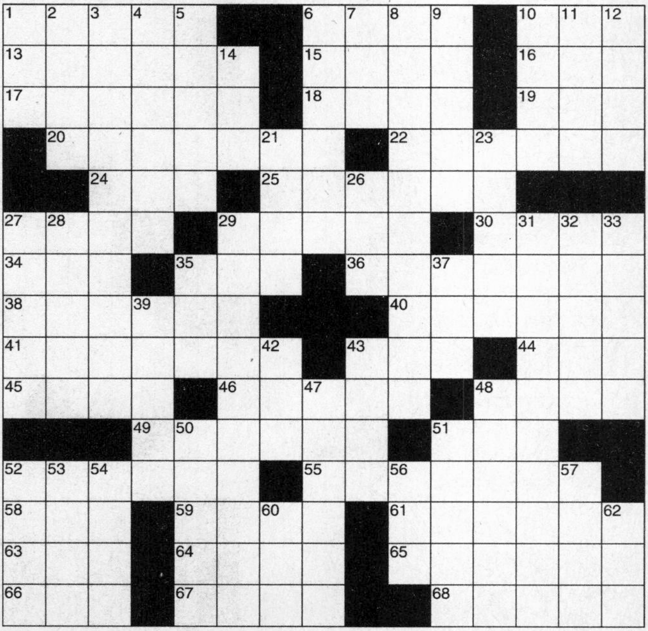

400 COMMAND MEN

by Dean Niles

ACROSS
1 Ran in the wash
5 Ran easily
10 Take it easy
14 Helper
15 Sound off
16 A Great Lake
17 Use the scissors
18 Dreadlocked cultist
19 Swedish soprano
20 Ray Charles song
23 Corrida cry
24 Boston ballplayers, familiarly
25 Weasel relative
28 MTV viewer, typically
30 French friend
33 Woody Allen film
36 Register drawer
37 Give a squeeze
38 Creole vegetable
39 *Star Trek* order
44 Hardwood tree
45 Advocate
46 Black-and-white snacks
47 __-Cat (winter vehicle)
48 Canadian prov.
49 Disillusioned one's lament
57 Cotton holder
58 Unaffiliated company
59 Sunscreen chem.
60 Radar image
61 Punctuation mark
62 Component
63 "__ Sides Now"
64 In the matter of
65 Becomes firm

DOWN
1 Baroque composer
2 Leslie Caron film
3 Redact
4 Cabinet grp.
5 Rhine siren
6 "__ Ben Jonson"
7 El __, TX
8 Singer James
9 Scroll site
10 Chill out
11 Actor Roberts
12 Swim alternative
13 Newsman Koppel
21 Sacred
22 Folk singer Mitchell
25 Eavesdroppers
26 Islamic deity
27 Palliative
28 Stocking shade
29 Omelet ingredients
30 Seek permission
31 *The Bells of St. __*
32 "__ Believer" ('66 tune)
34 Gangster
35 Jot down
36 *TV Guide* abbr.
40 Paul of *Scarface*
41 Nin's works, e.g.
42 Subject matter
43 Table scraps
47 Slender one
48 Pungent plant
49 By oneself
50 Got off
51 Soon
52 Out of commission
53 Musical composition
54 Tarzan's partner
55 Newspaper notice
56 Grub
57 Consumer org.

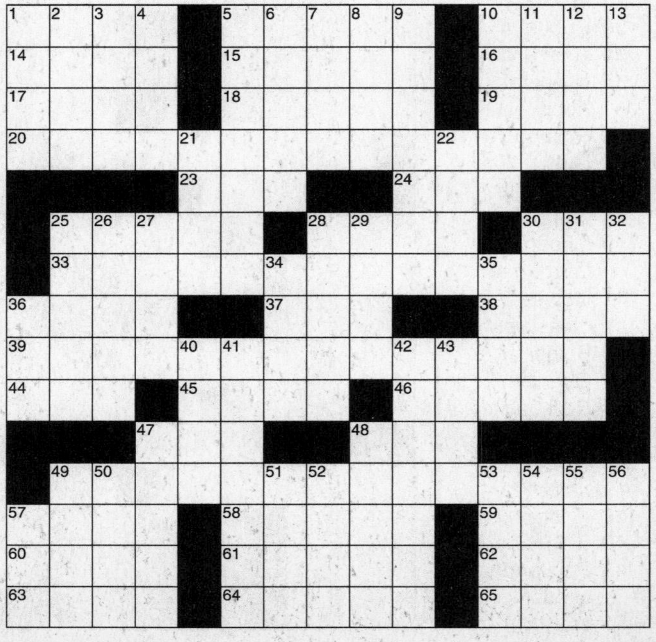

ANSWERS

1

L	O	G	I	C	■	C	U	M	■	T	E	S	L	A
A	R	U	B	A	■	R	N	A	■	I	N	C	A	S
M	E	T	E	R	M	A	I	D	■	M	A	R	Y	S
■	■	■	T	W	O	S	T	E	P	■	B	E	L	A
P	A	R	■	A	S	H	■	R	A	I	L	W	A	Y
A	G	H	A	S	T	■	J	E	R	K	E	D	■	■
T	E	E	T	H	■	Q	U	A	K	E	■	R	O	D
I	N	T	O	■	F	U	N	D	S	■	R	I	P	E
O	T	T	■	L	E	A	K	Y	■	R	A	V	E	N
■	■	B	O	V	A	R	Y	■	G	O	F	E	R	S
T	O	U	R	I	S	T	■	A	I	M	■	R	A	E
A	L	T	I	■	T	E	A	R	G	A	S	■	■	■
M	I	L	E	S	■	R	O	B	I	N	C	O	O	K
E	V	E	N	T	■	E	N	O	■	C	A	R	P	I
D	A	R	T	S	■	D	E	R	■	E	R	R	E	D

2

B	L	I	M	P	■	C	H	E	F	■	A	S	P	S
A	U	D	I	O	■	R	A	V	I	■	R	H	E	A
S	P	L	I	T	L	E	V	E	L	■	G	O	N	G
K	E	Y	■	H	A	T	E	■	T	R	Y	O	N	E
■	■	■	O	O	Z	E	■	S	H	E	L	F	■	■
W	A	G	G	L	Y	■	C	H	I	S	E	L	E	D
A	D	O	R	E	■	Q	U	I	E	T	■	Y	A	Y
L	I	F	E	■	T	U	B	E	R	■	A	P	S	E
L	E	O	■	P	R	I	E	D	■	B	R	I	E	R
S	U	R	F	E	I	T	S	■	C	A	M	E	L	S
■	■	B	O	L	A	S	■	S	O	U	S	■	■	■
M	E	R	I	T	S	■	J	I	N	X	■	O	D	E
I	D	O	L	■	S	C	A	T	S	I	N	G	E	R
L	I	K	E	■	I	O	N	E	■	T	I	L	E	S
D	E	E	D	■	C	O	E	D	■	E	X	E	R	T

3

W	E	B	S	■	I	R	M	A	■	■	C	A	R	P
A	L	A	I	■	R	E	A	L	M	■	O	M	O	O
R	A	N	G	■	K	A	R	M	A	■	N	O	T	E
E	L	A	N	D	■	P	E	A	J	A	C	K	E	T
■	■	N	E	E	D	S	■	■	O	L	E	■	■	■
N	E	A	T	E	R	■	H	E	R	O	I	C	S	■
E	S	S	■	R	U	M	O	R	■	E	T	H	E	R
S	T	E	W	■	M	I	N	O	R	■	S	O	T	O
T	E	A	R	S	■	M	E	S	A	S	■	P	T	A
■	S	T	E	M	M	E	D	■	H	E	N	S	O	N
■	■	■	C	U	E	■	■	A	S	S	E	T	■	■
M	I	L	K	G	L	A	S	S	■	S	W	I	S	H
O	D	E	A	■	E	R	U	P	T	■	E	C	H	O
O	L	E	G	■	E	E	R	I	E	■	S	K	I	P
T	Y	K	E	■	■	S	E	C	T	■	T	S	P	S

4

O	T	H	E	R	■	R	U	D	E	R	■	A	T	M
C	H	O	S	E	■	I	R	I	S	H	■	L	I	E
H	O	L	L	O	W	V	I	C	T	O	R	I	E	S
S	U	E	■	P	O	I	S	E	■	■	A	N	D	S
■	■	C	R	E	M	E	■	D	E	A	D	E	Y	E
S	C	A	N	N	E	R	S	■	B	I	A	S	E	D
H	O	R	S	■	N	A	T	■	B	R	R	■	■	■
E	N	D	■	■	■	S	A	T	■	■	■	P	I	P
■	■	■	P	I	U	■	R	O	W	■	B	I	K	E
C	A	R	I	N	G	■	R	O	A	D	S	T	E	R
H	E	A	V	E	H	O	■	L	I	R	A	S	■	■
A	R	N	O	■	■	P	A	S	T	A	■	T	C	U
L	A	S	T	D	I	T	C	H	E	F	F	O	R	T
E	T	O	■	A	F	I	R	E	■	T	E	P	E	E
T	E	M	■	R	A	C	E	D	■	Y	E	S	E	S

5

C	A	V	E	■	S	A	L	E	S	■	S	H	E	A
A	L	A	S	■	P	R	O	X	Y	■	E	A	R	P
F	I	L	E	F	O	L	D	E	R	■	A	M	I	E
E	V	E	■	F	R	E	E	R	■	A	C	M	E	S
S	E	T	T	L	E	S	■	C	A	N	O	E	■	■
■	■	■	H	A	S	■	G	I	F	T	W	R	A	P
B	E	F	I	T	■	C	A	S	T	E	■	O	B	I
A	G	I	N	■	H	O	M	E	S	■	Y	U	L	E
B	A	R	■	D	U	N	E	S	■	C	O	T	E	S
A	D	E	Q	U	A	C	Y	■	A	O	K	■	■	■
■	■	D	U	N	C	E	■	E	L	B	O	W	E	D
D	E	R	E	K	■	R	A	T	I	O	■	O	V	A
E	L	I	A	■	O	N	T	H	E	L	E	V	E	L
A	I	L	S	■	H	E	M	E	N	■	R	E	N	E
R	E	L	Y	■	O	D	O	R	S	■	A	N	T	S

6

C	O	T	E	S	■	S	H	A	M	S	■	D	A	D
O	R	A	T	E	■	C	A	N	O	E	■	I	R	A
B	R	U	C	E	B	A	N	N	E	R	■	C	I	I
■	■	■	■	D	E	N	S	E	■	I	N	K	E	R
S	O	P	H	I	E	S	■	■	G	A	N	G	L	Y
Q	U	E	U	E	S	■	C	H	O	L	E	R	■	■
U	T	T	E	R	■	J	O	U	R	S	■	A	I	R
I	R	E	S	■	K	I	R	B	Y	■	D	Y	N	E
D	E	R	■	R	O	V	E	S	■	M	I	S	T	S
■	■	P	I	E	C	E	S	■	C	A	V	O	R	T
B	L	A	N	C	H	■	■	B	A	N	A	N	A	S
L	O	R	N	E	■	C	O	O	P	T	■	■	■	■
A	S	K	■	D	I	A	N	A	P	R	I	N	C	E
Z	E	E	■	E	D	I	T	S	■	A	M	O	U	R
E	R	R	■	D	O	N	O	T	■	P	A	D	R	E

7

A	L	M	A	■	■	I	C	E	R	■	W	A	D	S
W	O	O	F	■	B	R	O	K	E	■	A	T	O	P
F	O	O	T	B	R	I	D	G	E	■	R	E	N	E
U	S	E	■	O	I	S	E	■	M	O	A	N	E	D
L	E	D	G	E	S	■	S	T	E	R	N	■	■	■
■	■	■	I	R	K	S	■	E	R	O	D	I	N	G
S	K	I	N	S	■	O	L	E	G	■	P	L	E	A
A	N	D	A	■	G	R	A	T	E	■	E	L	A	L
S	E	E	N	■	A	R	C	H	■	P	A	S	T	A
S	W	A	D	D	L	E	■	E	P	I	C	■	■	■
■	■	■	T	E	L	L	A	■	E	L	E	C	T	S
G	I	G	O	L	O	■	S	H	E	A	■	A	W	E
A	G	I	N	■	P	O	K	E	R	F	A	C	E	D
Y	O	G	I	■	E	W	E	R	S	■	S	T	A	G
E	R	I	C	■	R	E	D	S	■	■	P	I	K	E

8

D	E	C	A	F	■	A	L	E	C	■	T	S	A	R
O	L	A	N	D	■	P	U	L	L	■	A	L	I	A
O	B	S	E	R	V	A	T	I	O	N	P	O	S	T
R	A	H	■	■	I	R	E	■	S	U	P	P	L	E
■	■	B	A	D	A	T	■	G	E	N	E	S	E	S
S	H	O	V	E	L	■	P	O	U	N	D	■	■	■
S	A	X	E	S	■	H	E	L	P	■	■	K	E	A
T	H	E	R	I	T	E	O	F	S	P	R	I	N	G
S	A	S	■	■	A	W	N	S	■	L	I	B	Y	A
■	■	■	C	A	P	E	S	■	C	A	V	I	A	R
R	E	L	A	X	E	D	■	J	A	N	E	T	■	■
E	V	E	N	E	D	■	E	E	R	■	■	Z	E	D
M	I	D	D	L	E	A	G	E	S	P	R	E	A	D
U	T	I	L	■	C	L	A	P	■	A	O	R	T	A
S	A	N	E	■	K	I	D	S	■	M	E	S	S	Y

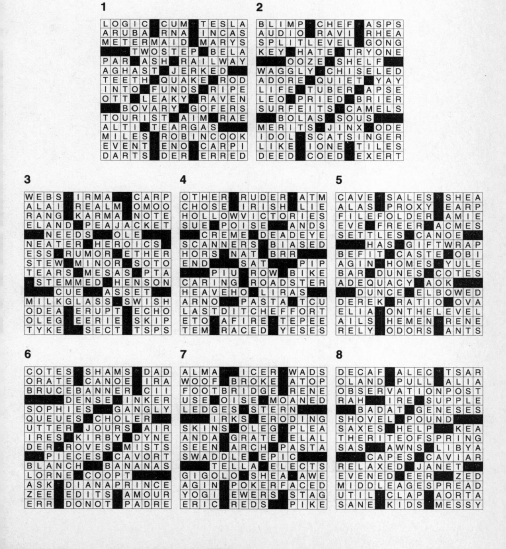

9

FAZE TAMP BALM
OXEN SAFES ISEE
OLDCOUNTRY KANT
LES MAD ECLIPSE
SEVE HAN
NEWAGEMUSICIANS
ANITA PACE DOT
BEDE POPES ALVA
ORE JADE FLIER
BORROWEDTROUBLE
INN HARM
STOPGAP ESC APE
ARLO BLUEPENCIL
REEF LANNY ALES
ASOF EYED PURE

10

CAR SOLD TAMPS
ADOS TREE OPART
FASTBREAK MEDIA
ENSILE REF MEET
SOIREE IRE
RAPIDTRANSIT
BADER ROREM IDO
USED SATED SLOB
SEW RUBEN SILLY
HASTYPUDDING
WEE CANADA
MALI RAH ERASED
ARENT QUICKLIME
RINGO URSA SAUL
EATEN ATOP NRA

11

SCRAM SPED CHOP
OHARA HARI HALO
LINER ALIE OWED
ENGAGEMENTRING
AYE CAR
MATURE POOH UMA
OBESE WINK INON
POPSTHEQUESTION
EVER OPUS ULTRA
DEE ANTE UNLESS
PIE AND
WILLYOUMARRYME
WADE BONA EIEIO
ELLA UZIS STAIN
BLED NETS SARIS

12

PAGAN SWAN BASE
ERASE CITE ANKA
TIGHTROPEWALKER
EASY HOE CULLEN
MET CORSET
PAPAYA TOMA
EXIST KITE LARD
ELEPHANTTRAINER
LESS BOLA JONNY
ASWE JANETS
MADMEN TUX
WARREN SAD ABBE
HUMANCANNONBALL
AVOW EWOK ALBUM
TERN SEWS PEERS

13

MARLA BAR SKATE
AXIOM ORO CORAL
CLIMBINGTHEWALL
HES USE CANTBE
ESL LEO
MOPTHEFLOORWITH
ASIA RILEY GEO
TAPS WEEDS ALMS
EKE SIETE DOPE
DARKENSONESDOOR
IAN RES
RANSOM ALL OSS
WINDOWENVELOPES
ASTON LEI ERECT
REEFS TED RENTS

14

RON ADIPOSE ACT
AMO SELECTS RAE
NOR SWEATYPALMS
DOWSE SLAM MEET
EON IFONLY
LIGHTFINGERS
OLIO ECOL ATRIA
RIA TRAVELS ERR
DENTS MANO SPAT
BAREKNUCKLES
BEFORE LII
EARN NANA OSCAR
GREENTHUMBS ARA
ALE RESTORE TEN
TYS CROSSAT EAT

15

ROTS ACED PESTO
AVOW CONE AVAIL
ZUNI THIS JOKED
OLYMPIADUKAKIS
REA RON LIME
CON ETNA BOA
ASIAN EWOK FRAN
MONTGOMERYCLIFT
ODDS RORY REESE
SAY BATS TUX
MALI SHE KOS
JACKSONPOLLOCK
PONCE NORM AREA
TENOR ASEA MEAT
SLAYS LYES BANE

16

APB OSAGE STRIP
SOO FINES TOOLE
TIA FRONTRUNNER
ESTEE TEED
RESENTS SEDATED
KEDGER DERATE
SRI SILOS DEBTS
PUPS FEMUR ALAI
UPPER SADAT ESS
REEVES NAMATH
SERENER NATIONS
DEAL TEPEE
JUMPERCABLE PEN
INGER EMEER EDS
MAMAS DEEDS RYE

17

ADDS IMAN TOSCA
DIRE CART OLEOS
SPILLEDTHEBEANS
SPLICE MAGNET
GAD COGS
COUCHPOTATO MAS
ONSET ONE CASK
STUN TROTS OMNI
TART HOT PLIED
SPY PEASHOOTERS
REIN IRS
ASPENS RASCAL
THEPUMPKINEATER
TENOR RING ROVE
NASTY EDGE EPIC

18

CZAR CHAMPS SCI
OATH OILERS TON
OPTIONPLAYS IRS
INN ANO ANTE
STOCKCHARACTER
IOU EEO LISZT
DADE AMASSED
APEX NICHE IHAD
TOUCHER COVE
ACTOR LIL MEW
WARRANTOFFICER
ALIT OAR ROM
ILK BONDSERVANT
TEE INGEAR EDIE
SRS GEORGE TEXT

19

RAM VOLT ALANON
AMO AROO ROTARY
DUCKSOUP CRADLE
ASHES SALADDAYS
REAGAN ZENO
RUB DEVELOP
ECCE MAP EVADE
ROLLSBACKPRICES
SMOKE SIR LEST
TAGSALE DOC
WASP SHEATH
EASYASPIE OLLIE
CREATE CUPOFTEA
HEALER KRIS ERR
OATERS SONY RST

20

SPAR YARD SUMS
PAREE ELIE ITAL
ADORN LION NINA
MEDIABLITZ CLOP
AMO SELLERS
HOLLERED LOA
ONE ORES NISEI
PUTTINONTHERITZ
ESTER SELA ATO
NAM BOTTOMED
RIPENER COS
ADAM DERSHOWITZ
MITE IGOT TAHOE
BORN CANE OLAND
OMIT SLAW ODDS

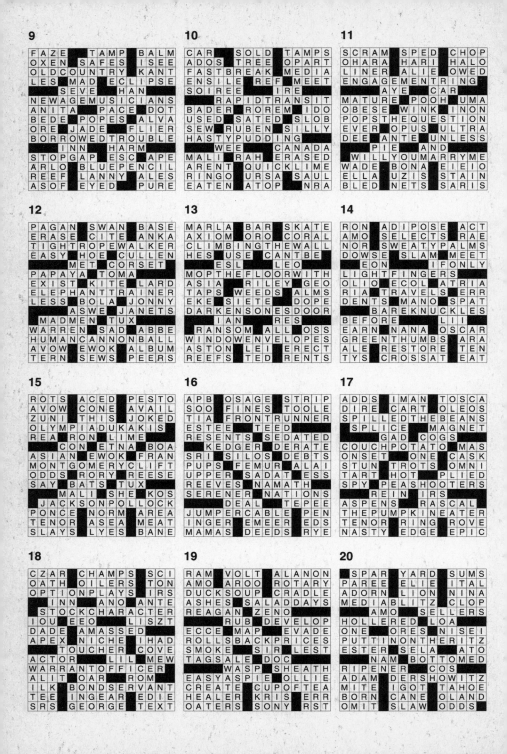

21

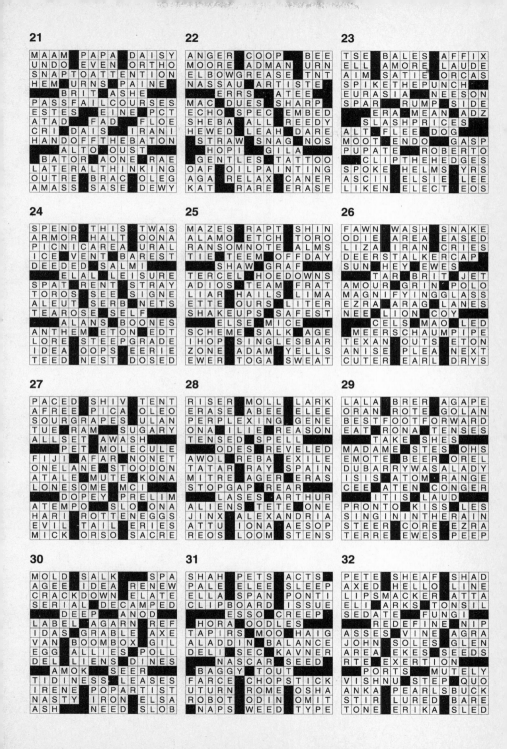

```
MAAM■PAPA■DAISY
UNDO■EVEN■ORTHO
SNAPTOATTENTION
HEM■URNS■PAINE■
■■■BRIT■ASHE■■■
PASSFAILCOURSES
ESTES■■EINE■PCT
ATAD■■FAD■■FLOE
CRI■DAIS■■IRANI
HANDOFFTHEBATON
■■■ALTO■OUST■■■
■BATOR■AONE■RAE
LATERALTHINKING
OUTRE■BRAC■OLEG
AMASS■SASE■DEWY
```

22

```
ANGER■COOP■■BEE
MOORE■ADMAN■URN
ELBOWGREASE■TNT
NASSAU■ARTISTE■
■■■ERRS■■ATEE■■
MAC■DUES■SHARP■
ECHO■SPEC■EMBED
SHEBA■ALL■REEDY
HEWED■LEAH■DARE
■STRAW■SNAG■NOS
■■HOPI■■GILA■■■
■GENTLES■TATTOO
OAF■OILPAINTING
AGA■RELAX■CANER
KAT■■RARE■ERASE
```

23

```
TSE■BALES■AFFIX
ELL■AMORE■LAUDE
AIM■SATIE■ORCAS
SPIKETHEPUNCH■■
EURASIA■■NEESON
SPAR■■RUMP■SIDE
■■■ERA■MEAN■ADZ
■■SLASHPRICES■■
ALT■FLEE■DOG■■■
MOOT■ENDO■■GASP
PUPATE■■ROBERTO
■■CLIPTHEHEDGES
SPOKE■HELMS■YRS
ASCII■ELSIE■LEE
LIKEN■ELECT■EOS
```

24

```
SPEND■THIS■TWAS
ARMOR■HALT■OONA
PICNICAREA■URAL
ICE■VENT■BAREST
DEEDED■SALMI■■■
■■■ELAL■LEISURE
SPAT■RENT■STRAY
TOROS■SEE■SIGNE
ALEUT■SERB■NETS
TEAROSE■SELF■■■
■■■ALANS■BOONES
ANTHEM■ETON■EDT
LORE■STEEPGRADE
IDEA■OOPS■EERIE
TEED■NEST■DOSED
```

25

```
MAZES■RAPT■SHIN
ALAMO■ETCH■TORO
RANSOMNOTE■ALMS
TIE■TEEM■OFFDAY
■■■SHAW■GRAF■■■
TERCEL■HOEDOWNS
ADIOS■TEAM■FRAT
LIAR■HAILS■LIMA
ETTE■OURS■LITER
SHAKEUPS■SAFEST
■■■ELSE■MICE■■■
SCHEME■SALK■AGE
IHOP■SINGLESBAR
ZONE■ADAM■YELLS
EWER■TOGA■SWEAT
```

26

```
FAWN■WASH■SNAKE
ODIE■AREA■EASED
LIZA■IRAN■CRIES
DEERSTALKERCAP■
SUN■HEY■EWES■■■
■■■TAR■BRIT■JET
AMOUR■GRIN■POLO
MAGNIFYINGGLASS
EZRA■ARAG■LANES
NEE■LION■COY■■■
■■■CELS■MAO■LED
■MEERSCHAUMPIPE
TEXAN■OUTS■ETON
ANISE■PLEA■NEXT
CUTER■EARL■DRYS
```

27

```
PACED■SHIV■TENT
AFREE■PICA■OLEO
SOURGRAPES■ULAN
TUE■RAM■■SUGARY
ALLSET■AWASH■■■
■■■PET■MOLECULE
FIJI■AFAR■NONET
ONELANE■STOODON
ATALE■MUTE■KONA
LONESOME■MCI■■■
■■■DOPEY■PRELIM
ATEMPO■■SLO■ONA
HARI■ROTTENEGGS
EVIL■TAIL■ERIES
MICK■ORSO■SACRE
```

28

```
RISER■MOLL■LARK
ERASE■ABEE■ELEE
PERPLEXING■GENE
ONA■ILIE■REASON
TENSED■SPELL■■■
■■■ODES■REVELED
AWOL■REBA■EXILE
TATAR■RAY■SPAIN
MITRE■AGER■ERAS
STOPGAP■REAR■■■
■■■LASES■ARTHUR
ALIENS■TETE■ONE
JINX■ALEXANDRIA
ATTU■IONA■AESOP
REOS■LOOM■STENS
```

29

```
LALA■BRER■AGAPE
ORAN■ROTE■GOLAN
BESTFOOTFORWARD
EAT■RONA■TENSES
■■■TAKE■SHES■■■
MADAME■STES■OHS
EMOTE■BEER■OREL
DUBARRYWASALADY
ISIS■ATOM■RANGE
CEE■ATEN■CONGER
■■■ITIS■LAUD■■■
PRONTO■KISS■LES
SINGININTHERAIN
STEER■CORE■EZRA
TERRE■EWES■PEEP
```

30

```
MOLD■SALK■■■SPA
AGEE■IDEA■RENEW
CRACKDOWN■ELATE
SERIAL■DECAMPED
■■■DEEP■■ANOD■■
LABEL■AGARN■REF
IDAS■GRABLE■AXE
VAN■BOOMBOX■GIL
EGG■ALLIES■POLL
DEL■LIENS■DINES
■■AMOK■■SEER■■■
TIDINESS■LEASES
IRENE■POPARTIST
NASTY■IRON■ELSA
ASH■■■NEED■SLOB
```

31

```
SHAH■PETS■ACTS■
PALE■ELEE■SLEEP
ELLA■SPAN■PONTI
CLIPBOARD■ISSUE
■■■■ESSO■CREEP■
■HORA■OODLES■■■
TAPIRS■MOO■HAIG
ALADDIN■BALANCE
DELI■SEC■KAVNER
■■■NASCAR■SEED■
■BAGGY■TOUT■■■■
FARCE■CHOPSTICK
UTURN■ROME■OSHA
ROBOT■ODIN■OMIT
■NAPS■WEED■TYPE
```

32

```
PETE■SHEAF■SHAD
AXED■HELLO■LINE
LIPSMACKER■ATTA
ELI■ARKS■TONSIL
SEDATE■■FUNGI■■
■■■REDEFINE■NIP
ASSES■VINE■AGRA
JOHN■SOLES■GLEN
AREA■EKES■SEEDS
RTE■EXERTION■■■
■■PORTS■■MUTELY
VISHNU■STEP■QUO
ANKA■PEARLSBUCK
STIR■LURED■BARE
TONE■ERIKA■SLED
```

33

TSP EAVES TIBET
EWE CRACK HOUSE
PARFORTHECOURSE
EMMA ODOR
EPITAPH SANCTUM
SST BOOR TYRANT
OUSTED ELIS
OFFTHESUBJECT
TGIF LINEUP
ALLEGE NEED RPS
JEERING STOREUP
VIAL ETTA
SHOWEDSOMECLASS
HAVEN PROVE KIM
EGADS SEPAL ENS

34

ALAN LODI ACRE
ROMA IRON STOOL
GOOSENECK HOLES
ONSALE STAND
MASC IRATER
BICKERER DELUGE
ASHER PORED RON
LOIN HAWED SKIT
BBC MELBA REESE
OAKIES ACRONYMS
ARENAS RHOS
NONET LITTLE
ATONE EAGLEEYED
TRUER ELEE ANNE
EATS NEER LEAN

35

SEWS PACE YORE
CLAM FURLS EMIR
OSLO CLOTH ANTI
WALKS DOORPRIZE
FETA KNEEL
FLYING DROWSY
ILO RILED UNITE
TOWS LEVEL GNAW
CREEL NABOB DRS
HARLEM TORSOS
LEECH MEOW
FLOORSHOW DOSES
LULU AUGER THAI
ABET STALE HOST
KEGS ENDS EPEE

36

MACAW CHET AGO
ABASE EURO ARID
TURKEYTROT NAVE
ESTE EELS IDLER
YESDEAR IDO
CHADEVERETT
DITTO UNEARTHS
ITHE SEEDS AREA
SCANTEST SNEER
CHINACLOSET
YRS CLEARER
CRUST FOAL COLE
RENO BURMASHAVE
ONIN ASAP PORES
PET GELS FOSSE

37

LOBE TOPS ASSET
ATIT RASH PUREE
SHAH URSA IMAGE
SESAMESTREET
IRENE DECODES
ESS THAW RETIES
OASIS ANNE
GASOLINEALLEY
NARC TEMPI
ELMORE DIEM OSS
TASTERS BATHE
FLAMINGOROAD
OPERA EDIE COMA
RILEY LENT ELAN
GAMES LAOS DENS

38

CHEAT CHAR SLIM
CAPRA HERA TUBE
CRIMINALCHARGES
PEC WASP VESTS
WADE HOES
MANANA TOWNSHIP
ANIN ARRAU ARE
GIVESABADREVIEW
ITE PRICE IGNI
CANAILLE BASSET
ENOL POLE
AWISE PIMA ACT
SHOOTSTHEBREEZE
SOAP SKIT MORAN
TAMS HOLY SNORT

39

RAFTS SCALA WAS
EFLAT HOREB IDE
CROCODILEDUNDEE
COWARD TRESS
ASK TESLA ASTI
DESKS ABA TEN
ENTAIL AMASS
TORTOISESHELL
LEFTS HERALD
OAK STA SAMBA
FRAY SLATE ISH
FERAL CAREEN
SNAKEINTHEGRASS
EAT TABOO ALTOS
TSE SNARE DEEDS

40

PICK CARET SCOT
ERIE ADORE TOME
SONGANDDANCEMAN
ONE BILE OVERT
MAINE GREED
CHASTE BRAD ICH
LUCIE BAITS AAA
ORES CREME SNIT
SOL CLARE FIBRE
EKE RUNS BARONS
BREED CALEB
SCRIP OATS HOE
PAINTINGTHETOWN
ARTS MELEE APED
RAYE PEERS MESS

41

BABA SALE AFTON
AMAS EVIL DIANE
TICKEDOFF OGDEN
ONO LANE INHALE
NONFAT RELIT
ITEM VISITOR
TASTE IDEA NOVA
ABET AMEND GRAF
OLEO LOOT SMELT
SYMBOLS SALA
ELIAS BADGER
STATEN ANON AXE
CILIA WROUGHTUP
ALGER EGON BODE
READY BEND OREL

42

TADA TIKI RABID
IGOR OLEG ELENA
NEWYORKPUNKBAND
NAM TAOIST
ASININE NON SIT
MONSTERSANDWICH
POG RAT LATKE
PROTESTER
OCULO APE SOP
FAMOUSAMOSTREAT
ALP LED THREATS
TWEEZE OAS
SWEETMIXEDDRINK
ARENT NIGH EDIE
LYNDE GTOS DEKA

43

CALIF AGNES LST
AVILA SEERS AHA
BELLCAPTAIN YET
STRIATE SURE
ALP OAR SAPPER
BOAT BETS BUSES
LUGOSI OILER
ETERNALTRIANGLE
RANEE AMELIA
STEER OMNI DAMS
CORNEA OSA DAY
AMAT CLAMORS
LAS THEGONGSHOW
ETE REFER UTILE
ROD ESTEE ESSES

44

JURIST ROC CHAR
ARISTA OUI HOME
INDIANCORN EVAN
TIGHTSQUEEZE
CHA DLI SCREW
NESTLECRUNCH
ONKEY HAIG MAD
TRIX WHORL BONO
EIN JOAD ARGON
TEENAGECRUSH
AFOOT NNE LEO
SUMMERSQUASH
STAT COUSCOUSES
TONI PHI TULANE
SNIT TOP STAYON

45

AURA BASAL CANE
CRAB LETME ONCE
EASYSTREET MEAL
SLASH INTHEWAY
SARAN SAL
HOT HER SIGNS
UPI NCO STEREO
MIDDLEOFTHEROAD
INAROW TAO STA
DELAY MUM SOS
GAS METAL
LOISLANE NODES
INST BEATENPATH
FLEE ERNIE ERNO
EYER ROTOR SEAT

46

DEFT GALS ASPIN
AERO IBET REUSE
BLOWAFUSE SALSA
LITTERS BLUR
DEFILE NEGATES
ELAN DAD GOGH
LADES SAMOA EDA
ATEST IRA DOPES
YET EASEL SPLAT
ODES SIC EURO
ALBERTA LARGER
PALS ALTOONA
INAIR SOUNDTAPS
SACRE OGRE OHIO
HIKES PASS RAND

47

CARP RASH ERAS
ARIA ELLEN RANT
RENT SMILE ETNA
RADIOCOMMERCIAL
OFUS ATOLL
LEA METALED
ATSEA SOS SETA
DAILYNEWSPAPERS
ETAL BEA VALUE
MAGNATE YET
SMELL PERT
TELEVISIONSHOWS
IDLE MANGO EVAS
NEER ALIEN SALT
TASS STES ELKS

48

TAP ADAPT SUSAN
IME DOBRO ATONE
NON ELBOW NAFTA
CRUISERWEIGHT
TAROT SRA SEE
SLYNESS NINETY
SWAP NOLTE
SUBMARINEBALLER
APRIL TARE
ROILED PERTEST
INT END HORNE
CARRIERPIGEON
MAHRE CLEAN CRO
IBEAM HELLO TEN
COSBY ESSES SRS

49

TRIM CROAK VICE
RENE HORSE AMOR
ATTA ARETE SPAR
COUNTRYSINGERS
ELITE REP OTS
DDT MALT DAPPER
APPEAL REDS
UNIONMEMBER
WANT SENDUP
ABASES STIR FIT
SUR SPA TERNS
STATESONESCASE
HIFI ACTED OMIT
OVUM KOREA LESS
GELS STORM ESTE

50

ASARAIL REPAIR
MADONNA DILEMMA
IWANNABEACOWBOY
MAIN RUE IKE
SHALE CENSOR
WAND PACT BEAS
END SORT FELLAS
ADEPTLY RESOLVE
REVERE SADE TOP
LETA GAGS OHIO
SPARSE EMERY
USA LES ODES
ROLEPLAYINGGAME
SNIGLET STEAMED
ASSOON TOSSERS

51

SLANT HELD ARAM
TENTH OLIO FATE
REDHERRING GTOS
IRE MUSEUM HEMS
DEADEN SARAH
EDNA SSS SINISE
BATHER DIKES
CAR ROADHOG ETS
AMUSE HEELED
VISTAS RAD ODES
HORAS INTERN
ECHO CHAISE MAE
GOOP RANCHHOUSE
GLUE ELKE RARER
YARD DEAR USERS

52

RAP PACS TAN
EVIL ABOUT DALI
POGO NEWSY EXEC
OWING SLAPSTICK
NEAT NOPE
STARLESS SACHET
TOP ASWAN STILE
ENOS TAROT STIR
PIKER GAMUT ADM
SCENES HEROINES
SEWS FOND
STRIKEOUT LEMON
LOIN LURID RIPE
AGOG LLAMA TSAR
MAT SLED SLO

53

HADJ FRET MORSE
ERIE LAME EVITA
LOOK EMIT SAGAS
PONYEXPRESS IVE
LEES WELDED
GELLED PRADO
ELO SEAMINESS
MOUNTWASHINGTON
SIDEWALKS TWI
MITTY ADJUST
THRONE ALOU
OOH BRONCOBILLY
WROTE POOH CIAO
ENDED ATRA ENID
DEALS LENS SERA

54

PUPS CRAMP SEGA
ASYE AUDIO APED
SUGARBEETS LIED
TAMTAM SETBACKS
ELY DEF POD
HONEYROASTED
SWOON DAUNT AVA
TEXT POSSE EXES
ORE MERIT IRISH
WENDYDARLING
AND END EPI
JAYWALKS CIGARS
ALAN EARTHANGEL
MORE RETIE ALEE
BEND SLAPS WENT

55

LIAR MAAM SCOT
EDNA ULNA PLACE
SIGHTSITE LASTS
SOL ASKS BATHES
TEEHEE DETECT
GOD TERESA
PEKOE TENTS COM
URNS CRASH CHAP
PRE WHERE WHETS
ATHENS CIA
ADRIFT MANTIS
DINERS TANG RUE
IDEAL CHICSHEIK
MEETS OOZE ANTE
EDDY DUEL SEED

56

AJAR SAM OGLALA
DUMA PIA XRATED
ADOS ORG TIPTOE
MYSTERYMEAT UNS
ALE ANITA
TSP IST GLIBBER
OLAF ARAL NORGE
ROMANCELANGUAGE
UMBRA KANE TIED
SOYMILK DUH DRY
SLEET TIS
PAM HORRORSTORY
ARAGON AMI IKEA
ALKALI MAN FRAN
ROOTED PRO FALK

57

SERF SHOP PASHA
AQUA PURE ALAIN
MUSS AFAR STYLE
BUTTERFLIES COW
ASSERT LAUGH
DRAIN SPEECH
ETC INDEBT NERO
LORDS ERA CASES
AREA RADISH EWE
LEANTO STEAM
MEATS CLASPS
LAP THEMILKYWAY
EXULT TUTU HORN
ALFIE TIED ERIC
DEFER ORME MESH

58

DAM HOPED APOD
IRA AMICE TRACY
SCREWBALL RISEN
MAJAS FALSE SLA
ADORES TACKROOM
YER RHO AKINTO
SAS ARP NEL
MOLLYCODDLE
LIE SRI EDA
OPTIMO DUH MUS
BRADPITT MOROSE
LOG ELIOT MANTA
AVERT NAILBITER
DENIS ESTER ORE
INDO STOVE NED

59

ROVER SASH SOLD
ANITA ELIA CLEO
HONOR MORT ADAM
ONELIFETOLIVE
LIST INDEED
JACLYN WET
ALAI DASH ASSES
GENERALHOSPITAL
SCENE MESH GAVE
TEA RANGED
PAPERS DEER
ALLMYCHILDREN
SLAB RUNT OVERT
TONE OLEO WIRED
EWER WARN SLOPS

60

TEAM LHASA TAG
LUCID EASES OWE
CRAZYEIGHTS PAN
DENY SETAPART
GTE EER RESIZES
REM SLIM ESS
ATIT EPIC ITSME
DRESSTOTHENINES
EASEL NEON LIDS
TOO RISE TIE
OLESTRA RIG CAN
RAKEHELL GASH
AMI FIVEANDTENS
TAN UDINE SYRIA
ERG LANDS ESPN

61

SACS LOGE DART
ASHE BONGO IGOR
FEET SHARP RULE
EARTH SWEETTALK
REED STRAY
AYEAYE ARISES
SGT DEGAS ENOLA
PAAR RADAR GUAM
APRON DARES RTE
RETAIN AVENGE
SLURS STIR
BITTEREND SCALE
ODIE SPIRE EPEE
PEER ELDER SEAL
SASS YEWS TSPS

62

FOOLS BEFIT BUT
INDIA ELAND ANE
SMOKYPLACES NBA
HERA LITE AJAR
BLAZEOFGLORY
EVILEYE FIAT
DANES AFFRONTS
GIT DANSE ORE
ENORMOUS CORAL
AINT ALABAMA
HEARTSONFIRE
AXLE CARE RTES
YUL BURNINGLOVE
EDO ISAAC AIMEE
SET LOTSA SNERD

63

BAGS CHEEK BOOK
ELLA HUMAN AXLE
GOODFIGURE LEER
ONO ILE LEBANON
TEMPLE DYLAN
LEAVE SACHET
MENU NATO LEERY
ALAS STAND BARN
PEROT SITE ELSE
SECRET LORCA
MEANS ARMADA
MELISSA TIE RIN
OVEN TOTALWOMAN
LIEU EMILE TONI
ELKS DINED TREE

64

BARD MACY CARPE
ASEA ALOE AMORE
WHAT ROLL TOTER
LOVELYTOLOOKAT
ERODE REN TED
DEW NAP DOTTIER
PIPED IRONY
PRETTYWOMAN
SALON SALEM
CRAFTED GEL HUB
HAT MEA ARENA
BEAUTIFULGIRLS
LIARS COLA SEEK
SAUTE EONS ESSE
UNSER STAT SYST

65

SSTS RATA AMES
OLEO KARAT TOLE
POPCONCERT FLIT
HOE SEEN ETUDES
SPECIE ANNUL
REST ADELINE
LUNAR RIME BREW
OPEC RARER LANE
WORK OVAL SANER
ENDORSE YAWS
FEELS CITIES
AMIDST TURN TRA
SARA THEBIGBANG
SLOW EAVED ALIE
TENN SEER RYES

66

SCARF REFS SPAS
LABOR ALEC QUIT
ARISE NIRO URSA
PRESSAGENT ELLY
CRY THESES
HOTPOT SOYUZ
INRI STAR LEGUP
STONY EVA ABASE
NONCE RONA OVEN
HAMMY SOXERS
FLOPSY EAR
RENE STAMPALBUM
EDEN TOTE NOONE
STAN IGOR GLACE
HOLY COZY EATAT

67

CLAP SPAR SCALD
HOSS POSE TOTIE
ATTY ELIE EVADE
CIRCLEOFLIFE
HOOHA STARDOM
ANS UPDO SNAILS
WREATH LADS
CHARITYBALL
DARE SEDERS
OTTAWA RENT RTS
HOSTAGE IDEAL
GLOBETHEATRE
UNSER BARE RIME
NEHRU EVIL TRAP
ITEMS DEPP SECY

68

SOWN TIMID RIIS
THAI SAIDA EDNA
ARID EMDEN TRIM
GETUP DECORATE
ISABEL ERAT
MAN GALE RACHEL
ORG OSLO DEERE
SAFE KAFKA DRAT
EROSE TATI BTU
SARTRE HERO EOS
LIEN ELINOR
TREMBLER ARISE
SOFA INONE AGER
POTT STAEL THAN
SKYE TODDY ETTE

69

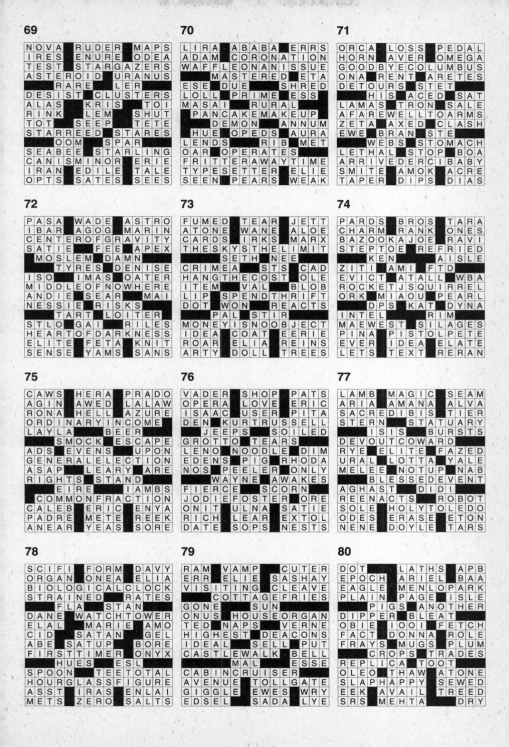

```
NOVA■RUDER■MAPS
IRES■ENURE■ODEA
TEST■STARGAZERS
ASTEROID■URANUS
■■■RARE■■LER■■■
DESIST■CLUSTERS
ALAS■■KRIS■■TOI
RINK■■LEM■■SHUT
TOT■■SEEP■■TETE
STARREED■STARES
■■■OOM■■SPAR■■■
SEABEE■STARLING
CANISMINOR■ERIE
IRAN■EDILE■TALE
OPTS■SATES■SEES
```

70

```
LIRA■ABABA■ERRS
ADAM■CORONATION
WAFFLEONANISSUE
■■■MASTERED■ETA
ESE■DUE■■■SHRED
LOLL■PRIME■ESS■
MASAI■■RURAL■■■
■PANCAKEMAKEUP■
■■■DEMON■■ANNUM
■HUE■OPEDS■AURA
LENDS■■■RIB■MET
OAR■OPERATES■■■
FRITTERAWAYTIME
TYPESETTER■ELIE
SEEN■PEARS■WEAK
```

71

```
ORCA■LOSS■PEDAL
HORN■AVER■OMEGA
GOODBYECOLUMBUS
ONA■RENT■ARETES
DETOURS■STET■■■
■■■HIS■ACED■SAT
LAMAS■TRON■SALE
AFAREWELLTOARMS
ZETA■AXED■CLASH
EWE■BRAN■STE■■■
■■■WEBS■STOMACH
LETHAL■STOP■BOA
ARRIVEDERCIBABY
SMITE■AMOK■ACRE
TAPER■DIPS■DIAS
```

72

```
PASA■WADE■ASTRO
IBAR■AGOG■MARIN
CENTEROFGRAVITY
SATIE■■FEE■APEX
■MOSLEM■DAMN■■■
■■■TYRES■DENISE
ISO■■IMAS■OATER
MIDDLEOFNOWHERE
ANDIE■SEAR■■MAI
NESSIE■RISKS■■■
■■■TART■LOITER■
STLO■GAI■■RILES
HEARTOFDARKNESS
ELITE■FETA■KNIT
SENSE■YAMS■SANS
```

73

```
FUMED■TEAR■JETT
ATONE■WANE■ALOE
CARDS■IRKS■MARX
THESKYSTHELIMIT
■■■■SETH■NEE■■■
CRIMEA■■STS■CAD
HANGTHECOST■OLE
ITEM■■VAL■■BLOB
LIP■SPENDTHRIFT
DOT■WON■■REACTS
■■■PAL■STIR■■■■
MONEYISNOOBJECT
IDEA■COAT■EERIE
ROAR■ELIA■REINS
ARTY■DOLL■TREES
```

74

```
PARDS■BROS■TARA
CHARM■RANK■ONES
BAZOOKAJOE■RAVI
STEPTOE■REFRIED
■■■KEN■■■■AISLE
ZITI■AMI■FTD■■■
EVICT■ATALL■WBA
ROCKETJSQUIRREL
ORK■MIAOU■PEARL
■■■DPS■KAT■DYNA
INTEL■■■■RIM■■■
MAEWEST■SILAGES
PINA■PISTOLPETE
EVER■IDEA■ELATE
LETS■TEXT■RERAN
```

75

```
CAWS■HERA■PRADO
AGIN■AWED■LALAW
RONA■HELL■AZURE
ORDINARYINCOME■
LAYLA■■■BEER■■■
■■■SMOCK■ESCAPE
ADS■EVENS■■UPON
GENERALELECTION
ASAP■■LEARY■ARE
RIGHTS■STAND■■■
■■■EIRE■■■IAMBS
■COMMONFRACTION
CALEB■ERIC■ENYA
PADRE■METE■REEK
ANEAR■YEAS■SORE
```

76

```
VADER■SHOP■PATS
OPERA■LOVE■ERIC
ISAAC■USER■PITA
DEN■KURTRUSSELL
■■JEEPS■■SOILED
GROTTO■TEARS■■■
LENO■NOODLE■DIM
EDENS■PIG■RHODA
NOS■PEELER■ONLY
■■■WAYNE■AWAKES
FIERCE■■SCORN■■
JODIEFOSTER■ORE
ONIT■ULNA■SATIE
RICH■LEAR■EXTOL
DATE■SOPS■NESTS
```

77

```
LAMB■MAGIC■SEAM
ARIA■AMANA■ALVA
SACREDIBIS■TIER
STERN■■STATUARY
■■■ISIS■■BURSTS
DEVOUTCOWARD■■■
RYE■ELITE■FAZED
URAL■LOTTA■YALE
MELEE■NOTUP■NAB
■■■BLESSEDEVENT
AGHAST■■DIDI■■■
REENACTS■■ROBOT
SOLE■HOLYTOLEDO
ODES■ERASE■ETON
NENE■DOYLE■TARS
```

78

```
SCIFI■FORM■DAVY
ORGAN■ONEA■ELIA
BIOLOGICALCLOCK
STRAINED■■RATES
■■■FLA■■STAN■■■
DANE■WATCHTOWER
ELAL■■MARIE■AMO
CID■■SATAN■■GEL
ABE■SATUP■■BORE
FIRSTTIMER■ONYX
■■■HUES■■ESL■■■
SPOON■■TEETOTAL
HOURGLASSFIGURE
ASST■IRAS■ENLAI
METS■ZERO■SALTS
```

79

```
RAM■VAMP■■CUTER
ERR■ELIE■SASHAY
VISITING■CLEAVE
■■■COTTAGEFRIES
GONE■■■■SUN■■■■
ONUS■■HOUSEORGAN
TED■NAPS■■VERNE
HIGHEST■DEACONS
IDEAL■■SELL■PUT
CASTLEWALK■BELL
■■■■■MAL■■■ESSE
CABINCRUISER■■■
AVENUE■TOLLGATE
GIGGLE■EWES■WRY
EDSEL■■SADA■LYE
```

80

```
DOT■■■LATHS■APB
EPOCH■ARIEL■BAA
EAGLE■MENLOPARK
PLAIN■PAGE■ISLE
■■■PIGS■ANOTHER
DIPPER■BLEAT■■■
OBIE■1001■FETCH
FACT■DONNA■ROLE
FRAYS■MUGS■PLUM
■■■CROPS■TRADES
REPLICA■TOOT■■■
OLEO■THAW■ATONE
SLAPHAPPY■SEWED
EEK■AVAIL■TREED
SRS■MEHTA■■■DRY
```

81

MAST BASTE MET
ALTAR AREAS AVE
SPARECHANGE TEN
COSTAR LOG RENT
ALES REVERTS
CLERMONT DAH
OUI LOOS SANKA
STRIKEUPTHEBAND
TEETH TERI NEO
EAR DARKAGES
ALUMNUS PENS
LENS MIT RATTLE
AMI SPLITSCREEN
MOT ALONE KARAN
ONE MESTA LAKE

82

ETE SCALA BASIS
MIX PANEL ELATE
IRE EVENT RATED
LITTLEWOMEN IRA
INERT ALE RAT
OGRE HOSNI RITE
MENU VASES
SHORTSHRIFT
ARTIE HOOP
PERT ASIDE IMRE
PGA ART SNEER
EAT SMALLCHANGE
ALIAS PEALE TAC
RIFLE LARUE ALT
SAYIT ENDER LES

83

BART SLUMP APES
AMOS PERIL SAVE
SOCK LANKA SLAW
INK RAPSESSIONS
EGOTIST TIS
FISH ELITISTS
FLARE PLACE WOW
LOGE SALTS MILA
EVE LUCIE LINDY
DESSERTS RUNG
OAF BATISTA
ALLTHATJAZZ HIP
POOH CAIRO LIAR
BOCA ELMER AFRO
SPOT SKIDS STAN

84

SPUD ASAP STS
TIMID MESAS CRY
APPLEPOLISH RON
RESUME LATITUDE
TANG ARAB
ESSENCES STUNT
AYE DENTS SPURN
CRAB ERA ERIE
HULAS SANDS SEW
PICAS PERTNESS
NOLA RARE
SIGNALED MIASMA
POW MOPUPACTION
ATA INEPT TENON
MAX SEES RENO

85

AUTOS GAIT BOSS
STENO ALSO LAPP
KEATS POEM ASIA
MOOSEHEADBEER
CCS ASA HASSLE
OUTLET RAN
STEAL SHAW COOS
TURTLENECKSHIRT
APSE VANE HINDU
BEG RENTED
CHASER STY MRS
HAWKEYEPIERCE
OBOE OREL HANDS
PIKE NILE ENTER
STET EELS ASSES

86

HONES CLUB CHIP
ADORN HIRE LANA
LEAGUEOFNATIONS
ESC FLOE MAPLES
CAFES BOER
ADOS MEXICAN
BRUIN ENOS PEI
CONFERENCECALLS
SPT PESO OCALA
WHATNOT HUEY
SERE RUBES
INLAWS SIRE IBM
DIVISIONOFLABOR
EDIT DEAL ALLIE
MESH EDGE YIELD

87

ADOBE SCI GRATE
CABAL TOR REPOT
THINKTANK AGENT
SLED ORC ACADIA
SIREE SIT
MAANDPAKETTLE
PRAWN THE ARIA
LAG SOO AWL ORT
EGIS FRA EAVES
BUCKETBRIGADE
IRE UNARM
ZOLTAN GIT IOTA
EXITS BUTTERTUB
RENEE ALI PATRI
ONERS MAO ALONE

88

AEGIS REHAB LPS
BRENT AROSE IOU
CANDYHEARTS ALE
STEELE SNIT RED
NERD ENMASSE
SECT BOLD AMP
ISR EGO SNOOTY
LAIC RENTA SKYE
TUMULT ERN EPA
ETA ARID ARES
MIASMAS ODER
ANN OUST ARREAR
RAW TRUSSBRIDGE
INA TARAS EVERY
EER ALERT DENIS

89

SHEAF SHES DASH
TORSI TONI ALPO
DEEPSEATED NAIL
SSS CPR ELAINE
THICKSKINNED
ELSIE HIKING
CAMERA NECK GEM
OVER GREEK BARE
NAE WRIT SLOGAN
POETIC ORATE
WIDEREACHING
ALASKA ENG ALI
FLUE BROADBASED
TENT LENT ONEAL
SRTA EVES WACKY

90

GEAR PLEAS PROW
AXLE TALIA ROBE
FUDGESWIRL ICER
FLEAS NOTE SKYE
STRIPS TOMBOY
NYET UNRIG
ZAPS WAITER ONE
ELI JETTING AGO
TIS ERASED ODES
ASTIR ROUX
ANKLES WRINGS
SECT IVES ADORE
ACHE NEAPOLITAN
WHIR UNTIL ZIPS
SOON STONE EPEE

91

JOBS KAPPA WHIG
OLIO AIRES HOSE
HEARTBREAKHOTEL
NOSTRUMS EYERS
UKE DODO
DEVILINDISGUISE
IVORY ALLY DIM
NITE CARLO TIED
ATE COLE SHONE
HARDHEADEDWOMAN
RIDS SOO
ORION ATTRACTS
FOLLOWTHATDREAM
FUEL IRATE ELMO
SEXY GIBED ALEG

92

SLAT MATH GAMES
LOCI ALOE ABASE
ADEN NAME REUSE
WIDESTSELECTION
DAR LOS
ARE BASTION ASS
TAMER HASP CLAW
INCREDIBLEVALUE
LEER ERLE ABATE
TEE TAKESON YET
POL CCC
LOWESTPRICEEVER
ASHES LULU AERO
SHAVE ABEL SNIT
HATES TEST EACH

93

LIED TOFU SEDGE
ENDO WALL POORS
ADIN ERIC ANDES
PICKLESPEAR GEE
SATEEN RESTERS
YESES SEED
REB TOTO RAVE
DEEP STRAP PRIG
AERO PART TAG
TORE YAYAS
SALLIES AGHAST
ALA BROKENARROW
NINJA LARK INRE
DECAL ANTE MITE
SNERD REED PEAT

94

MARC FRAY ARGON
ONOR LIDO TERRE
PAPADOCDUVALIER
STEVE ORBE INSO
ALEC INRE
CHIT CHEGUEVARA
LAD LOEW SHEKEL
ARISE TIE ADEPT
STOWED NLRB LAO
PETERROGET RAYS
EYES VETO
ABET AGUA DUTCH
MARIAMONTESSORI
IRISH ODOR ETAL
DACHA DORE DEBT

95

AWAY JACK DIGIT
RACE EVAN ALIVE
OXEN AIRE NIGER
MET ANDREAGASSI
ANIMUS RED
CYD OLDER APT
COATI CORN SNOW
ANCHORAGEALASKA
LEIS ELIA OBEYS
LSD ELAND REL
NNE HERALD
ALLAMERICAN DER
MIAMI ORAN MATE
INLET AMID EMUS
STORY MANY ASPS

96

OFA SCHEMER APT
RAD ORINOCO NEO
BLOODANDTHUNDER
SPRINT HOTAIR
BETRUE GRIT
ALE MSG PTA ONS
HYDE REARRANGE
SWEATSUIT
PHOTOSTAT MYRA
CAV NEA SCI OAT
TRIP ONEDGE
PSEUDO TOSEED
TEARSONMYPILLOW
ARC SNEERED ELK
ESS RESTORE RLS

97

MOST BAN FRO
IDEA FACTS SOAP
DOWNFORTHECOUNT
IRS ORTO ALONG
ELMER SANDY
HELLER BIN
MARIO SAD ISME
THROWINTHETOWEL
VAST SAY STARK
CRY CREATE
SAMOA WAITS
PROVE ORGS LAS
HITBELOWTHEBELT
URIS IDIOT UCLA
HOE DEN THIN

98

ATLAS PTA BID
COAXER RAN AGUE
EMPIRE OBTAINED
SANDPAINTING
HAP OOHS AETNA
ERIES NECK REAR
YELLOWSTONE
ALLAH ELTON
PEBBLEBEACH
SEAL TREE ATTAR
INGOT IVES HAS
GRAVELGERTIE
MATERIAL OVERLY
AGER ADE WARIER
ESS RED NODES

99

DREAM PIA ALLAY
REACT UNC BLEND
INREVERSE OBEYS
PENT GEE ERE
GEORGECOSTANZA
EDNA STAT NEUT
ESP SKAT SLO
CATSPAW STRATUM
ALA STAR EIN
NORA HIED ATUB
STATEOFDECLINE
HAS TAR HIRT
DEFOG BAROMETER
BLAME APT ORATE
LINER HEH BOSSY

100

DEFT ASTER HUGS
OGRE MAIZE ANEW
FREDROGERS IRMA
FEE ARARAT REST
STRATA RODE
WILMARUDOLPH
CAMEO ALONE IOU
OLES LYING ANNE
BOA NIOBE PIGGY
BETTYFRIEDAN
BEET UNTIES
STAN ALTARS CLU
CALS BARNEYFIFE
AXLE LOOTS ALID
MISS ESTES TYNE

101

ALPS SCRAM CAST
CALM QUOTA ONOR
INAUGURATIONDAY
DEN REED NADIR
GOAD ALTO
ATRISK BLAH ANT
TAILS ARON WOO
OFFTOAGOODSTART
NFL MEAN ARISE
EYE LAND PROTEM
PORT SLOT
MARIE DOIN DUD
BEGINTHEBEGUINE
BRED TAMER MATE
CEDE ODORS PLOP

102

CLAW OTIS EDNAS
LIMA PETE GRATE
ELAN ELSE GUILE
FINGERLAKES LAM
LEES SHREWS
INTENT RESEND
FAHD TOUT LAD
STU PALMOIL OLE
MEL DONS TWIN
BRAYER GRANDS
FLEECE SOAR
REL KNUCKLEHEAD
OVINE CLAD ELSA
SENAT LATE EMIT
TRAPS AMEN LOSE

103

LAGS JUAN DAME
ABOU MAGMA EVEN
BYEBYEBLACKBIRD
SENSEN INHOUSE
ENOS SOOT
PART THE SLITS
ADA STARE ANAME
CHICHIRODRIGUEZ
TOSEA EDGED PAR
CANNY EAT HERA
TAOS RITE
BRINGON RIALTO
MAUMAUREBELLION
ELSE REMUS TROT
TIES TROD HALO

104

AHAB IBIS SPIKE
MAMA TUNA TATER
PHINEASTBLUSTER
SANDAL OUI TOP
STY BRA
CASTS HIRE CAM
UCLA CLARABELLE
STAN OILER ROLL
HOWDYDOODY GNAT
YRS SINS POETS
TLC SUN
MAO ISA ABODES
BUFFALOBOBSMITH
ASTIN DUNE ISTO
TESTY AMER CHEW

105

■BMI■SADA■DOMO■
HEAR■ELAN■ERODE
MARKSDOWN■NINOS
ORK■PANG■SMEARS
■■ICING■CHAN■■■
CLEATS■SHORTAGE
LOPES■CHINK■CAN
ATON■TORTE■SCUD
ITS■ROVES■SIEGE
MOTHERED■FANNED
■■■OMAR■CRUET■■
FARRAH■GRIT■MET
ANEAR■TRADEMARK
STACK■RANG■BRIO
■IDES■ISEE■AKC■

106

ABUTS■MAST■TREK
CAROL■ASIA■OOZE
TRAFALGARSQUARE
ENLIVEN■ETERNAL
■■■VETO■NED■■■■
ACHE■■LAS■■WADS
BRA■OTIS■SPINET
BERMUDATRIANGLE
OTTERS■RENT■ELI
TEEN■■TAD■■FRAN
■■■■BOA■FATE■■■
MISCAST■ARRAIGN
ANTARCTICCIRCLE
ROUT■AONE■SNEER
ENDS■ROAD■HOSED

107

CODE■ELSE■PELTS
ABEL■TERN■ELIOT
ROBINHOOD■LITER
LESSON■■SAINT■■
■■■■LIFT■SCOLD■
■MANACLE■PARERS
SALON■ELLEN■JOE
WILT■RESIN■LONE
ALA■HASTE■COHEN
BENTON■AGROUND■
■DARLA■REEL■■■■
■■DELTA■■COSTAS
BLAME■FRIARTUCK
VALOR■RUIN■ANTI
DYERS■OMIT■REST

108

WEAK■STEVE■SHAG
ARON■TOTAL■NINE
WININAWALK■ETTA
ACETATES■HARPER
■■■■MEL■GOTTA■■
HASTEN■BAUM■YEA
ALTOS■TWIN■ADAM
SORE■BRAND■LITE
THIS■EONS■PARTS
OAK■TATA■FRITOS
■■EVERS■DRU■■■■
PAGODA■LIONIZES
ALOT■BREEZEHOME
PALE■LANGE■ONIT
ANDS■ENDON■PETS

109

ABBA■HISS■CASTS
BOUT■OREO■ASTRO
ONME■MOTHERHOOD
REP■GIN■ORR■PTA
TREELESS■ROI■■■
■■REAR■THATCHER
DECKS■TRON■YOYO
ARR■SEWARDS■RED
MOON■LOIS■TENDS
POPULIST■SORE■■
■■■TIC■SATURDAY
IAN■TIS■PAT■TWA
THEBATTERY■MOAN
BARON■ALIE■BARK
EBONY■GILD■ADDS

110

SIT■ACIDS■WADED
TOO■ROSIE■ICIER
ION■TOMSMOTHERS
LOYAL■■CIRC■■■■
TORPEDO■SCHWAS■
■■ABSURD■HEARTS
JAN■SOLED■SISAL
ALDO■SOFAR■NERO
MOATS■NOTES■NEW
BOLTED■GEMINI■■
■FLORID■SOMEONE
■■■■AVER■■MAHAL
JACKPALANCE■ANI
OLDIE■FREER■LCD
NERDS■TACOS■LYE

111

LAME■■DARN■TMAN
ERIC■ROLEO■RAVI
NASL■ASTER■ALEC
ABSENCEOFMALICE
■■■CAY■■■ABE■■■
RUSTY■SAG■YEMEN
ASTI■ACTORS■ILO
THECOLOROFMONEY
EEN■DEPEND■VOCE
DROOD■EEE■NERTS
■■■REP■■■OAR■■■
THEDROWNINGPOOL
ROVE■SHAKO■ANNA
AMER■SEVER■ICER
YENS■EYES■■DESK

112

PAULS■COB■MAYAN
POSIT■AVA■INUSE
SNEER■VAL■LIGHT
■EDGARALLANMOE■
■■■EWE■■■PEA■■■
ASPS■LETME■TATA
CUE■PIQUE■LOGON
HELENCURLYBROWN
IDEAS■INDUS■ONE
PEER■SPASM■ADES
■■■PAT■■■MIT■■■
■JOHNLARRYMORE■
PIVOT■MOO■ANODE
AMINO■OIL■GETGO
WIDEN■SLY■ESSES

113

MARE■SARA■■RAMP
UNIT■IRENE■APIE
STPAULMINNESOTA
HEE■BEEN■DAPPER
■■■SAND■EERY■■■
PATENT■ELMS■BEL
OWING■ALLI■PERI
LANSINGMICHIGAN
LINE■ORES■ELATE
STY■OVER■DALTON
■■■ELEE■SODS■■■
CHAPEL■SLUE■TOY
LINCOLNNEBRASKA
ALTO■ARIEL■CAIN
MOST■■ATTY■TREK

114

PAPA■CADS■RATON
ALAS■ATAN■ATONE
SIGH■VILA■TOUTS
SEETHELIGHT■COT
ENTREAT■■EACH■■
■■■EAT■TINNIEST
BEGET■WYNN■ADAM
ADO■HEARSAY■UKE
LEON■PLOT■ASPEN
ENDORSES■EWE■■■
■■TRIO■■AVENGES
AVA■SMELLEDARAT
PASTE■VIAL■TARA
ENTER■EMMY■OPEN
DEEDS■NOON■REDD

115

KEBAB■STAT■AMA■
IVANA■HERO■CADS
NADIR■USER■ERMA
■■■TOOTHANDNAIL
BANANA■■■ARTURO
ORA■ETC■DDE■DEN
INTOTHEWOODS■■■
LOON■■DIN■■AIDE
■■■ARMANDHAMMER
ADS■OAR■IAN■ALI
DITTOS■■■ICEMAN
ISAWTHELIGHT■■■
OPIE■EXAM■OHARA
SERE■REMI■RAKES
■LSD■SCAN■SNACK

116

DALI■SHALE■EDAM
AVON■EATEN■DELI
DEUS■ALONEAGAIN
ASTI■SENT■DELVE
■■■NCO■■■■ESTER
THECANDYMAN■■■■
ROVER■ROAD■CHAD
EWER■MAKOS■ROLE
ELSE■OPER■BASIL
■■■■AMERICANPIE
NEPAL■■■■RNA■■■
EXIST■ALDO■PRIM
WITHOUTYOU■PACE
SLOE■AIRES■LIEN
YENS■WEARE■ENDS

117

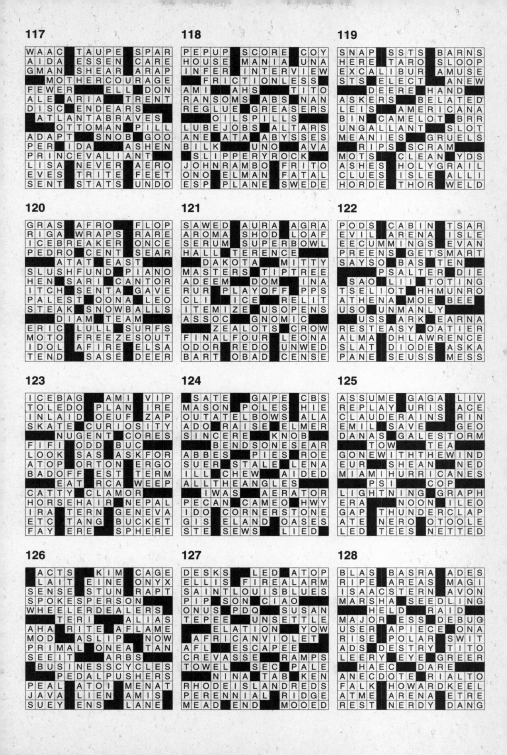

WAAC TAUPE SPAR
AIDA ESSEN CARE
GMAN SHEAR ARAP
MOTHERCOURAGE
FEWER ELL DON
ALE ARIA TRENT
DISC ENDEARS
ATLANTABRAVES
OTTOMAN PILL
ADAPT SNOB GOO
PER IDA ASHEN
PRINCEVALIANT
LISA NEVER AERO
EVES TRITE FEET
SENT STATS UNDO

118

PEPUP SCORE COY
HOUSE MANIA UNA
INFER INTERVIEW
FRICTIONLESS
AMI AHS TITO
RANSOMS ABS NAN
REGLUE GREASERS
OILSPILLS
LUBEJOBS ALTARS
ANE ATA ABYSSES
BILK UNO AVA
SLIPPERYROCK
JOHNRAMBO FRITO
ONO ELMAN FATAL
ESP PLANE SWEDE

119

SNAP SSTS BARNS
HERE TARO SLOOP
EXCALIBUR AMUSE
STS ELECT ANEW
DEERE HAND
ASKERS BELATED
LEIS AMERICANA
BIN CAMELOT BRR
UNGALLANT SLOT
MEANIES GRUELS
RIPS SCRAM
MOTS CLEAN YDS
ASHES HOLYGRAIL
CLUES ISLE ALLI
HORDE THOR WELD

120

GRAS AFRO FLOP
RIGA WRAPS RARE
ICEBREAKER ONCE
PEDRO CENT SEAR
ATAT EAST
SLUSHFUND PIANO
HEN SARI CANTOR
ITCH SENTA GAVE
PALEST OONA LEO
STEAK SNOWBALLS
DIAM TEAM
ERIC LULL SURFS
MOTO FREEZESOUT
IDOL AFIRE ELSA
TEND SASE DEER

121

SAWED AURA AGRA
AROMA SHOD LOAF
SERUM SUPERBOWL
HALL TERENCE
DAKOTA MITTY
MASTERS TIPTREE
ADEEM DOM INA
RUR PLAYOFF PPS
CLI ICE RELIT
ITEMIZE USOPENS
ASSOC GNOMIC
ZEALOTS CROW
FINALFOUR LEONA
ODOR REDO UNWED
BART OBAD CENSE

122

PODS CABIN TSAR
EVIL ARENA ISLE
EECUMMINGS EVAN
PREENS GETSMART
SAYSO BAS TEN
PSALTER DIE
SAO LII TOTING
TSELIOT HHMUNRO
ATHENA MOE BEE
USO UNMANLY
USS ARK EARNA
RESTEASY OATIER
ALMA DHLAWRENCE
SLAT DIODE ASKA
PANE SEUSS MESS

123

ICEBAG AMI VIP
TOLEDO PLAN IRE
INLAID OEUF ZAP
SKATE CURIOSITY
NUGENT CORES
FIFI ODD BUC
LOOK SAS ASKFOR
ATOP ORTON ERGO
BADOFF EST TERM
EAT RCA WEEP
CATTY CLAMOR
HORSEHAIR NEPAL
IRA TERN GENEVA
ETC TANG BUCKET
FAY ERE SPHERE

124

SATE GAPE CBS
MASON POLES HIE
OUTATELBOWS ALA
ADO RAISE ELMER
SINCERE KNOB
BENDSONESEAR
ABBES PIES ROE
SUER STALE LENA
ILL CHEW AIDED
ALLTHEANGLES
IWAS AERATOR
PECAN CAMEO HWY
IDO CORNERSTONE
GIS ELAND OASES
STE SEWS LIED

125

ASSUME GAGA LIV
REPLAY URIS ACE
CLAUDERAINS RIN
EMIL SAVE GEO
DANAS GALESTORM
TOW TEA
GONEWITHTHEWIND
EUR SHEAN NED
MIAMIHURRICANES
PSI COP
LIGHTNING GRAPH
ERA NOON ILEO
GAP THUNDERCLAP
ATE NERO OTOOLE
LED TEES NETTED

126

ACTS KIM CAGE
LAIT EINE ONYX
SENSE STUN RAPT
SPOKESPERSON
WHEELERDEALERS
TERI ALIAS
AHA RITE AFLAME
MOD ASLIP NOW
PRIMAL ONEA TAN
SEEIT ARBS
BUSINESSCYCLES
PEDALPUSHERS
PEAL ATOI MENAT
JAVA LIEN AMIS
SUEY ENS LANE

127

DESKS LED ATOP
ELLIS FIREALARM
SAINTLOUISBLUES
PIP SON CIAO
ONUS PDQ SUSAN
TEPEE UNSETTLE
ELATION YOW
AFRICANVIOLET
AFL ESCAPEE
CREVASSE RAMPS
TOWEL SEC PALE
NINA TAB KEN
RHODEISLANDREDS
PERENNIAL RIDGE
MEAD END MOOED

128

BLAS BASRA ADES
RIPE AREAS MAGI
ISAACSTERN AVON
MARSHA SEEDLING
HELD RAID
MAJOR ESS DEBUG
USER APIECE ONA
RISE POLAR SWIT
ADS DESTRY TITO
LEERY EYE GREER
HAEC DARE
ANECDOTE RIALTO
FALK HOWARDKEEL
ATME ARENA ETRE
REST NERDY DANG

129

```
GASH■SEGAL■FESS
IDLE■HAITI■LEAP
BEERBARRELPOLKA
ENDEARED■■LOSER
■■■■RED■THAR■■■
SIPPED■SOON■ARM
CORE■■STORE■BAA
ANYPORTINASTORM
RIO■FEELS■■IDEA
FAR■FEAT■COMERS
■■■PILL■LOA■■■■
ASSES■■LASTSTEP
CATCHERINTHERYE
ARIA■RAVEL■LEER
BARN■REEDY■LEST
```

130

```
GRAS■RAPS■RACES
LENO■ALAI■CRYME
ACEY■POND■ATRIA
SAABSISTER■FELT
SPREADS■BOSUN■■
■■■ABS■■■MILANO
PAYNE■GOFER■UAR
ONUS■LINES■SLOE
ENG■PYLON■PATHS
TOOTER■■■PIN■■■
■■BORIC■PREFACE
CALF■CAMEOROLLS
LEAFY■BOLT■RIIS
ARCED■OREO■DANE
POKES■TEEN■SSTS
```

131

```
MASK■USURY■AJAR
EREI■MAFIA■GALA
DONNYBROOK■ACTS
IMAGER■STEP■KOP
CATSPAW■STROP■■
SSE■■GAB■YOHOHO
■■■SCENES■ASTIR
AMATI■EAT■MASTS
MELON■DRESSY■■■
ALFRED■SAP■■EDS
■■REMAP■DRIBLET
EWE■AURA■ARRIVE
NOSE■BOBBYSOXER
DOCS■EMCEE■MIRE
SLOT■DOSED■OREO
```

132

```
WADE■SASS■HORSY
EDEN■ACHE■ALOHA
AMAN■AMEX■NEWEL
VITUSBERING■SSE
ETHIC■■BEAUT■■■
■■■■ROBERTPEARY
ROD■OBIT■■■AVOW
ALADDIN■HAWKISH
MEMO■■■PUMA■SEA
PONCEDELEON■■■■
■■■SCENA■■EARED
MEN■LIVINGSTONE
AROMA■INAN■ODDS
SINAI■ELBA■MEEK
SNEER■SYST■SODS
```

133

```
MONA■SARAH■BAWL
ORAL■ERODE■ASIA
SEVENDEADLYSINS
TOY■EGAD■POISES
■■■AGES■BMWS■■■
PAMPAS■DEAL■BBC
ABORT■COAT■PLEA
THREEMUSKETEERS
TONS■ARES■ASSET
YRS■KRIS■KNOTTS
■■■FAKE■LIDS■■■
ASSAYS■VINE■IQS
TENCOMMANDMENTS
MEAT■EASEL■SKIT
ERGS■NEEDY■TSPS
```

134

```
ESSES■SELF■GEMS
LUCRE■IDEO■ALIT
BERET■NEAR■MILA
ATE■THUNDERBOLT
■■WALES■■MILTIE
ROBBER■THANE■■■
OPAL■DARING■BOW
OILER■VAN■SARGE
MEL■EJECTS■DALE
■■■AVERT■AMAZED
STATUE■■SWAMI■■
WASHERWOMAN■LSU
ASWE■ERLE■TINAS
STAN■RIGA■LOUSE
HENS■STAR■ENTER
```

135

```
■EBRO■ALDA■REAP
SNEER■SEAS■ANYA
ITSYBITSYSPIDER
DOES■SISSIES■■■
EMT■FAN■■GLANCE
ABSORB■TUNE■OAR
■■■TEEDUP■■ANKA
■LITTLEBOYBLUE■
DINO■■PANELS■■■
OFF■UMPS■LOOKER
GEORGE■■TLC■ONO
■■■ALLEGRO■SOTS
WEEWILLIEWINKIE
OVAL■OLGA■LAIRS
WETS■WAIT■EPEE■
```

136

```
PELT■■MAIL■SWAT
ONOR■RANDY■IAGO
AONE■ASTER■STOP
CLEARTHEAIR■EGO
HARDER■■SCOUR■■
■■■LOANS■SANDER
FIFE■COAT■MOOLA
ARI■GERBILS■GET
LORNE■AIDE■ASEA
KNEELS■NEGEV■■■
■■BOILS■■IRIDIC
CAR■DOWNTOEARTH
ALAS■PAEAN■TAME
RANT■PLOPS■OMAR
ANDY■YENS■■RAYE
```

137

```
ANTE■STOOD■CHAD
COOT■ORIBI■RIGA
HIGHTAILIT■ITEM
ERASURES■TASTES
■■■■NED■LYMPH■■
CAMBER■BEBE■EDS
AWARD■CUTANDRUN
BAKE■SHRUG■ROLE
BREAKCAMP■PEACE
YET■OONA■MADDER
■■REBUT■SAO■■■■
STARER■STILETTO
COCO■GETAMOVEON
ARKS■ELATE■ELSE
BASE■SIRED■NESS
```

138

```
EBBS■BOARD■DDAY
RENE■ALLEY■ERIE
GEAR■NIECE■TURN
■FIELDOFDREAMS■
■■■NOS■■■SCI■■■
CAGER■PER■UNBAR
OCR■NAILED■ERGO
THEBADNEWSBEARS
TEAR■DENOTE■SEE
ASTOP■DAN■LOSES
■■■WIL■■■SLR■■■
■CASEYATTHEBAT■
MAGI■ROMEO■IRIS
OPEN■INANE■TUNA
BERG■CENTS■STEW
```

139

```
ACHE■■SPA■■CELT
NOOK■SPENT■ADAM
NINE■CRANE■NAVE
OLE■THECANDYMAN
■■YAHWEH■DUO■■■
DAHLIA■■REFUSAL
ATOMS■SMURF■USO
TONS■DAMNS■AGIN
ENE■WINES■BLADE
REYNARD■■POORER
■■■ERN■PLUSES■■
SWEETDREAMS■UAR
LARD■LETUP■OGRE
AKIN■SEARS■FAIL
MEET■■FLA■■FRAY
```

140

```
TWIG■PLEAD■EGGS
ORCA■LEASE■JILT
SAKSFIFTHAVENUE
SPY■RATS■DECAMP
■■■PONY■CHET■■■
ABJECT■BAER■JOB
CREAK■OLGA■GOBI
HILLSTREETBLUES
EELS■OBEY■LASSO
DRY■SNIP■LISTEN
■■■MEET■BETS■■■
AGEOLD■MOTH■CHI
MIDDLEOFTHEROAD
OBIE■ALOHA■DAZE
SEEM■FERAL■AXES
```

141

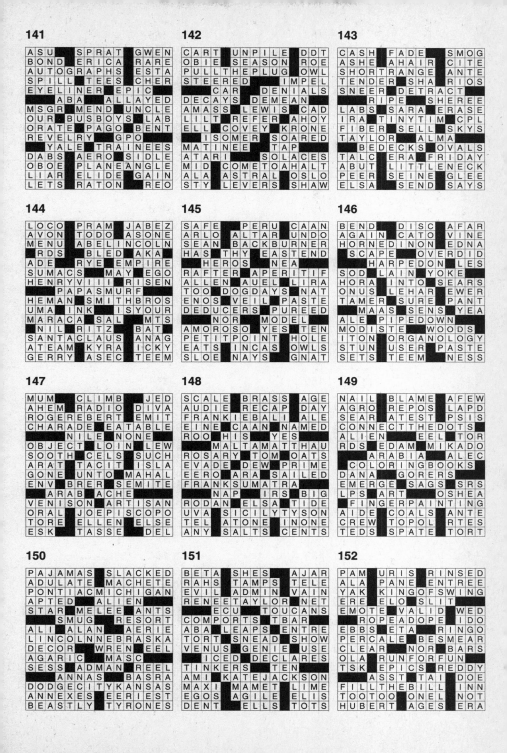

ASU SPRAT GWEN
BOND ERICA RARE
AUTOGRAPHS ESTA
SPILL TEES CHER
EYELINER EPIC
ABA ALLAYED
MSGR MEND UNCLE
OUR BUSBOYS LAB
ORATE PAGO BENT
REVELRY GPO
YALE TRAINEES
DABS AERO SIDLE
OBOE PLANEANGLE
LIAR ELIDE GAIN
LETS RATON REO

142

CART UNPILE DDT
OBIE SEASON ROE
PULLTHEPLUG OWL
STEERED IMPEL
CAR DENIALS
DECAYS DEMEAN
AMASS LEWIS CAD
LILT REFER AHOY
ELL COVEY KRONE
ISOMER SOARED
MATINEE TAP
ATARI SOLACES
MID COMETOAHALT
ALA ASTRAL OSLO
STY LEVERS SHAW

143

CASH FADE SMOG
ASHE AHAIR CITE
SHORTRANGE ANTE
TENDER SHA RIOS
SNEER DETRACT
RIPE SHEREE
LABS SARA ERASE
IRA TINYTIM CPL
FIBER SELL SKYS
TAYLOR ALMA
BEDECKS OVALS
TALC ERA FRIDAY
ABUT LITTLENECK
PEER SEINE GLEE
ELSA SEND SAYS

144

LOCO PRAM JABEZ
AVON TODO ASONE
MENU ABELINCOLN
RDS BLED AKA
ADE RYE EMPIRE
SUMACS MAY EGO
HENRYVIII RISEN
PAPASMURF
HEMAN SMITHBROS
UMA INK ISYOUR
MARACA SAL MTS
NIL RITZ BAT
SANTACLAUS ANAG
ATEAM KYRA ICKY
GERRY ASEC TEEM

145

SAFE PERU CAAN
ARLO ALTAR UNDO
SEAN BACKBURNER
HAS THY EASTEND
HEROS NEA
RAFTER APERITIF
ALLEN AUEL LIRA
TOO DOGDAYS NAT
ENOS VEIL PASTE
DEDUCERS PUREED
NOR MODEL
AMOROSO YES TEN
PETITPOINT HOLE
EATS INCAS OWLS
SLOE NAYS GNAT

146

BEND DISC AFAR
AGAIN CATO VINE
HORNEDINON EDNA
SCAPE OVERDID
HARPEDON LES
SOD LAIN YOKE
HORA INTO SEARS
ONUS LEHAR EWER
TAMER SURE PANT
MAAS SENS YEA
ALE PIPEDOWN
MODISTE WOODS
ITON ORGANOLOGY
STUN USER PASTE
SETS TEEM NESS

147

MUM CLIMB JED
AHEM RADIO DIVA
ROGEREBERT EMIT
CHARADE EATABLE
NILE NONE
OBJECT LOIN LEW
SOOTH CELS SUCH
ARAT TACIT ISLA
GONE UNTO MAHAL
ENV BRER SEMITE
ARAB ACHE
VENISON ARTISAN
ORAL JOEPISCOPO
TORE ELLEN ELSE
ESK TASSE DEL

148

SCALE BRASS AGE
AUDIE RECAP DAY
FRANKIEBALI ALE
EINE CAAN NAMED
ROO HIS YES
MALTAMATTHAU
ROSARY TOM OATS
EVADE DEW PRIME
EERO ARA SAILED
FRANKSUMATRA
NAP IRS BIG
RODAN ELSA TIDE
UVA SICILYTYSON
TEL ATONE INONE
ANY SALTS CENTS

149

NAIL BLAME AFEW
AGRO REPOS LAPD
SEAR ATEST PSIS
CONNECTTHEDOTS
ALIEN EEL TOR
RDS EDAM MIKADO
ARABIA ALEC
COLORINGBOOKS
DANA GORERS
EMERGE SAGS SRS
LPS ART OSHEA
FINGERPAINTING
AIDE COALS ANTE
CREW TOPOL RTES
TEDS SPATE TORT

150

PAJAMAS SLACKED
ADULATE MACHETE
PONTIACMICHIGAN
APTED ALIEN
STAR MELEE ANTS
SMUG RESORT
ALI ALAN AERIE
LINCOLNNEBRASKA
DECOR WREN EEL
AGARIC MASC
SESS ADMAN REEL
ANNAS BASRA
DODGECITYKANSAS
ANNEXES EERIEST
BEASTLY TYRONES

151

BETA SHES AJAR
RAHS TAMPS TELE
EVIL ADMIN VAIN
RENEETAYLOR NET
ECU TOUCANS
COMPORTS TBAR
ABA LEAPS ENTRE
TORT SNEAD SHOW
VENUS GENIE USE
ICED DECLARES
TINKERS TEN
AMI KATEJACKSON
MAXI MAMET LIME
EGOS AGILE ELIS
DENT ELLS TOTS

152

PAM URIS RINSED
ALA PANE ENTREE
YAK KINGOFSWING
ERE ELO SLIT
EMOTE VALID WED
ROPEADOPE IDO
EBBS ETA RINGO
PERCALE BESMEAR
CLEAR NOR BARS
OLA RUNFORFUN
TSK EPICS REDDY
ASST TAI DOE
FILLTHEBILL INN
TOOTOO ONEL NOT
HUBERT AGES ERA

153

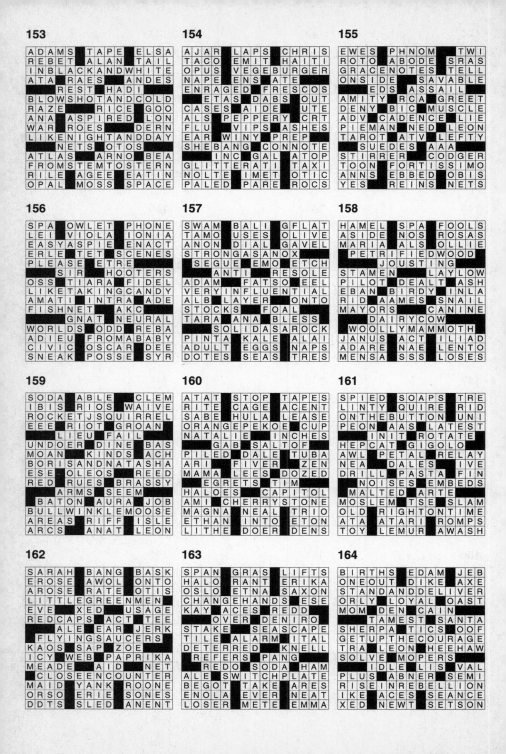

A	D	A	M	S	■	T	A	P	E	■	E	L	S	A
R	E	B	E	T	■	A	L	A	N	■	T	A	I	L
I	N	B	L	A	C	K	A	N	D	W	H	I	T	E
A	T	A	■	R	A	E	S	■	■	A	N	D	E	S
■	■	■	R	E	S	T	■	H	A	D	I	■	■	■
B	L	O	W	S	H	O	T	A	N	D	C	O	L	D
R	A	Z	E	■	■	■	R	I	C	E	■	G	O	O
A	N	A	■	A	S	P	I	R	E	D	■	L	O	N
W	A	R	■	R	O	E	S	■	■	■	D	E	R	N
L	I	K	E	N	I	G	H	T	A	N	D	D	A	Y
■	■	■	N	E	T	S	■	O	T	O	S	■	■	■
A	T	L	A	S	■	■	A	R	N	O	■	B	E	A
F	R	O	M	S	T	E	M	T	O	S	T	E	R	N
R	I	L	E	■	A	G	E	E	■	E	A	T	I	N
O	P	A	L	■	M	O	S	S	■	S	P	A	C	E

154

A	J	A	R	■	L	A	P	S	■	C	H	R	I	S
T	A	C	O	■	E	M	I	T	■	H	A	I	T	I
O	P	U	S	■	V	E	G	E	B	U	R	G	E	R
N	A	P	E	■	E	N	S	■	A	T	E	■	■	■
E	N	R	A	G	E	D	■	F	R	E	S	C	O	S
■	■	E	T	A	S	■	D	A	B	S	■	O	U	T
C	A	S	E	S	■	A	I	D	E	■	■	U	T	E
A	L	S	■	P	E	P	P	E	R	Y	■	C	R	T
F	L	U	■	■	V	I	P	S	■	A	S	H	E	S
E	A	R	■	W	I	N	Y	■	P	R	E	P	■	■
S	H	E	B	A	N	G	■	C	O	N	N	O	T	E
■	■	■	I	N	C	■	G	A	L	■	A	T	O	P
G	L	I	T	T	E	R	A	T	I	■	T	A	X	I
N	O	L	T	E	■	I	M	E	T	■	O	T	I	C
P	A	L	E	D	■	P	A	R	E	■	R	O	C	S

155

E	W	E	S	■	P	H	N	O	M	■	■	T	W	I
R	O	T	O	■	A	B	O	D	E	■	S	R	A	S
G	R	A	C	E	N	O	T	E	S	■	T	E	L	L
O	N	S	I	D	E	■	■	S	A	V	A	B	L	E
■	■	■	E	D	S	■	A	S	S	A	I	L	■	■
A	M	I	T	Y	■	R	C	A	■	G	R	E	E	T
D	E	N	Y	■	B	I	C	■	M	U	S	C	L	E
A	D	V	■	C	A	D	E	N	C	E	■	L	I	E
P	I	E	M	A	N	■	N	E	D	■	L	E	O	N
T	A	R	O	T	■	A	T	V	■	L	E	F	T	Y
■	■	S	U	E	D	E	S	■	A	A	A	■	■	■
S	T	I	R	R	E	R	■	■	C	O	D	G	E	R
T	O	O	N	■	F	O	R	T	I	S	S	I	M	O
A	N	N	S	■	E	B	B	E	D	■	O	B	I	S
Y	E	S	■	■	R	E	I	N	S	■	N	E	T	S

156

S	P	A	■	O	W	L	E	T	■	P	H	O	N	E
L	E	I	■	V	I	O	L	A	■	I	O	N	I	A
E	A	S	Y	A	S	P	I	E	■	E	N	A	C	T
E	R	L	E	■	T	E	T	■	S	C	E	N	E	S
P	L	E	A	S	E	■	E	T	R	E	■	■	■	■
■	■	■	S	I	R	■	■	H	O	O	T	E	R	S
O	S	S	■	T	I	A	R	A	■	F	I	D	E	L
L	I	K	E	T	A	K	I	N	G	C	A	N	D	Y
A	M	A	T	I	■	I	N	T	R	A	■	A	D	E
F	I	S	H	N	E	T	■	■	A	K	C	■	■	■
■	■	■	■	G	N	A	T	■	N	E	U	R	A	L
W	O	R	L	D	S	■	O	D	D	■	R	E	B	A
A	D	I	E	U	■	F	R	O	M	A	B	A	B	Y
C	I	V	I	C	■	O	S	C	A	R	■	D	E	E
S	N	E	A	K	■	P	O	S	S	E	■	S	Y	R

157

S	W	A	M	■	B	A	L	I	■	G	F	L	A	T
T	A	M	O	■	U	S	E	S	■	O	L	I	V	E
A	N	O	N	■	D	I	A	L	■	G	A	V	E	L
S	T	R	O	N	G	A	S	A	N	O	X	■	■	■
■	S	E	G	U	E	■	E	M	O	■	E	T	C	H
■	■	■	A	N	T	I	■	■	R	E	S	O	L	E
A	D	A	M	■	■	F	A	T	S	O	■	E	E	L
V	E	R	Y	I	N	F	L	U	E	N	T	I	A	L
A	L	B	■	L	A	Y	E	R	■	■	O	N	T	O
S	T	O	C	K	S	■	■	F	O	A	L	■	■	■
T	A	R	A	■	A	N	A	■	B	L	E	S	S	■
■	■	■	S	O	L	I	D	A	S	A	R	O	C	K
P	I	N	T	A	■	K	A	L	E	■	A	L	A	I
A	D	U	L	T	■	E	G	G	S	■	N	A	P	S
D	O	T	E	S	■	S	E	A	S	■	T	R	E	S

158

H	A	M	E	L	■	S	P	A	■	F	O	O	L	S
A	S	I	D	E	■	N	O	S	■	R	O	S	A	S
M	A	R	I	A	■	A	L	S	■	O	L	L	I	E
■	P	E	T	R	I	F	I	E	D	W	O	O	D	■
■	■	■	■	J	O	U	S	T	I	N	G	■	■	■
S	T	A	M	E	N	■	■	■	L	A	Y	L	O	W
P	I	L	O	T	■	D	E	A	L	T	■	A	S	H
E	B	A	N	■	B	I	R	D	Y	■	I	N	L	A
R	I	D	■	A	A	M	E	S	■	S	N	A	I	L
M	A	Y	O	R	S	■	■	■	C	A	N	I	N	E
■	■	■	D	A	I	R	Y	C	O	W	■	■	■	■
■	W	O	O	L	L	Y	M	A	M	M	O	T	H	■
J	A	N	U	S	■	A	C	T	■	I	L	I	A	D
A	D	A	R	E	■	N	A	E	■	L	E	N	T	O
M	E	N	S	A	■	S	S	S	■	L	O	S	E	S

159

S	O	D	A	■	A	B	L	E	■	■	C	L	E	M
I	B	I	S	■	R	I	O	S	■	W	A	I	V	E
R	O	C	K	E	T	J	S	Q	U	I	R	R	E	L
E	E	E	■	R	I	O	T	■	G	R	O	A	N	■
■	■	■	L	I	E	U	■	F	A	I	L	■	■	■
U	N	D	O	E	R	■	D	I	N	E	■	B	A	S
M	O	A	N	■	■	K	I	N	D	S	■	A	C	H
B	O	R	I	S	A	N	D	N	A	T	A	S	H	A
E	S	E	■	O	L	E	O	S	■	■	R	E	E	D
R	E	D	■	R	U	E	S	■	B	R	A	S	S	Y
■	■	■	A	R	M	S	■	S	E	E	M	■	■	■
■	B	A	T	O	N	■	A	U	R	A	■	J	O	B
B	U	L	L	W	I	N	K	L	E	M	O	O	S	E
A	R	E	A	S	■	R	I	F	F	■	I	S	L	E
A	R	C	S	■	■	A	N	A	T	■	L	E	O	N

160

A	T	A	T	■	S	T	O	P	■	T	A	P	E	S
R	I	T	E	■	C	A	G	E	■	A	C	E	N	T
S	A	B	E	■	H	U	L	A	■	L	E	A	S	E
O	R	A	N	G	E	P	E	K	O	E	■	C	U	P
N	A	T	A	L	I	E	■	■	I	N	C	H	E	S
■	■	■	G	A	B	■	S	A	L	T	O	F	■	■
P	I	L	E	D	■	D	A	L	E	■	T	U	B	A
A	R	I	■	■	F	I	V	E	R	■	■	Z	E	N
M	A	M	A	■	L	E	E	S	■	D	O	Z	E	D
■	■	E	G	R	E	T	S	■	T	I	M	■	■	■
H	A	L	O	E	S	■	■	C	A	P	I	T	O	L
A	M	I	■	C	H	E	R	R	Y	S	T	O	N	E
M	A	G	N	A	■	N	E	A	L	■	T	R	I	O
E	T	H	A	N	■	I	N	T	O	■	E	T	O	N
L	I	T	H	E	■	D	O	E	R	■	D	E	N	S

161

S	P	I	E	D	■	S	O	A	P	S	■	T	R	E
L	I	N	T	Y	■	Q	U	I	R	E	■	R	I	D
O	N	T	H	E	B	U	T	T	O	N	■	U	N	I
P	E	O	N	■	A	A	S	■	L	A	T	E	S	T
■	■	■	I	N	I	T	■	R	O	T	A	T	E	■
H	E	P	C	A	T	■	G	I	G	O	L	O	■	■
A	W	L	■	P	E	T	A	L	■	R	E	L	A	Y
N	E	A	■	■	D	A	L	E	S	■	■	I	V	E
D	R	I	L	L	■	P	A	S	T	A	■	F	I	N
■	■	N	O	I	S	E	S	■	E	M	B	E	D	S
■	M	A	L	T	E	D	■	A	R	T	E	■	■	■
M	O	S	L	E	M	■	T	S	E	■	S	L	A	M
O	L	D	■	R	I	G	H	T	O	N	T	I	M	E
A	T	A	■	A	T	A	R	I	■	R	O	M	P	S
T	O	Y	■	L	E	M	U	R	■	A	W	A	S	H

162

S	A	R	A	H	■	B	A	N	G	■	B	A	S	K
E	R	O	S	E	■	A	W	O	L	■	O	N	T	O
A	R	O	S	E	■	R	A	T	E	■	O	T	I	S
L	I	T	T	L	E	G	R	E	E	N	M	E	N	■
E	V	E	■	■	X	E	D	■	■	U	S	A	G	E
R	E	D	C	A	P	S	■	A	C	T	■	T	E	E
■	■	■	A	L	E	■	E	A	R	■	J	E	R	K
■	F	L	Y	I	N	G	S	A	U	C	E	R	S	■
K	A	O	S	■	S	A	P	■	Z	O	E	■	■	■
I	C	Y	■	W	E	B	■	P	A	P	R	I	K	A
M	E	A	D	E	■	■	A	I	D	■	■	N	E	T
■	C	L	O	S	E	E	N	C	O	U	N	T	E	R
M	A	I	D	■	Y	A	N	K	■	R	O	O	N	E
O	R	S	O	■	E	R	I	E	■	S	O	N	E	S
D	D	T	S	■	S	L	E	D	■	A	N	E	N	T

163

S	P	A	N	■	G	R	A	S	■	L	I	F	T	S
H	A	L	O	■	R	A	N	T	■	E	R	I	K	A
O	S	L	O	■	E	T	N	A	■	S	A	X	O	N
C	H	A	N	G	E	H	A	N	D	S	■	E	S	E
K	A	Y	■	A	C	E	S	■	R	E	D	D	■	■
■	■	■	O	V	E	R	■	D	E	N	I	R	O	■
S	T	A	K	E	■	■	S	E	A	S	C	A	P	E
T	I	L	E	■	A	L	A	R	M	■	I	T	A	L
D	E	T	E	R	R	E	D	■	■	K	N	E	L	L
■	R	E	F	E	R	S	■	P	A	N	G	■	■	■
■	■	R	E	D	O	■	S	O	D	A	■	H	A	M
A	L	E	■	S	W	I	T	C	H	P	L	A	T	E
B	E	G	O	T	■	T	A	K	E	■	A	R	E	S
E	N	O	L	A	■	E	V	E	R	■	N	E	A	T
L	O	S	E	R	■	M	E	T	E	■	E	M	M	A

164

B	I	R	T	H	S	■	E	D	A	M	■	J	E	B
O	N	E	O	U	T	■	D	I	K	E	■	A	X	E
S	T	A	N	D	A	N	D	D	E	L	I	V	E	R
O	R	L	Y	■	L	O	Y	A	L	■	O	A	S	T
M	O	M	■	D	E	N	■	C	A	I	N	■	■	■
■	■	■	T	A	M	E	S	T	■	S	A	N	T	A
S	H	E	R	P	A	■	T	I	C	S	■	O	O	F
G	E	T	U	P	T	H	E	C	O	U	R	A	G	E
T	R	A	■	L	E	O	N	■	H	E	E	H	A	W
S	O	L	V	E	■	M	O	P	E	R	S	■	■	■
■	■	■	I	D	L	E	■	L	I	S	■	V	A	L
P	L	U	S	■	A	B	N	E	R	■	S	E	M	I
R	I	S	E	I	N	R	E	B	E	L	L	I	O	N
I	K	E	■	A	C	E	S	■	S	E	A	N	C	E
X	E	D	■	N	E	W	T	■	S	E	T	S	O	N

165

OTHER ERA BIDS
CHINA VON MEDIA
TOTES ETC CRESS
OUT PUNCHACLOCK
HAIRS OBOE
ICEMEN BRAY JAL
VISOR SLAT HUGO
OLAV BEIGE AMIS
RICE APSE DUPLE
YAK ANTS RENTER
ONCE FIFTH
SKIPTOMYLOU ELK
ANNIE BOO SAGAN
FOCUS EGO ETUDE
EXAM RID DENSE

166

MBAS TCU OMITS
ALTA POLL PINOT
YAWN UNIT ESTEE
ANATOLEFRANCE
SCRAMS FALA RDA
NAG DIAPER
HAG IRANBARKLEY
OTOS PIE CARA
JILLIRELAND YEN
OLDPRO MIA
STS ESSE NYMETS
MICHAELJORDAN
BLINK PLEA MIRO
RETRO PEGS ONTO
ASHEN YRS MAST

167

HUGO COB SPASM
ASAP ORE THEDAY
SUPERMAN AERATE
PRECEPT PARLOR
SYR PLEASE YENS
JOE STRAW
ASTI TEAR CHUMS
SLAMMER ARTISAN
KARMA AIDE TACO
YEAST VIE
AERO NESTER CUP
STALAG BRAILLE
THISBE LOISLANE
RESEAL INN IRAN
OLAND PEG EKES

168

PIMA RAKE AMEN
ELAN EVES NEVIS
SKATESONTHINICE
TAM VINS AMULET
ROD TRA
TAKETHEPLUNGE
SHADE HERO NOLA
PARIS ERE OTTER
EROS EGOS CRIES
WITHINANACEOF
STY ELD
PESTLE ATNO RIO
ONTHERIGHTTRACK
TOLET DEAR IGOR
SONS ASWE GENA

169

TIP VERB RATES
LIRE OVAL ERODE
IDEA LARA TATAR
MASC CHERRYBOMB
ALTHEA REAP
YANK DEGREE
WORKROOMS DRAWN
ALOE SPEED ACED
RISES STRIPPERS
MOANED FORE
COTS COVERT
APPLESAUCE ILIE
BARED XMAS NAVE
ELITE CURE ETAS
TEXAS OPTS SEL

170

IQTEST HANDBOOK
SUITOR ARGUABLE
HOPALONGCASSIDY
LETA HIT
IFS HULLO FADE
BLURB GAY ENOS
MONARCHY GADGET
SKIPTOMYLOU
RAPIER VAPORIZE
AMOS LEN EASEL
MYTH DORIA HEM
BOG ASAP
JUMPINJACKFLASH
OPERAHAT ERODES
TIRESOME RODENT

171

SPAR PART SKATE
LAVE OBOE PILES
USIA LYNX ECLAT
SHARPASATACK
HANGARS NISSAN
UPI SHEA HBO
WISEASANOWL AHS
IDO SER ROE
SIB FREEASABIRD
POE REAR POO
STREET MENTORS
MADASAWETHEN
SNACK LONE LAMA
PUREE MSGR ERIK
ANTED SOYS RATE

172

CHIC ADZE ABBOT
LENO COIN NOONE
INCLEMENT TODAY
CROONERCROSBY
HYMNS AMY SIP
EVE JUMPY JUNO
UNIFY TORTS
FLASHGORDONSFOE
LEVEL NORTH
AVER ISAAC GAB
KIM ASP MAUVE
AUTHORLARDNER
HARPO NEONTETRA
AXIOM GAWK PEST
MEANS ELSA TREE

173

NOTE PASSE SWAM
AMIN ORCAS PESO
PILLOWTALK OTTO
ATTIRE NAIROBI
VALET MILL
SHELLS BONSAIS
ATON STRESS NRA
BETSY EAR ONKEY
INS IDREAM EENS
TOPPERS TODATE
ROLE TENOR
WINDSOR SONATA
TONI SHEETMETAL
URGE ETAGE SALT
BESS ROTOR STLO

174

BACH SPOT ENOS
ACRE TIBIA LAPP
THEMORNINGAFTER
HEW DIKE IDIOCY
BEVY STAN
REBATE BEAM SST
OPART BEAT INTO
DOGDAYAFTERNOON
ICES ASIS ELOPE
NHL BRIT AVATAR
MADE SLAW
SHEILA AHEM VII
MIDNIGHTEXPRESS
URIS EARLE ORAL
GEEK MALI TYKE

175

AVA MATES PHIL
LIMP ORALS RARE
ATOR DEBITHOMAS
MANORIAL ONSET
PEGGYFLEMING
REY ARI LOA
OGRE DAMNDEST
KRISTIYAMAGUCHI
LETSINON CHAT
AWE RID SET
KATARINAWITT
ALOON ACETONES
SONJAHENIE RONA
TATA ANGER KNAR
AMOK LEERS EMS

176

AJAR SCAM PLIES
ROSE TREE RIFLE
ITSSOEASY OLIVE
IMSOEXCITED
LAMAS SPREE SSS
ATONES DEL
BESS OKRA DAMS
SHESSOUNUSUAL
TELL SNAP DUOS
MAY SLEDGE
AKC VENOM IREST
YOURESOVAIN
EATER HESSOFINE
ALINE OTOE AVIS
RATED WANE TEXT

177

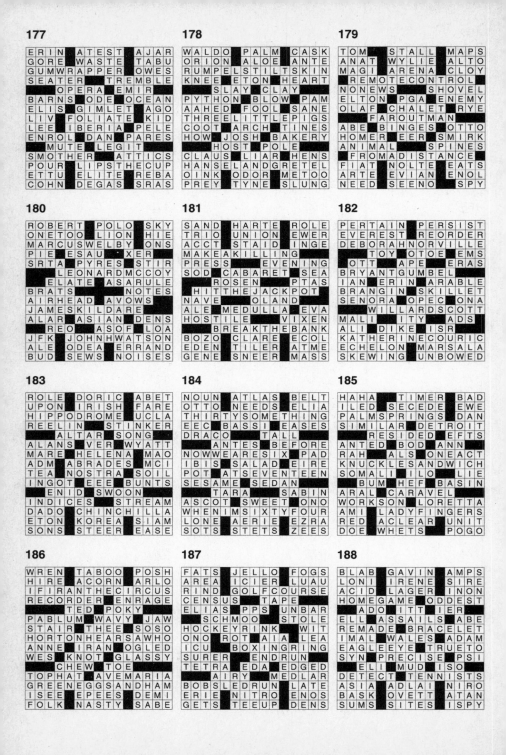

ERIN■ATEST■AJAR
GORE■WASTE■TABU
GUMWRAPPER■OWES
SEATER■■TREMBLE
■■■OPERA■EMIR■■
BARNS■ODE■OCEAN
ELIS■GIMLET■AGO
LIV■FOLIATE■KID
LEE■IBERIA■PELE
ENROL■DAN■PARES
■■MUTE■LEGIT■■■
SMOTHER■■ATTICS
POUR■LIPSTHECUP
ETTU■ELITE■REBA
COHN■DEGAS■SRAS

178

WALDO■PALM■CASK
ORION■ALOE■ANTE
RUMPELSTILTSKIN
KNEE■ETON■HEART
■■■SLAY■CLAY■■■
PYTHON■BLOW■PAM
AAHED■FOOL■SANE
THREELITTLEPIGS
COOT■ARCH■TINES
HOW■JOSH■BAKERY
■■■HOST■POLE■■■
CLAUS■LIAR■HENS
HANSELANDGRETEL
OINK■ODOR■METOO
PREY■TYNE■SLUNG

179

TOM■■STALL■MAPS
ANAT■WYLIE■ALTO
MAGI■ARENA■CLOY
■REMOTECONTROL■
NONEWS■■■SHOVEL
ELTON■PGA■ENEMY
OLAF■CHALET■RYE
■■■FAROUTMAN■■■
ABE■BINGES■OTTO
HOMER■EER■SMIRK
ANIMAL■■■SPINES
■FROMADISTANCE■
FIAT■NOLTE■EATS
ARTE■EVIAN■ENOL
NEED■SEENO■■SPY

180

ROBERT■POLO■SKY
ONETOO■LION■HIE
MARCUSWELBY■ONS
PIE■ESAU■■XER■■
SRTA■PYRES■STIR
■■LEONARDMCCOY
■■ELATE■ASARULE
BRATS■■■■■NOTES
AIRHEAD■AVOWS■■
JAMESKILDARE■■■
ALAR■ASIAN■DENS
■■REO■■ASOF■LOA
JFK■JOHNHWATSON
ALE■ODEA■ERRAND
BUD■SEWS■NOISES

181

SAND■HARTE■ROLE
TRIO■UNION■EWER
ACCT■STAID■INGE
MAKEAKILLING■■■
PRESS■■■EVENING
SOD■CABARET■SEA
■■■ROSEN■■■PTAS
■HITTHEJACKPOT■
NAVE■■■OLAND■■■
ALE■MEDULLA■EVA
HOSTILE■■■VIXEN
■■■BREAKTHEBANK
BOZO■CLARE■ECOL
EDEN■TILER■ATME
GENE■SNEER■MASS

182

PERTAIN■PERSIST
EVEREST■REORDER
DEBORAHNORVILLE
■■■TOY■OTOE■EMS
■OTT■■APE■■ERAS
BRYANTGUMBEL■■■
IAN■ERIN■ARABLE
BRANGIN■SKILLET
SENORA■OPEC■ONA
■■■WILLARDSCOTT
MALI■■ITY■■ADS■
ALI■DIKE■ISR■■■
KATHERINECOURIC
ECHELON■MARSALA
SKEWING■UNBOWED

183

ROLE■DORIC■ABET
UPON■IRISH■FARE
HIPPODROME■UCLA
REELIN■■STINKER
■■■ALTAR■SONG■■
ALANS■VER■WYATT
MARE■HELENA■MAO
ADM■ABRADES■MCI
TEA■NOSTRA■SOIL
INGOT■EEE■BUNTS
■■ENID■SWOON■■■
INDICES■■STREAM
DADO■CHINCHILLA
ETON■KOREA■SIAM
SONS■STEER■EASE

184

NOUN■ATLAS■BELT
OTTO■NEEDS■ELIA
THIRTYSOMETHING
EEC■BASSI■EASES
DRACO■■■TALL■■■
■■■ANTES■BEFORE
NOWWEARESIX■PAD
IBIS■SALAD■EIRE
POT■ATSEVENTEEN
SESAME■SEDAN■■■
■■■TARA■■■SABIN
ASCOT■SWEET■ONO
WHENIMSIXTYFOUR
LONE■AERIE■EZRA
SOTS■STETS■ZEES

185

HAHA■■TIMER■BAD
ILED■SECEDE■EWE
PALMSPRINGS■DAN
SIMILAR■DETROIT
■■■RESIDED■EFTS
ANTED■BOD■ANN■■
RAH■■ALS■ONEACT
KNUCKLESANDWICH
SOMALI■ILO■■LIE
■■BUM■HEF■BASIN
ARAL■CARAVEL■■■
WORKSON■LORETTA
AMI■LADYFINGERS
RED■ACLEAR■UNIT
DOE■WHETS■■POGO

186

WREN■TABOO■POSH
HIRE■ACORN■ARLO
IFIRANTHECIRCUS
RECORDER■ENRAGE
■■■■TED■POKY■■■
PABLUM■WAVY■JAW
STAIR■THEE■SOSO
HORTONHEARSAWHO
ANNE■IRAN■OGLED
WES■KNOT■GLASSY
■■■CHEW■TOE■■■■
TOPHAT■AVEMARIA
GREENEGGSANDHAM
ISEE■EPEES■DEMI
FOLK■NASTY■SABE

187

FATS■JELLO■FOGS
AREA■ICIER■LUAU
RIND■GOLFCOURSE
CENSUS■■TAPE■■■
ELIAS■PPS■UNBAR
■■SCHMOO■■STOLE
HOCKEYRINK■■WIT
ONO■ROT■AIA■LEA
ICU■■BOXINGRING
SURER■■ENDRUN■■
TETRA■EDA■EDGED
■■■AIRY■■MEDLAR
BOBSLEDRUN■LATE
ERIE■NITRO■ENOS
GETS■TEEUP■DENS

188

BLAB■GAVIN■AMPS
LONI■IRENE■SIRE
ACID■LAGER■INON
HOMEGAME■ODDEST
■■ADO■ITT■IER■■
ELL■ASSAILS■ABE
REMADE■BRACELET
IMAL■WALES■ADAM
EAGLEEYE■TRUETO
SYN■PRECISE■PSI
■■ELI■MUD■ISO■■
DETECT■TENNISTS
ASIA■ADLAI■NIRO
BASK■OVETT■ATAN
SUMS■SITES■ISPY

189

ECCE■ETTAS■BIAS
DOAS■DEARS■ANNE
DUSTJACKET■NATE
ANTHEM■ENSLAVES
STEER■CST■ANA■■
■■■REAR■■APACHE
CAWS■SEDANS■UAR
ASA■STOOLIE■URN
LES■CANNOT■AMES
MAHLER■■FARR■■■
■■BEN■FAT■ERIKA
FRONTIER■ADORES
LEAS■SWEEPSWEEK
INRE■LENDS■ENNE
PODS■ERASE■DEED

190

RICK■SPEND■SPAR
ASHE■EAGER■PATE
PLUMBCRAZY■ASEA
TEMPERED■DENTED
■■■■RED■MORSE■■
PARENT■DICE■BSA
IMAGE■KINK■GOAL
LIZA■SENDS■RANI
ETON■TREY■CARTE
SYR■MARS■MADDEN
■■BEANS■KID■■■■
SHARED■INTERACT
PICA■PAPERTIGER
ILKS■AISLE■TARA
NOSE■TROTS■ARTY

191

GAFFE■OHNO■OOPS
AWAIT■DOOR■CLAP
PRIVATEPRACTICE
EYRE■ITEM■RENEW
■■■CANS■ABUT■■■
ASSERT■AJAX■BOW
SHANE■USER■BOZO
CAPTAINKANGAROO
ALPS■SPIN■ASONE
PLY■PEON■BURNER
■■■WEEP■MILE■■■
AWARE■UPON■LIMP
GENERALHOSPITAL
OAKS■PAIR■RETIE
GNAT■ERLE■OFOLD

192

KISS■TWAS■JADED
ANTE■RAJA■OLIVE
PLIE■URAL■BAGEL
PENNANTRACES■■■
ATTACK■■DOT■BAH
■■■■OSLO■CHARGE
POLAR■OTTO■BAER
ABANNERHEADLINE
PEST■VEER■RENTS
ASSISI■RIPE■■■■
LEO■ETE■■EASTER
■■■STANDARDTIME
POSIT■DOOM■ABBA
AWARE■OMNI■PIER
NEWER■FEET■HARM

193

SHES■SWAIN■CAKE
EAVE■HORNE■ANNA
THELIONINWINTER
HALFNOTE■LOOSEN
■■■■TIS■TYNE■■■
MATRON■MOWS■CBS
ORBIT■PIKE■SALK
CROCODILEDUNDEE
HONK■ICON■NURSE
AWE■TSKS■ATBEST
■■■POKY■ERR■■■■
SCRIBE■INCUBATE
PLANETOFTHEAPES
RENT■TOWEL■LIRA
YOKO■EMERY■MENU

194

TILDE■POOR■■SRA
OCEAN■UPTO■STEP
TONYCURTIS■HAVE
SNOCONE■STERNER
■■■ARIES■EVILLY
TURRET■EUREKA■■
KNEE■EVER■REUPS
ODD■ESO■GIS■RAH
SOBER■WREN■AERO
■■UNREST■VALLEE
PATTON■EMIRS■■■
ATTIRES■AVIANCA
CROC■RINGOSTARR
TINE■GLEN■TIBET
SAS■■YOGA■OASES

195

ERA■JAVA■YAWNED
LOM■URIS■ADRIAN
ICESTATIONZEBRA
JOCASTA■UKES■■■
ACHY■■MISE■TACT
HOE■TWISTER■COO
■■■GRANT■■INLAW
■WATERCHESTNUT■
WAGON■■MAIZE■■■
EVE■DEBUSSY■TWO
BEEP■VEST■■WHEN
■■■LOIS■WINERED
STEAMLOCOMOTIVE
PASCAL■HOOT■VIC
ARTERY■EDNA■ELK

196

RIDE■■GASP■COMA
ANON■TABOO■OVER
CANDLEPINS■NANA
ENAMOR■EAT■CLUB
RESOUND■RATE■■■
■■■STARS■GARAGE
HART■LANTERNJAW
USA■■■WAY■■■ALE
LAMPOONING■PRES
APPEAR■LARGE■■■
■■■DRAG■NEATASA
MRED■CRO■EVADES
COLL■LIGHTERMEN
ABLE■ELLIS■DIME
NEER■SLED■■STER

197

BORG■■MAIM■BITS
ASIA■BELLA■ONIT
ISNT■ONAIR■BARA
RIGHTASRAIN■BEN
DESERT■MCNAIR■■
■■■RUMP■■EBBETS
EGGS■AREA■ONEAL
GEE■SNOWJOB■ZOO
ANTAL■WEAN■PEST
DEWIER■■REDO■■■
■■IMPOSE■EDUCES
PUN■TAKEBYSTORM
ALDA■SIREE■ERNE
INON■TRIED■ROIL
RAFT■STEP■■STET

198

ASSES■MARS■LETT
THEME■ALEC■OLIO
EATEN■RITA■GLEN
SPINDOCTOR■RARE
TENDER■■RENO■■■
■■■■REACT■ELATE
ORBS■GIL■POLLEN
REAP■OMEGA■EGAD
ENJOIN■AAR■RAMS
STAIR■ANTIS■■■■
■■■LEAD■■SPRINT
LESS■WARDHEELER
ALUM■AGEE■ABOVE
MAMA■SIDE■RUNES
ANON■HOOD■STARS

199

TOSCA■HEROD■SAO
ABHOR■ALIVE■ITS
LOONEYTUNES■LEA
LEON■EEL■REFLAG
■■■OMAR■CARRYME
FACTOR■RAGTOP■■
INRED■GENES■UFO
ETAS■ALOES■STEP
FEZ■CREWS■UTTER
■■YEOMAN■GRAYLY
SAHARAN■RAIN■■■
AMOUNT■OAR■DATA
DAR■FUNNYPAPERS
ASS■ERATO■MARIA
TSE■DEMON■STOMP

200

CHUG■ASMAD■CASA
ROSY■RUEDE■AUNT
AHEM■APTER■TRIO
BORNFREE■ERSATZ
■■■ALAR■SLOP■■■
RAISETHETITANIC
EMOTE■EXEC■WASH
NAW■■ERUPT■■MAI
ETAS■TORS■GLEAN
SINKTHEBISMARCK
■■■EWES■SPAN■■■
PARLOR■STANDPAT
EXIT■EATER■SULU
ALTO■AVERS■AMES
LEAN■LAPSE■TACK

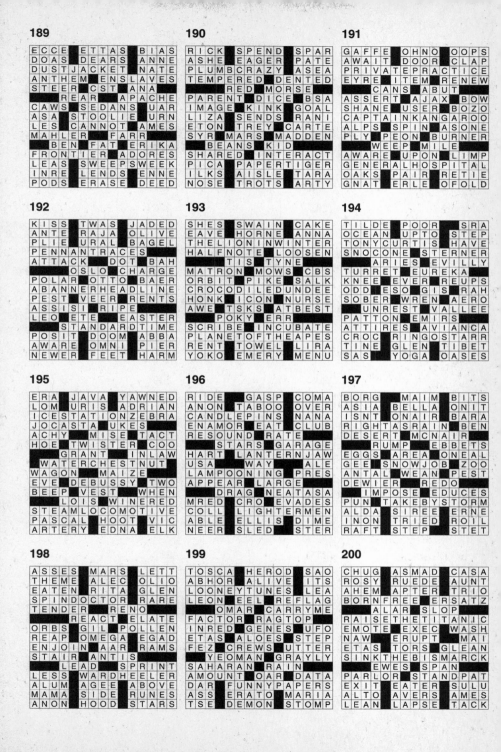

201

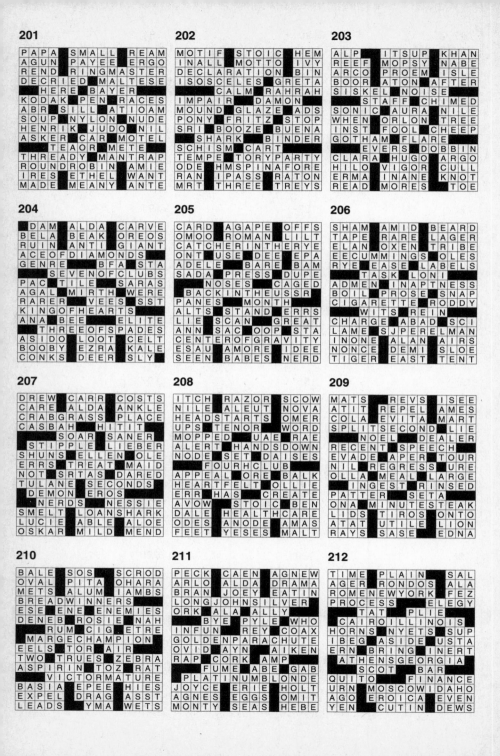

PAPA■SMALL■REAM
AGUN■PAYEE■ERGO
REND■RINGMASTER
DECRIED■MALTESE
■■HERE■BAYER■■■
KODAK■PEN■RACES
ABR■SILL■ATIOAM
SOUP■NYLON■NUDE
HENRIK■JUDO■NIL
ASKER■CAR■MOTEL
■■■TEAOR■METE■■
THREADY■MANTRAP
ROUNDROBIN■AMIE
IRES■ETHEL■WANT
MADE■MEANY■ANTE

202

MOTIF■STOIC■HEM
INALL■MOTTO■IVY
DECLARATION■BIN
ISOSCELES■GRETA
■■■■CALM■RAHRAH
IMPAIR■■DAMON■■
MOUND■GLAZE■ADS
PONY■FRITZ■STOP
SRI■BOOZE■BUENA
■■SHARK■■BINDER
SCHISM■CART■■■■
TEMPE■TORYPARTY
ODE■HMSPINAFORE
RAN■IPASS■RATON
MRT■THREE■TREYS

203

ALP■■ITSUP■KHAN
REEF■MOPSY■NABE
ARCO■PROEM■ISLE
BOOR■ATON■AFTER
SISKEL■NOISE■■■
■■■STAFF■CHIMED
SONIC■AURA■NILE
WHEN■ORLON■TREE
INST■FOOL■CHEEP
GOTHAM■FLARE■■■
■■■EVERS■DOBBIN
CLARA■HUGO■ARGO
HILO■VIGOR■CULL
ERMA■INANE■KNOT
READ■MORES■■TOE

204

■DAM■ALDA■CARVE
BELA■BEAK■OREOS
RUIN■ANTI■GIANT
ACEOFDIAMONDS■■
GENRE■■■BFA■STA
■■■SEVENOFCLUBS
PAC■TILE■■SARAS
AGAL■MIRTH■WERE
RARER■■VEES■SST
KINGOFHEARTS■■■
ANA■BEE■■■ELITE
■■THREEOFSPADES
ASIDO■LOOT■CELT
BOOBY■EZRA■KALE
CONKS■DEER■SLY■

205

CARD■AGAPE■OFFS
OMOO■ROMAN■LILT
CATCHERINTHERYE
ONT■USE■DEE■EPA
ADELE■■BARE■BAM
SADA■PRESS■DUPE
■■■NOSES■■CAGED
■BACKINTHEUSSR■
PANES■■MONTH■■■
ALTS■STAND■ERRS
LIE■SCAN■■GREAT
ANN■SAC■OOP■STA
CENTEROFGRAVITY
ESAU■AMORE■IDEE
SEEN■BABES■NERD

206

SHAM■AMID■BEARD
TAPE■RARE■LAGER
ELAN■OXEN■TRIBE
EECUMMINGS■OLES
RYE■EASE■LABELS
■■■TASK■LONI■■■
ADMEN■INAPTNESS
BOIL■PROSE■SNAP
CIGARETTE■RODDY
■■■WITS■REIN■■■
CHARGE■ABAD■SCI
LAME■SJPERELMAN
INONE■ALAN■AIRS
NONCE■DEMI■SLOE
TIGER■EAST■TENT

207

DREW■CARR■COSTS
CARE■ALDA■ANKLE
CRABGRASS■PLACE
CASBAH■■HITIT■■
■■■■SOAR■SANER■
■STIPPLE■LIEBER
SHUNS■ELLEN■OLE
ERRS■TREAT■MAID
NOT■SRTAS■DARED
TULANE■SECONDS■
■DEMON■EROS■■■■
■■NERDS■■NESSIE
SMELT■LOANSHARK
LUCIE■ABLE■ALOE
OSKAR■MILD■MEND

208

ITCH■RAZOR■SCOW
NILE■ALEUT■NOVA
HEADSTARTS■OMER
UPS■TENOR■■WORD
MOPPED■■UAE■RAE
ALERT■HANDSDOWN
NODE■SET■DAISES
■■■FOURHCLUB■■■
APPEAL■ORE■BALK
HEARTFELT■OLLIE
ERR■HAS■■CREATE
AVOW■■STOIC■BEN
DALE■HEALTHCARE
ODES■ANODE■AMAS
FEET■YESES■MALT

209

MATS■■REVS■ISEE
ATIT■REPEL■AMES
COLA■EVITA■MART
SPLITSECOND■LIE
■■■NOEL■■DEALER
RECENT■SPEECH■■
EVADE■APER■TOUR
NIL■REGRESS■URE
OLLA■MEAL■LARGE
■■INGEST■RINSED
PATTER■■SETA■■■
ONA■MINUTESTEAK
LIDS■TIROS■ONTO
ATAT■UTILE■LION
RAYS■SASE■■EDNA

210

BALE■SOS■■SCROD
OVAL■PITA■OHARA
METS■ALUM■IAMBS
BREADWINNERS■■■
ESE■ENE■ENEMIES
DENEB■ROSIE■NAH
■■■RUM■CIG■ETRE
■MARGECHAMPION■
EELS■TOR■AIR■■■
TWO■TRUES■ZEBRA
ASPIRIN■TOZ■RAT
■■■VICTORMATURE
BASIA■EPEE■HIES
EXPEL■DRAG■ASST
LEADS■■YMA■WETS

211

PECK■CAEN■AGNEW
ARLO■ALDA■DRAMA
BRAN■JOEY■EATIN
LONGJOHNSILVER■
ORK■ALA■ALLY■■■
■■■BYE■PYLE■WHO
INFUN■■REY■COAX
GOLDENPARACHUTE
OVID■AYN■■AIKEN
RAP■CORK■AMP■■■
■■■FUME■ABE■GAB
■PLATINUMBLONDE
JOYCE■ERIE■HOLT
AGNES■EGGS■OMIT
MONTY■SEAS■HEBE

212

TIME■PLAIN■■SAL
AGER■RONDOS■ALA
ROMENEWYORK■FEZ
PROCESS■■■ELEGY
■■■TAT■■PLIE■■■
■CAIROILLINOIS■
HORNS■NYETS■SUP
IBEG■ASIDE■USTA
ERN■BRING■INERT
■ATHENSGEORGIA■
■■■SCOT■■BAR■■■
QUITO■■■FINANCE
URN■MOSCOWIDAHO
AGO■EROICA■EVEN
YEN■■CUTIN■DEWS

213

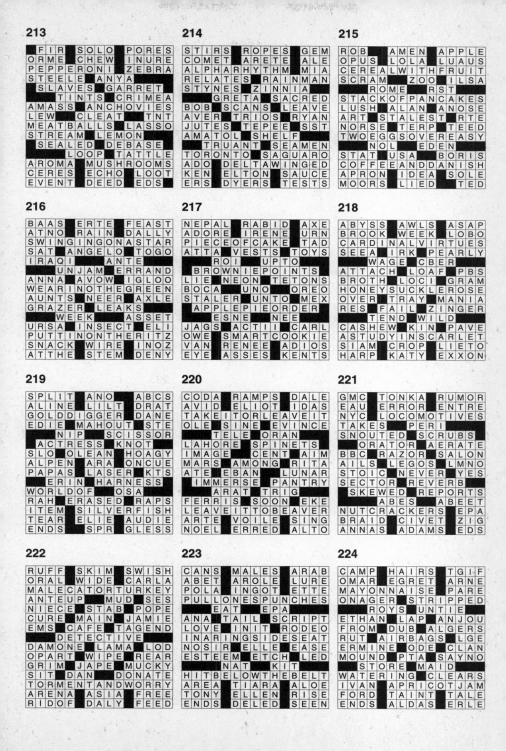

```
■FIR■SOLO■PORES
ORME■CHEW■INURE
PEPPERONI■ZEBRA
STEELE■ANYA■■■■
■SLAVES■GARRET■
■■■TINTS■CRIMEA
AMASS■ANCHOVIES
LEW■■CLEAT■■TNT
MEATBALLS■LASSO
STREAM■LEMON■■■
■SEALED■DEBASE■
■■■■LOOP■TATTLE
AROMA■MUSHROOMS
CERES■ECHO■LOOT
EVENT■DEED■EDS■
```

214

```
STIRS■ROPES■GEM
COMET■ARETE■ALE
ALPHARHYTHM■MIA
RELATES■RAINMAN
STYNES■ZINNIA■■
■■■GRETA■SACRED
BOB■SCANS■LEAVE
AVER■TRIOS■RYAN
JUTES■TEPEE■SST
AMATOL■SHELF■■■
■■TRUANT■SEAMEN
TORONTO■SAGUARO
ADO■DELTAWINGED
KEN■ELTON■SAUCE
ERS■DYERS■TESTS
```

215

```
ROB■■AMEN■APPLE
OPUS■LOLA■LUAUS
CEREALWITHFRUIT
SCRAM■■ZOO■ILSA
■■■ROME■■RST■■■
STACKOFPANCAKES
LUSH■ALAN■ANOSE
ART■STALEST■RTE
NORSE■TERP■TEED
TWOEGGSOVEREASY
■■■NOL■■EDEN■■■
STAT■USA■■BORIS
COFFEEANDDANISH
APRON■IDEA■SOLE
MOORS■LIED■■TED
```

216

```
BAAS■ERTE■FEAST
ATNO■RAIN■DALLY
SWINGINGONASTAR
SAT■ANGELO■TOGO
IRAQI■■■ANTE■■■
■■■UNJAM■ERRAND
ANNA■AVOW■IGLOO
WEARINOTHEGREEN
AUNTS■NEER■AXLE
GRAZER■LEAKS■■■
■■■WEEK■■■ASSET
URSA■INSECT■ELI
PUTTINONTHERITZ
SNACK■WIRE■INOZ
ATTHE■STEM■DENY
```

217

```
NEPAL■RABID■AXE
ADORE■IRENE■URN
PIECEOFCAKE■TAD
ATTA■VESTS■TOYS
■■■ROI■■UPTO■■■
■BROWNIEPOINTS■
LIE■NEON■TETONS
BOCA■■UNO■■OREO
STALER■UNTO■MEX
■APPLEPIEORDER■
■■■ESNE■■NEE■■■
JAGS■ACTII■CARL
OWE■SMARTCOOKIE
VAN■RENEE■ADIOS
EYE■ASSES■KENTS
```

218

```
ABYSS■AWLS■ASAP
BROOK■WEEK■LOBO
CARDINALVIRTUES
SEEA■IRK■PEARLY
■■■WAGE■CBER■■■
ATTACH■LOAF■PBS
BROTH■LOCI■GRAM
HONEYSUCKLEROSE
OVER■TRAY■MANIA
RES■FAIL■ZINGER
■■■TEND■WILD■■■
CASHEW■KIN■PAVE
ASTUDYINSCARLET
SIAM■CROP■LIETO
HARP■KATY■EXXON
```

219

```
SPLIT■ANO■■ABCS
ALINE■LILT■DRAT
GOLDDIGGER■DANE
EDIE■MAHOUT■STE
■■■NIP■■SCISSOR
■ACTRESS■KNOT■■
SLO■OLEAN■HOAGY
ALPEN■ARA■ONCUE
PAPAS■LASER■KTS
■■ERIN■HARNESS■
WORLDOF■■OSA■■■
RAH■ERASED■RAPS
ITEM■SILVERFISH
TEAR■ELIE■AUDIE
ENDS■■SPR■GLESS
```

220

```
CODA■RAMPS■DALE
AVID■ELIOT■IDAS
TAKEITORLEAVEIT
OLE■SINE■EVINCE
■■■TELE■ORAN■■■
LAHORE■SPINETS■
IMAGE■■CENT■AIM
MARS■AMONG■RITA
ATE■EBAN■■LUNAR
■IMMERSE■PANTRY
■■■ARAT■TRIG■■■
FERRIS■SOON■EKE
LEAVEITTOBEAVER
ARTE■VOILE■SING
NOEL■ERRED■ALTO
```

221

```
GMC■TONKA■RUMOR
EAU■ERROR■ENTRE
NYC■LOCOMOTIVES
TAKES■■PERI■■■■
SNOUTED■SCRUBS■
■■ORATOR■AERATE
BBC■RAZOR■SALON
AILS■LEGOS■LMNO
STOIC■NEVER■YES
SECTOR■REVERB■■
■SKEWED■REPORTS
■■■■ABES■■ABEET
NUTCRACKERS■EPA
BRAID■CIVET■ZIG
ANNAS■ADAMS■EDS
```

222

```
RUFF■SKIM■SWISH
ORAL■WIDE■CARLA
MALECATORTURKEY
ANTEUP■■MUD■SES
NIECE■STAB■POPE
CURE■MAIN■JAMIE
EMS■CAFE■TAGEND
■■■DETECTIVE■■■
DAMONE■LAMA■LOD
OPART■WIPE■REAR
GRIM■JAPE■MUCKY
SIT■DAN■■DONATE
TORMENTANDWORRY
ARENA■ASIA■FREE
RIDOF■DALY■FEED
```

223

```
CANS■MALES■ARAB
ABET■AROLE■LURE
POLA■INGOT■ETTE
PULLONESPUNCHES
■■■EAT■■EPA■■■■
ANA■TAIL■SCRIPT
LOVE■INIT■RODEO
INARINGSIDESEAT
NOSIR■ELLE■EASE
ESTEEM■ETCH■LED
■■■■NAT■■KIT■■■
HITBELOWTHEBELT
AREA■TIARA■ALOE
TONY■ELLEN■RISE
ENDS■DELED■SEEN
```

224

```
CAMP■HAIRS■TGIF
OMAR■EGRET■ARNE
MAYONNAISE■PARE
ONAGER■STRIPPED
■■■ROYS■UNTIE■■
ETHAN■LAP■ANJOU
FROM■DUB■ALGERS
RUT■AIRBAGS■LGE
ERMINE■ODE■CLAN
MOUND■PTA■SAYNO
■■STORE■MAID■■■
WATERING■CLEARS
IVAN■APRICOTJAM
FORD■TAINT■TALE
ENDS■ALDAS■ERLE
```

225

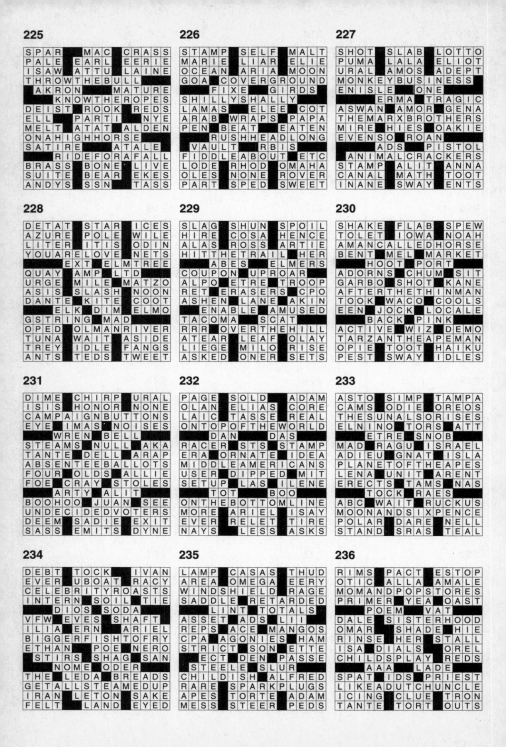

```
SPAR##MAC#CRASS
PALE#EARL#EERIE
ISAW#ATTU#LAINE
THROWTHEBULL###
#AKRON###MATURE
###KNOWTHEROPES
DEIST#ROOK#REDS
ELL##PARTI##NYE
MELT#ATAT#ALDEN
ONAHIGHHORSE###
SATIRE###ATALE#
###RIDEFORAFALL
BRASS#BONE#LIVE
SUITE#BEAR#EKES
ANDYS#SSN##TASS
```

226

```
STAMP#SELF#MALT
MARIE#LIAR#ELIE
OCEAN#ARIA#MOON
GOA#COVERGROUND
###FIXE##GIRDS#
SHILLYSHALLY###
LAMAS##ELEE#COT
ARAB#WRAPS#PAPA
PEN#BEAT##EATEN
###RUSHHEADLONG
#VAULT##RBIS###
FIDDLEABOUT#ETC
LODE#RHOD#OMAHA
OLES#NONE#ROVER
PART#SPED#SWEET
```

227

```
SHOT#SLAB#LOTTO
PUMA#LALA#ELIOT
URAL#AMOS#ADEPT
MONKEYBUSINESS#
ENISLE##ONE####
####ERMA#TRAGIC
ASWAN#AMOR#GENA
THEMARXBROTHERS
MIRE#HIES#OAKIE
EVENSO#ROAN####
####ADS##PISTOL
#ANIMALCRACKERS
STAMP#ALIT#ANNA
CANAL#MATH#TOOT
INANE#SWAY#ENTS
```

228

```
DETAT#STAR#ICES
AZURE#POLE#WILE
LITER#ITIS#ODIN
YOUARELOVE#NETS
####EXT#ELMTREE
QUAY#AMP#LTD###
URGE#MILE#MATZO
ASIS#SLASH#NOON
DANTE#KITE#COOT
###ELK#DIM#ELMO
GSTRING#MAD####
OPED#OLMANRIVER
TUNA#WAIT#ASIDE
TREY#IDLE#FANGS
ANTS#TEDS#TWEET
```

229

```
SLAG#SHUN#SPOIL
HIRE#COSA#HENCE
ALAS#ROSS#ARTIE
HITTHETRAIL#HER
###ABES##ELMERS
COUPON#UPROAR##
ALPO#ETRE#TROOP
RET#ERASERS#CPO
ASHEN#LANE#AKIN
##ENABLE#AMUSED
TACOMA##SCAT###
RRR#OVERTHEHILL
ATEAR#LEAF#OLAY
LIEGE#MILO#RISE
ASKED#ONER#SETS
```

230

```
SHAKE#FLAB#SPEW
TOLET#IOWA#NOAH
AMANCALLEDHORSE
BENT#MEL#MARKET
###HOOT#PORT###
ADORNS#CHUM#SIT
GARBO#SHOT#KANE
AFTERTHETHINMAN
TOOK#WACO#COOLS
EEN#JOCK#LOCALE
###BACK#PINK###
ACTIVE#WIZ#DEMO
TARZANTHEAPEMAN
OPIE#TOOT#HAIKU
PEST#SWAY#IDLES
```

231

```
DIME#CHIRP#URAL
ISIS#HONOR#NONE
CAMPAIGNBUTTONS
EYE#IMAS#NOISES
###WREN#BELL###
STEAMS#NULL#AKA
TANTE#DELL#ARAP
ABSENTEEBALLOTS
FOUR#OLDS#ALLIE
FOE#CRAY#STOLES
###ARTY#ALIT###
BOOHOO#JUAN#SEE
UNDECIDEDVOTERS
DEEM#SADIE#EXIT
SASS#EMITS#DYNE
```

232

```
PAGE#SOLD##ADAM
OLAN#ELIAS#CORE
LAIC#TASSE#REAL
ONTOPOFTHEWORLD
###DAN###DAS###
RACER#STS#STAMP
ERA#ORNATE#IDEA
MIDDLEAMERICANS
USER#DIPPED#MIT
SETUP#LAS#ILENE
###TOT###BOO###
ONTHEBOTTOMLINE
MORE#ARIEL#ISAY
EVER#RELET#TIRE
NAYS##LESS#ASKS
```

233

```
ASTO#SIMP#TAMPA
CAMS#ODIE#OREOS
THESUNALSORISES
ELNINO#TORS#ATT
###ETRE#SNOB###
MAD#RAGU#ISRAEL
ADIEU#GNAT#ISLA
PLANETOFTHEAPES
LENA#UNIT#ARENT
ERECTS#TAMS#NAS
###TOCK#RAES###
ABC#WAIT#RUCKUS
MOONANDSIXPENCE
POLAR#DARE#NELL
STAND#SRAS#TEAL
```

234

```
DEBT#TOCK##IVAN
EVER#UBOAT#RACY
CELEBRITYROASTS
INTERN#SOIL#TIE
###DIOS#SODA###
VFW#EVES#SHAFT#
ILIA#ERN##ARIEL
BIGGERFISHTOFRY
ETHAN##POE#NERO
#STIRS#SHAG#SAN
###NOME#ODER###
THE#LEDA#BREADS
GETALLSTEAMEDUP
IRAN#LETON#SAKE
FELT##LAND#EYED
```

235

```
LAMP#CASAS#THUD
AREA#OMEGA#EERY
WINDSHIELD#RAGE
SADDLE#RETARDED
###LINT#TOTALS#
ASSET#ADS#LII##
REPS#ACE#MANGOS
CPA#AGONIES#HAM
STRICT#SON#ETTE
##ECT#DEN#PASSE
#STEELE#SLUR###
CHILDISH#ALFRED
RARE#SPARKPLUGS
APES#TORTE#ADAM
MESS#STEER#PEDS
```

236

```
RIMS#PACT#ESTOP
OTIC#ALLA#AMALE
MOMANDPOPSTORES
PRIMER#YEA#OAST
###POEM##VAT###
DALE#SISTERHOOD
OMAR##SHADE#HIE
RINSE#HER#STALL
ISA#DIALS##OREL
CHILDSPLAY#REDS
###AAA##LADE###
SPAT#IDS#PRIEST
LIKEADUTCHUNCLE
ICING#CLUE#TRON
TANTE#TORT#OUTS
```

237

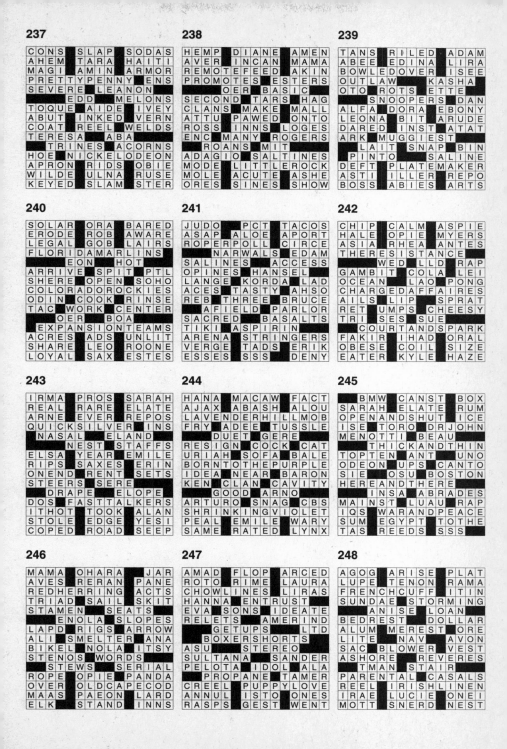

```
CONS■SLAP■SODAS
AHEM■TARA■HAITI
MAGI■AMIN■ARMOR
PRETTYPENNY■ENS
SEVERE■LEANON■■
■■■■EDD■■MELONS
TOQUE■AIDE■IVEY
ABUT■INKED■VERN
COAT■REEL■WELDS
TERESA■■ABA■■■■
■■TRINES■ACORNS
HOE■NICKELODEON
APRON■RIDS■OBIE
WILDE■ULNA■RUSE
KEYED■SLAM■STER
```

238

```
HEMP■DIANE■AMEN
AVER■INCAN■MAMA
REMOTEFEED■AKIN
PROMOTES■ESTERS
■■■■OER■BASIC■■
SECOND■TARS■HAG
CLANS■MAKE■MALL
ATTU■PAWED■ONTO
ROSS■INNS■LOGES
ENC■MANY■ROGERS
■■ROANS■MIT■■■■
ADAGIO■SALTINES
MODE■LITTLEROCK
MOLE■ACUTE■ASHE
ORES■SINES■SHOW
```

239

```
TANS■RILED■ADAM
ABEE■EDINA■LIRA
BOWLEDOVER■ISEE
OUTLAW■■■KASHA■
OTO■ROTS■ETTE■■
■■■SNOOPERS■DAN
ALFA■DORA■EBONY
LEONA■BIT■ARUDE
DARED■INST■ATAT
ARK■MUGGIEST■■■
■■LAIT■SNAP■BIN
■PINTO■■■SALINE
DEFT■PLATEMAKER
ASTI■ILLER■REPO
BOSS■ABIES■ARTS
```

240

```
SOLAR■ORA■BARED
ERODE■ROB■AWARE
LEGAL■GOB■LAIRS
FLORIDAMARLINS■
■■■■EON■■HOT■■■
ARRIVE■SPIT■PTL
SHERE■OPEN■SOHO
COLORADOROCKIES
ODIN■COOK■RINSE
TAC■WORK■CENTER
■■■OER■■BOA■■■■
■EXPANSIONTEAMS
ACRES■ADS■UNLIT
SHARE■LEO■ROONE
LOYAL■SAX■ESTES
```

241

```
JUDO■■PCT■TACOS
ASAP■ALOE■APORT
ROPERPOLL■CIRCE
■■■NARWALS■EDAM
SALINES■■ACCESS
OPINES■HANSEL■■
LANGE■KORDA■LAD
ACES■TASTY■AHSO
REB■THREE■BRUCE
■■AFIELD■PARLOR
SACRED■■BASALTS
TIKI■ASPIRIN■■■
ARENA■STRINGERS
VERGE■TADS■ERIK
ESSES■SSS■■DENY
```

242

```
CHIP■CALM■ASPIE
HALE■OPIE■MYERS
ASIA■RHEA■ANTES
THERESISTANCE■■
■■■■WED■LLD■RAP
GAMBIT■COLA■LEI
OCEAN■■LAO■PONG
CHARGEDAFFAIRES
AILS■LIP■■SPRAT
RET■UMPS■CHEESY
TRI■SES■SUE■■■■
■■COURTANDSPARK
FAKIR■IHAD■ORAL
OBESE■COIL■SIZE
EATER■KYLE■HAZE
```

243

```
IRMA■PROS■SARAH
REAL■RARE■ELATE
ARNE■EVER■REPOS
QUICKSILVER■INS
■NASAL■■ELAND■■
■■■■NEST■STAFFS
ELSA■YEAR■EMILE
RIPS■SAXES■ERIN
ONEND■RENT■SETS
STEERS■SERE■■■■
■■DRAPE■■ELOPE■
DOS■FASTTALKERS
ITHOT■TOOK■ALAN
STOLE■EDGE■YESI
COPED■ROAD■SEEP
```

244

```
HANA■MACAW■FACT
AJAX■ABASH■ALOU
LAVENDERHILLMOB
FRY■ADEE■TUSSLE
■■■DUET■GERE■■■
RESIGN■COCK■CAT
URIAH■SOFA■BALE
BORNTOTHEPURPLE
IDEA■NEAR■BARON
KEN■CLAN■CAVITY
■■■GOOD■ARNO■■■
ARTURO■SNAG■CBS
SHRINKINGVIOLET
PEAL■EMILE■WARY
SAME■RATED■LYNX
```

245

```
■■BMW■CANST■BOX
SARAH■ELATE■RUM
OPENANDSHUT■ICE
ISE■TORO■DRJOHN
MENOTTI■BEAU■■■
■■■THICKANDTHIN
TOPTEN■ANT■■UNO
ODEON■UPS■CANTO
SIE■■OSU■BOSTON
HEREANDTHERE■■■
■■■INSA■ABRADES
MAINST■LUAU■RAP
IQS■WARANDPEACE
SUM■EGYPT■TOTHE
TAS■REEDS■SSS■■
```

246

```
MAMA■OHARA■■JAR
AVES■RERAN■PANE
REDHERRING■ACTS
TRIAD■SAIL■SKIT
STAMEN■■SEATS■■
■■■ENOLA■SLOPES
LAPD■RIGS■ARROW
ALI■SMELTER■ANA
BIKEL■NOLA■ITSY
STENOS■WORDS■■■
■■STEWS■■SERIAL
ROPE■OPIE■PANDA
OVER■OLDCAPECOD
MAAS■PAEON■LARD
ELK■■STAND■INNS
```

247

```
AMAD■FLOP■ARCED
ROTO■RIME■LAURA
CHOWLINES■LIRAS
HANNA■ENTRUST■■
EVA■SONS■IDEATE
RELETS■■AMERIND
■■■GETUPS■■■LTD
■■BOXERSHORTS■■
ASU■■■STEREO■■■
SULTANA■■SANDER
PELOTA■IDOL■ALA
■■PROPANE■TAMER
CREEL■PUPPYLOVE
ANNUL■ISTO■ONES
RASPS■GEST■WENT
```

248

```
AGOG■ARISE■PLAT
LUPE■TENON■RAMA
FRENCHCUFF■ITIN
SUNDAE■STORMING
■■■ANISE■LOAN■■
BEDREST■■DOLLAR
ALUM■MEREST■ORE
LITE■■NAV■■AVON
SAC■BLOWER■VEST
ASHORE■■REVERES
■■TMAN■STAIR■■■
PARENTAL■CASALS
REEL■IRISHLINEN
IRAE■LUCIE■ONEI
MOTT■SNERD■NEST
```

249

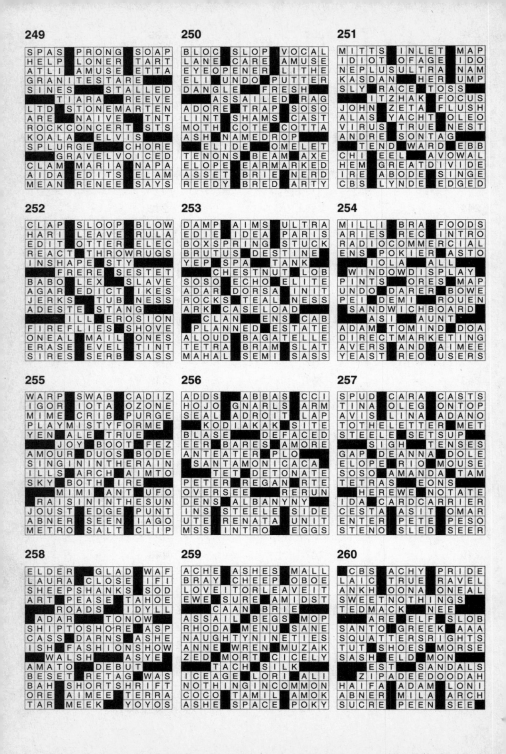

S	P	A	S		P	R	O	N	G		S	O	A	P
H	E	L	P		L	O	N	E	R		T	A	R	T
A	T	L	I		A	M	U	S	E		E	T	T	A
G	R	A	N	I	T	E	S	T	A	R	E			
S	I	N	E	S				S	T	A	L	L	E	D
			T	I	A	R	A			R	E	E	V	E
L	T	D		S	T	O	N	E	M	A	R	T	E	N
A	R	E			N	A	I	V	E			T	N	T
R	O	C	K	C	O	N	C	E	R	T		S	T	S
K	O	A	L	A			E	L	V	I	S			
S	P	L	U	R	G	E				C	H	O	R	E
			G	R	A	V	E	L	V	O	I	C	E	D
C	L	A	M		M	A	R	I	A		N	A	P	A
A	I	D	A		E	D	I	T	S		E	L	A	M
M	E	A	N		R	E	N	E	E		S	A	Y	S

250

B	L	O	C		S	L	O	P		V	O	C	A	L
L	A	N	E		C	A	R	E		A	M	U	S	E
E	Y	E	O	P	E	N	E	R		L	I	T	H	E
E	L	I		U	N	D	O		P	U	T	T	E	R
D	A	N	G	L	E			F	R	E	S	H		
			A	S	S	A	I	L	E	D		R	A	G
A	D	O	R	E		T	R	A	P		S	O	S	O
L	I	N	T		S	H	A	M	S		C	A	S	T
M	O	T	H		C	O	T	E		C	O	T	T	A
A	S	H		N	A	M	E	D	R	O	P			
		E	L	I	D	E			O	M	E	L	E	T
T	E	N	O	N	S		B	E	A	M		A	X	E
E	L	O	P	E		E	A	R	M	A	R	K	E	D
A	S	S	E	T		B	R	I	E		N	E	R	D
R	E	E	D	Y		B	R	E	D		A	R	T	Y

251

M	I	T	T	S		I	N	L	E	T		M	A	P
I	D	I	O	T		O	F	A	G	E		I	D	O
N	E	P	L	U	S	U	L	T	R	A		N	A	M
K	A	S	D	A	N			H	E	R		U	M	P
S	L	Y		R	A	C	E		T	O	S	S		
			I	T	Z	H	A	K		F	O	C	U	S
J	O	H	N		Z	E	T	A		F	L	U	S	H
A	L	A	S		Y	A	C	H	T		O	L	E	O
V	I	R	U	S		T	R	U	E		N	E	S	T
A	N	D	R	E		S	O	N	T	A	G			
		T	E	N	D		W	A	R	D		E	B	B
C	H	I		E	E	L			A	V	O	W	A	L
H	E	M		G	R	E	A	T	D	I	V	I	D	E
I	R	E		A	B	O	D	E		S	I	N	G	E
C	B	S		L	Y	N	D	E		E	D	G	E	D

252

C	L	A	P		S	L	O	O	P		B	L	O	W
H	A	R	I		L	E	A	V	E		R	U	L	A
E	D	I	T		O	T	T	E	R		E	L	E	C
R	E	A	C	T		T	H	R	O	W	R	U	G	S
I	N	S	H	A	P	E		S	T	Y				
			F	R	E	R	E		S	E	S	T	E	T
B	A	B	O		L	E	X			S	L	A	V	E
A	G	A	R		E	D	I	C	T		I	K	E	S
J	E	R	K	S			T	U	B		N	E	S	S
A	D	E	S	T	E		S	T	A	N	G			
				I	L	L		E	R	O	S	I	O	N
F	I	R	E	F	L	I	E	S		S	H	O	V	E
O	N	E	A	L		M	A	I	L		O	N	E	S
E	R	A	S	E		E	V	E	L		T	I	N	T
S	I	R	E	S		S	E	R	B		S	A	S	S

253

D	A	M	P		A	I	M	S		U	L	T	R	A
E	D	I	E		I	D	E	A		P	A	R	I	S
B	O	X	S	P	R	I	N	G		S	T	U	C	K
B	R	U	T	U	S		D	E	S	T	I	N	E	
Y	E	P		S	P	A			T	A	N	K		
			C	H	E	S	T	N	U	T		L	O	B
S	O	S	O		E	C	H	O		E	L	I	T	E
A	D	A	R		D	O	R	S	A		I	N	I	T
R	O	C	K	S		T	E	A	L		N	E	S	S
A	R	K		C	A	S	E	L	O	A	D			
		C	L	A	N			E	N	S		C	A	B
	P	L	A	N	N	E	D		E	S	T	A	T	E
A	L	O	U	D		B	A	G	A	T	E	L	L	E
T	E	T	R	A		B	R	A	M		S	L	A	T
M	A	H	A	L		S	E	M	I		S	A	S	S

254

M	I	L	L	I		B	R	A		F	O	O	D	S
A	R	I	E	S		R	E	C		I	N	T	R	O
R	A	D	I	O	C	O	M	M	E	R	C	I	A	L
E	N	S		P	O	K	I	E	R		A	S	T	O
			I	O	L	A			A	L	L			
	W	I	N	D	O	W	D	I	S	P	L	A	Y	
P	I	N	T	S			O	R	E	S		M	A	P
U	N	D	O		D	A	R	E	R		B	O	W	E
P	E	I		D	E	M	I			R	O	U	E	N
	S	A	N	D	W	I	C	H	B	O	A	R	D	
			A	S	I			A	U	N	T			
A	D	A	M		T	O	M	I	N	D		D	O	A
D	I	R	E	C	T	M	A	R	K	E	T	I	N	G
A	V	E	R	S		A	N	D		A	I	M	E	E
Y	E	A	S	T		R	E	O		U	S	E	R	S

255

W	A	R	P		S	W	A	B		C	A	D	I	Z
I	G	O	R		I	O	T	A		O	Z	O	N	E
M	I	M	E		C	R	I	B		P	U	R	G	E
P	L	A	Y	M	I	S	T	Y	F	O	R	M	E	
Y	E	N		A	L	E		T	R	U	E			
			J	O	Y		B	O	O	T		F	E	Z
A	M	O	U	R		D	U	O	S		B	O	D	E
S	I	N	G	I	N	I	N	T	H	E	R	A	I	N
I	L	L	S		A	R	C	H		A	I	M	T	O
S	K	Y		B	O	T	H		I	R	E			
			M	I	M	I		A	N	T		U	F	O
	R	A	I	S	I	N	I	N	T	H	E	S	U	N
J	O	U	S	T		E	D	G	E		P	U	N	T
A	B	N	E	R		S	E	E	N		I	A	G	O
M	E	T	R	O		S	A	L	T		C	L	I	P

256

A	D	D	S			A	B	B	A	S		C	C	I
H	O	J	O		G	N	A	R	L	S		A	R	M
S	E	A	L		A	D	R	O	I	T		L	A	P
		K	O	D	I	A	K	A	K		S	I	T	E
B	L	A	S	E				D	E	F	A	C	E	D
E	E	R		B	A	R	E	S		A	M	O	R	E
A	N	T	E	A	T	E	R		P	L	O			
	S	A	N	T	A	M	O	N	I	C	A	C	A	
			T	E	T		D	E	T	O	N	A	T	E
P	E	T	E	R		R	E	G	A	N		R	T	E
O	V	E	R	S	E	E				R	E	R	U	N
D	E	N	S		A	L	B	A	N	Y	N	Y		
I	N	S		S	T	E	E	L	E		S	I	D	E
U	T	E		R	E	N	A	T	A		U	N	I	T
M	S	S		I	N	T	R	O			E	G	G	S

257

S	P	U	D		C	A	R	A		C	A	S	T	S
T	I	N	A		O	L	E	G		O	N	T	O	P
A	V	I	S		L	I	N	A		A	D	A	N	O
T	O	T	H	E	L	E	T	T	E	R		M	E	T
S	T	E	E	L	E		S	E	T	S	U	P		
			S	I	G	H			T	E	N	S	E	S
G	A	P		D	E	A	N	N	A		D	O	L	E
E	L	O	P	E		R	I	O		M	O	U	S	E
S	O	S	O		A	M	A	N	D	A		T	A	M
T	E	T	R	A	S			E	O	N	S			
		H	E	R	E	W	E		N	O	T	A	T	E
I	D	A		C	A	R	D	C	A	R	R	I	E	R
C	E	S	T	A		A	S	I	T		O	M	A	R
E	N	T	E	R		P	E	T	E		P	E	S	O
S	T	E	N	O		S	L	E	D		S	E	E	R

258

E	L	D	E	R			G	L	A	D		W	A	F
L	A	U	R	A		C	L	O	S	E		I	F	I
S	H	E	E	P	S	H	A	N	K	S		S	O	D
A	R	T		P	E	A	S	E		T	A	H	O	E
			R	O	A	D	S			I	D	Y	L	L
	A	D	A	R				T	O	N	O	W		
S	H	I	P	T	O	S	H	O	R	E		A	S	P
C	A	S	S		D	A	R	N	S		A	S	H	E
I	S	H		F	A	S	H	I	O	N	S	H	O	W
		W	A	L	S	H				A	S	Y	E	
A	M	A	T	O			D	E	B	U	T			
B	E	S	E	T		R	E	T	A	G		W	A	S
B	A	H		S	H	O	R	T	S	H	R	I	F	T
O	R	E		A	I	M	E	E		T	E	R	R	A
T	A	R		M	E	E	K			Y	O	Y	O	S

259

A	C	H	E		A	S	H	E	S		M	A	L	L
B	R	A	Y		C	H	E	E	P		O	B	O	E
L	O	V	E	I	T	O	R	L	E	A	V	E	I	T
E	W	E		S	U	R	E		A	M	I	D	S	T
			C	A	A	N		B	R	I	E			
A	S	S	A	I	L		B	E	G	S		M	O	P
R	H	O	D	A		M	E	N	U		S	A	N	E
N	A	U	G	H	T	Y	N	I	N	E	T	I	E	S
A	N	N	E		W	R	E	N		M	U	Z	A	K
Z	E	D		M	O	R	T		C	I	C	E	L	Y
			T	A	C	H		S	I	L	K			
I	C	E	A	G	E		L	O	R	I		A	L	I
N	O	T	H	I	N	G	I	N	C	O	M	M	O	N
C	O	C	O		T	A	M	I	L		A	M	O	K
A	S	H	E		S	P	A	C	E		P	O	K	Y

260

	C	B	S		A	C	H	Y		P	R	I	D	E
L	A	I	C		T	R	U	E		R	A	V	E	L
A	N	K	H		O	O	N	A		O	N	E	A	L
S	W	E	E	T	N	O	T	H	I	N	G	S		
T	E	D	M	A	C	K			N	E	E			
			A	R	E		E	L	F		S	L	O	B
S	A	N	T	O		G	R	E	E	K		A	A	A
S	Q	U	A	T	T	E	R	S	R	I	G	H	T	S
T	U	T		S	H	O	E	S		M	O	R	S	E
S	A	S	H		E	L	D		M	O	N			
			E	S	T			S	A	N	D	A	L	S
		Z	I	P	A	D	E	E	D	O	O	D	A	H
H	A	I	F	A		A	D	A	M		L	O	N	I
A	B	N	E	R		M	I	L	A		A	R	C	H
S	U	C	R	E		P	E	E	N		S	E	E	

261

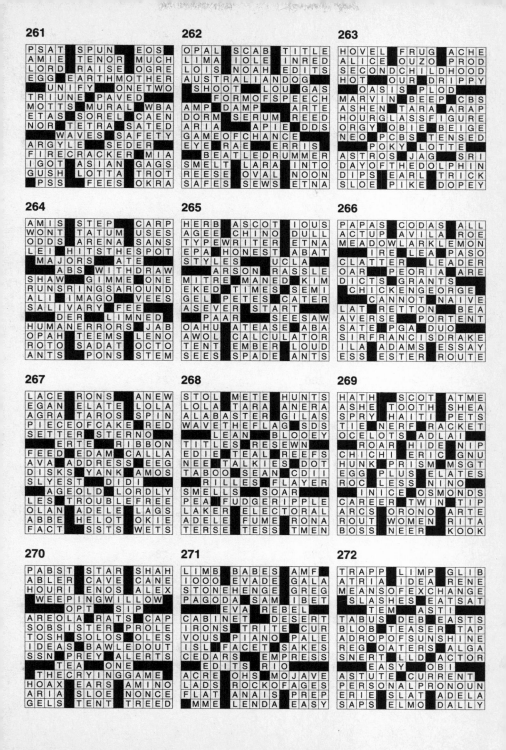

PSAT■SPUN■■EOS■
AMIE■TENOR■MUCH
LORD■RAISE■OGRE
EGG■EARTHMOTHER
■■UNIFY■■ONETWO
TRIUNE■PAVED■■■
MOTTS■MURAL■WBA
ETAS■SOREL■CAEN
NOR■TETRA■SATED
■■■WAVES■SAFETY
ARGYLE■■SEDER■■
FIRECRACKER■MIA
IGOT■ASIAN■GAGS
GUSH■LOTTA■TROT
■PSS■■FEES■OKRA

262

OPAL■SCAB■TITLE
LIMA■IOLE■INRED
LOIS■NOAH■EDITS
AUSTRALIANDOG■■
■SHOOT■■LOU■GAS
■■■FORMOFSPEECH
AMP■DAMP■■■ARTE
DORM■SERUM■REED
ARIA■■■APIE■DDS
GAMEOFCHANCE■■■
EYE■RAE■■ERRIS■
■■BEATLEDRUMMER
SMELT■LARA■INTO
REESE■OVAL■NOON
SAFES■SEWS■ETNA

263

HOVEL■FRUG■ACHE
ALICE■OUZO■PROD
SECONDCHILDHOOD
HOT■■OUR■DRIPPY
■■OASIS■PLOD■■■
MARVIN■BEEP■CBS
ASHEN■TARA■ARAP
HOURGLASSFIGURE
ORGY■OBIE■BEIGE
NEO■PCBS■TENSED
■■■POKY■LOTTE■■
ASTROS■JAG■■SRI
DAYOFTHEDOLPHIN
DIPS■EARL■TRICK
SLOE■PIKE■DOPEY

264

AMIS■STEP■■CARP
WONT■TATUM■USES
ODDS■ARENA■SANS
LEI■HITSTHESPOT
■MAJORS■■ATE■■■
■■■ABS■WITHDRAW
SHAW■■GIMME■ONE
RUNSRINGSAROUND
ALI■IMAGO■■VEES
SALIVARY■FEE■■■
■■■DER■■LIMNED■
HUMANERRORS■JAB
OPAH■TEEMS■LENO
ROTO■SADAT■OCTO
ANTS■■PONS■STEM

265

HERB■ASCOT■IOUS
AGEE■CHINO■DULL
TYPEWRITER■ETNA
EPA■HONEST■ABAT
STYLES■■■UCLA■■
■■■ARSON■RASSLE
MITRE■MANED■KIM
EKED■TIMES■SEMI
GEL■PETES■CATER
ASEVER■START■■■
■■PAAR■■■SEESAW
OAHU■ATEASE■ABA
AWOL■CALCULATOR
TENT■EMBER■LOUD
SEES■SPADE■ANTS

266

PAPAS■CODAS■ALL
ACTUP■AVILA■ROE
MEADOWLARKLEMON
■■■IRE■LEA■PASO
CLATTER■■LEADER
OAR■■PEORIA■ARE
DICTS■GRANTS■■■
■CHICKENGEORGE■
■■■CANNOT■NAIVE
LAT■RETTON■■BEA
AVERSE■■PORTENT
SATE■PGA■DUO■■■
SIRFRANCISDRAKE
ILA■ADAMS■ESSAY
ESS■ESTER■ROUTE

267

LACE■RONS■■ANEW
EGAN■ELATE■LOLA
AGRA■TAROS■SPIN
PIECEOFCAKE■RED
SETTER■STERNO■■
■■■ERTE■■RIBBON
FEED■EDAM■CALLA
AVA■ADDRESS■EEG
DISKS■YANK■AMOS
SLYEST■■DIDI■■■
■■AGEOLD■LORDLY
LES■TROUBLEFREE
OLAN■ADELE■LAGS
ABBE■HELOT■OKIE
FACT■■SSTS■WETS

268

STOL■METE■HUNTS
LOLA■TARA■ANERA
ALABASTER■GILAS
WAVETHEFLAG■SDS
■■■LEAN■■BLOOEY
TITLES■RESEWN■■
EDIE■TEAL■REEFS
NEE■TALKIES■DOT
TABOO■SEAN■CDII
■■RILLES■FLAYER
SMELLS■■SOAR■■■
PEA■FUDGERIPPLE
LAKER■ELECTORAL
ADELE■FUME■RONA
TERSE■TESS■TMEN

269

HATH■■SCOT■ATME
ASHE■TOOTH■SHEA
SPRY■HAITI■PETS
TIE■NERF■RACKET
OCELOTS■ADLAI■■
■■ROAR■HIDE■NIP
CHICHI■ERIC■GNU
HUNK■PRISM■MSGT
EGG■PLUS■ELATES
ROC■LESS■NINO■■
■■INICE■OSMONDS
CAREER■TWIN■TIP
ARCS■ORONO■ARTE
ROUT■WOMEN■RITA
BOSS■NEER■■KOOK

270

PABST■STAR■SHAH
ABLER■CAVE■CANE
HOURI■ENOS■ALEX
■WEEPINGWILLOW■
■■■■OPT■■SIP■■■
AREOLA■RATS■CAP
SOBSISTER■PROLE
TOSH■SOLOS■OLES
IDEAS■BAWLEDOUT
SSN■PREY■ALERTS
■■■TEA■■ONE■■■■
■THECRYINGGAME■
HOAX■EARS■AMINO
ARIA■SLOE■NONCE
GELS■TENT■TREED

271

LIMB■BABES■AMF■
IOOO■EVADE■GALA
STONEHENGE■GREG
PAGODA■SAM■IBET
■■■■EVA■REBEL■■
CABINET■■DESERT
IRONS■TRITE■CUR
VOUS■PIANO■PALE
ISL■FACET■SAKES
CEDARS■■EMPRESS
■■EDITS■RIO■■■■
ACRE■OHS■MOJAVE
LADS■ROCKOFAGES
FLAT■ANAIS■PREP
■MME■LENDA■EASY

272

TRAPP■LIMP■GLIB
ATRIA■IDEA■RENE
MEANSOFEXCHANGE
■SLASHES■EATSAT
■■■TEM■■ASTI■■■
TABUS■DEB■EASTS
BLOB■TEASER■TAP
ADROPOFSUNSHINE
REG■OATERS■ALGA
SNERT■LLD■ACTOR
■■■EASY■■OBI■■■
ASTUTE■CURRENT■
PERSONALPRONOUN
ERIE■SLAT■ADELA
SAPS■ELMO■DALLY

273

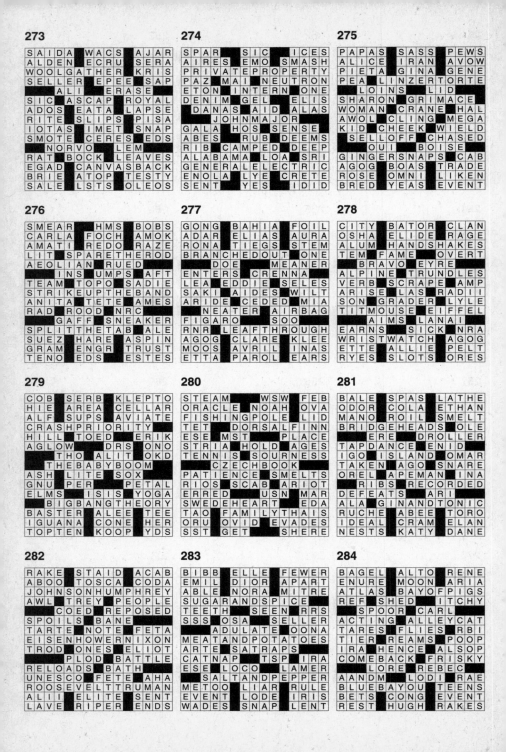

SAIDA WACS AJAR
ALDEN ECRU SERA
WOOLGATHER KRIS
SELLER EPEE SAP
ALI ERASE
SIC ASCAP ROYAL
ADOS EATA LAPSE
RITE SLIPS PISA
IOTAS IMET SNAP
SMOTE CERES EDS
NORVO LEM
RAT BOCK LEAVES
EGAD CANVASBACK
BRIE ATOP TESTY
SALE LSTS OLEOS

274

SPAR SIC ICES
AIRES EMO SMASH
PRIVATEPROPERTY
PAZ MAI NEUTRON
ETON INTERN ONE
DENIM GEL ELIS
DANAS AID ALAS
JOHNMAJOR
GALA HOS SENSE
ABES RUB DEEMS
RIB CAMPED DEEP
ALABAMA LOA SRI
GENERALELECTRIC
ENOLA LYE CRETE
SENT YES IDID

275

PAPAS SASS PEWS
ALICE IRAN AVOW
PIETA GINA GENE
PEA LINZERTORTE
LOINS LID
SHARON GRIMACE
WOMAN CRANE HAL
AWOL CLING MEGA
KID CHEEK WIELD
SELLOFF CHASED
OUI BOISE
GINGERSNAPS CAB
AGOG BOAS TRADE
ROSE OMNI LIKEN
BRED YEAS EVENT

276

SMEAR HMS BOBS
CARLA FOCH AMOK
AMATI REDO RAZE
LIT SPARETHEROD
AEOLIAN RUED
INS UMPS AFT
TEAM TOPO SADIE
STRIKEUPTHEBAND
ANITA TETE AMES
RAD ROOD NRC
GAFF SNEAKER
SPLITTHETAB ALE
SUEZ HARE ASPIN
GRAM ENGR TRUST
TENO EDS ESTES

277

GONG BAHIA FOIL
ADAR ELIAS AURA
RONA TIEGS STEM
BRANCHEDOUT ONE
DOE MEANER
ENTERS CRENNA
LEA EDDIE SELES
SAKI AIDES WILT
ARIDE CEDED MIA
NEATER AIRBAG
FIGARO SOO
RNR LEAFTHROUGH
AGOG CLARE KLEE
MOOS AVRIL INAS
ETTA PAROL EARS

278

CITY BATOR CLAN
OSHA ELIDE RAGE
ALUM HANDSHAKES
TEM FAME OVERT
BRAVO EYRE
ALPINE TRUNDLES
VERB SCRAPE AMP
ARISE LAS RADII
SON GRADER LYLE
TITMOUSE EIFFEL
AIMS LANAI
EARNS SICK NRA
WRISTWATCH AGOG
ETTE ALLIE PELT
RYES SLOTS ORES

279

COB SERB KLEPTO
HIE AREA CELLAR
ALF SUPS AVIATE
CRASHPRIORITY
HILL TOED ERIK
AGLOW DRS ONO
THO ALIT OKD
THEBABYBOOM
ASH LITE SOX
GNU PER PETAL
ELMS ISIS YOGA
BIGBANGTHEORY
BASTER ALEE TEE
IGUANA CONE HER
TOPTEN KOOP YDS

280

STEAM WSW FEB
ORACLE NOAH OVA
FISHINGPOLE LID
TET DORSALFINN
ESE MST PLACE
STRIA HOLD AGES
TENNIS SOURNESS
CZECHBOOK
PATIENCE SMELTS
RIOS SCAB ARIOT
ERRED USN MAR
SWEDEHEART EDA
TAO FAMILYTHAIS
ORU OVID EVADES
SST GET SHERE

281

BALE SPAS LATHE
ODOR COLA ETHAN
MANO ROIL SMELT
BRIDGEHEADS OLE
ERE DROLLER
TAPDANCE ENID
IGO ISLAND OMAR
TAKEN AGO SNARE
OREL APEMAN INA
RIBS RECORDED
DEFEATS ARI
ALA GINANDTONIC
RUCHE ABEE TORO
IDEAL CRAM ELAN
NESTS KATY DANE

282

RAKE STAID ACAB
ABOO TOSCA CODA
JOHNSONHUMPHREY
AWL TREY PEOPLE
COED REPOSED
SPOILS BANE
TARTE NOTE FETA
EISENHOWERNIXON
TROD ONES ELIOT
PLOD BATTLE
RELOADS BATH
UNESCO FETE AHA
ROOSEVELTTRUMAN
ALII ELITE SENT
LAVE RIPER ENDS

283

BIBB ELLE FEWER
EMIL DIOR APART
ABLE NORA MITRE
SUGARANDSPICE
TEETH SEEN RRS
SSS OSA SELLER
ADULATE OONA
MEATANDPOTATOES
ARTE SATRAPS
CATNAP TSP IRA
ESE LOCO LAMER
SALTANDPEPPER
METOO LIAR RULE
EVENT LODE IRIS
WADES SNAP LENT

284

BAGEL ALTO RENE
ENURE MOON ARIA
ATLAS BAYOFPIGS
REF SHED ITCHY
SPOOR CARL
ACTING ALLEYCAT
TARES FLIES RBI
TIER REAMS POOP
IRA HENCE ALSOP
COMEBACK FRISKY
LORE REBEC
AANDM LODI RAE
BLUEBAYOU TEENS
BETS CONG EVENT
REST HUGH RAKES

285

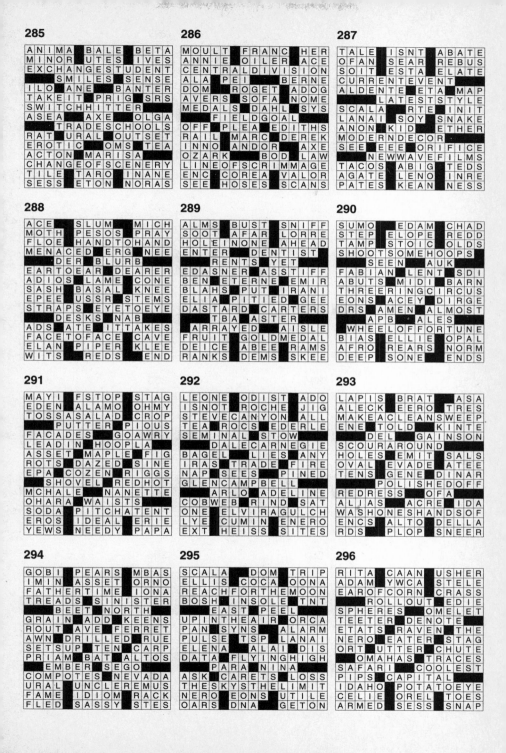

ANIMA BALE BETA
MINOR UTES IVES
EXCHANGESTUDENT
SMILES SENSE
ILO ANE BANTER
TAKEIT PRIG SRS
SWITCHHITTER
ASEA AXE OLGA
TRADESCHOOLS
RAT URAL OUTSET
EROTIC OMS TEA
ACTON MARISA
CHANGEOFSCENERY
TILE TARO INANE
SESS ETON NORAS

286

MOULT FRANC HER
ANNIE OILER ACE
CENTRALDIVISION
ALA PEI BERNE
DOM ROGET ADOG
AVERS SOFA NOME
MEDALS DAHL SYS
FIELDGOAL
OFF PLEA EDITHS
RAIL MARC DEREK
INNO ANDOR AXE
OZARK BOD LAW
LINEOFSCRIMMAGE
ENC COREA VALOR
SEE HOSES SCANS

287

TALE ISNT ABATE
OFAN SEAR REBUS
SOIT ESTA ELATE
CURRENTEVENT
ALDENTE ETA MAP
LATESTSTYLE
SCALA RTE INIT
LANAI SOY SNAKE
ANON KID ETHER
MODERNDECOR
SEE EEE ORIFICE
NEWWAVEFILMS
TACOS ABIG TEDS
AGATE LENO INRE
PATES KEAN NESS

288

ACE SLUM MICH
MOTH PESOS PRAY
FLOE HANDTOHAND
MENACED ERG NEE
DER BLURB
EARTOEAR DEARER
ADIOS LAME CONE
SASH BASAL KNEE
EPEE USSR STEMS
STRAPS EYETOEYE
DESKS NAB
ADS ATE ITTAKES
FACETOFACE CAVE
ELAN PIPER KLEE
WITS REDS END

289

ALMS BUST SNIFF
SOOT AFAR LORRE
HOLEINONE AHEAD
ENTER DENTIST
RENTS YET
EDASNER ASSTIFF
BEN ETERNE EMIR
BLAHS PUT IRANI
ELIA PITIED GEE
DASTARD CARTERS
TBA ASTER
ARRAYED AISLE
FRUIT GOLDMEDAL
DEICE ABEE RAMS
RANKS DEMS SKEE

290

SUMO EDAM CHAD
STEP ELOPE REDD
TAMP STOIC OLDS
SHOOTSOMEHOOPS
SEEN AUK
FABIAN LENT SDI
ABUTS MIDI BARN
THREERINGCIRCUS
EONS ACEY DIRGE
DRS AMEN ALMOST
APB ALES
WHEELOFFORTUNE
BIAS ELLIE OPAL
AFRO REARS NORM
DEEP SONE ENDS

291

MAYI FSTOP STAG
EDEN ALAMO OHMY
TOSSASALAD CROP
PUTTER PIOUS
FACADES GOAWRY
LEADIN HOOPLA
ASSET MAPLE FIG
ROTS DAZED SINE
EPA COZEN RIGGS
SHOVEL REDHOT
MCHALE NANETTE
OHARA WAISTS
SODA PITCHATENT
EROS IDEAL ERIE
YEWS NEEDY PAPA

292

LEONE ODIST ADO
ISNOT ROCHE JIG
STEVECANYON ALL
TEA ROCS EDERLE
SEMINAL STOW
DALECARNEGIE
BAGEL LIES ANY
IRAS TRADE FIRE
NAP SEES PINED
GLENCAMPBELL
ARLO ADELINE
COBWEB RIND SAT
ONE ELVIRAGULCH
LYE CUMIN ENERO
EXT HEISS SITES

293

LAPIS BRAT ASA
ALECK EERO TRES
MAKEACLEANSWEEP
ENE TOLD KINTE
DEL GAINSON
SCOURAROUND
HOLES EMIT SALS
OVAL EVADE ATEE
TENS GENE DINAR
POLISHEDOFF
REDRESS OFA
ALIAS ACRE IDA
WASHONESHANDSOF
ENCS ALTO DELLA
RDS PLOP SNEER

294

GOBI PEARS MBAS
IMIN ASSET ORNO
FATHERTIME IONA
TREADS SINISTER
BEET NORTH
GRAIN ADD KEENS
ROUT AVE FERRET
AWN DRILLED RUE
SETSUP TEN CARP
PRIAM BAT ALTOS
EMBER SEGO
COMPOTES NEVADA
URAL UNCLEREMUS
FAME IDIOM RACK
FLED SASSY STES

295

SCALA DOM TRIP
ELLIS COCA OONA
REACHFORTHEMOON
BOSH INSOLE TNT
EAST PEEL
UPINTHEAIR ORCA
PAN SYNS ALARM
PULSE TSP LANAI
ELENA ALAI DIS
DATA FLYINGHIGH
PARA NINA
ASK CARETS LOSS
THESKYSTHELIMIT
NERO EONS UTILE
OARS DNA GETON

296

RITA CAAN USHER
ADAM YWCA STELE
EAROFCORN CRASS
ROLLOUT EDIE
SPHERES OMELET
TEETER DENOTE
ETATS RAVEN THE
NERO EATER STAG
ORT UTTER CHUTE
OMAHAS TRACES
SAFARI COOLEST
PIPS CAPITAL
IDAHO POTATOEYE
CELIE OREL TOES
ARMED SESS SNAP

297

SASS APHID COOS
TROT ARENA PART
ECHO COLDTURKEY
WHOOSH MIAS SOX
LIES ABEE
HISPANIC ARARAT
ASWIM NATS GORE
SLAG CANOE LADD
TETE LISP RESOD
ASHORE TAPESTRY
NEAT ZINC
ACE EVEN STOKES
CHICKENOUT UNIT
TINA RETRO TERI
SPED STEEL SEER

298

HAGAR PLED BRAG
INANE ROLE LETO
PASTA OGLE ENTO
LICENSEPLATES
ALI HAT ERASE
WIGS ROCKET LTD
ETHOS RIATA
THEPLATTERS
OCEAN RAMBO
SAC UNDEAD BAIL
AROAR DUH ROD
DISHESTHEDIRT
ISTO WRAP MOSES
STAY AUNT OPERA
TASS BEGS METAL

299

BASIS SLAV SWAP
ABATE NINE RANI
MEDEA ENTR OTIS
STEMTHETIDE ETA
SEAR ULTRA
TOW RLS OGLES
SPARSE BUOYEDUP
PAVE BAR MOVE
SHELLOUT ANSWER
LEANS PRO NAT
GETME ECTO
PAN BEINTHESWIM
ORGS YSER PAIGE
ONTO ELIE AGLOW
HIHO DELL DEERS

300

TALC BAL BLAB
VIGOR URAL ROXY
ATONE FIRE ISEE
THREEOFAKIND
SEA PRESS BEATS
ASIT PAC LII
BIGWIG SUN KITT
ETERNALTRIANGLE
ZANY MAY SCONES
ELI SIM PEAT
LOESS POLED ASP
TRIPLEDECKER
SHEA CODA MARIE
TEAR ISIS IRONY
PERK TEE CANE

301

SHUT STES WHO
TAPES LITE CHOW
ASHEN UNDERLINE
TOPIARY SEALED
LETUP PASSED
INSECT LEWIS
BAT HOGAN TIDAL
ITEM SECTS COCA
DORIC NEAPS WRY
SLIER ATONES
LATINS STANG
COGENT TASTERS
OVERGROWN OMAHA
PENS OVID RADON
ERA SAGS NEWT

302

HAZY CHILI SCAM
OBIE HAVOC HALO
CLOSEONESEYESTO
KEN LOOS WALKON
DESI CALL
INLOVE GATE FCC
MAINE PURE AREA
PINONESEARSBACK
EVER VAST LOUIE
LEN HILT CUDDLY
HELM PAGE
ACCORD PANG PJS
THUMBONESNOSEAT
TOBE ERASE POPE
AWAY RAKES ANEW

303

CARP ABASH CHAR
ALOU BOCCI RENO
PAULNEWMAN ENTO
PRESET ENDEARED
ASST TUMMY
STETS AMY DOFFS
TALE PLO BEFORE
ALI BALLOON NEE
COWPER LLB SDAK
KNARS RYE TEAKS
LOOSE ODOR
ALLSTATE EDMUND
REAP GARYCOOPER
ANCE APLEA NORA
BOHR SEEPY SNOW

304

BLAH MIRED ABBA
OOZE ERASE TIER
SOURGRAPES ITEM
CPR LENT PALTRY
HYENAS BITTE
ARTHOUSE REV
HASTE INGE MELS
ERAT SCALD ANSI
ALLY OKIE INDEX
TOT ABERRANT
WILEY VEALER
SPARER STAR ONE
LUTE SWEETTOOTH
OMEN UINTA ASEA
PARE PATER SERB

305

AGES RAVES ATTA
MOLE ALIKE SWAB
PAIROFACES TIRE
STAIR NEST ANTS
AMISS EMIT
LADLES STAROF
EROS ABUT MEWLS
STU TWOTONE EEE
TIBER NAPE TRAM
ELAINE AGASSI
ERGO HELEN
ATTN OLEG NAILS
SOIE SINGINGDUO
POMS ELIOT ELMS
STET STENO REPO

306

CORN BASIC EPEE
ABOO AROMA SODA
MOUSETRAPS STIR
PEEWEE RETREATS
ELSA LEANT
TOGAS PAS SCORN
HURT HES SPECIE
ATE EARTHLY HOW
IDEALS ROY PITS
SONGS BOB TIPSY
AGILE OFIT
INCREASE RECAPS
TIRE BUNKERHILL
ONES ORDIE ERIE
NESS RESTS DYED

307

ALAS OHARA CHUB
SADE RATON HARI
SIMMERDOWN OLGA
ANAIL AMS FIFES
DENTISTS CURB
EAT FORBADE
LEE SEALED OKRA
ELMS AMEND YEAR
ABBE MIDDLE DBL
PARADED EDS
OWED BADGERED
TRIAL FAR ENOLA
MALL BOILEDOVER
EVEL RAZES RECT
NEDS AMENS ARTS

308

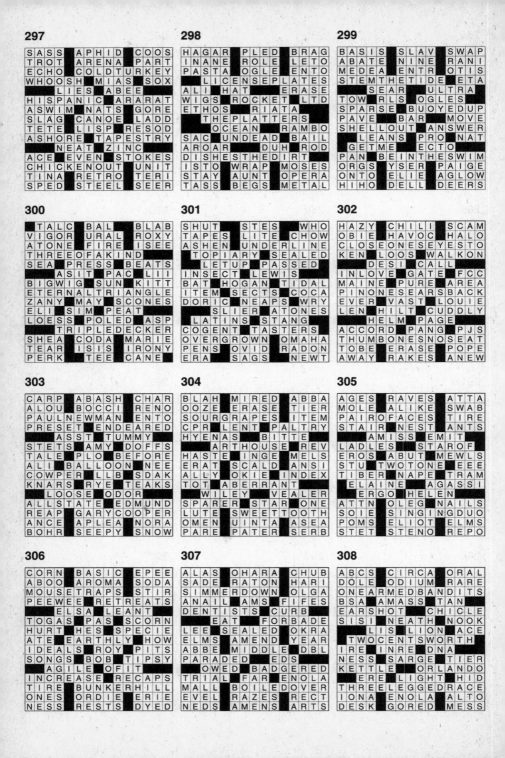

ABCS CIRCA ORAL
DOLE ODIUM RARE
ONEARMEDBANDITS
BSA AMASS TAN
EARSHOT CHICLE
SISI NEATH NOOK
LIS LION ACE
TWOCENTSWORTH
IRE INRE DNA
NESS SARGE TIER
KETTLE ORLANDO
ERE LIGHT HID
THREELEGGEDRACE
IONA ENOLA ALTO
DESK GORED MESS

309

ECHO MASON AJAR
FLOP ANKLE RULE
TAPE SNIDE TMEN
SPAN HEP PIPED
LIVE AZALEA
CLONED GERE TSP
RANGE MESTA TWO
EGGS MONTY SHES
SEC CONEY FEELS
TRA HOER ORACLE
SIESTA BACH
VISOR TAJ HAIG
EDIT LOIRE ENRY
LEDA STOIC SCAN
DAYS DONAT TENT

310

RIGEL PEER ABCS
ADORE ELEE PILE
GEORGESAND OLIN
SAP ATOM BALLOT
PTAS GAILY
SAMUEL BARROOMS
AGAPE KILOS COO
LIRA CONAN MERL
ELK CORDS CEASE
MESDAMES WARNED
TAMPA CANE
CORNEA ILSA TAN
AMAD DINAHSHORE
LONI RATS TIMEX
MODE ENOS ATEST

311

WEST AIMS HANS
HAIR WRIT HABIT
ACRE AONE ELENA
THEMORNINGAFTER
OSE RPM
SMART BOA OAST
ION IMPEND OFNO
DOGDAYAFTERNOON
OREO OTIOSE ORE
NELL PET VOTER
PSI CUR
NIGHTANDTHECITY
ANNIE ARIA HORA
STUNT PINS INON
HOSS EPEE DANK

312

BELL DEBS EBSEN
OLEO AERO LOTTO
BEACHHEAD LORAN
SERIAL ALIBI
RIAS ASONG
ANIMATE DOOGIE
IGORS EATEN BAN
ALOE SATES FEND
NED REMIT DRATS
SALTED NOTIONS
MEUSE GNAT
SLURP UTMOST
SHOAL ASTRODOME
COUNT CHOU CLOD
HOPES EYES LAGS

313

ESPY AGAL AGRA
THAI POLES ELAL
HAPPYEVENT GAIL
ERASER STOLIDLY
LES ATA IRISH
CHUCKLES ASA
RAJA RIN ABNER
IGOT EDITS IDLE
SAYSO FEE BSAS
ERR GLEECLUB
IDEAS STR ROC
ANDRETTI ZADORA
BAIO HORSELAUGH
INNS SPIER STAN
GAGS SSTS HENS

314

FLAIR MUTE LEST
OUNCE ARUT ACTI
GREENEGGSANDHAM
SEW DRIES ALONE
NEG LATE
FAKIR OVERT TAE
ALOE ONE GERUND
CLOCKWORKORANGE
TAKEIN SET REIN
SHY MELON MEDES
SODA AIR
ASIAN SHARK TAP
YELLOWSUBMARINE
EVEL HIRE DANTE
SEXY YELL OTTER

315

ASTA SWAMI AJAR
WHIM HELEN PALE
RUBBERBAND ICON
ALE TISSUE EKED
PATTON SNACK
INKED TRENDS
DEGAS LAGER IOU
EROS GIVER NFLD
ELL NOSIR BEETS
DEFIES TESLA
BRASS CARERS
ALAI ICEMAN LOA
POLS PAPERCLIPS
ABLE ELITE IDES
TESS RACES VERY

316

SLOPE HOBO MOLT
AIDAN EVEL OLEO
TRENT READ OMAN
EARTHWORMS NOVA
URN TASSEL
BRASSY BRENT
LOTTE SOURCREAM
TOMA GLOBS ULNA
STERILIZE SCION
SLIME TOKENS
REPELS EEL
ELLA SUNGLASSES
PAAR ASEA CUTIE
OTIC DEAD EVENT
SETH ERRS DAWES

317

REESE AMES MORT
CARTA NAVE AREA
ARGOT TREE TREX
POPEYEANDOLIVE
CREST KINER
ACCOST AMAN
CHOC GALOP IVY
MICKEYANDMINNIE
EPA MESTA UCLA
SASH ESTHER
AMATI SANER
DONALDANDDAISY
DROP ILED METER
LADE CARE UNITE
EYES KIDD STRIP

318

SPAS SIRS ROPED
PAST TRIP OPERA
ASHE RONA MATES
WHEELANDDEAL
NARROW SEMI SKI
USA INSPAN
ALERT SPARETIRE
SELA TEARS ANAP
WASHCYCLE BRENT
ARISES AMA
NNE COAT ELANDS
RINGSIDESEAT
SPOIL RAGU SERA
TARSI EROS EDIT
ATSEA ESTA TYNE

319

ASPS RENT STROP
ROLE EDIE PIANO
ALAN DANA IMPEL
MAYDAYMALONE
ICE VEE NESTLE
SERGE SAME RUIN
ERG ROI OBOE
SOSYOUROLDMAN
SABU SPA LOA
AKIN PAYS UNCLE
NEEDLE EGG AAR
HELPMERHONDA
COHEN LOGO PADS
AWAIT ANEW EPEE
PESTO TORN NERD

320

HICCUP VET
ORIOLE HERO TIM
DATING ANNO RCA
IFA GREENMAIL
ADZE MANES EVEL
PIEDPIPER DOERS
SON ODES HOWL
ENS PARSLEY ETC
ASPS RARE RHO
PARTY HARDNOSED
IRRA SOCKS NCAA
QUEBECOIS ASH
UBS TARN GREECE
EAT CRAG SITCOM
HEY TASKET

321

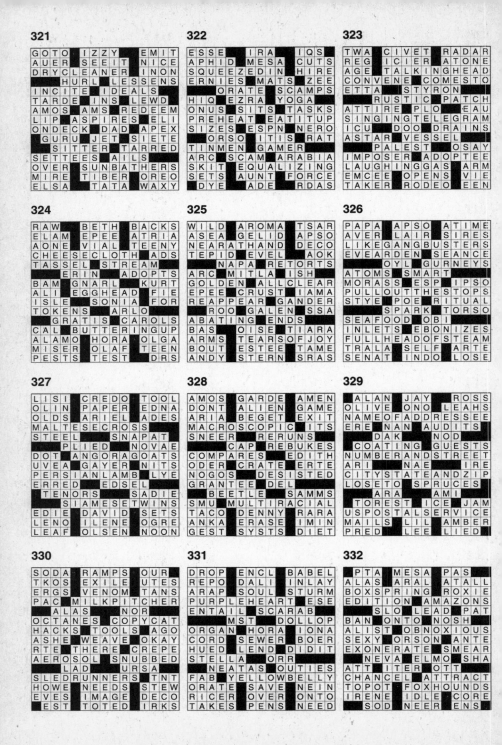

G	O	T	O	■	I	Z	Z	Y	■	■	E	M	I	T
A	U	E	R	■	S	E	E	I	T	■	N	I	C	E
D	R	Y	C	L	E	A	N	E	R	■	I	N	O	N
■	■	■	H	U	R	L	■	L	E	S	S	E	N	S
I	N	C	I	T	E	■	I	D	E	A	L	S	■	■
T	A	R	D	E	■	I	N	S	■	L	E	W	D	■
A	M	O	S	■	A	M	S	■	R	E	D	E	E	M
L	I	P	■	A	S	P	I	R	E	S	■	E	L	I
O	N	D	E	C	K	■	D	A	D	■	A	P	E	X
■	G	U	R	U	■	J	E	T	■	S	I	E	T	E
■	■	S	I	T	T	E	R	■	T	A	R	R	E	D
S	E	T	T	E	E	S	■	A	I	L	S	■	■	■
O	V	E	R	■	S	U	N	B	A	T	H	E	R	S
M	I	R	E	■	T	I	B	E	R	■	O	R	E	O
E	L	S	A	■	■	T	A	T	A	■	W	A	X	Y

322

E	S	S	E	■	■	I	R	A	■	■	I	Q	S	■
A	P	H	I	D	■	M	E	S	A	■	C	U	T	S
S	Q	U	E	E	Z	E	D	I	N	■	H	I	R	E
E	R	N	I	E	S	■	M	A	T	S	■	Z	E	E
■	■	■	O	R	A	T	E	■	S	C	A	M	P	S
H	I	Q	■	E	Z	R	A	■	Y	O	G	A	■	■
O	N	U	S	■	S	I	T	S	■	T	A	S	K	S
P	R	E	H	E	A	T	■	E	A	T	I	T	U	P
S	I	Z	E	S	■	E	S	P	N	■	N	E	R	O
■	■	O	R	S	O	■	I	T	I	S	■	R	A	T
T	I	N	M	E	N	■	G	A	M	E	R	■	■	■
A	R	C	■	S	C	A	M	■	A	R	A	B	I	A
S	K	I	T	■	E	Q	U	A	L	I	Z	I	N	G
S	E	T	S	■	A	U	N	T	■	F	O	R	C	E
■	D	Y	E	■	■	A	D	E	■	■	R	D	A	S

323

T	W	A	■	C	I	V	E	T	■	R	A	D	A	R
R	E	G	■	I	C	I	E	R	■	A	T	O	N	E
A	G	E	■	T	A	L	K	I	N	G	H	E	A	D
C	O	N	V	E	N	E	■	C	O	M	E	S	T	O
E	T	T	A	■	■	S	T	Y	R	O	N	■	■	■
■	■	■	R	U	S	T	I	C	■	P	A	T	C	H
A	T	T	I	R	E	■	P	L	O	■	■	E	A	U
S	I	N	G	I	N	G	T	E	L	E	G	R	A	M
I	C	U	■	■	D	O	O	■	D	R	A	I	N	S
A	S	T	A	R	■	V	E	S	S	E	L	■	■	■
■	■	■	P	A	L	E	S	T	■	■	O	S	A	Y
I	M	P	O	S	E	R	■	A	D	O	P	T	E	E
L	A	U	G	H	I	N	G	G	A	S	■	A	R	M
E	M	C	E	E	■	O	P	E	N	S	■	V	I	E
T	A	K	E	R	■	R	O	D	E	O	■	E	E	N

324

R	A	W	■	■	B	E	T	H	■	B	A	C	K	S
E	L	A	M	■	E	P	E	E	■	A	T	R	I	A
A	O	N	E	■	V	I	A	L	■	T	E	E	N	Y
C	H	E	E	S	E	C	L	O	T	H	■	A	D	S
T	A	S	S	E	L	■	S	T	R	E	A	M	■	■
■	■	■	E	R	I	N	■	■	A	D	O	P	T	S
B	A	M	■	G	N	A	R	L	■	■	K	U	R	T
A	L	I	■	E	G	G	H	E	A	D	■	F	I	E
I	S	L	E	■	■	S	O	N	I	A	■	F	O	R
T	O	K	E	N	S	■	■	A	R	L	O	■	■	■
■	■	G	R	A	T	I	S	■	C	A	R	O	L	S
C	A	L	■	B	U	T	T	E	R	I	N	G	U	P
A	L	A	M	O	■	H	O	R	A	■	O	L	G	A
M	I	S	E	R	■	O	L	A	F	■	T	E	E	N
P	E	S	T	S	■	T	E	S	T	■	■	D	R	S

325

W	I	L	D	■	A	R	O	M	A	■	T	S	A	R
A	S	E	A	■	G	E	L	I	D	■	A	P	S	O
N	E	A	R	A	T	H	A	N	D	■	D	E	C	O
T	E	P	I	D	■	E	V	E	L	■	■	A	O	K
■	■	■	N	A	P	A	■	R	E	T	O	R	T	S
A	R	C	■	M	I	T	L	A	■	I	S	H	■	■
G	O	L	D	E	N	■	A	L	L	C	L	E	A	R
E	P	E	E	■	C	R	U	S	T	■	I	A	M	A
R	E	A	P	P	E	A	R	■	G	A	N	D	E	R
■	■	R	O	O	■	G	A	L	E	N	■	S	S	A
A	B	A	T	I	N	G	■	E	N	D	S	■	■	■
B	A	S	■	■	O	I	S	E	■	T	I	A	R	A
A	R	M	S	■	T	E	A	R	S	O	F	J	O	Y
B	O	U	T	■	E	S	T	E	E	■	T	A	M	E
A	N	D	Y	■	S	T	E	R	N	■	S	R	A	S

326

P	A	P	A	■	A	P	S	O	■	A	T	I	M	E
A	V	E	R	■	L	A	I	R	■	S	I	R	E	S
L	I	K	E	G	A	N	G	B	U	S	T	E	R	S
E	V	E	A	R	D	E	N	■	S	E	A	N	C	E
■	■	■	■	O	Y	L	■	G	U	R	N	E	Y	S
A	T	O	M	S	■	S	M	A	R	T	■	■	■	■
M	O	R	A	S	S	■	E	S	P	■	I	P	S	O
P	U	L	L	O	U	T	T	H	E	S	T	O	P	S
S	T	Y	E	■	P	O	E	■	R	I	T	U	A	L
■	■	■	■	S	P	A	R	K	■	T	O	R	S	O
S	E	A	F	O	O	D	■	O	B	I	■	■	■	■
I	N	L	E	T	S	■	E	B	O	N	I	Z	E	S
F	U	L	L	H	E	A	D	O	F	S	T	E	A	M
T	R	A	L	A	■	S	E	L	F	■	A	R	T	E
S	E	N	A	T	■	I	N	D	O	■	L	O	S	E

327

L	I	S	I	■	C	R	E	D	O	■	T	O	O	L
O	L	I	N	■	P	A	P	E	R	■	E	D	N	A
O	L	D	S	■	A	R	I	E	L	■	A	D	E	S
M	A	L	T	E	S	E	C	R	O	S	S	■	■	■
S	T	E	E	L	■	■	■	S	N	A	P	A	T	■
■	■	■	P	L	I	E	D	■	■	N	O	V	A	E
D	O	T	■	A	N	G	O	R	A	G	O	A	T	S
U	V	E	A	■	G	A	Y	E	R	■	N	I	T	S
P	E	R	S	I	A	N	L	A	M	B	■	L	Y	E
E	R	R	E	D	■	■	E	D	S	E	L	■	■	■
■	T	E	N	O	R	S	■	■	■	S	A	D	I	E
■	■	■	S	I	A	M	E	S	E	T	W	I	N	S
E	D	I	E	■	D	A	V	I	D	■	S	E	T	S
L	E	N	O	■	I	L	E	N	E	■	O	G	R	E
L	E	A	F	■	O	L	S	E	N	■	N	O	O	N

328

A	M	O	S	■	G	A	R	D	E	■	A	M	E	N
D	O	N	T	■	A	L	I	E	N	■	G	A	M	E
A	R	I	A	■	B	E	G	E	T	■	E	X	I	T
M	A	C	R	O	S	C	O	P	I	C	■	I	T	S
S	N	E	E	R	■	■	R	E	R	U	N	S	■	■
■	■	■	■	C	A	P	■	R	E	B	U	K	E	S
C	O	M	P	A	R	E	S	■	■	E	D	I	T	H
O	D	E	R	■	C	R	A	T	E	■	E	R	T	E
N	O	G	O	S	■	■	D	E	S	I	S	T	E	D
G	R	A	N	T	E	E	■	D	E	L	■	■	■	■
■	■	B	E	E	T	L	E	■	■	S	A	M	M	S
S	M	U	■	M	U	L	T	I	R	A	C	I	A	L
T	A	C	O	■	D	E	N	N	Y	■	R	A	R	A
A	N	K	A	■	E	R	A	S	E	■	I	M	I	N
G	E	S	T	■	S	Y	S	T	S	■	D	I	E	T

329

■	A	L	A	N	■	J	A	Y	■	■	R	O	S	S
O	L	I	V	E	■	O	N	O	■	L	E	A	H	S
N	A	M	E	O	F	A	D	D	R	E	S	S	E	E
E	R	E	■	N	A	N	■	A	U	D	I	T	S	■
■	■	■	D	A	K	■	■	■	N	O	D	■	■	■
■	C	O	A	T	I	N	G	■	G	U	E	S	T	S
N	U	M	B	E	R	A	N	D	S	T	R	E	E	T
A	R	I	■	■	■	N	A	E	■	■	■	I	R	E
C	I	T	Y	S	T	A	T	E	A	N	D	Z	I	P
L	O	S	E	T	O	■	S	P	R	U	C	E	S	■
■	■	■	A	R	A	■	■	■	A	M	I	■	■	■
■	T	O	R	E	S	T	■	I	C	E	■	J	A	M
U	S	P	O	S	T	A	L	S	E	R	V	I	C	E
M	A	I	L	S	■	L	I	L	■	A	M	B	E	R
P	R	E	D	■	■	L	E	E	■	L	I	E	D	■

330

S	O	D	A	■	R	A	M	P	S	■	O	U	R	■
T	K	O	S	■	E	X	I	L	E	■	U	T	E	S
E	R	G	S	■	V	E	N	O	M	■	T	A	N	S
P	A	C	■	M	I	L	K	P	I	T	C	H	E	R
■	■	A	L	A	S	■	■	■	N	O	R	■	■	■
O	C	T	A	N	E	S	■	C	O	P	Y	C	A	T
H	A	C	K	S	■	T	O	O	L	S	■	A	G	O
A	S	H	E	■	W	E	A	V	E	■	O	K	A	Y
R	T	E	■	T	H	E	R	E	■	C	R	E	P	E
A	E	R	O	S	O	L	■	S	N	U	B	B	E	D
■	■	■	L	A	D	■	■	■	U	R	S	A	■	■
S	L	E	D	R	U	N	N	E	R	S	■	T	N	T
H	O	W	E	■	N	E	E	D	S	■	S	T	E	W
E	V	E	S	■	I	M	A	G	E	■	D	E	C	O
■	E	S	T	■	T	O	T	E	D	■	I	R	K	S

331

D	R	O	P	■	E	N	C	L	■	B	A	B	E	L
R	E	P	O	■	D	A	L	I	■	I	N	L	A	Y
A	R	A	P	■	S	O	U	L	■	S	T	U	R	M
P	U	R	P	L	E	H	E	A	R	T	■	E	S	E
E	N	T	A	I	L	■	S	C	A	R	A	B	■	■
■	■	■	■	M	S	T	■	■	D	O	L	L	O	P
O	R	G	A	N	■	H	O	R	A	■	I	O	N	A
C	O	R	D	■	S	E	W	E	R	■	B	O	E	R
H	U	E	D	■	L	E	N	D	■	D	I	D	I	T
S	T	E	L	L	A	■	■	O	R	R	■	■	■	■
■	■	N	E	A	T	A	S	■	O	U	T	I	E	S
F	A	B	■	Y	E	L	L	O	W	B	E	L	L	Y
O	R	A	T	E	■	S	A	V	E	■	N	E	I	N
R	I	C	E	R	■	O	V	E	R	■	O	N	T	O
T	A	K	E	S	■	P	E	N	S	■	N	E	E	D

332

■	P	T	A	■	M	E	S	A	■	P	A	S	■	■
A	L	A	S	■	A	R	A	L	■	A	T	A	L	L
B	O	X	S	P	R	I	N	G	■	R	O	X	I	E
E	D	I	T	I	O	N	■	A	M	A	Z	O	N	S
■	■	■	S	L	O	■	L	E	A	D	■	P	A	T
B	A	N	■	O	N	T	O	■	N	O	S	H	■	■
A	L	I	S	T	■	O	B	N	O	X	I	O	U	S
S	E	X	Y	■	O	R	S	O	N	■	A	N	T	E
E	X	O	N	E	R	A	T	E	■	S	M	E	A	R
■	■	N	E	V	A	■	E	L	M	O	■	S	H	A
A	T	T	■	I	T	E	R	■	O	T	T	■	■	■
C	H	A	N	C	E	L	■	A	T	T	R	A	C	T
T	O	P	O	T	■	F	O	X	H	O	U	N	D	S
I	R	E	N	E	■	I	D	L	E	■	C	O	R	E
■	■	S	O	D	■	N	E	E	R	■	E	N	S	■

333

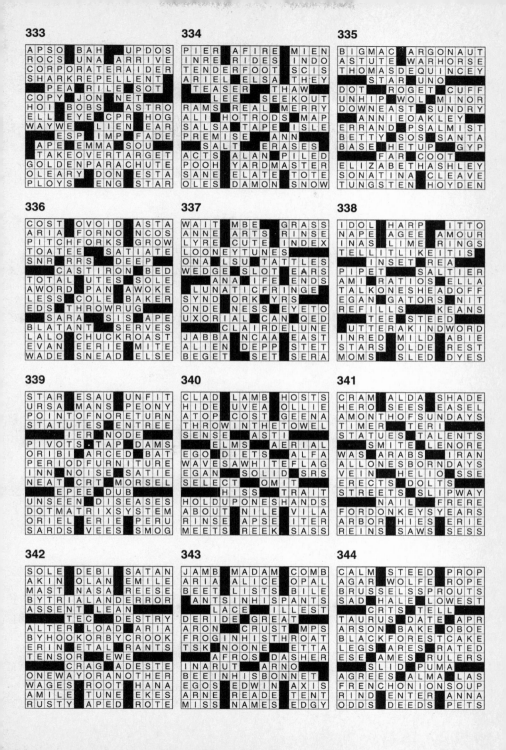

```
APSO■BAH■■UPDOS
ROCS■UNA■ARRIVE
CORPORATERAIDER
SHARKREPELLENT■
■■PEA■RILE■SOT■
COPY■JON■NET■■■
HOI■BOBS■■ASTRO
ELL■EYE■CPR■HOG
WAYWE■■LIEN■EAR
■■■ESP■IMP■FADE
■APE■EMMA■SOU■■
■TAKEOVERTARGET
GOLDENPARACHUTE
OLEARY■DON■ESTA
PLOYS■■ENG■STAR
```

334

```
PIER■AFIRE■MIEN
INRE■RIDES■INDO
TENDERFOOT■SCIS
ARIEL■ELSA■THEY
■TEASER■■THAW■■
■■■LEE■■SEEKOUT
RAMS■REAL■MERRY
ALI■HOTRODS■MAP
SALSA■TAPE■ISLE
PREMISE■■ANN■■■
■■SALT■■ERASES■
ACTS■ALAN■PILED
POOH■YARDMASTER
SANE■ELATE■TOTE
OLES■DAMON■SNOW
```

335

```
BIGMAC■ARGONAUT
ASTUTE■WARHORSE
THOMASDEQUINCEY
■■■STAR■UNO■■■■
DOT■■ROGET■CUFF
UNHIP■WOL■MINOR
DOWNEAST■SUNDRY
■■ANNIEOAKLEY■■
ERRAND■PSALMIST
BETTY■SOS■SANTA
BASE■HETUP■■GYP
■■■■FAR■COOT■■■
ELIZABETHASHLEY
SONATINA■CLEAVE
TUNGSTEN■HOYDEN
```

336

```
COST■OVOID■ASTA
ARIA■FORNO■NCOS
PITCHFORKS■GROW
TOATEE■■SATIATE
SNR■RRS■■DEEP■■
■■■CASTIRON■BED
TOTAL■UTES■SOLE
AWORD■PAN■AWOKE
LESS■COLE■BAKER
EDS■THROWRUG■■■
■■SARA■■SIS■APE
BLATANT■■SERVES
LALO■CHUCKROAST
EVAN■EERIE■MITE
WADE■SNEAD■ELSE
```

337

```
WAIT■MBE■■GRASS
ANNE■ARTS■RINSE
LYRE■CUTE■INDEX
LOONEYTUNES■■■■
ONA■LSU■TATTLES
WEDGE■SLOT■EARS
■■■ANA■IFE■ENDS
■LUNATICFRINGE■
SYND■ORK■YRS■■■
ONDE■NESS■EYETO
UXORIAL■CAN■QED
■■■■CLAIRDELUNE
JABBA■NCAA■EAST
ALIEN■DEPP■STET
BEGET■■SET■SERA
```

338

```
IDOL■HARP■■ITTO
NAPE■AGEE■AMOUR
INAS■LIME■RINGS
TELLITLIKEITIS■
■■■INSET■REA■■■
PIPET■■■SALTIER
AMI■RATIOS■ELLA
TALKONESHEADOFF
EGAN■GATORS■NIT
REFILLS■■■KEANS
■■■TEE■STEED■■■
■UTTERAKINDWORD
INRED■MILD■ABIE
STARS■OLDE■REST
MOMS■■SLED■DYES
```

339

```
STAR■ESAU■UNFIT
URSA■MANS■PEONY
POINTOFNORETURN
STATUTES■ENTREE
■■■■IER■NODE■■■
PIVOTS■TAP■DAMS
ORIBI■ARCED■BAT
PERIODFURNITURE
INN■NOISE■SATIE
NEAT■CRT■MORSEL
■■■EPEE■DUB■■■■
UNSEEN■DISEASES
DOTMATRIXSYSTEM
ORIEL■ERIE■PERU
SARDS■VEES■SMOG
```

340

```
CLAD■LAMB■HOSTS
HIDE■UVEA■OLLIE
ATOP■COST■GEENA
THROWINTHETOWEL
SENSE■■ASTI■■■■
■■■ELMS■■AERIAL
EGO■DIETS■■ALFA
WAVESAWHITEFLAG
EGAN■■SOLID■SRS
SELECT■■OMIT■■■
■■■■HISS■■TRAIT
HOLDUPONESHANDS
ABOUT■NILE■VILA
RINSE■APSE■ITER
MEETS■REEK■SASS
```

341

```
CRAM■ALDA■SHADE
HERO■SEES■EASEL
AMONTHOFSUNDAYS
TIMER■■TERI■■■■
STATUES■TALENTS
■■■SMITE■LENORE
WAS■ARABS■■IRAN
ALLONESBORNDAYS
VEIN■■HELIO■SSE
ERECTS■DOLTS■■■
STREETS■SLIPWAY
■■■■NAIL■■FRERE
FORDONKEYSYEARS
ARBOR■HIES■ERIE
REINS■SAWS■SESS
```

342

```
SOLE■DEBI■SATAN
AKIN■OLAN■EMILE
MAST■NASA■REESE
BYTRIALANDERROR
ASSENT■LEAN■■■■
■■■■TEC■■DESTRY
ALTER■LOAD■ARIA
BYHOOKORBYCROOK
ERIN■ETAL■RANTS
TENSOR■■EWE■■■■
■■■■CRAG■ADESTE
ONEWAYORANOTHER
WAGES■ROOT■HANA
AMILE■TUNE■EKES
RUSTY■APED■ROTE
```

343

```
JAMB■MADAM■COMB
ARIA■ALICE■OPAL
BEET■LISTS■BILE
■ANTSINHISPANTS
■■■LACE■■ILLEST
DERIDE■GREAT■■■
ARON■■CRUST■MPS
FROGINHISTHROAT
TSK■NOONE■■ETTA
■■■AFROS■DASHER
INARUT■■ARNO■■■
BEEINHISBONNET■
EGOS■EDWIN■AXIS
ARNE■READE■TENT
MISS■NAMES■EDGY
```

344

```
CALM■STEED■PROP
AGAR■WOLFE■ROPE
BRUSSELSSPROUTS
SAD■HALE■LOWEST
■■■CRTS■TELL■■■
TAURUS■DATE■APR
ARSON■BAKE■OBOE
BLACKFORESTCAKE
LEGS■ARES■RATED
ESE■AMES■RULERS
■■■SLID■PUMA■■■
AGREES■ALMA■LAS
FRENCHONIONSOUP
RIND■ENTER■ANNA
ODDS■DEEDS■PETS
```

345

HAIFA ADAM GARP
AGLOW LILI APAR
FAIRE PROD MACE
TREBLE TOPIECES
REST FOSTERS
RHEOSTAT ILE
TALKS BORNE KKK
ERLE TOPOT WINE
SPA SWOOP SHEER
BEE LEFTOVER
AWAITED DIAL
TOBLAZES BREADS
SOIL EVIL THROE
EDDY RIDE LOUSE
AYES SLED EGGED

346

COKE RANGE SLAT
ODIN IDOLS TARO
MOLD COLEPORTER
ARLENE ANCIENT
EMU FIN ETNAS
EMBITTER TLC
MARC RNA ROHMER
IKE BUSTOUT ELI
TOWERS ERN AYIN
LIT LAKEMEAD
ROPED AYN AIR
ICECAPS STABLE
TATTLETALE BEEN
ALEE NOVEL LEND
SARD TRAIL ERAS

347

ABASE WIT FASTS
RACER IDO UTTER
ALLIE NEW NORAS
BLAZINGSADDLES
LOSE ASTRO LAPS
ETS POP DEL MOI
MAMAS ODEON
TOWERINGINFERNO
OVALS TNOTE
GET EMS DTS ETO
ARCH CLAUS ALID
CHARIOTSOFFIRE
RAMBO WET IOTAS
EMAIL EAR COEDS
DENTE DRY ATSEA

348

CLAMP DROP SODA
PALER RAGE ALAN
OBESE OMEN DENT
SCALLOPEDEDGE
AILS ALL
SHASTA KNEECAP
OYSTERWHITE EVA
NETS HEN ADEN
INA CLAMDIGGERS
CARSEAT TOASTY
ANN TACT
LOBSTERSHIFTS
LORE ERIK NEALS
EVER RIPE TAROT
TESS NEED ORATE

349

PAP SOSO JUICE
ANA ETNA ARBOR
LYRE ERIK MIAMI
MARLAMAPLES RON
MIL SARI
MOSTLY NONCOMS
OHARE PODS EMIL
DATED OLA ADANO
ERIE ANDS LANCE
MANSARD DORIES
BAER RNS
OOP SPRUCEGOOSE
KNIFE ONUS FLEA
LENIN SIRS LAC
ALERT ANDY ASH

350

BARR SABRA ADZE
OPIE AILED SEEM
LENNYBRUCE PAST
ORDEAL REPRINTS
GREW STORM
SIREN ASS MEARA
TSAR FRI MADRID
ALY HANGMAN TAM
RECKON HOP SITE
ETHER CSA HUNAN
ANNUL BLOC
CORNERED INCHES
ABLE BRIANKEITH
NOEL AGAPE ERNE
TESS NYLON DEAD

351

MAAMS BABO OAFS
AGGIE REAM ARIA
CHINESECHECKERS
SANDMAN TRAINEE
ETTA TREADS
LAREDO SAAR
AGAR NACL ELIAS
RUSSIANROULETTE
DEPTS TIER NOME
TRIB ATONED
SARTRE ETNA
TSARINA EURASIA
INDIANWRESTLING
LEAP IRAN APACE
ERRS EYES NOMAD

352

ARC RAIDS ADES
BARB APRON BABA
OVER FEETOFCLAY
MEDEA NERO INS
BLOWSONESTOP
SIRE STRAPS
CHA ASSES OLIO
HAVENOTRUCKWITH
IDEA SALON THO
PARROT FLEE
PLAYBALLWITH
EPA AMOR TERRA
GOFLYAKITE RAIN
GORE LENIN STLO
SLOG EDGED ELI

353

AGHAST ADA LEA
SHRINER DIX INC
WOODYWOODPECKER
ALC AUTH AERO
NEER PHOEBESNOW
RAP TONE
ARISE GONNA DEE
THEPELICANBRIEF
EOS WRITS LARKS
AEON EST
THEPENGUIN ABCS
AONE SNOB IRE
SANDIEGOCHICKEN
TRI LYE AIRIEST
EDS LEM STRESS

354

HAHA AMEN HADIT
OVEN RAVE OLIVE
SALT THEBLUEMAX
TILL SAN ASSENT
SLOES LISLE
DROP NEO ABET
SRO ROUGE SHULA
DOLORES POMADES
ALLAY ISSUE DES
KEYS NNE RACY
PAGES RABAT
ELDERS SAM MUCH
DIRTYHARRY EDIE
IRATE TEAR ODDS
TATER EDNA NYSE

355

ARIA SABLES AHA
PEND TROLLS NOB
HPLOVECRAFT NAB
ILO EPSOM SEXY
DOVISH ACTOR
SWEETEST LIMITS
RANDY ICECAP
MAJ KIROV ERA
ADONAI ONEGA
DEHORN SIBILANT
NUDGE AZALEA
BOSN REARM OAR
IRA DEANRKOONTZ
TAU ARSINE ASEA
ELL SEEDER TORN

356

SLEW BAMBI SPAT
IOTA ARIAS PABA
MAUI RINSE ARON
PNIN REDHERRING
SHEL ESSES
BEACON SKATE
ACTON JAIL LOU
WHITECOLLARJOBS
LOT OMEN AEGIS
MSDOS VETOER
ABBEY REST
BLUERIBBON IFFY
YORK PEASE SIRE
SAKE SATIE OVEN
STER OTHER NETS

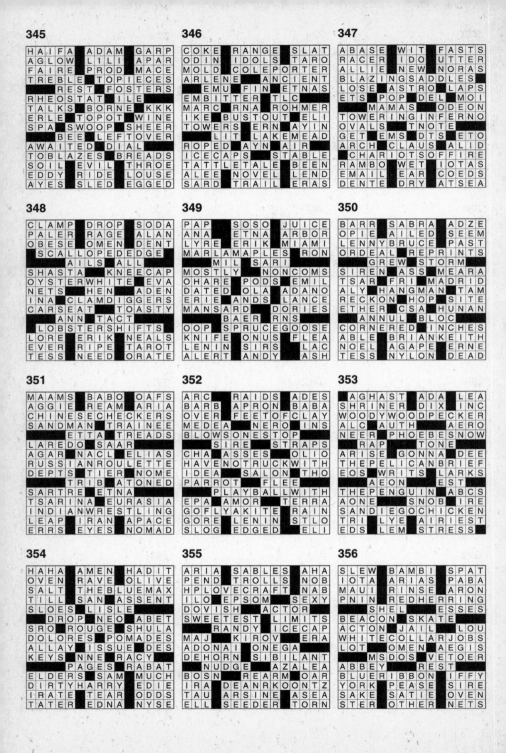

357

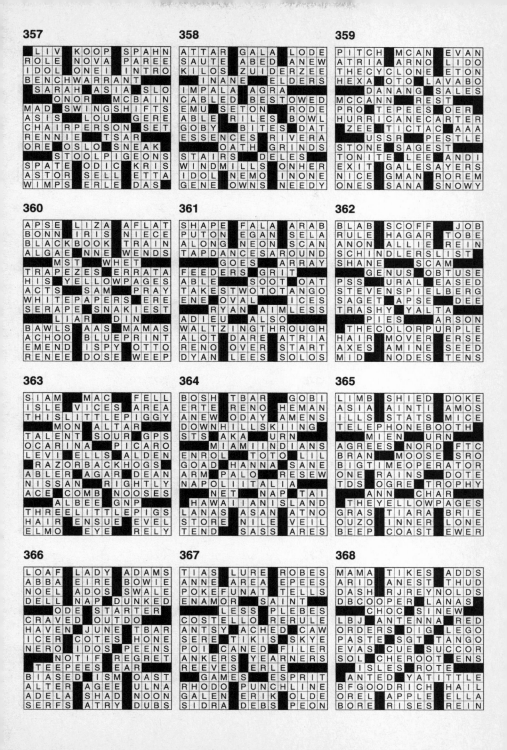

■	L	I	V	■	K	O	O	P	■	S	P	A	H	N
R	O	L	E	■	N	O	V	A	■	P	A	R	E	E
I	D	O	L	■	O	N	E	I	■	I	N	T	R	O
B	E	N	C	H	W	A	R	R	A	N	T	■	■	■
■	S	A	R	A	H	■	A	S	I	A	■	S	L	O
■	■	■	O	N	O	R	■	■	M	C	B	A	I	N
M	A	D	■	S	W	I	N	G	S	H	I	F	T	S
A	S	I	S	■	■	L	O	U	■	■	G	E	R	E
C	H	A	I	R	P	E	R	S	O	N	■	S	E	T
R	E	N	N	I	E	■	■	T	S	A	R	■	■	■
O	R	E	■	O	S	L	O	■	S	N	E	A	K	■
■	■	■	S	T	O	O	L	P	I	G	E	O	N	S
S	P	A	T	E	■	O	D	I	C	■	K	R	I	S
A	S	T	O	R	■	S	E	L	L	■	E	T	T	A
W	I	M	P	S	■	E	R	L	E	■	D	A	S	■

358

A	T	T	A	R	■	G	A	L	A	■	L	O	D	E
S	A	U	T	E	■	A	B	E	D	■	A	N	E	W
K	I	L	O	S	■	Z	U	I	D	E	R	Z	E	E
■	■	I	N	A	N	E	■	■	E	L	D	E	R	S
I	M	P	A	L	A	■	A	G	R	A	■	■	■	■
C	A	B	L	E	D	■	B	E	S	T	O	W	E	D
E	M	U	■	S	E	T	O	N	■	■	R	O	D	E
A	B	L	E	■	R	I	L	E	S	■	B	O	W	L
G	O	B	Y	■	■	B	I	T	E	S	■	D	A	T
E	S	S	E	N	C	E	S	■	R	I	V	E	R	A
■	■	■	■	O	A	T	H	■	G	R	I	N	D	S
S	T	A	I	R	S	■	■	D	E	L	E	S	■	■
W	I	N	D	M	I	L	L	S	■	O	N	H	E	R
I	D	O	L	■	N	E	M	O	■	I	N	O	N	E
G	E	N	E	■	O	W	N	S	■	N	E	E	D	Y

359

P	I	T	C	H	■	M	C	A	N	■	E	V	A	N
A	T	R	I	A	■	A	R	N	O	■	L	I	D	O
T	H	E	C	Y	C	L	O	N	E	■	E	T	O	N
H	E	X	A	■	O	T	O	■	L	A	V	A	B	O
■	■	■	D	A	N	A	N	G	■	S	A	L	E	S
M	C	C	A	N	N	■	■	R	E	S	T	■	■	■
P	R	O	■	T	E	P	E	E	S	■	O	E	R	■
H	U	R	R	I	C	A	N	E	C	A	R	T	E	R
■	Z	E	E	■	T	I	C	T	A	C	■	A	A	A
■	■	■	U	S	S	R	■	■	P	E	S	T	L	E
S	T	O	N	E	■	S	A	G	E	S	T	■	■	■
T	O	N	I	T	E	■	L	E	E	■	A	N	D	I
E	X	I	T	■	G	A	L	E	S	A	Y	E	R	S
N	I	C	E	■	G	M	A	N	■	R	O	R	E	M
O	N	E	S	■	S	A	N	A	■	S	N	O	W	Y

360

A	P	S	E	■	L	I	Z	A	■	A	F	L	A	T
B	O	N	N	■	I	R	I	S	■	N	I	E	C	E
B	L	A	C	K	B	O	O	K	■	T	R	A	I	N
A	L	G	A	E	■	N	N	E	■	W	E	N	D	S
■	■	■	M	S	T	■	■	W	H	E	T	■	■	■
T	R	A	P	E	Z	E	S	■	E	R	R	A	T	A
H	I	S	■	Y	E	L	L	O	W	P	A	G	E	S
A	C	T	S	■	■	S	A	M	■	■	P	R	A	Y
W	H	I	T	E	P	A	P	E	R	S	■	E	R	E
S	E	R	A	P	E	■	S	N	A	K	I	E	S	T
■	■	■	L	I	A	R	■	■	D	I	N	■	■	■
B	A	W	L	S	■	A	A	S	■	M	A	M	A	S
A	C	H	O	O	■	B	L	U	E	P	R	I	N	T
E	M	E	N	D	■	I	S	P	Y	■	O	T	T	O
R	E	N	E	E	■	D	O	S	E	■	W	E	E	P

361

S	H	A	P	E	■	F	A	L	A	■	A	R	A	B
P	U	T	O	N	■	E	G	A	N	■	S	E	L	A
A	L	O	N	G	■	N	E	O	N	■	S	C	A	N
T	A	P	D	A	N	C	E	S	A	R	O	U	N	D
■	■	■	■	G	O	E	S	■	■	A	R	R	A	Y
F	E	E	D	E	R	S	■	G	R	I	T	■	■	■
A	B	L	E	■	■	■	S	O	O	T	■	O	A	T
T	A	K	E	S	T	W	O	T	O	T	A	N	G	O
E	N	E	■	O	V	A	L	■	■	■	I	C	E	S
■	■	■	R	Y	A	N	■	A	I	M	L	E	S	S
A	D	I	E	U	■	■	A	L	S	O	■	■	■	■
W	A	L	T	Z	I	N	G	T	H	R	O	U	G	H
A	L	O	T	■	D	A	R	E	■	A	T	R	I	A
R	E	N	O	■	O	V	E	R	■	S	T	A	R	T
D	Y	A	N	■	L	E	E	S	■	S	O	L	O	S

362

B	L	A	B	■	S	C	O	F	F	■	■	J	O	B
R	U	L	E	■	H	A	G	A	R	■	T	O	B	E
A	N	O	N	■	A	L	L	I	E	■	R	E	I	N
S	C	H	I	N	D	L	E	R	S	L	I	S	T	■
S	H	A	N	E	■	■	■	S	C	A	M	■	■	■
■	■	■	G	E	N	U	S	■	O	B	T	U	S	E
P	S	S	■	■	U	R	A	L	■	E	A	S	E	D
S	T	E	V	E	N	S	P	I	E	L	B	E	R	G
S	A	G	E	T	■	A	P	S	E	■	■	D	E	E
T	R	A	S	H	Y	■	Y	A	L	T	A	■	■	■
■	■	■	P	I	E	S	■	■	■	A	R	S	O	N
■	T	H	E	C	O	L	O	R	P	U	R	P	L	E
H	A	I	R	■	M	O	V	E	R	■	E	R	S	E
A	X	E	S	■	A	M	I	N	E	■	S	E	E	D
M	I	D	■	■	N	O	D	E	S	■	T	E	N	S

363

S	I	A	M	■	■	M	A	C	■	■	F	E	L	L
I	S	L	E	■	V	I	C	E	S	■	A	R	E	A
T	H	I	S	L	I	T	T	L	E	P	I	G	G	Y
■	■	■	M	O	N	■	A	L	T	A	R	■	■	■
T	A	L	E	N	T	■	S	O	U	R	■	G	P	S
O	C	A	R	I	N	A	■	■	P	I	C	A	R	O
L	E	V	I	■	E	L	L	S	■	A	L	D	E	N
■	R	A	Z	O	R	B	A	C	K	H	O	G	S	■
A	B	L	E	R	■	A	G	A	R	■	D	E	A	N
N	I	S	S	A	N	■	■	R	I	G	H	T	L	Y
A	C	E	■	C	O	M	B	■	N	O	O	S	E	S
■	■	■	A	L	B	E	E	■	G	N	P	■	■	■
T	H	R	E	E	L	I	T	T	L	E	P	I	G	S
H	A	I	R	■	E	N	S	U	E	■	E	V	E	L
E	L	M	O	■	■	E	Y	E	■	■	R	E	L	Y

364

B	O	S	H	■	T	B	A	R	■	■	G	O	B	I
E	R	T	E	■	R	E	N	O	■	H	E	M	A	N
A	N	E	W	■	O	D	A	Y	■	A	M	E	N	S
D	O	W	N	H	I	L	L	S	K	I	I	N	G	■
S	T	S	■	A	K	A	■	■	U	R	N	■	■	■
■	■	■	M	I	A	M	I	I	N	D	I	A	N	S
E	N	R	O	L	■	■	T	O	T	O	■	L	I	L
G	O	A	D	■	H	A	N	N	A	■	S	A	N	E
A	R	M	■	P	A	L	O	■	■	R	E	S	E	W
N	A	P	O	L	I	I	T	A	L	I	A	■	■	■
■	■	■	N	E	T	■	■	N	A	P	■	T	A	I
■	H	A	W	A	I	I	A	N	I	S	L	A	N	D
L	A	N	A	S	■	A	S	A	N	■	A	T	N	O
S	T	O	R	E	■	N	I	L	E	■	V	E	I	L
T	E	N	D	■	■	S	A	S	S	■	A	R	E	S

365

L	I	M	B	■	S	H	I	E	D	■	D	O	K	E
A	S	I	A	■	A	I	N	T	I	■	A	M	O	S
I	L	L	S	■	S	T	A	T	S	■	M	I	C	E
T	E	L	E	P	H	O	N	E	B	O	O	T	H	■
■	■	■	M	I	E	N	■	■	U	R	N	■	■	■
A	G	R	E	E	S	■	N	O	R	D	■	F	T	C
B	R	A	N	■	■	M	O	O	S	E	■	S	R	O
B	I	G	T	I	M	E	O	P	E	R	A	T	O	R
O	N	E	■	R	A	I	N	S	■	■	D	O	T	E
T	D	S	■	O	G	R	E	■	T	R	O	P	H	Y
■	■	■	A	N	N	■	■	C	H	A	R	■	■	■
■	T	H	E	Y	E	L	L	O	W	P	A	G	E	S
G	R	A	S	■	T	I	A	R	A	■	B	R	I	E
O	U	Z	O	■	I	N	N	E	R	■	L	O	N	E
B	E	E	P	■	C	O	A	S	T	■	E	W	E	R

366

L	O	A	F	■	L	A	D	Y	■	A	D	A	M	S
A	B	B	A	■	E	I	R	E	■	B	O	W	I	E
N	O	E	L	■	A	D	O	S	■	S	W	A	L	E
D	E	L	L	■	N	A	P	■	D	U	N	K	E	D
■	■	■	O	D	E	■	S	T	A	R	T	E	R	■
C	R	A	V	E	D	■	O	U	T	D	O	■	■	■
H	A	V	E	N	■	J	U	N	E	■	T	B	A	R
I	C	E	R	■	C	O	T	E	S	■	H	O	N	E
N	E	R	O	■	I	D	O	S	■	P	E	E	N	S
■	■	■	N	O	T	I	F	■	R	E	G	R	E	T
■	T	E	E	P	E	E	S	■	E	A	R	■	■	■
B	I	A	S	E	D	■	I	S	M	■	O	A	S	T
A	L	T	E	R	■	A	G	E	E	■	U	L	N	A
A	D	E	L	A	■	S	H	A	D	■	N	O	O	N
S	E	R	F	S	■	A	T	R	Y	■	D	U	B	S

367

T	I	A	S	■	L	U	R	E	■	R	O	B	E	S
A	N	N	E	■	A	R	E	A	■	E	P	E	E	S
P	O	K	E	F	U	N	A	T	■	T	E	L	L	S
E	N	A	M	O	R	■	■	S	A	I	N	T	■	■
■	■	■	■	L	E	S	S	■	P	L	E	B	E	S
C	O	S	T	E	L	L	O	■	R	E	R	U	L	E
A	N	T	S	Y	■	A	C	H	E	D	■	C	A	W
S	E	R	E	■	T	I	K	I	S	■	S	K	Y	E
P	O	I	■	C	A	N	E	D	■	F	I	L	E	R
A	N	K	E	R	S	■	Y	E	A	R	N	E	R	S
R	E	E	V	E	S	■	E	R	L	E	■	■	■	■
■	■	G	A	M	E	S	■	■	E	S	P	R	I	T
R	H	O	D	O	■	P	U	N	C	H	L	I	N	E
G	A	L	E	N	■	E	R	I	K	■	O	L	D	E
S	I	D	R	A	■	D	E	B	S	■	P	E	O	N

368

M	A	M	A	■	T	I	K	E	S	■	A	D	D	S
A	R	I	D	■	A	N	E	S	T	■	T	H	U	D
D	A	S	H	■	R	J	R	E	Y	N	O	L	D	S
D	B	C	O	O	P	E	R	■	L	A	N	A	S	■
■	■	■	C	H	O	C	■	S	I	N	E	W	■	■
L	B	J	■	A	N	T	E	N	N	A	■	R	E	D
O	R	D	E	R	S	■	D	I	G	■	L	E	G	O
P	A	S	T	E	■	S	G	T	■	T	A	N	G	O
E	V	A	S	■	C	U	E	■	S	U	C	C	O	R
S	O	L	■	C	H	E	R	O	O	T	■	E	N	S
■	■	I	S	L	E	S	■	R	O	T	E	■	■	■
■	A	N	T	E	D	■	Y	A	T	I	T	T	L	E
B	F	G	O	O	D	R	I	C	H	■	H	A	I	L
O	R	E	L	■	A	P	P	L	E	■	E	L	L	A
B	O	R	E	■	R	I	S	E	S	■	R	E	I	N

369

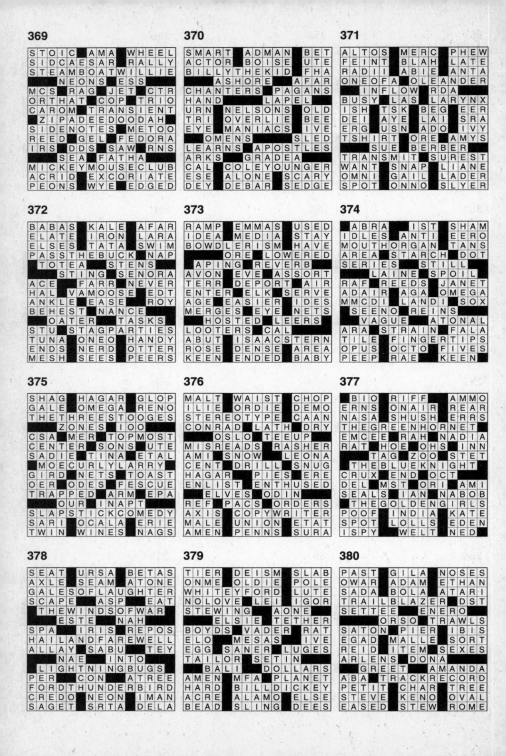

STOIC■AMA■WHEEL
SIDCAESAR■RALLY
STEAMBOATWILLIE
■■■NEONS■ESS■■■
MCS■RAG■JET■CTR
ORTHAT■COP■TRIO
CAROM■TRANSIENT
■ZIPADEEDOODAH■
SIDENOTES■METOO
REED■GEL■FEDORA
IRS■DDS■SAW■RNS
■■■SEA■FATHA■■■
MICKEYMOUSECLUB
ACRID■EXCORIATE
PEONS■WYE■EDGED

370

SMART■ADMAN■BET
ACTOR■BOISE■UTE
BILLYTHEKID■FHA
■■■ASHORE■■AFAR
CHANTERS■PAGANS
HAND■■■■LAPEL■■
URN■NELSONS■OLD
TRI■OVERLIE■BEE
EYE■MANIACS■IVE
■■OMENS■■■■SLED
LEARNS■APOSTLES
ARKS■■GRADEA■■■
CAL■COLEYOUNGER
ESE■ALONE■SCARY
DEY■DEBAR■SEDGE

371

ALTOS■MERC■PHEW
FEINT■BLAH■LATE
RADII■ABIE■ANTA
ONEOFA■OLEANDER
■■INFLOW■RDA■■■
BUSY■LAS■LARYNX
ISH■TSK■BEG■EER
DEI■AYE■LAI■SRA
ERG■USN■ADO■IVY
TSHIRT■ORE■AMYS
■■■SUE■BERBER■■
TRANSMIT■SUREST
WANT■SNAP■LIANE
OMNI■GAIL■LADER
SPOT■ONNO■SLYER

372

BABAS■KALE■AFAR
ELATE■IRON■LARA
ELSES■TATA■SWIM
PASSTHEBUCK■NAP
■TOTEA■■STENS■■
■■■STING■SENORA
ACE■■FARR■NEVER
HAL■VAMOOSE■EDT
ANKLE■EASE■■ROY
BEHEST■NANCE■■■
■■OATER■■TASKS■
STU■STAGPARTIES
TUNA■ONEO■HANDY
ENDS■NERD■OTTER
MESH■SEES■PEERS

373

RAMP■EMMAS■USED
IDEA■MEDIA■STAY
BOWDLERISM■HAVE
■■■■ORE■LOWERED
■APING■REVERB■■
AVON■EVE■ASSORT
TERR■DEPORT■AIR
ENTER■ELK■SERVE
AGE■EASIER■IDES
MERGES■EYE■NETS
■■HOSTED■LEERS■
LOOTERS■CAL■■■■
ABUT■ISAACSTERN
ROSE■DENSE■AREA
KEEN■ENDED■BABY

374

■ABRA■■IST■SHAM
IDLES■ANTI■EERO
MOUTHORGAN■TANS
AREA■STARCH■DOT
SERIES■■STILL■■
■■■LAINE■SPOIL■
RAF■REEDS■JANET
ADAIR■AGA■OMEGA
MMCDI■LANDI■SOX
■SEENO■REINS■■■
■■VAGUE■■ATONAL
ARA■STRAIN■FALA
TILE■FINGERTIPS
OPUS■OCTO■FIVES
PEEP■RAE■■KEEN■

375

SHAG■HAGAR■GLOP
GALE■OMEGA■RENO
THETHREESTOOGES
■■■ZONES■IOO■■■
CSA■MER■TOPMOST
CENTER■SONS■UTE
SADIE■TINA■ETAL
■MOECURLYLARRY■
GIRD■NETS■TOAST
OER■ODES■FESCUE
TRAPPED■ARM■EPA
■■■OUR■INAPT■■■
SLAPSTICKCOMEDY
SARI■OCALA■ERIE
TWIN■WINES■NAGS

376

MALT■WAIST■CHOP
ILIE■ORDIE■DEMO
STEREOTYPE■CAAN
CONRAD■LATH■DRY
■■■OSLO■TEEUP■■
MISREADS■RASHER
AMI■SNOW■■LEONA
CENT■DRILL■SNUG
HAGAR■■PIES■ERE
ENLIST■ENTHUSED
■■ELVES■ODIN■■■
REF■PACS■ORDERS
AXIS■COPYWRITER
MALE■UNION■ETAT
AMEN■PENNS■SURA

377

■BIO■RIFF■■AMMO
ERNS■ONAIR■REAR
NASA■SHUSH■ERRS
THEGREENHORNET■
EMCEE■RAH■NADIA
RAT■HOE■OHS■INN
■■■TAG■ZOO■STET
■THEBLUEKNIGHT■
CRUX■END■OCT■■■
DEL■MST■ORI■AMI
SEALS■IAN■NABOB
■THEGOLDENGIRLS
POOF■INDIA■KATE
SPOT■LOLLS■EDEN
ISPY■■WELT■NED■

378

SEAT■URSA■BETAS
AXLE■SEAM■ATONE
GALESOFLAUGHTER
SCAPE■■ASP■■EAT
■THEWINDSOFWAR■
■■■ESTE■■NAH■■■
SPA■■IRIS■REPOS
HAILANDFAREWELL
ALLAY■SABU■■TEY
■■■NAE■■INTO■■■
■LIGHTNINGBUGS■
PER■■CON■■ATREE
FORDTHUNDERBIRD
CREDO■NEON■IMAN
SAGET■SRTA■DELA

379

TIER■DEISM■SLAB
ONME■OLDIE■POLE
WHITEYFORD■LUTE
NOLOVE■LEI■IGOR
STEWING■■AONE■■
■■■ELSIE■TETHER
BOYDS■VADER■RAT
ELO■■MESAS■■IVE
EGG■SANER■LUGES
TAILOR■SETIN■■■
■■BALI■■DOLLARS
AMEN■MFA■PLANET
HARD■BILLDICKEY
ACRE■ALAMO■ELSE
BEAD■SLING■DEES

380

PAST■GILA■NOSES
OWAR■ADAM■ETHAN
SADA■BOLA■ATARI
TRAILBLAZER■DST
SETTEE■■ENERO■■
■■■■ORSO■TRAWLS
SATON■PIER■IBIS
EGAD■MALLE■SORT
REID■ITEM■SEXES
ARLENS■DONA■■■■
■■GREET■■AMANDA
ABA■TRACKRECORD
PETIT■CHAR■TREE
STEVE■KENO■OVAL
EASED■STEW■ROME

381

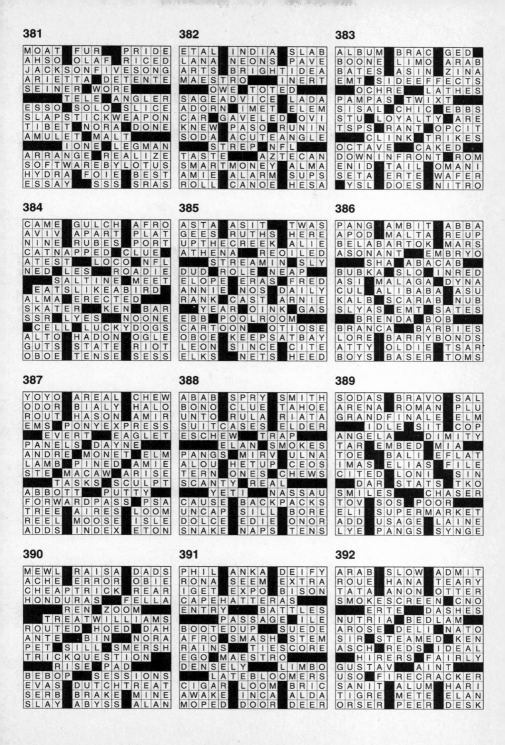

M	O	A	T		F	U	R			P	R	I	D	E
A	H	S	O		O	L	A	F		R	I	C	E	D
J	A	C	K	S	O	N	F	I	V	E	S	O	N	G
A	R	I	E	T	T	A		D	E	T	E	N	T	E
S	E	I	N	E	R		W	O	R	E				
				T	E	L	E		A	N	G	L	E	R
E	S	S	O		S	O	L	O		S	L	I	C	E
S	L	A	P	S	T	I	C	K	W	E	A	P	O	N
T	I	B	E	T		N	O	R	A		D	O	N	E
A	M	U	L	E	T		M	A	L	T				
				I	O	N	E		L	E	G	M	A	N
A	R	R	A	N	G	E		R	E	A	L	I	Z	E
S	O	F	T	W	A	R	E	B	Y	L	O	T	U	S
H	Y	D	R	A		F	O	I	E		B	E	S	T
E	S	S	A	Y			S	S	S		S	R	A	S

382

E	T	A	L		I	N	D	I	A		S	L	A	B
L	A	N	A		N	E	O	N	S		P	A	V	E
A	R	T	S		B	R	I	G	H	T	I	D	E	A
M	A	E	S	T	R	O				I	N	E	R	T
			O	W	E		T	O	T	E	D			
S	A	G	E	A	D	V	I	C	E		L	A	D	A
A	D	O	R	N		I	M	E	T		E	L	E	M
C	A	R		G	A	V	E	L	E	D		O	V	I
K	N	E	W		P	A	S	O		R	U	N	I	N
S	O	D	A		A	C	U	T	E	A	N	G	L	E
			S	T	R	E	P		N	F	L			
T	A	S	T	E				A	Z	T	E	C	A	N
S	M	A	R	T	M	O	N	E	Y		A	L	M	A
A	M	I	E		A	L	A	R	M		S	U	P	S
R	O	L	L		C	A	N	O	E		H	E	S	A

383

A	L	B	U	M		B	R	A	C		G	E	D	
B	O	O	N	E		L	I	M	O		A	R	A	B
B	A	T	E	S		A	S	I	N		Z	I	N	A
E	M	T		S	I	D	E	E	F	F	E	C	T	S
		O	C	H	R	E			L	A	T	H	E	S
P	A	M	P	A	S		T	W	I	X	T			
S	I	S	A	L		C	H	I	C		E	B	B	S
S	T	U		L	O	Y	A	L	T	Y		A	R	E
T	S	P	S		R	A	N	T		O	P	C	I	T
			C	L	I	N	K		T	R	I	K	E	S
O	C	T	A	V	E			C	A	K	E	D		
D	O	W	N	I	N	F	R	O	N	T		R	O	M
E	N	I	D		T	A	I	L		O	M	A	N	I
S	E	T	A		E	R	T	E		W	A	F	E	R
	Y	S	L		D	O	E	S		N	I	T	R	O

384

C	A	M	E		G	U	L	C	H		A	F	R	O
A	V	I	V		A	P	A	R	T		P	L	A	T
N	I	N	E		R	U	B	E	S		P	O	R	T
C	A	T	N	A	P	P	E	D		C	L	U	E	
A	T	E	S	T			L	O	C	O		N	F	L
N	E	D		L	E	S			R	O	A	D	I	E
			S	A	L	T	I	N	E		M	E	E	T
	E	A	T	S	L	I	K	E	A	B	I	R	D	
A	L	M	A		E	R	E	C	T	E	D			
S	K	A	T	E	R			K	E	N		B	A	R
S	S	R		L	Y	E	S			N	O	O	N	E
	C	E	L	L		L	U	C	K	Y	D	O	G	S
A	L	T	O		H	A	D	O	N		O	G	L	E
G	U	T	S		S	T	A	T	E		R	I	O	T
O	B	O	E		T	E	N	S	E		S	E	S	S

385

A	S	T	A		A	S	I	T			T	W	A	S
G	E	E	S		R	U	T	H	S		H	E	R	E
U	P	T	H	E	C	R	E	E	K		A	L	I	E
A	T	H	E	N	A			R	E	O	I	L	E	D
			S	T	R	E	A	M	I	N		S	L	Y
D	U	D		R	O	L	E		N	E	A	P		
E	L	O	P	E		E	R	A	S		F	R	E	D
A	N	N	I	E		N	O	S		D	A	I	L	Y
R	A	N	K		C	A	S	T		A	R	N	I	E
		Y	E	A	R		O	I	N	K		G	A	S
E	B	B		P	O	O	L	R	O	O	M			
C	A	R	T	O	O	N			O	T	I	O	S	E
O	B	O	E		K	E	E	P	S	A	T	B	A	Y
L	E	O	N		S	I	N	C	E		C	I	T	E
E	L	K	S			N	E	T	S		H	E	E	D

386

P	A	N	G		A	M	B	I	T		A	B	B	A
A	P	O	D		M	A	L	T	A		R	E	U	P
B	E	L	A	B	A	R	T	O	K		M	A	R	S
A	S	O	N	A	N	T			E	M	B	R	Y	O
			S	H	A		A	B	A	C	A	B		
B	U	B	K	A		S	L	O		I	N	R	E	D
A	S	I		M	A	L	A	G	A		D	Y	N	A
C	U	L		A	L	I	B	A	B	A		A	S	U
K	A	L	B		S	C	A	R	A	B		N	U	B
S	L	Y	A	S		E	M	T		S	A	T	E	S
		B	R	E	N	D	A		B	O	B			
B	R	A	N	C	A			B	A	R	B	I	E	S
L	O	R	E		B	A	R	R	Y	B	O	N	D	S
A	T	T	Y		O	L	D	I	E		T	S	A	R
B	O	Y	S		B	A	S	E	R		T	O	M	S

387

Y	O	Y	O		A	R	E	A	L		C	H	E	W
O	D	O	R		B	I	A	L	Y		H	A	L	O
R	O	U	T		H	A	S	O	N		A	M	I	R
E	M	S		P	O	N	Y	E	X	P	R	E	S	S
		E	V	E	R	T			E	A	G	L	E	T
P	A	N	E	L	S		D	A	Y	N	E			
A	N	D	R	E		M	O	N	E	T		E	L	M
L	A	M	B		P	I	N	E	D		A	M	I	E
S	T	E		M	A	C	A	W		A	R	I	S	E
			T	A	S	K	S		S	C	U	L	P	T
A	B	B	O	T	T			P	U	T	T	Y		
F	O	R	W	A	R	D	P	A	S	S		P	S	A
T	R	E	E		A	I	R	E	S		L	O	O	M
R	E	E	L		M	O	O	S	E		I	S	L	E
A	D	D	S		I	N	D	E	X		E	T	O	N

388

A	B	A	B		S	P	R	Y		S	M	I	T	H
B	O	N	O		C	L	U	E		T	A	H	O	E
U	N	T	O		R	U	L	A		R	I	A	T	A
S	U	I	T	C	A	S	E	S		E	L	D	E	R
E	S	C	H	E	W			T	R	A	P			
				E	L	A	N		S	M	O	K	E	S
P	A	N	G	S		M	I	R	V		U	L	N	A
A	L	O	U		H	E	T	U	P		C	E	O	S
T	E	R	N		O	N	E	S		C	H	E	W	S
S	C	A	N	T	Y		R	E	A	L				
			Y	E	T	I			N	A	S	S	A	U
C	A	U	S	E		B	A	C	K	P	A	C	K	S
U	N	C	A	P		S	I	L	L		B	O	R	E
D	O	L	C	E		E	D	I	E		O	N	O	R
S	N	A	K	E		N	A	P	S		T	E	N	S

389

S	O	D	A	S		B	R	A	V	O		S	A	L
A	R	E	N	A		R	O	M	A	N		P	L	U
G	R	A	N	D	F	I	N	A	L	E		E	L	M
			I	D	L	E		S	I	T		C	O	P
A	N	G	E	L	A				D	I	M	I	T	Y
T	A	R		E	M	B	E	D		M	I	A		
T	O	E			B	A	L	I		E	F	L	A	T
I	M	A	S		E	L	I	A	S		F	I	L	E
C	I	T	E	D		L	O	N	I			S	I	N
		D	A	R		S	T	A	T	S		T	K	O
S	M	I	L	E	S				C	H	A	S	E	R
T	O	V		S	O	S		P	O	O	R			
E	L	I		S	U	P	E	R	M	A	R	K	E	T
A	D	D		U	S	A	G	E		L	A	I	N	E
L	Y	E		P	A	N	G	S		S	Y	N	G	E

390

M	E	W	L		R	A	I	S	A		D	A	D	S
A	C	H	E		E	R	R	O	R		O	B	I	E
C	H	E	A	P	T	R	I	C	K		R	E	A	R
H	O	N	D	U	R	A	S			F	E	L	L	A
				R	E	N		Z	O	O	M			
		T	R	E	A	T	W	I	L	L	I	A	M	S
R	O	U	T	E	D		H	O	E	D		D	A	H
A	N	T	E			B	I	N			N	O	R	A
P	E	T		S	I	L	L		S	M	E	R	S	H
T	R	I	C	K	Q	U	E	S	T	I	O	N		
			R	I	S	E		P	A	D				
B	E	B	O	P			S	E	S	S	I	O	N	S
E	V	A	S		D	U	T	C	H	T	R	E	A	T
S	E	R	B		B	R	A	K	E		M	I	N	E
S	L	A	Y		A	B	Y	S	S		A	L	A	N

391

P	H	I	L		A	N	K	A		D	E	I	F	Y
R	O	N	A		S	E	E	M		E	X	T	R	A
I	G	E	T		E	X	P	O		B	I	S	O	N
C	A	P	E	H	A	T	T	E	R	A	S			
E	N	T	R	Y				B	A	T	T	L	E	S
				P	A	S	S	A	G	E		I	L	E
B	O	O	T	E	D	U	P			S	U	E	D	E
A	F	R	O		S	M	A	S	H		S	T	E	M
R	A	I	N	S			T	I	E	S	C	O	R	E
E	G	O		M	A	E	S	T	R	O				
D	E	N	S	E	L	Y				L	I	M	B	O
			L	A	T	E	B	L	O	O	M	E	R	S
C	I	G	A	R		L	O	O	M		B	R	I	C
A	W	A	K	E		I	N	C	A		A	L	D	A
M	O	P	E	D		D	O	O	R		D	E	E	R

392

A	R	A	B		S	L	O	W		A	D	M	I	T
R	O	U	E		H	A	N	A		T	E	A	R	Y
T	A	T	A		A	N	O	N		O	T	T	E	R
S	M	O	K	E	S	C	R	E	E	N		C	N	O
			E	R	T	E			D	A	S	H	E	S
N	U	T	R	I	A		B	E	D	L	A	M		
A	R	O	S	E		D	E	L	I		N	A	T	O
S	I	R		S	T	E	A	M	E	D		K	E	N
A	S	C	H		R	E	D	S		I	D	E	A	L
		H	I	R	E	R	S		F	A	I	R	L	Y
G	U	S	T	A	V			A	I	N	T			
U	S	O		F	I	R	E	C	R	A	C	K	E	R
S	A	N	I	T		A	L	U	M		H	A	R	I
T	I	G	R	E		M	E	T	E		E	L	A	N
O	R	S	E	R		P	E	E	R		D	E	S	K

393

LATHE BARR CLEF
ARRAY OPIE HARE
SLIME LAND AIDE
TECH PORKBARREL
SNEAKS OPT
NEIGHBOR ASI
GLADE ROOK GUTS
RIVEN ERN MORAL
AMID VASE OHARE
YES WATERLOO
PAC EGGNOG
PIGINAPOKE WORE
ONYX NOTA FITIN
ETRE CLAY FLEER
TOOL YOYO ADDLE

394

EMITS FRET ABCS
BERRA DELE ERLE
BRAINDRAIN RIAL
SENDER MAE OGRE
EROS STASHES
DAWN OLE SLOT
ALIT PIMA OLIVE
LAS EYEBROW DOE
INERT REID TELL
CENT RED EATS
CERTAIN SELA
OMAR NIP SARAHS
MICE SMARTMONEY
ILKA EBRO PONES
CEST LIED SMELT

395

MASS RITA GNP
ADIEU SUSHI RIO
OSCARWINNER ANS
BANGOR SCAT
TOGAS STEVIE
SILENTS SAMPAN
ARID EATS NIECE
LAV ISLANDS ROE
ADEPT ERIE BIRD
DEBRIS PATRONS
RASHES ROADS
STAY EVICTS
HUN FAITHHEALER
ABC ARTIE EMILY
HAH ASAN OPIE

396

PROS HIPPO CHAR
AUNT ODEON HALO
PECANROLLS IMAM
ARENAS TIECLASP
DIES STEIN
AWFUL ASH REDUB
HARP RIO PESETA
ACE REDUCES GIN
BOSSED SUN OGLE
HIP PER FUSES
ALFALFA BRUT
FARMYARD ARROWS
TRUE CORNFLAKES
EGIS EDICT GRIT
ROTE TYPOS EARS

397

PANSY RACER AWL
ALICE AGORA COE
POLARICECAP CPO
SEEM RINK SARAN
PLANTAR RATE
ALL USE TOUT
NEILL TOADIER
DEMOLITIONDERBY
REVERIE ERNIE
EDIT APR OSS
TAXI SOUREST
OWENS INGA AERO
PAN COSMOTOPPER
PRO ANTES PEEVE
SEN TESTY TRESS

398

SPARE FLED SPOT
HASAT RANI TOGA
ARTICHOKES EKES
DEAL ONE AGREES
WORD LEERS
SAHARA HALLOF
PLOYS HALO SANG
AOK OKINAWA COL
STEP INKS GRETA
YEASTS SEEDED
APERS LIST
GLORIA AIR IRAS
RAKE BACKSTROKE
AMES LIRE RESIN
BOYS EDEN IDENT

399

SARAH BUMP MAD
SPIRAL ESAU ONE
REVERE LAIR AKA
SENEGAL NECTAR
ROM LESSER
SOFT UPSET ADUB
CAR CPO ARIZONA
ATOAST EVENTS
LENGTHS RAY NIT
ESTA EPSOM LYLE
INCANT SOB
CORNER AIRPORT
ORO REEK PEKOES
KAT VERE INTOTO
ELS EKED TOKEN

400

BLED LOPED REST
AIDE ORATE ERIE
CLIP RASTA LIND
HITTHEROADJACK
OLE SOX
SABLE TEEN AMI
PLAYITAGAINSAM
TILL HUG OKRA
BEAMMEUPSCOTTY
ASH URGE OREOS
SNO ONT
SAYITAINTSOJOE
BOLL INDIE PABA
BLIP COLON UNIT
BOTH ANENT SETS